Business

KEITH ABBOTT, B.A. (Hons). MBA, Solicitor
Head of Business Studies
Hendon College
and
NORMAN PENDLEBURY, F.C.M.A., M.B.I.M.
Senior Lecturer in Law
Southampton Institute of Higher Education

5TH EDITION

DP PUBLICATIONS LTD
Aldine Place
142/144 Uxbridge Road
Shepherds Bush Green
London W12 8AW
1991

ACKNOWLEDGEMENTS

The authors wish to express their thanks to the following for permission to reproduce past examination questions:-

Chartered Association of Certified Accountants

Chartered Institute of Management Accountants

Institute of Chartered Secretaries and Administrators

First Edition 1982
Reprinted 1983
Reprinted 1984

Second Edition 1985

Third Edition 1986
Reprinted 1986
Reprinted 1987

Fourth Edition 1988
Reprinted November 1989 incorporating Employment Act 1988
and The Copyright, Designs & Patents Act 1988

Fifth Edition 1991
Reprinted September 1991 incorporating the Employment Act 1989,
Employment Act 1990 and Courts & Legal Services Act 1990

ISBN 1 870941 721

Typeset by
Alphaset,
65A The Avenue,
Southampton,
SO1 2TA

Printed in Great Britain by
The Guernsey Press Company Ltd.,
Braye Road, Vale,
Guernsey, Channel Islands.

Table of Contents

PART III THE LAW OF TORTS

PART IV COMMERCIAL LAW

PART V LABOUR LAW

Preface

This book is designed primarily for students sitting the following examinations:-

ACCA	Level 1.4	Law;
CIMA	Exemption Paper	Business Studies (Law);
CIMA	Stage 1	Business Law;
ICSA	Part 1	Introduction to English Law;
ICSA	Part 2	English Business Law;

It is also relevant to any other students who are taking an introductory law course, for example Legal Executives, AAT, IComA and BTEC students.

The basic requirement for passing any law examination is a good factual knowledge of the relevant law. The bulk of the text is therefore devoted to the presentation of rules of law in a style and format which will help students to assimilate the necessary facts. The remainder of the text serves three purposes:-

1. Chapters 1 and 2 recognise that examination success is not merely an indication of factual knowledge or even intelligence. Organisation in learning and examination technique are also being tested and therefore need to be practised as much as possible.

2. The Coursework and Revision Questions (most of which are actual past examination questions) provide the opportunity and incentive to undertake the practice which is essential to pass the examination. They are also an indication of the standard expected by the examiner. It is suggested that the Coursework Questions are attempted at appropriate times throughout the course whereas the Revision Questions (as their name implies) are best "saved" until the end of the course. Suggested answers are given to all of these questions (71 in all) in Appendices 1 and 2.

3. Appendix 3 is intended as a teaching aid. It consists of 30 more difficult questions without suggested answers. Lecturers may obtain from the publishers free of charge, provided the order is placed on college notepaper, notes to assist in discussion of these questions.

4. The Fifth Edition incorporates changes introduced by the Employment Act 1988, the Copyright, Designs and Patents Act 1988 and the Companies Act 1989. Several new cases have also been included.

The law is stated as at 1st September 1990.

Note on reprint 1991
This reprint, September 1991, incorporates amendments as a consequence of:
The Employment Act 1989
The Employment Act 1990
The Courts & Legal Services Act 1990

Syllabus Guide

Topic	ACCA	CIMA Exemption Paper	CIMA Stage 1	ICSA Pt.1	ICSA Pt.2
Sources of Law	✓	✓	✓	✓	✗
English Legal History	✓	✗	Background Reading	Background Reading	✗
The Courts, Tribunals, Arbitration	✓	✗	✓	✓	✗
The Personnal of the Law	✓	✗	✗	✓	✗
Procedure and Evidence	✗	✗	✗	✗	✗
The Law of Persons:-					
– Natural Persons	✓	✗	✗	✗	✗
– Companies	✓	✓	✓	✓	✗
– Partnerships	✓	✓	✓	✓	✗
– Trade Unions	✓	✗	✗	✓	✗
Property Law	✗	✗	✗	✓	✗
Trusts	✗	✗	✗	✓	✗
The Law of Contract	✓	✓	✓	✓ (Outline)	(Depth)
The Law of Tort:-					
– Negligence	✓	✓	✓	✓	✗
– Strict Liability	✗	✗	✓	✓	✗
– Nuisance	✗	✗	✗	✓	✗
– Trespass	✗	✗	✗	✓	✗
– Defamation	✗	✗	✗	✓	✓
– Conversion	✗	✗	✗	✓	✗
Agency	✓	✓	✓	✗	✓
Sale of Goods	✓	✗	✓	✗	✓
Consumer Credit	✓	✗	✓	✗	✓
Negotiable Instruments	✓	✗	✗	✗	✓
Insurance	✗	✗	✗	✗	✗
Carriage of Goods	✗	✗	✗	✗	✗
Lien and Bailment	✗	✗	✗	✗	✗
Bankruptcy	✗	✗	✗	✗	✗
Patents etc.	✗	✗	✗	✗	✓
Labour Law:-					
– In Outline	✓	✗	✗	✗	✗
– In Depth	✗	✗	✓	✗	✗

Table of Cases

xxiii

Table of Statutes

1 Methods of Learning

INTRODUCTION

1. ''The skills of learning are themselves learned, but seldom taught!'' In fact this chapter does not set out to teach a person how to learn. Learning is a very individual process and there is no set procedure which is best for everyone regardless of their personality. The contents of this chapter amount to a series of suggestions, some or all of which may be integrated into whatever method of learning a student has already developed. It therefore

    a. Outlines the various *resources* available to a student;

    b. Explains the essential *requirements* necessary to pass a law examination;

    c. Gives some advice on the approach to learning; and

    d. Suggests some methods of using the resources to achieve the requirements.

2. Resources

    a. Lectures and the lecturer.

    b. Lecture notes, both written and taped.

    c. Text books.

    d. Past questions.

    e. Suggested answers to past questions.

    f. Discussions with fellow students and arranged visits, for example, to the courts.

    g. This book.

3. Requirements. Three qualities are necessary to pass law examinations

    a. Understanding the principles of law,

    b. Learning the relevant legal facts, and

    c. Skill in applying the principles and facts to examination questions.

This chapter suggests the best available resources for attaining the requirements of understanding and learning. Chapter 2 deals with the third requirement of application.

4. Approach

    a. *Mental approach.* It is vital to neither underestimate nor overestimate your own ability or the standard of the examination. Both undue pessimism and overconfidence can be the cause of failure. The methods described below should minimise the risk of failure because of an unrealistic assessment of either personal ability or of what is expected by the examiner. The best approach is summed up in a Chinese proverb:-

> "That the birds of worry and care fly above your head,
>   This you cannot change,
>   But that they build nests in your hair,
>   This you can prevent."

b. *Physical approach*

   i.   *Timetabling.* When the course is nearing its conclusion, ie 6-8 weeks before the examination, it is generally advisable to prepare a revision timetable which allows roughly equal time for each paper that is to be taken. The timetable need not be complex, eg Mondays — Law; Tuesdays — Accounts; Wednesdays — Economics. A target number of hours should be set for each day, and if time is lost one day, it should be made good as soon as possible. Timetabling avoids time wasted deciding what to study each day, and it ensures that no subjects are neglected. The timetable may be changed occasionally if the revision time considered necessary for a particular subject changes as the examination draws near.

   ii. *When to work.* This is mainly a matter for personal preference. It is however generally accepted that chances of success are not improved by working so late at night that you get less sleep than you need. A more contentious question is whether or not you should work up to the "last minute" before an examination. The authors believe that you should do so. The evening before the examination is most usefully spent on revision rather than trying to relax watching television.

UNDERSTANDING

5. Law is Easy to Understand!

a.   Such a statement by an author or lecturer may appear to reveal a lack of sympathy with the problems faced by students. This is not the case. It is merely that our experience has shown that most people who fail law examinations do not do so because they are unable to understand the subject. Law is after all a human creation. It is relevant to everyday life, and the medium of expression is words. Subjects, such as mathematics, with abstract concepts and more indirect relevance are arguably more difficult to understand. All students can therefore approach law with confidence that they will not encounter unsurmountable difficulties in understanding the subject.

b.   If however you do encounter a principle, rule, or case that you do not understand you must never accept defeat. Read about it in several textbooks if necessary, ask your lecturer for a second explanation or discuss it with fellow students. Even if they have the same problem a discussion will almost certainly help. If a lack of understanding stems from not knowing the meaning of an individual word, then look it up in a dictionary. It seems an obvious solution, but it is rarely done.

6.   The Trap. Since law is often not difficult to understand, by its nature it lays a trap. A comparison with mathematics is again useful. If a mathematical concept is understood the answer can usually be worked out. In contrast the understanding of a legal rule does not, by itself, mean that the rule can be recalled in an examination. The trap is that understanding can be mistaken for an ability to recall, ie understanding can be mistaken for learning. They are related, but they are not synonymous. Understanding by itself will not enable you to succeed in a law examination, but it is the vital first step. Clearly you will not be able to learn or apply what you do not understand.

LEARNING

7.   Law is Difficult to Learn! Inadequate learning is the main reason why many students fail law examinations. It therefore follows that learning and memory are the main things which law examinations test. A good factual knowledge of the relevant law is therefore the basis for success. Acquiring this factual knowledge can at times be boring. It may involve repetition of well understood facts, and it is usually a solitary and rather unsociable activity. Every effort must therefore be made to minimise boredom and maximise interest and enthusiasm, whilst using the limited time as effectively as possible. The best two ways to do this are:-

    a.   Use as many different methods of study (ie resources) as possible, and

    b.   Constantly test yourself.

8.   The Use of Different Resources. If you have allocated a particular 2 hour period for the study of law, do not spend all of the time reading notes or a book, because your concentration will soon fade. It is much more productive to select a topic and then study it using 4 different methods. For example in 4 periods of ½ hour each:-

    a.   Read a textbook.

    b.   Read notes.

    c.   Test yourself on the notes, and

    d.   Write a timed answer (see below).

9.   Self-Testing. The main reason for self-testing is to avoid falling into the understanding/learning trap discussed above. If you test yourself you will find out whether or not you have learnt what you have understood. The actual method of self-testing will vary from person to person. For example:-

Select the 25 most important contract cases and write out their names and brief details. Cover the details with a sheet of paper and attempt a brief summary of the details on a separate sheet of paper. Compare your summary with the details and award yourself a mark out of 4 for each case and write this mark down. Repeat this for all the cases to arrive at a mark out of 100. Record this mark. A few days later repeat the procedure and see if your mark improves. Keep repeating the exercise until you achieve 80-90 out of 100. Even if you find the actual mechanics of learning rather tedious you may enjoy the challenge of improving on your previous mark.

10. The Usefulness of Individual Resources for Learning:-

a. *Textbooks*. It is not generally advisable to try to memorise facts from textbooks. Textbooks should only be referred to when a topic is not sufficiently understood, or when a break is needed from the other study methods. Conventional textbooks should not be used as a basic learning method.

b. *Lectures*. Lectures are primarily a time for the communication of the correct quantity of relevant information, and for increasing understanding by discussion and asking questions. The actual learning of this information will take place after the lecture.

c. *Lecture notes*. If lecture notes are "good", ie adequate in detail (not excessive) and without "gaps" they are probably the best resource for learning because they are personal to you. Read them regularly and if possible record them on cassette tapes. These cassettes should not be used as your basic learning method, but they will be useful if you feel that you need a short break from more traditional methods of study. When taking notes in lectures it is important

    i.   To be as neat as possible. — It is very difficult to learn from untidy notes.

    ii.   To space the notes out (rather like this book). — This assists the assimilation of facts.

    iii.   To only write on one side of each sheet of paper. The other side can then be used at a later date to expand on a difficult topic, or to write down a question on which a lecturer's comment is required.

d. *Past Questions*. It is essential to obtain past questions as soon as possible after the start of the course, so that the standard of the examination can be assessed at an early date, and a good mental approach adopted. There are two main ways in which these past questions can be used.

    i.   Writing *timed answers*. ie Without the assistance of notes, books, or suggested answers, write an answer in the same amount of time as would be available in the examination. Clearly it is preferable for a lecturer to assess your answer, and even if he has not set the question he should be prepared to mark it if requested to do so. At the times when lecturer assessment is not possible (eg shortly before the examination) it is nevertheless useful to write timed answers. You will then have to critically assess your own answer, perhaps awarding yourself a mark, or even re-writing the answer if you consider your attempt very poor.

ii.   Writing *model answers*. If a topic appears with regularity in the examination it is often worth writing an exam-length model answer, ie using all the available resources spend 1-2 hours writing the best possible answer that you can achieve. Lecturer assessment of such an answer would again be helpful. It is not suggested that you attempt to memorise every word of such an answer. It would however be possible to remember the structure of your answer, ie remember the number of paragraphs and general point which each paragraph deals with.

e.   *Suggested Answers*. These are helpful only if they are used responsibly. They will be of no help if you merely read the question, then glance at the answer and either:-

i.   Tell yourself (probably incorrectly) that you could write a similar answer in the examination, or,

ii.   Get depressed because you know that you cannot produce such an answer. Remember that these answers are not an indication of the standard that the examiner expects. Although they are ''examination-length'' each answer takes the author several hours to plan and write, – a much less competent answer would still achieve a good pass.

One must nevertheless aim high. Suggested answers help to achieve this aim by serving three purposes:-

i.   They illustrate the style, structure, and content necessary to answer the particular question. However they should not be regarded as the only possible correct answer. In most of the answers different cases will be just as acceptable as the cases quoted. Sometimes even a different conclusion is equally ''correct'', for example if a question asks your views on the value of trial by jury. The most important advice in connection with style and content is *write in your own words*. Never try to memorise word for word sentences or paragraphs from any suggested answer. Such attempts usually fail, even one wrong word can alter the meaning of a whole paragraph.

ii.   They are a valuable means of self-testing.

iii.   They provide an incentive to practice. *Practice* is just as important as self-assessment. You would not expect to pass your driving test if all you did was read about the brakes, steering wheel, and clutch in a book and then step into a car for the first time on the day of the test. Sitting a written examination is the same, practice is essential, and because suggested answers are a help in self-assessment they provide an incentive to practice, particularly at those times, eg shortly before the examination, when lecturer assessment is not possible.

f. ***This book.*** "Business Law" may be used either as a study manual or as a textbook.

i.   ***Use as a study manual.*** If you do not have a good and adequate set of notes then use this book as a study manual, making it your basic method of study. Read it and re-read it several times (excluding the chapters which are not part of your syllabus) as you would with notes and use the coursework questions and revision questions as part of your self-testing programme.

ii.   ***Use as a textbook.*** If you do have good notes you may nevertheless choose to use this book as a study manual, or you may decide to use it as a textbook or a casebook referring to the text or cases when the need arises for a source of legal facts, a description of the facts of a case, or clarification of a particular point of law. To facilitate use as a textbook a table of cases and an index is provided.

11. Mnemonics. A mnemonic is an aid to memory. Some students find that a code sentence or code word is a useful memory aid. For example a code word could be made from the seven requirements that Blackstone stated were necessary before a local custom could be accepted as law (see Chapter 4). His requirements, in the order stated in the text, are antiquity, continuity, peaceable enjoyment, obligatory force, certainty, consistency, and reasonableness. The initial letters are ACPOCCR. These could be rearranged to form CCC-POAR. If this code "word" could be remembered it should trigger-off recollection of the word which each letter represents, thus providing the basis for an answer.

12. Finally some advice is offered to those persons for whom something goes wrong. It may be illness, or accommodation problems, or perhaps just wasted time. — So if you have about 4 weeks left to the examination and you seem to be heading towards certain failure but have now decided to make a late attempt to pass, then your best chance of salvation is to predict from past questions which topics are most likely to be asked. These topics should then be learnt as thoroughly as possible. It is better to have a good knowledge of a few topics than a vague knowledge of everything. — You just have to hope that some of your predictions are correct.

2 Examination Technique

GENERAL POINTS

1. Introduction. This chapter contains both "golden rules", breach of which could mean the difference between success and failure, and useful hints which are comparatively less important, but which could nevertheless save a few vital marks. The points are dealt with in order of importance. The chapter assumes a 3 hour examination, giving a choice of 5 out of 8 questions.

2. Answer All Parts of All Questions. Never leave a question unanswered. The first 5 marks out of 20 are the easiest to obtain, the second 5 moderately easy, the third 5 more difficult and the final 5 almost impossible. Therefore if you find that you have only 10 minutes remaining in which to answer 2 questions it is best to spend 5 minutes on each question, writing down in note form as much of the relevant law as you can remember. In such a situation it will be necessary to use the time that you would normally spend reading through your answers for this purpose.

3. Never Leave the Examination Before the End. If you finish early check your answer paper carefully and re-read the question paper to make sure that you have not omitted part of any of the questions. Keep reading and re-reading the question paper and your answers until the last possible moment. You may find an error or remember a case or point of law which had previously eluded you. If you do then include it at the end of the answer book and cross-reference it with the remainder of your answer.

4. Time Allocation. The basic rule is that you should allocate equal time to each question, leaving 10-15 minutes at the end of the examination to read through your paper. If however you realise that you do not know enough to use all the time originally allocated to your fifth answer, whereas you could write in excess of your allocated time for your first answer, then deduct about 5 minutes from answer 5 and add it to answer 1.

5. The First Five Minutes. As you read the examination paper for the first time underline what appear to be the key words in each question. Also write down in the margin the names of any cases, statutes or mnemonics which may be relevant. This gives you two chances of recalling these details, once at the start and again as you write each answer.

6. Choice of Questions

a. Read through the whole paper "ticking" questions which you can definitely answer and "crossing" those which you cannot answer. If this does not produce exactly the correct amount of ticks, do not spend any further time on question choice at present — start your answers. — It will be easier later in the examination to delete excess ticks, or to choose your best question out of the remaining 4 than to choose your fifth best out of 8 at the start.

b.   General essay questions for example on common law and equity or precedent result in a narrower range of marks than problem questions, ie there will be less students falling in the 0-5 and 15-20 brackets. Therefore if you are aiming for a very high mark, it is advisable to choose problem questions, although if you miss the point of the problem the result will be very serious.

7.   Order of Answering Questions. Start with the question which you are best able to answer. It is definitely very poor technique to save your best questions to the end, because if you start with your "worst" question and make an error in timing, you may find that you have inadequate time to answer the questions on which your knowledge is greatest.

STYLE AND STRUCTURE

8.   Starting With a Conclusion. It is a bad and common error to start with a conclusion. Answers often commence, for example, "John will succeed in his negligence claim because . . .". This is a conclusion and it should therefore come at the end. If it comes at the start, and is wrong, the rest of the answer will be spent in an attempt to justify an incorrect conclusion, which often produces an answer where only one side of the argument is presented. The answer should be structured as follows:-

a.   State the relevant principles of law illustrating them where applicable with decided cases. If there are two sides to a problem both of them must be discussed, and not merely the argument which supports the conclusion which will eventually be reached. The names of the characters of the problem need not necessarily be mentioned at this stage.

b.   Apply the stated principles to the facts of the problem.

c.   Give your conclusion. It does not have to be 100% certain. It is acceptable to say ". . . therefore John will probably succeed" if there is some reasonable doubt as to his chances. You must however commit yourself one way or the other, do not finish by stating that "John has a 50/50 chance of success."

9.   Contradictory Conclusions. If you place your conclusion at the end this will help to avoid the danger of self-contradiction. If however on reading through your answer you find contradictory statements or conclusions, you must delete one of them. If you do not do this you will get the worst of both worlds rather than the best, ie even if one is correct it will not score any marks.

10. Repeating the Question. This is a very common fault, it never scores any marks, it wastes time, and it spoils the structure of the answer.

8

11. The Introduction. Often an answer on offer will start "A contract is a legally binding agreement between persons. In order to make a contract there must be an offer, an acceptance of that offer, consideration and an intention to create legal relations. An offer is . . ." The whole of this quotation, except the last three words although correct, is not sufficiently relevant to earn any marks. An introduction (if any) should be very brief, you should get to the point of the question as directly as possible. If you are stuck then start with the phrase "The relevant law is as follows . . ."

12. Format. Generally answers should be structured in un-numbered paragraphs. Occasionally it may be suitable to make several points under headings (a) (b) (c) etc in one particular paragraph. Even so this should not be the basic style of the answer. If however you have very little time remaining for a question it is better to write as many relevant points as possible in note form, rather than one or two paragraphs in perfect English.

13. Balance. Answers often tend towards one of two extremes. An answer may contain a list of principles of law, without any mention of cases, or it may consist of a number of case descriptions apparently unconnected by legal principles. Both these extremes are very poor. An answer should be well-balanced, containing both statements of principles of law, and case law illustrations of those principles.

14. Meaning. Many students fail to express what they wish to say. An example from a recent paper stated "Performance of a contract is only precise and exact". The examiner will probably realise that the student does in fact know the basic rule regarding performance of a contract. However the sentence, in its present form is meaningless, and probably would not obtain any marks. The sentence should of course read "Performance of a contract must be precise and exact".

It is not possible to become an expert at expressing your desired meaning merely by effort or determination, it is a very slow process. All you can do is (i) be as careful as possible, (ii) do not try to write too fast, and (iii) read through what you have written.

CONTENT

15. Names, Dates, and Facts of Cases. − Perhaps the most frequent question a law lecturer is asked is the importance of including names, dates, and facts of cases in an answer.

a. Facts without names. − If you cannot remember the name of a case, but you can recall the facts, then include the facts in your answer, but introduce them in some other way, eg "In a recent case . . .". It is far better to do this than to omit the case.

b. Names without facts. − Where a principle of law is derived from a case it is acceptable for the case name alone to follow the principle. Some case names must however be supported by facts otherwise the answer will not be "balanced".

9

c. Dates. – Dates are comparatively less important than names. It is not worth specifically learning dates, but if you do remember the date then include it in the answer.

d. Choice of cases. – Sometimes a number of cases are equally good illustrations of a legal principle. In this situation choose the case which can be described most concisely.

16. Jargon. Avoid the use of unnecessary "jargon". Do not for example start your final paragraph "After taking all the relevant law into consideration it is submitted that . . .". The simple "In conclusion . . ." is far better.

17. Latin Phrases. If you wish to say for example "X will make a quantum meruit claim against Y" you cannot assume that the examiner knows that you know what "quantum meruit" means. You should therefore add, perhaps in brackets – "a payment for work done proportionate to the contract price". The examiner then knows that you have remembered the meaning of the words as well as the words themselves.

18. Miscellaneous Points

a. Never use slang, or attempt to introduce humour into your answer. For example "X has not got a snowflakes chance in hell of success" would not impress the examiner.

b. Avoid the use of "I", "we", and "us". When asked in a question to "Advise X" do not write "You will fail in your claim", write "X will fail in his claim".

c. Never use red ink, even to underline cases. This causes confusion when two or more examiners read the script.

d. If you wish to cross-out anything that you have written use a single line drawn with a ruler. If you wish to reinstate words which you have previously crossed-out then draw a line of dots under the words deleted, and write "stet" in the margin. This means "let it stand".

e. Finally there is no need to emphasise words by underlining them or writing them in capitals. It is acceptable to emphasise case names or statutes in this way but not general words.

CONCLUSION

19. The final advice regarding the examination is "don't panic". This is of course easy advice to give, but it can be very difficult to put into practice. Perhaps the best antidote to possible panic is to consider the consequences of failure. – Failure of an examination does not necessarily mean that you follow an inferior path through life. It may mean that you follow a different path, but it is impossible to say, at the time of the examination, whether this different path will ultimately be for the better or the worse.

PART I   THE ENGLISH LEGAL SYSTEM

3 Introduction

THE NATURE OF LAW

1. Definition

a. The law of a particular state is the body of rules designed to regulate human conduct within that state. Broadly speaking there are three types of rule:-

    i. Rules which forbid certain types of behaviour under threat of penalty.

    ii. Rules which require people to compensate others whom they injure in certain ways.

    iii. Rules which specify what must be done to order certain types of human activity, e.g. to form a company, to marry, or to make a will.

b. Although it is inevitable that the courts will make some rules, Parliament is the sovereign body. It can therefore impose new rules or abolish any existing rules. The basic role of the courts is to interpret these rules, decide whether they have been broken and pass sentence or make an award of compensation.

2. Law and Morality

a. The law which is enforced by the courts must be distinguished from what is sometimes referred to as "natural" or "moral" law. In many cases the rules of law and morality clearly coincide. For example if a person murders another this offends both law and morality. The state will therefore punish the offender.

b. Sometimes however the rules of law and morality are not the same. For example homosexual behaviour in private between consenting adults is not illegal although many people would regard it as a breach of moral law.

c. The term "natural law" is sometimes used to refer to rules which although not enacted are accepted as part of the legal system. For example the right of both sides to be heard (or to remain silent), and the principle that an accused person is innocent until proven guilty.

3. Law and Justice.
The basic aim of law is the attainment of justice in society. However in some situations the degree of justice hoped for is not achieved. For example:-

a. Compensation for injuries usually depends on proving that someone else is at fault. If a person is injured due to his own fault, or in a "pure" accident where no-one is at fault, he will not receive compensation unless he is insured. This inequality is a result of the rules on negligence liability.

13

b. The rules regarding mistake and misrepresentation in the formation of a contract often operate to determine which of two innocent parties must bear all of the loss. The loss is not divided equally, for example **LEWIS v AVERAY (1971)** (Chapter 19.2).

c. Sentencing policies applied by magistrates in different areas often result in substantially different sentences for very similar offences.

4. Conclusion

a. It would therefore be an oversimplification to say that most people obey the law because it is just, or because it coincides with their view of which is morally correct. Law is also closely related to force and authority and these relationships would have to be examined in order to properly explain the intrinsic nature of law, and to find out why most people obey the law. Such analysis is beyond the scope of this book.

b. An alternative to explaining law by reference to its intrinsic nature is to explain it by reference to what it does. In the most general terms law classifies human behaviour. At one end of the classification there exists the infinite variety of behaviour and the end result is a clear decision between only two alternatives − "right" and "wrong", ie in criminal cases a verdict of "guilty" or "not guilty" and in civil cases a finding for the plaintiff or a finding for the defendant. Law is therefore the most ambitious and complex classification system devised by man.

THE CHARACTERISTICS OF ENGLISH LAW

5. There are several features which distinguish the English Legal System from foreign systems:-

a. *Continuity*. English law has developed since 1066 without any major changes in the system. Two factors have led to this:-

    i. England has not been conquered since 1066, and

    ii. Acts of Parliament and case law do not become inoperative merely due to old age. For example the *TREASON ACT 1351* was considered in **JOYCE v D.P.P. (1946)**.

b. *Absence of codification*. In some countries most of the law has been reduced to written codes which contain the whole of the law on a particular subject. Generally this is not so in England.

c. *The system of precedent*. This means that a judge is bound to apply rules of law formulated in earlier cases provided the facts of the case before him are sufficiently similar, and the earlier case was heard in a court of superior, or (subject to exceptions) equal status.

d. *The judiciary*. English judges are independent of both Parliament and the Civil Service. This is evident from the fact that they often give judgement against The Crown or a Government Department. In addition a judge will be immune from liability provided he acts honestly in the belief that he is within his jurisdiction. The judiciary is important because the judges of the superior courts have a great effect on development of the law. They do not merely apply statutory rules, they *make* law when interpreting statutes and by developing the doctrine of judicial precedent.

e. *Common law and equity.* English law is based on two complementary systems of law known as common law and equity. Common law was the first system to develop. Its rules were rigid and sometimes harsh. Equity evolved to supplement the common law with more flexible rules based on principles of good conscience and equality.

f. *The accusatorial procedure.* In both civil and criminal cases the court remains neutral and hears the arguments presented by each side. In countries where an inquisitorial procedure is used the court plays a more active part, itself questioning the witnesses.

CIVIL AND CRIMINAL LAW

6. There are many ways to classify law, the most fundamental distinction being that drawn between criminal and civil law.

7. Criminal Law

a. A crime is regarded as a wrong done to the State. Prosecutions are usually commenced by the State, although they may be brought by a private citizen. If the prosecution is successful the accused person (the defendant) is liable to punishment. Some crimes, for example rape, have specific victims. Others, for example treason or speeding, can be committed without causing loss to any particular person. If there is a victim he will not usually have a say in whether or not a prosecution is brought, nor will he benefit from a conviction, since fines are payable to the State.

b. Criminal and civil hearings take place in different courts with different rules of procedure. There is also a different standard of proof. In a criminal trial the prosecution must prove the accused's guilt *beyond reasonable doubt*. In a civil case the plaintiff must prove his case on the *balance of probabilities*.

8. Civil Law. Civil actions may be commenced by any person who seeks compensation for a loss which he has suffered. If the plaintiff is successful he will usually be awarded damages. The damages must be paid by the defendant. Their purpose is to compensate the plaintiff for his loss rather than to punish the defendant. There are many categories of civil law, for example:-

a. *Contract.* This determines whether promises made by persons are enforceable.

15

b. ***Tort.*** A tort is defined as the breach of a general duty imposed by law, for example the duty not to be negligent, and the duty not to trespass on another person's property.

c. ***Property law.*** This includes the law relating to freehold and leasehold land, and the ownership and possession of goods.

d. ***Company law.*** There is a need to regulate the relationship that a company has with its directors, shareholders, creditors, and employees.

e. ***Commercial law.*** This term covers contractual matters relating to business transactions, for example the law relating to sale of goods, consumer credit and cheques.

f. ***Labour law.*** This also involves contractual relationships, in this case between employer and employee. The term also includes redundancy, unfair dismissal and health and safety at work.

g. ***Family law.*** Marriage, divorce, nullity, guardianship and legitimacy are within the scope of family law.

9. Crime or Civil Wrong?

a. The distinction between a crime and a civil wrong is not found in the nature of the act itself, but in the legal consequences that follow it. Thus if a taxi driver crashes he may commit:-

    i. A breach of contract, ie failure to deliver the passenger to his destination.

    ii. A tort, ie negligence if he causes damage to any person or property.

    iii. A crime, for example dangerous driving.

b. In some situations the facts will therefore indicate both a criminal offence and a possible civil action. In such cases the victim will not be able to have both actions heard in the same court. He will have to start a civil action separate from any prosecution brought by the State. However *S.11. CIVIL EVIDENCE ACT 1968* provides that in any civil proceedings the fact that a person has been convicted of an offence shall be admissible to prove that he committed that offence. The effect is to raise a presumption that he committed the offence, unless the contrary is proved.

THE TITLE OF CASES

10. Criminal Cases

a. Prosecutions involving the more serious criminal offences, known as indictable offences, are brought in the name of The Queen. The case will then be known as, for example, "R v Jones", R being short for either Regina or Rex.

b.   Prosecutions for less serious offences, known as summary offences, are usually commenced in the name of the actual prosecutor (normally a police officer), for example "Evans v Jones".

c.   Where the offence is particularly serious or complex, for example murder or perjury, the Director of Public Prosecutions may investigate and prosecute. In addition some statutes require actions to be brought by the DPP, for example for election offences under the *REPRESENTATION OF THE PEOPLE ACT 1949.*

11.   Civil Cases

a.   The parties' names are used, the plaintiff's name being placed first, for example "Rylands v Fletcher". This is however traditionally pronounced "Rylands and Fletcher".

b.   Sometimes there will not be a plaintiff and a defendant, for example if an application has been made to the court to interpret Brown's Will the case would be known as "Re Brown".

12.   Appeal Cases. When a party appeals he is called the appellant, and the other party is the respondent. Since the appellant's name is always placed first, when a defendant appeals the name of the case will be reversed, thus Peek v Derry in the High Court, and on appeal, became Derry v Peek in the House of Lords.

4 The Main Sources of English Law

THE MEANING OF "SOURCES OF LAW"

1. The previous chapter classified the law into civil and criminal by reference to the subject matter of the dispute and the legal consequences which result from the dispute. Law may also be classified by reference to its source, ie the means by which the law is brought into existence. There are four *legal sources* of law, namely custom, judicial precedent, legislation, and European law.

2. Sometimes other meanings are attributed to the term "sources of law":-

a. The *literary source* describes where the law is physically found, ie in law reports and statutes.

b. The *formal source* describes the authority which gives force to the rules of law, ie the State.

c. The *historical sources* are generally regarded as common law and equity, although the term is sometimes used to refer to the reasons behind the creation of the law, for example a report by the Law Commission.

3. This chapter concentrates on the four legal sources, but since methods of classification of law are only matters of convenience, there is an inevitable overlap between these legal sources, civil and criminal law, and common law and equity.

CUSTOM

4. Uses of the Word "Custom". The word "custom" may be used in several different senses. In one sense it is the main source of English Law since it is the original source of common law. It would however be wrong to equate "common law" and "custom" today since most common law rules owe their origins to judicial decisions rather than ancient custom. In its second sense "custom" describes a conventional trade usage. Custom in this sense is not a source of law, but a means by which terms are implied into contracts.

5. Local Custom. The third use of custom is to describe rules of law which apply only in a particular area for example a county or parish. In this sense custom is a distinct source of law. In addition to the characteristic of restriction to a particular locality it must be an exception to the common law. For example under the custom of "Gavelkind", which operated in Kent, an intestate's property passed to his sons in equal shares, whereas over most of the country it would all pass to the eldest son. Gavelkind was abolished in 1925. A valid local custom may be limited to a class of persons within a locality such as fishermen, but it cannot apply to a class of persons throughout the country, since then it would not be an exception to common law, but a part of it.

6. Proof of Existence of a Local Custom. Local custom also differs from common law in that if an alleged custom is to be incorporated into the law it must be proved to exist in Court. It is then said to be "judicially noticed" and will be enforced by other courts. Thus a person who alleges the existence of a custom must prove its existence by satisfying the following tests laid down by Blackstone in 1765:-

a. *Antiquity.* Local custom must have existed since "time immemorial". This has been fixed by statute at 1189, the first year of the reign of Richard I. In practice proof back to 1189 is never possible, so the Court will accept proof of existence within living memory. If this is shown the person denying the existence of the custom must prove that it could not have existed in 1189.

In **SIMPSON v WELLS (1872)** Simpson, who had been charged with obstructing a public foot-way, by setting up a refreshment stall, alleged that he had a customary right to do so deriving from "statute sessions" (ancient fairs held for the purpose of hiring servants). It was shown that statute sessions were first authorised in the 14th century, so the right could not have existed in 1189.

b. *Continuity.* The *right* to exercise the custom must not have been interrupted. This does not mean that the custom itself must have been continuously exercised.

In **MERCER v DENNE (1905)** D owned a section of beach and wished to build on it. P, a fisherman, claimed a customary right to dry his nets on the beach and asked for an injunction to prevent the building. D's defence was that the custom was only exercised occasionally, and that before 1799 the beach ground was below the high water mark, and until recent times was unsuitable for use for drying nets.

It was held that the custom was valid. Its existence throughout living memory was proved, and the fluctuations in use were due to variations in wind and tide. However the fisherman had always claimed the right to use such ground as was available, and so the custom extended to the additional ground now available. (Throughout the text P = Plaintiff, D = Defendant).

c. *Peaceable enjoyment.* A custom can only exist by common consent. It must not have been exercised by the use of force, secrecy, or permission (Nec per vim, nec clam, nec precario).

d. *Obligatory force.* Where a custom imposes a specific duty that duty must be compulsory, not voluntary. Blackstone said:-

"a custom that all the inhabitants shall be rated towards the maintenance of a bridge will be good, but a custom that every man is to contribute thereto at his own pleasure is idle and absurd, and indeed no custom at all".

19

e. ***Certainty***. An alleged custom allowing tenants to take away turf "in such quantity as occasion may require" was held void for uncertainty. **(WILSON v WILLES (1806))**.

f. ***Consistency***. Customs are by their nature inconsistent with common law, but they cannot, in a defined locality, be inconsistent with one another.

g. ***Reasonableness***. A custom must be reasonable.

In **DAY v SAVADGE (1614)** a custom which allowed an Officer of the City of London Corporation to certify what customs were valid in matters in which the Corporation was interested was held to be invalid because it was unreasonable.

A custom cannot be reasonable if it conflicts with a fundamental principle of common law.

In **WOLSTANTON v NEWCASTLE-UNDER-LYME CORPORATION (1940)** the alleged custom allowed the landlord to undermine and remove minerals from his tenant's land without paying compensation for buildings damaged as a result. This was held to be unreasonable.

7. In recent years the tendency has been to standardise law by statute. This has led to the decline of custom as a source of law so that it is now almost extinct. The types of customary rights that do still exist are, for example, rights of way and rights to indulge in sports or pastimes on a village green.

JUDICIAL PRECEDENT

8. The History of Judicial Precedent

a. The doctrine of binding precedent did not become firmly established until the second half of the 19th century. In the common law courts the former practice was to apply the declaratory theory of common law, ie the law was contained in the customs of the land, and judges merely declared what it was. Thus although judges regarded precedents as persuasive they did not consider them to be binding. In **FISHER v PRINCE (1762)**, Lord Mansfield said:

"the reason and spirit of cases make law, not the letter of particular precedents."

b. As time passed judges paid more and more attention to previous decisions and in **MIREHOUSE v RENNELL (1833)**, Baron Parke said that notice must be taken of precedents. The court could not

"reject them and abandon all analogy to them".

c. In the Court of Chancery there was no declaratory theory, the judges merely tried to do justice in each individual case. This system lacked certainty and criticism was strong. From about 1700 the court began to pay increasingly greater respect to its previous decisions.

d.   The modern doctrine of binding precedent is about 120 years old. Its present form is due to two factors. Firstly in 1865 a Council was established by The Inns of Court and The Law Society to publish under professional control the decisions of the superior courts. Prior to this private reports were published, some were good, others were unreliable, and many cases were not reported at all. Secondly, the *JUDICATURE ACTS 1873-1875* established a clear court hierarchy. The doctrine of precedent depends for its operation on the fact that all courts stand in a definite relationship to one another.

9.   An Outline of the Doctrine. Despite the inevitable tendency of judges to create law, binding precedent is *based* on the view that it is not the function of a judge to make law, but to decide cases in accordance with existing rules. Two requirements must be met if a precedent is to be binding:-

a.   It must be a *ratio decidendi* statement, and

b.   The court must have a superior, or in some cases equal status to the court considering the statement at a later date.

If these requirements are met, and the material facts as found are the same the court is bound to apply the rule of law stated in the earlier judgement.

10.   The Ratio Decidendi

a.   Judgements contain:-

i.   *Findings of fact*, both direct and inferential. An inferential finding of fact is the deduction drawn by the judge from the direct, or perceptible facts. For example from the direct facts of the speed of a vehicle, the road and weather conditions, and the length of skid-marks, the judge may infer negligence. Negligence is an inferential finding of fact. Findings of fact are not binding. Thus even where the direct facts appear to be the same as those of an earlier case the judge need not draw the same inference as that drawn in the earlier case.

ii.   *Statements of law*. The judge will state the principles of law applicable to the case. Statements of law applied to the legal problems raised by the facts as found upon which the decision is based are known as *"ratio decidendi"* statements. Other statements, not based on the facts as found, or which do not provide the basis of the decision, are known as *"obiter dicta"* statements. For the purpose of precedent the ratio decidendi, which literally means "reason for deciding", is the vital element which binds future judges.

iii.   *The decision*. From the point of view of the parties this is the vital element since it determines their rights and liabilities in relation to the action, and prevents them from re-opening the dispute.

b.   Sometimes it is difficult to ascertain the ratio decidendi of a case. For example:-

i.   A statement intended by the judge to be the ratio is not accepted by a subsequent court as the ratio, however his other reasons are accepted.

ii.   In the Court of Appeal or House of Lords the different members of the court may reach the same decision, but for different reasons.

iii.   A judge may intend two rationes, one of which may be treated by a later judge as an obiter dicta statement because it was not essential to the decision.

11.   The Hierarchy of the Courts. The doctrine of precedent depends for its operation on the fact that each court stands in a definite position in relation to every other court.

a.   *The European Court.* Its decisions bind all British courts, but not its own future decisions.

b.   *The House of Lords.* Its decisions are binding on all English courts, however since 1966, following a statement by Lord Gardiner L.C. the House need not follow its own previous decisions.

c.   *The Court of Appeal (Civil Division).* In **YOUNG v BRISTOL AEROPLANE CO. (1944)** it was held that the court is bound by its own previous decisions unless

i.   There are two previous conflicting Court of Appeal decisions, in which case it may choose which to follow.

ii.   The previous decision conflicts with a later House of Lords judgement, or

iii.   The previous decision was given per incuriam. "Per incuriam" means through lack of care because some relevant statute or precedent was not brought before the court.

d.   *The Court of Appeal (Criminal Division).* The rules are the same as the Civil Division, except that the court need not follow its own previous decisions where this would cause injustice to the appellant. The reason is that where human freedom is at stake the need for justice exceeds the desire for certainty. − **R v GOULD (1968)**.

e.   *The High Court (Divisional Courts).* The High Court is bound by its own previous decisions subject to the rule in Young's Case and, in criminal cases, R v Gould.

f.   *The High Court (Judges at First Instance).* Their decisions are not binding on other High Court judges, but are of persuasive authority.

g.   *Inferior Courts.* Magistrates courts, county courts, and other inferior tribunals are not bound by their own previous decisions since they are less authoritative and are rarely reported.

12.   Persuasive Precedents. These are statements which a later court will respect, but need not follow. There are several kinds of persuasive precedent:-

a. *Obiter Dicta.* There are two types of obiter dicta:-

    i.   A statement based upon facts which were not found to exist.

    In **RONDEL v WORSLEY (1969)** the House of Lords stated an opinion that a barrister might be held liable in negligence when not acting as an advocate, and that a solicitor when acting as an advocate might be immune from action. Since the case actually concerned the liability of a barrister when acting as an advocate these opinions were obiter dicta.

    ii.   A statement which although based on the facts as found, does not form the basis of the decision, for example a dissenting (minority) judgement.

b. Ratio decidendi of inferior courts.

c. Ratio decidendi of Scottish, Commonwealth, or foreign courts, and statements of the Judicial Committee of the Privy Council.

13. Overruling and Reversing

a. Precedents can be overruled either by statute or by a superior court. Judges are usually reluctant to overrule precedents because this reduces the element of certainty in the law.

b. Overruling must be distinguished from reversing a decision. A decision is reversed when it is altered on appeal. A decision is overruled when a judge in a different case states that the earlier case was wrongly decided.

14. Distinguishing, Reconciling and Disapproving

a. A case is distinguished when the judge states that the material facts are sufficiently different to apply different rules of law.

b. Cases are reconciled when the judge finds that the material facts of both cases are so similar that he can apply the same rules of law.

c. A case is disapproved when a judge, without overruling an earlier case, gives his opinion that it was wrongly decided.

15. Advantages and Disadvantages of Precedent

a. *Advantages*

    i.   *Certainty.* It provides a degree of uniformity upon which individuals can rely. Uniformity is essential if justice is to be achieved. The advantage of certainty by itself outweighs the several disadvantages of precedent.

    ii.   *Development.* New rules can be established or old ones adapted to meet new circumstances and the changing needs of society.

    iii.   *Detail.* No code of law could provide the detail found in English case law.

iv.   *Practicality.* The rules are laid down in the course of dealing with cases, and do not attempt to deal with future hypothetical circumstances.

v.   *Flexibility.* A general ratio decidendi may be extended to a variety of factual situations. For example the "neighbour test" formulated in **DONOGHUE v STEVENSON (1932)** determines whether a duty not to be negligent is owed to a particular person whatever the circumstances of the case.

b.   *Disadvantages*

i.   *Rigidity.* Precedent is rigid in the sense that once a rule has been laid down it is binding even if it is thought to be wrong.

ii.   *Danger of illogicality.* This arises from the rigidity of the system. Judges who do not wish to follow a particular decision may be tempted to draw very fine distinctions in order to avoid following the rule, thus introducing an element of artificiality into the law.

iii.   *Bulk and complexity.* There is so much law that no-one can learn all of it. Even an experienced lawyer may overlook some important rule in any given case.

iv.   *Slowness of growth.* The system depends on litigation for rules to emerge. As litigation tends to be slow and expensive the body of case law cannot grow quickly enough to meet modern demands.

v.   *Isolating the ratio decidendi.* Where it is difficult to find the ratio decidendi of a case this detracts from the element of certainty.

16.   The Importance of Precedent Today

a.   It may appear that since the volume of statute law is increasing rapidly as government intervention in such areas as employment and consumer affairs increases, then the relative importance of case law much be decreasing. In fact the reverse is true, since as more Acts are passed, judges will more often be called upon to create new precedents when interpreting this new law. In addition some Acts deliberately and unavoidably vest a wide discretion in the judiciary. For example, the *UNFAIR CONTRACT TERMS ACT 1977* has the underlying theme that an exemption clause must be reasonable if it is to be valid, but it is, of course, left to the judge to decide what is reasonable in each particular case.

b.   In recent years the judges jurisdiction over common law and equity has given rise to some notable developments. For example Lord Denning's judgement in **CENTRAL LONDON PROPERTY TRUST v HIGH TREES HOUSE (1947)** has now been generally accepted as having created a new principle of equity, ie equitable estoppel. More recently in **SHAW v DPP (1962)** the House of Lords found Shaw guilty of "conspiracy to corrupt public morals," an offence previously unknown to the criminal law. Thirdly in **MILIANGOS v GEORGE FRANK TEXTILES (1976)** the House of Lords effected a major reform by deciding that courts could, in future, express their judgements in foreign currency.

c.   The traditional view that judges merely apply the law is useful to emphasise the fundamental feature of the constitution, namely the Sovereignty of Parliament, but it does not reflect reality, especially when a judge is faced with a "first impression" case where there is no existing precedent and no provision in an Act of Parliament. In such cases the judge must, of necessity create new law. Precedent is therefore a very important source of law, the other main source being legislation.

LEGISLATION

17. Introduction

a.   The most important source of law at the present day is legislation. Statutes are passed by Parliament which is the supreme law making body in the United Kingdom. In theory, at least, there is nothing which Parliament cannot do by statute. In practice statutes often amend, and sometimes abolish, established rules of common law or equity, overrule the effects of decisions of the courts, or make entirely new law on matters which previously have not been the subject of legislation.

b.   There are two types of legislation, parliamentary and delegated legislation. The functions of Acts of Parliament are as follows:-

    i.   *Law reform.* Relatively few statutes are concerned with changing substantive rules of law. Where such a change does take place it often follows from an unpopular decision of the House of Lords, or is based on a recommendation of the Law Commission.

    ii.   *Consolidation.* Where existing legislation is gathered into one Act this is known as consolidation.

    iii.   *Codification.* This takes place when all the law on a topic (both case law and statute law) is included in one Act.

    iv.   *Revenue collection.* The annual Finance Acts which implement the Budget proposals are the main revenue collection statutes.

    v.   *Special legislation.* These Acts are concerned with the day to day running of society, for example the *RENT ACT 1974.*

c.   An Act will come into force on the day on which it receives the Royal Assent, unless some other date is specified in the Act itself. It will cease to have effect only when it is repealed by another Act. Whilst in force an Act is presumed to be operative throughout the United Kingdom and nowhere else, unless the Act states otherwise.

18. The Need for Statutory Interpretation. Where the words of a statute are absolutely clear the need for statutory interpretation will not arise, because the persons affected by the statute will have no difficulty in conducting their affairs according to the statute. However where there is ambiguity or uncertainty interpretation is necessary.

a. *Ambiguity* is caused by an error in drafting whereby the words used are capable of two or more literal meanings.

b. *Uncertainty* arises when the words of a statute are intended to apply to various factual situations and the courts have to decide whether the case before them falls within the factual situations envisaged by the Act. Uncertainty is far more common than ambiguity.

19. Judicial Approaches to Interpretation. There are three recognised judicial approaches to statutory interpretation. The approach chosen will depend on the particular judge, so it is not possible to know in advance which will be used. They are known as ''rules'' although they are not rules in the accepted sense of the word.

a. *The literal rule.* This is the basic rule of interpretation. It states that the words used must be given their literal or usual meaning even if the result appears to be contrary to the intention of Parliament.

In **FISHER v BELL (1961)** the *RESTRICTION OF OFFENSIVE WEAPONS ACT 1959* made it an offence to *''offer for sale''* certain weapons including ''flick knives''. A shopkeeper who displayed these knives in his window was found not guilty of the offence, since although he had displayed the goods, accepted buyers' offers, and sold the goods he had not offered them for sale, because goods on display are not an offer to sell, they are an invitation to treat. (See Chapter 15).

b. *The golden rule.* This states that the literal must be followed unless to do so produces an absurd result. Where a statute permits two or more literal meanings application of the golden rule is not inconsistnt with the literal rule since the literal rule cannot be applied in such cases. However in rare cases a judge will apply the golden rule to a statute which has only one literal meaning:-

In **RE SIGSWORTH (1935)** the golden rule was applied to prevent a murderer from inheriting on the intestacy of his victim although he was, as her son, her only heir on a literal interpretation of the *ADMINISTRATION OF ESTATES ACT 1925*.

The golden rule may be criticised as being subjective, since a judge who decides that a literal interpretation is absurd, and therefore contrary to the intention of Parliament, must be ascertaining the intention of Parliament from a source other than the statute itself. This is strictly speaking beyond his function.

c. *The mischief rule.* Where an Act is passed to remedy a mischief the court must adopt the interpretation which will have the effect of remedying the mischief in question. For example the *AFFILIATION PROCEEDINGS ACT 1957* refers to a ''single woman''. This has been interpreted to include not only unmarried women, but any woman with no husband to support her, because the mischief which the Act was passed to remedy was the possibility of a woman having an illegitimate child with no means of supporting it.

20. Further Rules of Interpretation

a.   The statute must be read as a whole, and each section must be read in the light of every other section, especially an interpretation section.

b.   The Eiusdem Generis Rule. Where general words follow two or more particular words they must be confined to a meaning of the same kind (eiusdem generis) as the particular words. For example ''cats, dogs and other animals'' means other domestic animals.

c.   Where a criminal statute is uncertain or ambiguous it is generally interpreted in favour of the individual.

In **R v HALLAM (1957)** it was held that the offence of ''knowingly possessing an explosive'' required the accused to know, not only that he possessed the substance, but also that it was explosive.

Contrast **Re ATTORNEY-GENERAL'S REFERENCE (No. 1 of 1988)** where the accused received unsolicited information from an employee of a firm of merchant bankers, to the effect that there was to be a merger between two companies. He knew that if this information were generally known it would affect the price of the shares. He also knew that it was confidential information, however within ten minutes he had instructed his stockbroker to purchase shares in one of the companies. The merger was announced the following day and a few weeks later the accused sold the 6,000 shares that he had purchased at a profit of £3,000. He was accused under *S.1 COMPANY SECURITIES (INSIDER DEALING) ACT 1985* which, among other things, required him to ''knowingly obtain'' price sensitive information. He was originally acquitted on the basis that ''obtaining'' meant actively obtaining the information, rather than passively obtaining it. This interpretation was rejected by both the Court of Appeal and the House of Lords on the grounds that the approach would water down the effect of the legislation and also require the courts to make almost imperceptible factual distinctions. The House of Lords recognised the importance of the general rule that in a penal statute the words would normally be given their narrower meaner, but felt that this was not appropriate in the present case.

d.   Where a statute does not make an alteration of the law absolutely clear it will be presumed that Parliament did not intend to alter the law. For example prior to 1898 a wife was not permitted to give evidence against her husband. The *CRIMINAL EVIDENCE ACT 1898* made her competent to do so, but in the absence of express provision, it was held in **LEACH v R (1912)** that she could not be compelled to give evidence against her husband.

21. Statutory Interpretation and Judicial Precedent. Precedent and legislation are sometimes mistakenly regarded as separate sources of law. This is not the case because once a superior court in the hierarchy has interpreted the words of an Act an inferior court is bound to adopt that interpretation if faced with the same words in the same Act. Thus statutory interpretation forms a link between the sources of precedent and legislation.

22. Delegated Legislation

a. Delegated legislation comes into being when Parliament confers on persons or bodies, particularly Ministers of the Crown in charge of Government Departments, power to make regulations for specified purposes. Such regulations have the same legal force as the Act under which they are made.

b. *Types of delegated legislation*

    i. *Orders in council.* This is the highest form of delegated legislation, many Acts of Parliament being brought into operation in this way, the power to make the Order being contained in the Act. In theory an Order in Council is an order of the Privy Council, but in fact an Order in Council is usually made by the Government and merely approved by the Privy Council. This has the effect of conferring wide legislative power on government departments.

    ii. *Rules and regulations.* A statute may authorise a minister or a government department to make a wide variety of rules and regulations. These rules, and Orders in Council are collectively known as statutory instruments.

    iii. *By-Laws.* These are rules made by local authorities. Their operation is restricted to the locality to which they apply.

c. *Advantages of delegated legislation*

    i. It saves the time of Parliament, allowing Parliament to concentrate on discussing matters of general policy.

    ii. It can be brought into existence swiftly, enabling ministers to deal with urgent situations, such as a strike in an essential industry.

    iii. It enables experts to deal with local or technical matters.

    iv. It provides flexibility, in that regulations can be added to or modified from time to time without the necessity for a new Act of Parliament.

d. *Disadvantages of delegated legislation*

    i. Law making is taken out of the direct control of elected representatives and is placed in the hands of employees of government departments. This is in theory less democratic.

    ii. Parliament does not have enough time to effectively supervise delegated legislation or discuss the merits of the rules being created.

    iii. A vast amount of law is created, statutory instruments outnumbering by far the amount of Acts passed each year.

e. *Control of delegated legislation*

   i.   *Judicial control.* If a minister, government department, or local authority exceeds its delegated power its action would be held by the court to be *ultra vires* (beyond the powers of) and therefore void.

   ii.   *Parliamentary control.* There are several methods of parliamentary control. Some statutory instruments must be laid before Parliament and will cease to be operative if the House so resolves within 40 days. Others require a vote of approval from the House. In addition there are committees in both Houses whose function is to scrutinise statutory instruments with a view to seeing whether the attention of Parliament should be drawn to the instrument on one of a number of specified grounds, for example because the instrument is obscurely drafted.

LEGISLATION OF THE EUROPEAN COMMUNITY

23. The European Community and the Single Market

a.   The European Economic Community was set up by the First Treaty of Rome 1957. Its immediate aim was the integration of the economies of the member states, a more long term aim is political integration. In all there are three European Communities to which all 12 member states belong:

   i.   The European Coal and Steel Community (ECSC) set up in 1951

   ii.   The European Economic Community (EEC) set up in 1957

   iii.   The European Atomic Energy Community (EURATOM) also founded in 1957.

The term "European Community" (EC) is used to describe the three communities together.

b.   The six signatories to the Treaty of Rome were France, Germany, Italy, Belgium, Holland and Luxembourg. On 1st January 1973 Great Britain, Eire and Denmark joined as a result of the Brussels Treaty of Accession. Greece joined in 1981 and Spain and Portugal in 1986.

c.   The object of creating a common market goes back to the Treaty of Rome in 1957 which established the EEC. However, in 1985 E.C. Heads of Government committed themselves to progressively establishing a single market over a period expiring on 31st December 1992. This commitment has been included in a package of treaty reforms known as the *SINGLE EUROPEAN ACT 1986 (SEA)*. This Act, which came into operation on 1st July 1987, defines a single market as '*an area without internal frontiers in which the free movement of goods, persons, services and capital is ensured in accordance with the provisions of this Treaty''*. The Act will assist the free movement of goods by breaking down technical barriers (for example differing national product standards) national restrictions, subsidy policies and so on. The SEA also speeds up E.C. decision making by extending majority voting to most major areas of the single market programme. This replaces the unanimous voting requirements which applied before the Act came into force.

24. Community Institutions

a. *The Commission*

    i.   This is the executive body of the Community, and consists of 17 Commissioners appointed by mutual agreement of the member governments. There must not be more than two from any country, and the present practice is for the five larger countries — France, Germany, Italy, Spain and Britain to appoint two each, and the seven smaller countries one each.

    ii.   The Commission is responsible for the formulation of Community policy. It acts collectively, but individual commissioners specialise in particular areas such as agriculture, transport and social affairs.

    iii.   The Commission has wide legislative functions. It initiates and drafts most Community legislation, and puts its proposals before the Council for enactment. The Commission also has executive functions to ensure the enforcement of Council decisions.

    iv.   The Commission represents the E.C. in negotiations with non-member states and administers certain budgets and funds. In general it acts as the day-to-day executive of the E.C.

    v.   Each Commissioner is assisted by a small private staff whose members tend to be of the same nationality as the commissioner they serve. In addition the Commission has a staff of about 7,000, divided between various departments and auxiliary services.

b. *The Council*

    i.   The Council is the Community's decision making body. It agrees legislation on the basis of proposals put forward by the Commission.

    ii.   Each Council meeting will deal with a particular area of policy, for example agriculture, finance or industry and will be attended by the relevant Minister from each member state.

    iii.   There are three methods of decision making (a) unanimity (b) simple majority voting i.e. at least seven member states in favour, and (c) qualified majority (weighted) voting based on the relative population of member states. Most single market proposals are subject to qualified majority voting.

c. *The European Parliament*

    i.   This directly elected body has 518 members, 81 from the U.K. It has consultative and advisory functions which are exercised through standing committees dealing with specialist topics.

ii.   Under the E.C. Treaties its formal opinion is required on many proposals before they can be adopted by the Council. Most single market proposals are subject to the new co-operation procedure introduced by the SEA. This enables the Parliament to give an opinion when the Commission makes a proposal and again when the Council has reached agreement in principle, (known as a "Common Position"). Members of the European Parliament are elected for a period of five years.

d.   *The Court of Justice.* The European Court is a court of first instance from which there is no appeal. It consists of 13 judges, selected from persons whose independence can be relied on and who are either recognised legal experts or qualified for judicial office in their respective countries. The judges hold office for 6 years. They are assisted by 5 Advocates-General who present the cases in an unbiased manner. The decision of the Court is a single judgement, dissenting opinions are not expressed. Its decisions are binding on the national courts of member states. The jurisdiction of the Court includes:-

i.   Actions brought against member states either by other member states or by the Commission on the ground that Treaty obligations are not being fulfilled.

ii.   Actions brought against E.C. institutions by member states, private individuals, or coporate bodies.

iii.   Disputes between the Communities and their employees arising from the employee's contracts of employment.

iv.   Rulings on the interpretation of the Treaties or on the validity of any of the acts of the Community institutions.

25.   The Sources of Community Law

a.   *Treaties.* The primary sources of Community law are foundation treaties of Paris and Rome. The *TREATY OF PARIS 1951* established the European Coal and Steel Community (E.C.S.C.). The *TREATY OF ROME 1957* established the European Atomic Energy Community (EURATOM). A second *TREATY OF ROME 1957* established the European Economic Community (E.E.C.).

b.   *Community legislation.* This is mainly concerned with economic matters such as free trade, agriculture, and transport. The Treaties set out in broad terms the objectives to be achieved and leave many of the details to the Council and the Commission. These bodies have law making powers which they may exercise in accordance with the Treaties. The community instruments which may be classified as legislation are:-

i.   *Regulations.* These are of general application, binding in their entirety and directly applicable in all member states without the need for further legislation. They confer individual rights and duties which the national courts of the member states must protect. Their object is to obtain uniformity of law throughout the member states.

ii.   *Directives.* Unlike regulations, directives do not have immediate binding force in all member states. They are addressed to member states, requiring the national Parliament to make whatever changes are necessary to implement the directive within a specified time.

iii.   *Decisions.* These may be addressed either to a member state or to an individual or institution. They are a formal method of enunciating policy decisions and they are binding on those to whom they are addressed.

c.   *The legislative process*

i.   Community legislation is the result of lengthy and complex negotiations and consultations involving several Council and Commission working parties and other committees provided for by the Treaties.

ii.   Briefly the procedure is for the Commission to discuss the proposal with officials from member states and other interested parties before adopting it as a formal proposal. It is then submitted to the Council and the European Parliament. Parliament may give an opinion and, depending on the Article of the Treaty on which the proposal is based, the Council can either adopt the proposal or agree a common position by qualified majority voting. In the latter case the European Parliament may give a second opinion before the proposal is returned to the Council to be finally adopted as Community Law.

d.   *Interpretation of community legislation.* Community legislation is drafted in terms of broad principle, the courts being left to supply the detail by giving effect to the intention of the legislature. This can be ascertained because regulations, directives, and decisions are required to state the reasons on which they are based. Thus in the interpretation of Community legislation the "golden rule" and the "mischief rule" are applied, rather than the "literal rule".

26.   Acceptance of Community Law by the U.K.

a.   *THE EUROPEAN COMMUNITIES ACT 1972* provides that any enactment of the U.K. Parliament shall have effect subject to the directly applicable legislation of the Communities. "Directly applicable" means that a provision confers directly on individuals rights enforceable by them in the courts of a member state without the need for further legislation by that state. Thus U.K. legislation is repealed by subsequent directly applicable Community legislation to the extent that the two are inconsistent. Parliament has therefore been obliged to give up sovereignty so far as Community matters are concerned. It is however clear that the basic principle of Parliamentary Sovereignty has not been impaired.

Community law is only enforceable in the UK because the 1972 Act so stated and it was said in **MACARTHYS v SMITH (1978)** that "Parliament's recognition of European Community Law . . . by one enactment can be withdrawn by another."

b.   The E.C. is concerned primarily with economic and commercial matters, and the effect of U.K. entry is being felt initially in those fields. Company law is experiencing wide changes as movement is made towards a uniform set of rules applicable to business organisations throughout the E.C. Commercial law, particularly concerning monopolies and restrictive trade practices is also being affected. However criminal law, contract, tort, property law and family law will not be affected.

5 The Subsidiary Source of Law

1. The following sources are subsidiary in the sense that they are not currently responsible for the direct creation of law. They are either records of the law (the Law Reports), historical explanations of the existence of laws (Law Merchant, Roman Law or Canon Law), or opinions of what the law is or should be (text books and the Law Commission).

THE LAW REPORTS

2. The History of Law Reporting

a. *1272-1535.* The earliest reports were "Year Books", which were first compiled in the reign of Edward I. They dealt mainly with matters of procedure rather than rules of substantive law.

b. *1535-1865.* The year books ceased in about 1535, and were replaced by private sets of reports published under the name of the law reporter. The standard varied greatly, the most reliable reports being produced by Coke (1572-1616) and Burrow (1751-1772). Many of the private reporters were also judges.

c. *1865-Present day.* In 1865 a Council was established by the 4 Inns of Court and the Law Society to publish under professional control the decisions of the superior courts. Since incorporation in 1870 it has been known as The Incorporated Council of Law Reporting. The Council publishes "The Law Reports" and "The Weekly Law Reports". In addition to the Council's reports some private reports are published by Butterworths. There are also private reports on specialist areas for example "Simon's Taxes".

3. Law Reporting and Judicial Precedent

a. The doctrine of precedent is closely linked to law reporting. It was only after the Council of Law Reporting was formed that the Law Reports became completely reliable, and consequently, only then was precedent able to function efficiently.

b. There is however, no rule which states that a court may only rely on a precedent if it is reported. It is sufficient that the decision be vouched for by a member of the bar who was present when judgement was delivered. Nevertheless personal recollections by judges and barristers would be too haphazard to form the basis of a workable system, therefore precedents are almost always contained in law reports.

c. Although law reports are fundamental to the doctrine of precedent the courts themselves have never created a methodical system of producing law reports. This is left to private enterprise, so that even now there is an element of chance and individual preference in the choice of whether or not to report a case.

d.   Law reporters are barristers, and they must be present when judgement is delivered if their report is to be valid.

LAW MERCHANT

4.   The law of contract administered in the Common Law courts in the 13th and 14th centuries was very unsophisticated. In addition their jurisdiction was limited to claims involving less than 40 shillings. They were therefore badly equipped to deal with the increasing volume of disputes arising from England's growth as a trading centre. A new set of courts therefore evolved to deal with disputes between merchants. They were not common law courts since their rules originated partly in trade custom, and partly in international law.

5.   Courts Administering Law Merchant

a.   *Courts of Pie Poudre.* These were courts held at fairs and markets (where most trade was conducted). The power to hold the court would be granted by the King to officers of the borough in return for dues known as "tolls". The courts attracted the merchants because of their speed and simple procedure (in contrast with common law courts), and because they gave effect to the merchants' own customs. The 13th and 14th centuries were the heyday of these courts, thereafter various factors contributed to their decline. By the 18th century almost all of these courts had ceased to function. The name "pie poudre" comes from the French "pieds poudres", after the "dusty feet" of the traders who used the courts.

b.   *Staple Courts.* In order to facilitate the collection of taxes from foreign merchants, dealings in certain basic commodities such as wool and tin were confined to certain towns. In each of these "staple" towns was a court which had exclusive criminal and civil jurisdiction over merchants. These courts applied a mixture of common law and merchants' customs.

c.   *The High Court of Admiralty.* Mercantile law and maritime law have always been closely connected, both having their origins in mercantile custom. The High Court of Admiralty was created in the 14th century and originally had both civil and criminal jurisdiction over matters arising at sea. It later acquired jurisdiction over contracts made on land, but this was removed by Sir Edward Coke on his accession to the bench in 1606.

6.   The Content of the Law Merchant. Law merchant is responsible for the concept of negotiability, and is the basis of many of the rules of partnership, insurance, and agency. Over the years many of the rules of the law merchant were incorporated into the common law and later into statute, for example the *BILLS OF EXCHANGE ACT 1882* and the *SALE OF GOODS ACT 1893*.

CANON LAW

7.   Canon Law (the law of the Catholic church) influenced the growth of English Law in two ways.

a. ***Influence on common law and equity.*** For example the punishment of imprisonment, family rights, and the strong moral content of equity, are concepts which originated in Canon law.

b. ***Application in the Ecclesiastical Courts.*** Like the Pie Poudre and Staple courts these courts were independent of the common law courts. They dealt mainly with offences against morality, eg adultery, and slander. They also had jurisdiction over the law of succession. They kept this jurisdiction until 1857 when The Divorce Court and The Probate Court were established. Until about 1500 the ecclesiastical courts also tried all persons accused of felonies provided the accused person claimed "the benefit of the clergy" (See Chapter 6.12).

ROMAN LAW

8. Although it is the basis of most continental systems of law, Roman law is of little importance as a source of English law. Its influence was mainly felt in the ecclesiastical courts and, since the Church used to play a part in the distribution of a deceased person's property, in the rules relating to the requirements of a valid will. A soldier's privileged will (ie a verbal will) is an example of a current law which has Roman origins.

TEXT BOOKS

9. Early Text Books. Although they are not original sources of law early text books are sometimes regarded as authoritative statements of the law at that time. For example *Littleton's Tenures* (approximately 1480) and *Coke's Institutes* (1628). Coke was relied on in **REID v POLICE COMMISSIONER OF THE METROPOLIS (1973)**.

10. Modern Text Books. These are sometimes used by barristers in court, but are of little importance as a source of law since this function is fulfilled by the law reports and statutes. However some writers have had the distinction of court recognition of their work. For example *Pollock's* definition of consideration was accepted by the House of Lords in **DUNLOP v SELFRIDGE (1915)** and *Winfield's* definition of nuisance was accepted in **READ v LYONS (1947)**.

THE LAW COMMISSION

11. The Law Commission was established in 1965. It consists of solicitors, barristers, and academic lawyers who are appointed on a full-time basis by the Lord Chancellor. The Commission's function is to review areas of law where there is a need for reform, simplification or modernisation. It produces a steady flow of reports, recommendations and draft Bills, most of which have been enacted by Parliament, for example the *CRIMINAL LAW ACT 1967* and the *THEFT ACT 1968*.

6 English Legal History

THE ORIGINS OF THE COMMON LAW

1. Prior to 1066 there existed a primitive legal system based on local custom. The effect of the Norman conquest was to set in motion the unification of these local customs into one system of law with the King at its head. The system was common to all men and for this reason was known as "common law".

2. The ascendancy of the King's courts over the local courts took about 300 years, during which the King gradually assumed control through his itinerant justices, and established a central system of courts. The growth of the King's courts was resisted by the local barons, landowners and sheriffs whose jurisdiction (and revenue) was being diminished.

3. Many factors accounted for the growth of the King's courts and the decline of the local courts including:-

a. *The evolution of the writ system.* The King, as the source of justice, would grant a writ where there was a denial of justice in the local courts. These writs became standardised and provided specific rights which could be enforced in the King's courts. This led to a decline in the civil jurisdiction of the local courts, since most early writs were concerned with protecting rights in land, and disputes over land were the main business of the local courts.

b. The *STATUTE OF GLOUCESTER 1278.* This was passed in an attempt to limit the jurisdiction of the King's courts over personal actions. It actually provided that no action for less than 40 shillings could be commenced in the King's courts. It was however deliberately misinterpreted by the royal judges who took it to mean that no personal action for more than 40 shillings could be tried in the local courts.

THE COURTS OF THE COMMON LAW

4. The Curia Regis (King's Court). Although called a "court" it had legislative, administrative and judicial functions. It was therefore the predecessor of Parliament as well as the courts. It originally consisted of the King and his tenants-in-chief. These were men to whom land had been granted in return for some service such as the provision of men or arms. The King would travel the country, and the Curia Regis would meet wherever the King was. In medieval times a pattern developed whereby courts separated from the Curia Regis and eventually acquired a jurisdiction separate from it. The King however retained a residual judicial power which later led to other courts deriving their jurisdiction from him, notably The Court of Chancery and The Star Chamber. The common law courts which split from the Curia Regis were the courts of Exchequer, Common Pleas and King's Bench.

5.   The Court of Exchequer. This became a separate court in the reign of Henry I (approximately 1140) and originally dealt with the collection of royal revenue, and at a later date disputes over debts. The judges were known as Barons. It acquired jurisdiction over the writ of debt through the fiction of "Quominus". This depended on a fictitious allegation of a debt owned by the plaintiff to the Crown which he was unable to pay because of a debt owed to him by the defendant. The King's interest was thus involved and the royal court could try the substantive dispute between the parties.

6.   The Court of Common Pleas. Since it was impractical for litigants to follow the King around the country the *MAGNA CARTA 1215* provided that common pleas should be heard in a "certain plaee" which was fixed as Westminster. The judges were full-time lawyers and the court's jurisdiction extended to all disputes which did not concern the King's interest, for example personal actions of debt. It also tried actions for trespass where the title to land was concerned. It was the most widely used court, since it exercised jurisdiction over land, and most disputes concerned land, since only landowners could afford to use the courts.

7.   The Court of the King's Bench. This was the last of the three courts to break away from the Curia Regis, its first Chief Justice being appointed in 1268. Its original jurisdiction was exercised principally in civil matters, although its judges did have criminal jurisdiction in the assize courts. It also had, because of its association with the King, the jurisdiction to issue the prerogative writs of mandamus, prohibition, and certiorari, which restrain abuses of jurisdiction by inferior courts and public officials. In addition it had appellate jurisdiction over the Court of Common Pleas.

8.   These three royal courts all basically exercised a civil jurisdiction, with some overlap of their functions. They were abolished by the *JUDICATURE ACTS 1873-1875*. Most criminal matters were dealt with by the itinerant justices in the assizes.

9.   Assizes and Itinerant Justices

a.   It has always been impossible to administer justice on the basis of all trials taking place in London. The Normans therefore adopted the system of sending out royal justices to hold *"assizes"* or sittings of the Royal Courts. Their original main function was the supervision of local administration and tax collection. They also had some criminal jurisdiction. Later their powers were extended to civil proceedings. The system was so successful that in the 12th century the country was divided into circuits, and each was visited three or four times a year by the justices.

b.   The early justices were either judges of the common law courts, members of the clergy, or prominent laymen. They held office by reason of commissions issued by the King. The commission of *Oyer and Terminer* and the commission of *Gaol Delivery* conferred criminal jurisdiction. Civil jurisdiction was granted by the commission of *Assize*. Civil jurisdiction was however limited, most cases being heard at Westminster. This was inconvenient because of the difficulty of transporting local juries to Westminster. The *STATUTE OF NISI PRIUS 1285*, therefore extended the civil jurisdiction of the justices by providing that in certain civil actions, eg trespass, a jury should be summoned to Westminster on a certain day unless before (nisi prius) that date the case had been heard at a local assize.

c.   The itinerant justices were of considerable importance in the development of common law. At first they administered local customs ascertained with the help of a local jury. When not on circuit the justices would meet and discuss the merits of the various customs they had discovered. Some would be rejected, other gained general acceptance, and were gradually applied throughout the whole country. This formed the basis from which the common law was developed.

10. Quarter Sessions and Justices of the Peace

a.   The original function of J.P.s (approximately 1200) was administrative rather than judicial. However in the early 14th century their civil function declined and, since the assizes could not deal with the growing number of offenders, they were given a criminal jurisdiction.

b.   The original of the modern J.P. is the *STATUTE OF LABOURS 1361*. This provided for the appointment of lay justices and compelled them to hold sessions in each county four times a year (quarter sessions). In 1590 J.P.s were given jurisdiction over all criminal offences. It was not until 1842 that the jurisdiction of quarter sessions was limited to exclude treason, murder and some of the other more serious offences. Trial at quarter sessions was by jury.

c.   In the 15th century J.P.s were given statutory power to try the less important criminal cases outside quarter sessions. These sittings became known as "petty sessions". The jurisdiction of the petty sessions was entirely statutory, and the court sat without a jury. Such courts are now termed "magistrates' courts".

d.   The administrative function of J.P.s declined as their criminal jurisdiction grew. However certain functions remain to the present day, for example the power to issue warrants for arrest, and the task of conducting preliminary investigations into indictable offences (committal proceedings).

11. The General Eyre.

11. The General Eyre. A wider commission than was issued to itinerant justices and J.P.s was issued to the justices of the General Eyre. They were concerned to safeguard royal interests of all kinds, for example the collection of revenue and fines, trying prisoners in gaol, and the questioning of local officials. The Eyre was held once every 7 years, and was very unpopular. It ceased in about 1340.

THE ORIGINS OF EQUITY

12. The early common law was rigid and often harsh. This was to some extent reduced through the use of legal fictions. Fictions were used for three purposes:-

   a.   To reduce the severity of the criminal law. For example stolen property in fact worth more than one shilling would be valued by the court at less than one shilling, thus classifying the offence as a misdemeanour rather than a felony and consequently reducing the severity of the sentence. Another example is the "benefit of the clergy". — If a person could show that he was a member of the clergy he could be tried in the ecclesiastical courts where the penalties were less severe. The test to determine whether a person was a clergyman was whether he could read. To show ability to read he had only to recite a verse of Latin commonly supposed to have been Psalm 51 Verse 1 which most people therefore learnt by heart — just in case!

   b.   To extend the scope of writs beyond their literal scope.

   c.   To acquire jurisdiction from other courts, for example the fiction of "Quominus" (**5.** above). Such fictions cannot be explained by a desire to improve the common law, but by the fact that judicial salaries depended upon the number of cases heard.

13. Fictions were not however capable of remedying all the defects of the common law. For example

   a.   The plaintiff either had to fit his action into the framework of an existing writ, or show that it was similar to such a writ. If he could do neither he had no remedy.

   b.   In civil actions the only remedy which the common law courts could give was an award of damages.

   c.   There were elaborate rules governing the procedure which had to be followed in bringing a case, and any slight breach of the rules might leave a plaintiff who had a good case without a remedy.

14. In many of these cases dissatisfied persons would petition the King, since the Curia Regis was not subject to the limitations of the common law courts, and could exercise the royal prerogative as it thought fit. For a time the King determined these petitions himself, but he later delegated this function to his Chancellor. The Chancellor was one of the most important members of the Curia Regis. He was in charge of the Chancery which was responsible for the issue of writs. Since he was already concerned with the legal process it was logical that the Chancellor should preside at hearings of petitions. Initially the Chancellor issued decrees in the King's name. In 1474 a Chancellor first issued a decree in his own name. At this point in time the Court of Chancery was created. Like the common law courts it had now become independent of the King.

THE COURT OF CHANCERY

15. The early Chancellors were members of the clergy who were very concerned to order what was, as a matter of conscience, fair between the parties. The first lawyer to be appointed Chancellor was Sir Thomas More in 1529. At first there were no fixed rules on which the Court proceeded. Gradually the Court began to be guided by its previous decisions, and formulate general principles, known as the "maxims of equity", upon which it would proceed. Finally the Court of Chancery evolved a body of law the principles of which were as firm as those of the common law.

16. The Maxims of Equity. These are principles which the Court of Chancery followed when deciding cases, and which are applied today when equitable relief is claimed. There are many maxims, the following being some of the more well known examples:-

    a. *He who seeks equity must do equity.* A person who seeks equitable relief must be prepared to act fairly towards his opponent as a condition of obtaining such relief. For example a mortgagor who wishes to exercise his equitable right to redeem must give reasonable notice of his intention.

    b. *He who comes to equity must come with clean hands.* Not only must the plaintiff "do equity" by making proper present concessions to the defendant, he must also have acted properly in his past dealing with the defendant. For example **D.C. BUILDERS v REES (1966)** (Chapter 15).

    c. *Equality is equity.* For example since equity does not allow the remedy of specific performance to be invoked against a minor (a concession to his youth), it will also not allow a minor to claim the benefit of this remedy.

    d. *Equity looks at the intent rather than the form.* For example if an agreed damages clause in a contract is not a genuine pre-estimate of the loss that would result from a breach, equity would regard the clause as a penalty clause and treat it merely as a device to induce performance of the contract. The court would therefore enforce the contract as written, but would award the innocent party his actual loss.

17. The Achievement of the Court of Chancery. These were considerable, in particular the Court developed the law relating to trusts and mortgages, and discretionary remedies namely:-

    a. *Injunction* − An order of the court compelling or restraining the performance of some act.

    b. *Specific performance* − An order of the court compelling a person to perform an obligation existing under either a contract or trust.

    c. *Rectification* − The alteration of a document so that it reflects the true intention of the parties.

    d. *Rescission* − The restoration of the parties to a contract to their pre-contract state of affairs.

18. **The Defects of the Court of Chancery**

    a.   The Court inevitably bore the characteristics of the Chancellor. This was a good feature in that excellent lawyers such as Sir Thomas More and Sir Frances Bacon were able to contribute greatly to the development of equity. It was a bad feature when the shortcomings of other Chancellors brought the Court into disrepute, for example in the 17th century the sale of offices was widespread and in 1725 when Lord Macclesfield was Chancellor, a deficiency of about £100,000 was discovered in court funds. In addition it was clear that there was a variation in the standard of justice dispensed by different Chancellors.

    b.   The sale of offices resulted in an excessive number of court officials, who tended to try to extend the scope of their duties so as to increase their revenue. This meant that procedure became very slow and expensive.

    c.   In contrast to the excess of officials there was a scarcity of judges. At first the Chancellor was the only judge, but he was later assisted by his Chancery Masters. The chief of these was the Master of the Rolls, who was effectively a second judge. It was not until 1813 that the first Vice-Chancellor was appointed by Lord Eldon.

COMMON LAW AND EQUITY

19. **Similarities between Common Law and Equity**

    a.   Both common law and equity are law. In ordinary language "equity" means natural justice, but although inspired by these ideas, equity no longer represents the flexible concept of natural justice. It is now a branch of the law.

    b.   Common law and equity have both developed in an English context. They are not imported systems, and have only been subject to minimal foreign influence.

    c.   Both have been partly embodied in statute, for example the *SALE OF GOODS ACT 1979* (common law) and the *TRUSTEE ACT 1925* (equity).

    d.   Since the *JUDICATURE ACTS OF 1873-1875* both have been administered in the same courts.

20. **Differences between Common Law and Equity**

    a.   The most important difference is that common law was constructed as a complete and independent system, whereas equity developed to remedy the defects of the common law, and would be meaningless if considered in isolation, since it pre-supposes the existence of common law. For example the doctrine of equitable estoppel in contract developed as an exception to the arguably harsh rule of **PINNEL'S CASE (1602)** (Chapter 15).

b.   Historically each system had different procedural rules since, until 1875, they were administered in separate courts. In the common law courts an action was commenced by the issue of a writ, whereas in the Court of Chancery an action was commenced by a petition, which allowed a greater scope to the plaintiff.

c.   Although the administration of common law and equity has now been fused, their content nevertheless remains separate. Thus to say that a rule or remedy is "equitable" means that it must be interpreted in an equitable atmosphere, and that the principles of equity apply. Thus the equitable remedies, for example specific performance, and rescission are discretionary, whereas the common law remedy of damages exists as a right if a wrong is proved. A recent example of the exercise of this discretion was **MILLER v JACKSON (1976)** where although the plaintiff "won" the case the injunction he sought was refused. (See Chapter 28.5).

d.   By its nature the Court of Chancery was certain to come into conflict with the Common Law courts. For example the Chancellor would rescind a contract where the common law courts would enforce it as originally drawn. In such cases equity would have to prevail or it would be of no effect. This has been clear since 1615 when there was a dispute between Sir Edward Coke who was Chief Justice of the Common Pleas and Lord Ellesmere, the Lord Chancellor. This dispute was only resolved when King James I, after consulting the Attorney-General, (Sir Francis Bacon), decided in favour of the Court of Chancery.

THE REFORMS OF 1873-1875

21.   By the second half of the 19th century the court structure was coming under heavy criticism for several reasons:-

a.   Procedure was complex and out of date.

b.   The separate existence of common law courts and the Court of Chancery was not satisfactory. It has been said that one court was set up to do injustice and another to stop it.

c.   The appeals procedure was in need of reform.

22.   The necessary reforms were implemented by the *JUDICATURE ACTS OF 1873-1875* which came into operation together in 1875. Their main effect was to create a new Supreme Court of Judicature to which was transferred the jurisdiction of all the superior courts of law and equity. The Supreme Court was divided into two parts, The High Court and The Court of Appeal. The Judicature Acts did not affect the other courts. Thus, for example, the House of Lords and County Courts are not part of the Supreme Court. The Judicature Acts changed the court structure as follows:-

Before 1875	Created in 1875 **HIGH COURT**	Today
Court of Queens Bench Court of Common Pleas Court of Exchequer	Queens Bench Division Common Pleas Division Exchequer Division	Queens Bench Division (Merger in 1880)
Court of Chancery Court of Bankruptcy	Chancery Division	Chancery Division
Court of Probate Court of Admiralty Court of Divorce	Probate, Divorce and Admiralty Division	Family Division (Re-named by The Administration of Justice Act 1970)
Court of Appeal in Chancery Court of Exchequer Chamber	**COURT OF** **APPEAL** Split in 1966	The Court of Appeal (Civil Division) The Court of Appeal (Criminal Division)

23. The above changes had the effect of fusing the administration of common law and equity. It did not however fuse their content. It also enacted the established rule that in cases of conflict the rules of equity shall prevail.

24. Finally the Judicature Acts simplified procedure by creating a single set of rules to apply throughout the Supreme Court. This considerably reduced the chance of a case being lost due to an error in pleading.

7 The Courts

THE COURT STRUCTURE

1. The English court structure is fairly complex. It has 4 basic levels — the House of Lords; the Court of Appeal; the High Court (including the Crown Court); and the Inferior Courts (including County Courts and Magistrates Courts). Within this structure there is neither a clear division into criminal and civil courts, nor a division into first instance and appeal courts. For example the Queen's Bench Division of the High Court hears both civil and criminal cases and operates as both a first instance and an appeal court.

2. The following diagram may help to clarify the court structure.

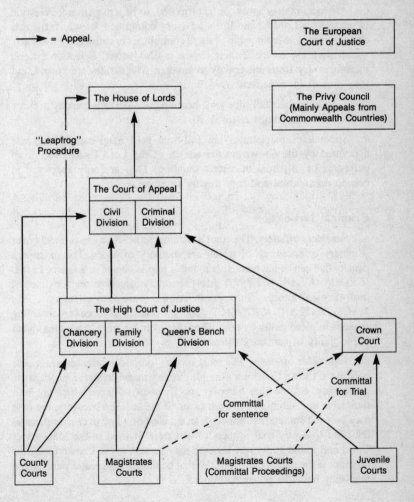

— = Appeal.

The European Court of Justice

The House of Lords

The Privy Council (Mainly Appeals from Commonwealth Countries)

"Leapfrog" Procedure

The Court of Appeal

Civil Division | Criminal Division

The High Court of Justice

Chancery Division | Family Division | Queen's Bench Division

Crown Court

Committal for Trial

Committal for sentence

County Courts

Magistrates Courts

Magistrates Courts (Committal Proceedings)

Juvenile Courts

MAGISTRATES COURTS

3. Composition

a. Magistrates courts are composed of Justices of the Peace. The court consists of at least 2, but not more than 7 justices (usually 3) or a stipendiary magistrate.

b. J.P.s (except stipendiary magistrates) are not legally qualified, but they must live within 15 miles of their commission area and they are required to undertake basic training in judicial science. Each court has a legally qualified Clerk to the Justices. He advises the justices on the law, but he does not assist them with their decision on the facts. There is no jury in magistrates courts.

c. Any person may apply, or be proposed, to be a magistrate. Selection is made by a Lord Chancellor's advisory committee, of which there is one per county. Membership of these committees is secret and the criteria which they use to make their choice is also secret. Selection criteria therefore vary from one county to another. Magistrates are unpaid, but they may claim expenses.

d. J.P.s keep their full-time jobs, hearing cases perhaps one day in every two weeks. They must retire at 70.

e. Stipendiary magistrates are full-time paid magistrates. They are appointed by the Crown on the advice of the Lord Chancellor, from barristers or solicitors of certain standing. They are only appointed in certain urban areas and they usually sit alone.

4. Criminal Jurisdiction

a. *Summary offences.* The court's criminal jurisdiction exists mainly over summary offences, all of which are statutory offences. The maximum penalty that can be imposed is six month's imprisonment or a fine of £1,000 (*CRIMINAL LAW ACT 1977*). Most summary offenders are convicted of motoring offences. Since convictions were so numerous, the *MAGISTRATES COURTS ACT 1957* introduced a procedure enabling persons to plead guilty by post. There are over 1½ million persons a year found guilty of summary offences.

b. *Indictable offences.* The most serious indictable offences are triable only in the Crown Court, for example murder, manslaughter, rape, bigamy, conspiracy. Statute does however specify some offences which are both indictable and summary. In such cases, if the accused consents, the case may be tried summarily, although an accused of 17 or over may demand the right to a jury trial in the Crown Court. If tried in the Magistrates Court and found guilty, the accused may be sent to the Crown Court for sentence if the magistrates consider that he deserves a greater punishment than they have the power to impose.

5. Examining Magistrates (Committal Proceedings). A person cannot be tried on indictment before a jury unless he is first brought before one or more magistrates so that they can hold a preliminary examination to decide whether or not a prima facie reasonable case can be made out against him. If such a prima facie (on the face of it) case is found to exist he will be committed for trial in the Crown Court.

6. Juvenile Courts

a.   Children (under 14) and young persons (14-16) must generally have their cases heard (not "tried") in a juvenile court. The *CHILDREN AND YOUNG PERSONS ACT 1963* specifies that the court must consist of three magistrates specially qualified to deal with juvenile cases. The court sits in private and must include a man and a woman among its members.

b.   Under the *CHILDREN AND YOUNG PERSONS ACT 1969* a child or young person may only be brought before the court in the following circumstances:-

   i.   If his health or development is being impaired,

   ii.   If he is exposed to moral danger,

   iii. If he is beyond parental control,

   iv. If he is not being educated properly, or

   v.   If he is guilty of an offence, and is in need of care and control.

Two points are worthy of note concerning the above circumstances:-

   i.   In many cases a child may be brought before the court even though he is in no way at fault.

   ii.   Under v. above a child may be found guilty of an offence without a trial as such. However the court must not find the "offence condition" satisfied unless it would have found him guilty of that offence in ordinary criminal proceedings, thus the usual onus of proof rules apply.

c.   The main principle of the 1969 Act is that children and young people should not be treated as criminals, but as subject to one of several orders. Thus if a child is found "guilty" of an offence, this finding is in no sense a conviction, and he is dealt with not as a criminal, but as a child or young person in need of help. The court may however order the detention of a child or young person in a "community home" in the limited circumstances where this is necessary for the protection of the public. The court may also make:-

   i.   A supervision order ie an order placing him under the supervision of a probation officer;

   ii.   A hospital order; or

   iii. A guardianship order.

7. Civil Jurisdiction. Magistrates civil jurisdiction is less important than their criminal jurisdiction, but it is varied and includes, for example:-

a.   The recovery of certain civil debts including income tax, electricity and gas bills and council rates.

b.   Domestic proceedings under the *DOMESTIC PROCEEDINGS AND MAGISTRATES COURTS ACT 1978* (see below).

c.   The granting of gaming and liquor licences.

8.   Domestic Courts

a.   These courts are constituted under the 1978 Act (see **7.**b. above) to hear domestic proceedings. "Domestic proceedings" is defined to include, for example, affiliation, adoption, guardianship and matrimonial proceedings.

b.   The only people allowed to be present at the hearing are the officers of the court, the parties and their legal representatives, witnesses and other persons directly concerned with the case, and other persons whom the court may permit to be present.

c.   Under the 1978 Act either party to a marriage may apply for an order on the ground that the other:-

i.   Has failed to provide reasonable maintenance for the applicant; or

ii.   Has failed to provide, or make a proper contribution towards, reasonable maintenance for any child of the family; or

iii.   Has behaved in such a way that the applicant cannot reasonably be expected to live with the respondent; or

iv.   Has deserted the applicant.

d.   If one of the above grounds is proved the court has a variety of orders available, for example:-

i.   Periodical payments and/or a lump sum (of up to £500) to or for the benefit of the applicant or any child of the family;

ii.   Orders for custody or access;

iii.   Orders committing children to the care of a local authority;

iv.   Orders excluding one spouse from the matrimonial home.

9.   The Advantages and Disadvantages of Lay Magistrates

a.   *Advantages*

i.   Public participation in the legal process reduces the remoteness of the law from the public.

ii.   The system is cheap since magistrates are not paid, but it nevertheless appears to attract high quality personnel.

iii.   Lay magistrates reduce the pressure on professional lawyers, leaving them to hear the more serious offences and most civil cases.

iv.   Although not legally qualified, magistrates may be better qualified in other respects, for example to hear childrens' cases. In addition the use of lay magistrates reduces the risk of the child perceiving himself as a young criminal.

b. *Disadvantages*

i. Magistrates tend to be drawn from a narrow background. The majority are male, middle-aged and middle class. For example less than 10% of magistrates are under 40.

ii. It has been argued, although not proved, that magistrates are too willing to accept police evidence.

iii. There is also evidence that sentencing policies differ widely from one area to another. A person convicted of an offence may have three or four times the chance of going to prison if he comes from an area where the magistrates prefer custodial sentences to alternative sentences such as community service, probation and fines.

THE CROWN COURT

10. Creation. The Crown Court was created by the *COURTS ACT 1971*. It replaced the Assizes and Quarter Sessions and was made part of The Supreme Court of Judicature. The Assizes and Quarter Sessions were local courts, but in contrast the Crown Court is a single court which has buildings throughout the country and may sit anywhere in England and Wales, its jurisdiction is in no sense local. When sitting in the City of London it is known as The Central Criminal Court (The Old Bailey).

11. Judges

a. Crown court judges are either

i. High Court judges, usually of the Queen's Bench Division; or

ii. Circuit judges ie full-time judges appointed from the ranks of barristers or solicitors of 10 years standing, or from recorders of at least 3 years standing.

iii. Recorders ie part-time judges who are either barristers or solicitors of 10 years standing.

b. The judge will usually sit alone unless an appeal is being heard from a Magistrates Court, when the judge will be joined by 2, 3, or 4 lay magistrates. The court, sitting in this form, also exercises a limited civil jurisdiction, mainly over appeals concerning liquor and gaming licences.

12. Criminal Jurisdiction

a. The criminal jurisdiction of the Crown Court concerns all cases above the level of Magistrates Courts. The more serious offences are tried by the High Court judges and the less serious by the circuit judges and recorders.

b. When hearing appeals from the Magistrates Courts, the court may allow the appeal, reduce the sentence, or increase the sentence up to the maximum that could have been imposed by the Magistrates Court.

13. The Jury. The court sits with a jury of 12, and a majority verdict of 10-2 will be sufficient to convict the accused.

COUNTY COURTS

14. Introduction

a. County courts were created by the *COURTS ACT 1846* to try civil cases involving small sums of money. Originally the upper limit of their jurisdiction was fixed at £20. This limit has been extended on many occasions so that today they deal with the majority of the country's civil litigation.

b. Jurisdiction is however limited in 3 respects:

i. It is entirely statutory, so that if in any matter statute provides no jurisdiction then none exists;

ii. They have no appellate jurisdiction;

iii. Jurisdiction is local, so there must be a connecting factor between the action and the county court district in which it is tried.

c. There are about 400 county court districts grouped into circuits, each of which is presided over by one or more circuit judges. The term "county court" is misleading since these circuits are not based on county boundaries.

15. Jurisdiction

a. The extent of county court jurisdiction was extended considerably from 1 July 1991 by the *COUNTY COURT JURISDICTION ORDER 1991* under the provision of the *COURTS AND LEGAL SERVICES ACT 1990*. The Order abolished many existing financial limits, resulting in many cases being triable in either the county court or the High Court.

In general terms the extent of the county court jurisdiction is:-

i. Contract and tort (actions for less than £25,000 shall normally be tried in a county court and actions for £50,000 and over in the High Court). Actions which fall in the middle range or have no quantifiable value can be tried in either court.

ii. Personal injury claims unless the claim is worth £50,000 or more.

iii. Equity and probate when an estate has a value of not more than £30,000.

iv. Mortgages − up to £30,000 amount owing.

v. Enforcement of payment of fines.

vi. Action to recover solicitors' costs up to £5,000.

b. In addition some courts outside London have bankruptcy jurisdiction which is unlimited in amount. The courts with such jurisdiction also have the power to wind-up companies where the paid-up capital is less than £120,000. Some courts in coastal areas also have Admiralty jurisdiction limited to £5,000 (£15,000 in salvage cases).

16. Composition

a. A county court is presided over by a circuit judge.

b. The *COURTS ACT 1971* contains provisions enabling judges of the Court of Appeal and High Court and recorders to sit in the county court. The judge usually sits alone, without a jury, although in some cases, for example fraud, there is provision for trial by a jury of 8.

c. Each county court also has a registrar who acts as an assistant judge. He must be a solicitor of at least 7 years standing. In his administrative capacity he maintains the court records, arranges for the issue and service of summonses, deals with money paid into court, and a large number of similar functions. In practice much of his work is delegated to clerks and bailiffs. The registrar's judicial function is narrower than that of the judge. He may hear undefended cases, cases where the amount at stake does not exceed £1,000 and (if the judge and parties agree) other cases involving up to £2,000.

17. Importance. The practical importance of the County Courts is that they deal with the majority of the country's civil litigation. Over 1½ million actions are commenced each year, although only about 5% result in trials since most actions are discontinued or settled out of court before the trial stage is reached. Several factors may however prevent County Courts being as effective a means of resolving small disputes as was originally intended. These factors may be expressed as 3 questions:-

a. Does X know that he has suffered a wrong which entitles him to a legal remedy? He may, for example, be unaware that an exemption clause is invalidated by the *UNFAIR CONTRACT TERMS ACT 1977*.

b. Does X wish to involve the law? He may see the law as a middle or upper class institution, which is "not for me".

c. Can X afford to risk losing his case, possibly incurring expenses in excess of his original claim?

This may be a particularly difficult decision to take if the potential defendant is an institution or company with resources to employ the best lawyers to fight the case regardless of cost.

THE HIGH COURT

18. Creation and Composition

a. The High Court was established by the *JUDICATURE ACTS 1873-1875*. Prior to 1971 it sat in the Royal Courts of Justice in London, although when the judges tried a case on assize they constituted a court of the High Court. The *COURTS ACT 1971* abolished all courts of assize, but provided that sittings of the High Court could take place anywhere in England or Wales. The centres where sittings are held are determined by the Lord Chancellor.

b.   The High Court is divided into 3 divisions, namely the Queen's Bench Division, the Chancery Division, and the Family Division. Each division has a head and a number of puisne judges.

c.   High Court judges are appointed by the Queen on the advice of the Lord Chancellor. They must be barristers of not less than 10 years standing. The division to which they are appointed depends on the practice followed prior to appointment. The maximum number of High Court judges is fixed by Order in Council at 80.

d.   The trial is usually before a judge sitting alone, or before 2 or 3 judges in appeal cases. A jury may sit in defamation, false imprisonment, and fraud cases.

19.   The Queen's Bench Division

a.   The jurisdiction of the Queen's Bench Division is wider than that of the other two divisions. It is both civil and criminal, and original and appellate.

b.   The most important aspect of its business is its *original civil jurisdiction*, mainly over contract and tort actions. Jurisdiction over commercial matters is exercised by a Commercial Court which is part of the Division. It sits in London, Liverpool and Manchester. The Division also has an Admiralty Court which deals with claims for damage, loss of life, or personal injury arising out of collisions at sea, claims for loss or damage to goods carried in a ship, and disputes concerning the ownership or possession of ships.

c.   The *appellate civil jurisdiction* of the Division is relatively minor. A single judge has jurisdiction to hear appeals from some tribunals, for example the Pensions Appeal Tribunal. A divisional court, consisting of 2 or more judges may hear appeals by way of "case stated" from magistrates courts, the Crown Court, and from the Solicitors' Disciplinary Tribunal.

d.   The *criminal jurisdiction* of the High Court is exercised exclusively by the Queen's Bench Division. This is entirely appellate and is exercised by the divisional court, usually consisting of 3 judges, and often including the head of the division, the *Lord Chief Justice*. The jurisdiction is over appeals by way of "case stated" from magistrates courts and the Crown Court.

e.   The divisional court also exercises a *supervisory jurisdiction*. It may issue the prerogative writ of habeas corpus, and it may make orders of mandamus, prohibition, and certiorari by which inferior courts and tribunals are compelled to exercise their powers properly, and are restrained from exceeding their jurisdiction.

f.   Finally the jurisdiction of Queen's Bench Division judges extends to hearing trials in the Crown Court. Judges of the Division spend about half their time "on circuit" and half their time in the Royal Courts.

g.   About 50 judges are appointed to the Queen's Bench Division.

20. The Chancery Division

a.   The nominal head of the division is the *Lord Chancellor*, although he never sits in first instance cases.

b.   The jurisdiction includes trusts, mortgages, bankruptcy, company law and partnership, and contentious probate business. There is some overlap of jurisdiction with the Queen's Bench Division. For example **ESSO PETROLEUM LTD v HARPER'S GARAGE (STOURPORT) LTD (1966)** was tried in the Queen's Bench Division, whereas **PETROFINA (GREAT BRITAIN) LTD v MARTIN (1965)** was tried in the Chancery Division. (These cases are very similar, and will be discussed in Chapter 19.)

c.   The Chancery Division currently has about 15 judges.

21. The Family Division

a.   This division, set up in 1970, deals with defended divorces, wardship, adoption, guardianship, legitimacy, disputes concerning the matrimonial home, and non-contentious probate cases. It also hears appeals from Magistrates and County Courts on family matters.

b.   The head of the Division is the *President*, and he is assisted by about 20 puisne judges.

THE COURT OF APPEAL

22.   The Court of Appeal was split into civil and criminal divisions in 1966. The head of the civil division is the *Master of the Rolls* and the head of the criminal division is the *Lord Chief Justice*.

23.   There are 18 Lord Justices of Appeal, Appeals are normally heard by 3 judges, but certain cases may be heard by 2 judges and occasionally a "full court" of 5 or more judges will sit for an important case. For example **YOUNG v BRISTOL AEROPLANE CO (1944)** (Chapter 4.11) was heard by a court of 6 judges. A majority decision is sufficient and a dissenting judgement is expressed.

24.   The appeal takes the form of re-hearing the case by drawing on the judge's notes and the official shorthand writer's transcript and by listening to arguments from counsel. Witnesses are not heard again nor is fresh evidence usually admitted. The court may uphold or reverse the decision in whole or part, it may alter the amount of damages awarded and it may make a different order as to costs. If new evidence is discovered it may order a new trial.

THE HOUSE OF LORDS

25. The House of Lords is the final court of appeal for all internal cases. There are 11 Lords of Appeal in Ordinary. The minimum number to hear an appeal is 3, but 5 judges usually sit. As in the Court of Appeal, a majority decision is sufficient and dissenting judgements are expressed. The Law Lords are, of course, professional lawyers, not lay members of the House of Lords.

26. The leapfrog procedure was introduced in 1969 because it was thought that two appeals from the High Court the Court of Appeal and then to the House of Lords were unnecessary. Appeal direct from the High Court to the House of Lords is allowed if

    a. The trial judge grants a certificate on the ground that the case involves a point of law of general importance, for example a matter of statutory interpretation

    b. The parties consent

    c. The House of Lords grants leave for a direct appeal.

Since its introduction in 1969 the leapfrog procedure has rarely been used.

27. *ARTICLE 177(3)* of the *TREATY OF ROME* affects the jurisdiction of the House of Lords. It provides that a court of a member state against whose decisions there is no judicial remedy under national law must refer certain questions to the European Court for a preliminary ruling, and having obtained the ruling is bound to follow it. The questions concern:-

    a. The interpretation of a Treaty; or

    b. The validity and interpretation of acts of the institutions of the Community; or

    c. The interpretation of the statutes of bodies established by an act of the Council of Ministers.

8 Tribunals and Arbitration

TRIBUNALS AND INQUIRIES

1. Statutory Tribunals

a. Statutory tribunals (also called administrative tribunals) are specialised courts established by statute to deal with disputes between government agencies and individuals or between two individuals in a less formal manner than is normal in a court.

b. Tribunals have developed because the growth of social legislation in the 20th century has resulted in many new types of dispute. These disputes are often well suited to a procedure which is comparatively cheap, quick and informal. They are also far to numerous to be dealt with by the ordinary courts. Important statutory tribunals include:-

i. *Social Security Tribunals* — to hear the claim of a person refused a social security benefit;

ii. *Rent Tribunals* — to fix fair rents between landlord and tenant;

iii. *Rating Tribunals* — to determine the proper rateable value for houses, shops and other properties;

iv. *The Lands Tribunals* — to determine disputes concerning the amount of compensation payable when land is compulsorily purchased.

v. *Industrial Tribunals* — with jurisdiction over unfair dismissal, redundancy pay, equal pay and sex discrimination;

vi. *Commissioners of Income Tax* — who hear appeals by tax payers against assessments made by the Inland Revenue.

c. The main difference from the ordinary courts is their composition, their members being lawyers, judges, or laymen with a specialised knowledge of the field in which the tribunal operates.

d. In recent years the control of tribunals, in particular by the courts, has increased. The *TRIBUNALS AND INQUIRIES ACT 1971* provides that in the case of certain specified tribunals the chairman is to be selected from a panel appointed by the Lord Chancellor. In addition there is a Council on Tribunals which keeps under review the working of tribunals and reports on them from time to time. Tribunals subject to the scrutiny of the council include, for example the Lands Tribunal, National Insurance Tribunals, and Rent Tribunals.

2. Some private or professional associations have tribunals to resolve disputes between members or exercise control and discipline over them. The jurisdiction of these tribunals is based on contract in that by becoming a member of the association a person accepts the jurisdiction of the governing tribunal. In some cases the powers of the tribunal are defined by statute, for example The Solicitors Act 1974 and The Medical Act 1978 define the powers of the Solicitors

Disciplinary Tribunal and the Professional Conduct Committee of the General Medical Council respectively. There is normally an appeal from such tribunals to the High Court. If the powers of the tribunal are based solely on contract, for example the tribunals of trade unions or private clubs there is no appeal to the courts, although the High Court may declare that the tribunal has acted beyond its contractual powers and that its action is void.

3. Tribunals of Inquiry. Parliament may, on occasion, set up tribunal to inquire into a matter of urgent public importance. The tribunal will usually be given many of the procedural powers of the High Court, such as summoning witnesses, requiring the production of documents and examining witnesses on oath. The tribunal will sit in public unless the public interest requires otherwise. Persons appearing before the tribunal may, at the discretion of the tribunal be represented by a barrister or solicitor.

4. Local Statutory Inquiries. Many statutes confer jurisdiction upon Ministers to hold local inquiries. Such inquiries often arise when an order made by a local or public authority is submitted to a Minister for confirmation, for example an order for the compulsory acquisition of land. The inquiries are conducted by local inspectors but ultimate responsibility lies with the Minister. Procedure is governed by the statute under which the inquiry is held. However the *TRIBUNALS AND INQUIRIES ACT 1958* requires the Minister to give the reasons for his decision if requested to do so.

5. The Criminal Injuries Compensation Board. Sometimes tribunals are set up to determine an individual's right to compensation from public funds. Thus the Criminal Injuries Compensation Board was established in 1964 to provide compensation to victims of crimes of violence (or if the victim dies, his dependants). Compensation is assessed on the same basis as common law damages and is paid as a lump sum.

6. Control by the Courts

    a. The Donoughmore Committee in 1932 recommended four types of safeguard:-

        i. Against excess of jurisdiction.

        ii. Against failure to observe natural justice ie both sides must be heard, and no person may be the judge of his own case.

        iii. Through publication of reports of tribunals. (This was implemented by the *TRIBUNALS AND INQUIRIES ACT 1958*).

        iv. Through the exercise of supervisory and appellate jurisdiction.

    b. The supervisory control of the courts over tribunals is exercised in two ways:-

        i. By the issue of the prerogative orders of mandamus, certiorari, and prohibition. *Mandamus* is an order compelling the performance of a duty by a person or body of persons. *Prohibition* is the opposite, it is an order to prevent something from being done. *Certiorari* is an order to bring before the High Court a case which has been adjudicated upon, or which is in progress so that the High Court can decide whether or not the inferior court has acted in excess of its jurisdiction, or contrary to natural justice.

ii.   By allowing an individual to bring an action against the officers of the tribunal claiming an injunction or a declaration as to his rights.

c.   *Appeals from tribunals.* The *TRIBUNALS AND INQUIRIES ACT 1971* provides for any party to appeal or to require the tribunal to state a case on a point of law to the High Court. However there is often no right to appeal from the decision of a local inquiry.

7.   Advantages and Disadvantages of Tribunals

a.   *Advantages*

i.   Tribunals specialise in a particular field and use personnel with specialised knowledge and experience.

ii.   They are as informal as is consistent with the proper conduct of their affairs.

iii.   They are less expensive than the courts.

iv.   They are able to meet by appointment, and therefore act more quickly than the courts.

b.   *Disadvantages*

i.   As a result of their flexibility decisions can be inconsistent and difficult to predict.

ii.   Some tribunals do not give reasons for their decisions and others hear cases in private.

iii.   In some cases there is no representation by professional lawyers.

ARBITRATION

8.   Introduction

a.   In the field of commerce in particular many parties prefer to refer their disputes to arbitration rather than have them resolved in court. The main advantages of arbitration are speed, cheapness, and privacy.

b.   An agreement to refer disputes to arbitration is a contract, and is therefore subject to the ordinary law of contract. If the provision attempts to oust the jurisdiction of the courts it is void as being contrary to public policy. The parties may however include a **"SCOTT v AVERY (1856)** clause". Such a clause makes reference to arbitration a condition precedent to a court action. The court may therefore stay proceedings until an arbitrator has first heard the case.

9.   Procedure

a.   Procedure is governed by the *ARBITRATION ACTS 1950 AND 1979* and the ordinary rules of English Law. The arbitrator has an implied power to examine witnesses, order the inspection of documents and so on.

b. Under *S.5. ARBITRATION ACT 1979* if a party fails to comply with an order made by an arbitrator in the course of the reference the High Court may extend his powers to allow him to deal with the default in the same way as a High Court judge in civil proceedings.

c. Under *S.3-4 ARBITRATION ACT 1979* once the arbitration has commenced the parties may enter into an "exclusion agreement". There will then be no power for the High Court to consider a question of law arising during the arbitration, nor will there be a right of appeal. Note that in general an exclusion agreement entered into before the arbitration has commenced will be ineffective.

d. The decision of the arbitrator is known as an "award" and it will deal with all the issues on which reference was made. The award may order the payment of money or costs or it may order specific performance.

10. Appointment of Arbitrators

a. Where an agreement refers a dispute to arbitration it will be presumed that this means reference to a single arbitrator, but where a specific provision is made for 2 arbitrators they must appoint an umpire who, if they cannot agree, will break the deadlock.

b. The parties may appoint any person they wish to act as arbitrator. Lawyers are often appointed, but in some cases a person with relevant technical knowledge is appointed. The High Court has the power to appoint arbitrators in default of appointment by the parties, and to revoke the authority of an arbitrator on the ground of delay, bias or improper conduct.

11. Appeal and Enforcement

a. Under *S.1. ARBITRATION ACT 1979* a party may appeal on any question of law arising out of an award made on an arbitration agreement (unless there is a valid "exclusion agreement"). It is however necessary either for the court to grant leave to appeal or all the parties must consent.

b. The High Court also has jurisdiction to determine (with the consent of the arbitrator or all the parties) any question of law arising in the course of the reference.

c. There is an appeal from the High Court to the Court of Appeal only
    i.   With leave of both of the above courts, and
    ii. Provided the High Court certifies that the question of law is of general public importance.

d. An arbitration award may, with leave of the High Court, be enforced in the same way as a judgement of that court. Alternatively an action may be brought on the award as a contract debt.

9 The Personnel of the Law

1. This chapter deals with solicitors, barristers, judges and juries. Both lay and stipendiary magistrates are personnel of the law, but they are discussed in Chapter 7. The police could also be included under this heading, however a study of their role is beyond the scope of this book.

SOLICITORS

2. Functions of Solicitors

a. There are about 40,000 solicitors practising in the UK. They perform a wide variety of work including conveyancing, probate, divorce, company and commercial matters and general litigation. Some solicitors, particularly in the city centres, are specialists, concentrating for example on company law or maritime law. Many others are general practitioners, deriving most of their income from conveyancing and general litigation, but prepared to undertake most work requested by their clients.

b. If a person wishes to seek a legal remedy or use the facilities of the law for example to sell his house or make a will he will usually consult a solicitor. If a barrister's services are needed, either to present a case in court or to give an expert opinion, the solicitor will instruct the barrister. A layman cannot, in general, instruct a barrister direct. Solicitors are not involved exclusively in office work. They have a right of audience in magistrates and county courts and many solicitors specialise in advocacy.

c. There is no legal obligation to employ a solicitor when seeking a legal remedy. A person may conduct his own case in any court in the land. He can do his own conveyancing, draw up his own will, and conduct his own divorce provided he has the time and common sense to understand and apply the basic procedures involved.

3. The Law Society

a. The solicitors' governing body is the Law Society. Its main functions are:-

i. To control entry requirements to the profession.

ii. To make rules governing the handling of client's money by solicitors.

iii. To protect the public against work by unqualified persons.

iv. To administer the legal aid scheme.

b. Solicitors are liable to the general criminal law, and to a solicitors disciplinary tribunal consisting of the Master of the Rolls, solicitor members, and lay members. Solicitors however cannot be sued for negligence in their conduct of a case in court.

4. Legal Executives. Solicitors usually employ legal executives. They work under the control and authority of the solicitor, and usually specialise in a particular field, for example conveyancing. The governing body of legal executives is the Institute of Legal Executives. It sets its own examinations, however qualification as a legal executive does not entitle a person to practise on his own account.

BARRISTERS

5. Functions of Barristers. Only a minority of qualified barristers practise at the bar. The rest work in industry or education. Barristers work includes advocacy in all courts, and giving written opinions on their specialist areas. They take their instructions only from solicitors and not directly from the client. A successful barrister will usually "take silk" ie become a Queen's Counsel. His work will then be exclusively advocacy. Barristers have a right to be heard in any court, but they may not form partnerships, nor may they sue for their fees.

6. Liability of Barristers

    a. Barristers may not be sued for negligence as a result of their conduct of a case in court.

        In **RONDEL v WORSLEY (1969)** P contended that D, a barrister, had been negligent in the conduct of his case. The claim was struck out as disclosing no cause of action. The main reason given was that if a barrister could be sued for negligence it would mean a re-trial of the original case. This would open the door to every dissatisfied litigant and lead to dozens of pointless actions.

    b. Barristers are not immune from action as a result of pre-trial acts or omissions. The immunity is confined to work which "is intimately connected with the conduct of the case in court" (**SAIF ALI v SYDNEY MITCHELL (1978)**).

7. The Bar Council. This is the barristers governing body. It was formed in 1894. Its purpose is to maintain the standards and independence of the bar. It also deals with questions of professional etiquette, but it has no disciplinary powers.

8. Fusion of the Legal Profession

    a. The division of the legal profession into two branches has been a topic of much discussion in recent years. The Royal Commission established in 1976 to investigate every aspect of legal services considered it at length, eventually concluding (as generally expected) in favour of maintaining the status quo. The main arguments for and against fusion are as follows:

    b. *Arguments against fusion*

        i.   The service provided to the public. – It is argued that if fusion took place the specialist barristers would join the large firms and the client's of small firms would accordingly to be denied access to such specialists. This would result in the decline of small firms of solicitors.

ii.   The service provided to judges. – In a judicial system that relies heavily on oral trials judges need clear argument and guidance to lead them to the correct decision. Such a service can only be provided by a select group of professional advocates.

c.   *Arguments in favour of fusion*

i.   Functions overlap in the present system, both in advocacy and in specialisation in subject matter. – Many solicitors are advocates and spend much of their working life in Magistrates and County Courts and, particularly in the larger firms, many solicitors are highly specialised.

ii.   The present system is inefficient since it involves duplication of effort, and the quality of work is affected because responsibility is divided. Also the custom whereby a barrister only receives his brief one or two days before the trial is seriously prejudicial to the client.

iii.   Cost. – The client will usually have to pay two experts to bring his case to court, and if a Queen's Counsel is employed three lawyers would have to be paid.

d.   A number of reforms have been suggested, for example solicitors could be given a full right of audience in all courts, all barristers could be permitted to form partnerships with solicitors. Alternatively all lawyers could qualify in the same way and then practise as they please, in partnership or alone, taking instructions from lay clients or other lawyers. One class of lawyers would exist, some would be specialists and others general practitioners. Each lawyer could adjust his own practice to the needs of his clients, and his own preferences. The decisions as to which lawyers to use, and in what combinations could then be taken by the client in his own best interests. It is now clear that no unification of the profession will take place in the foreseeable future.

MINISTERS OF THE CROWN

9.   The United Kingdom does not have a Minister of Justice. The link between Parliament and the Judiciary is provided by 4 ministers:-

a.   *The Lord Chancellor.* He is a member of the House of Lords, appointed by the Crown on the advice of the Prime Minister. He is chosen from eminent lawyers or judges who support the party in office and he has a seat in the Cabinet. The Lord Chancellor:-

i.   Is Head of the Judiciary;

ii.   Presides over the House of Lords in both its legislative and judicial capacities;

iii. Is responsible for advising the Crown on the appointment of High Court (puisne) judges;

iv. Is Head of the Chancery Division of the High Court;

v. Is responsible for the work of the Law Commission, the Land Registry, The Public Trustee and the Public Record Office;

vi. Acts as general legal advisor to the Government and as its spokesman in the House of Lords.

b. *The Home Secretary.* He is a member of the House of Commons and of the Cabinet. His responsibilities include:-

i. The Prison, Borstal and Probation services;

ii. The Police;

iii. The administration of the Metropolitan Courts; and

iv. Advice to the Government on the treatment of offenders and on the prerogative of pardon.

c. *The Attorney-General.* He is a barrister and a member of the House of Commons. As senior law officer of the Crown he represents the Crown in important civil and criminal matters. He appoints and supervises the Director of Public Prosecutions.

d. *The Solicitor-General.* He is also a barrister and member of the House of Commons. He assists and deputises for the Attorney-General both in the Commons and in Court.

NB. The *Director of Public Prosecutions (D.P.P.)* is a barrister or solicitor with at least 10 years experience. He is appointed by the Home Secretary and assisted by a staff of professional lawyers and civil service administrators. His role concerns the administration of criminal justice and his duty is to institute proceedings:-

i. When the offence is punishable by death;

ii. When a case is referred to him by a government department; and

iii. In other cases where he considers that his intervention is needed.

JUDGES

10. Appointment

a. Judges above puisne judges are appointed by the Crown on the advice of the Prime Minister. Two posts deserve special mention:-

i. *The Lord Chief Justice.* He is the head of the Criminal Division of the Court of Appeal and the Queen's Bench Division.

ii. *The Master of the Rolls.* He is the head of the Civil Division of the Court of Appeal. He also has duties in connection with the admission of solicitors.

b. High Court (puisne) judges, circuit judges, and recorders are appointed by the Crown on the advice of the Lord Chancellor.

i.   *Puisne judges* must be barristers of at least 10 years standing. They are usually appointed to the division of the High Court in which they practised, but they may sit in any division. There are 80 puisne judges. Appointment is by invitation. On retirement a knighthood is automatic.

ii.   *Circuit judges* number about 340. Any barrister of at least 7 years standing may apply to become a circuit judge, but in practice these judges are appointed from the middle ranks of barristers. The top barristers do not apply because either they are unwilling to take a drop in salary or they hope to be invited to become a puisne judge (there is no career progression from circuit judge to puisne judge).

iii.   *Recorders* must be barristers or solicitors of at least 3 years standing. They are part-time judges who sit in the county court for about 20 days each year. At present there are about 500 recorders.

c.   Judges can only be removed on an address by both Houses of Parliament. No judge has been removed from office since before 1700. Puisne judges retire at 75, and circuit judges at 72.

11. Constitutional Position

a.   Judges are not under the control of Parliament, or the Civil Service. The independence of the judiciary is a fundamental principle of constitutional law. Closely related to judicial independence is the doctrine of judicial immunity. In **SIRROS v MOORE (1975)** it was held that any judge will be immune from action provided he acts honestly and in the belief that he is within his jurisdiction.

b.   Judicial immunity extends to the parties, witnesses, advocates, the verdict of the jury and fair, accurate and contemporaneous newspaper reports.

12. The Function of Judges

a.   The traditional function of judges is to apply existing rules of law to the case before them. It is however being increasingly accepted that judges are capable of ''making law'' both through the interpretation of statutes and the doctrine of precedent. Furthermore it is clear that when an Act of Parliament makes no provision for the case in question and there is no existing precedent, the judge must, of necessity, create new law.

b.   In the following notable cases the judiciary went beyond the application of existing legal rules:-

i.   In **CENTRAL LONDON PROPERTY TRUST v HIGH TREES HOUSE (1947)** Denning J. (as he then was), in the view of many writers, created a new rule of equity, namely equitable estoppel.

ii.   In **SHAW v DPP (1962)** Shaw published a directory of prostitutes. He was found guilty of ''conspiracy to corrupt public morals'', an offence previously unknown to the criminal law.

63

    iii. In **MILIANGOS v GEORGE FRANK TEXTILES (1975)** the House of Lords effected an important reform by holding that English courts have power to give judgements expressed in foreign currency.

  c. Judges also exercise certain administrative functions, for example:-

    i. The Court of Protection (Chancery Division) supervises the affairs and administers the property of persons of unsound mind.

    ii. A rule committee chaired by the Lord Chancellor makes rules to govern procedure in the Supreme Court.

JURIES

13. The History of the Jury

a. The trial of criminals by jury evolved in the 13th century to replace trial by ordeal which the church condemned in 1215. Most civil cases were also tried by jury until 1854.

b. Juries were originally summoned for their local knowledge, but by the 15th century their function had changed from witnesses to judges of fact. Nevertheless it was not until **BUSHELL'S CASE (1670)** that it was established that jurors could not be punished for returning a verdict contrary to the direction of the trial judge.

c. Until the present century the jury was widely regarded as one of the chief safeguards of the individual against the abuse of prerogative and judicial power. However, particularly in civil cases, juries were unpredictable and liable to make errors. In 1854 the *COMMON LAW PROCEDURE ACT* therefore provided that in civil cases the trial could be heard by a judge sitting alone if both parties consented.

    In 1933 the *ADMINISTRATION OF JUSTICE (MISCELLANEOUS PROVISIONS) ACT* abolished civil juries in most cases, the main exceptions being fraud and defamation. The jury has also declined in criminal cases, but the loss of faith in the criminal jury has been far less marked.

14. The Present Day Jury

a. Jurors are summoned by the Lord Chancellor and selection is by random ballot. An incomplete jury may be completed by summoning any person in or near the court to serve. A juror is in contempt of court if he refuses to serve or if he is drunk. MPs, lawyers, doctors, the clergy, some ex-prisoners, and the mentally unsound do not qualify for jury service.

b. Juries used to be criticised because the property-ownership qualification produced a jury that was not representative of the population. However the property qualification was abolished in 1972, and now any registered elector resident for 5 years or over, between 18 and 65, may be summoned for jury service.

c. The jury sits in private and a majority verdict of 10-2 is necessary for a conviction.

15. Criticisms of the Jury

a. To some people the whole idea of a jury seems absurd. 12 individuals usually with no prior contact with courts are chosen at random to listen to evidence, often of a highly technical nature. They are given no training, they deliberate in secret, they do not give reasons for their verdict, and they are responsible to no one but themselves. After making a decision affecting the liberty of another individual they merge back into the community.

b. More specific criticisms are

i. Jurors are thought to be biased towards the motorist in motoring offences, and against newspapers in libel cases.

ii. Jurors can be taken in by skilled speakers, and are not experienced in weighing evidence.

iii. The system is not popular with jurors since attendance is compulsory and unpaid.

iv. In a comprehensive study published in 1979, John Baldwin and Michael McConville found that the jury was representative of the population in terms of age and social class, but unrepresentative in terms of sex and race. Their research did not however find a consistent relationship between the composition of the jury and its verdict. A more important aspect of their study was to look at "questionable" convictions and acquittals. They found that the incidence of such decisions was sufficiently high to "shake the dogmatic and complacent attitudes that tend to characterise opinions about the jury system".

16. Defence of the Jury

a. There are many passionate defenders of the jury. The argue that it is a check upon unpopular laws, that it is the best means for establishing the truth, that it serves an important political function by involving laymen in the administration of justice, and most important that it is a safeguard of liberty. Lord Devlin wrote:-

"No tyrant could afford to leave a subject's freedom in the hands of 12 of his countrymen. So that trial by jury is more than an instrument of justice and more than one wheel of the constitution: it is the lamp that shows that freedom lives".

b. It is also clear that in general the jury enjoys the confidence of the public, the judiciary, lawyers, and the police, and although Baldwin and McConville show that its verdicts are questionable more often than was previously thought, it may well be that it reaches the right decision as often as can reasonably be expected of any tribunal.

10 Procedure and Evidence

"Procedure" and "Evidence" are both topics of considerable substance and complexity. This chapter does not attempt to explain these topics in detail. It merely explains some of the basic rules, procedures and terminology. It is primarily intended to indicate that particular rules exist rather than describe their detailed content.

CIVIL PROCEDURE

1. **Introduction.** The term "procedure" covers all the steps necessary to turn a legal right into a satisfied judgement, it does not merely refer to the trial itself. The proceedings prior to trial, particularly in larger civil cases usually take many months and often result in a settlement being reached before any trial takes place. Proceedings after trial may also take many months, for example appeals procedure and the enforcement of the judgement. This section will be concerned with bringing an action in the Queen's Bench Division of the High Court, which may be regarded as the standard procedure. There are however many variations from this where an action is brought, for example, in bankruptcy. Procedure in the Queen's Bench Division is governed by the Rules of the Supreme Court. These rules are delegated legislation and are made by a Rule Committee under powers conferred by the *JUDICATURE ACT 1925*. It is important to note that these rules are purely procedural and will be declared ultra vires if they attempt to deal with substantive rules of law.

2. **Summary.** The basic steps involved are as follows:-

    a. The action is begun by issuing and serving a writ.

    b. The defendant acknowledges service.

    c. An exchange of pleadings takes place.

    d. Preparation is made for the trial, including discovery and inspection of documents.

    e. The trial.

    f. If there is no appeal the matter is concluded by enforcement of the judgement.

3. **Commencement of Proceedings**

    a. *Writs.* — The usual method of commencing an action is to issue a writ. This places the matter on official record. A copy of the writ must be served on each defendant either personally or by some other means such as service on his solicitor.

    b. *Petitions.* — Some actions are commenced by a petition rather than a writ, for example a divorce or a company liquidation.

c. ***Acknowledgement of service.*** – If a person on whom a writ is served proposes to enter a defence he must, within 14 days of service of the writ, deliver an acknowledgement. The form of acknowledgement is served by the plaintiff with the writ. After acknowledging service the defendant has a further 14 days in which to file a defence.

4. Pleadings

a. The object of pleadings is to define the area of contention between the parties. A pleading must contain a brief statement of the facts relied on, but not the evidence by which they will be proved. If a matter is not included in the pleadings it cannot usually be raised at the trial.

b. The pleadings are:-

i. The *statement of claim*. This is the first pleading and it is made by the plaintiff.

ii. The *defence*, ie the defendant's answer. If the defendant has a complaint against the plaintiff he may include a *counterclaim* with his defence.

iii. The *reply*. This is the plaintiff's answer to the defence.

c. A typical series of pleadings may appear as follows:-

In the Queen's Bench Division of the High Court.

Between

ACME BUILDERS LTD   *Plaintiff*

and

JOHN BROWN   *Defendant*

Particulars of Claim

The Plaintiff's claim is for the balance of the agreed price for materials supplied and work done at the Defendant's factory at 30 Newton Street, Luton, between November 1987 and June 1988.

Particulars

Agreed price of work	£20,000
Received on account	£16,000
Balance	£4,000
And the Plaintiff claims:	£4,000

Defence and Counterclaim

1. The Defendant admits that the Plaintiff agreed to build an extension to the Defendant's factory for the sum of £20,000 to a specification prepared by the Plaintiff and agreed by the Defendant in a letter dated 30th September 1987.

2. It is admitted that the Plaintiff purported to carry out the work contracted for and that the sum of £4,000 is outstanding therefor. The Defendant will seek to set off his counterclaim in extinction of the sum due to the Plaintiff.

Counterclaim

3. It was a term of the contract the the Plaintiff would carry out the work in a workmanlike manner.

4. In breach of contract certain work has been carried out in a defective manner and not in accordance with the agreed specification.

5. Particulars of the defects are shown on the attached schedule. The total estimated cost of rectification shown therein is £5,000.

And the Defendant Counterclaims: £5,000

Reply and Defence to Counterclaim

1. The Plaintiff admits the facts and matters set out in the Defence.

2. Paragraph 3 of the counterclaim is admitted. Paragraph 4 is denied. It is denied that any of the work is defective or fails to comply with the specification.

---

   d. If either party needs more information he may ask for "further and better particulars" of specific matters.

5. Default Judgements. If the defendant fails to acknowledge service or if he fails to serve a defence the plaintiff may obtain a default judgement without the necessity of restoring to a trial.

6. Summary Judgements. If the plaintiff feels that there is no defence to the action he may apply for a summary judgement. The application will be dealt with by a Master of the Court. He is an official who has most of the powers of a judge. His decision can be set aside on appeal to the judge.

7.   Procedure from Close of Pleadings to Trial

a.   Between close of pleadings and trial much preparatory work must be done by the parties' solicitors.

b.   *Discovery and inspection of documents.* Discovery refers to the requirements of each side to disclose to the other all documents which are relevant to the dispute. Certain privileged documents need not be disclosed, for example letters between the party and his solicitor and experts' reports.

c.   *Summons for directions.* The interlocutory proceedings (proceedings until trial) are concluded by the taking out by the plaintiff of a summons for directions. A Master will hear the summons for directions. He will fix such matters as the date and venue of the trial and the numbers of expert witnesses that may be called by each side.

8.   Trial

a.   In the High Court the parties are usually represented by barristers although they may appear in person. Solicitors have a right of audience in the County Court and in Magistrates Courts but not in the High Court.

b.   The trial starts with the plaintiff's barrister outlining the issues involved and calling witnesses. The defendant's barrister then outlines his case and calls the evidence for the defence. Next the defendant's barrister and then the plaintiff's barrister will make a closing speech. Finally the judge gives the decision in the form of a reasoned judgement which may be delivered as soon as the case is concluded, or reserved to a later date if the judge wishes to consider the case further.

9.   Enforcement of the Judgement. The final stage is enforcement of the judgement. If the defendant does not pay a judgement debt there are several ways by which the judgement creditor can obtain payment. The most important of these is the writ of *fieri facias* (fi fa) which orders the sheriff to seize the debtor's goods and, if necessary, sell them to pay the plaintiff out of the proceeds. The creditor may also be able to obtain a *charging order* on the defendant's land. If the debt is not paid the creditor will eventually be able to have the land sold and recover the judgement debt from the proceeds.

10.   Proceedings in County Courts are broadly similar to High Court actions, although rather less formal and complex.

CRIMINAL PROCEDURE

11. Procedure before Trial

a.   Where the offence is not serious and the accused is likely to appear when required a summons is issued informing him of the time, date and place of the trial.

b.   If the offence is more serious and there is a possibility that the accused will not appear voluntarily a warrant for his arrest will be issued. A warrant is a written order addressed to the police ordering them to secure the person to whom it refers.

12. Summary Trial

a.   A summary trial is a trial by magistrates without a jury.

b.   The Clerk to the Justices will read the charge and ask the accused to plead it. If the accused pleads not guilty or if he remains silent the trial will commence with the prosecutor addressing the court and then calling his evidence. The defence may then address the court and call evidence. Both prosecution and defence witnesses may be cross-examined, as in civil cases. The prosecution may then call further evidence (if appropriate) to rebut the defence, and the defence may also be given a second opportunity to address the court. If the defence has been granted this second opportunity to speak the prosecution will be given the final right of reply.

c.   The magistrates will then make their decision. If they find the accused guilty they may consider previous convictions or evidence of previous good character before deciding on the sentence. If the court consider that the accused should receive a greater punishment than they have power to impose the accused may be referred to the Crown Court for sentence.

d.   Prior to 1957 the accused had to appear in court in person. The *MAGISTRATES' COURTS ACT 1957* introduced a procedure whereby the accused can plead guilty by post in cases where his appearance at court would be a mere formality, if not a waste of time and money. The procedure has been successful and is widely used, particularly in motoring cases.

13. Trial of an Indictable Offence

a.   First it is necessary to establish whether there is a prima facie case against the accused. This is the function of committal proceedings before examining magistrates. (Chapter 7.5.)

b.   If it is decided to commit the accused to the Crown Court for trial the magistrates then have to decide whether to remand him in custody or release him on bail. In making this decision they will consider, in particular, the nature of the offence and the character of the accused.

c.   Between committal and trial a document called an *indictment* is prepared. This is a brief statement of the nature of the offence. This is read to the accused at the start of the trial. He then pleads "guilty" or "not guilty". If the plea is "not guilty" a jury must be summoned. From this point the procedure is basically similar to the summary procedure outlined in **12.**b. above.

EVIDENCE

14. Definition

a. *Evidence* is the means by which the facts in issue are proved.

b. A *fact in issue* is any fact which is presented to the court as fundamental to the court. For example if a person is accused of murder it must be proved that he unlawfully killed the deceased and he did so with malice aforethought. These are the facts in issue. If the defence of insanity is raised, the accused's sanity would also be a fact in issue.

15. The Burden of Proof

a. The general rule is that the burden (or onus) of proving a fact falls on the person seeking to rely on that fact.

b. In criminal cases the accused is presumed to be innocent until he is proved to be guilty. In order to prove him guilty the prosecution must prove its case beyond *reasonable doubt*.

c. In civil cases the burden of proof is less onerous. It is sufficient that the facts are proved on the *balance of probabilities*.

d. There are several exceptions to the general rule whereby certain matters do not require affirmative proof:-

    i. **Formal admissions.** Facts which are formally admitted in civil or criminal cases need not be proved.

    ii. **Judicial notice.** In both civil and criminal cases the court will recognise the existence of certain facts without the need for proof. Such facts are said to be "judicially noticed". For example

       In **BRYANT v FOOT (1868)** the rector of a parish claimed that 13 shillings (65 pence) was the customary fee for the celebration of a marriage in the parish. In order to prove the existence of a valid custom it must be shown that the custom dates from "time immemorial" (fixed by statute at 1189) and that it is reasonable. A custom cannot be reasonable if it would obviously have been unreasonable in 1189. The court were prepared to take judicial notice of the fact that the value of money had declined since 1189, ie this fact did not need to be proved. It was therefore held that the customary right did not exist because the amount claimed would have been unreasonable in 1189.

    iii. **Presumptions.** Sometimes certain facts will be presumed in favour of a party, who will therefore not need to prove them. Some presumptions cannot be denied. These are said to be irrebuttable. For example the *CHILDREN AND YOUNG PERSONS ACT 1963* provides that "It shall be conclusively presumed that no child under the age of 10 years can be guilty of any offence". However most presumptions are rebuttable, ie they will be set aside if there is actual evidence

71

to the contrary. The effect of such a presumption is therefore to shift the burden of proof from the party in whose favour the presumption operates to his opponent. For example there is a rebuttable presumption that any alterations to a will were made after its execution.

16. Relevance and Admissibility

a. Two types of facts are relevant:-

i. Facts in issue, and

ii. Other facts from which the facts in issue may be inferred. This is known as circumstantial evidence.

b. Problems are more likely to arise when determining whether a fact is relevant as circumstantial evidence than when trying to decide whether a fact is, or is not, a fact in issue. It will be up to the judge to decide in each case. For example it has been held that if the speed of a vehicle at a given moment is a fact in issue, evidence of its speed a few moments earlier is admissible as circumstantial evidence (**BERESFORD v ST ALBANS JUSTICES (1905)**). Similarly in a prosecution for murder evidence that the accused purchased the gun which fired the bullet which killed the deceased is admissible as circumstantial evidence.

c. Some evidence, which would probably be regarded by a layman to be relevant is regarded by the law as irrelevant and therefore inadmissible. For example:-

i. *Similar facts*. Evidence that a person behaved in a certain way on other occasions is not admissible to prove that he behaved in a similar way on the occasion in question. For example:-

In **R v RODLEY (1913)** the Court of Appeal quoshed a conviction of burglary (with intent to ravish) because evidence had been wrongfully admitted that the accused had entered another house by the chimney later the same night and had intercourse with the consenting occupant.

The court will not however ignore ''striking resemblances'' which if ignored, would be an affront to common sense.

ii. *Character*. The fact that a person is of good or bad character is generally irrelevant to whether or not he has performed a certain act on the occasion in question. In addition such evidence could be prejudicial to a fair trial. If Mr X gives evidence of his good character a jury may be persuaded to find in his favour even though his arguments are not adequately supported by facts. If his opponent, Mr Y, also produces evidence of good character the trial could be diverted from investigation of the facts by examination of witnesses to a comparison of the supposed characters of Mr X and Mr Y. Thus evidence as to character is generally inadmissible. There are many exceptions to this rule, for example reputation, which is one aspect of character, is a fact in issue in defamation.

17. The Means of Proof

a. Once it has been decided what facts may be proved and on whom the burden of proving them falls the question arises of the means by which these facts are to be proved. There are three methods:-

i. By the evidence of witnesses;

ii. By documentary evidence;

iii. By real evidence.

b. *Witnesses*

i. The general rule is that all persons including children and mentally disordered persons are both competent and compellable as witnesses. There are several exceptions to this general rule, for example the Sovereign, ambassadors and various grades of diplomatic staff are not compellable; the spouse of the accused in a criminal case is competent but not compellable for the defence and is incompetent for the prosecution; the accused person is not a competent witness for the prosecution in a criminal case; and very young children may be incompetent simply because of immaturity.

ii. The general rule is that all witnesses must give evidence on oath. In civil proceedings the oath is:-

"I swear by Almighty God that the evidence which I shall give shall be the truth, the whole truth, and nothing but the truth."
(S.2. OATHS ACT 1909).

iii. There are two basic rules which relate to the testimony of witnesses:-

Firstly evidence should be given orally and in open court. There are many exceptions to this rule, for example provisions enabling evidence to be taken before trial, and in some cases given by affidavit.

Secondly evidence must be confined to facts which the witness personally perceived. This rule excludes opinions and hearsay evidence. (These are discussed below).

c. *Documentary evidence.* A person who wishes to rely on the contents of a document as a means of proving a fact must prove:-

i. What the document in question contains. This is usually done by producing the original of the document, although there are several exceptional circumstances in which a copy is admissible.

ii. That the document on which he relies is authentic or has been duly executed. In most cases it will not be necessary for a party to prove all the documents in his possession since many of them will be formally admitted by his opponent. When a document is not admitted it may be proved by handwriting, attestation, or presumption. *Handwriting* is the commonest method of proving the validity or execution of a document and may be proved by ordinary or expert witnesses. The usual method of proof is to put the document before the writer in the witness box. *Attestation* is the signature of a document as a witness to the signature of one of the parties to the document. Proof by attestation involves calling one of the attesting witnesses, or if none of them are available, by proof of the handwriting of one of them. The main category of documents which require attestation are wills and codicils. *Presumption* applies to documents more than 20 years old. Provided such documents are produced from proper custody, (ie from a place where the document would be expected to be kept, for example a bank or a solicitor's office), there is a presumption that the document is validly executed *(S.4 EVIDENCE ACT 1938)*.

d.   *Real evidence.* This refers to the inspection of physical objects (other than documents) by the court. There are three main types of real evidence:-

i.   Material objects produced for inspection by the court, for example an alleged murder weapon, or goods alleged to have been stolen. These are referred to in court as "exhibits".

ii.   The physical appearance of persons. For example a person's wounds may be inspected by the court when it is necessary to assess damages for personal injury.

iii.   A view is real evidence, ie an inspection outside the court of a place or object where the physical characteristics of that place or object are relevant facts.

18.   Means of Proof which are Generally Inadmissible

a.   *Opinions.* The basic rule is that a witness may only testify as to facts which he has directly perceived. He may not state his opinion on how those facts should be interpreted. The reason for this rule is that it is the function of the court, not of the witnesses, to draw conclusions from the proven facts. Opinion as a means of proof must be distinguished from opinion as a fact in itself, which is not excluded. For example if a man is accused of having unlawful sexual intercourse with a girl under 16 his opinion that she was over 16 is admissible as part of his defence. The main exception to the rule excluding proof by opinion relates to expert witnesses who may give an opinion based on impression or inference, although the court is not bound to accept the inference.

b.   *Hearsay.* Hearsay evidence is basically "second hand" evidence of what another person said or wrote. The general rule is that a person can give evidence of what he heard or saw, however he cannot give evidence of what he heard another person say. For example "I heard X say that he had seen Y steal the car" would be inadmissible. The reason is that it would be unfair to admit a statement (X's statement) which was not made under oath and which cannot be tested by cross-examination. Hearsay evidence may be oral or written. Thus for example a birth certificate is hearsay evidence of a date of birth (although it is admissible as an exception to the rule). There are many other exceptions to the hearsay rule which are beyond the scope of this book.

11 The Law of Persons

INTRODUCTION

1.   A legal person is a being that is regarded by the law as having rights and duties.

2.   There are two basic types of legal person — natural persons and corporations. A corporation is an artificial person which is recognised in law as a separate legal entity once the formalities for its creation have been complied with. A corporation must be distinguished from an unincorporated association, which does not have a legal identity separate from that of its members. The most significant types of corporation and unincorporated association are limited companies and partnerships respectively. The discussion below will therefore concentrate on these two forms of business organisation, in addition to considering natural persons, and the concepts of nationality, domicile and residence.

NATURAL PERSONS

3.   Human beings generally have full legal capacity, and consequently are potentially subject to any rule of law. The actual rules to which a person is subject depends on the factual situation in which he finds himself. These factual situations which affect a persons rights and capacities are called statuses. One person may have many statuses, for example husband, father, employer. Other examples include infant, guardian, wife, and mentally disordered person.

4.   **Husband and Wife.** In HYDE v HYDE (1866) marriage was defined as the ''voluntary union for life of one man and one woman to the exclusion of all others''. The main legal consequences of marriage are:-

    a.   Both spouses are under a duty to cohabit.

    b.   The husband has a duty to maintain his wife.

    c.   Both spouses can sue each other in contract and tort.

    d.   Both have rights regarding succession on death.

    e.   Under *S.17. MARRIED WOMAN'S PROPERTY ACT 1882* either spouse may apply to the court for the determination of any dispute arising between them as to the title or possession of property.

    f.   Both have a right to occupy the matrimonial home.

    g.   A wife takes her husband's domicile.

5.   **Infants.** In addition to the contract and tort rules applicable to infants which are dealt with in Chapter 16 and Chapter 25 respectively the following points should be noted:-

a.   An infant cannot marry under 16, and requires his parent's consent to marry under 18.

b.   He cannot vote, or become a Member of Parliament.

c.   He cannot hold a legal estate in land, but he can hold an equitable interest.

d.   He cannot make a will.

e.   He cannot take part directly in civil litigation, but must sue through his "next friend" and defend through his "guardian ad litem" — usually his father in both cases. An infant may however defend himself if he is charged with a crime.

f.   Under the *CHILDREN AND YOUNG PERSONS ACT 1963* an infant below the age of 10 cannot be guilty of a crime. Between the ages of 10 and 14 there is a rebuttable presumption that he does not have the intention (ie the mens rea) necessary to hold him liable.

g.   There are many other rules concerning, for example driving, films, drinking, smoking, school attendance, and work that affect infants.

LIMITED COMPANIES

6.   **Introduction.** There are various types of corporation including:-

a.   *Corporation sole.* ie An official position which is filled by one person who is replaced from time to time. For example the Public Trustee and the Treasury Solicitor.

b.   *Chartered corporations.* These are usually charitable associations and bodies such as the Law Society, the Institute of Chartered Accountants and the Association of Certified Accountants.

c.   *Statutory corporations.* For example the British Railways Board and the National Coal Board.

d.   *Registered companies.* The *COMPANIES ACT 1985* provides for the registration of unlimited companies, companies limited by guarantee and companies limited by shares. The latter are by far the most numerous and the remainder of this part (7-15) is devoted to them. Recently the *COMPANIES ACT 1989* has made a number of major changes to Company Law concerning for example company accounts, company auditors, the capacity of companies and company administration.

7.   **Consequences of Registration**

a.   The most important consequence of registration is that a company becomes a legal person distinct from its members.

In **SALOMON v SALOMON LTD (1897)** S formed a limited company with other members of his family, and sold his business to the company. He held 20,001 of the 20,007 shares which had been issued by the company, and £10,000 of debentures (documents acknowledging that the company owed S money). About a year after its formation the company was wound-up. The assets were at that time worth about £6,000. The persons claiming these assets were (a) Creditors to the value of £7,000 and (b) S, as holder of £10,000 debentures. The creditors claimed that they should have priority because S and the company were in effect the same person. The House of Lords however held that S and the company were separate legal entities and that since debenture holders generally have priority over creditors in a winding-up, S was entitled to the £6,000 assets.

b.   Some of the consequences of the separate legal entity of a company are:-

    i.   It can make contracts, sue, and be sued in its own name.

    ii.   It can own property and the members have no direct or insurable interest in its property.

    In **MACAURA v NORTHERN ASSURANCE CO. (1925)** M owned a timber estate. He formed a limited company and sold the timber estate to it. Like Salomon he was basically a "one man company". Before he sold the estate to the company it had been insured in his own name. After the sale to the company he neglected to transfer the insurance policy to the company's name. The estate was destroyed by fire. It was held that M could not claim under the policy because the assets that were damaged belonged to a separate legal entity. ie M, as shareholder, had no insurable interest in the assets of the company.

    In contrast to Salomon's case, this case shows that the separate legal entity theory does not always operate in the shareholder's favour.

    iii.   It has perpetual succession, ie its existence is not affected by the death of some, or even all of its members.

c.   In some circumstances the law will ignore the separate legal personality of the company, and will "lift the veil of incorporation" to hold the members personally responsible for the actions of the company. eg

    i.   If the company is being used to evade legal obligations.

    In **GILFORD MOTOR CO. v HORNE (1933)** An employee convenanted that after the termination of his employment he would not solicit his employer's customers. Soon after the termination of his employment he formed a company, which then sent out circulars to the customers of his former employer. The court were prepared to lift the "veil of incorporation", granting an injunction which prevented both the former employee *and his company* from distributing the circulars, even though the company was not a party to the covenant.

    ii.   If the controllers of the company are alien enemies.

    In **DAIMLER v CONTINENTAL TYRE AND RUBBER CO. (1916)** CTR sued Daimler for money due in respect of goods supplied.

Daimler's defence was that since CTR's members and officers were German, to pay the debt would be to trade with the enemy, even though CTR was a company registered in England. This defence succeeded.

iii. If it appears that business has been carried on with intent to defraud creditors, members who are party to the fraud are personally liable for the company's debts.

8. Public and Private Companies — Definition

a. *Public companies* must

   i. Be registered as public companies;

   ii. Have at least 2 members; and

   iii. State in their memorandum that they are public companies.

b. *Private companies* are limited companies having at least two members, and which are not registered as public companies. ie A company will be private unless it is specifically registered as public.

9. The Main Differences Between Public and Private Companies

a. *Purpose.* Public and private companies fulfil different economic purposes. The purpose of a public company is to raise capital from the public to run the enterprise. This ability to offer shares to the public is now the only advantage of a public company. The purpose of a private company is to confer separate legal personality on the business of a sole trader or partnership.

b. *Issue of Capital.* A private company may not raise capital by issuing its securities to the public. There is no restriction on the offer of securities by a public company. A public company must however issue a prospectus (a document which gives minimum essential information to potential members) and comply with Stock Exchange rules to obtain a listing of the securities.

c. *Transferability of Shares.* The shares of a public company are freely transferable on the Stock Exchange. A private company will, in contrast, wish to remain under the control of the "family" or "partners" concerned. Its articles will therefore contain a clause restricting the right to transfer shares. The restriction may be:-

   i. An absolute power vested in the directors to refuse a register a transfer; and/or

   ii. A right of pre-emption (first refusal) granted to existing members when another member wishes to transfer his shares.

d. *Minimum Share Capital.* A public company must have a minimum allotted share capital of £50,000. A private company has no minimum share capital.

e.   *Company Name.* The name of a public company must end with the words ''Public Limited Company'', which may be abbreviated to ''P.L.C.'' A private company's name must end with ''Limited''. This may be abbreviated to ''Ltd''.

f.   *The Memorandum.* A public company's memorandum must state that ''The company is to be a public company''.

g.   *Payment for Shares.* There are a number of differences in the rules relating to the consideration given in return for shares. For example if a public company issues shares in return for the transfer of a non-cash asset, that asset must be independently valued to ensure that the company is receiving an asset of a value at least as great as the value of shares issued in return. In a private company there is no requirement to obtain a report on the value of non-cash consideration received as payment for shares.

h.   *Dividends.* There are detailed rules which differentiate between the ability of public and private companies to distribute their profits as dividends.

i.   *Company Administration.* The *COMPANIES ACT 1989* made a number of changes designed to help small businesses by cutting the burden of regulation. Thus a private company may pass an *elective resolution* (this must be agreed by all members entitled to attend and vote at the meeting) if it wishes, for example (a) to dispense with the requirement to lay accounts and reports before the company in general meeting (b) to dispense with the requirement to hold an AGM or (c) to dispense with the requirement to appoint auditors annually.

j.   *Written Resolutions.* The 1989 Act also introduced a written resolution procedure for private companies. Anything which may be done by resolution of a private company in general meeting may now be done by a written resolution signed by or on behalf of all members.

k.   *Other Differences.* There are numerous other differences concerning, for example, directors, the secretary, commencement of business, and accounts.

10.   The Memorandum and Articles

a.   On the creation of a company the promoters must file certain documents with the Registrar of Companies. These include the Articles of Association and the Memorandum of Association. The Articles contain details of how the company will be run from day to day, for example the duties of directors, the rights of each class of shares, and procedure at meetings. The memorandum lays down the constitution of the company, for example its name, authorised capital, and objects.

b.   Prior to the *COMPANIES ACT 1989* the objects clause was regarded as very important because it defined the limits of the company's contractual capacity and any act beyond those limits was ultra vires and void.

Companies tried to avoid the ultra vires rule by drafting long and detailed objects clauses allowing them to do almost anything that they could ever wish to do.

The effect of the 1989 Act is to considerably reduce the importance of the objects clause. It does this in two ways.

> i.   It provides that it will be sufficient for the memorandum to state that the object of the company is to carry on business as a general commercial company. This will allow the company (a) to carry on any trade or business whatsoever and (b) to do all such things as are incidental or conducive to the carrying on of any trade or business by it.

> ii. It also provides that the validity of an act done by a company shall not be called into question on the ground of lack of capacity by reason of anything in the company's memorandum. Consequently a completed act will have total protection from the ultra vires rule and will be enforcable by both the company and an outsider.

The Act does retain the power of members to bring proceedings to restrain ultra vires acts. However it is most unlikely that a company taking advantage of the provision described in (i) above will ever make an ultra vires contract.

11. The Raising and Maintenance of Capital

a.   The acceptance of limited liability has led to a need to protect the capital contributed by the members since the members cannot be required to contribute funds to enable the company to pay its debts once they have paid for their shares in full. The capital therefore represents a guarantee fund for creditors. It is protected in 2 basic ways (b. and c. below).

b.   There are provisions designed to prevent the capital being "watered down" as it comes in to the company. For example

> i.   The provision requiring an independent valuation of a non-cash asset accepted by a public company as payment for its shares.

> ii. A company may not pay underwriters a commission of more than 10% of the issue price of shares. Underwriters are persons who agree to take any shares not taken up by the public on a public issue of shares. They receive a commission which means that, in effect, they pay less than the full price for any shares which they have to take.

> iii. Subject to exceptions, a person must pay the full price for his shares if called upon to do so.

c.   Other rules are designed to prevent the capital going out of a company once it has been received. For example:-

> i.   Dividends may only be paid out of profits and not out of capital.

> ii. A company may not purchase its own shares. (If it buys its own shares from "Member X" it will have less money available to pay Creditors X, Y, and Z.)

d.   Creditors are also protected by many other rules not connected with the maintenance of capital. For example the rule that "PLC" or "Ltd" must be the last word of the name warns creditors that they do not have access to the private wealth of the members to pay their debts.

12. Company Securities

a.   There are 2 basic types of company security, *shares* and *debentures*.

b.   *Differences between shares and debentures*

   i.   A shareholder is a member of the company. He therefore has an *interest in* the company. Ownership of a share gives a person rights in and obligations to a company. It does not however constitute part ownership of the assets of the company since the company, as a separate legal entity, owns its own assets. A debentureholder is a person who has lent money to a company. His status is that of a creditor. He therefore has a *claim against* the company rather than an interest in it.

   ii.   Since debentures are not "capital", none of the rules of capital maintenance apply to them. Thus, for example a company may purchase its own debentures since this merely amounts to early repayment of a loan.

c.   *Similarities between shares and debentures*

   i.   The typical debenture is one of a series or "class" similar to a class of shares.

   ii.   Usually debentureholders (like normal mortgagees) will not be able to claim their money back on demand. The loan will only be repayable after a date several years in the future.

   iii.   Debentures are transferable. The same form is used as for a transfer of shares.

   iv.   Debentures may be quoted on the Stock Exchange and when debentures are issued to the public a prospectus is required.

13. Company Officers

a.   Directors are the persons to whom management of a company is entrusted. Together with the secretary and the managers they are the "officers" of the company.

b.   Directors may be appointed and removed by a simple majority vote of the members. Since they are in a position of trust where they control large sums of other peoples' money, and in a position whereby it is relatively easy to abuse this trust, directors are subject to a wide variety of statutory and non-statutory rules which try to ensure that directors do not abuse their position. For example:-

   i.   A company cannot transfer to or acquire from a director any property the value of which exceeds £50,000 or 10% of the company's net assets without prior approval of the shareholders.

ii.   Subject to exceptions, a company may not lend money to its own directors.

iii. Any "golden handshake" payments on retirement must first be disclosed to and approved by the members.

iv.   A director must not make any undisclosed profit from his position.

c.   The Articles of the company will usually authorise the directors to appoint one of their number as *managing director* on such terms as they think fit. He will usually be given a service contract for a fixed period of years. His rights and duties will depend on the terms of this contract.

d.   Every company must have a *secretary*. The secretary is usually appointed by the directors. He is the chief administrative officer of the company and on matters of administration he has authority to make contracts on behalf of the company, for example hiring office staff. He cannot however bind the company on a trading contract.

14. Liquidation, Receiverships and Administration

a.   The *liquidation* or *winding-up* of a company is the process whereby its life is ended and its property administered for the benefit of its creditors and members. A liquidator takes control of the company, collects its assets, pays its debts and distributes any surplus among the members. There are two main types of liquidation. A *compulsory liquidation* is under an order of the court, and usually follows a petition by unpaid creditors. A *voluntary liquidation* is initiated by a resolution of the company, although the underlying reason is usually the same, ie pressure from creditors.

b.   A *receiver* is a person appointed by the debentureholders in the event of, for example, non-payment of interest. His basic duty is to collect in the assets which provide the security for the loan, to realise those assets and to pay the debentureholders the amount due to them, accounting to the company for the surplus. A receivership will not necessarily lead to a liquidation, but in many cases the appointment of a receiver will induce the creditors to petition to wind-up the company.

c.   *Administration* is a new procedure introduced in the *INSOLVENCY ACT 1985* as an alternative to receivership. The basic purpose of an administration order is to freeze the debts of a company in financial difficulties to assist an administrator to save the company, or at least achieve the better realisation of its assets. It is not a procedure designed for creditors to enforce their security. It is not yet known whether the procedure will be a success. This will depend on the answer to two questions:

i.   Will debentureholders block the procedure by appointing a receiver who then vetoes the appointment of an administrator? This will probably happen in very many cases.

ii.   If an administrator has been appointed, how willing will people be to trade with the company?

d.   The *INSOLVENCY ACT 1985* also introduced *minimum qualifications for insolvency practitioners*. Prior to the Act neither liquidators nor receivers had to have any professional qualifications or practical experience. This no doubt contributed to some illegal and unethical practices by a minority of liquidators, usually to the detriment of creditors. Under the Act an insolvency practitioner, ie a liquidator, administrator or receiver will only be able to act if he is authorised to do so by:-

i.   A recognised professional body; or

ii.   The "relevant authority" to be set up by the Secretary of State.

e.   The statutory provisions on liquidation, receivership and administration are now contained in the *INSOLVENCY ACT 1986*. Like the *COMPANIES ACT 1985* it did not create any new rules, it repealed the *INSOLVENCY ACT of 1985* and consolidated all the insolvency provisions in that Act and in the *COMPANIES ACT 1985*.

15.   Conclusion. The law relating to limited companies is complex and detailed. Its purpose is to provide a framework for the fair and efficient operation of business enterprise. In particular it attempts to achieve the following aims:-

a.   To preserve the principle of majority rule, while ensuring that the controlling majority do not abuse their power;

b.   To protect the general body of shareholders from abuse of power by the directors; and

c.   To protect the capital of the company, since this is the fund on which the creditors rely for payment of their debts.

PARTNERSHIPS

16.   Introduction. Unincorporated associations consist of a number of persons who have come together for a matter of common interest, for example a sports club, a trade union, or a partnership. The associations do not have a separate legal entity from their members. Thus the property of an association is regarded as belonging to the members jointly, and if a wrong is committed by a member the general rule is that he alone is liable for what he has done. There are exceptions to this rule, in particular in connection with partnerships.

17.   Definition

a.   A partnership is defined by the *PARTNERSHIP ACT 1890* as "a relation which subsists between persons carrying on a *business* in common with a *view to profit*".

b.   "Business" includes any trade, occupation or profession.

18. Creation

a.   No formalities are necessary, although for practical reasons writing is usually used.

b.   The maximum number of partners is 20, except for certain professional partnerships, for example solicitors and accountants, where there is no maximum.

c.   The partners may trade under any name they please, except that the word "limited" must not be the last word of the name.

d.   Any partnership agreement will usually deal with the following matters:-

   i.   The firm's name

   ii.   The place and nature of the business

   iii. The date on which the partnership is to commence and its duration. If there is no fixed period then it is a partnership at will.

   iv.   The proportions in which capital is to be provided, and whether interest is to be paid on capital before profits are divided.

   v.   Details of the firm's bank account, including who is allowed to sign cheques.

   vi.   Whether all or only some of the partners shall manage the business and whether all partners shall give their whole time to the business.

   vii. How profits are to be shared, and provisions for drawings.

   viii. Provisions for keeping regular accounts and the preparation of an annual profit and loss account and balance sheet.

   ix.   What shall happen on the death or retirement of a partner. In the absence of an agreement to the contrary the death of a partner automatically dissolves the partnership.

   x.   An arbitration clause.

19. The Relationship of Partners to Outsiders

a.   Every partner is an agent of the firm and therefore has *implied authority* to bind the firm by transactions entered into by him in the *ordinary course of business*. Thus an outsider who contracts with a partner within the scope of that implied authority may treat the firm as bound, despite any restriction on the authority of that partner to which the partners have agreed, unless the outsider knew of the restriction.

b.   In a trading partnership the following acts are within the implied authority of a partner:-

   i.   Borrowing money and giving security;

   ii.   Signing cheques;

   iii. Employing a solicitor to defend an action.

c. The following acts are outside a partner's implied authority:-

    i.   Consenting to a judgement against the firm;

    ii.   Executing a deed;

    iii. Giving a guarantee in the absence of a trade custom to do so;

    iv. Referring a dispute to arbitration;

    v.   Accepting property other than money in payment of a debt.

d. ***Liability for torts.*** On the usual principle of vicarious liability (since each partner is an agent of the others) all the partners are liable for a tort committed by a partner in the ordinary course of the firm's business, or with the authority of his co-partners.

20. The Relationship of Partners to Each Other

a. ***Good faith.*** There is a duty of utmost good faith once the partnership is established, although the contract of partnership is not itself uberrimae fidei. Thus:-

    i.   Partners are bound to render true accounts and full information on all matters affecting the partnership;

    ii.   A partner must account for any profit made by him without the consent of the others from using the firm's property, name, or trade connections;

    iii. A partner may have a separate account unless he has agreed to the contrary, but a partner must account for any profit made in a business of the same kind as, and competing with, the firm.

b. ***Management***

    i.   Subject to contrary agreement every partner is entitled to access to partnership books and may take part in the management of the business.

    ii.   Decisions on ordinary matters connected with the partnership business are by majority of the general partners. If there is a deadlock the views of those opposing any change will prevail, but unanimity is required for matters relating to the constitution of the firm, for example to change the nature of the partnership business or to admit a new partner.

c. ***Capital, profits and losses***

    i.   Profits and losses are shared equally in the absence of contrary agreement. However if the partnership agreement states that profits are to be shared in certain proportions then, prima facie, losses are to be shared in the same proportions.

    ii.   No interest is paid on capital except by agreement. However a partner is entitled to 5% interest on advances beyond his original capital.

d.   **Indemnity.** The firm must indemnify any partner against liabilities incurred in the ordinary and proper conduct of the partnership business, or in doing anything necessarily done for the preservation of the partnership property or business.

e.   **Partnership property.**

i.   The *initial* property of the partnership is that which the partners, expressly or impliedly agree shall be partnership property. It is quite possible that property used in the business should not be partnership property, but should, for example, be the sole property of one of the partners, it depends entirely on the intention of the partners.

ii.   Property *afterwords* acquired is governed by the same principle, but clearly it will be partnership property if it is bought with partnership money.

21. Dissolution

a.   Dissolution occurs:-

i.   By effluxion of time, if the partnership was entered into for a fixed term.

ii.   By termination of the adventure, if entered into for a single adventure.

iii.   By the death or bankruptcy of a partner, unless the partnership agreement otherwise provides.

iv.   By subsequent illegality, ie an event which makes it unlawful to continue the business.

v.   By notice of a partner.

vi.   By order of the court, for one of several reasons, for example the permanent incapacity of a partner, or because it is just and equitable to order dissolution.

b.   **Misrepresentation.** When a partner is induced to enter into a partnership by misrepresentation he remains liable to creditors for obligations incurred while a partner, but he has several remedies against the maker of the statement including, for example, rescission and /or damages.

c.   The authority of the partners after dissolution continues so far as is necessary to wind-up the partnership affairs and complete transactions already begun.

d.   On dissolution any partner can insist on realisation of the firm's assets, (including goodwill), payment of the firm's debts, and distribution of the surplus, subject to any contrary agreement.

22. Companies and Partnerships Compared

a.   The main *differences* between companies and partnerships are as follows:-

i.   A company is created by registration under the *COMPANIES ACT 1985*. A partnership is created by the express or implied agreement of the partners, no special form being required, although writing is usually used.

ii.   A company is an artificial legal person with perpetual succession. It may own property, make contracts, and sue and be sued. It has a legal personality distinct from its members. In contrast a partnership is not a separate legal person, although it may sue and be sued in the firm's name. The partners own the property of the firm and are liable on its contracts.

iii.   Shares in a public company are freely transferable, whereas a partner cannot transfer his share without the consent of all of his partners. He may assign the right to his share of the profits, but the assignee does not become a partner.

iv.   A company must have at least 2 members and there is no upper limit on membership. A partnership must not consist of more than 20 persons although there are some exceptions, for example solicitors, accountants, auctioneers and estate agents.

v.   Members of a company may not take part in its management unless they become directors, whereas all partners are entitled to share in management, unless the partnership agreement provides otherwise.

vi.   A member of a company is not an agent of the company, and he therefore cannot bind the company by his acts. A partner however is an agent of the firm, therefore it will be bound by his acts.

vii.   The liability of a member of a company may be limited by shares or by guarantee. The liability of a general partner is unlimited, although it is possible for one or more partners to limit their liability provided there remains at least one general partner. The advantage of limited liability is unlikely to be real for many small companies since lenders will usually require a personal guarantee of their loan from the directors and/or majority shareholders.

viii.   The power and duties of a company are closely regulated by the Companies Acts and by its constitutional documents. In contrast partners have much more freedom to make their own arrangements with regard to the running of the firm.

b.   The main *similarity* between companies and partnerships is that they are both methods of carrying on a business. Many companies are of course large and impersonal, having many institutional shareholders. Small private companies are however often founded on the same basis as a partnership, ie a relationship of mutual trust and confidence.

c.   ***Conclusion.*** Despite the greater degree of legal regulation affecting the registered company, it is undeniable that the advantages of incorporation — separate legal personality, limited liability, transferability of shares, and possible tax advantages have induced many partners and sole traders to convert their businesses into corporate form. However partnership remains important, and in many cases mutual trust and confidence are more highly regarded than the benefits of incorporation. Thus, subject to a few exceptions, partnership is the compulsory form of association for many professional persons, for example solicitors and accountants. This preserves the principle of individual professional accountability towards the client — a policy which is central to professional ethics.

NATIONALITY

23. Nationality is the relationship between a person and a particular state or political unit. It is a person's political status and is important in determining the applicability of immigration law and certain other rights and duties such as the right to vote and the duty to serve on a jury.

24. The British Nationality Act 1981. This Act created 3 new categories of citizenship to replace Citizenship of the United Kingdom and Colonies. The new categories are:-

a.   *British Citizenship,* ie persons born, registered, adopted or naturalised in the UK. This category has the right of abode in the UK and freedom from immigration control.

b.   *Citizenship of the British Dependent Territories,* ie persons who held a UK passport before 1981 and who were born, registered or naturalised in a British dependency, for example Hong Kong, Bermuda, Gibraltar and The Falklands. Such persons have no automatic right of entry to the UK.

c.   *British Overseas Citizenship,* ie granted to pre-1981 passport holders in East Africa, India and Malaysia.

25. A person may acquire British Citizenship by naturalisation. The conditions are:-

a.   Residence in the UK for the preceding 12 months plus 4 of the 7 years preceding that year.

b.   Full age ie 18.

c.   Good character.

d.   Ability to speak English.

e.   Intention to remain resident in the UK.

26. British citizenship may be lost:-

a.   By *renunciation* — the declaration of renunciation must be made. This will be registered by the Secretary of State provided he is satisfied that the person will acquire some other citizenship or nationality.

b.   By *deprivation* — the main ground is that the Secretary of State is satisfied that registration or naturalisation was obtained by fraud or misrepresentation.

DOMICILE

27.   A precise definition of domicile is impossible, but broadly a person is domiciled in a territory if he has his permanent home there. Domicile implies a link with a particular system of law, in contrast to nationality which involves allegiance to a particular sovereign.

28.   No person can be without a domicile, and no person can have more than one domicile at one time. The types of domicile are:-

a.   *Domicile of origin.* This attaches to a person at birth.

i.   If he is legitimate he will take the domicile of his father.

ii.   If illegitimate it will be that of his mother.

b.   *Domicile of choice.* A person over 16 may adopt a domicile of choice. This has two elements:-

i.   The fact of living in a territory, and

ii.   The intention to stay there. All relevant factors will be taken into account in determining this intention, for example whether or not a house has been purchased.

c.   *Domicile of dependence.* This type of domicile applies to children under 16. The dependent domicile of a legitimate child under 16 is that of his father, ie if the father's domicile of origin changes then the child's domicile also changes. Similarly if the mother of an illegitimate takes a new domicile that domicile will become the dependent domicile of the child. If the father of a legitimate child dies the dependent domicile of the child will usually be the domicile of the mother.

29.   The main importance of domicile is that it governs jurisdiction in many family matters, for example marriage and divorce.

RESIDENCE

30.   Residence is a question of fact to be determined by the courts. The word implies a degree of permanence. The residence of a wife is prima facie that of her husband.

31. Residence is relevant in determining domicile, liability to taxation, and the jurisdiction of the courts, but it is not the only factor in each case.

12 Property Law

CLASSIFICATION

1. Property is anything that can be owned. It is divided into real property (realty) and personal property (personalty or chattels). Property is classified into real and personal according to the historical action necessary to recover it:-

a. If dispossessed of real property the plaintiff had a right to get back the very thing he had lost. This was known as a right in rem (a right in the thing) and was enforced by a real action.

b. If dispossessed of anything else (including leasehold land) a person's only right was to monetary compensation from the person who had dispossessed him. This was known as a right in personam and was enforced by a personal action.

2. *Real property* consists of all freehold (as opposed to leasehold) interests in land.

3. *Personal property* is sub-divided into:-

a. Chattels real, ie leasehold interests in land, and

b. Chattels personal (pure personalty). These are further sub-divided between:-

i. Choses in possession, ie tangible, moveable objects such as a car, wristwatch, or the family pet. It is possible to enjoy a right over such objects by physical possession.

ii. Choses in action, ie rights such as debts, patents and copyrights which may only be enforced or protected by bringing a legal action. Other examples are trade marks, stocks and shares, business goodwill and cheques.

LEGAL ESTATES AND LEGAL INTERESTS

4. Since the Norman conquest in 1066 it has been accepted that only the Crown may "own" land in the absolute way that other property may be owned. Other persons hold an estate or interest in land which gives them certain rights over that land for a definite or indefinite period of time. These rights may be broadly classified as legal estates, legal interests, and equitable interests. Since the *LAW OF PROPERTY ACT 1925* only two legal estates can now exist:-

a. Fee simple absolute in possession (or freehold estate) and

b. Term of years absolute (or leasehold estate).

5. Fee Simple Absolute in Possession

a. The meaning of this term may be clarified as follows:-

91

i.   *Fee.* This means that the estate is capable of being inherited. It may devolve to any person under the deceased's will, or if he died without leaving a will it would devolve to his relatives. A fee estate would end if a person died leaving no will and no relatives. In such a case the land would revert to the Crown. A fee estate must be distinguished from a life estate. For example land bequeathed ''to A for life remainder to B'' is not a fee estate because A cannot bequeath the land in his will.

ii.   *Simple.* This means without a provision as to tail. Thus a fee simple may pass to any relative or anyone else under a will, whereas a fee tail can only pass to lineal descendants. It cannot pass, for example to a brother or parent, or as a gift in a will.

iii.   *Absolute.* This means not subject to any conditions.

iv.   *In possession.* ie The person is entitled to immediate physical possession, although he will still hold the freehold (ie be regarded as in possession) where he grants a lease of the land in return for a rental.

b.   The distinctive characteristic of a freehold estate is that it is of uncertain duration since it cannot be known when the estate will revert to the Crown.

6.   A Term of Years Absolute

a.   This is an estate which, in contrast to a freehold estate, is of a certain duration, for example 99 years, 5 years or 1 month. It does not matter if the period is for less than a year provided the lease has a certain duration, nor does it matter if the estate does not take effect immediately, since there is no requirement that it must be ''in possession''.

b.   A tenancy agreement made on a weekly or monthly basis is not a legal estate since there is no certainty as to duration. It is an equitable interest.

7.   The *LAW OF PROPERTY ACT 1925* also provided for the creation of *legal interests*. The most important of these are easements and mortgages.

a.   An *easement* is a right to use or restrict the use of another person's land in some way. For example a right of way or a right of light.

b.   A *mortgage* is a form of security for a loan. It involves the transfer of an interest in land from the borrower (or mortgagor) to the lender (or mortgagee) with a provision for redemption on repayment of the loan.

EQUITABLE INTERESTS

8.   The two legal estates referred to above must be distinguished from equitable interests. There are several different equitable interests. Their common factor is that they can only exist as the result of an express or implied trust.

For example A conveys his property ''to B for the use of an in trust for C''. The common law took no notice of A's intention that B (the trustee) should hold the land for C (the beneficiary). C's only protection was in equity. Equity acknowledged that at common law the legal estate was vested in B, but as a matter of conscience compelled B to act in accordance with A's intentions.

9. The distinction between legal estates (and interests) and equitable interests is important because:-

a. If a person purchases land which is subject to a legal estate or legal interest of which he is not aware he is nevertheless bound by the legal estate or interest, but

b. If he is a bona fide purchaser for value of a legal estate, which is subject to an equitable interest, he will take the estate free from the equitable interest if he had no notice (actual or constructive) of it.

For example — A, the owner of the fee simple of "Courtlands" grants by deed a lease to B over part of the land. (This creates a legal estate). A also grants by means of a written contract a lease to C over another part of the land. (Since this lease is not by deed it only creates an equitable interest). While A retains the fee simple both B and C have remedies against him, although C's remedies being equitable are discretionary. If however A sells his fee simple to D, who is a bona fide purchaser for value without notice of C's equitable interest, or B's legal estate, then D will take the land free from C's interest, but subject to B's estate. C's interest in the land is said to be "overreached", ie converted to an interest in the sale proceeds, and A must account to him with an amount of the sale proceeds equal to the value of his interest.

c. Note the meaning of "constructive notice". This refers to the ability to fix the whole world with notice of an equitable interest by registering it at HM Land Charges Registry. All persons are then deemed to have notice (ie have constructive notice) of the interest regardless of whether or not they have actual notice of it.

OWNERSHIP AND POSSESSION

10. The law has not developed concise definitions of these terms. Both however are relationships between persons and property.

11. *Possession* has two elements:-

a. The means to exercise control over the thing by direct or indirect means, for example through an employee, and

b. The intention to exclude others.

If a person has a. above, but not b. he has custody of the property.

12. A problem arises when considering whether or not a person can possess something which he does not know is on his person or on his land. The answer depends on the context:-

a.   If unknown to an occupier something is buried on his land, he will possess it for the purposes of the civil law of trespass and he will be able to sue any person who wrongfully disturbs it.

b.   If however the thing buried is a dangerous drug, an occupier without knowledge of its presence will not be criminally liable as possessor of the drug.

c.   It was held in **R v HALLAM (1957)** that the offence of "knowingly possessing an explosive" requires knowledge on the part of the accused that the substance possessed is explosive, not merely that he possessed the substance.

13. *Ownership* has been defined by Pollock in his book "Jurisprudence" as "The entirety of the powers of use and disposal allowed by law."

This definition illustrates that a person's rights over the property he owns are limited by law. For example:-

a.   Planning permission is necessary to build on land, or to change the use of land.

b.   Gold and silver found under land belong to the Crown.

c.   Adjoining land has a natural right to support.

d.   Buildings or trees may be subject to preservation orders.

e.   A person cannot use his land in such a way that it constitutes a nuisance.

f.   Land may be subject to a compulsory purchase order.

14. Ownership may be acquired in the following ways:-

a.   Originally by

i.   Creating something, for example a painting.

ii.   Receiving the benefit of a transaction that creates something, for example an inventor is granted a patent.

iii.   Occupation, ie taking possession of something that has no owner, such as a wild animal.

iv.   Accession, ie something new is added to something already owned, for example a cat has a kitten.

b.   Derivatively, ie acquired from a previous owner who intends ownership to pass, for example a gift, or a sale.

c.   Succession, ie by reason of the death of the previous owner.

THE ASSIGNMENT OF CHOSES IN ACTION

15. A chose in action is a personal property right which can only be protected or enforced by bringing a legal action. A chose may be legal, for example a simple debt, or equitable, for example a beneficiary's interest in a trust fund. Assignments of choses in action are possible both at law, and in equity.

16. Assignments at Law

a.   A legal assignment of a legal chose must comply with *S.136. LAW OF PROPERTY ACT 1925* if it is to be valid. This section requires:-

   i.   That the assignment is in writing and signed by the assignor, and

   ii.   That it is absolute, ie the whole of the interest is transferred to the assignee, and

   iii.   That written notice is given to the debtor.

b.   The effect of such an assignment is that the assignee becomes the legal owner of the chose, and can sue the debtor without making the assignor a party to the action. Consideration for the assignment is not required by *S.136*.

17. Assignments in Equity

a.   Equitable assignments of both legal and equitable choses are possible. For example an attempted legal assignment will take effect as an equitable assignment if it does not comply with *S.136* because, for example, only part of a debt is assigned. In general equity looks at the intent rather than at the form and will therefore enforce an assignment provided there is:-

   i.   Intention to assign,

   ii.   Identification of the chose, and

   iii.   Communication to the assignee.

b.   Writing is not necessary for the equitable assignment of a legal chose, but by *S.53. LPA 1925* an equitable assignment of an equitable chose must be in writing and signed by the assignor.

c.   Notice to the debtor is not necessary to complete an equitable assignment, although it is advisable to prevent the debtor paying the assignor. The effect of the assignment is to enable the assignee to sue the debtor in his own name, except where the assignment is non-absolute, in which case equity requires the assignor to join in the action.

13 Trusts

INTRODUCTION

1. **Definition**

   a.   A trust is a relationship in which a person called a *trustee*, in whom the legal title of property is vested, holds that property for the benefit of another person called a *beneficiary*.

   b.   There may be several trustees and/or several beneficiaries in respect of the same trust. In many cases a trust corporation will be appointed to act as trustee.

   c.   A trust must be distinguished from:-

   i.   A *bailment*. A trustee is usually the legal owner of the property and can therefore pass good title to a bona fide purchaser on an unauthorised sale. A bailee generally can pass no title.

   ii.   A *contract*. A contract creates legal, rather than equitable rights. It is an agreement either under seal or supported by consideration, and it can generally only be enforced by a person who was party to it. A trust creates equitable rights, it can be created without any agreement and it can be enforced by a beneficiary who was not a party to its creation, and even though he was not born when the trust was created.

   iii.   *Agency*. In general an agent is not a trustee for his principal. Therefore if the agent owes money to his principal the principal's remedy is a common law action for recovery of money. However an agent may become a trustee of money received from his principal for a particular purpose, for example investment.

2. **Classification**

   a.   The two main classes of trusts are:-

   i.   *Private*, ie they are for the benefit of an individual or class irrespective of the public at large and are enforceable by the beneficiaries.

   ii.   *Public* (charitable), ie the object is to promote the public welfare. Such trusts are often enforced by the Attorney-General.

   b.   Trusts may also be classified as follows:-

   i.   *Express*. For example A declares himself to be trustee of property for B or conveys it to T on trust for B.

   ii.   *Implied*, ie from the presumed intention of the owner of property. For example if A pays for property which is conveyed by the vendor to B, the general rule is that B is presumed to be trustee for A.

iii.   *Constructive*, ie where independent of the intention of the owner it would be an abuse of confidence for him to hold the property for his own benefit. For example if a trustee were to obtain renewal in his own name of a lease held by him as trustee.

EXPRESS PRIVATE TRUSTS

3.   Formalities. Some form of written evidence is sometimes required for the declaration of a trust:-

a.   Trusts of *land* to take effect *inter vivos* (within the lifetime of the settlor). − Here the terms must be contained in some written evidence signed by the settlor.

b.   Trusts of *pure personalty* to take effect *inter vivos*. − A verbal declaration is sufficient.

c.   Trusts of *any property* to arise on the settlor's death but irrevocable until then must be declared by a duly executed will.

4.   The main requirements for the creation of an express private trust are as follows:-

a.   The *"three certainties"* must be present, namely

i.   *Certainty of words*, ie the settlor must have intended to create a binding duty to carry out his wishes and must have shown this intention by the words used. Thus the use of words such as "hope" and "in full confidence" will not create a trust.

In **RE ADAMS AND KENSINGTON VESTRY (1884)** a testator left property to his widow "in full confidence that she will do what is right as to the disposal thereof between my children". It was held that the words were not sufficiently certain to create a trust, therefore the widow took beneficially.

ii.   *Certainty of subject matter*, ie of both the *property* to which the trust is to attach and to the *beneficial interest*.

iii.   *Certainty of objects*. ie the beneficiaries must be adequately identified. In general every beneficiary must be initially ascertainable, but in a discretionary trust it is only necessary that the beneficiary, on exercise of the discretion, should be within a defined class. **(McPHAIL v DOULTON (1971))**.

b.   The trust must be *completely constituted*.

i.   A trust is completely constituted when the legal ownership of the trust property is effectively vested in the person who is intended to act as trustee of it. This may be done by a declaration of trust if the settlor intends to act as trustee himself, otherwise a conveyance to trustees in the form appropriate to the property must be made by the settlor. Examples of incompletely constituted trusts would be if a defective conveyance is used, or where a share transfer to the trustee does not follow the correct procedure.

ii.   If a trust is completely constituted it may be enforced by the beneficiaries whether or not they have given value to the settlor in return for the creation of the trust. If the trust is not completely constituted a beneficiary cannot enforce the trust unless he has given value. ie If value has been given an imperfect conveyance will be treated as a contract to convey and specific performance may be granted. This is an application of the maxim *"Equity looks upon that as done which ought to be done"*.

iii.   In contrast to the above maxim another maxim of equity is that *"Equity will not perfect an imperfect gift"*. ie If a settlor attempts to make a gift (ie no value is given) of property and the transfer fails because of some technical defect equity will not assist the intended beneficiary to compel the settlor to perfect the gift.

iv.   *"Value"* in the above context not only includes money and money's worth but it includes transfer made in consideration of marriage. For example if Bill is about to marry Mary when he transfers property to trustees to hold for "Mary and any children of the marriage" both Mary and any children born to Bill and Mary are within the marriage consideration and can therefore enforce the trust even if it is incompletely constituted.

5.   Setting Trusts Aside

a.   Once constituted a trust is irrevocable unless there is fraud, duress, mistake or the settlor has reserved a power to revoke.

b.   The *INSOLVENCY ACT 1986* provides for setting aside any transaction that is a preference of one creditor over the other creditors and transactions at an undervalue.

i.   A *preference* occurs when a person does anything that puts a creditor in a better position in the event of that person's bankruptcy than he would have been if that thing had not been done.

ii.   A *transaction at an undervalue* includes gifts, transactions where the consideration received is worth significantly less than that provided and transactions in consideration of marriage.

A transaction at an undervalue may be set aside by the trustee in bankruptcy if the settlor becomes bankrupt within five years. In the case of a preference not at an undervalue the period is two years if the beneficiary is related to the settlor, in other cases the period is six months. However if the preference is fraudulent the period is five years rather than two years or six months.

Where there is a preference or a transaction at an undervalue the court has wide powers to make orders restoring the status quo and protecting the position of persons prejudiced.

PUBLIC (CHARITABLE) TRUSTS

6. In order to be charitable a trust must satisfy 3 requirements. It must be

   a. Of a charitable nature;

   b. For the public benefit; and

   c. Exclusively charitable.

7. Charitable Nature. The modern definition of charitable trusts comes from Lord Macnaughten's judgement in **COMMISSIONERS OF INCOME TAX v PEMSEL (1891)**, namely trusts for:-

   a. *The relief of poverty*. "Poverty" does not mean destitution, it includes having to "go short" regard being had to the person's status in life.

   b. *The advancement of education*. "Education" includes general education and includes the foundation of lectureships and scholarships and aesthetic education such as appreciation of music and drama.

   In **INCORPORATED COUNCIL OF LAW REPORTING v ATTORNEY-GENERAL (1972)** it was held that the Council is a charity because law reports, although used for commercial purposes, did serve to advance legal education.

   c. *The advancement of religion*. "Religion" includes any religion not subversive of morality, and its advancement includes the maintenance of places of worship or of all the graves in a churchyard, but not of one tomb in a churchyard. A gift to a charitable persona or body as such creates a charitable trust if the objects are not specified, because the recipient must devote the property to charitable purposes.

   In **RE GARRARD (1907)** a gift to a vicar "to be applied in his sole discretion as he thinks fit" was held to be a gift to the vicar in his capacity as vicar and it was therefore charitable.

   Contrast **FARLEY v WESTMINSTER BANK (1939)** where the gift was for "Parish work". It was held that where the objects are not specified the trust is not charitable unless those objects are exclusively charitable. Since "Parish work" could include non-charitable ends the gift as a whole was not charitable.

   d. *Other purposes beneficial to the community*, for example relief of the aged, or preservation of places of historic interest. Note that:-

      i. A trust for the protection of animals will be a charitable trust if its execution involves a benefit to the public.

      In **RE MOSS (1949)** a gift "for work in care of cats and kittens needing protection" was held to be charitable because it developed the better side of human nature.

      Contrast **I.R.C. v NATIONAL ANTI-VIVISECTION SOCIETY (1948)** where it was held that the society was not a charity firstly because it was political (ie it campaigned for changes in the law) and secondly because it was for animal benefit not public benefit.

ii.   The mere encouragement of a sport is not of itself charitable.

In **RE NOTTAGE (1895)** a trust for the provision of prizes for yacht racing was held to be not charitable.

However the *RECREATIONAL CHARITIES ACT 1958* declares charitable the provision of facilities for recreation or other leisure time occupation if the facilities are provided in the interests of social welfare.

8.   Public Benefit

a.   The trust must benefit the public or a section of the public.

In **GILMOUR v COATS (1949)** a trust for the benefit of a convent of cloistered and contemplative nuns was not held to promote a public benefit.

b.   It is sufficient that there is a benefit to a section of the public, for example the residents of a particular area, but a class of person defined by a test of relationship with a specified person or body (for example a testator's relations or the employees of a company) is not a section of the public. There is an exception — a trust for the relief of poverty may be charitable although the objects are confined to such a class of persons.

9.   Exclusively Charitable. Where the words of a trust are such that the objects could be charitable, but could also be non-charitable the trust will be a private trust.

In **CHICHESTER DIOCESAN FUND v SIMPSON (1944)** a gift for "charitable or benevolent purposes" was held not to be a charitable trust. (It also failed as a private trust for uncertainty of objects).

10.   Differences between Charitable and Private Trusts

a.   A charitable trust will not fail for uncertainty of objects. For example a trust "for such charities as my executors shall select" is good.

b.   Charitable trusts are partly exempt from the perpetuity rules. These rules are rather complex. The basic requirement is that a gift must vest absolutely in some person within the perpetuity period. This period is either a life in being plus 21 years, or if specified in the trust instrument, a fixed period not exceeding 80 years. A non-charitable trust is void unless it is bound to terminate within the perpetuity period. A first (or only) charitable gift must also take effect within the perpetuity period, but a gift to one charity followed by a gift over to another charity is valid however remote the time at which the gift over may take effect. For example a gift to Charity A with a gift over to Charity B if the tomb is not kept will not fail even if the gift over takes effect outside the perpetuity period (**RE TYLER (1891)**). In fact if the property given is substantial Charity A will no doubt ensure that the tomb is maintained to avoid the gift over taking effect.

c.   Charitable trusts have advantages over private trusts in respect of taxation.

11. The Cy-Pres Doctrine

a. This doctrine allows the application of a fund for purposes which are not precisely those the donor provided for but which as nearly as possible fit his intention. (Cy-pres means as near as).

b. The requirements are

i. That the donor has shown a paramount charitable intention, ie an intention to benefit charity in any event, and

ii. *S.13. CHARITIES ACT 1960* has been complied with. This section specifies several circumstances when the cy-pres doctrine may apply, for example if the original purposes have been fulfilled or cannot be carried out, or if there is a surplus after carrying them out.

IMPLIED OR RESULTING TRUSTS

12. These are implied by equity to give effect to the presumed intention of the parties. There are many situations when such trusts will be implied, for example:-

a. If a settlor conveys property to trustees on trusts which do not exhaust the whole beneficial interest, subject to the interests effectually created, the trustees hold the property on a resulting trust for the settlor or his estate.

b. Where a person purchases in the name of another there is a presumption of resulting trust to the real purchaser. ie If X pays for property which is conveyed by the vendor to Y, the general rule is that Y is presumed to be trustee for X.

CONSTRUCTIVE TRUSTS

13. These are trusts imposed by equity on grounds of conscience, independently of any presumed intention. For example:-

a. If a stranger to the trust, who is not a bona fide purchaser for value, receives trust property without notice of the trust he is a constructive trustee of such part of the property as he possesses when he receives notice of the trust.

b. A similar liability will be incurred by a person who knowingly assists in a fraud by the trustee.

TRUSTEES

14. Appointment

a. By *S.20. LAW OF PROPERTY ACT 1925* the appointment of an infant as a trustee is void.

b. For a trust of land the maximum number of trustees is 4. There is no maximum for a trust of pure personalty. There is no minimum, but a sole trustee (other than a trust corporation) cannot give a valid receipt for the sale of land.

c.   The settlor normally appoints the original trustees. New trustees may be appointed either under an express power in the trust instrument or under *S.36. TRUSTEE ACT 1925*:-

  i.   *In place of* a former trustee who is *dead*; or *remains* out of the UK for more than 12 months or refuses to act; or is *unfit* to act; or is an *infant* or incapable of acting; or *desires* to be discharged. (Mnemonic: DRUID)

  ii.   *In addition to* the existing trustees as long as no trust corporation is acting and the number of trustees is not increased beyond 4.

d.   Note that "equity never wants for a trustee". ie Equity will never allow a valid trust to fail on account of the absence or incapacity of a trustee. Thus for example if all the trustees disclaim, the settlor will hold as trustee, and if all the trustees die, the personal representatives of the last survivor will hold as trustees.

15.   Disclaimer. A trustee may disclaim the trust at any time before he has done anything to indicate acceptance. Disclaimer may be by words or conduct, but it must relate to the whole trust. Failure to assume trusteeship for a considerable time is evidence of disclaimer.

16.   Retirement. A trustee may only retire when there is an express provision in the trust instrument or

a.   Under *S.36. TRUSTEE ACT 1925* on the appointment of a new trustee

b.   Under *S.39. TRUSTEE ACT 1925* provided the retirement is by deed with the consent by deed of the co-trustees and 2 trustees or a trust corporation are left acting

c.   By consent of the beneficiaries if they are of full age and capacity

d.   By removal by the court.

17.   Duties of Trustees. These are obligations imposed by the trust, by statute, or by the rules of equity. They must be performed strictly and a trustee is liable for breach of duty without proof of negligence. Examples of the duties are:-

a.   *To reduce trust property into possession.* The property must be put under the joint control of the trustees so that it cannot be dealt with without the agreement of all. Bearer securities should be deposited in a bank in the names of all the trustees.

b.   *To choose authorised investments.* When investing trust funds the trustees must choose investments authorised by the *TRUSTEE INVESTMENTS ACT 1961*. The powers conferred by this Act are however in addition to and not in derogation from the powers conferred by the trust instrument.

c. *To keep accounts*, and produce them to the beneficiaries when required.

d. *Not to delegate their duties*, although in some circumstances their duties may be performed through agents. For example

    i.   By *S.23. TRUSTEE ACT 1925* a trustee may appoint a solicitor or other agent to do any act required in the carrying out of the trust and he will not be liable for the agent's default if he was appointed in good faith.

    ii.   By *S.8. TRUSTEE ACT 1925* a trustee lending money on mortgage may employ an independent surveyor or valuer.

    iii.   By *S.29. LAW OF PROPERTY ACT 1925* trustees holding land on trust for sale may revocably delegate in writing to the life tenant their powers of leasing, accepting surrenders of leases and management.

e. *Not to profit from the trust*. Thus for example:-

    i.   If a trustee of a leasehold obtains a renewal of the lease for himself he is a constructive trustee of the new lease for the beneficiaries **(KEECH v SANDFORD (1726))**.

    ii.   If a trustee speculates with trust property for his own advantage, he bears any losses and is a constructive trustee of any profits that he makes.

    iii.   A trustee may not buy the trust property without the permission of the court or a power in the trust instrument, but he may buy the beneficial interest of a beneficiary if he can prove that the transaction was in good faith and for full value and that he made full disclosure of the material facts known to him.

    iv.   If a trustee obtains a post (for example as company director) by virtue of exercising any power which he acquired by virtue of his office he is a constructive trustee of the remuneration.

    v.   A trustee is not entitled to remuneration as such, but will usually be granted remuneration either by a power in the trust instrument; by agreement with all the beneficiaries, or by order of the court if the trust is especially onerous. A trustee is however entitled to indemnity for his proper out-of-pocket expenses.

18. Powers of Trustees. The *TRUSTEE ACT 1925* gives a number of discretionary powers to trustees, for example concerning the sale, insurance, and mortgage of trust property. Note in particular

a. *The power of maintenance*. By *S.31. TRUSTEE ACT 1925* where trustees hold money on behalf of an infant they may apply the *income* from the property for his maintenance, education or benefit.

b. *The power of advancement*. By *S.32. TRUSTEE ACT 1925* where a beneficiary has an interest in the *capital* of a trust fund the trustees may apply up to one half of his vested or presumptive share for his advancement or benefit, (which includes maintenance and education).

19. Liability for Breach of Trust

a.   A trustee is responsible only for his own acts and omissions where he has committed a breach of duty or exercised a discretion otherwise than with good faith or reasonable prudence.

b.   A trustee is not responsible for the acts of his co-trustee unless his own neglect or default contributed to the breach.

c.   The main remedy of the beneficiaries is to obtain indemnity from the trustee personally. The measure of indemnity is the loss to the estate. If the trustee has made a profit from the breach the beneficiary may claim it.

COURSEWORK QUESTIONS 1-8
THE ENGLISH LEGAL SYSTEM

1.   Trace the history of the common law until the Judicature Acts of 1873-1875, and explain why these Acts were passed.

2.   What are the main sources of English law today?
ACCA Level 1 June 1986

3.   How and why are laymen involved in the administration of justice?

4.   a.   Define "statute law" and discuss the advantages and disadvantages of statutes as a source of law.   *(8 marks)*

b.   Explain the rules which govern the interpretation of statutes.
(12 marks)
ACCA Level 1 December 1984

5.   "Once a corporation has come into being it forms an entirely separate entity from the individuals who compose it." Discuss. In what ways may corporations be created?
ACCA Foundation December 1978

6.   Summarise the jurisdiction of Magistrates' Courts. How important are these courts in the judicial system?

7.   What is meant by a "trust"? How does it come into existence? What are the main functions and duties of a trustee under a trust?
ICSA Part 1 December 1980

8.   What is the basis of the legal distinction between real and personal property and what are the main differences between them as regards their creation and transfer.
ICSA Part 1 June 1987

PART II   THE LAW OF CONTRACT

14 The Concept of a Contract

1. A contract is an agreement which legally binds the parties. Sometimes contracts are referred to as "enforceable agreements". This is rather misleading since one party cannot usually force the other to fulfil his part of the bargain. The usual remedy is damages.

2. The underlying theory is that a contract is the outcome of "consenting minds", each party being free to accept or reject the terms of the other. However to speak of consenting minds is no longer accurate because, for example:-

a. Parties are judged by what they have said, written, or done, not by what is in their minds, ie an objective standard is applied.

b. Mass production and nationalisation have led to the standard form contract. The individual must usually "take it or leave it", he does not really agree to it. For example, the customer has to accept his supply of electricity on the electricity board's terms — he is not likely to succeed in negotiating special terms.

c. Public policy sometimes requires that the freedom of contract should be modified. For example, the *RENT ACT 1968*, and the *UNFAIR CONTRACT TERMS ACT 1977*.

d. The law will sometimes imply terms into contracts because the parties are expected to observe certain standard of behaviour. A person is bound by these terms even though he has never agreed to them, or never even thought of them. For example *SECTIONS 12-15 SALE OF GOODS ACT 1979*.

e. The law of agency enables the agent to bind his principal provided the agent acts within the scope of his apparent authority, even if he goes beyond his actual authority. As a result a principal may find himself bound by a contract that he did not intend to make.

3. The essential elements of a contract are:

a. That an *agreement* is made as a result of an *offer and acceptance*.

b. The agreement contains an element of *value known as consideration*, although a gratuitious promise is binding if it is made by deed.

c. The parties *intend to create legal relations*.

4. The validity of a contract may also be affected by the following factors:

a. *Capacity*. Some persons, e.g. children have limited capacity to make contracts.

b. *Form*. Most contracts can be made verbally, but others must be in writing or by deed. Some verbal contracts must be supported by written evidence.

c. ***Content***. The parties may generally agree any terms, although they must be reasonably precise and complete. In addition some terms will be implied by the courts, custom or statute and some express terms may be overridden by statute.

d. ***Genuine consent***. Misrepresentation, mistake, duress and undue influence may invalidate a contract.

e. ***Illegality***. A contract will be void if it is illegal or contrary to public policy.

5. A contract that does not satisfy the relevant requirements may be void, voidable or unenforceable.

a. A *void* contract has no legal effect. The expression "void contract" is a contradiction in terms since if an agreement is void it cannot be a contract. However the term usefully describes a situation where the parties have attempted to contract, but the law will not give effect to their agreement because, for example there is a common mistake on some major term (such as the existence of the subject matter). When a contract is void ownership of any property "sold" will not pass to the buyer, so he will not be able to sell it to any one else. The original seller (i.e. the owner) will therefore be able to recover the property from the person in possession.

b. When a contract is *voidable* the law will allow one of the parties to withdraw from it if he wishes, thus rendering it void. Voidable contracts include some agreements made by minors and contracts induced by misrepresentation, duress or undue influence. A voidable contract remains valid unless and until the innocent party chooses to terminate it. Therefore if the buyer resells the goods before the contract is avoided, the sub-buyer will become the owner and will be able to keep the property, provided he took it in good faith.

c. An *unenforceable* contract is a valid contract and any goods or money transferred cannot be recovered, even from the other party to the contract. However if either party refuses to perform his part of the contract the other party cannot compel him to do so. A contract will be unenforceable when the required written evidence of its terms is not available e.g. the written evidence for a contract for the sale of land.

15 The Formation of a Contract

INTRODUCTION

1. The method by which the courts determine whether an agreement has been reached is to enquire whether one party has made an offer which the other party has accepted. For most types of contract the offer and acceptance may be made orally or in writing, or they may be implied from the conduct of the parties. The person who makes the offer is known as the *offeror* and the person to whom the offer is made is the *offeree*.

2. In addition to offer and acceptance the law imposes the requirements of consideration (value) and intention to create legal relations. These are elements in the formation of a contract and are dealt with in this chapter. The other requirements are contractual capacity and legality of object which are considered later.

OFFER

3. Definition

a. An offer is a definite promise to be bound on certain specific terms. It cannot be vague as in **GUNTHING v LYNN (1831)**, where the offeror promised to pay a further sum for a horse if it was "lucky". However if an apparently vague offer is capable of being made certain, either by implying terms or by reference to previous dealings between the parties, or within the trade, then it will be regarded as certain. Thus in **HILLAS v ARCOS (1932)**, a contract for the sale of timber "of fair specification" between persons well acquainted with the timber trade was upheld.

b. An offer may be made to a particular person, or class of persons, or to the public at large as in **CARLILL v CARBOLIC SMOKEBALL CO. (1893)** (Paragraph **4.** below.)

c. An offer must not be confused with the answer to a question or the supplying of information.

> In **HARVEY v FACEY (1893)** P telegraphed D
> "Will you sell us Bumper Hall Pen? Telegraph lowest cash price."
> D telegraphed the reply
> "Lowest price for Bumper Hall Pen £900."
> P then telegraphed
> "We agree to buy Bumper Hall Pen for £900 asked by you."

D then decided that he did not wish to sell Bumper Hall Pen to P for £900, and P claimed that a contract had been made, the second telegraph being an offer. The court held that there was no contract, the second telegram being merely an indication of what D would sell for, if and when, he decided to sell. It was supplying of information in response to a question.

4.   Invitations to Treat. An offer must be carefully distinguished from an invitation to treat, which is an invitation to another person to make an offer. The main distinction between the two is that an offer can be converted into a contract by acceptance, provided the other requirements of a valid contract are present, whereas an invitation to treat cannot be "accepted". There are several types of invitations to treat:-

a.   *The exhibition of goods for sale in a shop.* For example **FISHER v BELL (1961)** (Chapter 4 Paragraph **19.**)

Also **PHARMACEUTICAL SOCIETY OF GREAT BRITAIN v BOOTS CHEMISTS (1953)** where by statute certain drugs had to be sold in the presence of a qualified pharmacist. Boots operated a self service shop, with a qualified pharmacist present at the check-out, but not at the shelves on which the drugs were displayed. The precise location of the place of sale was therefore relevant to determine whether or not an offence had been committed. It was held that the display was an invitation to treat, the customer's tender of the drugs was the offer, and the taking of the money by the pharmacist was the acceptance. The sale therefore took place at the check-out, and Boots therefore did not commit an offence.

b.   *General advertising of goods.* Thus a newspaper advertisement that goods are for sale is not an offer. Also in **GRAINGER v GOUGH (1896)** it was held that the circulation of a price-list by a wine merchant was only an invitation to treat.

However advertisements of rewards for the return of lost or stolen property are offers since they clearly show an intention to be bound without the need for further negotiation. Similarly the promise to pay money in return for an act has been held to be an offer.

In **CARLILL v CARBOLIC SMOKEBALL CO (1893)** the defendant company manufactured a patent medicine, called a "smokeball". In various advertisements they offered to pay £100 to any person who caught influenza after having sniffed the smokeball three times a day for two weeks. They also stated that they had deposited £1,000 at The Alliance Bank in Regent Street to show their "sincerity". Mrs C used the smokeball as advertised, and contracted influenza after more than two weeks treatment, and while still using the smokeball. She claimed her £100. The company raised several defences:-

i.   The advertisement was too vague since it did not state a time limit in which the user had to contract influenza.

    – The court said that it must at least protect the user during the period of use.

ii.   It was not possible to make an offer to the whole world, or to the public at large.

    – The court made a comparison with reward cases, and stated that such an offer was possible.

iii.   Acceptance was not communicated.

− Not necessary in such cases. A comparison was made with reward cases where no communication is necessary.

iv.   The advertisement was a mere gimmick or "puff" and there was no intention to create legal relations.

− The deposit of £1,000 would indicate to a reasonable man that there was an intention to create legal relations.

v.   C provided no consideration.

− It was held that the actual act of sniffing the smokeball was consideration. (The purchase price was not consideration for a contract with the manufacturer, it was consideration for the contract with the retailer.)

c.   *An invitation for tenders*. A tender is an estimate submitted in response to a prior request. An invitation for tenders does not amount to an offer to employ the person quoting the lowest price.

d.   *An auctioneer's request for bids*. An advertisement stating that an auction is to be held, or a request for bids is an invitation to treat, and no an offer to sell to the highest bidder. The bid is the offer, and the fall of the auctioneer's hammer is the acceptance. Until this happens the bidder may retract his bid. *(S.57(2) SALE OF GOODS ACT 1979)*

e.   In some cases it is not absolutely clear what amounts to an an offer and what is an invitation to treat. For example:-

i.   Buses. It is probable that the bus itself is the offer **(WILKIE v LONDON TRANSPORT (1947))** since if the bus were an invitation to treat, and the passenger's tender of the fare an offer, then a passenger could board a bus and, not having seen the conductor, get off again without being in breach of contract.

ii.   "Pay on exit" carparks.

In **THORNTON v SHOE LANE PARKING (1972)**. A ticket to a carpark was dispensed by an unattended machine. The court held that the offer was the sign "Parking" outside the garage, and the acceptance was the customer placing his car on the spot which caused the automatic machine to operate. In this case the precise time at which the contract was made was important, since it determined whether or not conditions printed on the ticket dispensed by the machine were a part of the contract. In this case there had been an offer and acceptance before the ticket was issued. The conditions printed on the ticket therefore come too late to be incorporated into the contract.

5.   **Termination of Offer.** An offer may be terminated in the following ways.

a.   *Revocation*, ie withdrawal of the offer. Note that

i.   A promise to keep an offer open for a fixed period does not prevent its revocation within that period. However a person may buy a promise to keep an offer open for a fixed period, ie he may buy an option to purchase. The offer cannot then be revoked without breach of this "option contract".

ii.   Revocation is ineffective until communicated to the offeree. Thus revocation by post is ineffective until it reaches the offeree. However if the offeree must know that the offer has been revoked he cannot accept it, even if he obtained his information through a third party.

In **DICKENSON v DODDS (1876)** D offered to sell a house to P for £800, and the offer was to be left open until 9 am Friday. On Thursday D sold the house to a Mr Allan, and a Mr Berry told P of this sale. P nevertheless wrote a letter of acceptance which he handed to D before Friday 9 am. It was held that there was no contract, the offer having been withdrawn before acceptance and communication by a third party being valid. An offer to sell a particular item is withdrawn by implication if that item is sold to another person.

iii.   Where the offer consists of a promise to pay money for the performance of an act the offer cannot be revoked once performance has commenced. For example if a promise is made to pay £100 to the first person to swim the English Channel 4 times non-stop, the offer cannot be revoked once the swim has commenced.

b.   *A refusal or a counter offer.*

i.   In **HYDE v WRENCH (1840)** D offered his farm to P for £1,000. P wrote saying he would give £950 for it. D refused this, and P then said he would pay £1,000 after all. D had by now decided that he did not wish to sell to P for £1,000. P sued for breach. His action failed because his offer of £950 was a counter offer which terminated D's offer of £1,000, thus when P purported to accept at £1,000 there was no offer in existence, and therefore no contract was formed.

ii.   A counter offer must be distinguished from a request as to whether or not other terms would be acceptable, since such a request does not, by itself, terminate an offer.

In **STEVENSON v McLEAN (1880)** D offered to sell iron to P for cash. P wrote and asked for 4 months credit. This inquiry was not held to be a counter offer, but a request for information. It did not therefore terminate D's offer.

c.   *Lapse of time.* The offer will terminate at the end of the period stated in the offer, or if no period is fixed, it will terminate after a reasonable time.

In **RAMSGATE VICTORIA HOTEL v MONTEFIORE (1866)**. In June 1864 D offered to take shares in P's hotel. P did not reply to this offer, but in November he allotted shares to D, which D refused to take. It was held that the refusal was justified, since P's delay had caused D's offer to lapse.

d. *Failure of a condition subject to which the offer was made.*

In **FINANCINGS LTD v STIMSON (1962)** D who wished to purchase a car signed a hire-purchase form on the 16th of March. This was the offer. The form stated that the agreement would only become binding when the finance company signed the form. On the 24th of March the car was stolen from the dealer's premises, and it was recovered badly damaged. On the 25th March the finance company signed the form. It was held that D was not bound to take the car. There was an implied condition in D's offer that the car would be in substantially the same condition when the offer was accepted as when it was made.

e. *Death.* The position depends on who dies.

   i.   If the offeree dies the offer lapses.

   ii. If the offeror dies the offer lapses if the offeree knows of the death at the time of his purported acceptance, or if the contract requires personal performance by the offeror, for example playing in an orchestra.

ACCEPTANCE

6. **What Amounts to Acceptance**

   a.   The acceptance may be in writing, or oral, or it may be inferred from conduct, for example by dispatching goods in response to an offer to buy.

   b.   The acceptance must be unqualified and must correspond to the terms of the offer. Accordingly:-

   i.   A counter offer is insufficient and, as stated above, causes the original offer to lapse.

   ii. A conditional assent is not enough, for example when an offer is accepted "subject to contract".

   c.   Where it is intended to make a contract by means of sealed competitive bids, a submission by one bidder of a bid dependant for its definition on the bids of others is invalid.

   In **HARVELA INVESTMENTS** the **ROYAL TRUST COMPANY OF CANADA (1985)** a seller of shares (Royal Trust (RT)) had by a telex dated 15 September agreed to accept the highest bid made by HARVELA (H) or OUTERBRIDGE (O). H bid $2,175,000 Canadian dollars. O's bid was as follows "$2,100,000 Canadian dollars or $101,000 Canadian dollars in excess of any other offer which you may receive . . . which ever is higher". On 29 September RT telexed O stating that in the circumstances they were bound to accept O's offer. H objected and commenced this action. The House of Lords had to decide two issues:-

   i.   was the status of the telex of the 15 September such that a contract had been formed between RT and H?

ii.   was there a second contract (as claimed by O) as a result of the telex of the 29 September?

It was held that the telex of 15 September was not an invitation to treat, but a unilateral offer, conditional upon the happening of a specified event. Such an event could only be done by one of the promisee's, not both. Since the intention was to create a fixed bidding sale, the court rejected the referential bid (O's bid) and held (reversing the Court of Appeal) that a binding contract existed between RT and H. Any other decision would recognise a means by which sealed competitive bidding could be wholly frustrated. Concerning the second contract it was held that no such contract had been formed because there was no intention on the part of the parties. RT's only intention, manifested in the telex of the 28 September was to perform the legal obligation that it mistakenly thought it had incurred.

7.   The Communication of Acceptance – General Rules

a.   Acceptance is not effective until communicated to and received by the offeror. Thus if an acceptance is not received because of interference on a telephone line, or because the offeree's words are too indistinct to the heard by the offeror, there is no contract.

b.   Acceptance must be communicated by the offeree or by someone with his authority.

In **POWELL v LEE (1908)** P applied for the post of headmaster of a school. He was called for interview and the managers (D being one) passed a resolution appointing him, but they did not make any arrangements for notifying him. However one of the managers, without authority, informed P that he had been appointed. The managers subsequently re-opened the matter and appointed another candidate. It was held that P failed in his action for breach of contract since acceptance had not been properly communicated to him.

c.   The offeror may expressly or impliedly prescribe the method of communicating acceptance, although there will be valid acceptance if the offeree adopts an equally expeditious method, unless the offeror has made it clear that no method other than the prescribed method will be adequate.

d.   A condition that silence shall constitute acceptance cannot be imposed by the offeror without the offeree's consent.

In **FELTHOUSE v BINDLEY (1863)** P was engaged in negotiations to purchase his nephew's horse. There was some confusion as to the price so P wrote to his nephew saying:-

"If I hear no more about him I consider the horse is mine at £30 15s."
The horse was at time in the possession of D, an auctioneer. The nephew, wishing to sell at £30 15s therefore told D not to sell the horse, but D sold the horse by mistake. P therefore sued D in conversion (a tort alleging wrongful disposal of the plaintiff's property by the defendant). D's defence was that the horse did not belong to P, since there was no valid

114

contract between P and his nephew, because the condition that silence constituted acceptance was ineffective. This defence succeeded.

e.   Acceptance is not effective if communicated in ignorance of the offer. However, if a person knows of the offer, the fact that he has a motive for his acceptance, other than that contemplated by the offeror, does not prevent the formation of a contract.

f.   There is no contract if two offers, identical in terms, cross in the post. For example, A offers to sell his car to B for £500 and B offers to buy A's car for £500. There is no contract because although there are "consenting minds" there is no acceptance.

8.   The Communication of Acceptance − Exceptions

a.   *Unilateral contracts.* These are contracts where the offer consists of a promise to pay money in return for the performance of an act. In such cases performance of the act is sufficient acceptance, however consideration is not complete until performance has finished.

b.   *Postal rules.* Where the parties contemplate acceptance by post, acceptance is complete when the letter is posted, even if the letter is lost in the post.

In **HOUSEHOLD FIRE INSURANCE CO. v GRANT (1879)** D applied for shares in the company. A letter of allotment (the acceptance) was posted to him, but it never arrived. The company later went into liquidation and D was called upon to pay the amount outstanding on his shares. It was held that he had to do so. There was a contract between the company and himself which was completed when the letter of allotment was posted, regardless of the fact that it was lost in the post.

Note that:-

i.   If the letter is lost or delayed in the post because the offeree has addressed it incorrectly the "post rule" will not apply.

ii.   "Posted" means put into the control of the post office in the usual manner, and not for example, by handing it to a postman.

iii.   The post rule applies to telegrams, but not to telex or telephone.

CONSIDERATION

9.   Definition. A promise is only legally binding if it is made in return for another promise or an act (either a positive act or something given up), ie if it is part of a bargain. The requirement of "something for something" is called consideration. It may be defined as some benefit accruing to one party, or some detriment suffered the other. There have been several case law definitions, for example from **CURRIE v MISA (1875)**:-

"Some right interest profit or benefit accruing to one party, or some forbearance, detriment, loss or responsibility given suffered or undertaken by the other".

10. Executory, Executed, and Past Consideration. Consideration may be executory or executed, but it may not be past.

a. *Executory consideration.* Here the bargain consists of mutual promises. The consideration in support of each promise is the other promise and not a performed (executed) act.

For example A orders a greenhouse from B to be paid for when it is delivered next week. There are two promises for the law to enforce, B's promise to deliver the greenhouse and A's promise to pay for it.

b. *Executed consideration.* Here the consideration for the promise is a performed, or executed act. For example, fertiliser is ordered and paid for, and it is agreed that delivery will take place within 10 days. If delivery is late the buyer may sue, putting forward his executed act, (ie payment) as consideration. Similarly a person who returns a lost dog, having seen an offer of reward may claim the reward. His act of returning the dog is executed consideration. The sequence of events in both examples is first the promise, and subsequently the act.

c. *Past consideration.* If the act put forward as consideration was performed before any promise of reward was made it is not valid consideration.

For example X promises to give Y £10 because Y dug X's garden last week. Y cannot sue because when X's promise was made Y's act was in the past.

In **ROSCORLA v THOMAS (1842)** P purchased a horse from D. After the sale was complete D gave an undertaking that the horse was not vicious. This proved to be wrong. P sued on this undertaking. He failed since his consideration was in the past. The act put forward as consideration, ie the payment of the price, was complete before the undertaking was given. P therefore gave nothing new in return for the undertaking. It is not possible to sue in a "something for nothing" situation.

In deciding whether consideration is past the courts do not always take a strictly chronological view. If the consideration and the promise are substantially the same transaction it does not matter in which order they are given. Thus manufacturers may give guarantees to persons who buy their products from retailers. The buyer then sends a card to the manufacturer to claim the benefit of the guarantee, and he usually does this after he has bought the goods.

d. *Exceptions to the past consideration rule*

i.   Past consideration will support a bill of exchange (*S.27. BILLS OF EXCHANGE ACT 1882*). (Chapter 35-18)

ii.   Where a subsequent promise is made to pay for services rendered at the defendant's request. The explanation is that when the request was made there was an implied understanding that there would be some payment, and the subsequent promise merely fixed the amount.

In **LAMPLEIGH v BRAITHWAIT (1615)** D killed a man and asked P to obtain for him a royal pardon. P did so and D then promised to pay him £100. D broke this promise and P sued him. P succeeded in this action because P's request was regarded as containing an implied promise to pay, and the subsequent promise to pay £100 was merely fixing the amount.

11. "Consideration Must Move from the Promisee". This maxim represents an alternative way of stating the basic rule of privity of contract. It means that the only person who can sue on a contract is the person who paid the price. For example if John orders flowers to be sent to Mary, who is in hospital, and those flowers are not sent, then it is John who is entitled to a remedy against the shop. Although Mary was to have had the benefit of the flowers, she cannot sue because she did not pay the price.

12. Consideration Must be of Some Value

a. As long as some value is given the court will not ask whether it is proportionate in value to the thing given in return. In other words there is no remedy for someone who makes a bad bargain.

In **THOMAS v THOMAS (1842)** executors agreed to convey the matrimonial home to a widow provided she paid £1 per year rent and kept the house in repair. In an action on the promise to convey it was held that the promise of payment and doing the repairs were valuable consideration.

b. Some acts, although arguably of some value, have been held to be no consideration:-

    i. Payment on the day that a debt is due of less than the full amount of the debt is not consideration for a promise to release the balance (**PINNEL'S CASE (1602)**). However if the creditor agrees to take something different from what he is entitled to, or if payment is made at his request at an earlier date there is sufficient consideration.

In **D.C. BUILDERS v REES (1945)** D owed P £482 and knowing that they were in financial trouble offered them £300 in full settlement of the debt. P accepted this cheque, but later sued for the balance of £182. P succeeded because:-

    a. D paid P a cheque, and the court did not consider this as different from the cash to which P was entitled.

    b. The payment was made at D's suggestion and not at P's request.

    c. Equitable estoppel was not an available defence for D, because she had attempted to take advantage of P's financial difficulties and had not therefore come to equity with "clean hands".

    ii. A promise to do what the promisee can already legally demand.

In **STILK v MYRICK (1809)** P was a seaman who had agreed to work throughout a voyage for £5 per month. During the voyage two of the crew of eleven deserted, and the captain promised to divide their wages between the rest of the crew if they would complete the voyage. On completion of the voyage P requested his share, and was refused. His legal action failed on the grounds that he was already contractually bound to complete the voyage and did not therefore provide any consideration for the promise of the deserters' wages.

Contrast **HARTLEY v PONSONBY (1857)** where 17 out of a crew of 36 deserted. The remainder were promised an extra £40 each to work the ship to Bombay. P, a seaman, had to sue to recover his £40. He succeeded, mainly because the large number of desertions made the voyage more dangerous, and this had the effect of discharging the original contract. (It was now fundamentally different from the voyage bargained for.) This left P free to enter into a new contract under which his promise to complete the voyage constituted consideration for the promise to pay £40.

Contrast also **WILLIAMS v ROFFEY (1989)** where D engaged P to carry out carpentry work in a block of flats at an agreed price of £20,000. P soon realised that the price was too low for him to operate satisfactorily and make a profit. D was concerned that P would not complete the work on time and therefore made an oral agreement to pay P a further sum of £10,300. Seven weeks later, after D had paid P only a further £1,500 P ceased work and later sued D for the additional sum promised. The Court of Appeal held that where D promised to pay P a sum of money additional to that already agreed as the contract price, in return for P's promise to perform his existing obligations on time, the resultant benefit to D was capable of being consideration for D's promise to make the additional payment (provided there was no economic duress or fraud). The court considered that this did not contravene the principle in Stilk v Myrick (1809), but merely limited its application. P was therefore successful in obtaining the additional amount promised.

iii.   A promise to discharge a duty imposed by law.

In **COLLINS v GODEFROY (1831)** P was called by subpoena to give evidence in a case involving D. He afterwards alleged that D had promised to pay him six guineas for his loss of time. P failed in his action since he was bound by law to attend the trial (this is the effect of the subpoena) and he did not therefore do anything for D that he was not already bound to do. P therefore had not provided any consideration.

13. Equitable Estoppel

a.   Strict application of the rule in **PINNEL'S CASE (1602)** could cause hardship to a person who relies on a promise that a debt will not be enforced in full. Equitable estoppel mitigates this harshness. It may be expressed as follows:-

If X, a party to a legal relationship, promises Y, the other party, that

118

he (X) will not insist on his full rights under that relationship, and this promise is intended to be acted upon by Y, and is in fact acted upon, then X is estopped (stopped because of his own previous conduct) from bringing an action against Y which is inconsistent with his promise, even if Y gives no consideration. ie Y can use the principle of equitable estoppel as a defence against X and X attempt to enforce his original rights.

In **CENTRAL LONDON PROPERTY TRUST v HIGH TREES HOUSE (1947)** P leased a block of flats from D. Due to the war he was unable to sub-let the flats, and so P agreed to accept half rent. 6 months after the war P claimed the full rent for the post-war period. This claim succeeded. However the court also considered whether P would have succeeded if he had claimed the full rent back to the start of the war. Denning, J. (as he then was), said that he would not have been successful because he would have been estopped in equity from going back on his promise.

b.   Note that

i.   The effect of equitable estoppel is suspensory. ie When circumstances change, so as to remove the reasons for the promise, the original rights of the promisor become enforceable again as in the High Trees Case.

ii.   The principle acts as "a shield and not a sword" — Birkett L. J. Thus it only prevents the promisor from insisting on his strict legal rights when it would be unjust to allow him to do so, it does not enable the promisee to sue on an action unless he has given consideration.

In **COMBE v COMBE (1951)** A husband during divorce proceedings promised to pay his wife an annual allowance. The wife, relying on this promise, forbore from applying to the court for a maintenance order, and later sued to enforce the husband's promise. At first instance her claim succeeded on the authority of the High Trees case. The Court of Appeal reversed this decision because:-

a.   Equitable estoppel may only be used when a person who promises not to enforce his strict legal rights goes back on this promise. It does not give effect to a new contract. Any new contract must be supported by consideration in the usual way.

b.   The wife had not supplied consideration since her forbearance to apply for a maintenance order was not at the husband's request.

INTENTION TO CREATE LEGAL RELATIONS

14.   Where the parties have not expressly denied an intention to create legal relations, what matters is not what the parties had in their minds, but the inferences that reasonable people would draw from their words or conduct, ie it is an objective test. **CARLILL v CARBOLIC SMOKEBALL CO. (1893)** (Paragraph **4.** above). The decision in this case might have been different if there had been no deposit of money to show sincerity.

119

15. Where there is a commercial agreement it is presumed the parties intend to create legal relations. However if the parties expressly deny intention by stating that negotiations are "subject to contract" or that any agreement is to be "binding in honour only" then there is no contract.

In **JONES v VERNONS POOLS (1938)** P claimed that he had sent D a football coupon on which the draws he had predicted entitled him to a dividend. D denied having received the coupon. They relied on a clause printed on the coupon which stated that the transaction should not "give rise to any legal relationship . . . but . . . be binding in honour only." It was held that this clause was a bar to an action in court.

16. Where there is a domestic agreement the presumption is that legal relations are not intended. For example an agreement by a man to pay his wife £50 per week "housekeeping" money. However it is possible for a man to make a binding contract with his wife, for example as part of a separation agreement.

In **MERRITT v MERRITT (1970)** A husband left his wife and when pressed by her to make arrangements for the future agreed that if she would pay the outstanding mortgage instalments he would, when all the payments had been made, transfer the house into her name. It was held that there was a binding contract since the presumption that legal relations are not intended does not apply if husband and wife are separated or about to separate.

17. Where adult members of a family (other than husband and wife) share a household, the financial arrangements which they make may well be intended to have contractual effect.

In **PARKER v CLARK (1960)** a young couple were induced to sell their house and move in with elderly relations by the latter's promise to leave them a share of the home. It was held that legal effect was intended, otherwise the young couple would not have taken the important step of selling their own home.

18. An agreement between persons who share a household, but which has nothing to do with the management of the household will probably be intended to be legally binding.

In **SIMPKINS v PAYS (1953)** Three ladies who lived in the same house took part in a fashion competition run by a newspaper. They agreed to send their entries on one coupon and to share any prize money. The court rejected the contention that the agreement to share was not intended to be legally binding since the contract had nothing to do with the routine management of the household.

16 Capacity to Contract

In order for an agreement to be a valid contract both parties must have capacity to contract. In general all persons have full power to enter into any contract they wish. Different rules apply to infants, corporations, mental patients and drunks. The law relating to mental patients and drunks is relatively unimportant and will not be discussed. Infants and corporations are considered, but for more detail on corporations please refer to Chapter 11.

INFANTS

1. Introduction

a. An infant (or minor) is a person who has not yet reached his 18th birthday. When the age of majority was reduced from 21 to 18 in 1969 the practical importance of the rules governing infants' contracts was reduced since most of the decided cases concerned persons aged between 18 and 21. Problems today are most likely to arise with contracts of employment and hire purchase agreements.

b. The law governing infants' contracts shows how the law must compromise between two principles. The first, and more important is that the infant must be protected against his own inexperience. The second is that in pursuing this object the law should not cause unnecessary hardship to those who deal with infants. The compromise between these principles results in certain contracts with infants being valid, (contracts for necessaries and contracts of service), others are void or voidable, and in some cases the infant may be liable in tort, or in equity. These categories are considered below:-

2. Contracts for Necessaries

a. *S.3. SALE OF GOODS ACT 1979* provides that an infant must pay a reasonable price for necessaries sold and delivered. The section also defines necessaries as

> "goods suitable to the condition in life of such minor and to his actual requirements at the time of sale or delivery."

b. Note that:-

i.   The term "necessaries" is not confined to goods but also includes necessary services and, if the infant is married, necessaries for his family.

ii. The infant is only bound to pay a reasonable price, and not the contract price.

iii. If the necessaries are sold but not delivered (ie if the contract is executory, the adult not having performed his part) the infant is not bound.

iv. If the goods are delivered, but not paid for the infant is bound because the goods are "sold and delivered". The time of payment is not relevant in deciding whether or not a sale has been made.

c. The burden of proving that the goods are necessaries lies on the seller.

i. Firstly he must show that they are capable of being necessaries. Items of mere luxury, eg a racehorse can never be necessaries, but in **PETERS v FLEMING (1840)**, it was shown that a luxurious item of utility such as a gold watch may be a necessary. This broad definition of necessaries was clearly not adopted for the benefit of the infant, but to give protection to suppliers who gave credit to young men from wealthy families.

ii. Secondly the seller must show that the goods are in fact necessary for the particular infant in question.

In **NASH v INMAN (1908)**, a tailor sued an infant for the price of clothes, including 11 waistcoats. His action failed because he could not show that the infant was not already adequately supplied. An infant is not liable if he has an adequate supply, even if the supplier did not know this.

3. Contracts of Service

a. A contract of service or apprenticeship is binding on an infant if, looked at as a whole, in the light of the circumstances when it was made, it is for his benefit. He may be bound even if some of the clauses of the contract do not turn out to be to his advantage.

In **CLEMENTS v L and NW RAILWAY (1894)** An infant porter agreed to join an insurance scheme to which his employers contributed, and to give up any claim for personal injury he might have under the Employers' Liability Act 1880. The scheme covered a wider range of injuries than the Act but the scale of compensation was lower. The infant was injured in such a way that would have entitled him to compensation under the Act, but it was held that the contract was binding on him since, looked at a whole, in the light of the circumstances when it was made, the insurance scheme was more beneficial to him than the Act.

b. An infant will therefore not be bound if the contract is on the whole harsh or oppressive.

In **DE FRANCESCO v BARNUM (1890)** A girl was apprenticed for stage dancing by a contract which provided that she should be entirely at the disposal of her master; that she would only be paid if he actually employed her (which he was not bound to do); that she could not marry during the apprenticeship; that he could end the contract if he found her unsuitable; and that she could not accept any professional engagement without his consent. She accepted a professional engagement with D without the master's (P's) consent. It was held that P could not sue D in the tort of inducing a breach of contract since, as the contract was unreasonably harsh, it was invalid.

4. Voidable Contracts

a. "Voidable" means that the contract will bind both parties, unless it is avoided by the infant before, or within a reasonable time after, reaching 18. In **EDWARDS v CARTER (1893)** 4½ years after reaching the age of majority (at that time 21) was held to be an unreasonable delay. The other party cannot avoid the contract.

b. Voidable contracts include those by which the minor acquires an interest in subject matter of a permanent or continuing nature, such as land, shares in a company, or contracts of partnership.

c. When an infant avoids a contract he escapes liabilities such as rent which are not yet due, but he can be sued for liabilities (again rent is a possible example) which have accrued.

d. Avoidance will not entitle the infant to recover money paid by him under the contract unless there has been a total failure of consideration, ie unless he has received absolutely nothing for his money.

In **STEINBERG v SCALA (1925)** An infant purchased some shares in a company. When she was required to pay the balance of the purchase price she attempted to avoid the contract, and recover the money that she had already paid. It was held that she did not have to pay the balance, but she could not recover what she had already paid, because she had received some benefits, such as the right to vote at company meetings, and the right to receive dividends. There had not been a failure of consideration since she had received something for her money.

Contrast **CORPE v OVERTON (1833)** An infant agreed to enter into a partnership to be formed in the future. He paid £100 in advance. He later changed his mind, and attempted to recover the £100. His action succeeded because, since the partnership had not yet been formed, he had received absolutely nothing for his money, ie there was a total failure of consideration.

5. Other Contracts – Common Law

a. At common law a contract which was neither valid nor voidable did not bind the infant. It nevertheless had three legal effects:-

   i. It bound the other party.

   ii. The infant could not recover money paid or property transferred unless there had been a total failure of consideration.

   iii. It bound the infant if he ratified it after reaching full age. This had been changed by statute (see below).

b. An infant will therefore not be bound by a trading contract.

In **MERCANTILE UNION GUARANTEE CORPORATION v**

BALL (1937) an infant purchased on hire-purchase a lorry for use in his haulage contractor business. It was held that this was a trading contract rather than a contract for necessaries and so the infant was not bound.

6.   The Minors Contracts Act 1987. The Infants Relief Act 1874 made the following provisions:

    a.   The following contracts were absolutely void:

        i.   Contracts for the repayment of money lent or to be lent to an infant.

        ii.   Contracts for goods supplied, or to be supplied to an infant (other than necessaries).

        iii.   All accounts stated, ie admissions that money is due such as an I.O.U.

    b.   The following contracts were made unenforceable:

        i.   A fresh promise after full age to pay a debt contracted during minority.

        ii.   Any ratification after full age of any promise made during minority.

    c.   The *MINORS CONTRACTS ACT 1987* repealed the Infants Relief Act and therefore the position reverts back to that of common law (see **5.** above).

    d.   The Act also repealed the *BETTING & LOANS (INFANTS) ACT 1892* which made unenforceable any new agreement after majority and any security given to repay a previous loan. Therefore the effect is to enable a former minor to ratify a previous debt, repay a previously unenforceable loan and perform a previously unenforceable contract.

    e.   The Act repeals the rule under which a guarantee by an adult of a void contract or one repudiated after majority was equally void.

    f.   The common law rule whereby property could not be recovered from defaulting minors under unenforceable contracts is altered. The creditor is now allowed, when it is "just and equitable", to obtain a court order for the return of property by a minor, or "any property representing it." It would appear that not only is property recoverable but also identifiable proceeds of the sale of that property.

    g.   The Act also extends the enforceability of guarantees of minors contracts to contracts made under regulated credit agreements under the *CONSUMER CREDIT ACT 1974*.

7.   Liability in Tort. An infant cannot be made indirectly liable on a void contract through being sued in tort, but he can be sued in tort if his act is of a kind not contemplated by the contract.

In **BURNARD v HAGGIS (1863)** an infant hired a horse subject to a condition that he was not to use it for jumping. He broke this provision, and the horse died in a jumping accident. In this case the owner's tort action succeeded because the infant had done an act not contemplated by the contract, and had thus taken himself out of the scope of the law of contract, and the protection it affords to infants.

Contrast **JENNINGS v RUNDALL (1799)** when an infant hired a horse for "riding" and rode it so hard that it was injured. He was held not liable in tort because all he did was an act contemplated by the contract, ie riding, although in an excessive manner. Since he was not liable in contract, he could not be made indirectly liable on the contract by bringing a tort action.

8. The Effect of Equity on Infants' Contracts

a. *Subrogation.* − If an infant borrows money to buy necessaries and he actually spends money for this purpose, the lender may "step into the shoes" of the seller and recover from the infant the reasonable price which the seller could have recovered. The lender is said to subrogated to the rights of the seller.

b. *Restitution.* − If an infant obtains non-necessary goods or money by fraudulently misrepresenting his age, equity will compel him to restore them. However if he has ceased to possess them, it seems that he will not be compelled to restore their value, or any proceeds of sale, or other articles for which they have been exchanged.

c. *Specific performance.* − This will not be granted to an infant, since equity will not grant it against an infant. The equitable maxim "equality is equity" applies.

CORPORATIONS

9. There are three types of Corporation, classified according to their mode of creation:-

a. *Chartered corporations.* A corporation created by Royal Charter has power to do whatever an individual can do. If it makes a contract which offends the spirit of the Charter the contract is valid, although the Charter may be withdrawn.

b. *Statutory corporations.* They have only the powers expressly or impliedly conferred on them by the creating statute.

c. *Companies registered under the Companies Act 1985.*
   i.   When a company is registered it must file various documents with the Registrar of Companies. One of these documents is its Memorandum of Association. This contains the company's "objects clause" which lays down the permitted range of activities which the company can follow.

ii.   Prior to the Companies Act 1989 the basic rule was that an act outside the objects clause was *ultra vires* and void and therefore could not be enforced by the company or by an outsider. This was unpopular with companies (for whom it could be inconvenient to have restricted powers) and outsiders (who might find that their contract could not be enforced). This was generally the case even if the outsider did not actually know of the restriction on the company's power, because of the doctrine of *constructive notice*, by which everyone was deemed to know of the contents of the company's registered documents.

iii.   Companies therefore sought to avoid the ultra vires rule by drafting lengthy objects clauses allowing them to do almost anything they could ever wish to do. They also usually included general powers allowing anything incidental to any of their other objects and powers.

iv.   The 1989 Act reduces the importance of the objects clause in two ways:-

(a)   It provides that it will be sufficient for the memorandum to state that the object of the company is to carry on business as a general commercial company. This will allow the company (a) to carry on any trade or business whatsoever and (b) to do all such things as are incidental or conducive to the carrying on of any trade or business by it.

(b)   It also provides that the validity of an act done by a company shall not be called into question on the ground of lack of capacity by reason of anything in the company's memorandum. Consequently a completed act will have total protection from the ultra vires rule and will be enforcable by both the company and an outsider.

v.   The Act does retain the power of members to bring proceedings to restrain ultra vires acts. However it is most unlikely that a company taking advantage of the provision described above will ever make an ultra vires contract.

17 Form of Contracts

1. The general rule is that a contract may be in writing, or oral, or inferred from conduct, or a combination of any of these. It is a common mistake to think that a binding contract must be in writing. Writing makes it easier to prove the contents of the contract, but it is not usually necessary. There are however three categories of exceptions.

2. Contracts which must be by Deed

a. A conveyance or transfer of a legal estate in land (including a mortgage) or the grant of a lease for three or more years must be by deed. A conveyance is the document which transfers the title of unregistered land. A transfer is the document which transfers title to registered land.

b. Consideration is not necessary for a deed. Therefore a binding gratuitous promise can be made by deed. The essentials of a deed are:-

i.   Writing.

ii. Signature.

iii. Seal. This means intention that the document be executed as a deed. No wax or red stick-on seal is necessary.

iv. Delivery. This means conduct indicating that the person executing the deed intends to be bound by it. No physical transfer of possession is necessary.

c. The effect of non-compliance with the above is that the contract is void. Therefore any money paid or property transferred can be recovered. However an unsealed lease operates in equity as an agreement to enter into a lease. It will therefore bind the parties, but it will not bind a third party who purchases the landlord's interest without notice of the tenant's interest. (A properly sealed lease would bind such a purchaser).

3. Contracts which must be in Writing

a. The main types are:-

i.   The transfer of shares in limited companies.

ii. The sale or disposition of an interest in land.

iii. Bills of exchange and cheques.

iv. Consumer credit contracts.

v.   Policies of marine insurance.

vi. Legal assignments of choses in action.

b. The effect of non-compliance varies, depending on the type of agreement. Usually the contract will be void, but in the case of consumer credit transactions the effect of non-compliance by the seller is to make the agreement unenforceable against the debtor unless the creditor (seller) obtains a court order − *S.127. CONSUMER CREDIT ACT 1974*. The debtor may therefore keep the goods if they are already in his possession.

4.   Contracts which must be Evidenced in Writing. A contract of guarantee must be evidenced in writing to be legally enforceable, although the contract itself may be oral.

a.   *Nature of the contract.* For example is A contracts to buy goods from B, and C promises to pay B if A does not, a contract of guarantee is formed. This should be distinguished from a contract of indemnity in which the person giving the indemnity makes himself primarily liable by saying, for example, 'I will see that you are paid'. A guarantor however does not expect to be approached for payment. He may say 'If he does not pay you then I will'.

b.   *Written Evidence.* Any signed note of the material terms of the contract is sufficient. Besides the signature of the guarantor other evidence must include the names or identification of the parties, a description of the subject matter and any other material terms. Any consideration need not be stated. The evidence may be contained in several separate documents.

18 The Contents of Contracts

1. A contract may contain three types of clause, namely express terms (other than exemption clauses), implied terms, and exemption clauses (which are always expressly agreed).

EXPRESS TERMS

2. A statement may be an express term of the contract or a representation inducing its formation. The importance of the distinction is that different remedies are available if a term is broken or a representation is untrue. Which it is depends on the intention of the parties (objectively assessed). It may be helpful to consider:-

    a. The stage of negotiations at which the statement was made. − The later it was made the more likely it is to be a term.

    b. Whether the statement was reduced to writing after it was made. − If it was so reduced it is clearly regarded as more important, and is therefore probably a term of the contract.

    c. Whether the maker of the statement possessed special skill or knowledge as compared with the other party.

    In **OSCAR CHESS v WILLIAMS (1975)** D, a private individual, sold to P, car dealers, for £280 a car honestly described as a 1948 Morris 10. It was in fact a 1939 model worth £175. The statement that it was a 1948 model was held not to be a term of the contract, since D had himself been sold the car as a 1948 model, being given a forged log book. D thus had no special knowledge as to the age of the car, whereas P, being a dealer was in at least as good a position as D to know whether the statement was true.

    Contrast **DICK BENTLEY PRODUCTIONS v HAROLD SMITH MOTORS (1965)** A dealer sold a Bentley car stating that it had only done 20,000 miles since a replacement engine, whereas it had in fact done 100,000 miles since then. This statement was held to be a warranty since the dealer was in a better position to know the mileage than the purchaser.

3. There are two basic types of express term:-

    a. A *condition* is a vital term, going to the root of the contract, breach of which normally entitles the innocent party to treat the contract as at an end (ie to repudiate the contract) and to claim damages.

    b. A *warranty* is a term which is subsidiary to the main purpose of the contract, breach of which only entitles the innocent party to damages.

Classification as a condition or warranty depends on the intention of the parties, but in many cases their intention is not expressed and the clause will not obviously be a condition or a warranty. Such terms are called *intermediate terms*. They remain unclassified until the seriousness of a breach can be judged. If the breach goes to the root of the contract, depriving the plaintiff of the major benefits of the contract, the relevant term will be classified as a condition.

In **HONG KONG FIR SHIPPING CO. v KAWASAKI KISEN KAISHA (1962)** a ship delivered under a 24 month charterparty was unseaworthy, and took 7 months to repair. The court said that many contractual undertakings could not be categorised simply as ''conditions'' or ''warranties'', and the innocent party should be entitled to rescind only if the effect of the breach is to substantially deprive him of the benefit of the contract. Since the ship was available for 17 out of 24 months rescission was not granted.

The use by the parties of ''condition'' or ''warranty'' is not conclusive. If breach of a term expressed to be a condition can only produce a very small loss it may be held that the breach will not justify rescission.

In **WICKMAN v SCHULER (1974)** it was a ''condition of a four year agreement that a representative of the plaintiff should visit six named customers once a week to solicit orders.'' The plaintiff failed to make some of the required visits and the defendant terminated the contract. The court held that the plaintiff could recover damages for wrongful termination. It was not likely that the parties intended that failure to make a few visits out of a total of over 1,400 visits should justify rescission.

4.   Incomplete Contracts

a.   A legally binding agreement must be complete in its terms.

In **SCAMMELL v OUSTON (1941)** an agreement for the purchase of a van provided for the balance of the price to be paid over two years ''on hire purchase terms''. It was held that there was no agreement since it was uncertain what terms of payment were intended. Hire purchase terms may vary over intervals between payments, rate of interest, etc.

However the parties may leave an essential term to be settled by specified means outside the contract. For example it may be agreed to sell at the ruling open market price (if there is a market) on the day of delivery, or to invite an arbitrator to determine a fair price. It is also possible for the price to be determined by the course of dealing between the parties.

In **HILLAS v ARCOS (1932)** a contract for the supply of timber in 1930 contained an option for the purchaser to buy a quantity of timber in 1931, but made no reference to the price. It was held that the missing terms of the 1931 purchase could be deduced from the conduct of the parties in their 1930 transaction when the price was determined by reference to an official price list.

c.   If the parties used non essential words, for example standard printed conditions some of which are inappropriate, such words may be disregarded.

In **NICOLENE v SIMMONDS (1953)** a contract provided that the
"usual conditions of acceptance apply". However there were no usual
conditions of acceptance. It was held that this phrase was non essential
and meaningless. It could therefore be ignored.

5. Standard Form Contracts

Many agreements are not individually negotiated, indeed it would be impossible for business to cope if every agreement had to be negotiated by the parties.
Standard form contracts are usually used by large organisations in their contracts
with consumers, for example British Telecom. They are also often used in
commercial transactions. There are two main ways in which a problem with
the agreed terms can arise.

a.   There will be a problem of consistency when blank parts of a standard
term contract are completed in a way that is inconsistent with the printed
words. However the basic rule of construction is that the particular override the general, thus the written words inserted in the contract override
inconsistent printed words.

b.   The second problem occurs when both parties have their own standard
terms. A buyer will order on his standard terms but the seller will purport
to accept on his standard terms which of course will be inconsistent with
those of the buyer.

In **BUTLER MACHINE TOOL COMPANY v EX-CELL-O
CORPORATION (1979)** the seller offered machine tools subject to certain
terms and conditions which "shall prevail over any terms and conditions
in the buyer's order". The conditions included a price variation clause.
The buyer replied by placing an order for the machine on terms and
conditions which were materially different from those put forward by the
seller and which, in particular, made no provision for a variation of price.
At the foot of the buyer's order there was a tear-off acknowledgement
of receipt of the order stating that "we accept your order on the terms
and conditions stated thereon". The seller completed the acknowledgement and returned it to the buyer. When the seller came to deliver the
machine they claimed that the price had increased by about £2,900. The
buyer refused to pay the increased price and contended that the contract
had been concluded on his rather than the seller's terms and therefore
constituted a fixed price contract. The judge found for the seller and buyer
appealed. The Court of Appeal found for the buyer because:-

i.   applying the rules of offer and acceptance, the buyer's order was
a counter offer which destroyed the offer made in the seller's quotation. The seller by completing and returning the acknowledgement
form, accepted the counter offer on the buyer's terms.

ii.   the documents comprising a "battle of forms" were to be
considered as a whole. If the conflicting terms and conditions of both
parties were irreconcilable, then the acknowledgement of the order

was the decisive document since it made it clear that the contract was on the buyer's and not the seller's terms.

IMPLIED TERMS

6. Terms may be implied by custom, the courts, or by statute.

7.   Custom. The parties are presumed to have contracted by reference to the customs prevailing in the trade or locality in question, unless they have shown a contrary intention.

In **BRITISH CRANE HIRE v IPSWICH PLANT HIRE (1974)** both firms were in the business of hiring out cranes and heavy plant. D urgently needed a crane for work on marshy ground and agreed to hire such a crane from P. The method of payment was agreed but the hire conditions were not. P then sent D a copy of their standard conditions (which were similar to those used throughout the trade) which provided that the hirer would be liable for all expenses arising out of the crane's use. Before these conditions were signed the crane sank into the marshy ground, and P incurred expenses in recovering it. P claimed these expenses from D. Their action succeeded since both parties were in the same trade, and had equal bargaining power, and the evidence was that they both understood that P's standard conditions of hire would apply.

8.   The Courts

a.   The courts will imply two types of terms into contracts. Firstly terms which are so obvious that the parties must have intended them to be included. These are called terms implied in fact. Secondly terms which are implied to maintain a standard of behaviour, even though the parties may not have intended them to be included. These are called terms implied in law.

b.   *Terms implied in fact.* The implied term must be both obvious and necessary to give "business efficacy" to the contract. The courts will not imply a term merely because it is reasonable to do so. The test used is known as the "officious bystander" test. ie If when the parties were making the contract and officious bystander had asked "Is X a term of the contract?" and if he would have received the reply "Yes, obviously" then the term will be implied.

In **THE MOORCOOK (1889)** D, who were wharf owners contracted to allow P to unload their ship at the wharf. The ship grounded at low water, and was damaged by settling on a ridge of hard ground. D were held to be in breach of an implied term that the wharf was safe.

In **EYRE v MEASDAY (1986)** P underwent a sterilisation operation. The surgeon had advised her that the operation was irreversible and consequently P believed that she would be sterile. The fact that there was a slight risk of pregnancy after the operation was not pointed out. Later the plaintiff became pregnant and gave birth to a son. It was held that the word "irreversible" did not amount to a guarantee of success, it merely indicated that the procedure could not be reversed, which is quite different. Applying the "officious bystander" test the courts said that although it would be reasonable for P to assume that she was sterile, it would not be reasonable for her to think that she had been given a guarantee that she was sterile. If she had wanted such a guarantee she should have asked for it. P was therefore unsuccessful.

c.   *Terms implied in law*. Terms implied in law cover many classes of contract. Thus in a contract of employment the employee impliedly undertakes, for example, to faithfully serve his employer, and that he is reasonably skilled. The employer impliedly undertakes that he will not require the employee to do an unlawful act, and that he will provide safe premises. Similarly in a tenancy agreement the landlord impliedly covenants that his tenant shall have quiet possession, and the tenant impliedly agrees not to commit waste.

In **LIVERPOOL CITY COUNCIL v IRWIN (1977)** it was held that where parts of a building have been let to different tenants, and where rights of access over the parts of the building retained by the landlord eg the stairs, have been granted to these tenants, then a term could be implied that the landlord would keep these parts reasonably safe.

9.   **Statute.**

a.   The most well known examples are the terms implied by *S. 12-15 SALE OF GOODS ACT 1979*:-

i.   That the seller has the right to sell.

ii.   That in a sale by description the goods shall correspond with the description.

iii.   That the goods supplied are of merchantable quality, and fit for the purpose for which they are required.

iv.   That where the goods are sold by sample the bulk will correspond with the sample.

b.   Recently the *SUPPLY OF GOODS AND SERVICES ACT 1982* has given similar protection to persons who are supplied with (as opposed to sold) goods, and to persons who are supplied with services.

These two Acts are considered in more detail in Chapter 33.

EXEMPTION CLAUSES

10.   An exemption clause is a term in a contract which seeks to exempt one of the parties from liability, or which seeks to limit his liability to a specific sum if certain events occur, such as a breach of warranty, negligence, or theft of goods.

11. An exemption clause may become a term of the contract by signature or by notice.

a. If a person signs a document he is bound by it even if he does not read it.

In **L'ESTRANGE v GRAUCOB (1934)** P, who was the proprietor of a cafe, purchased a cigarette vending machine. She signed, without reading, a sales agreement which contained a large amount of "small print". The machine was defective but the vendors were held to be protected by an exemption clause contained in that small print.

b. A person may not be bound by a signed document if the other party misrepresented its terms.

In **CURTIS v CHEMICAL CLEANING CO. (1951)** P took a white satin wedding dress, trimmed with beads and sequins to the cleaners. The assistant gave her a form to sign, and when asked about its contents said that it excluded the company's liability for damage to the beads and sequins. The plaintiff then signed the form, which in fact contained a clause excluding the company from all liability. When the dress was returned it was badly stained. The company attempted to rely on their exemption clause but it was held that they could not do so since the assistant had misrepresented (albeit innocently) the effect of the form.

c. Where a document is not signed the exemption clause will only apply if

   i. The party knows of the clause, or if

   ii. Reasonable steps are taken to bring it to his notice before the contract is made.

In **OLLEY v MARLBOROUGH COURT (1949)** P booked in at the D's hotel. When she went to her room she saw a notice on the wall stating that the hotel would not be liable for articles lost or stolen unless they were handed in for safe keeping. P left some furs in the bedroom, closed the self-locking door, and hung the key on a board in reception. The furs were stolen. It was held that the exemption clause was not effective. The contract was completed at the reception desk, and accordingly a notice in the bedroom came too late to be incorporated into the contract.

d. The court will not enforce an exemption clause unless the party affected by it was adequately informed of it when he accepted it. Thus the exemption clause must be put forward in a document which gives reasonable notice of the liability conditions proposed by it.

In **CHAPELTON v BARRY UDC (1940)** there was a pile of deck chairs and a notice saying "hire of chairs 2d per session of 3 hours". P took two chairs, paid for them and received two tickets. One of the chairs collapsed and he was injured. The Council relied on a notice on the back of the tickets by which it disclaimed liability for injury. It was held that the notice advertising chairs for hire gave no warning of limiting conditions and it was not reasonable to communicate them on a receipt. The disclaimer of liability was not effective.

Contrast **THOMPSON v LMS RAILWAY (1930)** where an elderly lady who could not read asked her neice to buy her a railway excursion ticket on which was printed "Excursion. For conditions see back". On the back it was stated that the ticket was issued subject to conditions contained in the company's timetables. These conditions excluded liability for injury. It was held that the conditions had been adequately communicated and therefore accepted.

NB A further distinction between the two cases is that in Chapelton's case the ticket was a mere receipt, it did not purport to set out the conditions for the hire of the chair, it only showed the time for which it was hired and that a fee had been paid. However in Thompson's case it would have been obvious to a reasonable person that the ticket had contractual effect since tickets of that kind generally contain contract terms.

e.   If the parties have had long and consistent dealings on terms incorporating an exemption clause, then the clause may apply to a particular transaction, even if the usual steps to incorporate it were not taken. If there are only a few transactions spread over a long period it would not be reasonable to assume that the person has agreed to the term.

In **HOLLIER v RAMBLER MOTORS (1972)** on three or four occasions over a period of five years H had had repairs done at the garage. On each occasion he had signed a form by which the garage disclaimed liability for damage caused by fire to customers' cars. On the latest occasion he did not sign the form. The car was damaged by fire caused by negligence of garage employees. The garage contended that the disclaimer had by course of dealing, become an established term of any contract made between them and H. It was held that the garage was liable. There was insufficient evidence to show that H knew of and agreed to the condition as a continuing term of his contracts with the garage.

12.   Limitations on the Use of Exemption Clauses

a.   In considering the validity of exemption clauses the courts have had to strike a balance between:-

i.   The principle that parties should have complete freedom to contract on whatever terms they wish, and

ii.   The need to protect the public from unfair exemption clauses in standard form contracts used by large business enterprises.

b.   The use of exemption clauses by large organisations to abuse their bargaining power is clearly indefensible. Nevertheless exemption clauses do have a proper place in business. They can be used to allocate contractual risk, and thus determine in advance who is to insure against that risk.

They also make it possible for a contracting party to quote different rates according to the risk borne by him. Thus between businessmen of similar bargaining power exemption clauses are a legitimate device, but limitations on their use have been necessary in contracts involving the public. The main limitations are now contained in the *UNFAIR CONTRACT TERMS ACT 1977*, and in the past were exercised through the doctrine of fundamental breach.

13.   The Unfair Contract Terms Act 1977

a.   The Act uses two techniques for controlling exemption clauses — some types of clause are stated to be ineffective, whereas others are subject to a test of reasonableness.

b.   The contract and tort provisions of the Act, (with the exception of *S.6.*)

    i.   Are limited to liability which arises in the course of a business, and

    ii.   Do not apply to contracts made before 1st February 1978.

The main provisions of the Act are:-

c.   *S.2.* Exclusion of negligence liability.

    i.   A person cannot by reference to any contract term restrict his liability for death or personal injury resulting from negligence.

    ii.   In the case of other loss or damage a person cannot restrict his liability for negligence unless the term is reasonable.

d.   *S.3.* Standard term contracts and consumer contracts. The party who imposes the standard term contract or who deals with the consumer cannot, unless the term is reasonable,

    i.   Restrict his liability for his own breach, or

    ii.   Claim to be entitled to render substantially different performance, or no performance at all.

e.   *S.6.* (as amended) Sale of goods.

    i.   *S.12. SALE OF GOODS ACT 1979* cannot be excluded.

    ii.   *S.13-15 SALE OF GOODS ACT 1979* cannot be excluded in a consumer sale, but can be excluded in a non-consumer sale if the exemption clause is reasonable.

f.   *S.11.* The requirement of reasonableness. The term must be a fair and reasonable one having regard to all the circumstances which were, or ought reasonably to have been known to or in the contemplation of the parties when the contract was made. The burden of proving reasonableness lies on the person seeking to rely on the clause. In contracts for the sale of goods guidelines have been laid down for determining reasonableness, for example:-

    i.   The strength of the bargaining positions of the parties relative to each other.

136

ii.   Whether the customer received an inducement to agree to the term. — If he did the term is more likely to be reasonable.

iii.   Whether the goods were manufactured to the special order of the customer. — If they were the term is again more likely to be reasonable.

A very common situation was recently considered by the House of Lords.

In **SMITH v ERIC BUSH (1989)** P wished to purchase a house. She approached the Abbey National for a mortgage and paid for a survey including a valuation report by the surveyor hired by the Building Society (Eric Bush). In view of her limited resources P did not hire her own surveyor, but relied on the building society's valuation. However the surveyor had negligently failed to notice that the removal of the chimney breasts had left the chimneys in a dangerous state. A few months after P moved in they collapsed, causing considerable damage. Although P was allowed to see the valuation report, the mortgage application form stated that neither the Abbey National nor the surveyor gave any warranty that the report was accurate, and that it was supplied without responsibility on their part. The House of Lords held that this disclaimer of responsibility was unreasonable in circumstances where they surveyor knows that the borrower will be supplied with a copy of the report and would be likely to rely on it despite the disclaimer. P was successful in her action.

When considering all of the relevant circumstances the question for the court is limited to whether the clause satisfied the requirement of reasonableness *in relation to the particular contract*, not every contract in which it might be used.

In **PHILLIPS PRODUCTS v HYLAND (1984)** Philips hired a JCB, plus driver (Hyland) from a plant hire company. An exclusion clause in the contract stated "when a driver or operator is supplied by the owner to work the plant, he shall be under the direction and control of the hirer. Such drivers or operators shall for all purposes in connection with their employment in the working of the plant be regarded as their servants". Hyland nevertheless made it clear to Philips that he would not tolerate interference in the way he operated his machine. He then drove it negligently causing over £3,000 of damage to Philips' buildings. It was held that the exclusion clause was not reasonable the plaintiff hire company were therefore liable for Hyland's negligence.

g.   *S.12.* The definition of consumer. A person deals as a consumer if

i.   He neither makes the contract in the course of a business, nor holds himself out as doing so, and

ii.   The other party does make the contract in the course of a business, and

iii.   The goods are of a type ordinarily supplied for private use or consumption.

The person who claims that the other party does not deal as a consumer must show that he does not.

Where a business engages in an activity (for example buying a car) that is merely incidental to their business (for example as shipping brokers) that activity will not be "in the course of" the business unless it is an integral part of it, and it will not be an integral part unless it is carried on with a degree of regularity **(R & B CUSTOMERS BROKERS v UNITED DOMINIONS TRUST (1988)).**

14. The Requirement of Reasonableness and the End of Fundamental Breach

a.   It has now become clear that the statutory requirement of reasonableness has replaced the common law rules on fundamental breach. The problem was that some breaches were so serious that they amounted to totally different performance or no performance at all. There used to be a rule that an exemption clause could not apply to such a fundamental breach. In 1967 this was changed by the House of Lords and it was said that if a clause was sufficiently well constructed it was possible to exclude liability for a fundamental breach. For example:-

In **PHOTO PRODUCTIONS v SECURICOR TRANSPORT (1980)** P engaged D to provide a visiting patrol service to their factory at a charge of £8.75p per week. One night an employee of D intentionally started a fire at the factory causing damage of £615,000. D sought to avoid liability by relying on a clause which stated:-

"Under no circumstances shall the company (Securicor) be responsible for any injurious act or default by any employee of the company unless such act or default could have been foreseen and avoided by the exercise of due diligence on the part of the company as his employer."

It was not suggested that D could have foreseen and avoided the act of their employee. However the Court of Appeal held that there was a fundamental breach to which the exemption clause did not apply. The House of Lords unanimously reversed the decision, holding that as a matter of construction, the words of the exemption clause clearly relieved D from the liability which they would have otherwise incurred.

b.   The case that finally laid to rest the doctrine of fundamental breach was decided by the House of Lords in 1983. It was the first time that the House had had to consider a statutory provision giving power to override on exemption clause.

In **GEORGE MITCHELL v FINNEY LOCK SEEDS (1983)** P, who was a farmer, ordered 30 lb. of cabbage seed from D, who were seed merchants. The purchase price was about £200. D's standard term contract limited their liability for the supply of defective goods to replacement or refund of the amount paid by P. P planted the seed over a wide acreage but when the crop came up it was not fit for human consumption but consisted of unusable weeds. P claimed about £61,500 damages and

138

about £30,500 interest. P's arguments were based both on the common law ground of fundamental breach and on the statutory ground of reasonableness. It was held that at common law the exemption clause would have protected D, but the court decided in favour of P, relying exclusively on the statutory ground. Lord Bridge said that fundamental breach had been "forcibly evicted" from our system. Thus it will no longer be necessary to use this artificial method of analysing contract terms now that it is possible for the court to set aside the term if it does not satisfy the requirement of reasonableness. It is hoped that the application of this test will lead to less uncertainty.

Note: Since the contract in the above case was made before 1/2/78 (when the Unfair Contract Terms Act came into force) the provision which applied was *S. 55 of SCHEDULE 1 of the SALE OF GOODS ACT 1979*. This applies to contracts made between 18/5/1973 and 1/2/1978 and it adopts a requirement of reasonableness very similar to the *UNFAIR CONTRACT TERMS ACT*.

19 Vitiating Factors

These are factors which affect the validity of an otherwise effective contract.

MISTAKE

1. It is considered to be in the interest of business generally that apparent contracts be enforced. Thus most mistakes, for example as to the quality of a product, will not affect the validity of the contract. The common law rules on mistake, if applicable, render the contract void, but these rules are exercised within narrow limits. In equity the rules have a wider scope, but their effect is less drastic. If a document is signed by mistake special rules apply.

2.   Common Law. The following types of mistake render a contract void, provided the mistake actually induces the contract.

    a.   Mistake as to the existence of the subject matter.

    In **GALLOWAY v GALLOWAY (1914)** a man and a woman made a separation agreement, believing that they were married. In fact they were not married because, unknown to them, at the time of their marriage ceremony the man's wife was still alive. The separation agreement was held to be void for mistake because the "marriage" which was the basis for the agreement was void.

    b.   Mistake as to the possibility of performing the contract.

    In **SHEIK BROS v OCHSNER (1957)** a contract was made for the exploitation of sisal grown on a specific plot of land. The contract provided for an average delivery of 50 tons of sisal per month. The contract was held to be void because the land was not capable of producing 50 tons per month.

    c.   Mistake as to the identity of the subject matter.

       i.   For example A intended to buy product X, but B intended to sell product Y.

    In **RAFFLES v WICHELHAUS (1864)** P agreed to sell to D a consignment of cotton which was to arrive "ex Peerless from Bombay". There happened to be two ships called Peerless sailing from Bombay, one in October and one in December. P was thinking of one ship and D of the other. It was held that there was no contract.

       ii.   It is important to be able to distinguish a mistake as to identity from a mistake as to quality.

    In **SMITH v HUGHES (1871)** P was shown a sample of oats by D, and thinking that they were old oats he bought them. They were in fact new oats, and he refused to accept them. It was held that his mistake did not invalidate the contract. The parties were at cross-purposes, but not to such an extent that there was no agreement at all. The mistake was only one of quality, and as such does not operate to render the contract void.

iii.   A mistake as to quality will only invalidate the contract if it is a mistake as to the fundamental quality by which the thing is identified not if it is a mistake as to one of the various other qualities of the product.

d.   Mistake as to the identity of the other party. It is clear that such a mistake cannot be made when parties deal face to face. In such a situation a person can only make a mistake as to the attributes (ie the quality) of the other party, and not his identity. An agreement apparently made between X and and Y will be void if X can prove:-

i.   That at the time of the agreement he regarded the identity of the other party as of importance.

ii.   That he did not intend to contract with Y, but with a different existing person — Z, and

iii.   That this fact was known to Y.

In **CUNDY v LINDSAY (1878)** L, who manufactured handkerchiefs, received an order from a crook called Blenkarn, who gave his address as 37 Wood Street. He signed his name to make it look like Blenkiron and Co, who were a respectable firm who traded at 123 Wood Street. L then sent the goods to "Blenkiron and Co, 37 Wood Street" where Blenkarn took possession of them. Blenkarn, who had obtained the goods on credit, then sold them to C for cash and absconded with the proceeds without paying L. It was held that there was no contract between L and Blenkarn, since L intended to deal with someone else. Thus the title to the handkerchiefs did not pass to Blenkarn, and so he could not pass title to C. C therefore had to return the handkerchiefs to L.

Contrast **LEWIS v AVERAY (1971)** P advertised his car for sale, and was induced to accept a cheque from a crook who said he was the famous actor Richard Greene. The cheque was dishonoured. P then claimed the car from D who had bought it in good faith from the crook. The claim failed because his contract with the crook was not void for mistake, since the presumption that he intended to contract with the person physically before him had not been overcome. P's mistake was as to the credit-worthiness of the other party, and not as to his identity. The contract between P and the crook was voidable for fraud. Voidable however means valid until avoided, and P had not avoided by the time the crook sold the car to D. The contract was therefore valid, and the crook was able to pass title to D.

In **KINGS NORTON METAL v EDRIDGE MERRETT (1897)** P received an order for wire from "Hallam and Co." The letterhead depicted a large factory and described Hallam and Co as a substantial firm. In fact Hallam and Co did not exist, being merely an alias for a crook named Wallis. P sent the goods to "Hallam and Co" on credit. Wallis took possession of them and re-sold them to D. It was held that as Wallis and "Hallam and Co" were the same person, P had not made a mistake as to identity, but had intended to contract with the writer of the letters. Thus the contract was only voidable for fraud, and since Wallis sold to D before P avoided the contract D obtained title to the goods.

e. Mistake as to the terms of the contract of which the other party is aware.

In **HARTOG v COLIN AND SHEILDS (1939)** A seller of hare skins mistakenly offered them at a price "per pound" instead of "per piece", there being about three pieces to the pound. The buyer, knowing of the mistake, accepted the offer, and later sued the seller for non-delivery. His action failed since he knew that the seller did not intend to contract on the terms stated.

3. Equity. Equity will in limited situations relieve a party from the effects of his mistake where the common law would hold him to the contract. There are two equitable remedies:-

a. *Rescission.* The circumstances when this remedy will be granted have never been precisely defined. In general it will only be granted if the party seeking to rescind was not at fault, and provided justice can be done to the other party by imposing conditions.

In **GRIST v BAILEY (1966)** The contract concerned the sale of a house which was occupied by a tenant. Both parties believed that the house was subject to rent control, and they agreed a price of £850. In fact the house was not subject to rent control, and so was worth £2,250. The contract for sale at £850 was rescinded in equity, with the condition imposed that the vendor should give the purchaser first option to buy the house at the correct market price.

b. *Rectification.* Where there has been a mistake, not in the actual agreement, but in its reduction into writing, equity will rectify the written document so that it coincides with the true agreement of the parties provided:-

i.   The terms were clearly agreed between the parties

ii. The agreement continued unchanged up to the time it was put into writing, and

iii. The writing fails to express the agreement of the parties.

In **WEEDS v BLANEY (1976)** P orally agreed with D to sell him a farmhouse and some land. P's solicitor in error prepared a contract which included further land owned by P. The error was not noticed and the land was transferred to D who became the registered owner. It was held that P was entitled to rectification of the contract and the transfer.

4.   Non Est Factum (It is not my act). The general rule concerning signed documents is that a person is bound even if he does not read or understand the document (**L'ESTRANGE v GRAUCOB (1934)**, Chapter 18, Paragraph 11). However an apparent signed contract will be regarded as void if a party can successfully plead the defence of non est factum. Three conditions must be satisfied:-

a.   The signature must have been induced by fraud.

b.   The document must be fundamentally different from that thought to be signed. A mistake as to the contents is not sufficient to allow non est factum to be raised.

c.   The party seeking to avoid liability must prove that he acted with reasonable care.

In **LEWIS v CLAY (1897)** D was induced to sign two promissory notes by the fraudulent misrepresentation that his signature was required as a witness. The rest of the document apart from the space for the signature was covered by blotting paper, D being told that the documents were of a private nature. It was held that the defence of non est factum applied even though D could not say precisely what type of document he thought he had signed.

Contrast **SAUNDERS v ANGLIA BUILDING SOCIETY (1970)** The original plaintiff (a Mrs Gaillie who died before 1970) wanted to help her nephew, Parkin, to raise money on the security of her leasehold house, provided she could continue to live there rent free for the rest of her life. Parkin did not want to raise the loan or become owner of the house himself as he feared this would enable his wife (from whom he was separated) to enforce a claim for maintenance against him. He therefore arranged that his friend — Lee, should raise the money on a mortgage of Gaillie's house, and then give the money to him. Before Lee could mortgage the house it had to be transferred to him. An assignment was prepared under which the lease of the house was transferred to Lee for £3,000 (a reasonable price was included in the assignment so as not to subsequently arouse the Building Society's suspicions). When Gaillie was asked to sign the assignment she did not read it because her glasses were broken, but Lee told her it was a deed of gift to Parkin (who witnessed the document). Lee then raised money by mortgaging the property to The Anglia Building Society, but he did not pay any money to Parkin, nor did he pay the £3,000 to Gallie.

It was held that non est factum did not apply to Gaillie's signature of the assignment, since her mistake was not sufficiently serious. She believed the document would enable Parkin to raise money on the security of the house, and the document was designed to achieve this aim, though by a different method than that contemplated by Gaillie. It was also stated that Mrs. Gallie's carelessness prevented her from relying on non est factum.

MISREPRESENTATION

5.   General Definition. A misrepresentation is an untrue statement of fact which is one of the causes which induces the contract. Note that

a.   It must be a statement (either written, spoken, or by conduct) of fact and not a statement of law, intention, or opinion.

b.   Silence is not usually misrepresentation except

i.   When a statement made in the course of negotiations subsequently becomes false and is not corrected, or

ii.   When silence distorts a literally true statement.

In **R v KYLSANT (1931)** A company when inviting the public to subscribe for its shares, stated that it had paid a regular dividend throughout the years of the depression. This clearly implied that the company had made a profit during those years. This was not the case since the dividends had been paid out of the accumulated profits of the pre-depression years. The company's silence as to the source of the dividends was held to be a misrepresentation since it distorted the true statement that dividends had been paid.

iii.   Where the contract is of utmost good faith (uberrimae fidei).

c.   The misrepresentation must induce the contract. The plaintiff therefore cannot avoid the contract if

i.   He knew the statement was false, or

ii.   He would have made the contract despite the misrepresentation, or

iii.   He did not know that there had been a misrepresentation.

In **HORSFALL v THOMAS (1862)** The vendor of a gun concealed a defect in the gun (a misrepresentation by conduct). The buyer purchased the gun without examining it. Therefore the concealing of the defect could not have affected his decision as to whether or not to purchase it. His action therefore failed.

6.   Fraudulent Misrepresentation

a.   Definition — A statement which is known to be false, or made without belief in its truth, or recklessly, not caring whether it is true or false.

In **DERRY v PEEK (1889)** A company had a power conferred by a special Act of Parliament to run trams by animal power and with Board of Trade consent by steam or mechanical power. The company invited applications for shares from the public and stated in the prospectus that they had power to run trams by steam power. They had assumed that Board of Trade permission would be granted, but in the event it was not. As a result the directors were sued for fraud. The court formulated the definition of fraud stated above and held that the directors were not liable since they honestly believed their statement to be true.

b.   Assuming that it does not induce an operative mistake, fraud makes the contract voidable, and whether the contract is avoided or not, gives the innocent party a right to damages for the tort of deceit.

c.   When a contract is voidable, it will generally be valid until the other party is informed of the avoidance. However where the seller has a right to avoid for fraud he does so if, on discovering the fraud, he takes all reasonable steps to recover the goods.

In **CAR AND UNIVERSAL FINANCE v CALDWELL (1964)** A person was induced by fraud to sell his car to a crook. The crook's cheque was dishonoured, and the crook could not be found. Immediately the cheque was dishonoured the former owner informed the police and the Automobile Association, and asked them to find his car. It was held that since he had done all he could in the circumstances he had successfully avoided the contract. It is clearly vital to avoid a contract induced by fraud as soon as possible. Since fraud makes a contract voidable, (and not void), if the crook sells the goods to a third party before avoidance he passes a good title and the original owner bears the loss. If the crook "sells" after avoidance he cannot pass title, thus the third party to whom he has "sold" must bear the loss.

7.   **Innocent Misrepresentation.** An innocent misrepresentation is a statement which the maker honestly believes to be true. The law on this topic represents an attempt to strike a balance between two innocent parties, the maker of the statement and the person who has been induced to make a contract in reliance on that statement. It is in such situations that the law often becomes very complex. This is true of innocent misrepresentation where the rules originate from three sources, common law, equity and statute. The topic will be dealt with in four sections. The relevance of 1967 is that this is the date of the *MISREPRESENTATION ACT*, which modified both common law and equity.

a.   *Common law before 1967*. No remedy existed unless

   i.   The representation had become a term of the contract, in which case the maker of the statement could be sued for breach of contract, or

   ii.   A tort action was possible under the principle in **HEDLEY BYRNE v HELLER (1964)**. (Chapter 26.3)

b.   *Common law after 1967*.

   i.   The innocent party has a right to damages for misrepresentation if he has suffered loss. However if the maker of the statement proves that he had reasonable grounds for believing, and in fact did believe, up to the time the contract was made that the facts represented were true then he has a defence. − *S.2(1) MISREPRESENTATION ACT 1967*.

   ii.   If this defence does not succeed, but the misrepresentation was not fraudulent then it is said to be negligent misrepresentation.

In **F AND H ENTERTAINMENTS v LEISURE ENTER-PRISES (1976)** P purchased the lease of a club premises from D for £23,100 having been told that the rent was £2,400 per year, and that no rent review notices had been served. P went into occupation and spent £4,000 on re-equipping and preparing the premises for use. The landlords then requested the revised rent of £6,500 (valid rent review notices had in fact been served). P vacated the premises and sought rescission and damages. It was held that damages under *S.2(1)* would be awarded and that they would include compensation for expenditure properly and not prematurely incurred, ie the £4,000. Rescission was also granted.

c. *Equity before 1967.* The contract was voidable at the option of the innocent party. He could therefore

    i.   Insist on performance.

    ii.   Do nothing and resist an action for specific performance.

    iii.   Commence proceedings for rescission, claiming in addition an indemnity for expenses necessarily incurred as a result of the contract. The right to rescission was however lost if the representation was incorporated into the contract.

d. *Equity after 1967.* The Act affected the equitable remedy of rescission. The innocent party's three options remain the same however

    i.   The right to rescission is no longer lost if the representation is later incorporated into the contract (*S.1.*).

    ii.   The court has a discretion to award damages in lieu of rescission if it thinks it equitable to do so. (*S.2(2).*). These damages may be awarded even if the *S.2(1)* defence of reasonable belief is available, but they may not be awarded in addition to rescission since the section specifies "in lieu of rescission", ie instead of rescission.

8.   Bars to Rescission. The remedy of rescission will not be available in the following situations:-

a.   If the innocent party, with knowledge of his rights, affirms the contract.

In **LONG v LLOYD (1958)** P was induced to buy a lorry from D after hearing representations as to its condition, and a statement that it would do eleven miles to the gallon. P then drove the lorry home from Hampton Court to Sevenoaks. The next Wednesday P drove to Rochester, and during the journey the dynamo ceased to function, an oil leak developed, a crack appeared in one of the wheels, and petrol consumption was five miles per gallon. He complained to D who offered to pay half the cost of a new dynamo, and this offer was accepted. The next day the lorry broke down on a journey to Middlesbrough, and P asked for his money back. A subsequent examination by an expert showed that the lorry was unroadworthy. It was held:

146

i.   That the representations as to the condition of the lorry were innocent.

ii.   The journey to Rochester was not affirmation because P had to have an opportunity to test the vehicle in a working capacity.

iii.   The acceptance of the offer to pay half of the cost of the dynamo, and the subsequent journey to Middlesbrough, did amount to affirmation and therefore rescission could not be granted.

If this case had been heard after 1967 P may have succeeded under *S.2(1) MISREPRESENTATION ACT 1967*. It is unlikely that D could have proved that he had reasonable grounds for believing that the lorry was in good condition.

b.   Lapse of time.

i.   Where the misrepresentation is fraudulent lapse of time does not itself bar rescission because time only begins to run from discovery of the truth.

ii.   Where the misrepresentation is innocent lapse of time may bar rescission.

In **LEAF v INTERNATIONAL GALLERIES (1950)** P was induced to buy a painting by an innocent misrepresentation that it was by John Constable. 5 years later he discovered the truth and immediately claimed rescission. He could not therefore have affirmed the contract but his claim was held to be barred by lapse of time.

Two further points of interest were made in Leaf's case. Firstly the contract was not void for mistake, the mistake being merely as to quality. Secondly Lord Denning said that a claim to rescind for innocent misrepresentation must be barred when the right to repudiate for breach of condition is barred ie when there is "acceptance" within the meaning of *S.35. SALE OF GOODS ACT 1893*. (Now *S.35. SGA 1979)*

c.   If restitutio in integrum is impossible. ie If restoration to the pre-contract state of affairs is impossible, because for example a partnership's capital has been converted into shares in a limited company as in **CLARKE v DICKSON (1858)**. A more obvious example of impossibility of restoration is where the subject matter is food which has been eaten. A modern tendency is for the courts to award rescission if the substantial identity of the property remains even though the parties cannot be precisely restored to their pre-contract position, financial adjustments being made if necessary.

d.   The intervention of third party rights. Thus a person cannot rescind an allotment of shares in a company after the company has gone into liquidation, since at this point third party rights intervene because the assets of the company have to be collected to distribute among the company's creditors.

9.   Exempting Liability for Misrepresentation. If a contract purports to take away any liability or remedy for misrepresentation that provision is of no effect unless it satisfies the requirement of reasonableness as defined by *S.11. UNFAIR CONTRACT TERMS ACT 1977.*

10.   Trade Descriptions. Note that the *TRADE DESCRIPTIONS ACT 1968* which prohibits mis-descriptions of goods relates to criminal law, not the law of contract.

DURESS AND UNDUE INFLUENCE

11.   Duress. This is a common law doctrine, and its effect if proved is that the contract is voidable. It is limited in scope to illegal violence or threats of violence to the person of the contracting party. To threaten a person's property is not duress, but to threaten unlawful imprisonment is duress.

In **CUMMING v INCE (1847)** An old lady was threatened with unlawful confinement in a mental home if she did not transfer certain property rights to one of her relatives. The subsequent transfer was set aside since the threat of unlawful imprisonment amounted to duress.

12.   Undue Influence

a.   In developing this doctrine equity recognised that consent may be affected by influences other than physical ones. Its effect is to make the contract voidable. The burden of proof of undue influence will depend on the relationship between the parties.

b.   If there is no special relationship the party seeking to avoid must prove that he was subjected to influence which excluded free consent.

In **WILLIAMS v BAYLEY (1866)** A father agreed to mortgage his property to a bank if the bank would return to him promissory notes on which his son had forged his signature. The bank had hinted at prosecution and "transportation" of the son if the father did not agree to execute the mortgage. The agreement to execute the mortgage was set aside because undue influence had been proved.

c.   Where a confidential relationship exists between the parties it is for the party in whom confidence is placed to show that undue influence was not used. Examples of such relationships are trustee/beneficiary, solicitor/client, parent/child, however the presumption applies whenever the relationship is such that one of them is by reason of the confidence placed in him able to take unfair advantage of the other.

In **TATE v WILLIAMSON (1866)** D became financial adviser to an extravagant Oxford undergraduate. The undergraduate sold his estate to D for about half its value, and died of alcoholism at the age of 24. His executors were successful in having the sale of the estate set aside.

d.   A transaction will not be set aside on the ground of undue influence unless it can be shown that the transaction is to the manifest disadvantage of the person subjected to undue influence. Also a presumption of undue influence will not arise merely because a confidential relationship exists, provided the person in whom confidence is placed keeps within the boundaries of a normal business relationship.

In **NATIONAL WESTMINSTER BANK v MORGAN (1985)** a wife (W) signed a re-mortgage of the family home (owned jointly with her husband H) in favour of the bank to prevent the original mortgagee from continuing with proceedings to re-possess the home. The bank manager told her in good faith but incorrectly, that the mortgage only secured liability in respect of the home. In fact it covered all H's debts to the bank. W signed the mortgage at home in the presence of the Manager, and without taking independent advice. H and W fell into arrears with the payments and soon afterwards H died. At the time of his death nothing was owed to the bank in respect of H's business liabilities. The bank sought possession but W contended that she had only signed the mortgage because of undue influence from the bank and therefore it should be set aside. The House of Lords held, reversing the Court of Appeal, that the Manager had not crossed the line between explaining an ordinary business transaction and entering into a relationship in which he had a dominant influence, furthermore the transaction was not unfair to W, therefore the bank was not under a duty to ensure that W took independent advice. The order for possession was granted.

e.   Where there is a commercial relationship it appears that the courts are prepared to recognise the existence of economic duress as part of the concept of undue influence.

In **THE ATLANTIC BARON (1979)** the parties reached agreement on the purchase price to be paid for a ship. There was then a currency devaluation and as a result the vendor claimed a 10% increase in price. The purchaser refused to pay. The vendor then stated that if the extra was not paid he would terminate the contract and amicable business relations would not continue. Due to this threat the purchaser agreed to the increase in price. It was later held that the threat to terminate the contract and discontinue amicable business relations amounted to undue influence. The contract was therefore voidable.

In **ATLAS EXPRESS v KAFCO (IMPORTERS AND EXPORTERS) (1989)** D made a contract with Woolworths for the delivery of its goods to about 800 Woolworths stores. D then made a contract with P, a well known company of forwarders, for carriage of the goods. P later decided that the carriage charge was too low and presented D with a revised invoice showing higher carriage charges. They also refused to accept any goods for delivery unless invoice showing the higher charges was signed. D protested the increase, but since they were committed to Woolworths (who would probably withdraw their business if the goods were not delivered) they signed the invoice. They subsequently refused to pay the increased rate of charges. When sued by P they pleaded economic duress.

149

This defence was accepted by the court. It was also held that P had provided no consideration for the second agreement. Contrast **WILLIAMS v ROFFEY (1989)** Chapter 15.12.

ILLEGALITY

13. Introduction. The law will clearly refuse to give effect to a contract if it involves the commission of a legal wrong, or if it is invalidated by statute. Also classed as illegal contracts are contracts which do not involve the commission of a crime or tort, but which are not enforced by the courts because they are contrary to public policy. The most important of these are contracts in unreasonable restraint of trade.

14. Classification. There are many different ways to approach the classification of illegal contracts. For convenience the following categories will be used:-

    a.   Contracts involving the commission of a legal wrong.

    b.   Contracts illegal by statute.

    c.   Contracts contrary to public policy.

15. Contracts Involving the Commission of a Legal Wrong. The following are examples only and not a complete list:-

    a.   Where the object is to commit a crime or a civil wrong as in **NAPIER v NATIONAL BUSINESS AGENCY (1951)**, where the contract was drawn up so as to deceive the Inland Revenue.

    b.   A contract to pay money on the commission of an unlawful act.

16. Contracts Illegal by Statute. For example:-

    a.   Wagering contracts.

        i.   *S.18. GAMING ACT 1845* makes all contracts of wagering void and provides that no action can be brought to recover any money or valuable thing alleged to be won on a wager.

        ii.   A wagering contract is a contract by which two persons professing to hold opposite views as to the outcome of a future uncertain event agree that, dependent on the determination of such event, one shall win and the other shall lose, a sum of money or other stake; neither of the parties having any interest in the contract other than such sum or stake, there being no other consideration by either. It is essential that each party may either win or lose.

    b.   Restrictive trade agreements. The *RESTRICTIVE TRADE PRACTICES ACT 1976* does not make such agreements automatically void, but provides machinery whereby their validity is tested.

    c.   Statutes in general. If one party in performing a contract does an act, prohibited by statute, the act only may be illegal, or the whole contract may be illegal. It depends on whether or not the statute was intended to prohibit the whole contract.

In **ARCHBOLDS v SPANGLETT (1961)** D contracted to carry whisky belonging to P in a van which was not licensed to carry goods which did not belong to him. In carrying the whisky D therefore committed a statutory offence. The whisky was stolen on the journey and P sued for damages. D pleaded the illegality for his defence. The Court of Appeal rejected this defence because:-

    i.   The Act in question did not prohibit the contract expressly or by implication, and

    ii.   P did not know that D did not have the correct licence.

17. **Contracts in Contravention of Public Policy.** For example:-

    a.   Contracts promoting sexual immorality.

In **PEARCE v BROOKS (1866)** a contract to hire out a carriage to a prostitute for the purposes of her profession was held to be illegal.

    b.   Contracts which detract from the institution of marriage. For example:-

    i.   Marriage brokage contracts.

    ii.   Contracts in restraint of marriage.

    iii.   Contracts for the future separation of husband and wife.

    c.   Sales of offices and honours.

In **PARKINSON v COLLEGE OF AMBULANCE (1925)** A contract to obtain a knighthood was held to be illegal since it could lead to corruption and was "derogatory to the dignity of the Sovereign". It has since been made a criminal offence to make such a contract.

    d.   Contracts made with an enemy in wartime.

    e.   Contracts which involve doing an illegal act in a friendly foreign country.

In **FOSTER v DRISCOLL (1929)** A contract was made to smuggle whisky into the USA during the period when the sale of liquor in the USA was forbidden. This contract was held to be illegal.

    f.   Contracts in unreasonable restraint of trade (see below).

18. **Restraint of Trade.** A contract in restraint of trade is one which restricts a person from freely exercising his trade or profession. Such contracts are prima facie illegal. However some types of restraint can be justified if they are reasonable so far as the parties are concerned, and provided they are not contrary to public interest. When assessing the validity of contracts in restraint of trade the courts have had to balance the desire to allow complete freedom to contract with the fact that most restraints (especially restrictive trade practices) are contrary to public interest because they restrict the choice or bargaining power of the public. There are four types of contract in restraint of trade which may be held to be valid depending on the circumstances:-

151

a.   **Restraints imposed on ex-employees**.

i.   If the restraint is to be reasonable between the parties it must be no wider than is necessary to protect the promisee's trade secrets or business connections. Therefore a restraint imposed on an employee who has no knowledge of his employer's secrets or influence over his customers will be illegal, as it would be an attempt to prevent competition. However if trade secrets and business connections are legitimately protected the fact that the restraint incidentally reduces the ex-employee's power to compete does not invalidate it.

ii.   The court will also consider any time limits imposed by the restraint and/or the area it covers.

In **MASON v PROVIDENT CLOTHING (1913)** A canvasser employed to sell clothes in Islington covenanted not to enter into similar business within 25 miles of London for 3 years. The restraint was held to be void because the area of the restraint was about 1,000 times as large as the area in which he had been employed.

In **FITCH v DEWES (1921)** a lifelong restraint on a solicitor's managing clerk not to practise within 7 miles was upheld. In contrast to the previous case, the main objection concerned the duration of the restraint rather than the area covered. However a solicitor's business is one to which clients are likely to resort for a long time, thus the lifetime restraint was not unreasonable. If the business to be protected is of a more fluctuating nature, long restraints will not be upheld.

iii.   The court may grant judgement for a person against an association of employers who do not have a contractual relationship with the person concerned, but whose rules place an unjustified restraint on his liberty of employment.

In **GREIG v INSOLE (1978)** the Test and County Cricket Board sought to ban World Series cricketers from Test and County cricket by means of a change of their rules. The change of rules was held to be ultra vires since it was an unreasonable restraint of trade.

b.   **Restraints imposed on the vendor of a business**. The restraint will only be effective if:-

i.   There is a genuine sale of the goodwill of the business.

In **VANCOUVER MALT AND SAKE BREWING CO. v VANCOUVER BREWERIES (1934)** A company which was licensed to brew beer, but which did not in fact brew any, agreed to sell its business, and to refrain from manufacturing beer for 15 years. Since the company was not actually brewing beer the purchaser could only have paid for the tangible assets, because there were no intangible assets (ie goodwill) to sell. The purchaser had not therefore bought the promise not to brew beer, and so he could not enforce it.

ii.   The restraint must be no more than is necessary to protect the particular business bought by the purchaser. In assessing the reasonableness of the restraint the area covered, the duration of the restraint, and the type of business are again important. However it is possible even for a worldwide restraint to be upheld.

In **NORDENFELT v MAXIM NORDENFELT (1894)** the owner of an armaments business sold it to a company and covenanted not to carry on a similar business for 25 years except on behalf of the company. The covenant was held to be valid although it prevented competition anywhere in the world.

c. *Agreements between traders by which prices or output are regulated*

i.   Such agreements were usually valid at common law, since they were generally made between persons of equal bargaining power, and were of benefit to both parties. They were however often contrary to the public interest. Parliament has therefore passed several Acts to protect the consumer.

ii.   The *RESTRICTIVE TRADE PRACTICES ACT 1976* requires certain types of restrictive trading agreements to be registered with the Director General of Fair Trading. After registration the agreement is brought before the Restrictive Practices Court to determine whether the restriction is contrary to the public interest. If it is then the offending provisions are void. Failure to register a registrable agreement also renders the restrictions in it void. Any restriction is presumed to be contrary to the public interest unless it falls within one or more of 8 "gateways" referred to in the Act, for example the agreement benefits the public because it reduces the risk of injury.

iii. The *RESALE PRICES ACT 1976* provides that if an agreement between a supplier and a dealer seeks to establish a minimum price to be charged by the dealer such a provision will be void. However there is a power for the Restrictive Practices Court to grant exemption in certain cases.

d. *Solus agreements.* This is the name given to a contract by which a trader agrees to restrict his orders to one supplier. A solus agreement may be part of a mortgage or lease. The duration of the restraint is the most important factor in assessing the reasonableness, and thus the legality of these agreements.

In **ESSO PETROLEUM v HARPER'S GARAGE (1967)** D, who owned two garages, entered into solus agreements with P in respect of each garage. He agreed only to sell petrol supplied by P, to keep the garage open at all reasonable times, and not to sell the garage without ensuring that the purchaser entered into a similar agreement with P. One solus agreement was for a period of 4½ years, and the other (which was contained in a mortgage of his land to P) was for 21 years. The House of Lords held that the 4½ year agreement was valid, but that the 21 year agreement was invalid since it was of unreasonable duration, and was contrary to the public interest. In addition the obligation to sell only to a purchaser who was willing to enter into a similar solus agreement made the garage unsaleable.

In **PETROFINA v MARTIN (1966)** Martin's agreement with Petrofina was almost identical to Harper's agreement with Esso. In this case, however, the duration of the restraint was 12 years. D broke the agreement by selling other makes of petrol, and P sought to enforce it by means of an injunction preventing D from doing this. It was held that the restraint was invalid because it was of unreasonable duration.

19. Consequences of Illegality

a. *Contracts illegal as formed.* ie The contract is incapable of lawful performance, or is intended to be performed illegally as in **PEARCE v BROOKS (1866)**. Such contracts are void and unenforceable. Therefore money paid or property handed over usually cannot be recovered.

b. *Contracts illegal as performed.* ie Legal at the outset, but later used for an illegal purpose.

    i.   The guilty party has no remedies.

    In **COWAN v MILBOURN (1867)** D agreed to let rooms to P. He later discovered that P was going to use the rooms to give blasphemous lectures, which was an illegal purpose. D therefore refused to carry out the contract. P failed in his claim for possession since he was the guilty party.

    ii.   The innocent party has his normal contractual remedies, except in respect of anything done by him after he learns of the illegal purpose.

c. *Contracts in contravention of public policy.* Many such contracts, for example contracts in restraint of trade may not fall simply into the categories specified above, but will contain many different promises. These contracts will not be wholly void, but void in so far as public policy is contravened. The court may therefore sever the illegal part of the contract, leaving the remainder valid provided:-

    i.   The void promise is not substantially the whole consideration given by the party making it.

    ii.   The contract can be construed as severable without destroying the main substance of what was agreed.

    In **LOUND v GRIMWADE (1888)** D, who had committed a fraud making him both criminally and civilly liable, promised to pay P £3,000 if P promised not to take "any legal proceedings" in respect of the fraud. P's claim for the £3,000 failed as a substantial part of the consideration for the promise to pay it was his own illegal promise to stifle a criminal prosecution.

In **GOLDSOLL v GOLDMAN (1915)** D sold his business in imitation jewellery to P, and agreed that he would not for two years deal in real or imitation jewellery in the UK or specified foreign countries. The restriction was held to be too wide in area, since D had never traded abroad, and in respect of subject matter since he had hardly ever dealt in real jewellery. It was however held that the references to foreign countries and real jewellery could be severed, so that D could be restrained from dealing in imitation jewellery in the UK for two years.

20 Discharge of Contracts

1. There are four ways by which the rights and obligations of the parties may come to an end, namely performance, agreement, frustration, and breach.

PERFORMANCE

2. **General Rule.** When both parties have performed their obligations the contract is extinguished. Generally performance must be complete and exact, thus a party who does not precisely perform the contract will be in breach.

In **RE MOORE AND LANDAUER (1921)** A supplier of tinned fruit agreed to supply the goods in cases containing 30 tins each. When he delivered the goods about one half were packed in cases of 24 tins each. The correct total amount of tins were delivered, and the market value of the goods supplied was unaffected, however there was a breach of contract (*S.13(1) SALE OF GOODS ACT 1893*) and this entitled the buyer to reject the whole consignment.

3. **Exceptions.** There are six exceptions to this rule:-

   a. *Severable contracts.* Where a contract may be divided into several parts, payments for parts that have been completed can be claimed. Whether a contract is severable or not depends on the intention of the parties. In the absence of evidence as to intention the courts are reluctant to construe the contract so as to require complete performance before any payment becomes due.

   In **ROBERTS v HAVELOCK (1832)** P agreed to repair a ship. The contract did not state when payment was to be made. It was held that P was not bound to complete the repairs before claiming some payment.

   b. *Acceptance of part performance.* Where A has accepted the partial performance of B, having an option to reject, a promise to pay is implied and a quantum meruit may be claimed by B. A quantum meruit action is a claim for a percentage of the contract price in direct proportion to the percentage of work done.

   In **SUMPTER v HEDGES (1898)** P agreed to build a house for D for £565. He partially erected the building, doing work to the value of £333. He then stopped the job because he ran out of funds. D, using P's materials that had been left on the site, finished the job himself. P claimed £333 for work done plus the value of his materials used by D. He failed in his claim for the £333 because although D had "accepted" P's part performance D had no option to reject. It is impossible to reject a half-built house since the status quo cannot be restored. P however obtained judgement in respect of his materials that D had used to complete the house.

   c. *Prevention of performance.* Where one party is prevented by the other from completely performing the contract he may bring a quantum meruit action to claim for the work done.

156

In **PLANCHÉ v COLBURN (1831)** P agreed to write a book on costume and armour which was to appear in serial form in D's periodical. P was to be paid £100 on completion. After P had done some research, and written some of the book, but before he had completed it, D stopped publishing the periodical. It was held that P had been wrongfully prevented from performing the contract, and he was entitled to a quantum meruit.

d.   *Substantial performance.* Where a contract has been substantially performed an action lies for the contract price less a reduction for the deficiencies. This exception only applies when the defect relates to the quality of performance. If the defect concerns quantity, for example of goods supplied, the general rule applies.

In **HOENIG v ISAACS (1952)** P agreed to decorate and furnish D's flat for £750. The furniture had several defects which could have been made good for £55. D argued that P was only entitled to reasonable remuneration for work done under the contract. The court however held that P was entitled to the full contract rate, less the cost of making the defects good, since he had substantially performed the contract.

Contrast **BOLTON v MAHADEVA (1972)** A plumber agreed to install a central heating system for £560. His work was defective in that the system did not heat adequately and it gave off fumes. The defects cost £174 to repair. The plumber failed in his action to recover the price less a reduction of £174, since he could not be said to have substantially performed the contract. He therefore recovered nothing and the defendant got a £560 heating system for £174. The decision may seem unfair. However the court must draw the line so as not to encourage bad workmanship. It would also be unfair to allow every workman who did not complete a job to be paid pro rata for work done.

e.   Where the *LAW REFORM (FRUSTRATED CONTRACTS) ACT 1943* applies (see below).

f.   *Time of performance.* At common law a party who failed to perform his obligations within a given time was in breach of contract. The equitable rule, which now prevails, is that time is only of the essence of the contract if:-

i.   The parties expressly state, or if

ii.   A party who has been guilty of undue delay is notified by the other party that unless he performs within a reasonable time, the contract will be regarded as broken.

In **RICKARDS v OPPENHEIM (1950)** A contract for the sale of a car provided for delivery on March 20. The car was not delivered on that date but the buyer continued to press for delivery. On June 29 he told the seller he must have the car by July 25 at the latest. It was held that the buyer could not have refused delivery merely because the original date had not been met, but he could do so on giving the seller a reasonable time to deliver. Here the notice did give a reasonable time, so the buyer was justified in refusing delivery after July 25.

4. Tender of Performance

a.   Where an obligation under a contract is to deliver goods or render services, tender of the goods or services, which is refused, discharges the party tendering from further obligation and entitles him to damages for breach.

b.   Where money is tendered it must be "legal tender" and it must be the exact sum (change cannot be required). If such a tender is refused it does not release the debtor from his obligation to pay, but if he is sued he may pay the money into court, and the creditor will have to pay the costs of the action.

c.   If the debtor sends money in the post and it is lost he will have to pay again unless

    i.   the mode of delivery was requested by the creditor, and

    ii.   the debtor took reasonable care.

d.   *Appropriation of payments*. When a debtor makes a payment to his creditor which is insufficient to discharge all amounts outstanding, the payment is appropriated as follows:

    i.   The debtor may tell the creditor which debt or debts should be discharged by the payment.

    ii.   If the debtor does not do this then the creditor may appropriate the payments to debts as he chooses, including statute-barred debts.

    iii.   If the debtor pays the exact amount of a particular debt, it is presumed that the payment is in discharge of the debt of that amount.

    iv.   If there is a current account it is presumed that the payments are appropriated to the oldest debts first.

AGREEMENT

5.   The basic rule is that an agreement to discharge a contract is binding only if it is under seal, or if it is supported by consideration. It is not necessary for this type of agreement to be reached by means of an offer from one party which is accepted by the other. The legal position depends on whether the discharge is bilateral or unilateral.

6.   **Bilateral Discharge.** ie The contract is executory or partly executory on both sides (both parties have obligations outstanding).

a.   The consideration requirement is automatically present since both parties will surrender something of value − ie the right to insist on the other party's performance.

b.   Cases of waiver, ie forbearance, for example of the right to insist on performance at the agreed time, fall within the principle of equitable estoppel established in **CENTRAL LONDON PROPERTY TRUST v HIGH TREES HOUSE (1947)**. Therefore a voluntary concession granted by one party, upon which the other has acted, remains effective (ie binding on the promisor) until it is made clear by reasonable notice that the strict obligations of the contract are to be restored.

7.   **Unilateral Discharge.** ie Only one party has rights to surrender.

a.   Where one party has completely performed his side of the contract, ie it is wholly executed on one side, any release by him of the other party must be under seal, or supported by fresh consideration.

b.   Where there is a release supported by fresh consideration there is said to be "accord" and "satisfaction".

   i.   The accord is the agreement by which the obligation is discharged.

   ii.   The satisfaction is the consideration which makes the agreement effective.

   iii.   The satisfaction may be executory.

8.   There are two further ways in which a contract may be discharged by agreement.

a.   *Novation.* For example A owes B £100 and B owes C £100. A agrees to pay C, if C will release B from his obligation to pay him. All three parties must agree to the arrangement.

b.   *Condition subsequent.* Sometimes a clause in a contract will provide for its discharge if a particular event occurs in the future ie subsequent to the formation of the contract.

FRUSTRATION

9.   **The Basis of the Doctrine**

a.   The general rule is that if a person contracts to do something he is not discharged if performance proves to be impossible.

In **PARADINE v JANE (1647)** A tenant who was sued for rent pleaded that he had been dispossessed of the land for the last 3 years by the King's enemies. His plea failed. It was said:

"When a party by his own contract creates a duty or charge upon himself, he is bound to make it good, notwithstanding any accident by inevitable necessity, because he might have provided against it by his contract."

b.   This severe rule is mitigated by the doctrine of frustration, which, if it applies, automatically discharges the contract.

c.   In general if an event is to frustrate a contract it must be:-

i.   Not contemplated by the parties when the contract was formed.

ii.   One which makes the contract fundamentally different from the original contract.

iii.   One for which neither party was responsible.

iv.   One which results in a situation to which the parties did not wish originally to be bound.

10.   The Application of the Doctrine. Frustration occurs:-

a.   If the whole basis of the contract is the continued existence of a specific thing which is destroyed.

In **TAYLOR v CALDWELL (1863)** D contracted to let a music hall to P for four days, Before the first day the music hall was accidentally burnt down. P claimed damages, but it was held that D was discharged from his obligation when the music hall burned down. The contract was frustrated.

b.   If either party to a contract of personal service dies, becomes seriously ill, or is called up for military service.

In **CONDOR v BARRON KNIGHTS (1966)** P was the drummer in a pop group. Owing to illness he was forbidden by his doctor from performing more than a few nights per week. Since the nature of the work required him to be present seven nights a week the contract was held to be frustrated.

c.   If the whole basis of the contract is the occurrence of an event which does not occur.

In **KRELL v HENRY (1903)** D hired a flat in Pall Mall for the purpose of viewing the coronation procession of Edward VII, although this was not expressly stated in the contract. He paid £25 at the time of the agreement and was to pay a further £50 two days before the procession was to take place. Before the £50 had been paid the procession was cancelled due to the illness of the King. The contract was held to be frustrated. Performance was not physically impossible, but the court said that frustration was not limited to such cases but included "the cessation or non-existence of an express condition or state of things going to the root of the contract, and essential to its performance". P's claim for the balance of £50 therefore failed, as did D's counter-claim for return of the £25 already paid. D's claim would now be subject to the *LAW REFORM (FRUSTRATED CONTRACTS) ACT 1943*.

Contrast **HERNE BAY STEAMBOAT CO. v HUTTON (1903)** A boat was hired "for the purpose of viewing the naval review and for a day's cruise round the fleet". The review was to form part of Edward VII's coronation celebrations, but it was cancelled due to his illness. The fleet was however still assembled. The contract was not frustrated, since it was construed merely as a contract for the hire of a boat, which could still be performed even when one of the motives of the hirer was defeated.

The above two cases are very difficult to reconcile. A clue may be found in a passage in one of the judgements from Krell v Henry. It was stated that a contract for the hire of a cab to go to Epsom on Derby day would not be frustrated if the Derby was cancelled. The contract would be construed as one to get the passenger to Epsom and not the Derby. In Krell v Henry the contract was not construed as one merely to provide a flat since it was extremely unusual for flats to be let by the day for very high rents. Contracts to carry passengers to Epsom are however often made on days other than Derby days.

d. If the government prohibits performance of the contract for so long that to maintain it would impose on the parties fundamentally different obligations from those bargained for. All the circumstances are relevant, for example both the duration of the contract and the duration of the interruption.

In **TAMPLIN STEAMSHIP CO. v ANGLO-MEXICAN PETROL (1916)** A ship was requisitioned by the government for use as a troop-ship. The charterparty under which the ship was hired was for 5 years, and there were 19 months left to run. The owners claimed that the contract was frustrated so that they, and not the hirers, would obtain the government compensation (which exceeded what they would receive under the charterparty). It was held that the contract was not frustrated since there may have been months during the remaining period during which the ship would be available, and because the charterers were still prepared to pay the agreed price.

e. If the performance of the main object of the contract subsequently becomes illegal.

In **BAILY v DE CRESPIGNY (1869)** a landlord covenanted that neither he nor his successors in title would permit building on a paddock which adjoined the land let. The paddock was then compulsorily acquired for a railway, and a station was built. It was held that the landlord was not liable for breach of the covenant because it was impossible for him to secure performance of it.

11. The Limits to the Doctrine

a. A contract is not frustrated if it becomes unexpectedly more expensive or burdensome to one of the parties. If the contract is to be discharged performance must become "radically different".

In **DAVIS CONTRACTORS v FAREHAM UDC (1956)** P agreed to build 78 houses at a price of £94,000 in 8 months. Labour shortages caused the work to take 22 months at a cost to P of £115,000. P wished to claim that the contract was frustrated so that they could then claim for

161

their work on a quantum meruit. Lord Radcliffe however said that hardship, material loss, or inconvenience did not amount to frustration, the obligation must change such that the thing undertaken would, if performed, be a different thing from that contracted for.

b.   A party cannot rely on a self-induced frustration, ie frustration due to his own conduct.

   i.   The doctrine of frustration clearly does not protect a person whose own breach is actually the frustrating event.

   In **THE EUGENIA (1964)** a charterer in breach of contract ordered a ship into a war zone. The ship was detained. It was held that the charterer could not rely on the detention as a ground for frustration.

   ii.   Deliberate failure to perform a condition precedent may not amount to a self induced frustration. In each case the position must be determined in accordance with the proper construction of the contract.

   In **GYLLEHAMMER v SOURBRODOGRADEVNA IN-DUSTRILA (1989)** the parties had an outline agreement for the construction of a bulk carrier. The contract was subject to several conditions precedent (i.e. conditions that had to be complied with before the contract could be regarded as valid). One of these provided that the contract would be void if the shipbuilders did not obtain bank performance guarantees. When it appeared that a change in economic climate would render the building uneconomic, the shipbuilders did not seek the relevant guarantees. They then argued that their absence rendered the contract void. The purchasers claimed that it was not open to the other party to frustrate the inception of a contract by failing to take steps to allow conditions precedent to be fulfilled. The court held that this was not the case. It was clear that there would be no contract in the absence of bank guarantees and that their absence could be pleaded by the shipbuilders, whatever the reason for that absence.

   iii.   It is probable that negligence prevents a party claiming frustration. Thus if the fire in **TAYLOR v CALDWELL** had been started due to the defendant's negligence their plea of frustration would have failed.

c.   Frustration will not apply where the parties have expressly provided for a contingency which has occurred. It is a means by which risk is allocated, and loss apportioned in circumstances which neither party has foreseen.

12.   The Effect of Frustration

a.   The contract is discharged automatically as to the future, but it is not made void from the beginning.

b.   At common law the loss lay where it fell, ie money paid before the frustration could not be recovered (**KRELL v HENRY (1903)**) and money payable before the frustration remained payable, unless there was a total failure of consideration.

In **FIBROSA v FAIRBAIRN (1942)** A purchaser of machinery for £4,800 paid £1,000 on placing the order. The machinery was to be delivered in Poland. Shortly after the contract was made war broke out and Poland was occupied by Germany. It was therefore impossible to deliver the machinery. The plaintiff succeeded in his action to recover the £1,000 since he had received absolutely nothing in return for his £1,000, ie there was a total failure of consideration.

c.   The position is now governed by *THE LAW REFORM (FRUSTRATED CONTRACTS) ACT 1943* whereby

i.   Money paid before the frustrating event is recoverable and money payable before the frustrating event ceases to be payable, but if one party has incurred expenses the court may allow him to retain or be paid an amount not exceeding the amount of the expenses.

ii.   If one party has obtained a valuable benefit (other than money) because of something done by the other party in performance of the contract, he can be ordered to pay a just sum for it, not exceeding the amount of the benefit.

BREACH

13.   **Definition.** Breach occurs:

a.   If a party fails to perform one of his obligations under a contract, for example he does not perform on the agreed date, or he delivers goods of inferior quality, or

b.   If a party, before the date fixed for performance, indicates that he will not perform on the agreed date. This is an anticipatory breach.

14.   **Effect of Breach.** Breach does not automatically discharge the contract

a.   Breach of warranty only entitles the innocent party to damages.

b.   Breach of condition entitles the innocent party to damages, and gives him an option to treat the contract as subsisting or discharged.

15.   **Affirmation of the Breach**

a.   If the innocent party elects to treat the contract as still subsisting, and can complete his side without the co-operation of the other, he is entitled to do so, and claim the whole sum due under the contract.

In **WHITE AND CARTER (COUNCILS) v McGREGOR (1961)** P agreed to advertise D's business for 3 years on plates attached to litter-bins. D repudiated the contract on the same day that it was made. P nevertheless manufactured and displayed the plates as originally agreed, and claimed the full amount due under the contract. A majority of the House of Lords upheld the claim, their reason being that a repudiation does not, of itself, bring the contract to an end. Its effect is to give the innocent party a choice of whether or not to determine the contract. If he chooses to affirm the contract it remains in full effect.

b.   Affirmation does not of itself exclude a finding of reasonableness in relation to any exemption clause *S.9(2) UNFAIR CONTRACT TERMS ACT 1977*. This prevents the court being forced into a situation where it would feel compelled to find an exemption clause unreasonable, so as not to exclude an innocent party's remedies when he had affirmed a contract that he could have terminated.

16. Termination

a.   If the innocent party elects to end the contract he is not bound to accept further performance, and he may sue for damages at once.

b.   Where if it is to be valid, an exemption clause has to satisfy the requirement of reasonableness, it may be found to do so, and be given effect, even though the contract has been terminated by the innocent party. *S.9(1) UNFAIR CONTRACT TERMS ACT 1977*. ie A valid termination of a contract does not terminate an exemption clause. Clearly if it did exemption clauses would be useless in every case of a breach which entitled the innocent party to end the contract.

17. Anticipatory Breach

a.   Where there is an anticipatory breach, and the innocent party elects to treat the contract as discharged, he can sue for damages at once.

In **HOCHSTER v DE LA TOUR (1853)** D agreed to employ P as a courier for 3 months commencing on June 1. Before this date D told P that his services would not be required. This was to be an anticipatory breach of contract, and it entitled P to sue for damages immediately.

This decision could lead to difficulties, especially if the trial takes place before the date fixed for performance. For example if X contracts to deliver goods to Y in 2 years time, and then indicates that he does not intend to perform, Y's damages are in general quantified by reference to the market price at the time fixed for performance. Clearly if the trial takes place before this date the market price cannot be known.

b.   If the innocent party elects to treat the contract as still subsisting, he keeps it alive for the benefit of both parties, so that frustration may intervene to release the party at fault from further liability.

In **AVERY v BOWDEN (1855)** D chartered a ship from P to carry goods from Odessa. The charter allowed 45 days for loading. During this period D's agent told the captain (P's agent) that he had no cargo and that he would be wise to leave. The captain however remained in Odessa and pressed for performance. Before the 45 days had expired the Crimean War broke out and frustrated the contract. If P had accepted D's anticipatory breach immediately he could have sued for damages. Since he did not do so, he kept the contract alive for the benefit of both parties, so the frustration operated to relieve D from liability. P's claim for damages therefore failed.

c. The doctrine of anticipatory breach is important because

i.   It helps to minimise the total loss, because if the plaintiff could not sue immediately he would be more likely to keep himself available for performance. Whereas, since he may sue at once he has an incentive to abandon the contract and avoid the extra loss that he might have suffered had he waited.

ii.   It protects a person who has paid in advance for future performance. It would be unfair if such a person could not sue until the time fixed for performance, since his advance payment may have reduced his ability to make an alternative contract.

18. Instalment Contracts. If in an instalment contract there is a breach with regard to one or some instalments the main tests as to whether the breach entitles the innocent party to treat the contract as at an end are

a. The ratio that the breach bears to the contract as a whole, and

b. The degree of probability that the breach will be repeated.

In **MAPLE FLOCK CO. v UNIVERSAL FURNITURE PRODUCTS (1934)** the contract provided for 100 tons of rag flock to be delivered in instalments of 1½ tons at the rate of three instalments a week. The sixteenth instalment was defective and the buyers claimed to be entitled to rescind. Their claim failed mainly because the single instalment was a small quantity when compared with the contract as a whole.

21 Remedies for Breach of Contract

1.   There are both common law and equitable remedies for breach of contract.
The common law remedies are damages, an action for an agreed sum, and a
quantum meruit claim. The equitable remedies are specific performance and
injunction. By far the most commonly sought remedy is damages.

DAMAGES

2.   A claim for damages raises two questions

a.   For what kind of damage should the plaintiff be compensated? ie
Remoteness of damage.

b.   What monetary compensation should the plaintiff receive in respect
of damage which is not too remote? ie Measure of damages.

3.   Note carefully the distinction between damage and damages. Damage is
the loss suffered by the plaintiff. Damages are the financial compensation awarded to him. It is very important to use the correct word. For example
"Remoteness of damages" is a meaningless phrase.

4.   **Remoteness of Damage**

a.   Damage is not too remote if it is

"such as may fairly and reasonably be considered either as arising
naturally, ie according to the usual course of things from the breach
itself, or such as may reasonably be supposed to have been in the
contemplation of both parties at the time they made the contract, as
the probable result of the breach".

In **HADLEY v BAXENDALE (1854)** P's mill shaft broke and had
to be sent to the makers at Greenwich to serve as a pattern for a replacement. D agreed to transport the shaft to Greenwich, but in breach of contract delayed delivery causing several days loss of production at the mill.
P claimed £300 in respect of lost profit. Alderson B. stated the rule quoted
and applied it as follows:-

i.   The loss did not arise naturally since D could not foresee that his
delay would stop the mill. It was quite possible that P might have had
a spare shaft or been able to get one.

ii.   The loss could not have been contemplated by both parties at the
time of the contract as the probable result of the breach. If D had been
told that delay would stop the mill such loss would have been in his
contemplation and he may then have sought to limit his liability,
however he did not have this information.

b.   The above rule can be analysed into two parts, briefly summarised
as loss "naturally arising" and loss "in the contemplation of both

parties . . . as the probable result of the breach''. An example of the application of the first part is **PINNOCK v LEWIS (1923)**. The distinction between the two parts is illustrated by **PILKINGTON v WOOD (1953)**.

In **PINNOCK v LEWIS (1923)** the seller of poisonous cattle food was held liable for the loss of the cattle to which it was fed. This loss arose naturally from his breach.

In **PILKINGTON v WOOD (1953)** P bought a house in Hampshire, his solicitor, D, failing to notice that the title was defective. D was held liable for the difference between the value of the house with good title and with defective title − this was loss "naturally arising". However P's job shortly moved to Lancashire and he wished to sell his house. The defective title made the sale difficult and meant that P was delayed in paying off his bank overdraft out of the sale proceeds. D was held not liable for this additional loss as he could not have anticipated that P would shortly want to move, nor did he know that P had an overdraft, ie the loss was not, and could not reasonably be supposed to have been in his contemplation.

c.   Hadley v Baxendale broadly speaking represents the law today. It was considered by the House of Lords in **KOUFOS v CZARNIKOW (1969)** when all five law lords approved the rule, although saying that the loss must be contemplated as ""'a real danger" or "a serious possibility" rather than as "the probable result of the breach".

In **KOUFOS v CZARNIKOW (1969)** a ship was chartered to carry sugar from Constanza to Basrah. The charterer intended to sell the sugar immediately on its arrival. The shipowner did not know this, but he did know that there was a market for sugar at Basrah. In breach of contract the shipowner deviated and arrived 9 days late during which time the market value of the sugar had fallen by about £4,000. The House of Lords unanimously upheld P's claim for this amount, approving the rule in Hadley v Baxendale subject to the qualifications mentioned above. The case is interesting in that although there was a roughly equal chance of the price of sugar rising or falling, the fact that it fell was nevertheless foreseeable as "a serious possibility".

d.   When the breach of contract consists of failure to pay a sum of money the general rule is that only the sum of money, not interest or damages can be recovered, **(LONDON, CHATHAM AND DOVER RAILWAY v SOUTH EASTERN RAILWAY (1893))**. This rule is considered to be unsatisfactory and there are a number of exceptions. In particular it does not apply to claims for special damages under the second limb of the rule in **HADLEY v BAXENDALE**. For example:-

In **INTERNATIONAL MINERALS AND CHEMICALS CORPORATION v HELM (1986)** a debt was due to be paid to an American plaintiff in Belgium francs. Between the due date and the judgement date the value of Belgium francs as against US dollars had fallen by 40%. It was held that the loss was recoverable since D knew that such a loss was not an improbable consequence of their default.

e.   Note that the contract and tort tests for remoteness differ. In tort the loss must be the "reasonably foreseeable" result of the tort. The tort test is therefore more generous to the plaintiff.

5.   Measure of Damages

a.   The general rule is that the plaintiff recovers his actual loss (in respect of damage which is not too remote). ie He is placed in the same position as if the contract had been performed. Therefore in assessing damages for breach of contract to pay a pension, or up to £10,000 damages for wrongful dismissal, (Income and Corporation Taxes Act 1970, as amended), regard must be had to the plaintiff's liability to taxation.

b.   *SECTIONS 50 AND 51 SALE OF GOODS ACT 1979* provide respectively that in an action for damages for non-acceptance or non-delivery, where there is an available market, the measure of damages is the difference between the contract price and the market price on the date fixed for acceptance or delivery or, if no date was fixed, at the time of refusal to accept or deliver. The provisions of these two sections are only prima facie rules and may not be applied if they would not indemnify the plaintiff for his loss.

In **THOMPSON v ROBINSON GUNMAKERS (1955)** D purchased a "Standard Vanguard" car from P and later refused to accept delivery of it. P's profit on the sale would have been £61, but D argued that they were not liable for this amount, since the profit would still be made when the car was sold to another customer. The court rejected this argument since the supply of this model exceeded the demand. Therefore if P had found another customer he could have sold a car to him in addition to selling a car to D.

Contrast **CHARTER v SULLIVAN (1957)** D refused to accept delivery of a "Hillman Minx" car that he had bought from P. P claimed £97 15s loss of profits. In contrast with the above case his claim failed, because the demand for Hillman Minx cars exceeded the supply. He could therefore sell every car that he could obtain from the makers and had accordingly not lost a sale.

c.   In assessing the award of damages the court may take into account inconvenience and annoyance.

In **JARVIS v SWAN TOURS (1973)** P paid £63 for a two week winter sports holiday. It differed vastly from what was advertised. There was very little holiday atmosphere, the hotel staff did not speak English, and in the second week he was the only guest at the hotel. P recovered £125 damages for his upset and annoyance due to having his holiday spoilt.

d.   The defence of contributory negligence under the *LAW REFORM (CONTRIBUTORY NEGLIGENCE) ACT 1945* (chapter 26.9) cannot be used to justify a proportionate reduction in damages for breach of contract (**BASILDON DISTRICT COUNCIL v LESSER (1984)**). However the plaintiff's negligence may result in his claim being defeated.

In **LAMBERT v LEWIS (1982)** P used a trailer coupling after realising that it was clearly defective. This negligent action relieved the supplier from contractual liability for the loss that occurred as a result of the ensuing accident.

6.   Mitigation

a.   The above rules are subject to the limitation that the plaintiff must do what is reasonable to mitigate his loss, and cannot recover any part of it which the defendant can prove has resulted from failure to mitigate. ie The plaintiff cannot recover for a loss that he ought to have avoided.

In **DARBISHIRE v WARREN (1963)** P owned a car of which he was particularly proud. Although it was old he maintained it in excellent condition. It had a market value of about £85. The car was damaged by D's negligence and P was advised it would cost him £192 to get it repaired. P went ahead with the repairs and claimed £192 from D (less the money he had received from his insurance company, and plus the cost of hiring a car while the repairs were carried out). His claim failed. The court held that the expenditure on repairs was not justified. P should have mitigated his loss by buying a replacement vehicle on the open market.

b.   **WHITE & CARTER (COUNCILS) v McGREGOR (1962)** (Chapter 20, Paragraph **15.**) illustrates that mitigation is only relevant to a claim for damages and not to a claim for an agreed sum.

7.   Liquidated Damages and Penalties

a.   Where no provision for damages is made in the contract then the court will assess the damages payable. These are unliquidated damages. However the courts recognise that within the basic right of freedom to contract there is a right to specify the damages to be paid in the event of a breach. Equity however gives relief in circumstances where this right is abused by a party who has attempted to take an unfair advantage of his stronger bargaining position.

b.   Where the parties have agreed in a contract how much is to be payable on a breach, this sum is recoverable if it is liquidated damages, ie a genuine pre-estimate of the loss, but not if it is a penalty, ie an amount fixed as a threat to prevent a breach.

c.   Where it is a penalty the plaintiff can only recover his actual loss in respect of damage which is not too remote.

In **LAMDON TRUST v HURRELL (1955)** D purchased a car from P on hire-purchase. The hire-purchase price was £558. After he had paid

£302 D defaulted and P re-possessed the car, and resold it for £270. A provision in the hire-purchase agreement provided that if it was terminated due to a hirer's default, the hirer must pay as compensation the difference between the sums paid (in this case £302) and £425, ie £123. Since P had already received £572 for the car (£302 plus £270), D objected to their claim for £123. The court held that the compensation clause was a penalty and since P had already received more than the original price of the car D was not liable to pay him any more compensation. The effect of P's clause could be more vividly seen if D had defaulted after payment of £10. D could have claimed £415 under their compensation clause and resold the car probably for at least £500, giving them a total compensation of £915. Clearly this is not a genuine estimate of loss.

d.   Whether a particular sum is liquidated damages or a penalty depends on the parties' intentions. The words used by the parties are not conclusive evidence of intention, the courts will look at the following tests

    i.   Is the sum stipulated extravagant in comparison with the greatest loss which could have followed from the breach? If so it is a penalty.

    In **KEMBLE v FARREN (1829)**, an actor's contract provided that if either he or the theatre management broke their contract then the party in breach must pay the other £1,000 as "liquidated damages". This was held to be a penalty clause because it was disproportionate both to the actor's daily fee of £3 6s 8d, and to the greatest possible loss that would result from the breach.

    ii.   Where a lump sum is payable on the occurrence of certain events, some of which are serious and some of which are not, the lump sum is presumed to be a penalty, but where a precise estimate of the consequences of the breach is impossible the court may regard the lump sum as a genuine pre-estimate.

    In **DUNLOP PNEUMATIC TYRE CO. v NEW GARAGE AND MOTOR CO. (1915)** P offered a trade discount to dealers who promised:
    a.   not to sell below certain list prices;
    b.   not to supply certain named persons;
    c.   not to exhibit any of the goods; and
    d.   to pay £5 "by way of liquidated damages and not as a penalty" for each breach of the agreement. This clause was held to be enforceable since £5 was not an excessive figure to place on a breach the actual loss from which would be impossible to forecast.

OTHER COMMON LAW REMEDIES

8.   Action for an Agreed Sum. A contract will often provide for the payment by one party of an agreed sum in exchange for performance by the other, for example goods sold for a fixed price. Provided the duty to pay the price has arisen the innocent party may sue the contract breaker for the agreed sum. Such action is different from an action for damages, since the plaintiff recovers the agreed sum, neither more nor less. Therefore questions of remoteness and measure cannot arise.

9.   Quantum Meruit. Quantum meruit means "as much as he deserves". It is a claim for reasonable payment for work done or goods delivered. It is distinct from an action for damages and will arise if in a contract for the performance of work there is no expressly agreed rate of remuneration. Similarly if a contract for the sale of goods does not specify the price *S.8(2) SALE OF GOODS ACT 1979* states that the buyer must pay a reasonable price.

EQUITABLE REMEDIES

10. Specific Performance. Specific performance is a decree issued by the court which orders the defendant to carry out his obligations. It is a remedy which

a.   Is discretionary, although the discretion must be exercised within well established principles.

b.   Is not normally awarded if damages would be an adequate remedy. It is most likely to be awarded in contracts for the sale of land.

c.   Must be available to either party. Thus it is not available to an infant in respect of a contract not enforceable against him.

d.   Is not available in respect of certain types of contract, such as those requiring personal services, for example as a butler, or contracts which require extensive supervision, for example building contracts.

11. Injunction

a.   A *mandatory injunction* orders a person to take action to undo a breach of contract. For example he may be ordered to take down an advertising sign erected in breach of contract.

b.   A *prohibitory injunction* is an order of the court which prohibits a person from doing something. Such an injunction could be granted to prevent the breach of a reasonable restraint of trade clause.

In **WARNER BROTHERS v NELSON (1936)** D, an actress, agreed to act for P and undertook that she would not act for anyone else during the period of the agreement without P's written consent. It was held that she could be restrained by an injunction from breaking this undertaking. This did not of course force her to act for P, nor did it prevent her from obtaining different types of work.

12. Rescission and rectification are also equitable remedies. They were discussed in Chapter 19.

LIMITATION OF ACTIONS

13. The *LIMITATION ACT 1980* lays down periods of 6 years for a simple contract, and 12 years for a deed. Time runs from the date when the breach occurred and failure to discover the breach does not usually stop time running. There are two exceptions to this rule:-

    a. Where the action is based on the fraud of the defendant, or the breach is concealed by the fraud of the defendant, and

    b. Where the action is for relief from the consequences of a mistake.

In the above cases time runs from when the fraud or mistake was, or ought to have been discovered (whichever is the earlier).

14. If at the time the cause of action accrued the plaintiff was an infant or a mentally disordered person, the action must be commenced within six years of the cessation of the disability. Provided there is no interval between two disabilities, for example an infant becomes mentally ill, then the two disabilities can be added together. However if the disabilities are separated by an interval time will not be stopped from running by the second disability.

15. Where a claim is made for a contract debt time starts running afresh if before, or after, the limitation period has expired:-

    a. A written acknowledgement of the debt is given by the debtor to the creditor, or

    b. A payment of part of the debt is made.

The Limitation Act does not apply to equitable remedies, but the maxim "delay defeats equity" may apply.

In **POLLARD v CLAYTON (1855)** D agreed to sell P all the coal that he raised from a particular mine. In breach of the agreement he sold the coal elsewhere and 11 months later P sought specific performance of the contract. It was held that the right to this equitable remedy was barred by the unreasonable length of time that had elapsed since the breach.

22 Privity of Contract

1. The Basic Rule. The common law doctrine of privity of contract states that no one can sue or be sued on a contract to which he is not a party. This was clearly illustrated in the following two House of Lords' decisions.

In **SCRUTTONS v MIDLAND SILICONES (1962)** A shipping company agreed to carry drums of chemicals belonging to P from America to England, the contract limiting their liability to $500 per drum. The shipping company hired a firm of stevedores (D) to unload the ship, and due to D's negligence the chemicals were damaged to the value of $1,800 per drum. P were successful in their tort action against D, recovering their full loss. The court held that D could not rely on the exemption clause in the contract between P and the shipping company because they were not a party to this contract, nor were they protected by a similar exemption clause in their contract with the shipping company because P were not a party to this contract.

In **BESWICK v BESWICK (1967)** A Mr Beswick (B) entered into an agreement with his nephew (also Mr Beswick), the defendant in this case (D), whereby D was to take over B's business in return for a payment of £6.50p per week to B during his life, and after his death £5 per week to his widow. When B died D stopped the payments. B's widow sued D both in her personal capacity and in her capacity as administratix of his estate. She failed in her personal capacity, but succeeded as administratix and was awarded a decree of specific performance against D.

If a person dies leaving a will he will name an executor in the will. If a person leaves no will his affairs will be handled by an administrator who is usually his nearest relative. A female administrator is called an administratix.

2. Exceptions

   a. *Statutory exceptions*

      i. The *MARRIED WOMANS PROPERTY ACT 1882* provides that a man (or woman) may insure his (or her) life for the benefit of his wife (or husband) and children. On his death the insurance company becomes a trustee of the money due to his wife, and she as a beneficiary may sue to recover it, although she was not a party to the insurance contract.

      ii. The *ROAD TRAFFIC ACT 1972* provides that in certain cases an injured third party may proceed directly against the insurance company.

      iii. The *BILLS OF EXCHANGE ACT 1882* provides that certain persons who come into possession of a cheque may sue the drawer of the cheque, even though they have no contract with him.

   b. *Equitable exceptions.* Occasionally equity may confer a benefit on a third party by using the device of an implied trust.

In **GREGORY AND PARKER v WILLIAMS (1817)** P, who owed money to both G and W, agreed with W to transfer his property to him if W would pay his (P's) debt due to G. The property was duly transferred but W refused to pay G. The common law doctrine of privity prevented G from suing on the contract between P and W. Equity however held that P could be regarded as a trustee for G, and that G could therefore bring an action, jointly with P against W.

c.   *Covenants*

i.   At common law the assignee of a lease takes it with the benefits of, and subject to the burdens of, the assignor. Although there is no contract between the lessor and the assignee there is "privity of estate" and the assignee may therefore sue and be sued by the lessor.

ii.   In equity the case of **TULK v MOXHAY (1848)** established that restrictive covenants run with the land, i.e. a purchaser is bound by a covenant entered into by a previous owner if he has notice of the covenant.

iii.   Distinguish covenants in leases, which may be positive, eg to pay rent, or negative, for example not to keep a dog, from restrictive covenants which may apply to freehold land, for example not to build within fifteen feet of the road.

d.   *Price maintenance agreements*

i.   In the past manufacturers often attempted to stipulate a minimum price at which retailers would sell their goods. The difficulty was that there was usually no contract between the manufacturer and the retailer. The manufacturer would sell to a wholesaler who resold to a retailer. Various attempts were made to overcome this difficulty, but in general the courts were reluctant to find exceptions to the rule of privity.

In **TADDY v STERIOUS (1904)** P was a tobacco manufacturer who wanted to prevent retailers selling his goods below a certain minimum price. He therefore attached to each packet a notice stating that tobacco was sold on the express condition that it was not to be resold below the price specified. P sold the tobacco to a wholesaler, who subsequently resold to D, a retailer, who then sold at below the specified price. It was held that P's condition could not bind D, with whom he had no contract.

ii.   This area is now of less practical importance since the *RESALE PRICES ACT 1976* makes void any term by which a supplier of goods fixes a minimum price which must be charged on the sale of those goods.

e.   *Collateral contracts.* A collateral contract arises when a statement that is not part of the main contract is nevertheless part of another contract related to the same subject matter.

In **SHANKLIN PIER v DETEL PRODUCTS (1951)** P hired contractors (X) to paint Shanklin Pier. They specified that X use paint to be purchased from D, because D had assured P that the paint would last 7 to 10 years. X purchased and used the paint but it only lasted 3 months. P successfully sued D on the basis of their assurance that the paint would last 7 years even though the contract for the sale of the paint was from D to X. It was held that there was a collateral contract between P and D. The consideration given by P was that they caused X to make the contract with D.

The same principle applies when a person buys goods and is given a manufacturer's guarantee. The basic contract is between the customer and the retailer but the guarantee amounts to a collateral contract between the customer and the manufacturer.

3. **Conclusion.** The case of **BESWICK v BESWICK** is important because in the Court of Appeal the doctrine of privity was challenged by Lord Denning. He had said that the widow could also sue in her own right because the doctrine of privity was "at bottom . . . only a rule of procedure" and could be overcome if the intended beneficiary joined the promisee in the action.

The House of Lords did not consider it necessary to comment on this view since they already had sufficient reason to find the widow's favour. However the speeches all assume the correctness of the generally accepted view that a contract can only be enforced by the parties to it.

Thus in **BESWICK v BESWICK** the House of Lords affirmed the continued existence of the doctrine of privity in the face of critics who have suggested that a remedy should be provided for a party who has been given specific rights under a contract, and despite Lord Denning's attempt to give effect to this suggestion.

COURSEWORK QUESTIONS 9-16
THE LAW OF CONTRACT

9. a. *In what circumstances will a contract in restraint of trade be held to be valid?*

   b. *Alec was employed by Blackacres, a firm of estate agents in Oldtown, as a negotiator. In this capacity he had contact with customers wishing to buy or sell houses. His contract of employment provided, inter alia, that if he ceased at any time to work for the firm, he would not:*

   i.   within 5 years of leaving the employment, take employment with any other firm of estate agents within 50 miles of Oldtown;

   ii. canvass the present or future customers of Blackacres, or deal with them;

   iii. open an estate agency anywhere in England and Wales which might compete with Blackacres.

Consider which if any of these restraints might be held to be enforceable against Alec.

ICSA Part 1 June 1986

10. a.   *In what circumstances will a court grant or order:*
    i.   *an injunction to restrain a breach of contract?*
    ii. *specific performance of a contract?*   *(12 marks)*

    b.   i.   *John agrees to sell a painting to Dave for £200. The painting needs a new frame and John tells Dave that the painting will be ready for him to collect in a fortnight. However, when Dave comes to collect and pay for the painting John refuses to give it to him. Advise Dave.*   *(5 marks)*
      ii. *Would your answer be any different if Dave was a minor?*

(3 marks)
(20 marks)
ACCA Foundation June 1980

11. *When parties enter into a contract it is virtually impossible for them to include express terms to cover every eventuality. If a dispute later arises it may then be necessary for terms to be implied into the contract.*

Explain

    a.   *when these implied terms will be introduced*
      i.   *by the courts, and*
      ii. *by statute;*   *(12 marks)*

    b.   *the extent to which it is possible to exclude or vary these terms at the time of contracting.*   *(8 marks)*

(20 marks)
CIMA Stage 1 May 1987

12. a.   *What must a plaintiff prove in order to satisfy a court that he has been induced to enter into a contract as a result of a misrepresentation? If he succeeds, what remedies will then be available to him?*

(14 marks)

    b.   *Whilst negotiating to sell his business to Ivan, Henry made a true statement which gave total figures for turnover and profits for the previous five years. This created an impression that the business was in a healthy state. Henry did not disclose, nor did Ivan request, a breakdown of figures which would have revealed a steady decline in profitability over this period. Ivan, having purchased the business, discovered the true state of affairs.*
    What remedies, if any, does Ivan have?   *(6 marks)*

(20 marks)
CIMA Foundation May 1986

13. a.   *Explain the effect of mistake upon the validity of a contract.*

(12 marks)

b. **David agrees to insure his premises with ERC Insurance after ERC Insurance has told him that he would be comprehensively covered against all risks. The contract includes a clause that David's cover will only continue if he obtains an annual fire certificate to the effect that all reasonable precautions against fire are being taken. David signs the contract without reading it and consequently does not obtain the requisite fire certificates each year.**

Some years later the premises are destroyed by fire and ERC Insurance refuses to reimburse David for his loss.

Advise David. *(8 marks)*

(20 marks)

CIMA Foundation November 1985

14. **a.** **In what circumstances will a contract be discharged through frustration?** *(12 marks)*

b. **i.** **Bill books a room in an hotel in London in order to visit a Jazz Festival which is to be held in Hyde Park. The Festival is cancelled and Bill wishes to cancel his reservation.**
Advise Bill. *(4 marks)*

ii. **Peter accepts an engagement to play the piano at the O.K. Club in Newtown for two weeks commencing 1 June 1981. On 30 May, he is arrested by the police for being in possession of drugs and is held in custody by them until 3 June. The O.K. Club now refused to engage Peter.**
Advise Peter. *(4 marks)*

(20 marks)

ACCA Foundation June 1981

15. **a.** **When, if ever, does payment of a smaller sum discharge a debt owed to a creditor?** *(10 marks)*

b. **D owned a fleet of lorries.**
i. **He agreed with E to deliver E's grain to his warehouse. E then asked D to deliver the grain to a different destination 50 miles away, and offered him extra remuneration. E did not pay the extra remuneration.**

ii. **He agreed with F to deliver F's steel to G. G agreed to assist D with unloading the steel. When the steel was delivered G refused this assistance.**
Advise D. *(10 marks)*

(20 marks)

ACCA Level 1 June 1987

16. **Explain, with reasons, whether or not the following are valid and enforceable agreements:**

a. **where the agreement contains a clause excluding the jurisdiction of the courts;**

177

b.   where a lease is granted with an option to renew on terms to be agreed later by the parties;

c.   where a transport concern agrees to take all its petrol from a particular garage without any reference to price but with a clause providing for arbitration in the event of a dispute arising;

d.   where an offer to sell goods states that the offer will be deemed to have been accepted unless there is notification to the contrary.

CIMA Foundation May 1980

PART III   THE LAW OF TORTS

23 The Nature of a Tort

1.   A tort cannot be defined by reference to a particular act or omission. It is only possible to define it by reference to the origin of the rule and the legal consequences of its breach. Professor Winfield stated that "Tortious liability arises from the breach of a duty primarily fixed by law: such duty is towards persons generally and its breach is redressible by an action for unliquidated damages." (Unliquidated damages are damages determined by the court, and not previously agreed by the parties.)

2.   The law of tort deals with a wide variety of wrongs, for example

    a.   Intentionally or negligently causing physical injury to another, (trespass to the person and negligence).

    b.   Interfering with the enjoyment of another's land, (nuisance, trespass to land and the tort known as "Rylands v Fletcher").

    c.   Defamation, (libel and slander).

3.   A tort must be distinguished from:-

    a.   *A breach of contract*, where the obligation of which a breach is alleged arose from the agreement of the parties.

    b.   *A breach of trust*, where the duty broken is known only to equity and not to common law and where the remedy is equitable or discretionary and not the common law right to damages.

    c.   *A crime*, where the object of proceedings is to punish the offender rather than compensate his victim.

4.   Each individual tort has its own particular rules governing liability, but in general the plaintiff must prove the following:-

    a.   That the defendant's conduct has been intentional or negligent, ie liability is usually based on fault. There are however some instances of "strict liability", ie liability irrespective of fault.

    b.   That the tortious act or omission caused some damage to the plaintiff. However some torts are actionable "per se" (without proof of loss), for example trespass and libel.

5.   Malice in Tort

    a.   Malice means acting from a bad motive. The general rule is that the defendant's motives are irrelevant. Therefore a good motive will not excuse a tortious act, and a bad motive will not turn an otherwise innocent act into a tortious one.

       In **BRADFORD CORPORATION v PICKLES (1895)** in an effort to induce the Corporation to buy his land, D sank a well on his land and abstracted water which would have otherwise reached the Corporation's reservoir. It was held that an injunction would not be granted to the Corporation. The right to abstract water is not (like the right to make noise on one's land) limited by the requirement of reasonableness. It is an absolute right and an element of malice could not make it a nuisance.

b.   There are several exceptions to the general rule stated above:-

i.   The plaintiff must prove malice in the torts of malicious prosecution and injurious falsehood.

ii.   In the tort of defamation if the plaintiff can prove malice this will prevent the defences of qualified privilege and fair comment.

iii.   In nuisance the plaintiff will sometimes succeed if he shows that the defendant's malice turned an otherwise reasonable act into an unreasonable one.

In **HOLLYWOOD SILVER FOX FARM v EMMETT (1936)** D, a developer, felt that a notice board inscribed "Hollywood Silver Fox Farm" was detrimental to his neighbouring development. When P refused to remove the notice D caused his son to discharge guns on his land to interfere with the breeding of the foxes. It was held that his action constituted a nuisance.

24 General Defences

INTRODUCTION

1.   A defence need only be argued by the defendant once the basic requirements of the tort have been established by the plaintiff. The general defences described in this chapter are not usually the "first line of defence" for a defendant. Initially he will probably try to refute the allegation that he has committed the tort. For example:-

> "I did not commit the tort of negligence because the plaintiff has failed to prove that I did not act as a reasonable man. I was reasonable because . . ."

If the plaintiff does establish that the tort has been committed then, and only then, need the defendant argue a defence. For example:-

> "I accept that I was negligent, but the loss the plaintiff has suffered is not sufficiently closely related to my negligent act"

This is the defence of remoteness. The distinction is illustrated by the following case.

In **WOOLDRIDGE v SUMNER (1963)** the plaintiff was a professional photographer. He was standing inside a show jumping arena when a horse ridden by D galloped off the course and into him. The judge found that there was an error of judgement by D. P's negligence action against D failed because this error of judgement did not amount to a breach of D's duty of care to P. The tort of negligence had not therefore been committed. The rider did not therefore have to argue that P consented to run the risk of injury by standing inside the arena.

VOLENTI NON FIT INJURIA (CONSENT)

2.   The general rule is that a person has no remedy for harm done to him if he has expressly or impliedly consented to suffer the actual harm inflicted, or if he has consented to run the risk of it. Thus, for example, a boxer could not sue as a result of a broken jaw suffered in the ring.

3.   **The Meaning of "Consent"**

a.   Mere knowledge does not necessarily imply consent. The plaintiff must both appreciate the nature of the risk of injury and consent to run that risk.

In **SMITH v BAKER (1891)** P, who worked in a quarry, was injured when a stone fell from a crane which his employers negligently used to swing stones above his head. When sued his employers pleaded the defence of volenti. They were able to show that P knew of the risk of injury, but they could not show that he freely consented to run that risk. — He may have continued to work under the crane through fear of losing his job. P's action succeeded.

b.   Consent need not be expressly given. It is sufficient that the plaintiff voluntarily agrees to the risk of injury.

In **ICI v SHATWELL (1965)** P and his brother, who were experienced in handling explosives, disregarded their employer's instructions and tested some detonators without taking adequate precautions. P was injured due to his brother's negligence, and sued ICI (the employers) claiming that they were vicariously liable for his brother's negligence. ICI's defence of volenti succeeded.

P knew the risk he was taking, but he took the risk voluntarily. Note that P could have chosen to sue his brother. If he had done so the brother could have successfully pleaded volenti.

c.   A consent given under protest is no consent, as where an employee has the choice between incurring a risk, or giving up a job which is not normally dangerous.

In **BOWATER v ROWLEY REGIS CORPORATION (1944)** D ordered one of their employees (P) to take out a horse which they knew was unsafe. P was injured. D's defence of volenti failed because P took out the horse because he was in fear of losing his job. His consent was not therefore freely given.

d.   An apparent consent may be negated by statute. For example:-

i.   The *ROAD TRAFFIC ACT 1972* makes void any agreement between a driver and passenger whereby the passenger travels at his own risk since the Act makes passenger insurance compulsory.

ii.   The *UNFAIR CONTRACT TERMS ACT 1977* provides that a person cannot by reference to any contract term exclude or restrict his liability for death or personal injury resulting from negligence.

4.   Rescue Cases

a.   If a defendant who has placed a third party, or himself, in a position of danger is sued by the plaintiff in respect of injuries suffered while taking steps to effect a rescue, he cannot plead volenti as a defence. The plaintiff's moral duty to effect a rescue excludes any real consent by him.

In **HAYNES v HARWOOD (1935)** A boy threw a stone at a horse which had been left unattended, causing the horse to bolt into a crowded street. P, a policeman, was injured when he tried to stop the horse. P's action against the owners of the horse succeeded. They could not claim the defence of volenti since he was acting under a duty to effect a rescue, and had not therefore freely consented to run the risk of injury.

b.   The general principle is similar where injuries are suffered in an attempt to rescue property, although the risks to which a plaintiff may reasonably expose himself are less than when life is endangered.

c.   If there is no immediate danger, only inconvenience, the defence of volenti is likely to succeed.

In **CUTLER v UNITED DAIRIES (1933)** P attempted to catch a horse which had bolted into an empty field. In this case the owner's defence of volenti succeeded since, as no person was in danger, P was not effecting a rescue but was acting voluntarily.

REMOTENESS OF DAMAGE

5. Causation and Remoteness

a. Before the question of remoteness arises, the plaintiff must show that the defendant's conduct was a substantial factor in bringing about his injury. Thus if the plaintiff would have suffered the same injury despite the defendant's conduct he will not receive compensation.

In **BARNETT v CHELSEA HOSPITAL MANAGEMENT COMMITTEE (1969)** P went to the hospital complaining of vomiting and was sent away to see his own doctor without being given a proper examination. Shortly afterwards P died of arsenic poisoning. P's widow's negligence action failed because P would have died whatever action the hospital doctor had taken. The careless examination was not the *cause* of the death.

b. Causation and remoteness are different parts of the same series of events. For example the causes and consequences of a car accident can be represented as follows:-

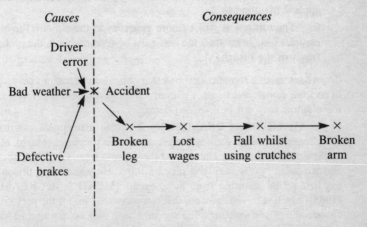

Causation is concerned with factors to the left of the dotted line, and remoteness with the consequences shown to the right of the line.

6. The Test for Remoteness

a. When causation has been established and the basic elements to the tort have been proved, the defendant may be able to escape payment of some or all of the damages claimed by showing that there is not a sufficiently close connection between his behaviour and the damage suffered by the plaintiff, ie that the loss is too remote.

b. The test for remoteness is *"Reasonable foreseeability"*, ie the defendant is only liable for the consequences of his act that a reasonable man would have foreseen. This test was established in **OVERSEAS TANKSHIP (UK) v MORTS DOCKS (THE WAGON MOUND) (1961)**, which overruled **RE POLEMIS (1921)**, a case which stated that the defendant was liable for all loss which was the "direct result" of his tort.

In **THE WAGON MOUND (1961)** an action was brought by the owners of a wharf against the owners of The Wagon Mound (a ship). The ship had discharged oil into Sydney harbour which ignited when hot metal from welding operations being carried on in the harbour fell onto a piece of cotton waste floating in the oil. The court held that damage to the wharf by fouling was foreseeable, but not damage by fire, since oil on water does not usually ignite. The ignition of the oil only occurred because the hot metal fell on to highly combustible cotton waste. Such an event was not reasonably foreseeable.

c. Note that

i. The test is objective. ie What matters is not what the defendant actually foresaw, (ie his subjective foresight), but what a reasonable man would have foreseen as the consequences of the tort, had he applied his mind to it.

ii. The tort test is wider (more generous to the plaintiff) than the contract test. In contract the loss must be foreseeable as the probable result of the breach.

d. An interesting recent case shows that policy considerations play a part in deciding remoteness issues, i.e. even if the loss is regarded as foreseeable the plaintiff may not be awarded damages.

In **MEAH v McCREAMER No 2 (1986)** a negligent car driver (McCreamer) crashed, causing head injuries to his passenger (Meah). Meah underwent a personality change and three years later sexually assaulted and wounded two women and raped a third. He was sent to prison. In the first action resulting from these events (**MEAH v McCREAMER (1985)**) Meah received damages that compensated him for the personality change and prison sentence. The second action was a claim against Meah for damages by his victims. Liability was admitted and £17,000 was awarded. In the final action (**MEAH v McCREAMER No 2 (1986)**) Meah sought to recover this £17,000 from McCreamer. The judge regarded this as a problem of remoteness. He pointed out that:-

i. The defendant must take his victim as he finds him even if he has an "eggshell personality" i.e. he was the worst possible person to receive an injury of this type.

ii.   The remoteness rules did not require the precise nature of the damage to be foreseeable, only the general type of damage.

iii.   Policy considerations would have to be taken into account when deciding whether a particular loss should be recoverable.

Meah's barrister argued that as the claim for imprisonment was successful then it followed that he must be able to recover the damages that he had to pay to his victims. The judge however said that there was a distinction between imprisonment of and injuries to Meah himself, and indirect loss suffered as a result of having to compensate someone else. Furthermore it was necessary to draw the line somewhere. It would not for example be reasonable to impose on the driver (McCreamer) liability to support any child born to the victim of the rape. It was held that the damage was too remote and the case was dismissed.

7.   Novus Actus Interveniens

a.   When a chain of events results from a tort sometimes the loss suffered is not within the scope of compensation merely because it is not reasonably foreseeable. For example:-

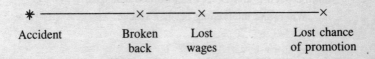

| Accident | Broken back | Lost wages | Lost chance of promotion |

Unless there was a very good chance of promotion the third consequence would probably be too remote.

b.   In other cases the chain of events is said to be "broken" by an intervening event known as a *novus actus interveniens*. This may be an act of the plaintiff himself or the act of a third party over whom the defendant had no control.

In **LAMB v CAMDEN BOROUGH COUNCIL (1981)** Council workmen broke a water main, causing serious damage to L's house. In fact the house became unsafe and the tenant to whom it was let moved out pending repairs. Squatters then moved into the empty house and caused £30,000 damage. The Court of Appeal awarded P damages in respect of damages due to flooding (liability was admitted by the Council) but rejected the claim for damage caused by squatters because this was not a reasonably foreseeable result of the Council's breach.

In **KNIGHTLY v JOHNS (1982)** D, a motorist negligently crashed his car, blocking a one-way traffic tunnel. A police inspector then told

P, a police constable to ride the wrong way down the tunnel to stop more motorists from entering. P was injured when he struck a vehicle that was entering the tunnel. It was held that D was not liable for P's injuries since P's accident was not a reasonably foreseeable result of D's negligence.

c.   To refer to a novus actus interveniens is in fact merely another way of saying that the loss is not reasonably foreseeable. In the example given in **5.**b. above it could be said that the broken arm is too remote because it is not reasonably foreseeable or because the fall from crutches is a novus actus interveniens.

d.   Some intervening acts (even if not foreseeable) will not break the chain of events which links the defendant's tort with the plaintiff's loss. For example:-

   i.   An act done "in the agony of the moment" created by the defendant's tort.

   In **SCOTT v SHEPHERD (1773)** D threw a lighted firework into a crowded market place. Several people threw the firework away from their vicinity until it exploded in P's face. D claimed that the onward throwing of the firework was a novus actus interveniens. The court however held that the onward throwing was an instinctive act, done in the "agony of the moment". It did not therefore break the link between P and D. P was awarded damages.

   ii.   Where the intervening act is a rescue.

8.   "Thin Skull" Cases. The Wagon Mound decision does not alter the common law rule applicable in "thin skull" cases. Thus the defendant must still take his victim as he finds him, he cannot plead the medical condition of his victim as a defence, even if this condition means that the loss suffered is not reasonably foreseeable.

   In **SMITH v LEECH BRAIN (1962)** P was injured at work when due to the negligence of one of D's employees a piece of molten zinc hit him on the lip. Most people would have been burned and nothing more, but P was susceptible to cancer and the accident brought it on − P died. The court applied the rule that the defendant must take his victim as he finds him, and his estate was awarded full compensation for the loss. The loss was clearly outside the scope of "reasonable foreseeability", but the judge made it clear that he did not think the Wagon Mound decision was intended to alter the common law rule applicable in "thin skull cases".

9.   Strict Liability Torts. In torts of strict liability, ie breach of statutory duty and "Rylands v Fletcher" the reasonable foreseeability test does not apply. The defendant will have to compensate the plaintiff for all the damage which is the direct result of his tort.

OTHER GENERAL DEFENCES

10. Mistake. The general rule is that mistake is no defence to a tort action. There are 3 exceptions. In each case the success of the defence depends on whether or not the defendant acted reasonably in making the mistake.

a. False imprisonment. — If a policeman without a warrant arrests somebody who has not committed a crime when he reasonably believes that they have.

b. Malicious prosecution. — If the person who commenced the prosecution (the defendant in the present tort action) was under the mistaken belief that the plaintiff was guilty of a crime.

c. Defamation. — See Chapter 30.7 (unintentional defamation).

11. Inevitable Accident

a. It has been said that a defendant is not liable if he can prove that damage is due to an "inevitable accident", ie that he is "utterly without fault".

In **STANLEY v POWELL (1891)** D fired his gun at a pheasant but the bullet hit a tree, and ricochetted into P. D was held to be completely blameless and not therefore liable in negligence.

b. Professor Winfield has suggested that the defence has very little relevance since the decision in **FOWLER v LANNING (1959)** which pointed out that since the burden of proving fault lies with the plaintiff, a defence which involves the defendant proving that he is without fault is superfluous.

c. In any event the plea of inevitable accident cannot be raised in cases of strict liability.

12. Act of God. This means circumstances which no human foresight can guard against. Act of god differs from inevitable accident since

a. It is available as a defence in strict liability cases; and

b. The "act" must be caused by the forces of nature without human intervention.

13. Self Defence. A person may use reasonable force to defend himself, or his property, or another person against unlawful force. What is reasonable depends on the facts of each case, however retaliation will never be reasonable.

14. Necessity

a. This defence may be used where the defendant has inflicted loss on an innocent plaintiff while attempting to prevent a greater loss to himself.

In **COPE v SHARPE (1912)** A fire broke out on P's land. D, a gamekeeper on adjoining land, entered P's land and burnt some of the heather to form a firebreak to prevent the fire spreading to his employer's land. When sued for trespass his defence of necessity succeeded (even though the firebreak had proved to be unnecessary), since there was a real threat of fire, and D had acted reasonably.

b.   The difference between self defence and necessity is that self defence is used against a plaintiff who is a wrongdoer, and necessity is used against an innocent plaintiff.

15. Statutory Authority

a.   Absolute statutory authority, (ie where the statute has expressly authorised the thing done, or the thing done is a necessary consequence of what is authorised), is a complete defence, provided the defendant can prove he used all proper care.

In **ALLEN v GULF OIL (1981)** a 450 acre oil refinery dominated the small village of Waterston near Milford Haven, causing both noise and smell. P's nuisance action was one of 53 brought by local residents. D's defence was that their activities were authorised by the *GULF OIL REFINING ACT 1965*. After some disagreement between the Court of Appeal and the House of Lords on the extent of authority granted by the statute the House of Lords held that it authorised both the construction and use of a refinery together with its vast complex of jetties and railway lines. Furthermore it operated as a complete defence to an action for private nuisance. It is perhaps unfortunate that the House did not take the view of the majority of the Court of Appeal and Lord Keith in the House of Lords. They were of the opinion that although the statute enable Gulf to make the installation and operate it, (ie an injunction could not be granted), it did not excuse them from paying compensation for injury done to those living in the neighbourhood.

b.   Conditional statutory authority, (ie where the injury is not a necessary consequence of what is authorised), is no defence.

25 Capacity

PARTIES TO WHOM SPECIAL RULES APPLY

1. Generally any person can sue or be sued, but there are exceptions.

2. **The Crown**

   a. The *CROWN PROCEEDINGS ACT 1947* preserves the immunity of Her Majesty in her private capacity from any legal process, but provides machinery whereby (with some exceptions) the Crown can be sued in respect of the torts of subordinates.

   b. Actions under the Act are brought against the appropriate government department.

3. **The Post Office**

   a. No proceedings in tort lie against the Post Office for any act or omission of its servants in relation to a postal packet or telephonic communication *(POST OFFICE ACT 1969)*.

   b. However the Post Office is liable for loss or damage to a registered inland letter if caused by a wrongful act or omission of an employee or agent of the Post Office.

4. **Infants**

   a. An infant can sue in tort, although proceedings must be brought through his "next friend", ie his nearest adult relative.

   b. Minority is generally no defence, however,

   i. Extreme youth may be relevant in cases where some special mental element is needed, such as malice, or in considering the standard of care to be expected.

   ii. An infant cannot be sued in tort where this would be an indirect way of enforcing a contract on which he is not liable. Contrast **BURNARD v HAGGIS (1863)** with **JENNINGS v RUNDALL** (Chapter 16. 7.)

   c. A parent is not liable as such for his child's tort, but he may be liable on other grounds. For example:-

   i. If he employs the child he may be vicariously liable as employer;

   ii. If he expressly authorises the tort; or

   iii. If he negligently allowed his child the opportunity of causing harm, for example by allowing a young child to possess a dangerous weapon.

5. **Husband and Wife**

   a. A husband is not affected if his wife is sued and vice versa.

b. Each may sue the other as if they were not married.

6. Corporations

a. They can sue for such torts as can be committed against them and not, for example, for trespass to the person.

b. They can be sued for the torts of an employee committed whilst he was acting in the course of his employment.

7. Unincorporated Organisations

a. Such bodies have no legal existence separate from that of their members and cannot therefore sue or be sued, although members who committed or authorised the tort are liable.

b. Where the tort arises from the use of the organisation's property a representative action may be brought against one member of the organisation, representing himself and the other members.

c. There are provisions for partnerships to sue and be sued in the firm's name.

VICARIOUS LIABILITY

8. "Vicarious liability" means liability for the torts of others, and arises because of a relationship between the parties. The relationship may be either

a. Employer/independent contractor, or

b. Employer/employee (master/servant)

9. Liability for the Torts of Independent Contractors

a. An independent contractor is a person who undertakes to produce a given result, and who in the actual execution of the work is not under the control of the person for whom he does it.

b. The general rule is that an employer is not liable for the tort of his independent contractor.

In **PADBURY v HOLLIDAY AND GREENWOOD (1912)** An employee of a contractor engaged to fit windows negligently left a hammer lying on a window sill. A gust of wind caught the window which, as it moved, knocked the hammer onto P, a passer-by. D were not held liable since the tort was committed by an employee of their independent contractor.

c. Exceptions:-

i. Strict liability under the rule in Rylands v Fletcher;

ii. Where the employer was negligent in the hiring of the independent contractor;

iii. Where the work is "extra hazardous". For example

In **HONEYWILL AND STEIN v LARKIN BROTHERS (1934)** an independent contractor used magnesium flares to take pictures of the inside of a cinema. The negligence of the contractor caused a fire to start. In this case the employer of the contractor was held liable since he had ordered the performance of what was regarded as a hazardous activity.

10. Liability for the Torts of Servants

a. A person is a servant if his employer retains a right to control not only the work he does, but also the way in which he does it. The test is the right of control, not how much control was in fact exercised. This is the traditional test, but difficulties arise when applying it to professional persons such as doctors. In such cases it may be necessary to consider such criteria as payment of salaries and the power of dismissal.

b. The rule is that a master is vicariously liable for the torts of his servant that are committed within the *course of his employment*. The tortious act must be a wrongful way of doing what the employee is employed to do.

In **LIMPUS v LONDON GENERAL OMNIBUS CO. (1862)** A bus driver whilst racing a bus caused an accident. His employers were held liable because he was doing what he was employed to do, ie driving a bus, although in an improper way.

Contrast **BEARD v LONDON GENERAL OMNIBUS CO. (1900)** A bus conductor attempted to turn a bus around at the end of its route and in doing so he caused an accident. His employers were not liable since he was employed only to collect fares and not to drive buses.

i. The employer may be liable even if the employee acts contrary to clear instructions.

In **ROSE v PLENTY (1976)** D was a milkman. His employer did everything possible to stop the common practice of taking young children on the van and paying them to help deliver the milk. A notice at the depot said

"Children must not in any circumstances be employed by you in the performance of your duties."

Contrary to this instruction D employed P. While moving from one delivery point to another the boy had one leg dangling from the van so that he could jump off quickly. D drove negligently and P's foot was crushed between the van and the kerb.

It was held that D's employer was liable because D had been acting within the scope of his employment, ie delivering milk and collecting empty bottles, although in an improper way.

ii. Sometimes a prohibition imposed by an employer on an employee will limit the scope of employment. Thus in **TWINE v BEAN'S EXPRESS (1944)** a prohibition against drivers giving lifts to hitch-hikers was held to limit the scope of employment. However this was not considered relevant to Rose v Plenty since Rose was not a mere passenger being given a lift, but he was the method by which Plenty did his job.

iii.   An employee may be within the course of his employment even though he has acted fraudulently.

In **LLOYD v GRACE, SMITH (1912)** The defendants were solicitors who employed a managing clerk to do conveyancing. The managing clerk fraudulently induced P to convey two cottages to him by representing that this was necessary in order to sell the cottages. The clerk then resold the cottages and absconded with the sale proceeds. The solicitors were held liable on the grounds that by allowing him to perform conveyancing transactions they had given him apparent authority to act as he did. He was acting within the scope of his employment even though his act was fraudulent.

ix.   When an employee who is on a journey deviates from the authorised route, it is a question of degree whether he has started on a fresh journey (''a frolic of his own'') which relieves the employer from liability.

c.   Where the employer is held liable for his employee's tort, the employee is also generally liable, but if a blameless employer is held liable for his employee's tort, a term is implied in their contract that the employee will indemnify the employer. (**LISTER v ROMFORD ICE (1957)**).

26 Negligence

1. Basic Requirements. If he is to succeed in a negligence action the plaintiff must prove:-

    a. That the defendant owed to him a legal duty of care, and

    b. That the defendant has been guilty of a breach of that duty, and

    c. That damage has been caused to the plaintiff by that breach.

Note in particular that the burden of proof is placed on the plaintiff. Each of these requirements is now considered in turn.

THE DUTY OF CARE

2. The Neighbour Test

    a. The courts have always taken the view that a careless person should not have to compensate all the people who suffer as a result of his conduct. For example when a van driver is injured due to the negligence of another driver several people may also be affected. There may be a witness to the accident who suffers nightmares as a result of his experience and a trader to whom the driver was delivering goods may lose profits because of inadequate stock. In such cases the task of the court is to consider the interests of the victims whilst being fair to the careless person. This is achieved by asking two questions:-

        i. Is there a sufficient relationship of *proximity* between the plaintiff and the defendant?

        ii. If so are there any *policy* reasons for negating or reducing the class of persons to whom a duty is owned?

If these questions are applied to the above example the result will be compensation for the van driver, but for policy reasons the witness and trader are unlikely to be compensated.

    b. "Proximity" does not mean physical proximity, it is based on reasonable foreseeability and is generally known as the *"neighbour test"*. The first case to establish this principle of proximity was in 1932.

In **DONOGHUE v STEVENSON (1932)** P's friend purchased a bottle of ginger beer manufactured by D and gave it to P. P drank most of the bottle, but then noticed the decomposed remains of a snail in the bottom of the bottle. P subsequently became ill and sued D in negligence. D's defence was that he did not owe a duty of care to P because there was no contract between D and P (the purchaser having been P's friend).

The court however held that a contractual link should no longer be the test for determining whether or not a duty of care was owed. The House of Lords stated that a duty of care is owed to any person who we can reasonably

195

foresee will be injured by our acts or omissions. Such persons the court described as "neighbours". It was held that D could reasonably foresee that somebody apart from the original purchaser may consume his product and he was therefore held liable to P.

c.   The neighbour test has been applied in numerous cases since 1932, for example:-

In **KING v PHILLIPS (1952)** D carelessly drove his taxi over a boy's cycle. The boy, who was not on the bicycle, screamed. His mother (P) heard the scream and on looking out of the window saw the crushed bicycle, but not her son. As a result she suffered shock which made her ill. She failed in her action against D because it was held that a driver could only reasonably foresee that his carelessness would affect other road users and not persons in houses. He did not therefore owe a duty of care to P.

In **TUTTON v WALTER (1985)** P kept bees on land near to D's farm. D had a crop of oil seed rape which, when in flower, is particularly attractive to bees. Despite clear written instructions to the contrary D sprayed his crop while it was in flower, with a pesticide that was fatal to bees. His defence to P's action was that no duty was owed because he was doing on his own land something that he was entitled to do, and that the bees came on to the land without permission and were basically trespassers. The judge did not accept these arguments. It was held that the duty was owed under the neighbour principle and it had been broken. P therefore received compensation for the loss of his bee colony.

In **HOME OFFICE v DORSET YACHT CO. (1970)** it was held that the Home Office owed a duty of care to the Yacht Club in respect of the detention of Borstal trainees who had escaped from an institution and caused damage to P's yachts. The duty to people whose property might be damaged in an escape was based on the control which the Home Office has over Borstal trainees.

d.   In certain situations the courts will not apply the neighbour test without qualification. The main areas concern negligent statements, economic loss, and nervous shock, each of which are considered below (paragraphs 3-5). In addition a plaintiff who is within the neighbour test may not receive compensation:-

i.   Where the defendant is guilty of an omission which results in foreseeable harm, for example by failing to save a small child drowning in shallow water. This exception will only apply if there is a "pure omission", ie if the defendant's prior conduct gives rise to a duty, the fact that an omission is the direct cause of the harm will not save the defendant from liability − clearly a car driver cannot avoid liability by claiming that the accident was caused by his omission to apply the brake.

ii.   Where a barrister is sued for professional negligence as a result of his conduct of a case in court (**RONDEL v WORSLEY (1969)** Chapter 9.6).

iii.   If a person is the occupier of land and the injured person is a trespasser. (The extent of the duty is defined by the *OCCUPIERS LIABILITY ACT 1984*).

iv.   If the injured person is an accomplice in crime.

In **ASHTON v TURNER (1981)** D, a burglar driving a get-away car caused an accident in which P, his accomplice, was injured. Both P and D were drunk. It was held for public policy reasons that D was not liable.

3.   **Economic Loss**

a.   Where negligent conduct causes economic loss (ie financial loss that it not consequential upon physical injury to person or property) the courts have been generally unwilling to hold that a duty of care exists.

In **MUIRHEAD v INDUSTRIAL TANK SPECIALISTS (1986)** P established a lobster farm. He intended to purchase lobsters cheaply in the summer, keep them alive until Christmas, and then sell them at a higher price. A constant supply of circulating sea water was needed to keep the lobsters alive. He installed the necessary tanks and pumps. Unfortunately the pump motor (supplied by a French firm) could not cope with the fluctuations in English voltage and a large number of lobsters were lost as a result of a pump failure. P claimed compensation for the loss of lobsters and loss of potential profit. It was held that he could recover for the loss of the lobsters and any financial loss suffered in direct consequence, but could not recover for any loss of profit.

b.   Numerous economic loss cases have concerned the liability of persons involved in the design, approval and construction of buildings. The position was recently reviewed by the House of Lords.

In **MURPHY v BRENTWOOD DISTRICT COUNCIL (1990)** P claimed £35,000 from D as compensation for the reduction in the value of his house which suffered as a result of defects in the design. The defective design had been approved by the Council. P relied on a 1977 case (**ANNS v MERTON LBC**) where, in a similar situation, the plaintiff had been successful. However a 7 member House of Lords unanimously overruled the Anns' decision on the grounds that it did not proceed on the basis of established principles, but introduced a potentially indeterminate liability covering a wide range of situations. In Murphy's case the court held that such loss was purely economic (not physical) and was not therefore within the scope of the duty of care owed by D to P. They made it clear that the right to recover for pure economic loss, not flowing from physical injury, must be determined by the principle in Hedley Byrne v Heller (see 4. below).

c.   Hedley Byrne has been applied on many occasions. Recent examples include **SMITH v ERIC BUSH** (Chapter 18.13) and **HARRIS v WYRE FOREST DISTRICT COUNCIL (1989).**

In **HARRIS v WYRE FOREST DISTRICT COUNCIL** P paid a valuation fee to the Council in connection with a loan application. On the basis of the valuation report the Council lent P £8,500 out of a purchase price of £9,000. P did not personally see the valuation report. Serious settlement was later discovered which required extensive repair. The House of Lords held that D was liable since although P had not seen the valuation report it was reasonable for him to assume that the surveyor conducting the valuation had not found any serious defects.

Unfortunately the **SMITH** and **HARRIS** decisions are arguably inconsistent with **MURPHY v BRENTWOOD DC,** in that a surveyor who carries out a negligent valuation is liable to a purchaser who suffers economic loss (the **SMITH** and **HARRIS** cases) but a surveyor who negligently approves defective plans or foundations will not be liable to a purchaser (**MURPHY'S** case).

d.   The more cautious approach exemplified in **DONOGHUE v STEVENSON** and **MURPHY v BRENTWOOD DC** is also illustrated by another important recent economic loss case.

In **CAPARO INDUSTRIES v DICKMAN (1989)** P sued two directors of Fidelity plc and the accountants Touche Ross & Co, the auditors of Fidelity. P had taken over Fidelity and alleged that the profits were much lower than could be expected from the audited accounts, consequently they had suffered financial loss. The question of actual negligence by Touche Ross was not considered by the court. The court was concerned with the preliminary issue of whether an auditor of a public company owes a duty of care to either individual shareholders and/or potential investors. The Court of Appeal stated that to establish a duty of care three elements had to be proved (i) forseeability of loss (ii) proximity of P and D and (iii) that it was fair and reasonable that D should owe a duty to P. The House of Lords unanimously rejected this approach stating that the question of whether or not a duty of care is to be imposed should be determined "incrementally and by analogy with established categories". They held that P's action failed. The court stated that no duty of care was owed by auditors to members of the public, lenders or ordinary creditors who rely upon company accounts or buy or sell shares. This would impose liability "in an indeterminate amount for an indeterminate time to an indeterminate class".

4.   Negligent Statements

a.   The usual rules of liability apply when the negligent statement results in physical injury. For example

In **CLAY v CRUMP (1963)** D, an architect, stated that a wall on a demolition site was safe and could be left standing. It later collapsed injuring P. P succeeded in his action against D for his negligent statement.

b.   Where the negligent statement results in financial loss different rules of liability apply. The difference concerns the persons to whom a duty of care is owed. Instead of the "neighbour test" laid down in **DONOGHUE v STEVENSON (1932)** the courts initially formulated in **HEDLEY BYRNE v HELLER (1964)**, a much narrower test based on a "special relationship" between the parties.

In **HEDLEY BYRNE v HELLER (1964)** D were bankers and P were advertising agents. They had a mutual client E Ltd. who wished to place advertisements on television. E requested credit from P, so P asked D for references. D stated that E was a respectably constituted firm and was considered good, although the statement was made without responsibility on their part. P therefore incurred personal liability on several advertising contracts. E then went liquidation and P were unable to recover over £17,000 owed to them. P therefore sued D on his negligent statement. It was held that he did have a possible action, and he would have succeeded, but for the disclaimer of responsibility. In order to succeed in such a case the plaintiff must show a special relationship by proving that:-

i.   He relied on the special skill and judgement of the defendant, and

ii.   The defendant knew or ought to have known of this reliance and thus accepted responsibility for making the statement carefully.

c.   In some exceptional situations a plaintiff may succeed even if he does not rely on any statement by the defendant, although in such cases there must be close proximity between the plaintiff and the defendant.

In **ROSS v CAUNTERS (1979)** D was a solicitor. One of his clients bequeathed some property to the plaintiff. At the time the will was executed D had failed:-

i.   To tell the testator that the will must not be witnessed by the spouse of any beneficiary;

ii.   To check that the will had been properly executed;

iii.   To notice that P's husband had witnessed the will; and

iv.   To draw the testator's attention to this fact. (It was admitted that if the testator had been told of the error he would have put it right).

As a result of iii. above P was prevented from inheriting under the will. She was however successful in her negligence action against D, despite the fact that she clearly had not relied on any statement by D. The judge did not adopt the "reasonable foreseeability" test or the "special relationship" test. He chose a point between the two, in effect there must be a *close proximity* between P and D – *P individually (or as a member of a specific and limited class) must be in the defendant's direct contemplation as someone likely to be closely and directly affected by his acts*. This requirement was satisfied in Ross v. Caunters because

i.   P was named in the will;

ii.   The proximity was in no way accidental or unforeseen, but arose out of D's duty to his client. In fact the aim of the transaction between D and his client was to confer a benefit on P.

d.   If there is a subsequent contract between the plaintiff and the defendant, based wholly on a negligent statement made by the defendant, the plaintiff will not be confined to contractual remedies, but may also have a remedy in tort.

In **ESSO PETROLEUM v MARDON (1976)** In 1961 Esso found a site for a filling station on a busy main road. A company executive with 40 years experience of the petrol trade estimated that sales would be 200,000 gallons per year by the third year, (assuming access to the main road), so Esso bought the site. However planning permission was then refused for direct access to the main road, thus reducing potential sales. Despite this the executive later represented to M that sales would be 200,000 gallons per year. Even though M's own estimate was 100,000-150,000 gallons per year he accepted a tenancy relying on the accuracy of the executive's statement. His rent was based on expected sales of 200,000 gallons per year. In the first 15 months sales were only 78,000 gallons and M could not therefore pay the rent. He was sued by Esso. In return he brought a counter-claim against Esso, claiming damages in contract for breach of warranty and damages in tort for a negligent statement. It was held by the Court of Appeal.

i.   On the contract point:- That since the party making the statement had expertise it could be interpreted as a warranty (ie a term of the contract rather than a mere representation inducing the contract) breach of which entitled the innocent party to damages.

ii.   On the tort point:- That if a man professing to have special knowledge or skill makes a representation which induces the other to contract with him he is under a duty to take reasonable care to see that the representation is correct. Esso were therefore liable in damages. Esso's defence to the tort claim was that **HEDLEY BYRNE v HELLER** could not apply since it was concerned solely with liability in tort, and not where a pre-contract statement made in negotiations later resulted in a contract — in which case the law of contract provides the plaintiff's only remedies. This defence clearly failed.

e.   A disclaimer of responsibility by the defendant (as in Hedley Byrne v Heller) will be sufficient to exclude the duty of care. However since the *UNFAIR CONTRACT TERMS ACT 1977*. The exemption clause must satisfy the requirement of reasonableness. See **SMITH v ERIC BUSH (1989)** (Chapter 18.13).

5. Nervous Shock

a. The courts have been very reluctant to regard a duty as owed to persons who suffer nervous rather than physical injuries. There are several reasons for this:-

   i.   Fear of fraudulent claims;

   ii.   The difficulty of fixing a monetary value to such loss;

   iii.   Unfairness to defendants if damages become out of proportion to the negligent conduct complained of.

b. It used to be thought that to claim for nervous shock the plaintiff must fear injury to himself or a near relative and that the shock must result from actually seeing the accident itself rather than the aftermath. However recent cases have extended the basis for a claim.

In **CHADWICK v BRITISH RAILWAYS BOARD (1967)** The Board were held liable in negligence for a serious railway accident in which 90 people died. P was a voluntary rescue worker who worked all night in the wreck. As a result he later suffered from neurosis which necessitated hospital treatment. P succeeded in his action against BRB. It was held that in the circumstances injury by shock to volunteer rescue workers was foreseeable. Accordingly a duty was owed to such persons and damages could be awarded even though the shock did not arise from fear of injury to himself or his family.

In **McLOUGHLIN v O'BRIEN (1982)** P's husband and three children were injured in a car accident caused by D's negligence. One of the children died almost immediately. At the time of the accident P was at home about two miles away. About an hour later the accident was reported to her by a neighbour who said that he thought her son was dying. The neighbour then drove her to hospital where her fourth child (who was not in the accident) told her that her youngest daughter aged three, was dead. At the hospital she saw through a corridor window her other daughter (aged seven) crying, with her face cut and covered in dirt and oil, she could also hear her son (aged seventeen) shouting and screaming. As a result of seeing these injuries and the distressing way in which she learned of them P suffered a severe shock, depression and a change of personality. The House of Lords awarded damages since the loss was reasonably foreseeable and the injury was an illness rather than "normal" grief and sorrow. The House was not impressed by the public policy argument that such a decision "would open the flood gates".

c. It is not possible to define a clear principle for all nervous shock cases, however the shock must be an identifiable psychiatric illness not just grief and sorrow and it must be reasonably foreseeable. When deciding when it is reasonably foreseeable the court will consider the relationship of the plaintiff and defendant, the whereabouts of the plaintiff at the time of the accident and the way in which the plaintiff found out about the accident.

THE STANDARD OF CARE

6. The defendant will discharge his duty if he takes reasonable care. This is an objective test. ie The test is "Did the defendant exercise the care that a reasonable man would have exercised?" It is not "Did he do his best?"

The care which a reasonable man would show varies with the circumstances. Some relevant factors may be:-

a. The magnitude of the foreseeable risk.

In **LATIMER v A.E.C. (1953)** A thunderstorm flooded D's factory, making the floor slippery. D did all they could to clear the water and make the factory safe. P nevertheless slipped and was injured. P alleged negligence, claiming that the factory should have been closed. It was held that the risk of injury did not justify such a drastic measure. P's claim failed.

b. The known characteristics of the party exposed to the risk.

In **PARIS v STEPNEY B.C. (1951)** P, who only had one eye, worked for the council as a vehicle welder. He was blinded completely when a spark flew into his one good eye. He sued his employers for negligence claiming that he should have been supplied with goggles. The evidence was the goggles were not thought necessary for two-eyed welders. However since the loss of a person's only good eye is far more serious that the loss of one of two good eyes, goggles should have been supplied to P. The council had broken their duty of care.

c. Whether the defendant was faced with an emergency.

In **WATT v HERTFORDSHIRE C.C. (1954)** P, a fireman, was injured when a jack slipped in a lorry while going to an accident. The lorry was not equipped to carry the jack, but it had been used because the fire brigade were faced with an emergency. P's action failed, the council had not broken its duty of care.

d. Whether a special relationship exists, such as that of competitor to spectator as in **WOOLDRIDGE v SUMNER (1963)** (Chapter 24.1).

e. The state of health of the defendant. If the defendant causes a road accident he will only escape liability if his actions at the relevant time were wholly beyond his control, as in a case of sudden unconsciousness.

In **ROBERTS v RAMSBOTTOM (1980)** D collided head on with a parked vehicle, causing injury to its occupants. D claimed that he was not liable because 20 minutes earlier he had unknowingly suffered a stroke.

This affected his mind so that he could not drive properly. It also meant that he could not appreciate the he was unfit to drive. He did however have sufficient awareness of his surroundings and traffic conditions to continue to control the car, although in an inadequate way. It was held that where a driver retains some control, even if imperfect, he must be judged by the objective standard of a reasonable driver. In this case, even though D was not morally to blame because of the nature of the disabling symptoms, D had fallen below this objective standard and was liable.

f.   In addition to any statutory and contractual duties owed by an employer to his employee an employer has a common law duty to act with reasonable care towards his employees. To assess whether he has discharged this duty it will be necessary to consider, among other things, whether he has provided:-

    i.   A competent staff,

    ii.   Proper tools, machinery and premises, and

    iii.   A safe system of work and supervision.

Where work is done on another person's premises the employer's duty is less onerous, although he must still show reasonable care.

In **WILSON v TYNESIDE WINDOW CLEANING CO. (1958)** the employer discharged his duty of care by telling window cleaners employed by him to take reasonable care, and not to clean windows if it was dangerous to do so.

7.   Res Ipsa Loquitur

a.   In some situations the plaintiff will not need to prove a breach of the duty of care. This is where the maxim res ipsa loquitur (the thing speaks for itself) applies.

b.   The maxim applies when:-

    i.   The "thing" is under the control of the defendant;

    ii.   The defendant has knowledge denied to the plaintiff; and

    iii.   The damage is such that it would not normally have happened if proper care had been shown by the defendant.

c.   If these requirements are fulfilled there is prima facie evidence of a breach of duty. The burden of proof is then shifted to the defendant, who must prove that he did show reasonable care.

d.   The maxim does not apply when the facts are sufficiently known because it depends on an absence of explanation.

e. "Res Ipsa Loquitur" was considered in the following 4 cases. In the first two it was held to apply in the latter two it did not apply. However even when it does apply (ie b. i.-iii. are present) it does not guarantee success for the plaintiff. It merely shifts the burden of proof to the defendant, who may be able to show that despite the facts he acted as a reasonable man at all times.

In **BYRNE v BOADLE (1863)** A barrel of flour fell from D's warehouse injuring P, a passer-by. No explanation could be given by D for the incident and P was in no position to prove a breach of duty by D. The court therefore placed the burden of proof on D, who had to show that he had not broken his duty of care. He was unable to do this and P therefore succeeded in his action.

In **MAHON v OSBORNE (1939)** A swab was left in a patient's body after an operation. Clearly the patient could not prove a breach of duty, since he was under an anaesthetic. However the presence of the swab raised the inference of a breach of duty (res ipsa loquitur). The surgeon was unable to show that he had used reasonable care and was accordingly held liable.

In **FISH v KAPUR (1948)** P's jaw was found to be broken after D, a dentist, had extracted a tooth. It was held that this was not a res ipsa loquitur situation since there were reasons other than the dentist's breach of duty which could have accounted for the broken jaw. For example P may have had a weak jaw. P was therefore compelled to prove the three requirements of negligence in the usual way.

In **TURNER v MANSFIELD CORPORATION (1975)** P was a driver of a corporation dustcart. For some reason, which was never explained, the movable body of the cart rose and hit a bridge, causing the cab section to rise from the ground and jamming the dustcard under the bridge. P jumped from the cab and was injured in his fall to the ground. The Court of Appeal held that this was not a case to which res ipsa loquitur applied. It was for P who was in control of the dustcart to give an explanation of the accident. Since he could not do this his action failed.

DAMAGE

8.   The plaintiff must show that as a result of the breach of duty he has suffered some damage. If a person's unreasonable conduct fortunately injures no one then that person cannot be liable in negligence (although he may be guilty of a criminal offence, e.g. careless driving). The rules on damage have already been covered, but are summarised below.

a.   The damage must be *caused* to a substantial extent by the defendant's conduct.

b.   The damage must be sufficiently closely related to the negligent act, ie it must not be too *remote*.

c.   In most cases the damage must be either physical injury to the plaintiff's person or property or economic loss consequential upon physical injury, e.g. lost wages as a result of a broken leg.

d.   In cases of identifiable psychiatric illness the courts may award damages if such illness is reasonably foreseeable, but considerations of public policy limit the scope of such damages.

e.   If the damage is economic loss unaccompanied by any injury to person or property a "special relationship", based on reliance, must exist between the plaintiff and the defendant. **(HEDLEY BYRNE v HELLER (1964))**.

CONTRIBUTORY NEGLIGENCE

9.   a.   At common law if the plaintiff was guilty of any negligence which contributed to the cause of the accident, he recovered nothing.

b.   Since 1945 by virtue of the *LAW REFORM (CONTRIBUTORY NEGLIGENCE) ACT 1945* where a person suffers damage partly as a result of his own fault, and partly due to the fault of another, the damages recoverable will be reduced according to his share of responsibility.

c.   A person can be guilty of contributory negligence if his conduct while in no way contributing to the accident itself, contributed to the nature and extent of his injuries.

In **O'CONNELL v JACKSON (1971)** D, a car driver, knocked P off his moped, the accident being entirely D's fault. P suffered severe head injuries which the evidence showed would have been less serious if he had been wearing a crash helmet. It was held that the plaintiffs damages would be reduced by 15%.

d.   The court does not approach the problem by saying "What injuries would he have suffered if he had been wearing a crash helmet – we shall compensate him for such injuries". The court says – "Given that he has suffered injuries X, Y and Z what was his percentage of fault either in causing the accident or contributing to such injuries – his damages shall be reduced by this percentage".

e.   To prove contributory negligence it is not necessary for the defendant to show that the plaintiff owed him a duty of care, only that he failed to take reasonable care for his own safety. For example:-

In **FROOM v BUTCHER (1976)** it was held that failure to wear a seat belt amounted to contributory negligence.

In **OWENS v BRIMMELL (1977)** P's damages were reduced by 20% because he accepted a lift in D's car knowing that D was drunk.

OCCUPIERS' LIABILITY TO LAWFUL VISITORS

10. The duty of occupiers of premises towards lawful visitors is governed by the *OCCUPIERS' LIABILITY ACT 1957*.

a. An *"occupier"* is a person who has some degree of control over the premises. He need not necessarily be the owner. It is also possible for there to be more than one occupier.

b. *"Premises"* includes land, buildings, fixed, or movable structures such as pylons and scaffoldings; and vehicles, including ships and aeroplanes.

c. *"Visitors"* are persons lawfully on the premises, such as customers in shops and factory inspectors. A trespasser will be deemed to be a lawful visitor for the purposes of the Act if the occupier has granted him implied permission by habitual acquiescence in his known trespass.

11. The extent of the duty is laid down in *S.2(2)* of the Act:-

"A duty to take such care as in all the circumstances of the case is reasonable to see that the visitor will be reasonably safe in using the premises for the purpose for which he is permitted by the occupier to be there".

This duty is merely an enactment of the common law duty to act as a reasonable man (see **6.** above). The Act states that all the circumstances of the case are relevant in determining the duty owed. Therefore the occupier:-

a. Must be prepared for children to be less careful than adults. In the case of very young children the occupier is entitled to assume that they will be accompanied by an adult.

b. May expect a person who is doing his job to guard against the ordinary risks of his job.

In **ROLES v NATHAN (1963)** The plaintiffs, who were chimney-sweeps, were employed by D to block up holes in the flues of a coke-fired heating system. Despite a warning from D they attempted to do this while the coke fire was lit, and they were both killed by carbon monoxide gas. Their executor's action failed since it was a risk incidental to their job which they should have foreseen and guarded against.

Contrast **SALMON v SEAFARERS RESTAURANTS (1983)** when a fire broke out at D's fish and chip shop due to the negligence of one of the employees. The fire melted a seal of a gas meter, gas escaped and there was an explosion. P, a fireman, was injured. D contended that they were only liable if a fireman was injured as a result of some foreseeable but nevertheless exceptional risk, not risks ordinarily incidental to the job of a fireman. It was held that the duty was not limited in this way, the duty owed was the same as that owed to any other visitor. In this case it was foreseeable that fireman would be needed and that such an explosion might result from the fire. D was therefore liable.

c.   Will not be liable if the injury results from the faulty work of an independent contractor, provided the occupier took reasonable steps to ensure that the contractor was competent, and that the work was properly done.

d.   May be able to escape liability by giving an adequate warning of any danger.

12.   The Act preserves the right of the occupier to plead the defence of volenti non fit injuria in respect of risks "willingly accepted" by the visitor.

13.   The *DEFECTIVE PREMISES ACT 1972* provides that any person who undertakes work for, or in connection with the provision of a dwelling owes a duty of care to:-

a.   The person who orders the work; and

b.   Any person who subsequently acquires an interest in the dwelling.

OCCUPIERS' LIABILITY TO TRESPASSERS

14.   The *OCCUPIERS' LIABILITY ACT 1984* has now replaced the common law rules governing the duty of occupiers of premises to persons other than visitors. The Act covers not only trespassers but also persons using rights of way who fall outside the meaning of "visitor" under the *OCCUPIERS' LIABILITY ACT 1957*.

15.   For several years prior to 1984 the occupier's duty to trespassers was to act with common sense and humanity. This required all the surrounding circumstances to be considered, for example the seriousness of the danger, the type of trespasser likely to enter, and in some cases the resources of the occupier.

In **BRITISH RAILWAYS BOARD v HERRINGTON (1972)** BRB's electrified railway ran near a park used by children. The fences on each side of the railway were in poor condition and BRB knew that people used to climb through the broken fence to take "short-cuts" across the railway. H, aged 6, got through the fence and was seriously injured when he touched the live rail. The House of Lords held that the old rules relating to liability towards trespassers no longer applied, and although an occupier does not owe the same duty of care to a trespasser as he owes to a visitor, he must act by standards of common sense and humanity and warn or exclude, within reasonable limits, those likely to be injured by a known danger. BRB were therefore held liable.

16.   The main provisions of the 1984 Act are:-

a.   *Duty owed.* The occupier owes a duty if:-

i.   He is aware of the danger or has reasonable grounds to believe that it exists; and

ii.   He knows, or has reasonable grounds to believe, that someone is in (or may come into) the vicinity of the danger; and

iii.   The risk is one against which in all the circumstances of the case he may reasonably be expected to offer that person some protection.

b.   ***Duty broken.*** The duty is to take such care as is reasonable in all the circumstances to see that the person to whom the duty is owed does not suffer injury on the premises by reason of the danger concerned.

c.   ***Damage.*** The occupier can only be liable for injury to the person. The Act expressly provides that the occupier incurs no liability in respect of any loss of or damage to property.

d.   ***Warnings.*** The duty may be discharged (in appropriate cases) by taking reasonable steps to give warning of the danger. The Act also preserves the right of the occupier to plead the defence of volenti.

17.   The new Act does not significantly change the law, all the circumstances remain relevant, including what the occupier does know and ought to know both about the existence of the danger and the likelihood of trespassers. It is therefore very unlikely that Herrington's case or the other cases described below would be decided differently under the Act, and it will still be rather difficult to predict the outcome of many cases, contrast for example the cases of Penny and Harris.

In **HARRIS v BIRKENHEAD CORPORATION (1975)** P, aged 4, fell from the upper window of a derelict vandalised house. The house had been acquired for demolition by the council. Due to an administrative oversight the doors and windows had not been boarded up in the usual way. It was held that the council were liable because the house was a dangerous and tempting place for young children, therefore a humane and commonsense person should take precautions.

In **PENNY v NORTHAMPTON BOROUGH COUNCIL (1974)** a trespasser threw an aerosol can into a fire started by boys on a council tip. The can burst and injured an eight-year old trespasser. It was held that the council were not liable.

In **PANNETT v McGUINNESS (1972)** D, who were demolition contractors, were burning rubbish on a demolition site. They appointed three workmen to supervise the fire and keep a lookout for children. P, aged 5, fell into the fire while the men were away and was badly burned. Although P was a trespasser, and the men had on many occasions in the past chased children away, D was held liable since he had failed to keep a proper lookout.

Contrast **WESTWOOD v THE POST OFFICE (1974)** P, an adult employee of the post office, was injured when he entered an unlocked room which had warning of danger on the door. Although the room should have been locked P's claim failed since a notice of danger is regarded as adequate warning to an adult.

27 Strict Liability

1. Strict liability is liability which arises without fault. There are two torts dealt with in this chapter. The first is known as the tort of "Rylands v Fletcher" the second is "Breach of Statutory Duty".

RYLANDS v FLETCHER

2. The rule stated by Blackburn. J. is

"The person who for his own purposes brings on his lands and collects and keeps there anything likely to do mischief if it escapes, must keep it at his peril, and if he does not do so is prima facie answerable for all the damage which is the natural consequence of its escape."

In **RYLANDS v FLETCHER (1868)** The defendant, a mill owner, employed independent contractors to build a reservoir on his land for the purpose of supplying water for his mill. During the work the contractors found some disused mine shafts which unknown to them connected with the plaintiff's mines under adjoining land. The contractors failed to seal these shafts and when the reservoir was filled with water, the water escaped through these shafts and flooded the plaintiff's mine. Blackburn. J. held that the defendant was liable. Note that:-

a. Since the defendant employed competent workmen and did not know of or suspect the existence of the disused mine shafts, it follows that liability is absolute (strict) and does not depend on negligence.

b. The words of the rule make it clear that the defendant's liability was personal, not merely vicarious liability for the negligence of his independent contractor.

3. The rule applies to water, animals, chemicals, filth, industrial use of gas or electricity, and exceptionally humans.

In **ATTORNEY-GENERAL v CORKE (1933)** D allowed gypsies to occupy his land, living in caravans and tents. The gypsies fouled and caused damage to adjoining land. It was held that Rylands v Fletcher applied since although it was lawful to allow gypsies onto land, it was not a natural use of land, and therefore the owner had to bear the risk of damage due to this non-natural use.

Following **PAGE MOTORS v EPSOM BOROUGH COUNCIL (1980)** it is clear that where gypsies are concerned an action in nuisance is more appropriate (See Chapter 28.4.).

4. There must be a non-natural use of land, ie some special use bringing with it increased danger to others. The rule does not therefore apply to:-

a. Damage due to things naturally on the land, although in such cases an action may lie in nuisance (See **LEAKEY v NATIONAL TRUST (1980)** (Chapter 28.2.)).

b.   Damage due to a natural use of the land, for example domestic gas, electricity or water.

In **RICKARDS v LOTHIAN (1913)** D was the occupier of business premises and P was the lessee of the second floor. One evening an unknown person deliberately blocked a sink on the fourth floor and turned on the tap. Consequently P's stock was found next morning badly damaged. P's Rylands v Fletcher action against D failed because

i.   domestic water was not a non-natural use of the land, and

ii.   because the escape was caused by the deliberate act of an unknown person.

5.   There must be an escape beyond the boundaries of the defendant's land.

In **READ v J. LYONS (1947)** P was employed as an inspector of munitions factories. She was injured by a shell which exploded while being manufactured. She claimed under the rule in Rylands v Fletcher, but failed because there had been no escape of the dangerous thing over the boundaries of the defendant's land.

6.   **Defences**

a.   The escape was caused by:-

i.   The plaintiff.

ii.   Act of God.

iii.   The deliberate act of a third party over whom the defendant had no control as in **RICKARDS v LOTHIAN (1913)**.

b.   The accumulation was made:-

i.   With the plaintiff's express or implied consent (volenti).

In **PETERS v PRINCE OF WALES THEATRE (BIRMINGHAM) (1943)** D leased to P a shop in the same building that contained the theatre. The theatre had installed (and P knew this) a sprinkler system as a fire precaution. During a frost the water in the sprinkler system's pipes froze, cracking the pipes. In the following thaw P's shop was flooded and his stock damaged. There was no liability under Ryland v Fletcher because the sprinkler system was for the common benefit of both the theatre and P's shop, and because P had impliedly consented to run the risk of accidents involving the system.

ii.   With absolute statutory authority.

BREACH OF STATUTORY DUTY

7.   Whether or not a tort action is possible by a person injured due to a breach of statutory duty depends on the construction of the particular statute.

Generally an action will lie, unless it is clear from the statute, or the pre-existing law that this was not intended. However no action will lie if:-

210

a.   It is clear that the penalty provided by the Act was intended to be the
only remedy.

In **ATKINSON v NEWCASTLE WATERWORKS (1877)** P's
timber yard was destroyed by fire because there was insufficient water
pressure in the mains to put it out. The *WATERWORKS CLAUSES ACT
1874* provided a £10 penalty if a waterworks company allowed the pressure
to fall below a specified minimum. The pressure was below this minimum.
However P's action to recover his full loss did not succeed, since the statute
did not disclose a cause of action by individuals for damage of this kind,
because this would amount to the waterworks company providing a
gratuitous fire insurance service. It was clear that the £10 penalty was the
only penalty intended to be imposed by the Act.

b.   The Act was passed for the benefit of the public generally rather than
particular individuals, for example the *TRADE DESCRIPTIONS ACT 1968*.

c.   The Act was passed for the benefit of a section of the public of which
the plaintiff is not a member.

In **HARTLEY v MAYOH AND CO. (1954)** P, a fireman, was electrocuted while fighting a fire at D's premises. His electrocution was due
to D's breach of statutory regulations. P however failed to recover
compensation because the regulations were expressed to be for the benefit
of "employees" and he was not a member of this class of persons.

d.   The plaintiff suffered damage different from that which the statute
was intended to prevent.

In **GORRIS v SCOTT (1874)** In a storm sheep were swept from the
deck of a ship because they were not in pens. However the purpose of
the statutory requirement of "penning" sheep was to prevent the spread
of infection and not to stop them being washed overboard. The plaintiff
therefore recovered nothing.

8.   The statutory duty may be absolute, or to take reasonable care, depending
on the construction of the statute. If it is absolute (ie liability is strict) then
contributory negligence is an available defence, but it will be no defence to plead

a.   Volenti non fit injuria.

b.   That the duty has been delegated to a competent person, or

c.   That reasonable care was taken.

9.   The fact that the statutory penalty is applied for the benefit of the injured
party does not exclude a remedy in tort.

In **GROVES v LORD WIMBORNE (1898)** P, a factory employee, was
injured when he caught his hand in machinery which by statute should have
been fenced. The statute provided that an employer must pay a fine for breach
of this statutory duty, and also provided that the fine may be applied for the

benefit of the injured party. P therefore received "double compensation" he was awarded damages in tort for breach of statutory duty (he did not, of course, have to prove fault only that the statute had been broken and that he had been injured) and he had the fine imposed by the criminal law given to him.

PRODUCT LIABILITY
THE CONSUMER PROTECTION ACT 1987

10. Introduction

a.   Consumer groups have argued for some time that the law governing civil liability for damage due to defective goods is unfair. For a consumer to sue a manufacturer he must either proceed via a chain of contractual actions (possibly being defeated by an exemption clause) or he must sue for negligence and prove fault. This means that the law often fails to regulate the conduct of those responsible for the damage.

b.   Industrial groups have opposed strict product liability on the ground that insurance would be prohibitively expensive and some smaller businesses could be forced to close.

c.   After many years of deliberation the EC issued a directive on product liability in July 1985. This has been implemented in the *CONSUMER PROTECTION ACT 1987*. The Act has 3 main parts dealing with product liability, consumer safety and misleading price indications. Only Part I on product liability is discussed here.

11. Basic Rule *(S.2)*

a.   Where damage is caused wholly or partly by a defect in a product a producer or importer shall be liable for the damage.

b.   A supplier will also be liable if he fails to identify the producer or importer when requested to do so.

c.   The effect of this section is that in future liability will no longer be decided by reference to the fault of the manufacturer or some other person, but by reference to the state of the product in question.

d.   A 'product' must be moveable and industrially produced, eg. cars are products, buildings are not. Products of the soil, stock farming and fishing are not products unless subjected to industrial process, eg. potatoes are not, but potato crisps are products.

12. The Meaning of "Defect"

a.   There are 3 types of product defect:-

i.   A *manufacturing defect* occurs when a product fails to comply with the manufacturer's product specifications and consequently deviates from the norm. The frequency of such defects can be calculated fairly accurately and the producer will be able to spread the risk via insurance and pricing.

ii.   A *design defect* occurs when the product specifications are themselves at fault and present a hazard. This type of defect is far more serious and has led to major claims for compensation, particularly in defective drug cases, for example the Thalidomide case.

iii.   A *duty to warn defect* refers to the producer's responsibility to provide appropriate warnings and instructions to enable the consumer to use the product safely.

b.   *S.3* lays down the criteria for judging defectiveness. There is a defect in a product if the safety of the product is not such as persons generally are entitled to expect, taking all circumstances into account, including:-

i.   The presentation of the product, including instructions and warnings.

ii.   The use to which it could reasonably be expected to be put.

iii.   The time when the product was supplied.

c.   The above test is satisfactory in respect of manufacturing and duty to warn defects, but it is less appropriate for design defects. This is because it is based on consumer expectations and consumers will not know what to expect because they will not usually know how safe it is possible to make the product.

d.   The omission of "reasonably" from the phrase "entitled to expect" suggests a stricter standard than that normally applied in tort. However reasonableness is retained in the factors that the court must take into account.

13.   Defences *(S.4)*

a.   Any person has a defence if he can show:-

i.   That the defect is attributable to compliance with any enactment.

ii.   That he did not at any time supply the product.

iii.   That the supply was otherwise than in the course of a business.

iv.   That the defect did not exist in the product at the time of supply.

v.   That the state of scientific and technical knowledge at the relevant time was not such that the producer might be expected to have discovered the defect.

vi.   That the defect constituted a defect in a product in which the product in question had been comprised and was wholly attributable to the design of the subsequent product.

vii.   More than 10 years has elapsed since the product was first supplied.

b.   The most important defence is v. above, since it directly challenges the basic concept of strict liability for product defects. It is known as the *"state of the art"* defence. It is particularly significant in the area of drugs where new products are constantly being developed on the boundaries of medical and scientific knowledge. A defect in a new drug could affect thousands of users but they would not be compensated if the defect was unknowable at the time of the product's circulation.

c.   The impact of the "state of the art" defence will depend on the attitude of the courts. There are two possible approaches:-

i.   The stricter approach is based on the assumption that the producer will be aware of all the available information and technology relating to his product at any given time. There will be two issues for the court. Firstly was the knowledge available? Secondly whether the producer applied the knowledge.

ii.   The second approach pays more regard to the practicalities of the situation and would allow the producer to escape liability if the product was as safe as possible bearing in mind cost, utility, consumer expectations, the availability of safe alternatives and so on. Thus a producer would not be expected to make a product safe if to do so would be prohibitively expensive or if it would reduce the product's utility.

14. Conclusion

Defectiveness will in future be the most important factor in product liability. However design defects will be difficult to prove (although res ipsa loquitur may help) especially in view of the "state of the art" defence. Critics therefore claim that the Act is a very weak end product for nearly 10 years deliberation.

28 Nuisance

PRIVATE NUISANCE

1. A private nuisance is an unlawful interference with the use or enjoyment of another person's land. It will not usually be an unlawful activity. The interference may consist of:-

    a. Actual injury to property, for example fumes killing shrubs, or roots undermining a wall.

    b. Interference with health or comfort, for example noise, smoke, or smell.

    c. Interference with easements or natural rights.

2. Whatever the type of harm it does not follow that any harm constitutes a nuisance. Regard must be had to the rule of "give and take" between neighbours. It may therefore be relevant to consider:-

    a. How far the act complained of is unusual or excessive.

    In **FARRAR v NELSON (1885)** D bred and kept pheasants on his land. Had he kept only a reasonable number the inconvenience caused to his neighbour would not have constituted a nuisance. D however kept an excessive amount of pheasants and this was held to amount to a nuisance.

    d. Duration. − The longer the duration of an interference the more likely it is to be a nuisance. An isolated act cannot be a private nuisance.

    In **BOLTON v STONE (1951)** D hit a cricket ball out of the ground hitting P. The evidence was that on only about 8 occasions had balls been struck out of the ground in 35 years. P sued in negligence and nuisance.

    P's negligence action failed because she was not owed a duty of care. Injury to passers by was only foreseeable as a remote possibility, it was not reasonably foreseeable.

    It was held not to be a nuisance because it was an isolated act. A private nuisance must be a continuing state of affairs.

    c. The defendant's intention. − An act that would not otherwise the actionable may become a tort if it is done with intention to injure or annoy as in **HOLLYWOOD SILVER FOX FARM v EMMETT (1936)** (Chap 23.5).

    d. The character of the neighbourhood. − A person in a town cannot expect silence and clean air. Thus the standard of comfort protected by the law varies from place to place. However the character of the neighbourhood is only relevant where the interference is to health and comfort and not where actual damage to property is caused. If actual damage is caused it is a nuisance regardless of the neighbourhood.

    e. Sensitivity. − The law gives no special protection to abnormally sensitive persons or property. Thus no remedy lies if sensitivity is the sole reason for the damage.

In **ROBINSON v KILVERT (1889)** Heat which rose from D's flat damaged exceptionally sensitive paper stored by P in the above flat. There was no suggestion that the heat was excessive. P did not receive compensation because the paper was only damaged because it was very sensitive.

f.   The defendant's lack of care.

i.   If lack of care allows an annoyance to become excessive the defendant may be liable.

In **ANDRAE v SELFRIDGE (1938)** P, a hotel owner, recovered damages from D, who was demolishing the adjoining premises. Although building and demolition do not usually constitute a nuisance, since they are socially desirable, if the amount of noise and dust created is unnecessarily great, as in this case, a nuisance will be committed.

ii.   If a landowner's lack of care allows his land to encroach upon his neighbour's land he may be liable in either nuisance or negligence.

In **LEAKEY v NATIONAL TRUST (1980)** soil and tree stumps had fallen onto P's land from a natural mound on D's land, the movement being caused by natural subsidence due to weather and soil conditions. It was held that an occupier of land owes a general duty of care to neighbouring occupiers to take reasonable steps to prevent the natural or non-natural state of the land from causing damage to neighbours. In such cases it does not matter whether the action is brought in negligence or nuisance. It was suggested by D that the rule in Rylands v Fletcher indicated that there was no liability for the natural state of the land. It was however held that although liability under Rylands v Fletcher is restricted to non-natural use of the land it does not exclude or deny liability for natural hazards.

3.   **Persons Who Can Sue**

a.   Since the interference must be with the enjoyment or use of land it follows that the only person who can usually sue is the occupier of the land, not his lodger, guest or wife.

In **MALONE v LASKEY (1907)** M occupied a house which was leased by D to his (M's) employers. M's wife (the plaintiff) was injured when a lavatory cistern fell on her due to being loosened by vibrations from D's electric generator which was in adjoining premises. P's nuisance claim failed since she was not D's tenant, and in nuisance it is the tenant who must sue and no other persons on the premises.

b.   A reversioner can also sue if there is a permanent injury to his interest in the property. (A reversioner is an owner of freehold property who has granted a lease. His interest is called the freehold reversion. He may also be called a lessor or landlord.)

4. Persons Who Can be Sued

a. The person who created the nuisance may be sued even if he has vacated the land.

b. The person in possession may be sued unless:-

    i. The nuisance was caused by an independent contractor, *except* where the work necessitated special precautions by the occupier.

    In **BOWER v PEATE (1876)** P and D owned adjoining houses, each having a right of support from the other. D hired an independent contractor to pull down and rebuild his house, and the contractor undertook to support P's house while the work was in progress. The contractor was however negligent, and P's house was damaged. D was held liable because the duty to support his neighbour's house could not be delegated by D. – If D wished to work on his house then he must himself accept the risk of damage to P's house. (The nuisance in this case was the interference with an easement, ie the right of support that each could expect from his neighbour.)

    ii. The nuisance was caused by a trespasser, or

    iii. The nuisance existed before the occupier acquired the property, except where the occupier failed to take reasonable steps to abate it.

c. An occupier will be liable for a nuisance committed by a trespasser if he adopts the nuisance.

    In **SEDLEIGH-DENFIELD v O'CALLAGHAN (1940)** A trespasser (the county council) entered D's land and laid a drainage pipe in a ditch. The council protected the end of the pipe with grating so that it would not get blocked with leaves. The grating was unsatisfactory and every few months one of D's employees used to un-block the grating. On one occasion a blockage caused the flooding of P's land (which adjoined D's land). Usually proof that a nuisance was caused by a trespasser is a defence. However in this case D had, on finding out about the nuisance, acquiesced in its presence and continued it himself. He was therefore held liable.

    In **PAGE MOTORS v EPSOM BOROUGH COUNCIL (1980)** D leased P land for use as a car showroom and garage. At the start of the lease there were a few gypsies on D's adjoining land, but the number rapidly increased. D had a statutory duty to provide adequate sites for gypsies in the area, but they did not do so. P alleged that the gypsies were a nuisance – there was smell from bonfires, uncontrolled dogs, obstruction of access and customers and suppliers had become reluctant to visit the garage. Eventually, over 3 years after the lease was granted, sites were established and the gypsies left the area. It was held that although D had not caused the nuisance they had allowed it to continue for far too long and were liable for any loss suffered by P. The judge appreciated that the council had difficulties because of the lack of alternative sites and pressure from the

Department of the Environment not to move gypsies needlessly. However he pointed out that his decision was just in that it had the effect of sharing the burden of a local problem among the whole community on whose behalf the council was acting rather than allowing it to fall on one individual.

d.   A landlord out of possession is not liable, unless he permits his tenant to commit the nuisance.

5.   Defences

a.   Volenti non fit injuria.

b.   Absolute statutory authority.

c.   The nuisance was caused by a stranger and the defendant could not possibly have known of it.

d.   Long use, ie 20 years, provided the nuisance is capable of forming the subject matter of an easement.

e.   It may be a defence to establish that commission of a nuisance is in the public interest. There are however two conflicting Court of Appeal cases on this point.

In **MILLER v JACKSON (1977)** a majority of the Court of Appeal (Geoffrey − Lane and Cumming − Bruce L.JJ.) held that a cricket club were guilty of negligence and nuisance in allowing cricket balls to be struck out of the ground into P's adjoining premises, but a different majority (Lord Denning M.R. and Cumming − Bruce L.J.) refused an injunction and awarded damages on the basis that the greater interest of the public in being able to play cricket on a ground where it had been played for over 70 years should prevail over the hardship of a few individual householders, who had recently purchased their houses, and were deprived of the use of their gardens while the game was in progress.

Contrast **KENNAWAY v THOMPSON (1980)** where the nuisance complained of was noise from motor boat racing and water-skiing. The Court of Appeal held that a nuisance existed and they granted an injunction which limited the number of days on which large scale activities could take place and limited the noise level on other occasions. They refused to follow Miller v Jackson, feeling that it was wrong to allow a nuisance to continue merely because the wrongdoer is willing and able to pay for any injury he may inflict. The court felt that the two reasons for refusing to grant an injunction in Miller v Jackson (i. the public interest and ii. that the plaintiff "came to the nuisance") were contrary to earlier authority and were not binding on the court.

6.   Ineffective Defences

a.   That the plaintiff came to the nuisance.

In **STURGES v BRIDGEMAN (1879)** D had for many years been manufacturing sweets in premises adjoining P's garden. P, a doctor, then built a consulting room that adjoined the manufacturing premises. He then sued D in nuisance, due to the noise and vibrations caused by D's machinery. D's defence was in effect ''I was here first''. However this defence is ineffective, and particularly in view of the area (Wimpole Street) the noise and vibrations were held to constitute a nuisance. D also claimed that he had acquired a right to commit the nuisance through long use. It was held that this was not possible – any right acquired through long use (20 years) must be capable of forming the subject matter of an easement.

b.   That reasonable care has been taken.

In **RAPIER v LONDON TRAMWAYS (1893)** D kept about 200 horses in stables adjoining the P's land. Although D took reasonable measures to minimise any nuisance a certain amount of noise and smell was caused by the horses. D were held liable in nuisance – it was no defence to say that they had done everything possible to prevent it.

c.   That the defendant's conduct would not have amounted to a nuisance had it not been for the contributory acts of others.

7.   Abatement of Nuisances. In addition to the usual remedies of damages and/or an injunction the law will sometimes allow the remedy of abatement, ie removal of the nuisance.

a.   If there are two ways of abating a nuisance the less mischievous must be selected.

b.   Entry onto the land of a third party is not permissible.

c.   Notice should be given to the occupier of the land in which the nuisance arises except:-

   i.   Where abatement is possible without entry, or

   ii.   In cases of emergency, such as a fire.

d.   Abatement allows a person to cut off the branches of his neighbour's trees which overhang his land.

e.   Abatement is also applicable to public nuisance.

PUBLIC NUISANCE

8.   A public nuisance is an unlawful act or omission which endangers the health, safety, or comfort of the public (or some section of it) or obstructs the exercise of a common right, for example selling contaminated food, or obstructing a highway.

9.   It differs from private nuisance in that:-

a.   It is a crime as well as a tort.

b.   An isolated act may be a public nuisance.

c.   It need not involve an interference with the use of enjoyment of land.

d.   Several people at least must be affected.

In **R v MADDON (1975)** D dialled 999 and informed the telephonist that there was a 200 lb bomb at the local steel works. The call was a hoax and D was charged with the offence of commiting a public nuisance. The only people who knew of the call and its contents were the telephonist, eight security guards, and the police − who conducted an hour long search until the hoax was discovered. It was held that the offence of public nuisance had not been committed since not enough people were affected.

e.   A right to commit a public nuisance cannot be acquired by long use.

10. Potentially the same people may sue and be sued as in private nuisance, except that a private individual may only sue if he has suffered some special damage different from that suffered by the class of persons affected.

In **CAMPBELL v PADDINGTON CORPORATION (1911)** The Council erected a stand in Burwood Place, London so that council members could view King Edward VII's funeral procession. P owned a flat in Burwood Place which she often let for the purpose of viewing public processions. The Council's stand obstructed this view, so that she could not let her flat. Since the stand was a public nuisance, and since she had suffered special damage in excess of that suffered by the public at large, she was successful in her action against the Council.

11. If the same act is both a public and private nuisance the right of a private individual to sue for private nuisance is not affected.

12. Highway Nuisances. Common examples of public nuisances are obstructions on highways or dangerous premises adjoining the highway. Principles of "give and take" also apply to public nuisance. Thus a temporary obstruction, if reasonable in its size and duration, may be permissible. However:-

a.   Liability is strict for the collapse of an artificial projection over the highway, for example a lamp. If the projection is natural the occupier will be liable only if he knew or ought to have known of the danger.

In **NOBLE v HARRISON (1926)** The branch of a tree on D's land that overhung the highway suddenly fell and damaged a passing coach. The owner of the land was not held liable, because a reasonable examination would not have revealed the tree's defect.

b.   If something projects above the highway this will not constitute a public nuisance if no obstruction is caused.

c.   If a local authority allows a highway to become dangerous it may be liable unless it can be shown that reasonable care has been taken having regard to various matters such as the expected volume of traffic, and the standard of maintenance appropriate to such a highway.

13. Remedies

a. Criminal aspect. − A prosecution, or an application for an injunction by the Attorney General.

b. Civil aspect. − An application for an injunction and/or damages by the person suffering loss.

29 Trespass and Conversion

TRESPASS TO THE PERSON

1.   Definition. A trespass to the person is an intentional interference with the person or liberty of another. It was formerly thought that an action for trespass to the person could be brought where personal injuries were caused negligently though directly. However since **LETANG v COOPER (1965)** it has been clear that the phrase "trespass to the person" is restricted to intentional acts. Where an unintentional act causes physical injury the correct action is negligence. Trespass to the person is actionable per se (without proof of loss) unless the defendant establishes that his act was justified. It may take three forms — assault, battery and false imprisonment.

2.   Assault

a.   An assault is an act of the defendant which causes the plaintiff reasonable fear of an immediate battery on him by the defendant.

b.   Words are no assault, but they may prevent the act that they accompany from being an assault.

In **TUBERVELL v SAVAGE (1669)** during an argument D brandished his sword saying, "If it were not assize time I would not take such language from you".

However since it was assize time, (ie the local criminal courts were in session), these words prevented the brandishing of the sword from being an assault.

c.   It has been suggested that if a person rounds a corner and is confronted by a motionless gunman, the gunman may commit an assault if he does not move the gun barrel away from the other person. However it is generally accepted that some movement is necessary to commit an assault.

In **INNES v WYLIE (1844)** A policeman stood motionless in order to block a doorway. This was held not to be an assault.

3.   Battery

a.   Battery is the intentional application of force to another person. The amount of harm inflicted is relevant to the amount of damages awarded, but not to the determination of liability.

b.   It is a battery to throw something, eg water, at the plaintiff so that it hits him; or to remove a chair from under him; or to set a dog on him; or to drag him away from something for his own good.

c.   Consent is a defence to battery, but the defence will not apply if the defendant does some act which was not contemplated by the plaintiff.

In **NASH v SHEEN (1953)** P went to the hairdresser for a permanent wave, but was instead given a tone-rinse which changed the colour of her hair and caused a rash over the rest of her body. The hairdresser was held to have committed a battery.

d.   It is not a battery to touch a person to attract his attention.

4.   False Imprisonment

a.   This is the infliction of bodily restraint not authorised by law.

b.   The restraint must be total.

In **BIRD v JONES (1845)** D closed off the public footpath over one side of Hammersmith Bridge, and charged people admission to his enclosure to watch the Boat Race. P climbed into the enclosure from one side, and was prevented from leaving from the other side. He was however told that he could go out the same way that he came in. It was held that there was no false imprisonment since the restraint was not total.

c.   The plaintiff need not know that he is being detained.

In **MEERING v GRAHAME – WHITE AVIATION CO. (1919)** P was suspected of thefts from his employers, although he did not know that he was a suspect. When he was asked to answer some questions concerning the thefts he voluntarily agreed – he still did not realise that he was a suspect. He later found out that while he was being questioned there were two of the works security guards outside the door who would have prevented him leaving if he had attempted to do so. He succeeded in his false imprisonment action, not on the grounds of his discomfort, but because of the injury to his reputation caused by his employer's action.

d.   It is no tort to refuse to allow a person to leave premises when he does not fulfil a reasonable condition subject to which he entered them.

In **ROBINSON v BALMAIN NEW FERRY CO. (1910)** The terms of a contract to travel on a ferry provided that the passenger must pay one penny on entering the wharf and a further penny on leaving. P paid his penny to enter, but just missed the ferry. He attempted to leave without paying another penny, but was restrained from doing so until he had paid. He failed in his false imprisonment action. The court said there was no duty on a person to make exit from his premises gratuitous, where a person had entered on the basis of a definite contract which involved their leaving in another way.

e.   In addition to the usual remedy of damages the remedies of self help, (ie breaking out), and an application for a writ of habeas corpus are available. Habeas corpus is a prerogative writ designed to provide a person, who is kept in confinement without legal justification, with a means of obtaining release. An application may be made, for example, by the parents of a child who is being kept in an institution against their wishes.

5.   Justification of Trespass to the Person:-

a.   Defence of person or property. Reasonable force may also be used

223

to remove a trespasser.

b.   Parental authority. Reasonable and moderate punishment may be administered.

c.   Lawful arrest. A person arrested without warrant must be told of the reason for the arrest, and taken to a magistrate or police station as soon as possible.

d.   Judicial authority.

e.   Necessity.

In **LEIGH v GLADSTONE (1909)** P, who was on hunger strike in prison was forcibly fed by warders in order to save her life. The defence of necessity was successfully raised against her action for battery.

f.   Inevitable accident. (See **STANLEY v POWELL (1891)** Chapter 24.11).

TRESPASS TO LAND

6.   Trespass to land is the *direct interference* with the *possession* of another person's land without lawful authority. It is a tort actionable per se.

7.   Possession. − Since trespass is a wrong done to the possessor only he rather than the owner can sue. Possession includes not only physical occupation, but occupation through servants and agents. Mere use, for example as a lodger, is not possession.

8.   Interference

a.   This must be direct, either by

i.   Entering on land, or

ii.   Remaining on land after permission to stay has ended. An exception is a lessee, who if he remains at the end of his lease retains possession and therefore does not become a trespasser.

iii.   Placing objects on land.

b.   If a right to enter is abused this may be a trespass.

In **HARRISON v THE DUKE OF RUTLAND (1893)** the Duke owned a grouse moor. A road led across this moor which he allowed the public to use. P however abused this right of entry by deliberately frightening the grouse just as the Duke and his party were about to shoot. P was physically restrained by members of the shooting party and he brought an action for false imprisonment. His action failed because proportionate and reasonable force may be used to restrain or eject a trespasser and P, because he had abused his right of entry, was a trespasser.

c.   Entry below the surface is a trespass, as is entry into airspace, if it takes place within the area of ordinary use.

In **KELSEN v IMPERIAL TOBACCO CO. (1957)** P and D occupied adjoining premises, D however occupied a taller building than P. D attached an advertising sign to their wall which projected a few inches into the airspace about P's premises. P was successful in obtaining a court order compelling D to remove the sign since it was a trespass.

d. *S.40. CIVIL AVIATION ACT 1949* exempts civil aircraft flying at a reasonable height from liability for trespass, but it imposes strict liability on the owner of the aircraft for all damage caused by things falling from it.

e. If a person enters in exercise of a common law or statutory right and abuses the right by a positive act he is deemed to be a trespasser from the moment he entered the premises, ie a trespass ab initio (from the beginning).

In **THE SIX CARPENTERS CASE (1610)** six carpenters entered a public house and consumed a quantity of wine and bread. They then refused to pay the price. They were not held to be trespassers ab initio since their act was a non-feasance (an omission) and not a misfeasance.

9. Defences

a. The general defences of volenti, necessity, inevitable accident, self defence and statutory authority all apply, but mistake is no defence.

b. Entry to exercise a common law right. For example A enters B's land to re-possess his goods that B has wrongfully taken onto his land.

c. Entry by licence. For example theatre guests. When the licence expires the person becomes a trespasser when he does not leave, in contrast to a lessee who remains in possession.

d. Jus tertii. − There is a rule which states that a person claiming land from another who is in possession of it can succeed only by showing a stronger title than the person in possession. If the land rightfully belongs to neither of them, but to a third party, the person in possession will have the defence of jus tertii.

In **DOE d. CARTER v BARNARD (1849)** P was wrongfully turned off certain land by D. In her action to recover possession it became evident that neither P nor D were entitled to the land. P's action to recover the land therefore failed since she could not show a better title than D. D could therefore claim the defence of jus tertii.

10. Remedies.

The remedies available to the plaintiff depend on whether or not he is in possession of the land. If an owner has been wrongfully dispossessed he cannot sue for trespass since he is not in possession.

a. Remedies available to the person in possession:-

  i. Damages, nominal or compensatory.

  ii. Injunction.

  iii. Ejection of the trespasser. Reasonable and proportionate force may be used. (ie Proportionate to the amount of force that the trespasser is using to prevent ejection).

b.   Remedies available to an owner who has been wrongfully dispossessed:-

i.   Re-entry, however the re-entry must be peaceful.

In **HEMMINGS v STOKE POGES GOLF CLUB (1920)** P refused to leave his cottage when his tenancy had been lawfully ended by notice to quit. The landlords, using reasonable force, removed P and his furniture and re-entered the premises. It was held that they were entitled to do this. (The law regarding tenants has now been changed so that it is illegal to remove a tenant without first obtaining a court order. Reasonable force may however be used to remove a licencee remaining on premises after the termination of his licence.)

ii.   An action for the recovery of land. The limitation period for this remedy is 12 years.

iii.   Having recovered possession as above, such person is deemed by the doctrine of Possession by Relation to have been in possession since the moment his right to possession accrued. He can therefore maintain an action for mesne profits, ie profits lost to the plaintiff while the defendant was wrongfully in possession.

TRESPASS TO GOODS

11. A trespass to goods is the direct interference with the possession of goods. The interference must be direct and not consequential, although in some cases physical contact is not necessary, for example to chase cattle is a trespass to goods. Generally the interference will take one of 3 forms:-

a.   Taking the goods,

b.   Damaging goods, or altering their physical condition,

c.   Interfering with goods, for example moving them about.

12. Only persons in possession (ie having immediate physical control) can sue. Some persons not in actual possession are deemed to have possession for this purpose. For example a master who has given custody of his goods to his servant, or the personal representative of a deceased person, is deemed to be in possession.

13. Of the available defences three deserve special mention:-

a.   Inevitable accident

In **NATIONAL COAL BOARD v EVANS (1951)** in the course of excavating the foundations of a building D damaged a cable belonging to the NCB. It was held that since the presence of the cable was unforeseeable D was not liable, having the defence of inevitable accident.

b.   Reasonable defence of person or property. For example injuring a dog which is attacking somebody.

226

c. Pursuance of a legal right or legal process. For example levying distress for rent.

CONVERSION

14. Definition

Conversion is some dealing by the defendant in relation to the plaintiff's goods which is a denial of the plaintiff's right to possess and use those goods. It is the main method by which rights in personal property are protected.

15. The Wrongful Act

a. The defendant may be liable in conversion even if he never possessed the goods provided his dealing constituted an unjustifiable denial of title.

In **VAN OPPEN v TREDEGARS (1921)** P delivered goods by mistake to a firm. D purported to sell the goods to the firm. The firm disposed of the goods in the course of their business. D was held liable.

b. The defendant will not be liable if he merely moves goods without any denial of title.

In **FOULDES v WILLOUGHBY (1841)** D moved P's horses from D's ferry, hoping that this would also induce P to leave. P remained and was ferried across the river. It was held that there is no conversion since there had been no denial of P's title to the horses.

c. The usual form of conversion is an abuse of existing possession by for example:-

i.   Destroying goods;

ii. Altering their nature;

iii. Wrongfully refusing to return them;

iv. Selling and delivering them to the third party, even if the defendant dealt innocently with the goods. (Note the exceptions in *S22, 24 and 25 SALE OF GOODS ACT 1979* (Chapter 33)).

In **HOLLINS v FOWLER (1875)** D, a broker, sold and delivered cotton belonging to P. He was acting on behalf of a crook although he did not know this at the time. He was held liable in conversion because he had sold and delivered goods in denial of P's title.

d. Involuntary receipt of goods is not conversion, although the recipient must not willfully damage or destroy them unless they become a nuisance. However a person who receives unsolicited goods will be entitled to deal with them as if they were a gift if the sender fails to take them back within six months, or at some earlier date if the recipient gives notice to the sender *(UNSOLICITED GOODS AND SERVICES ACT 1971)*.

e. Conversion may arise in situations where a seller of goods includes a term in his contract reserving title until payment.

227

In **CLOUGH MILL v MARTIN (1985)** a contract for the sale of yarn had a reservation of title clause stating that the ownership of the yarn remained with the seller until the seller had received payment in full, or the yarn was sold by the buyer in a bona fide sale at full market value. When a receiver was appointed the seller claimed a quantity of the yarn. The receiver refused to return it. The seller's claim was upheld and the receiver was held personally liable in conversion.

16. The Plaintiff's Rights

a.   At the time of the conversion the plaintiff must have been in possession of the goods, or have had a right to immediate possession.

b.   Where the plaintiff has been deprived permanently of the goods the measure of damages is their market value at the time of the conversion unless:-

i.   The defendant has the goods and refuses to deliver them, in which case it is their value at the time of refusal;

ii.   The value has increased since the date of the conversion, in which case the measure may be the value at the date of judgement (provided the plaintiff sues promptly).

30 Defamation

1. A defamatory statement is a false statement that tends to injure the plaintiff's reputation, or causes him to be shunned by ordinary members of society. There are two forms of defamation namely libel and slander.

2. Distinctions Between Libel and Slander

a. A defamatory statement is libel if it is in permanent form, or if it is for general reception. For example writing, pictures, films, radio, television, the theatre, records, or waxworks. If the statement lacks permanence it will be slander. For example spoken words or gestures.

b. Libel is a crime as well as a tort, whereas slander is only a tort.

c. Libel is actionable per se, slander is not unless:-

   i. It imputes a crime punishable by imprisonment.

   ii. It imputes certain existing diseases, such as venereal disease or aids.

   iii. It imputes unchastity, adultery, or lesbianism in a woman.

   iv. It is calculated to damage the plaintiff in any office, trade, or profession held or carried on by him.

3. If the plaintiff is to succeed in a defamation action he must show three things

   a. That the statement is defamatory;

   b. That it refers to the plaintiff;

   c. That it has been published by the defendant.

In addition to the above requirements in most cases of slander (ie where it is not actionable per se) the plaintiff must prove damage. ie Material loss capable of monetary evaluation, such as loss of employment, and not mere loss of friends or reputation.

Each of the 3 main requirements is now considered in turn.

4. The Meaning of "Defamatory"

a. A useful guide was laid down by Lord Atkin in **SIM v STRETCH (1936)**. He said

"Would the words tend to lower the plaintiff in the estimation of right thinking members of society generally".

In **SIM v STRETCH (1936)** a housemaid left P's employment, and went to work for D, for whom she had worked in the past. D then sent P the following telegram.

"Edith has resumed her services with us today. Please send her possessions and the money you borrowed, also her wages".

P alleged this telegram was defamatory in that it implied he was in financial trouble, having to borrow off a housemaid, and not having paid her wages. The House of Lords held that the telegram was not defamatory, since if a statement has a number of good interpretations, it is unreasonable to seize upon a bad one to give a defamatory sense to the statement.

b.   A statement would satisfy Lord Atkin's test if it

i.   Reflects on a person's trading or professional ability.

ii.   Imputes dishonesty, criminality or immorality.

iii.   Imputes insanity, certain diseases, or that the plaintiff has been raped.

In **YOUSSOUPOFF v M.G.M. PICTURES LTD. (1934)** M.G.M. made a film about the life of Rasputin. In the film Rasputin was represented as having raped a Princess Natasha. In the film Princess Natasha was also represented as being in love with the man who was eventually to murder Rasputin.

In real life the plaintiff, a Russian Princess (whose name was not Natasha) was married to a man who was undoubtedly concerned with the murder of the real-life Rasputin. P alleged that because of her marriage reasonable people would think it was she who had been raped. P succeeded in her libel action.

It appears rather illogical that it is defamatory to accuse a person of something, which if it had happened, would have been actively resisted by that person, for example rape, or the catching of certain diseases. It does however probably reflect the reality of life in that so called "reasonable people" may in fact shun a person who has been raped or who is ill.

c.   A statement is not defamatory if the plaintiff's reputation suffers in the eyes of only a section of the community in circumstances where the majority of the community would approve of his action.

In **BYRNE v DEANE (1937)** D was the proprietor of a golf club and P was a member. There were some illegal gaming machines in the clubhouse, P informed the police of this and the machines had to be removed. A few days later a poem appeared on the wall near where the machines had been. The poem referred to the machines and ended as follows:-

"But he who gave the game away,
May he Byrne in hell and rue the day".

P alleged that this was defamatory, in that it showed that he was disloyal to his fellow members. It was held that the words were not defamatory because "right-thinking members of society" would not think less of a person who upheld the law. It was not sufficient that he was shunned by the members of the golf-club.

d.   A problem may arise if the words used are not prima facie defamatory. In this case an innuendo is required if the plaintiff is to succeed. An

230

innuendo is a statement by the plaintiff of the meaning that he attributes to the words.

In **TOLLEY v J.S. FRY AND SONS LTD (1931)** D, a chocolate manufacturer, published an advertisement showing a picture of P, and a poem including P's name and D's name. P was a well known amateur golfer and he had not given his consent for his name and picture to be used in this way. The picture and poem were not by themselves defamatory. However P brought a libel action alleging an innuendo. He alleged that reasonable people would think that he had been paid for the use of his name and that he therefore was not a genuine amateur golfer. It was held that this was a reasonable inference. He succeeded in his libel action.

In **CASSIDY v DAILY MIRROR (1929)** D published a picture of Cassidy and a young woman with a statement that their engagement had been announced. This information was given to the paper by Cassidy himself. Cassidy was however already married and his wife brought a libel action claiming that the photograph and statement contained an innuendo to those who knew her that she was not married to her husband, and was accordingly "living in sin" with him. The evidence was that some people who knew her were given this impression. She therefore succeeded in her action. Note that:

    i.   The young woman would probably have succeeded if she had brought an action. The innuendo would have been that she was the type of person who went out with married men. This would have been the thoughts of people who knew Cassidy was already married.

    ii.   If the case had occurred after 1952 the paper may have been able to succeed in the defence of unintentional defamation. (See below)

e.   The statement must also be false. The legal presumption is that it is false. Thus the defendant has to prove its truth, rather than the plaintiff its falseness.

5. Reference to the Plaintiff

a.   The plaintiff need not necessarily be named.

In **J'ANSON v STUART (1789)** A newspaper, speaking of a swindler (without naming him) described him as follows: "He has but one eye, and is well known to all persons acquainted with the name of a certain noble circumnavigator".

The plaintiff was able to succeed in his defamation action because he only had one eye and a name similar to that of a famous admiral.

b.   Except where a plea of unintentional defamation succeeds, it is no defence to say:-

    i.   That the defendant did not intend to refer to the plaintiff.

In **HULTON v JONES (1910)** A humorous newspaper article described the immoral life of a fictitious churchwarden from Peckham called Artemus Jones. There existed however a real Artemus Jones, who was a barrister. The evidence was that the people who knew him thought the article referred to him. Artemus Jones was awarded damages of £1,750.

ii. That the words were intended to refer to a third person of whom they were true.

In **NEWSTEAD v LONDON EXPRESS (1939)** the newspaper published a statement that Harold Newstead a thirty-year old Camberwell man had been convicted of bigamy. Unfortunately there were two thirty-year-old Harold Newstead's in Camberwell, and whilst the statement was true in respect of one of them it was untrue of the other. The Harold Newstead who had not been convicted of bigamy therefore recovered damages.

6. Publication by the Defendant. The plaintiff must prove that the statement was published ie communicated to at least one person other than himself. However:-

a. A person is not liable if publication occurs only as a result of an act which is not reasonably foreseeable by him, for example, a letter being opened by the plaintiff's butler. (It is however reasonably foreseeable that a letter will be opened by the plaintiff's wife).

b. Two or more persons may be responsible for the same publication, for example, the author, printer, publisher, and bookseller. The bookseller will have a defence if he did not know of the libel and could not be expected to know of it.

7. Defences

a. *Justification.* The defence of justification is available if the statement is true in substance. Small inaccuracies do not defeat this defence.

In **ALEXANDER v N.E. RAILWAY CO. (1865)** P had been convicted of failing to pay his rail fare. The railway published a poster stating that his sentence was a fine or three weeks imprisonment. In fact the alternative was two weeks imprisonment. It was held that this small inaccuracy did not defeat the defence of justification.

Note that:-

i. A defendant can plead inconsistent defences. For example if an innuendo is alleged, the defendant could plead firstly that there is no possible innuendo, and secondly that if there is then it represents the truth.

ii. If, for example, A says, "B said C is a thief". Then to succeed in the defence of justification he must prove that C is a thief, and not just that B said C is a thief.

iii. An honest belief that the statement is true is no justification.

iv. By *S.5. DEFAMATION ACT 1952* where the words complained of contain two or more distinct charges against the plaintiff the defence does not fail merely because the truth of each charge is not proved if the charge not proved to be true does not materially injure the plaintiff's reputation having regard to the true charges. For example if A calls B "a thief and a murderer" and B is a murderer, but not a thief, B would be unlikely to succeed in a defamation action against A since a murderer's reputation can hardly be lowered by being called a thief, albeit incorrectly.

b. *Fair comment.* This defence will apply where the statement is a fair comment made in good faith on a matter of public interest. Note that:-

i.   The subject matter must be of public interest, for example the conduct of politicians, or crime reporting.

ii. The statement must be opinion not fact.

iii. The comment must be based on facts which, if stated with the comment, must be true.

iv. The comment must be fair, ie an honest expression of the defendant's opinion. It cannot therefore be motivated by malice.

v.   An example of fair comment would be "Mr X raped Miss C — he is a disgrace to the community". The second part of the quotation is a comment on the first, it is also opinion. Since crime is a public interest, if Mr X did rape Miss C the defence would be available to the maker of the statement.

c. *Absolute privilege.* No action lies for defamation, however false or malicious the statement, if it is made:-

i.   In Parliament;

ii. In parliamentary papers;

iii. In the course of state communications;

iv. In judicial proceedings;

v.   In newspaper reports of judicial proceedings, provided they are fair accurate and contemporaneous. "Newspaper" in this context includes weekly but not monthly publications.

d. *Qualified privilege.* The defence will be available in the following situations, provided the statement was not published more widely than necessary, and provided it was not motivated by malice:-

i.   Where A makes a statement to B about C and A is under a legal, social or moral duty to make the statement to B, and B has an interest in receiving it.

In **WATT v LONGSDON (1930)** D, a company director, received allegations of drunkenness, dishonesty, and immorality by P, who was an employee of the company. He showed these allegations to the chairman of the company and to P's wife. The communication to the chairman was held to be subject to qualified privilege since both the duty to make the statement, and an interest in receiving it were present.

233

It was held however that he had no legal, social or moral duty to communicate the allegations to P's wife. Thus in respect of the communication to her the defence of qualified privilege failed.

ii.   Where A makes a statement to B about C and A has an interest to protect and B has a duty to protect it.

In **SOMERVILLE v HAWKINS (1851)** D told two servants that he had dismissed P for robbing him. D could plead the defence of qualified privilege because he had an interest to protect, ie his own property.

iii.   For fair and accurate reports of judicial or parliamentary proceedings, whether or not they are in a newspaper, and whether or not they are contemporaneous.

iv.   For fair and accurate reports in a newspaper or broadcast on various matters, such as public meetings (*S.7. DEFAMATION ACT 1952*). The *S.7.* definition of "newspaper" includes monthly publications.

v.   For professional statements between solicitor and client.

e.   *Unintentional defamation (S.4. DEFAMATION ACT 1952)*. This defence only applies to words published innocently. ie Where:-

i.   The publisher did not intend to refer to the plaintiff, and

ii.   The words were not prima facie defamatory, and the publisher did not know of any possible innuendo, and

iii.   The publisher was not negligent.

Where the above conditions are satisfied the publisher may make an "offer of amends". ie An offer of a suitable correction and apology, and an offer to take reasonable steps to notify persons who have received copies of the alleged defamatory words. If the offer is accepted the matter is closed. If the offer is refused the publisher has a defence if he can prove:-

i.   That the words were published innocently

ii.   That the offer was made as soon as possible, and

iii.   That the author wrote them without malice.

8.   **Mitigation.** The defendant may mitigate his payment of damages by:-

a.   Apology.

b.   Proof of provocation.

c.   Evidence of the plaintiff's bad reputation prior to the publication of the defamation.

31 Remedies and Limitation Periods

REMEDIES

1. Damages. It will be clear from the previous chapters that the main remedy for the victim of a tort is an award of damages. Damages are a sum of money payable by the defendant. The defendant may however choose, or be required by law, to insure against the payment of damages. Tort damages are always unliquidated, ie they clearly cannot be fixed by prior agreement between the parties. There are 3 main types of damages:-

2. Compensatory Damages

a. Their purpose is to put the plaintiff so far as money can do, in the position that he was in before the tort was committed. This sum must take into account future loss, since usually only one action may be brought. The damages awarded will be itemised under several "heads", for example,

   i. Loss of amenity;

   ii. Pain and suffering;

   iii. Loss of expectation of life;

   iv. Loss of income.

b. The relationship between iii. and iv. has recently been reviewed by the House of Lords.

In **PICKETT v BRITISH RAIL ENGINEERING (1980)** the court held that a plaintiff, (provided he survived the tort), could recover damages for loss of income on the basis of his pre-accident life expectancy. This overrules the Court of Appeal decision in Oliver v Ashman (1962) which decided that damages for future loss of income should be awarded only for the period during which the plaintiff is expected to remain alive.

3. Nominal Damages. If a tort is actionable per se, and the plaintiff proves the elements of the tort without showing actual loss, he will be awarded a small sum of money, for example £1 in recognition of the fact that he has suffered a wrong.

4. Exemplary Damages. These are granted in rare cases, their purpose being to punish the defendant in addition to compensating the plaintiff. They may be awarded for:-

a. Oppressive acts of public officials, or

b. When the defendant's conduct has been calculated to make a profit for himself.

In **CASSELL v BROOME (1972)** D published a book, knowing that it was defamatory of P, because they thought that any damages awarded

235

to P would be less than the profits of the book. The court however awarded exemplary damages against D, awarding P more than his actual loss to ensure that D did not profit from his tort.

5. The Effect of Death on an Award of Damages

a. At common law if either the plaintiff or defendant died any right of action died with him. Since the *LAW REFORM (MISCELLANEOUS PROVISIONS) ACT 1934* rights of action now survive in favour of a deceased plaintiff and against the estate of a deceased defendant, except that:

  i. Actions for defamation do not survive, and

  ii. Exemplary damages cannot be awarded to the estate of a deceased plaintiff.

b. The above rule must be carefully distinguished from the rule in **BAKER v BOLTON (1808)** ie That the death of a human being cannot be complained of as an injury in a civil court. Thus if A, by killing B, causes loss to C, tort action is not possible by C. This rule is subject to the exceptions created by the *FATAL ACCIDENTS ACTS 1846-1976*, whereby if the deceased would have had a cause of action had he survived his personal representatives may sue on behalf of certain of his dependants. The dependants include husband and wife, parent or grandparent, child or grandchild, and any person who is, or is the child of, a brother, sister, uncle or aunt of the deceased person.

c. Two claims may be brought in respect of the same fatal accident, one under the 1934 Act and one under the Fatal Accidents Act 1976, however the dependant cannot receive double compensation. ie An award made under the 1934 Act must be taken into account when assessing the amount to be paid under the 1976 Act.

6. Injunction

a. An injunction is an equitable remedy. It may be an order of the court commanding something to be done (a *mandatory injunction*) or it may forbid the defendant from doing something (a *prohibitory injunction*). Like other equitable remedies, the award of an injunction is at the court's discretion. A recent example of the exercise of this discretion is **MILLER v JACKSON (1977)** (Chapter 28) when although the plaintiff "won" the case he was not granted the injunction that he badly wanted.

b. A valuable feature of this remedy is the power of the court to grant an *interlocutory* (until trial) *injunction*. Thus a temporary remedy may be obtained within days or even hours of the complaint arising. The matter must however be serious, and the judge must consider that there would be a high change of success for the plaintiff at a full hearing of the case.

7. Other Remedies.
Other remedies may be appropriate for particular torts, for example

a.   Abatement of nuisance;

b.   Escape from false imprisonment;

c.   Ejection of trespassers;

d.   Application for a writ of habeas corpus.

LIMITATION OF ACTIONS

8.   Time limits for action in tort are governed by the *LIMITATION ACT 1980* and the *LATENT DAMAGE ACT 1986.*

a.   An action for the recovery of land must be brought within 12 years. *(S.15. LA 1980).*

b.   An action for damages in respect of personal injury caused by negligence, nuisance, or breach of duty must be brought within 3 years *(S.11. LA 1980).*

c.   An action under the Fatal Accidents Act 1976 must be brought within 3 years *(S.12. LA 1980).*

d.   An action for a claim not involving personal injury may not be brought later than 6 years from the date on which the cause of action accrued or 3 years from when the plaintiff knew or ought to have known about the damage. There is an overriding time limit of 15 years from the date of the defendant's breach of duty.

e.   There is a special 3 year time limit in cases of libel and slander (subject to an extension of one year by the High Court *(ADMINISTRATION OF JUSTICE ACT 1985)).*

9.   The Point When Time Starts to Run

a.   Where a tort is actionable per se, time runs from the moment of the wrongful act.

b.   Where a tort is actionable only on proof of damage, time runs from the moment damage was first suffered. Problems have occurred in cases of "latent damage" ie damage which does not manifest itself until some time after the act or omission which causes it. In such cases time does not begin to run until such time as the plaintiff discovers the damage, or ought, with reasonable diligence, to have discovered it.

c.   Where a cause of action is based on or concealed by fraud, time does not begin to run until the plaintiff discovers the fraud, or could with reasonable diligence have done so.

d.   Where a tort is of a continuing nature, for example nuisance or false imprisonment, a fresh cause of action arises daily, and an action lies for such instances of the tort as lie within the statutory period.

10. Discretion to Exclude Time Limits

a. By *S.33 LA 1980* the court is given a discretion to "disapply" the time limits specified in *S.11* and *12* of the Act. In the words of Ormrod L.J. "Parliament has now decided that uncertain justice is preferable to certain injustice, in other words certainty can be brought at too high a price". When deciding whether or not to override the time limits in *S.11.* and *S.12.* the court must consider all the circumstances, for example

i.   The period of, and reasons for, the delay.

ii. The difficulties that will be suffered by witnesses when they are asked to recall facts.

iii. The conduct of the defendant after the cause of action arose, including the extent to which he responded to reasonable requests for information from the plaintiff.

b. There have been many cases in the past 10 years on what is now *S.33.*

In **BUCK v ENGLISH ELECTRIC (1978)** P contracted pneumoconiosis from work in 1959. By 1963 he was sufficiently disabled to realise that he had a cause of action. By 1973 he was so disabled that he had to give up work. He died in 1975 shortly after issuing a writ. It was held that although the action was statute barred by the delay (from 1963-1975) that discretion to override what is now *S.11.* would be exercised in favour of P. The main reason was that D would not be prejudiced because there were other similar claims against them and it was unlikely that their evidence would be less cogent.

In **WALKLEY v PRECISION FORGINGS (1979)** by virtue of a solicitor's negligence P failed to prosecute a claim under a writ issued in 1971. In 1976 a fresh writ was issued bringing the same cause of action. It was held that *S.2.* (now *S.33.*) had no application in such a case. The prejudice to P was not to the time limits imposed by the Act but was due to the negligence of the solicitors.

COURSEWORK QUESTIONS 17-24
THE LAW OF TORTS

17. *a.   What is meant by res ipsa loquitur in the law of tort?*

b.   Harry is driving his car when suddenly the brakes fail. He is unable to stop and crashes into a motorcycle ridden by Susan, damaging the motorcycle and injuring Susan. Advise Harry as to his civil liability.

18. *a.   Define public nuisance and distinguish it from private nuisance.*

b.   The noise and vibrations from the Acme Plastics Ltd's factory annoy all the residents of Park Road. One of the residents, Mr Evans, is particularly annoyed because on one occasion a piece of hot plastic waste material from one of the factory chimneys fell on to his house causing damage to the roof. Advise the residents and Mr Evans.

19. Advise Thomas whether an action for negligence is likely to succeed against each of the parties in the following cases, explaining the relevant principles of law involved.

   a. Albert, a practising accountant, upon whose advice Thomas made an investment which proved to be worthless.

   b. Bernard, a barrister, who represented Thomas in a recent case and who conducted the case badly.

   c. Charles, a car driver, whose car skidded and crossed on to the wrong side of the road where it collided with Thomas's car.

   d. David, a demolition worker, who carelessly injured a fellow worker thereby causing Thomas, who was passing at the time to suffer nervous shock.

   CIMA Foundation November 1977

20. a. What is the distinction between libel and slander, and why is it important?

   b. Mike, a radio journalist, recorded a private interview on his tape-recorder with one Quip, a prominent politician, in which Quip accused Red, a political opponent, of being a traitor to his country and that he had "sold out to the Russians". Is this statement defamatory, and if so, is it libel or slander? Would your answer be the same if Mike broadcast the interview from the radio station for which he works?

   ICSA Part 1 June 1986

21. What is meant, in the law of tort, by "strict liability" and when will such liability arise?

   ICSA Part 1 June 1980

22. Mr. Adams and Mrs. Barker are neighbours. Mr. Adams has, in the last two years, done the following things on Mrs. Barker's land without her permission:

   a. he has allowed the roots of his tree to extend into Mrs. Barker's garden, where they have undermined the foundations of Mrs. Barker's house;

   b. he has moved the boundary fence which he shares with Mrs. Barker one metre into Mrs. Barker's land;

   c. he has dug a hole in Mrs. Barker's garden, and taken soil from it for his own garden.

What torts, if any, has Mr. Adams committed?

   ICSA Part 1 December 1985

239

23.   a.   **What is meant in the law of torts by a "novus actus interveniens"?**

   b.   **Arthur is employed by A B Ltd. Because of his employer's negligence Arthur sustains a broken leg. Consider A B Ltd's liability if**
      i.   **Arthur is left with a severe limp because of an error made by the surgeon who set his leg in plaster.**
      ii.   **Arthur's workmates, believing that he has merely dislocated a joint attempt to manipulate his leg back into place. This makes Arthur's injury much worse and it becomes necessary to amputate his leg.**

24.   **How is a tort distinguished from:**

   a.   **a crime,**

   b.   **a breach of contract?**

PART IV   COMMERCIAL LAW

32 Agency

INTRODUCTION

1. An agent is a person who is used to effect a contract between his principal and a third party. The agent may be an employee of his principal, for example a salesman in a shop, or he may be an independent contractor, for example an estate agent. Whatever the type of agent the distinctive characteristic of the relationship is that the agent has the power to make a binding contract between his principal and a third party without himself becoming a party to the contract.

2. There are several different types of agent, the more important being considered later. However all agents will fall into one of three general categories:-

    a. A *special agent*. His authority is limited to the performance of a specific act, such as buying a particular car.

    b. A *general agent*. He has authority to perform any of the duties which are normally within the scope of the business entrusted to him, for example a solicitor.

    c. A *universal agent*. Such an agent is appointed by a deed known as a "power of attorney". He has unlimited authority and may perform any acts that his principal could have performed including the execution of a deed on his behalf.

3. Since an agent does not contract on his own behalf he need not possess full contractual capacity – he may, for example, be an infant. His principal however must have full capacity to make the contract in question.

4. In everyday language the word "agent" is often used to describe anybody who buys and sells goods. For example a car dealer may be described as the "sole agent" for a particular make of car. This does not mean that the dealer acts as the legal agent of the manufacturer when he sells the car to a customer. In practice the dealer acts on his own account when he buys from the manufacturer and sells to the customer. This wider use of the word "agent" must be distinguished from the narrow legal usage. In law an agent is someone whose purpose is to make a contract between his principal and a third party.

APPOINTMENT OF THE AGENT

5. Agency may be created in the following 4 ways.

6. **Express Agreement.** The agent may be appointed verbally or in writing, unless he is authorised to execute a deed, in which case his appointment must be by deed.

7. Implication

a.   Agency will arise when, although there is no specific agreement, a contract can be implied from the conduct or relationship of the parties.

b.   The test is objective and agency may therefore be implied even if the principal and agent did not recognise the relationship themselves (**GARNAC GRAIN CO. v H.M. FAURE (1967)**.)

c.   If an alleged agent is a partner in a firm, he will be held to be acting as the agent of his co-partners if the contract that he made is within the usual scope of the partnership business.

d.   Cohabitation (rather than marriage) raises a presumption that the woman has authority to pledge the man's credit for necessaries. In defining necessaries regard is had to the man's style of living rather than to his actual means. The presumption can be rebutted by evidence that, for example, the trader had been told not to supply goods to the woman on credit, or that the woman had sufficient funds to purchase necessaries.

e.   An implied agency may arise by estoppel. Thus if a person by his words or conduct represents another as having authority to make contracts on his behalf, he will be bound by such contracts as if he had expressly authorised them. ie He is *estopped* by his conduct from denying the existence of an agency.

In **PICKERING v BUSK (1812)** A broker was employed by a merchant to buy hemp. After he had completed the purchase the broker retained the hemp at his wharf, at the request of the merchant. He then sold the goods. The purchaser was held to have obtained a good title to the goods because the broker was apparently an agent to sell, and the merchant was estopped by his conduct from denying the agency.

8. Necessity.
Agency of necessity is formed by operation of law (ie automatically). Thus the principal may be bound to a contract made on his behalf without authority and which he refuses to ratify. 3 conditions must be satisfied:-

a.   There must be an emergency, making it necessary for the agent to act as he did.

In **PRAGER v BLATSPIEL (1924)** A bought skins as agent for P but was unable to send them to P because of prevailing war conditions. Since A was also unable to communicate with P he sold the skins before the end of the war. It was held that A was not an agent of necessity, because he could have stored the skins until the end of the war. There was no real emergency.

b.   It must be impossible to get instructions from the principal.

In **SPRINGER v GREAT WESTERN RAILWAY (1921)** A consignment of fruit was found by the carrier to be going bad. The carrier sold the consignment locally instead of delivering it to its destination. It was held that the carrier was not an agent of necessity because he could have obtained new instructions from the owner of the fruit. He was therefore liable in damages to the owner.

c.   The agent must have acted in good faith, and in the interests of all the parties.

In **GREAT NORTHERN RAILWAY v SWAFFIELD (1874)** A horse was sent by rail and on its arrival at its destination there was no one to collect it. GNR incurred the expense of stabling the horse for the night. It was held that GNR was an agent of necessity who had implied authority to incur the expense in question.

9.   Ratification

a.   If a duly appointed agent exceeds his authority, or a person having no authority purports to act as agent, the principal is not bound.

b.   The principal may however adopt the contract at a later date, provided:-

i.   The agent named his principal and specifically informed the third party that he was contracting as agent.

ii.   The principal had contractual capacity at the date of both the contract and the ratification, and if the principal is a company, it must have been incorporated at the time of the contract.

In **KELNER v BAXTER (1866)** P sold wine to D who purported to act as agent for a company which was about to be formed. When it was formed the company attempted to ratify the contract made by D. It was held that it could not do so, since it was not in existence when the contract was made. D was therefore personally liable to pay for the wine.

iii.   The principal had full knowledge of all material facts, or was prepared to ratify in any event.

c.   A void contract cannot be ratified, for example if the directors of a company purport to make a contract which is ultra vires the company. Similarly a forged signature cannot be ratified because forgery is an illegal act, and because a forger does not purport to act as an agent.

In **BROOK v HOOK (1871)** a man forged his uncle's signature on a promissory note. When a third party came into possession of the note and discovered the forgery, he intended to bring proceedings against the forger. The uncle then purported to ratify his nephew's act by signing the note, but later refused to honour it. It was held that the ratification was ineffective and the promissory note was therefore void.

d.   If A, who has no authority to do so, contracts with X, on behalf of P, any ratification by P relates back to the making of the contract by A.

In **BOLTON PARTNERS v LAMBERT (1888)** the managing director of a company acting as an agent of the company, but without authority to do so, accepted an offer by the defendant for the purchase of company property. The defendant later withdrew his offer, but the company then ratified the manager's acceptance. It was held that D was bound by the contract as the ratification was retrospective to the time of the manager's acceptance.

THE RELATIONSHIP BETWEEN PRINCIPAL AND AGENT

10. The Duties of an Agent

a.   He must carry out his principal's lawful instructions, unless he is acting gratuitously.

In **TURPIN v BILTON (1843)** an insurance broker, in return for a fee, agreed to effect insurance on P's ship. He failed to do so and the ship was lost. The broker was held liable to P.

b.   He must exercise reasonable care and skill in the performance of his duties. The degree of skill expected of him depends on the circumstances. More skill is expected of a professional person than of a layman who merely advises a friend. If a payment is made this will also be taken into account in assessing the care and skill expected but even an unpaid agent may be liable in tort for negligence if he gives bad advice. (**HEDLEY BYRNE v HELLER (1964)**) (Chapter 26).

c.   He must act in good faith and for the benefit of his principal.

i.   He must not let his own interests conflict with his duty to his principal. It does not matter that the contract is made without intent to defraud, for example if an agent appointed to buy sells his own property to the principal at a proper market price. The reason for the rule is to prevent the agent from being tempted not to do the best for his principal.

In **ARMSTRONG v JACKSON (1917)** P employed D, a stockbroker, to buy some shares for him. In fact D sold his own shares to P. It was held that P could rescind the contract. The agent's interest as seller was to sell at the highest possible price, whereas his duty as agent was to buy at the lowest possible price − clearly a conflict of interest and duty.

ii.   He must not make a secret profit. ie He must not use his position to secure a benefit for himself.

In **LUCIFERO v CASTEL (1887)** an agent appointed to purchase a yacht for his principal bought the yacht himself and then sold it to his principal at a profit, the principal being unaware that he was buying the agent's own property. The agent had to pay his profit to the principal. (This case also illustrates i. above).

The agent must pay the profit to the principal even if the principal could not have earned the profit himself.

In **READING v ATTORNEY GENERAL (1951)** A sergeant in the British Army in Egypt agreed to accompany lorries carrying illicit spirits. He was paid £20,000 so that his presence in uniform would ensure that the vehicles were not searched. It was held that as he made his profit through the use of his position, he had to account to the Crown as his employer. (The sergeant was not strictly an agent, but he was held to have a fiduciary relationship with his employer similar to a principal/agent relationship.)

iii. He must not misuse confidential information regarding his principal's affairs.

iv. Certain employees owe fiduciary duties to their employer, e.g. the managing director of a company. Sometimes senior managers are also regarded as having an agency type of relationship with their employer. Such persons generally have a duty to disclose their own breaches of duty and any breaches by other employees.

In **CYBRON CORPORATION v ROCHEM (1983)** a "European Zone Controller" received on retirement a generous package of benefits. It was then discovered that he had, with other employees, set up a rival business and participated in large scale commercial fraud. The company sued to recover the money paid to him on his retirement. The court held that even if the person concerned had no duty to disclose his own breach (this was not made clear) he was under a duty to disclose breaches by other employees. Such a duty does not apply to all employees in all situations, it depends on the particular employee and the circumstances in general, however it clearly applies to a zone controller who is responsible for a large section of his employer's business. The company was therefore successful and the agreement concerning payments on retirement was voidable for non-disclosure.

v. A breach of duty by the agent may result in the agent losing his right to remuneration, but this will not be the case if the right to remuneration accrued before the principal exercised his right to terminate the contract for breach.

In **ROBINSON SCAMMELL v ANSELL (1985)** an estate agent had been engaged to sell P's house. The agent found purchasers, but when P's own house purchase fell through A informed the purchasers that the sale might not proceed and suggested alternative properties for them to look at. On discovering this P informed A that the agency was terminated. They then contacted the original purchasers and successfully completed the sale to them. The agents claimed their fee and their client refused to pay. It was held that the right to remuneration accrued before the breach. The estate agents were therefore awarded their commission. The Court of Appeal based their decision on **KEPPEL v WHEELER (1927)** where although the plaintiff was awarded damages for breach, the agent received his commission because the breach was not sufficiently serious to justify termination of the agency agreement.

d. He must not delegate the performance of his duties, unless the principal expressly or impliedly authorises the agent to appoint a sub-agent. An agent does not however "delegate" by instructing his own employees to do necessary acts in connection with the performance of his duty.

e. He must not mix his own financial affairs with those of his principal, for example by paying money received on behalf of his principal into his own account. In addition he must render accounts to the principal when required.

11. Duties of the Principal

a. He must pay the agent the commission or other remuneration that has been agreed. If nothing has been agreed the agent is entitled to what is customary in the particular business, or in the absence of custom, to reasonable remuneration. The exact point in time at which the right to commission arises depends on the terms of the contract between the principal and the agent. This has given rise to difficulty, particularly in cases concerning estate agents.

In **LUXOR (EASTBOURNE) v COOPER (1941)** The contract provided that the vendor of land should pay the estate agent his commission "on completion of sale". A prospective purchaser was introduced by the agent. He was ready, willing and able to buy, but the sale did not take place because the owner refused to deal with him. It was held that the agent was not entitled to commission.

Contrast **SCHEGGIA v GRADWELL (1963)** A similar contract provided that the vendor should pay commission as soon as "any person introduced by us enters into a legally binding contract to purchase". It was held that an agent was entitled to his commission when the purchaser signed a binding contract, although the vendor later rescinded the contract because of the purchaser's breach.

b. He must indemnify the agent for losses and liabilities incurred by him in the course of the agency.

In **ADAMSON v JARVIS (1827)** an auctioneer sold goods on behalf of his principal, being unaware that the principal had no right to sell. The auctioneer was held liable to the true owner in conversion, but was entitled to an indemnity from the principal.

It has been held that an agent may be indemnified when he makes a payment on behalf of his principal which is not legally enforceable by the third party, but which is made as a result of some moral or social pressure.

In **READ v ANDERSON (1884)** an agent was employed to bet on a horse. The horse lost and the agent paid the bet. It was held that he was entitled to an indemnity from the principal since if he had not paid he would have been recorded as a defaulter.

THE AUTHORITY OF THE AGENT

12. Express, Implied and Apparent Authority

a.   Where the agent is given *express authority* an act performed within the scope of this authority will be binding on the principal and the third party.

b.   Where an agent is employed to conduct a particular trade or business he has *implied authority* to do whatever is incidental to such trade or business. This is the case even if the principal told the agent that he did not have such authority, unless the third party knew of the lack of authority.

In **WATTEAU v FENWICK (1893)** the manager of a public house was instructed by D, the owner, not to purchase tobacco on credit. P, who was not aware of this restriction sold tobacco to the manager, and the manager was unable to pay for it. P then successfully sued D. It was held that the purchase of tobacco was within the usual authority of a manager of a public house, and it was this authority upon which the seller was entitled to rely.

c.   If a person's words or conduct lead another to believe that an agent has been appointed and has authority, he will usually be estopped from denying the authority of the agent, even though no agency was agreed between the principal and agent. The agent is said to have *apparent authority*.

13. Breach of Warranty of Authority

a.   A person who professes to act as agent, and who either has no authority from the alleged principal, or has exceeded his authority, is liable in an action for breach of warranty of authority at the suit of the party *with whom he professed to make the contract*.

b.   The agent is not liable if the third party knew of his lack of authority at the time the contract was made.

c.   The agent is liable whether he acted fraudulently or innocently. For example where his authority is terminated without his knowledge by the death or insanity of his principal.

In **YONGE v TOYNBEE (1910)** A solicitor was conducting litigation on behalf of a client who went insane. After this happened, but before the solicitor heard of it, he took further steps in the action. As a result the other party to the litigation incurred further costs. It was held that he could recover these costs from the solicitor since the solicitor had continued the action after the agency had been ended by the client's insanity. It made no difference that the solicitor had acted in good faith and with reasonable care.

WHO CAN SUE AND BE SUED

14. The question of whether or not the agent can sue or be sued by the third party depends on the parties intention. If their intention is not clear the following rules apply:-

15. If the Agent Names the Principal. The agent generally incurs neither rights nor liabilities, and drops out as soon as the contract is made. Only the principal can sue and be sued.

16. If the Agent Discloses the Existence but not the Name of the Principal. Again the general rule is that the agent can neither sue nor be sued, but a contrary intention is more easily inferred than when the principal is named. Regardless of whether or not the principal is named, in the following exceptional cases the agent may be personally liable:-

    a. If he signs his own name to a deed in which his principal is not named.

    b. If he signs a negotiable instrument in his own name without adding words indicating that he is signing as agent.

    c. If the custom of the particular trade makes him liable.

    d. If he agrees to be liable.

17. If the Agent does not Disclose the Existence of the Principal

    a. The agent may sue and be sued on the contract.

    b. The undisclosed principal may also sue on the contract provided:-

        i.   The agent's authority to act for him existed at the date of the contract, and

        ii. The terms of the contract are compatible with agency.

        In **HUMBLE v HUNTER (1842)** An agent entered into a charter-party and signed it as "owner". It was held that the word "owner" was incompatible with an agency relationship. Evidence was not admissible to show that another was principal. The principal could not therefore sue on the contract.

    c. On discovering the principal, the third party may choose to sue him instead of the agent. The commencement of proceedings against either the principal or agent does not necessarily amount to a conclusive election so as to bar proceedings against the other. (**CLARKSON, BOOKER v ANDJEL (1964)**). A judgement against one is however a bar to an action against the other.

TYPES OF AGENT

18. The following are examples of the more important types of agent.

19. Auctioneers

    a. An auctioneer is an agent to sell goods at a public auction.

b.   He has authority to receive the purchase price and can sue for it in his own name.

c.   He has a lien on the goods for his charges.

d.   He has implied authority to sell without a reserve price and even if he sells below a reserve price specified by the owner the contract will be binding. If however he declares that the sale is "subject to a reserve" then a sale below the reserve price is not binding on the owner.

20. Factors

a.   A factor is an agent "employed to sell goods or merchandise consigned or delivered to him by or for his principal for a compensation". (Story, Agency).

b.   His powers are:-

  i.   To sell in his own name;

  ii.   To give a warranty, if it is usual in the course of the business;

  iii.   To receive payment for goods sold, give valid receipts, and grant reasonable credit;

  iv.   To pledge the goods under the Factors Acts. (To pledge means to deposit as security).

c.   In addition a factor has a lien on the goods for his charges, and he has an insurable interest in the goods.

21. Brokers.
A broker has been defined by Story as "An agent employed to make bargains and contracts in matters of trade, commerce or navigation between other parties for a compensation commonly called brokerage". In contrast with a factor:-

a.   He rarely has possession of goods and therefore has no lien on them.

b.   He does not buy and sell in his own name, unless there exists a trade custom enabling him to do so.

c.   He has no power to pledge the goods.

22. Stockbrokers.
A member of the Stock Exchange has an implied authority to make contracts for his principal in accordance with the rules of the Exchange. These rules bind the principal even if he is not aware of them, provided they are neither illegal or unreasonable.

23. Del Credere Agents.
An agent who guarantees to his principal that the purchasers he finds will pay for the goods sold to them is called a del credere agent. Therefore if the buyer does not pay the principal the agent will have to do so. A del credere agent does not guarantee that a buyer will accept delivery, so if the buyer does not accept delivery, the agent is not liable.

TERMINATION OF AGENCY

24. By the Act of the Parties

a. The parties may at any time mutually agree to terminate the agency.

b. The principal may revoke the agent's authority at any time, subject to the following restrictions:-

i. If the agent is also an employee then proper notice must be given to terminate his contract of employment.

ii. The principal should give notice of the revocation to third parties with whom the agent has dealt, otherwise he will be estopped from denying the capacity of the agent, should the agent make subsequent contracts with these third parties.

iii. A termination in breach of contract will entitle the agent to damages.

In **TURNER v GOLDSMITH (1891)** G, a shirt manufacturer, employed T as an agent to sell such goods as should be forwarded to him. The agency was for 5 years, determinable by either party at the end of that time by notice. After two years G's factory was burned down and he ceased business. T's action for loss of commission succeeded since there was a definite agency agreement for 5 years and this contract was not frustrated merely because the factory in which G manufactured shirts was burnt down.

iv. Where the principal has given the agent an authority coupled with an interest he cannot revoke. For example if the agent is authorised to collect debts on behalf of his principal and retain a part of the sum collected.

c. If an agent commits a serious breach of an express or implied duty for example making a secret profit by failure to disclose the correct selling price of the principal's goods, the principal may terminate the agency agreement without notice and sue for damages. If the agent has made a secret profit the principal is entitled to it even if he could not have made the profit himself.

25. By Operation of Law

a. On the death or insanity of either the principal or the agent.

b. On the bankruptcy of the principal.

c. If the subject-matter or the operation of the agency agreement is frustrated or becomes illegal, for example if the principal becomes an alien enemy.

26. By Completion of the Agency Agreement

a. Either the period fixed for the agreement comes to an end, or

b. The purpose for which the agreement was created is accomplished.

33 Sale of Goods

INTRODUCTION AND DEFINITIONS

1. A sale of goods is the most common type of commercial transaction. Most of the common law relating to the sale of goods was first codified by the *SALE OF GOODS ACT 1893*. This was amended by the *SUPPLY OF GOODS (IMPLIED TERMS) ACT 1973* and the law has now been consolidated by the *SALE OF GOODS ACT 1979*. References in this chapter to sections are to sections of the 1979 Act, unless otherwise stated. It is convenient that most of the section numbers of the 1979 Act correspond to those of the 1893 Act.

2. The *UNFAIR CONTRACT TERMS ACT 1977* is also very important to contracts for the sale of goods. In addition to the statutory rules the ordinary principles of contract law are also applicable, for example the rules relating to mistake, misrepresentation, offer, acceptance and agency.

3. Contract of Sale Distinguished From Other Transactions

a. "A *contract of sale of goods* is a contract whereby the seller transfers or agrees to transfer the property in goods to the buyer for a money consideration called the price". *(S.2(1))*.

b. A *mortgage* is the transfer of the general property in the goods from the mortgagor to the mortgagee to secure a debt.

c. A *pledge* is the delivery of goods by one person to another to secure payment of a debt. It differs from a mortgage because a mortgagee obtains the general property in the goods whereas a pledgee only obtains a special property necessary to secure his rights, ie only possession passes, coupled with a power to sell. By *S.62(4)* the Act does not apply to a transaction in the form of a contract of sale which is intended to operate by way of mortgage, pledge, or other security.

d. A contract for *work and labour* is sometimes difficult to distinguish from a sale of goods. The test is whether the substance of the contract is the skill and labour exercised for the production of the item.

In **ROBINSON v GRAVES (1935)** it was held that a contract with an artist to paint a picture was not a sale of goods because the substance of the contract was the skill and experience of the artist and it was immaterial that some paint and canvas would also pass to the purchase. Similarly a contact for the repair of a car is not a sale of goods even if the repairs involve fitting some new parts.

e. A sale presupposes a "price". Therefore if the consideration is goods alone the contract is one of *exchange* and the Act will not apply.

4. Sale and Agreement to Sell Distinguished

a. The term *"contract of sale"* in the Act includes both actual *sales* and *agreements to sell. (S.61(1))*

    i.   Where under a contract of sale, the property in goods is passed from the seller to the buyer, the contract is called a *"sale" (S.2(4))*.

    ii.   Where the transfer of the property in the goods is to take place at a future time or subject to some condition later to be fulfilled the contract is called an *"agreement to sell" (S.2(5))*.

    iii.   An agreement to sell becomes a sale when the time elapses or the conditions are fulfilled subject to which the property in the goods is to be transferred *(S.2(6))*.

b.   The distinction is important because several consequences follow from the passing of property:-

    i.   Unless otherwise agreed the risk passes with the property. (See **25.** below)

    ii.   If the property has passed to the buyer the seller can sue for the price.

    iii.   If the seller re-sells the goods after the property has passed to the buyer, the second buyer acquires no title unless he is protected by one of the exceptions to the "nemo dat" rule. (See **27.** below). Similar principles apply if the buyer re-sells goods before the property has passed to him.

c.   "Property" means the right of ownership. It is of course possible to transfer possession of goods without transferring the ownership of them, for example hire purchase contracts and contracts whereby the seller has reserved his title as in **ALUMINIUM INDUSTRIE B.V. v ROMALPA (1976)**. (See **22.** below).

5.   **Goods**

a.   *"Goods"* means "All chattels personal other than things in action and money". The definition includes industrial growing crops, and has been held to include a ship and a coin sold as a collector's item.

b.   The Act also distinguishes between:-

    i.   *"Specific goods"*, ie "goods identified and agreed upon at the time a contract of sale is made" e.g. "My Ford Escort G123 ABC".

    ii.   *"Future goods"*, ie "goods to be manufactured or acquired by the seller after the making of the contract of sale" e.g. A Wedding Cake.

    iii.   *"Unascertained goods"*, ie goods defined only by a description applicable to all goods of the same class or goods forming part of a larger consignment e.g. 6 bottles of Chateau Laffite 1961 or e.g. half of that lorry load of sand.

c.   The distinction between specific and unascertained goods is important because, for example *S.6.* and *7* only apply to specific goods (see **26.** below) and because the rules governing the passing of property are different.

CAPACITY, FORM, SUBJECT MATTER AND PRICE

6. Capacity

a.   Capacity is regulated by the general law concerning capacity to contract, but where necessaries are sold and delivered to an infant, or a person who by reason of mental incapacity or drunkenness is incompetent to contract, he must pay a reasonable price for them *(S.3.)*.

b.   "Necessaries" are goods suitable to the condition of life of the infant or other incompetent person, and to his actual requirements at the time of sale and delivery. (See Chapter **16.**).

7. Form.
Subject to various statutory provisions a contract of sale may be in writing, by word of mouth, or implied from conduct *(S.4)*.

8. Subject Matter.
The goods may be existing goods, owned or possessed by the seller, or future goods *(S.5.)*.

9. The Price

a.   The price must be in money. It may be:-

  i.   Fixed by the contract;

  ii.   Left to be fixed in the manner agreed in the contract; or

  iii.   Determined by the course of dealing of the parties.

b.   If it is not determined as above the buyer must pay a reasonable price *(S.8.)*, however the absence of agreement as to price may render the contract void for uncertainty.

c.   Where the contract specifies that the price shall be fixed by the valuation of a third party and the third party does not make the valuation the contract is avoided. If however the goods or part of them have been delivered to and appropriated by the buyer he must pay a reasonable price for them. If the failure to value is the fault of the buyer or seller that party is liable to pay damages. *(S.9.)*.

THE TERMS OF THE CONTRACT

10. The following questions, which were considered in Chapter 18, are also relevant to sales of goods:-

a.   Is a statement made in negotiations a mere representation inducing the contract, or a term which is part of the contract?

b.   If it is a term, is it a condition or a warranty?

c.   If a term has not been expressly agreed, can it be included in the contract by implication?

d.   Are any exemption or limitation clauses valid?

255

11. Conditions and Warranties

a.   Of the 4 questions stated above, that relating to conditions and warranties merits revision and further discussion.

b.   A *condition* is a vital term, going to the root of the contract, breach of which normally entitled the innocent party to repudiate the contract and claim damages.

c.   A *warranty* is a subsidiary term, breach of which only entitles the innocent party to damages.

d.   The intention of the parties determines whether a clause is a condition or warranty, but in the absence of evidence of intention the courts will consider the commercial importance of the term, or less usually, the effects of the breach as in **HONG KONG FIR SHIPPING v KAWASAKI KISEN KAISHA (1962).**

e.   In the above case it was stated that many contracted undertakings could not be categorised simply as "conditions" or "warranties". It has since been held that the division into conditions and warranties is not exhaustive. A term may be an "intermediate term" in which case the remedy would depend upon the nature of the breach rather than the status of the term. If the breach goes to the root of the contract repudiation is justified, in other cases repudiation is not justified.

In **CEHAVE NV v BREMER (1975)** the buyers (B) agreed to purchase for £100,000 a shipment of animal feed. The contract between the sellers (S) and B provided that the goods should be "shipped in good condition". When the shipment arrived at its destination it was unloaded into containers. It was then discovered that some of the goods had been damaged in transit and B refused to accept delivery. The container owners applied to court and it was ordered that the goods be sold. In "somewhat strange circumstances" they were sold to an importer for £30,000 who then re-sold them to B the same day for £30,000. The Court of Appeal held that there was a breach of the term that the goods be "shipped in good condition" but this term was neither a condition nor a warranty, but an "intermediate term". Since breach of this term did not go to the root of the contract B was not entitled to reject the goods. The Court also decided that B could not reject for breach of the implied condition as to merchantable quality, it being concluded that the goods were merchantable.

12. The Treatment of Conditions as Warranties

a.   By *S.11(2)* a buyer may waive a breach of condition by the seller, or elect to treat it as a breach of warranty.

b.   By *S.11(4)* a buyer *must* treat a breach of condition as a breach of warranty where the contract is *non-severable* and he has *accepted* the goods or some of them. Note that:-

i.   *S.11(4)* does not apply to a breach of *S.12(1)* (see below).

ii.   The meaning of non-severable contracts and acceptance is discussed below – *S.31.* and *S.34-35.*

iii.   *S.11(4)* is important since it affects buyers' rights.

13.   Stipulations as to Time

a.   By *S.10.* unless a different intention appears from the terms of the contract, stipulations as to *time of payment* are not deemed to be of the essence of the contract. Whether any other stipulation as to time is of the essence of the contract depends on the terms of the contract.

b.   Where a party has waived a stipulation, for example as to the time for delivery, which was of the essence of the contract, he may again make that stipulation of the essence by giving the other party reasonable notice of his intention to do so. (**RICKARDS v OPPENHEIM (1950)** (Chapter 20.3)).

14.   The implied terms of the Act were outlined in Chapter 18. They will now be considered in more detail.

15.   Title

a.   By *S.12(1)* there is an implied *condition* that the seller has the right to pass good title to the goods.

In **NIBLETT v CONFECTIONERS' MATERIALS CO. (1921)** cans of condensed milk were labelled in a way that infringed the trade mark of a third party. The third party could therefore have restrained the sale by S to B by obtaining an injunction. It was held that S were in breach of the implied condition that they had the right to sell the cans. This case shows that *S.12* will be broken not only where the seller lacks the right to pass the property in the goods to the buyer, but also where he can be stopped by process of law from selling the goods.

b.   By *S.12(2)* there is an implied *warranty* that the goods are free of any encumbrance not made known to the buyer, and the buyer will enjoy quiet possession of the goods except so far as it may be disturbed by the owner or other person entitled to the encumbrance disclosed.

In **MICROBEADS v VINHURST ROAD MARKINGS (1975)** S sold to B road marking equipment. At the time of the sale, unknown to S, a third party had applied for a patent in respect of the equipment. At the time of the sale the third party could not have objected to B's use of the equipment. 2 years after the sale, the third party, who had now been granted patent rights informed B that he was infringing a patent. B then sued S for breach of *S.12(1)* and *S.12(2)* . It was held that there was no breach of *S.12(1)* since at the time of sale S could not have been prevented by injunction from selling the goods. However there was a breach of *S.12(2)* . The activities of the third party amounted to an infringement of B's quiet possession of the goods. S was therefore liable even though he did not know of the patent application.

c.   Since the essence of a contract is the transfer of property, if the seller breaks *S.12(1)* there will be a total failure of consideration and the buyer will be entitled to recover the whole price with no deduction for his use.

In **ROWLAND v DIVALL (1923)** B purchased a car from S for £334. Both B and S dealt in good faith. Four months later it was discovered that the car was stolen and B had to return it to the true owner. B sued to recover the price paid to S. S argued that since B had accepted the car he was limited by *S.11(4)* to a claim for damages for breach of warranty, and that in assessing these damages an allowance should be made for his use. Both these arguments failed. Atkin L.J. said that there could not be acceptance if there was nothing (ie no title) to accept, and that since B had paid for the property in the car and not merely the right to use it, there had been a total failure of consideration, entitling him to recover the whole purchase price without any set off for the use of the car. This has been criticised in that it is unrealistic to say that considertion has failed totally when B had 4 months use of the car before he had to return it.

16. Description

a.   Where goods are sold by description there is an implied *condition* that:-

   i.   The goods will correspond with the description *(S.13(1))*, and

   ii.   If the sale is by sample, as well as by description, the bulk of the goods will also correspond with the sample *(S.13(2))*.

In **GRANT v AUSTRALIAN KNITTING MILLS (1936)** A buyer of underpants contracted dermatitis because of an excess of sulphite in the garment he purchased. It was held:-

   a.   A sale may be "by description" even if the buyer has seen the goods before buying them provided he relied essentially on the description, and any discrepancy between the description and the goods is not apparent. There was therefore a breach of *S.13*.

   b.   Reliance on the seller's judgement is readily inferred in retail sales because a buyer will go into a shop with confidence that the seller has selected his stock with skill.

   c.   The buyer did not need to specify his purpose because it is obvious and therefore may be implied. *S.14.* was therefore also broken.

b.   A sale of goods is not prevented from being a sale by description solely because goods being exposed for sale are selected by the buyer *(S.13(3))*.

c.   A sale by description may include such matters as measurements and methods of packing, for example **RE MOORE AND LANDAUER (1921)** (Chapter 20.2.).

17. Quality or Fitness

a.   By *S.14(1)* there is no implied condition or warranty as to quality or fitness for a particular purpose of the goods sold, except as provided by the following sub-sections, or by *S.15*. This sub-section preserves the basic rule of caveat emptor (let the buyer beware).

b.   *Merchantable Quality*

   i.   By *S.14(2)* where goods are sold in the *course of business* there is an implied *condition* that those goods are of merchantable quality unless the defects
   — are brought specifically to the buyer's attention before the contract is made, or
   — if the buyer examines the goods before the contract is made, as regards defects which that examination ought to reveal.

   In **THORNETT AND FEHR v BEERS AND SONS (1919)** A purchaser of glue bought several barrels without inspecting their contents, although he did inspect the barrels themselves. If he had looked inside the barrels he would have discovered that the glue was defective. It was held that he could not rely on *S.14(2)* because the proviso on examination applied. The seller was not liable.

   ii.   *S.14(2)* covers goods "supplied" as well as goods "sold".

   In **WILSON v RICKETT COCKERELL (1954)** S supplied B with a ton of "coalite". The consignment included a detonator, which later exploded. S argued that the contract goods, ie the "coalite" was of merchantable quality and so the detonator, which was not part of the contract, could be disregarded. This argument failed. The implied condition as to merchantable quality is not confined to goods "sold", but includes all goods "supplied under the contract".

   iii.   By *S.14(6)* goods are of merchantable quality if they are as fit for the purpose or purposes for which goods of that kind are commonly bought as is reasonable to expect having regard to any description applied to them, the price (if relevant), and all the other relevant circumstances.

c.   *Fitness for Purpose*

   i.   By *S.14(3)* where goods are sold in the *course of a business* and the buyer makes known to the seller the purpose for which the goods are being bought there is an implied *condition* that the goods are reasonably fit for that purpose, except where the circumstances show that the buyer does not rely, or that it is unreasonable for him to rely, on the skill or judgement of the seller.

   In **ASHINGTON PIGGERIES v CHRISTOPHER HILL (1972)** B asked S to compound food for minks in accordance with a recipe supplied by B. The recipe included herring meal, which is toxic to minks. S compounded the food, which was later fed to the minks with the result that many died. S argued that they were not liable because B had supplied the recipe, and B and themselves were in the same line of business. S were however held liable. The court said that reliance on the seller's skill and judgement need not be total but it must be substantial and effective.

ii.   Where the purpose for which the goods are required is obvious, it need not be made known expressly because it is clearly implied.

In **GODLEY v PERRY (1960)** a 6 year old boy purchased a toy plastic catapult. The catapult broke whilst being used and the boy lost an eye. His action against the shopkeeper who sold it to him was successful. There was no need for the boy to make known the purpose of his purchase since it was known by implication.

iii.   The section applies to second-hand goods, but the standard of fitness expected is lower.

18.   Sale by Sample

a.   *S.15.* provides that where there is a sale by sample, *conditions* are implied that

i.   The bulk will correspond with the sample;

ii.   The buyer will have a reasonable opportunity of comparing the bulk with the sample; and

iii.   The goods shall be free from any defect rendering them unmerchantable, which would not be apparent on reasonable examination of the sample.

b.   If a sale is by sample and description the goods supplied must correspond with both the sample and the description.

In **NICHOL v GODTS (1854)** The seller sold "foreign refined rape oil warranted only equal to sample". When it was delivered the bulk did correspond with the sample but the sample was not "foreign refined rape oil". It was held that both *S.13.* and *S.15.* were broken because if the sale is by sample and description there is an implied condition that the goods correspond with both sample and description.

19.   Exemption Clauses.
The acceptability of exemption clauses is governed by the *UNFAIR CONTRACT TERMS ACT 1977*. This was considered in more detail in Chapter 18. *S.6.* of the Act (as amended) refers to contracts for the sale of goods and states that:-

a.   *S.12. SGA 1979* cannot be excluded.

b.   *S.13-15. SGA 1979* cannot be excluded in a consumer sale, but can be excluded in a non-consumer sale if the exemption clause is reasonable.

THE TRANSFER OF THE PROPERTY IN THE GOODS TO THE BUYER

20. Property (ownership) and possession must be distinguished since the property in goods sold may pass to the buyer although the seller retains possession of the goods. The moment property passes is important for several reasons. (See **4**.b. above).

21. By *S.16*. where there is a contract for the sale of *unascertained goods*, (ie goods defined by description only, and not identified until after the contract is made), no property passes to the buyer unless and until they are ascertained. Thus if a large consignment of goods are handed to a carrier who is directed to set aside the contractual goods, no property passes until the carrier has done so because until then the goods are unascertained.

In **HEALY v HOWLETT AND SONS (1917)** B ordered 20 boxes of fish from S. S consigned 190 boxes by rail and directed railway officials to set aside 20 boxes for B's contract. The train was delayed and the fish had deteriorated before 20 boxes had been appropriated for B. It was held that since property did not pass until appropriation for B. It was held that since property did not pass until appropriation the fish were at S's risk at the time of deterioration and B was not therefore liable to pay the price.

22. By *S.17* if the contract is for the sale of *specific or ascertained* goods the property passes when the parties intend it to pass. Intention is ascertained from the terms of the contract, the conduct of the parties, and the circumstances of the case. This section enables the parties to agree to "reserve title" to the goods until the buyer's outstanding debts are paid.

In **ALUMINIUM INDUSTRIE BV v ROMALPA (1976)** The plaintiffs, who were sellers of aluminium provided in their conditions of sale that "The ownership of the material to be delivered by AIV will only be transferred to the purchaser when he has met all that is owing to AIV no matter on what grounds."

After having taken delivery of a consignment of aluminium the purchaser went into liquidation. S who had not received the purchase price sought to enforce the above provision so as to secure payment prior to the distribution of B's assets to the general creditors. It was held that S could recover the consignment.

This decision has created a new remedy for an unpaid seller in addition to those provided by *S.39. SGA*. This remedy of possession is wider than the remedy of lien since a lien is for the price only, whereas the Romalpa remedy may be exercised until "all that is owing" has been paid. It is also wider than stoppage in transit since the right to stop in transit ends when transit ends, whereas the Romalpa remedy may be exercised after delivery of the goods. However a Romalpa clause will not apply where the material is subjected to a manufacturing process. For example

In **RE PEACHDART (1983)** leather was sold on reservation of title terms.

The intention was that it be used in the manufacture of handbags. It was held that the supplier's title ceased to exist when the leather had been made into handbags.

To increase the protection afforded by a reservation of title clause it is advisable for the supplier

    a.   To require that the material in question be kept separate from the buyer's other stock; and

    b.   To reserve a right of access to the buyer's premises.

23. Where the parties have not shown a definite intention at the time of contracting *S.18.* states that the following ''rules'' shall be applied to decide the time at which property shall pass.

    a.   *Rule 1.* Where there is an unconditional contract for the sale of specific goods in a deliverable state the property passes when the contract is made, and it is immaterial whether the time of payment or delivery or both are postponed.

        In **TARLING v BAXTER (1827)** B purchased a haystack. Before he took it away it was destroyed by fire. B was held liable to pay for the haystack because the property passed when the contract was made.

Note that:-

        i.   If, after the contract has been made, the parties agree that the property will pass at a certain time, the agreement will be ineffective if the property has already passed under Rule 1.

        In **DENNANT v SKINNER & COLLOM (1948)** a crook purchased a car at an auction. He was allowed to take the car away on payment of a cheque on condition that he signed a document whereby it was agreed that the property would not pass until the cheque had cleared. The crook then re-sold the car to the defendant. The cheque was later dishonoured. It was held that the defendant got good title to the car because property has passed to the crook under Rule 1 before the agreement was signed. The agreement was therefore of no effect.

        ii.   ''Deliverable state'' means such a state that the buyer would under the contract be bound to take delivery of them *(S.61(5)).*

    b.   *Rule 2.* Where the contract is for specific goods and the seller is bound to do something to the goods to put them into a deliverable state, the property does not pass until this has been done and the buyer has notice thereof.

        In **UNDERWOOD v BURGH CASTLE BRICK AND CEMENT SYNDICATE (1922)** the contract was for the sale of an engine, weighing 30 tons. At the time of sale it was imbedded in a concrete floor. Whilst being detached from its base and loaded into a railway truck the engine was damaged. The seller nevertheless sued for the price. It was held that the goods were not in a deliverable state when the contract was made so that the property did not pass under Rule 1. Also property would not pass under Rule 2 until the engine had been safely loaded into the truck.

c. **Rule 3.** Where the specific goods are in a deliverable state but the seller has still to do something, such as weighing, measuring or testing the goods, the property does not pass until such act has been done and the buyer has notice thereof.

    i.   For example B purchases a sack of potatoes from S. The price of potatoes is 25 pence per pound, but the total weight of the sack is not known. If it is agreed that the seller will weigh the potatoes to ascertain the total price payable property does not pass until this is done and the buyer has notice of it.

    ii.   Both Rule 2 and Rule 3 are confined to acts done by the seller. If the buyer is to do the act, the property would pass on making the contract.

d. **Rule 4.** Where goods are delivered on approval or on sale or return the property passes

    i.   When the buyer signifies his approval or acceptance to the seller, or

    ii.   When he does any other act adopting the transaction, such as pawning the goods, or

    iii.   If he does not signify approval or acceptance, property passes when he retains the goods beyond the agreed time or, if no time was agreed, beyond a reasonable time.

In **POOLE v SMITH'S CAR SALES (BALHAM) LTD (1962)** P left his car with D on "sale or return" terms in August 1960. After several requests D returned the car in November 1960 in a badly damaged state due to use by D's employees. It was held that since the car had not been returned within a reasonable time the property in the car had passed to D and he was accordingly liable to pay the price agreed.

e. **Rule 5.(1).** Where there is a contract for the sale of unascertained or future goods by description the property passes when the goods of that description and in a deliverable state are unconditionally appropriated to the contract by one party with the express or implied assent of the other.

In **PIGNATARO v GILROY (1919)** S sold 140 bags of rice to B. 15 bags were appropriated by S for the contract and B was told where he could collect them. The bags were then stolen through no fault of S before B was able to collect them. B failed in his action to recover the price paid for the 15 bags. It was held that S's appropriation of the bags for the contract, without any objection by B, constituted transfer of title to those bags. They therefore belonged to B when they were stolen.

f. **Rule 5.(2).** A seller who delivers goods to the buyer or to a carrier for transmission, without reserving a right of disposal, is deemed to have unconditionally appropriated the goods to the contract.

In **EDWARDS v DDIN (1976)** S filled B's petrol tank and B drove off without paying. It was held that B was not guilty of theft because the property has passed to him. It was impossible for the seller to reserve a right of disposal to petrol which at the point of delivery is mixed with the petrol already in B's tank. At that point the petrol is unconditionally appropriated to the contract with the consent of both parties. (B would now be guilty of the offence of making off without payment — *S.3. THEFT ACT 1978*).

Note that:-

> i.   Rule 5 must be considered in conjunction with *S.16*. Under *S.16*. no property passes until the goods are ascertained. Rule 5 shows when goods are ascertained.

> ii.   An example of an implied assent to appropriation would be where B orders goods to be sent by post. When S dispatches the goods this amounts to appropriation by S with B's consent.

24. By *S.19*. the seller may reserve the right of disposal of the goods until certain conditions are fulfilled and the property will not then pass until the conditions imposed by the seller are fulfilled.

25. Risk *(S.20.)*

a.   The general rule has already been stated, ie that the risk "follows" the property. Thus the owner must bear any accidental loss.

b.   This rule may be varied by trade usage or by agreement.

In **STERNS v VICKERS (1923)** S agreed to sell 120,000 gallons of spirit out of a tank containing 200,000 gallons which was on the premises of a third party. A delivery warrant was issued to B, but he did not act on it for some months, during which time the spirit deteriorated. It was held that although no property had passed (because there had been no appropriation) the parties must have intended the risk to pass when the delivery warrant (ie the authority requiring the third party to release the spirit to B) was issued to B. B therefore remained liable to pay the price.

c.   If delivery is delayed through the fault of either party the goods remain at the risk of that party as regards any loss which might not have occurred but for the delay.

In **DEMBY HAMILTON v BARDEN (1949)** S agreed to send 30 tons of apple juice by weekly consignments to B. B delayed in taking delivery of some of the juice which as a result went bad. B was held liable to pay the price since the loss was his fault.

26. Perishing of Goods

a.   Where there is a contract for the sale of *specific* goods, and the goods without the knowledge of the *seller* have perished at the time the contract is made, the contract is void. *(S.6.).* The section is limited to specific goods, but also applies where part of a specific consignment of goods has perished before the contract is made.

In **BARROW LANE AND BALLARD v PHILLIPS (1929)** S sold 700 bags of nuts. Unknown to the sellers 109 bags had already been stolen at the time of sale. It was held that the specific consignment of 700 bags had perished because a substantial part of it was missing.

b.   Where there is an agreement to sell *specific* goods and subsequently the goods, without any fault on the part of the seller or buyer, perish before the risk passes to the buyer, the agreement is thereby avoided. *(S.7.).*

c.   Note that:-

   i.   *S.6.* is a partial enactment of the common law rules relating to mistake in the formation of a contract.

   ii.   *S.7.* is an enactment of the common law rule relating to frustration when there is a sale of specific goods. *S.7.* cannot apply if the risk passes to the buyer at the time of sale, ie if *S.18.* Rule 1 applies.

   iii.   *S.6* and *7* do not apply to sales of unascertained goods.

SALE BY A PERSON WHO IS NOT THE OWNER

27.   The basic common law rule is *nemo dat quod non habet*. Literally translated this means "no man gives that which is not his own". This common law rule is enacted in *S.21.* which provides that where goods are sold by a person who is not the owner, the buyer acquires no better title than the seller had unless:-

a.   The seller had the authority or consent of the owner, or

b.   The owner is precluded by his conduct from denying the seller's authority to sell. For example

In **EASTERN DISTRIBUTORS v GOLDRING (1957)** M owned a van and he wanted to buy a car from C. However he did not even have enough money for a hire-purchase deposit. M and C therefore devised a scheme whereby C would pretend to a finance company (ED) that he owned both the car and the van — he would sell them both to ED, and then buy both back on hire-purchase. In order to convince ED that C owned both the car and the van M signed a form to this effect. C then sold the van to ED, but ED did not accept the car. However C told M that the *whole deal* had fallen through. Neither C nor M paid any of the hire-purchase instalments for the van. M, who had been in possession of the van all the time, then sold it to G (M believed he was the owner since C had told him that the deal had fallen through). ED then sued to recover the van from G. It was held that since M had acted as if C was the true owner of the van (by signing a form to this effect so as to trick ED) he was estopped from denying C's right to sell. ED therefore acquired a good title to the van from C. M therefore had no title to pass to G. ED therefore succeeded in their action to recover the van from G.

Note that:-

i.   Where there is an estoppel the effect is to pass title to the buyer.

ii.   The mere fact that the owner gives possession of the goods to a third party does not estop him from denying that person's authority to sell.

In **CENTRAL NEWBURY CAR AUCTIONS v UNITY FINANCE (1957)** A agreed with B that A would sell a car to a finance company, which would then let it to B on hire-purchase. A then handed the vehicle and registration book to B before the arrangements with the finance company had been completed. The finance company then refused B's application for hire purchase. B however was a crook and he had in the meantime sold the car to C. It was held that C did not get title to the car because B had no title to pass to him, and A's conduct in handing over the car and its registration book did not estop him from disputing B's authority to sell.

28. Apart from the two general exceptions contained in *S.21.* there are several other exceptions (**29-34** below).

29. Market Overt

a.   By *S.22.* where goods are sold in *market overt*, according to the usage of the market the buyer acquires a good title provided he buys in good faith.

b.   It is essential to such a sale that:-

i.   It takes place in an open, public and legally constituted market, or in a shop in the City of London. It cannot therefore take place in a private room. Since it must be "open" all of the goods and not merely a sample must be exposed for sale.

ii.   It takes place between sunrise and sunset (**REID v METROPOLITAN POLICE COMMISSIONER (1973)**).

iii.   The goods are of a kind usually sold in the market.

In **BISHOPSGATE MOTOR FINANCE v TRANSPORT BRAKES (1949)** The hirer of a car under a hire-purchase agreement, in breach of the agreement, took it to Maidstone market where he attempted to sell it in a car auction. This attempt failed, but later that day he sold it, in the market, to TB, who purchased in good faith. It was held that TB got a good title because Maidstone market was a market overt, having been constituted by royal charter and established since 1747. It was not material that the sale was by private treaty rather than auction.

30. Sale Under a Voidable Title

a.   Under *S.23.* where a seller of goods has a *voidable title*, but this title has not been avoided at the time of sale, the buyer acquires a good title provided he buys in good faith without notice of the seller's defect in title.

b.   This provision only applies to contracts which are voidable, for example for fraud, and not those which are void for mistake. Contrast **LEWIS v AVERAY** with **CUNDY v LINDSEY**. Note also **CAR AND UNIVERSAL FINANCE v CALDWELL** (Chapter 19.2 and 19.6).

31.   Mercantile Agents

a.   Under *S.2. FACTORS ACT 1889* any sale, pledge, or other disposition by a mercantile agent in possession of goods or documents of title with the consent of the owner, and in the mercantile agent's ordinary course of business to a bona fide purchaser for value without notice of any defect in his authority is as valid as if expressly authorised by the owner.

b.   A mercantile agent is an agent having in the customary course of his business authority to sell goods, or raise money on the security of goods. This definition includes an auctioneer or broker, but not a clerk or warehouseman.

c.   It has been held that in the case of second-hand vehicles to be within "the ordinary course of business" the sale must be accompanied by delivery of the registration book. (**PEARSON v ROSE AND YOUNG (1951)**).

32.   Dispositions by a Seller Who Remains in Possession after a Sale

a.   By *S.24.* where a person having sold goods continues in possession of them or documents of title to them the delivery or transfer by him, or by a mercantile agent acting for him, of the goods or documents under any sale, pledge or other disposition, is as valid as if authorised by the owner, provided the second buyer takes in good faith without notice of the previous sale.

b.   The usual sequence of events would be:-

  i.   A sale by X to Y under which the property passes, but X remains in possession.

  ii.   A second sale by X to Z and delivery to Z.

c.   For the section to apply the seller must continue in actual physical possession of the goods after the first sale, but not necessarily as seller. He may retain possession as, for example, a hirer or a trespasser.

  In **WORCESTER WORKS FINANCE v COODEN ENGINEER-ING (1971)** A sold a car to B, B paying by cheque. B re-sold the car to C but remained in possession of it. When B's cheque was dishonoured A went to B to re-possess the car and B allowed A to take it away. When C discovered this he sued A in conversion. It was held that although B was not a seller (since he never had title to the car) but a trespasser, the section nevertheless applied to him since continuity of physical possession was the vital factor, not the character of that possession. Note also that "other disposition" was widely contrued so as to include a retaking of the goods with the seller's consent. This case clearly does not follow the usual sequence referred to above.

d.   Consider the following example:-

X, who wishes to raise some money, sells his car to a finance company for £1,000, and then takes it back on hire purchase, paying a deposit and the balance by instalments. Throughout the transaction X keeps possession of the car. X then sells the car to Y for £900. Advise Y. *S.24.* is the correct advice and Y may keep the car. The finance company could have avoided this result by requiring the car to be delivered to them, and then immediately delivering it back to X. X would not then have "continued in possession".

e.   *S.24.* gives no protection to the seller, he remains liable to the first buyer.

33.   Dispositions by a Buyer Who Obtains Possession After an Agreement to Sell

a.   By *S.25.* where a person having bought or agreed to buy goods obtains possession of the goods or documents of title with the seller's consent the delivery or transfer by that person or by a mercantile agent acting for him of the goods or documents under any sale, pledge or other disposition to a person receiving them in good faith and without notice of any lien or other right of the original seller has the same effect as if the person making the delivery or transfer were a mercantile agent in possession of the goods or documents with the owner's consent.

b.   The usual sequence is:-

i.   X agrees to sell to Y and Y is given possession of the goods although the property in the goods has not yet passed.

ii.   Y "sells" and delivers the goods to Z who takes them in good faith.

c.   The person making the disposition must have bought or agreed to buy the goods, the section does not apply to someone who only has an option to purchase as in a hire purchase agreement (**HELBY v MATTHEWS (1895)**), nor does it apply to someone who has taken the goods on approval or on sale or return.

d.   The disposition must have been one which could have been made by a mercantile agent acting in the ordinary course of business (**NEWTONS OF WEMBLEY v WILLIAMS (1964)**).

e.   The section is not intended to take title away from an owner from whom goods have been stolen. In **NATIONAL MUTUAL AND GENERAL INSURANCE ASSOCIATION v JONES (1988)** thieves stole a car. They sold it to A, who sold it to B, who sold it to C, who sold it to D, who sold it to Jones. All the parties (A,B,C,D and Jones) were innocent and unaware of the defect in title. C and D were car dealers. It was held that Jones did not obtain title to the car because A did not make a contract of sale with B, and A and B could not properly be described as "seller" and "buyer". Thus A did not deliver the goods to B "under a sale" as required by the section, because a contract of sale supposed that the seller had, or was going to have, a general property in the goods.

f.   Recently there was an interesting case involving both Section 25 and reservation of title clauses.

In **FOUR POINT GARAGE v CARTER (1985)** Carter purchased a new car from X Limited. X Limited did not have the car in stock so it arranged to buy the car from Four Point who delivered it direct to Carter (who was unaware of Four Point's involvement). The contract between Four Point and X Limited reserved title to the car until the price had been paid. A few days after Carter had taken delivery X Limited went into liquidation without having paid Four Point. Four Point claimed that they were entitled to recover the car under their reservation of title clause. Carter claimed the protection of Section 25. As regards Section 25 it was held that there was no difference between a delivery direct to a sub-purchaser and a delivery to a buyer who then delivered to a sub-purchaser. X Limited would be regarded as having taken constructive delivery, therefore Four Point delivered to Carter as X Limited's agent. Concerning the reservation of title clause it was held that the basic form of clause used did not preclude implication of a term authorising the garage to sell the car in the ordinary course of business. Carter was therefore successful on both arguments.

34.   The final exception is where there is a disposition under a common law or statutory power of sale, or under a court order.

35. Conclusion. The reasons for the general rule and its exceptions were summed up by Lord Denning in Bishopsgate Motor Finance v Transport Brakes. He said:-

"In the development of our law two principles have striven for mastery. The first is the protection of property. No one can give a better title than he himself possesses. The second is the protection of commercial transactions. The person who takes in good faith for value without notice should get a good title. The first principle has held sway for a long time, but it has been modified by common law itself and by statute so as to meet the needs of our times."

PERFORMANCE OF THE CONTRACT

36. Delivery

a.   Delivery is the physical transfer of possession from one person to

269

another. It does not necessarily mean transportation. Delivery may be actual or constructive, for example when the keys to a warehouse in which the goods are stored are handed to the buyer.

b.   It is the duty of the seller to deliver the goods and the buyer to accept and pay for them *(S.27.)*

c.   Payment and delivery are concurrent conditions unless otherwise agreed, for example if the sale is on credit. *(S.28.)*

37. Place of Delivery *(S.29.)*

a.   Except where there is a provision in the contract the place of delivery is the seller's place of business, unless the contract is for specific goods, which to the knowledge of the parties are in some other place, in which case that other place is the place of delivery.

b.   If the goods are in the possession of a third party there is no delivery until the third party acknowledges to the buyer that he holds the goods on his behalf.

c.   If goods are to be sent, the seller must send them within a reasonable time, and demand or tender of delivery must be made at a reasonable hour to be effective.

38. Incorrect Delivery *(S.30.)*

a.   If the seller delivers a larger or smaller quantity of goods than ordered the buyer may

   i.   Reject the whole, or

   ii.   Accept the whole, or

   iii. Accept the quantity ordered and reject the rest.

If he chooses ii. or iii. above he must pay for the goods at the contract rate.

b.   If the seller delivers the contract goods mixed with other goods the buyer may:-

   i.   reject the whole, or

   ii.   accept the contract goods.

He cannot accept the incorrect goods. He will only be able to accept them if the seller first offers to sell them to him.

39. Instalment Deliveries *(S.31.)*

a.   The buyer is not bound to accept delivery by instalments unless so agreed.

b.   Where a contract provides for delivery in stated instalments which are to be separately paid for, and the seller makes defective deliveries, or the buyer fails to take delivery of, or pay for one or more instalments, it is a question of construction whether this amounts to a repudiation of the whole contract or to a severable breach giving a right to compensation, but not a right to treat the whole contract as at an end. The tests to be used in applying this section were laid down in **MAPLE FLOCK v UNIVERSAL FURNITURE PRODUCTS (1934)** (Chapter 20.18) as follows:-

    i.   The ratio quantitatively which the breach bears to the contract as a whole, and

    ii.   The degree of probability that the breach will be repeated.

c.   If instalments are to be separately paid for the contract is more likely to be construed as severable.

S.11(4) is relevant to severable and non-severable contracts. As a result of this section if an instalment contract is non-severable and the buyer accepts the first instalment this will prevent his rejection of later defective deliveries, and will limit his remedy to damages for breach of warranty.

40. Acceptance

a.   By *S.34.* where goods are delivered to a buyer which he has not previously examined, he is not deemed to have accepted them until he has had a reasonable opportunity of examining them to ascertain conformity with the contract. The seller is bound to afford this opportunity if so requested.

b.   By *S.35.* the buyer accepts the goods when he:-

    i.   Intimates to the seller that he has accepted them; or

    ii.   (Unless *S.34.* otherwise provides) does any act to the goods which is inconsistent with the ownership of the seller, such as sub-selling and delivering the goods; or

    iii.   Retains the goods, after the lapse of a reasonable time without intimating to the seller that he has rejected them.

    In **BERNSTEIN v PAMSONS MOTORS (1986)** P bought a new car from D. A defect caused the engine to seize up three weeks after purchase, the car having only covered 140 miles. P sought rescission. It was held that the car was neither of merchantable quality, nor reasonably fit for its purpose. However P's claim was rejected because he was deemed to have accepted the car under Section 35. He was therefore limited to damages for breach of warranty. The judge clearly took the view that "lapse of reasonable time" meant reasonable time to try out the goods generally, it did not mean reasonable time to discover the defect. Thus presumably the result would have been the same even if the plaintiff had not used the car at all. It is suggested that it is unsatisfactory and that the judge's decision was borderline.

c.   The words in brackets in ii. above were originally added by *S.4(2) MISREPRESENTATION ACT 1967.* Thus now an act which is "inconsistent with the seller's ownership" will not destroy the buyer's right to reject the goods unless and until he has had a reasonable opportunity of examining them. This prevents the type of injustice which occurred in the following case.

In **HARDY v HILLERNS AND FOWLER (1923)** B purchased a quantity of wheat from S. On the same day that it was delivered to him B sold part of it to a third party. Two days later B discovered that the wheat did not conform with the contract and he attempted to reject the whole consignment. It was held that although at the time of the purported rejection a reasonable time for examination had not elapsed, the sale and delivery to the third party was an act that was inconsistent with S's ownership of the goods, and under *S.35.* it was therefore deemed to be an acceptance.

THE RIGHTS OF THE UNPAID SELLER

41. Lien. *(S.41-43.)*

a. A lien is the right to retain possession of goods (but not to resell them) until the contract price has been paid.

b. The unpaid seller's lien is for the price only. When the price is tendered it does not enable him to retain possession for any other purpose, for example to recover the cost of storing the goods during the exercise of the lien.

42. Stoppage in Transit. *(S.44-46.)*

a. After the seller has parted with the possession of the goods to a carrier for transmission to the buyer he can stop the goods and retake possession on the buyer becoming insolvent (ie if the buyer is unable to pay his debts as they fall due).

b. The period of transit operates from the time when the goods are handed to the carrier until the time when the buyer takes delivery of them. Transit is also terminated if:-

    i. The buyer obtains delivery before the arrival of the goods at the agreed destination, for example because the carrier hands them to the buyer's agent during transit; or

    ii. If, on reaching the agreed destination, the carrier acknowledges to the buyer that he is holding the goods to the buyer's order; or

    iii. If the carrier wrongfully refuses to deliver the goods to the buyer.

43. Resale of Goods.
The general rule is that lien and stoppage in transit do not give the unpaid seller any right to re-sell the goods. By *S.48* the exceptions are:-

a. Where they are of a perishable nature; or

b. Where the buyer, after being given notice by the seller that he intends to resell, does not pay for them within a reasonable time; or

c. Where the seller has expressly reserved the right to resell if the buyer defaults in payment.

44. Repossession of Goods

a. If the seller has reserved title to the goods until the contract price, or any other debt owing to him by the buyer is paid, then he may re-possess the goods if the buyer, being a company, goes into liquidation or receivership. (**ALUMINIUM INDUSTRIE BV v ROMALPA (1976) 22.** above).

b. The right to re-possess from a buyer who is a private individual would arise:-

i. If he were adjudged bankrupt, or

ii. If it were intimated in some other way that the goods would not be paid for.

45. Remedies Against the Buyer. The above remedies are all enforced against the goods. The remedies against the buyer are:-

a. An action for the contract price, provided the property in the goods has passed to the buyer.

b. An action for non-acceptance. *S.50.* provides that in an action for damages for non-acceptance, where there is an available market the measure of damages is, *prima facie*, the difference between the contract price and the market price on the date fixed for acceptance, or if no date was fixed, at the time of refusal to accept.

THE REMEDIES OF THE BUYER

46. The buyer may:-

a. Sue for non-delivery. *S.51.* provides that in an action for damages for non-delivery, where there is an available market the measure of damages is, *prima facie*, the difference between the contract price and the market price on the date fixed for delivery, or if no date was fixed, at the time of refusal to deliver.

b. Sue to recover any money paid to the seller.

c. Repudiate the contract for breach of a condition by the seller, unless:-

i. He has waived the breach, and elected to treat it as a breach of warranty; or

ii. The contract is non-severable and he has accepted the goods or part of them. *(S.11(4))*.

d. In respect of a breach of warranty:-

i. Set up the loss in diminution of the price, or

ii.   Sue for damages.

THE SUPPLY OF GOODS AND SERVICES ACT 1982

47. The Act has two main parts. Part I amends the law with respect to terms
implied in certain contracts for the supply of goods. Part II codifies the common
law rules applicable when a person agrees to carry out a service.

48. Part I

a.   Many modern commercial transactions where property is transferred
do not fall within the definition of a sale of goods. For example:-

i.   Contracts for work and materials e.g. building, car repair, and
contracts to install central heating or double glazing.

ii.   Part exchange contracts e.g. when a secondhand car is traded in
part-exchange for a new car the consideration for the new car is partly
money and partly goods. This is defined as a barter not a sale of goods.

iii.   "Free Gifts". If a buyer is given a gift of "product x" if he buys
10 units of "product y" he will own product x although it was not
sold to him.

iv.   Contracts for the hire of goods.

b.   The problem was that Sale of Goods Act protection did not apply to
goods supplied under such contracts. This could be unfair. For example
when someone supplied work and materials his obligations in respect of
the materials were those implied at common law, but if he only supplied
the materials he would be subject to the more stringent requirements of
the Sale of Goods Act.

c.   This anomaly has been remedied by the 1982 Act. The Act applies
to "contracts for the transfer of property in goods" and "contracts for
the hire of goods". Sections 2-5 provide for statutory implied terms on
the part of the seller similar to those in *S.12-15 SALE OF GOODS ACT
1979*. Thus:-

i.   By *S.2* there is an implied condition that the transferor has the
right to transfer the property in the goods.

ii.   By *S.3* there is an implied condition that the goods will correspond
with their description.

iii.   By *S.4* there are implied conditions relating to quality and fitness
for purpose.

iv.   By *S.5* there is an implied condition that where the transfer is by
reference to sample the bulk will correspond with the sample.

d.   Contracts for the hire of goods are defined in *S.6* and *S.7-10* provide
for statutory implied conditions similar to *S.12-15 SALE OF GOODS ACT
1979*.

49. Part II

a.   In October 1981 the National Consumer Council published a report entitled "Service Please". This reported widespread dissatisfaction with regard to consumer services, the main areas of complaint concerned poor quality workmanship, delays in carrying out work and complaints about the price charged. These problems are clearly very important because of the vast number of service contracts made each day, involving for example storage, repairs, cleaning, transport, holidays, banking, dentistry, law, accounting and advertising. The purpose of the Act is to codify the common law relating to the three areas mentioned above, namely skill, time and price.

b.   The Act applies to contracts "under which a person agrees to carry out a service". However it does not apply to contracts of employment, apprenticeships, services rendered to a company by a director and the services of an advocate before a court or tribunal.

c.   By *S.13* there is an implied term that where the supplier is acting in the course of a business he will carry out the service with reasonable care and skill.

d.   By *S.14* there is an implied term that where the supplier is acting in the course of a business and the time for the service to be carried out is not fixed by the contract or determined by the course of dealings between the parties, the supplier will carry out the service within a reasonable time.

e.   By *S.15* there is an implied term that where the consideration is not determined by a contract or in a manner agreed in the contract or by the course of dealing between the parties, the party contracting with the supplier will pay a reasonable price.

50. Exclusion of Liability. *S.7 UNFAIR CONTRACT TERMS ACT 1977* (as amended by the *SUPPLY OF GOODS AND SERVICES ACT 1982*) deals with contracts for the supply of goods other than contracts of sale or hire purchase. *S.2* of the 1977 Act is relevant to Part II of the 1982 Act.

a.   If the exclusion clause relates to title it will be void *(S.7(3A) UCTA 1977)*.

b.   If the exclusion clause relates to description, quality, fitness or sample.

i.   If the buyer deals as a consumer the clause is void *(S.7(2))*.

ii.   If the buyer does not deal as a consumer the exclusion clause must satisfy the requirement of reasonableness *(S.7(3))*.

c.   If the exclusion clause relates to poor quality work, ie a breach of *S.13* the clause must satisfy the requirement of reasonableness (unless the negligent work causes personal injury or death, in which case it is void) *(S.2 UCTA 1977)*.

d.   If there is a complaint in a consumer contract for work and materials it will be necessary to discover the exact nature of the complaint. If it concerns defective materials the exclusion clause will be void. On the other hand if the materials are acceptable but the workmanship is negligent the exclusion clause will have to satisfy the reasonableness test. *S.2* of the 1977 Act does not distinguish between consumer and non-consumer contracts, however recent cases have shown that it is becoming more difficult for a trader to exclude liability for negligence when he deals with a consumer. For example:-

In **WOODMAN v PHOTO TRADE PROCESSING (1981)** (a test case supported by the Consumers Association), P took some film of a friend's wedding to a shop for developing. The shop displayed a notice limiting their liability to the cost of the film. Due to the processors negligence the film was ruined. It was held that the exemption clause in the shop was unreasonable and P was awarded £75 to compensate him for his disappointment.

34 Consumer Credit

INTRODUCTION: THE CONSUMER CREDIT ACT 1974

1. The consumer credit industry is regulated by the *CONSUMER CREDIT ACT 1974*.

2. The purposes of the Act are:-

    a. To introduce a uniform system of statutory control over the provision of credit. It therefore repeals the *HIRE PURCHASE ACT 1965*, and the *MONEYLENDERS* and *PAWNBROKERS ACTS*.

    b. To protect the interests of consumers by introducing a new system of licencing those who offer credit, and by increasing the protection of purchasers of credit by redressing bargaining inequality, controlling trading malpractices and regulating the remedies for default.

3. Previous credit legislation has imposed different rules according to the status of the creditor and the type of lending. The Act treats all lenders alike and regulates in the same way, so far as possible, all forms of credit, for example a cash loan, a sale of goods on credit, a credit card transaction, or a hire-purchase deal. It provides hirers of goods with similar protection to credit purchasers of goods, recognising that hire is often an alternative to credit. It also recognises that:-

    a. Prior to entering into an agreement the consumer needs an adequate supply of information to make an informed choice;

    b. The imposition of trading standards and the provision of consumer protection is needed at every stage of the transaction; and

    c. The credit industry is not made up of creditors only but also a wide range of ancilliary businesses for example debt collectors, debt counsellors, credit reference agencies, and brokers — either a "broker" in the traditional sense, or a retailer offering the financial services of a creditor in order to sell his goods.

4. The responsibility for the operation of the Act rests with the Director General of Fair Trading, whose duties include:-

    a. Supervision of the working and enforcement of the Act, and

    b. Administration of the licencing system.

5. The Act reforms the consumer credit industry within a framework of new and different terminology. The Act applies to *"regulated agreements"*. A regulated agreement may be either a *consumer credit agreement* or a *consumer hire agreement*.

6.   Consumer Credit Agreements

a.   A consumer credit agreement is a credit agreement by which the creditor (who may be an individual or a corporation) provides the debtor (who must be an individual) with credit not exceeding £15,000. The term "individual" is defined to include partnerships and other unincorporated bodies even though they are not usually thought of as "consumers".

b.   *S.10.* provides that credit may be either

  i.   *"Running Account"* credit, ie credit up to an agreed limit, for example a bank overdraft or a credit card; or

  ii.   *"Fixed Sum"* credit, ie credit of a definite amount, for example a bank loan or a hire purchase agreement.

c.   *S.11.* provides for the classification of credit agreements according to the purpose for which the credit is given. It refers to

  i.   *Restricted-use credit.* − The credit facility may be used for a stipulated purpose only, for example a hire-purchase agreement or a shop budget account.

  ii.   *Unrestricted-use credit.* − The debtor may use the loan as he pleases, for example an overdraft facility or an "Access" card if it is used to obtain cash.

d.   *S.12.* and *S.13.* provide a further type of classification based on the relationship between the creditor and the supplier:-

  i.   *Debtor-Creditor-Supplier* agreements, ie where credit is provided to finance a transaction between a debtor and a supplier. If the supplier of the goods also supplied the credit it is still a debtor-creditor-supplier agreement. The usual type of hire purchase transaction involving a consumer, a dealer and a finance company is a debtor-creditor-supplier agreement (see below).

  ii.   *Debtor-Creditor* agreements. − In effect any agreement to supply credit which is not a debtor-creditor-supplier agreement, for example a personal bank loan.

  iii.   The categorisation between debtor-creditor-supplier and debtor-creditor agreements is necessary because under the Act the creditor under a debtor-creditor agreement does not incur any liability for the quality of goods supplied, whereas the creditor who finances sales of goods directly, or in the course of an agreement with the supplier, does have such liability.

e.   The Act also regulates *credit-token* agreements. A credit-token is, for example an "Access" or "Barclaycard", a Cash Dispenser Card, or a credit card issued by a retailer. A number of special rules, which are beyond the scope of this book, apply to such agreements.

7.   Consumer Hire Agreements.

A consumer hire agreement is a bailment of goods to an individual for a period of more than 3 months, for not more than £15,000, and which is not a hire-purchase agreement. (A hire-purchase agreement is a consumer credit agreement).

HIRE-PURCHASE – PRELIMINARY MATTERS

8. Probably the most common method of obtaining the possession and use of goods before making full payment is to enter into a hire-purchase agreement. A hire-purchase is a bailment of goods (ie a delivery of possession of goods) plus the grant of an option to purchase the goods. The consumer does not "agree to buy" the goods at the time of the contract. Therefore if he sells the goods before he has exercised his option to purchase he does not pass title to them.

In **HELBY v MATTHEWS (1895)** the owner of a piano hired it to a bailee. The agreement provided that the bailee should pay monthly instalments, he could terminate by delivering the piano to the owner, and if he paid all the instalments punctually he would become the owner of the piano, but until such time the piano would be the property of the owner. Before paying all the instalments the bailee pledged the piano with a pawnbroker as security for an advance. It was held that the owner could recover the piano from the pawnbroker because the bailee had not "agreed to buy" the piano, he merely had an option either to purchase the piano by paying all the instalments, or to return the piano. Consequently he could not pass title to the pawnbroker.

9. The Role of the Finance Company. Usually when a consumer wishes to purchase goods on hire-purchase the dealer himself does not provide the credit. The dealer sells the goods to a finance company for cash. The finance company (now the owner) then hires the goods to the consumer, the rights and obligations being between the finance company and the consumer, rather than between the dealer and the consumer.

10. Obligations in Relation to Hire-Purchase Contracts

   a. *Obligations of the creditor (owner)*

      i.   The *SUPPLY OF GOODS (IMPLIED TERMS) ACT 1973* imposes obligations relating to title, description, quality and fitness for purpose, and sample very similar to those imposed by the *SALE OF GOODS ACT 1979*. The creditor also has an obligation to deliver the goods at the agreed time, or if no time is agreed, within a reasonable time.

      ii.   The restrictions on the use of exemption clauses imposed by the *UNFAIR CONTRACT TERMS ACT 1977* apply to hire-purchase in the same way as they apply to sale of goods.

      iii. If the creditor breaks an express or implied *condition* of the contract the bailee can treat the contract as at an end and claim damages. He is entitled to re-payment of all the instalments that he has paid, but he must allow the creditor to re-possess the goods. If the creditor breaks a *warranty* the bailee may claim damages.

279

iv.   By *S.56.* if a dealer arranges with a consumer for goods to be sold to a finance company the dealer is deemed to have conducted the negotiations as agent for the creditor. Thus the creditor will be liable for any representations or contractual promises made by the dealer.

b.   *Obligations of the dealer (credit-broker)*

i.   Although the usual type of hire-purchase contract will create a contractual relationship between the finance company (the owner) and the consumer, the dealer may be liable on an implied collateral contract.

In **ANDREWS v HOPKINSON (1956)** a car dealer said of a second-hand car "It's a good little bus; I would stake my life on it; you will have no trouble with it." A hire purchase agreement was entered into. A week later P was injured in a collision caused by a serious defect in the car. P could not sue the finance company because of an effective exemption clause, but he was successful in his action against the dealer, the court holding that there was an implied contract between P and D and express term of which was "you will have no trouble with it". Since this term was broken P received damages. This case is not affected by *S.56.* (above) since that section also preserves the personal liability of the dealer.

ii.   The dealer is deemed to be the agent of the creditor for the purposes of receiving any notice of revocation, cancellation or rescission, and where such notice or payment is received he is deemed to be under a contractual duty to transmit the notice or payment to the creditor.

c.   *Obligations of the debtor*

i.   To take delivery of the goods.

ii.   To take reasonable care of the goods. The debtor is not liable for fair wear and tear, but he will be liable for damage caused by his own negligence, or if he deals with the goods in a manner which is clearly unauthorised by the creditor. If the goods are stolen the agreement will be discharged by frustration and both parties will therefore be free from further liability.

iii.   To pay the instalments, unless the debtor has exercised his option to terminate (see below).

11.   Hire-Purchase, Conditional Sale, and Credit Sale Agreements. In addition to the more common hire-purchase agreements the Act also regulates conditional sale and credit sale agreements.

a.   A *conditional sale* is an agreement for the sale of goods whereby the price is payable by instalments and ownership remains with the seller until fulfilment of all conditions governing payment of instalments and other matters specified in the agreement. The "buyer" under a conditional sale agreement is not regarded as a person who has bought or agreed to buy the goods. Thus he will be treated the same way as a debtor under a hire-purchase agreement and will not be able to pass good title to the goods.

b.   A *credit sale* is an agreement for the sale of goods, the purchase price being payable by 5 or more instalments, not being a conditional sale agreement. Under such agreements the ownership of the goods passes to the buyer at once, and he may therefore pass on good title to another person.

FORMATION OF THE AGREEMENT

12. Licensing

a.   Any person who wishes to carry on a consumer credit or consumer hire business must first obtain a licence from the Director General of Fair Trading, who must be satisfied that the applicant is a fit person to engage in such business.

b.   A person who engages in activities for which a licence is required when he does not have a licence commits a criminal offence and in general the agreement will be unenforceable against the debtor or hirer.

13. Seeking Business

a.   *Advertising of credit.* An advertisement must give a fair and reasonably comprehensive picture of the credit offered, for example the "true" rate of interest. An offence is committed if the advertisement:-

i.   Gives information which is false or misleading in a material respect.

In **METSOJA v NORMAN PITT (1989)** a car dealer advertised a new car with a 0% credit facility. The dealer also operated a part exchange facility, however the part exchange allowance was lower if a new car was bought on credit than it would be if the car were purchased for cash. It was held that the lower allowance on part exchange for persons purchasing on credit was a hidden charge for credit contrary to the Act.

ii.   Fails to comply with the regulations that are from time to time in force.

iii.   Advertises restricted-use credit where the person offering the credit does not hold himself out as prepared to sell the goods or services for cash.

b.   *Canvassing.* It is an offence:-

i.   To solicit entry by an individual into a regulated debtor-creditor agreement *off trade premises*, unless in response to a written request.

ii.   To send an unsolicited credit-token.

iii.   To send a circular to a minor soliciting the use of credit or hire facilities.

14. Formal Requirements

a.   Prior to making the agreement certain information must be disclosed to ensure that the debtor is aware of his rights and duties, the amount and rate of the total charge for credit, and the protection and remedies available to him under the Act.

b.   The agreement itself must:-

i.   Be in writing;

ii.   Contain all express terms in a clearly legible form;

iii.   Be signed by the debtor personally and by or on behalf of the creditor or owner;

iv.   Comply with the current regulations as to form and content; and

v.   In the case of a cancellable agreement, contain a notice in the prescribed form indicating the right of the debtor to cancel the agreement, including how and when the right is exercisable and the name and address of a person to whom notice of cancellation may be given.

c.   *Copies of the agreement.* The debtor must receive:-

i.   Immediately upon signing — a copy of the form that the debtor signs.

ii.   Within 7 days — a second copy of the completed agreement. This second copy is only necessary if the agreement was not completed by the debtor's signature (ie if the creditor has not previously signed it). In the case of a cancellable agreement this copy must be sent by post and must contain details of the debtor's right to cancel.

iii.   Within 7 days (if no second copy is required) — a notice sent by post giving details of rights concerning cancellation of cancellable agreements.

d.   Non-compliance with the required formalities renders the agreement unenforceable against the debtor except on a court order. In some situations, for example if the creditor fails to give notice of the right to cancel, the court must refuse to enforce the agreement.

15.   The Debtor's Right to Cancel

a.   A regulated agreement is cancellable:-

i.   If its prior negotiations included oral representations made in the presence of the consumer by the owner, or creditor, or by a person acting on their behalf, and

ii.   Provided the consumer signed the agreement at a place *other than the place of business* of the owner, creditor, or person acting on their behalf.

b.   Notice of cancellation must be given before the end of the 5th day following the day on which the consumer received the second copy (where necessary) or, if there was no second copy, notice of his cancellation rights. Thus if the consumer signs an unexecuted agreement (ie not yet signed by the creditor) on 1st May, and receives his second copy on 7th May, the cancellation or "cooling off" period will expire at midnight on 12th May.

c.   Notice of cancellation must be in writing and may be served on either

>   i.   The creditor;
>
>   ii.   The credit-broker (for example a garage in a tripartite hire-purchase agreement for the sale of a car) or supplier who negotiated the agreement; or
>
>   iii.   Any person specified in the notice of cancellation rights.

d.   Notice of cancellation is effective when posted, even if it is lost in the post.

e.   The effect of cancellation is that the agreement is treated as if it had never been entered into. Therefore any deposit paid, or goods handed over in part exchange by the consumer must be returned to him, and he has a lien on the goods in his possession until this is done. The consumer need not send the goods back himself, but he must retain them and permit their collection in response to a written request. He has a duty to take reasonable care of the goods for 21 days, but thereafter owes no duty of care unless he has unreasonably refused to comply with a request to permit collection, in which case the duty continues until such request is complied with.

f.   Non-cancellable agreements include non-commercial restricted-use credit arranged to finance the purchase of land, or arranged in connection with a bridging loan, (ie a loan to enable the purchase of a house prior to the sale of the purchaser's previous house), and all agreements signed *on business premises*.

g.   The debtors rights to cancel was recently extended by the *CONSUMER PROTECTION (CANCELLATION OF CONTRACTS CONCLUDED AWAY FROM BUSINESS PREMISES) REGULATIONS 1987.* These give the consumer the right of cancellation not only if the contract is made during the trader's visit, but also if during the visit, the consumer makes an offer which is subsequently accepted by the trader. Even where the trader's visit was requested by the consumer, the agreement will still be cancellable if the consumer requested a visit in connection with a possible supply of a particular type of goods or service and the resulting agreement is for a different type of goods or service which the consumer, when requesting the visit, could not reasonably have known was part of the trader's business.

The Regulations except certain types of agreement, for example agreements for the sale of land, to finance the purchase of land, agreements for building work, agreements for the supply of food and drink, and insurance and investment agreements. Also excepted are agreements where the total payments to be made by the consumer do not exceed £35.

MATTERS ARISING DURING THE AGREEMENT

16. The main obligations of the creditor, dealer and debtor have already been considered. However there are a number of other matters which may arise during the period of a consumer credit agreement.

17. Additional Information. The debtor is entitled to receive, in return for a request in writing and a payment of 15 pence, another copy of his agreement and a statement of the current financial position of his account.

18. Appropriation of Payments. A consumer might have two or more agreements with the same creditor and tender a payment insufficient to discharge the total amount due under all the agreements. In such a case

a.   The consumer may allocate his payment between the various agreements as he thinks fit.

b.   In the absence of allocation by the consumer the creditor must appropriate the payment towards the various sums in due proportion that they bear to one another. He cannot appropriate them to the agreements that would best serve his interests.

19. Early Payment by the Debtor. The debtor is entitled, at any time, by notice to the creditor and payment of all amount outstanding, to discharge his indebtedness.

20. Variation of Agreements. Where, under a power conferred by the agreement, the creditor varies the agreement, for example by increasing the rate of interest payable, the variation does not take effect until notice of it is given to the debtor in the prescribed manner.

21. Death of the Debtor

a.   If the agreement is fully secured the creditor may not take action.

b.   If it is unsecured or partly secured the creditor may take action on an *order of the court* provided he can prove that he has been unable to satisfy himself that the present and future obligations of the consumer are likely to be discharged.

DEFAULT AND TERMINATION

22. Default Notices. Whenever a consumer defaults a creditor is stopped from taking any action to enforce the agreement unless he has first served on the consumer a "default notice" which must specify

a.   The alleged breach;

b.   The action required to put it right if it is capable of remedy; and if not −

c.   What sum, if any, is required to be paid as compensation; and

d.   The date by which such action must be taken, which must be not less than 7 days after the service of the default notice.

23. Further Restriction on Remedies for Default

a.   Where goods are bought on hire purchase *S.90.* provides that once one-third or more of the total price of the goods has been paid the creditor cannot recover possession of them except on an order of the court. Such goods are known as "protected goods".

b.   The section does not apply if the debtor voluntarily surrenders the goods.

c.   If goods are recovered by the creditor in contravention of *S.90.* the agreement will terminate and the debtor is released from all liability. In addition he is entitled to recover from the creditor all sums paid under the agreement.

d.   Entry on to any premises by the creditor to take possession of goods subject to hire-purchase, conditional sale, or consumer hire agreements is prohibited except by court order. Clearly this is of importance if the goods are not protected under *S.90.*

e.   The charging of default interest at a higher rate than the basic rate of interest is prohibited.

24. Termination

a.   The debtor may, at any time before the final payment falls due, terminate a *hire-purchase* or *conditional sale agreement* by giving notice in writing to any person authorised to receive the sums payable under the agreement.

b.   The debtor's liability is to pay the sums which have accrued due, plus the amount, if any, by which one half of the total price exceeds the total of the sums paid, or such lesser amount as may be specified in the agreement. He is also liable to compensate the creditor for any damage to the goods if he has failed to take reasonable care of them.

c.   If any contract term is inconsistent with these provisions, for example a term which imposes additional liability on the debtor, such term is void. The contract may however grant the debtor more favourable terms for termination than those provided by the Act.

d.   Different rules apply to the termination of a *consumer hire agreement*. Termination does not affect any liability which has already accrued. The right to terminate does not arise until the agreement has been in existence for 18 months, unless the agreement itself provides for a shorter period. The period of notice which must be given is one instalment period or 3 months, whichever is less. The right to terminate a consumer hire agreement does not apply:-

   i.   Where the total hire payments exceed £300 per year; or

285

ii.   Where the goods are hired for a business, and are freely chosen by the hirer from a supplier, and the hiring arrangement is not made until the goods have been chosen; or

iii. Where the hirer obtained the goods so that he could in turn hire them out in the course of his business.

JUDICIAL CONTROL

25. Judicial control over the provisions of the Act is exercised by the County Court.

26. Enforcement Orders

a.   In several situations, for example if the agreement is "improperly executed" the Act provides that, before he can enforce the agreement, the creditor must obtain a court order, ie an *"enforcement order"*.

b.   As a general rule the court must dismiss the application if in all the circumstances justice appears to require this. In some cases the court has no choice but to dismiss the application, for example where the agreement was a cancellable one, but the consumer was not given proper notice of his right to cancel it.

27. Time Orders. On an application for an "enforcement order", or on an application to recover possession of goods after service of a default notice, the court may grant a *"time order"*. This gives the consumer more time to pay, or to do something else he should have done, such as maintaining any security in good repair. While a time order is in force the consumer is protected against the consequences of his default, thus a security cannot be enforced, and the goods cannot be recovered by the creditor.

28. Return and Transfer Orders

a.   Where a creditor seeks to recover, because of a breach by the consumer, goods which he has let on hire-purchase, the court may order the consumer to return the goods under a *"return order"*. Where it thinks fit, the court may suspend the return order so long as the consumer keeps up revised payments under a "time order".

b.   As an alternative (in cases where goods may be divided up) the court may make a *"transfer order"* giving ownership of part of the goods to the consumer and returning the rest to the creditor, depending on how much the consumer has already paid in respect of the total price of all the goods.

29. Extortionate Credit Bargains

a.   If the court finds that a credit bargain is extortionate it may re-open the agreement so as to do justice between the parties. Thus it can relieve the consumer of liability to go on paying money, or it can order the return of money already paid by him. The court will consider whether the total charge for credit is exorbitant, and whether the credit agreement and other transactions taken together, grossly contravene ordinary principles of fair dealing. The court will look at, for example:-

i.   The interest rates prevailing at the time the agreement was made;

ii. The degree of financial pressure that the consumer was under; and

iii. The risk to the creditor.

In **KETLEY v SCOTT (1981)** a moneylender agreed to lend £20,500 at 48% interest to a housebuyer who urgently needed the money to complete a purchase. The borrower's application to his bank had been rejected, but the moneylender supplied the money at a few hours notice, and with precarious security. The borrower later claimed that the transaction was extortionate, but the court was not prepared to hold that 48% was excessive in the circumstances. Clearly 48% is a far higher rate than that charged by building societies, but they operate in the "safe" sector of the market. Moneylenders expect more bad debts and are known to charge higher rates. Also the borrower was experienced in business matters, he was not under threat of homelessness and he had not made full disclosure of his own financial position.

b.   If the debtor alleges that a credit bargain is extortionate the creditor must prove that this is not the case.

35 Negotiable Instruments

INTRODUCTION

1. **Choses in Action**

    a. A chose in action is a property right which cannot be enjoyed by physical possession, but which can only be enforced by legal action, for example a debt, patent or copyright.

    b. Most types of chose in action are assignable, (See Chapter 12) but

    i.   Notice to the debtor is always advisable and sometimes essential; and

    ii. The assignee can obtain no better rights than the assignor.

    c. Through customary usage certain types of chose in action have evolved to which these restrictions do not apply. These are known as negotiable instruments.

2. **Negotiable Instruments**

    a. A negotiable instrument is therefore a chose in action which has certain distinguishing characteristics, namely:-

    i.   Title passes by delivery, (if the instrument is payable to "bearer"), or by delivery and indorsement.

    ii. A transferee can obtain a good title even though the transferor had no title or a defective title, provided the instrument was in a negotiable state and the transferee took it in good faith, for value and without notice of any defect in title.

    iii. The holder can sue in his own name.

    b. The negotiability of an instrument can be established by proof that it is universally regarded as such by mercantile usage. Negotiable instruments include:-

    i.   Bills of Exchange;

    ii.   Cheques;

    iii. Promissory notes, including bank notes;

    iv.   Treasury bills;

    v.   Debentures payable to bearer;

    vi.   Share warrants;

    vii. Dividend warrants; and

    viii. Bankers' drafts.

    c. Postal orders, money orders, IOUs, and share certificates are not negotiable instruments.

BILLS OF EXCHANGE

3. The Purposes of a Bill of Exchange. The use of bills of exchange in domestic transactions is now comparatively uncommon. They are however frequently used in foreign trade. Cheques (which are a particular type of bill of exchange) are of course very important both in commercial and consumer transactions. The purposes of a bill can be illustrated by an example:-

If B (a buyer) owes S (a seller) £5,000 for goods supplied, by using a bill of exchange he can request F (probably a financier or agent) to pay the debt, B having given or agreed to give F the necessary funds. At the same time the bill can be used to enable B to obtain a period of credit, whilst S will nevertheless receive prompt payment (although of a slightly smaller amount). The bill of exchange may be drawn as follows:-

---

London 2nd January 1988

To: F

Three months after date pay S or order the sum of
Five Thousand Pounds (£5,000), value received.

Signed: B

Thus B has drawn a bill requiring F to pay £5,000 to S or to the order of S. Note that:-

a. The bill is payable at a fixed date in the future, but it could have been made payable *"on demand"*.

b. The bill is payable to "S or order". A bill may however be made payable to *"bearer"*.

c. S will have to *"present"* the bill to F since F will not have an obligation to pay until he has *"accepted"* the bill by signing his name on the face of it. By accepting the bill F becomes primarily liable to pay the bill on the agreed date.

d. S may keep the bill until the agreed date, ie until maturity, and then present it to F for payment or he may sell (ie *negotiate*) it. The buyer will pay less than £5,000 for the bill because he will have to wait until maturity to collect the money. The buyer is said to have *"discounted"* the bill.

e. The bill may be negotiated several times before payment. Negotiation is effected by the holder signing his name on the back of the bill. This is known as *indorsement*.

f. Although the acceptor (F) is primarily liable to pay, the drawer (B) and any indorser may also be liable on the bill. By signing the bill each indorser acts as a surety for the acceptor, although each indorser can claim an indemnity from the drawer or a previous indorser.

g. If F refuses to pay the bill when it is presented for payment on the agreed date it is said to be *"dishonoured"* and the holder will be able to sue F, or as stated above he may sue the drawer or a subsequent indorser.

4. The Parties to a Bill of Exchange. It will be useful at this stage to summarise the parties to a bill, and to introduce 2 new terms (h. and i. below).

a. *Drawer.* The person who orders money to be paid on his behalf.

b. *Drawee.* The person to whom the order is given.

c. *Payee.* The person to whom the money will be paid.

d. *Indorser.* The holder of an order bill who signs the back when transferring it.

e. *Indorsee.* The person to whom an order bill is indorsed.

f. *Bearer.* The person in possession of a bearer bill.

g. *Holder.* The payee or indorsee who is in possession of an order bill or the person in possession of a bearer bill (the bearer).

h. *Holder for value.* A holder who has given, or who is deemed to have given value.

i. *Holder in due course.* A holder who has taken a bill

   i. Complete and regular on the face of it;

   ii. Before it was overdue;

   iii. Without notice of previous dishonour by non-payment;

   iv. In good faith;

   v. For value;

   vi. Without notice of any defect at the time of negotiation.

Note that:-

   i. The payee cannot be a holder in due course because the bill is made *payable* to him, it is not *negotiated* to him. (**JONES v WARING & GILLOW (1926)**).

   ii. The difference between a holder for value and a holder in due course is important because a holder for value can only acquire the same title as his transferor, whereas a holder in due course can sometimes acquire a better one. An example is given at **20.** below.

THE STATUTORY DEFINITION OF A BILL OF EXCHANGE

5. Sufficient background information has now been given to introduce the definition of a bill of exchange. The definition appears in the *BILLS OF EXCHANGE ACT 1882* and any references to sections in this chapter are references to this Act, unless otherwise stated.

6. By *S.3*. "A *bill of exchange* is an unconditional order in writing addressed by one person to another signed by the person giving it, requiring the person to whom it is addressed to pay on demand or at a fixed or determinable future time a sum certain in money to, or to the order of, a specified person or to bearer".

7. The Act also defines a cheque. By *S.73*. "A *cheque* is a bill of exchange drawn on a banker payable on demand". In relation to cheques the definition of a bill of exchange may be re-drafted as follows:-

A cheque is an unconditional order in writing, addressed by one person *to a banker*, signed by the person giving it, requiring *the banker* to pay on demand a sum certain in money to or to the order of a specified person or to bearer.

Note that:-

a. The words "or at a fixed or determinable future time" have been omitted.

b. The "drawee" is the banker on whom the cheque is drawn, ie the *paying bank*.

c. The bank which collects payment for its customer (the payee) who pays in the cheque for the credit of his account is known as the *collecting bank*.

8. To comply with the definition of either a bill or a cheque the instrument must fulfil the following conditions:-

a. It must be an *order* and not a mere request.

b. The order must be *unconditional* as between the drawer and the drawee.

In **BAVINS v LONDON AND SOUTH WESTERN BANK (1900)** the direction of the drawer was to pay "on the attached receipt being signed". This was held to impose a condition on the drawee. The instrument was not therefore a bill.

Contrast **NATHAN v OGDENS (1905)** where at the foot of the instrument it was stated that "the receipt on the back must be signed". It was held that these words were addressed to the payee rather than the drawee. The instrument was therefore unconditional as between drawer and drawee and was therefore a valid bill.

c. The order must be in *writing*. "Writing" includes printing, although the bill or cheque need not necessarily be drawn on a printed form.

d. The order must be addressed by *one person to another*. "Person" in the Act includes a body of persons whether incorporated or not. Thus it includes both limited companies and partnerships. The drawer and the drawee may be the same person. The best known example is a *banker's draft* which is an order addressed by the bank to itself. Banker's drafts are usually used to pay for a purchase of land because the amount of money

291

involved is such that the vendor would not be prepared to accept a cheque. The fact that the order is signed by the bank itself makes it a safer method of payment than an order signed by any other person. A customer who requires the issue of a draft has to sign a draft request form. The bank then debit his account with the amount and give him the draft.

e.   The order must be *signed by the drawer*. The drawer need not sign at the time the bill is drawn, but until this is done the bill is of no effect. The drawer need not sign with his own hand, but may do so by a duly authorised agent. It appears that a mechanically produced signature is also acceptable.

f.   The order must be to *pay money*, which includes foreign currency.

g.   The order must be to *pay a sum certain*. *S.9*. provides that a sum is certain although it is required to be paid:-

   i.   With interest;

   ii.   By stated instalments;

   iii.   By stated instalments with a provision that upon default in payment of any instalment the whole shall become due;

   iv.   According to an indicated rate of exchange.

Where the sum payable is expressed in words and also in figures and there is a discrepancy between the two, the sum denoted by the words is the amount payable (*S.9(2)*.).

h.   *On demand*. A bill is payable on demand if expressed to be payable on demand or at sight or on presentation or if no time for payment is expressed. (*S.10.*) A cheque does not contain any indication that it is payable on demand, but it is so payable as a result of this section.

i.   At a *fixed or determinable future time*. By *S.11*. this means

   i.   At a fixed period after date or sight; or

   ii.   On or at a fixed period after the occurrence of a specified event which is certain to happen, though the time of happening may be uncertain.

"Sight" means when the drawee signifies his acceptance.

j.   *To, or to the order of, a specified person*. Unless the bill is payable to bearer, the payee must be named or indicated with reasonable certainty. A bill may be payable to two or more persons jointly, or to the holder of a particular office, for example "Pay the County Treasurer". The bill must however be payable to a person. Therefore a *"Pay Cash"* instrument is not a valid bill. A bill may however be made payable to the drawer. *"Pay self"* is therefore adequate for a bill or cheque. The term *"order bill"* refers to a bill which is payable to, or to the order of, a specified person without words prohibiting further transfer, for example Pay X; or Pay X or order; or Pay X indorsed "Pay Y signed X". An order bill requires a valid indorsement to complete transfer.

k.   *To bearer.* By *8(3)* a bill is payable to bearer if it is drawn as such, or if the only or last indorsement is in blank. When the holder of an order bill signs the back without adding words indicating to whom the bill is indorsed the bill is said to be *indorsed in blank*. A bearer bill may be transferred by delivery, no indorsement being required.

l.   *Dating*

    i.   By *S.3.* a bill is not invalid because it is not dated.

    ii.   By *S.13.* a bill may be ante-dated, post-dated, or dated on a Sunday.

CAPACITY, SIGNATURE AND DELIVERY

9.   Capacity

a.   By *S.22.* capacity to incur liability on a bill is co-extensive with capacity to contract.

b.   A minor is never liable on a bill **(RE SOLTYKOFF (1891))**.

c.   A trading company has an implied power to draw and indorse.

d.   Although a drawer or indorser lacking capacity is not liable, a holder can enforce a bill against any other party. For example A draws a cheque on B Bank in favour of C who is a minor. C indorses the cheque to D. This can be expressed diagrammatically

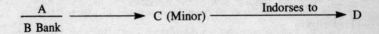

D can sue A when the cheque is dishonoured, but he cannot sue C.

10.   Signature

a.   By *S.23.* no person is liable as drawer or indorser who has not signed as such.

b.   By *S.56.* if a person signs a bill otherwise than as a drawer or indorser he is liable as an indorser to a holder in due course. This may occur when, for example, the director of a company adds his signature to a bill because the other party to a contract considers that the "signature" of the company is inadequate security. The director is said to have *"backed"* the bill and he is known as a *quasi-indorser*.

c.   *Agents*

    i.   The signature of any party to a bill may be written on it by some other person with his authority.

ii.   A signature by procuration, for example, "X per pro Y", operates as a notice that the agent has limited authority, and if he exceeds his authority his principal is not bound. *(S.25.)*.

In **MORRISON v KEMP (1912)** A clerk was authorised to draw cheques "per pro" his employer for the employer's business. He drew a cheque in this form in favour of a bookmaker in settlement of a private debt. The bookmaker cashed the cheque. It was held that the employer was not bound, and could recover the money from the bookmaker.

iii.   Where an agent signs a bill in his own name he is personally liable on the bill unless he adds the words making it clear that he is signing in the *capacity of agent*.

iv.   If however a person merely adds the words *describing himself as agent* he will not be exempt from personal liability. In cases of doubt the construction most favourable to the validity of the bill must be adopted.

In **ELLIOTT v BAX-IRONSIDE (1925)** a bill was addressed to F Ltd. It was accepted by F Ltd as follows:-
"Accepted . . . . . H. Bax-Ironside, R. Mason, directors, F Ltd."
The bill was also signed on the back:-
"F Ltd., H. Bax-Ironside, R. Mason, directors".

The payee sued the directors personally on the bill. It was held that they were liable since if the company were regarded as indorsing a bill which it had already validly accepted nothing would be added to its value by the indorsement. The most favourable construction for the validity of the bill was therefore to regard the indorsement as the personal indorsement of the directors.

11. Delivery

a.   Delivery is the transfer of possession from one person to another.

b.   Every contract on a bill is incomplete and revocable until delivery *(S.21.)*.

c.   Delivery must be made with the authority of the party assuming liability, but note the following presumptions:-

i.   Where a bill is no longer in possession of a signatory a valid delivery by him is presumed until disproved.

ii.   If the bill reaches a holder in due course a valid delivery of the bill by all parties prior to him so as to make them liable is conclusively presumed.

INCOHATE BILLS

12. *S.20.* provides that where a bill is wanting in any material particular the person in possession has prima facie authority to fill up the omission in any way he thinks fit.

13. In order to be enforceable against any person who became a party *prior to its completion*, the bill must be filled in:-

    a.   Within a reasonable time:

    In **GRIFFITHS v DALTON (1940)** the date of a cheque was filled in 18 months after the cheque was issued. It was held that this was an unreasonable delay and the payee could not enforce payment against the drawer.

    b.   Strictly in accordance with the authority given.

14. If, *after completion*, a bill is negotiated to a holder in due course, there is an estoppel in his favour as regards points a. and b. above. ie He can enforce it as if it had been completed within a reasonable time and in accordance with the drawers instructions. For example if a principal (P) gives his agent (A) a blank cheque, (with both the payee's name and the amount omitted), and instructions to purchase particular goods using the cheque P will, prima facie, not be liable if A uses the cheque to discharge his own private debts. If however the cheque is later negotiated to a holder in due course (who by definition will be unaware that the cheque has been filled up contrary to instructions) he will be able to enforce it against P.

15. Although the payee cannot be a holder in due course he may be able to rely on common law estoppel if he has changed his position in reliance on the drawer's signature.

    In **LLOYDS BANK v COOKE (1907)** D signed a blank paper and gave it to one of P's customers with authority to complete it as a promissory note for £250 payable to P. The purpose of the transaction was to enable the customer to use the note as security for an advance by P. The customer fraudulently filled up the promissory note for £1000 and obtained an advance of this amount from P. It was held that P could not succeed against D under *S.20.* because he was the original payee. However since P did not know of the fraud and because he had altered his position in reliance on D's signature D was estopped from denying the validity of the promissory note and was liable to P for £1000.

16. *S.20.* only applies where the instrument is *delivered* for the purposes of completion, and not where it is *stolen* before completion (**BAXENDALE v BENNETT (1878)**).

CONSIDERATION

17. The liability of a party to a bill is contractual in its nature and depends on the presence or absence of consideration. Any consideration sufficient to support a simple contract constitutes valuable consideration for a bill *(S.27.)*.

18. The rules as to consideration for a bill however differ from those for a simple contract because:-

a.   Consideration may be past, ie an "antecedent debt or liability" *(S.27.)*. Thus if S sells goods to B and several days later B gives S a cheque as payment for the goods, the consideration for the cheque is an "antecedent debt", but due to *S.27.* this is acceptable. The "antecedent debt" or liability will usually be that of the drawer. However if it is the debt of some other person the holder must show that he has given some normal consideration to the transferee of the bill if he is to enforce payment against him.

In **OLIVER v DAVIS AND WOODCOCK (1949)** D owed money to O. Being unable to pay he asked W to draw a cheque in favour of O to discharge his debt. This was done, but W stopped the cheque before payment and denied that O had give value. O produced two arguments in his attempt to claim to be a holder for value, and therefore entitled to payment:-

i.   There was an antecedent debt or liability and this was sufficient consideration;

ii.   He had provided consideration by forbearing to sue D.

He failed on both arguments, on the first because there was not a sufficient relationship between O and W. He failed on the second because of lack of evidence for an agreement not to sue.

b.   Consideration is presumed in favour of a plaintiff on a bill until the defendant proves the absence of it *(S.30.)*.

c.   Consideration need not move from the promisee. If value has at any time been given for a bill the holder is deemed to be a holder for value as regards all parties to the bill who became parties prior to that time. *(S.27(2))*.

d.   By *S.27(3)* where the holder of a bill has a lien on it, arising either from contract or by implication of law, he is deemed to be a holder for value to the extent of the sum for which he has a lien. For example a banker has a lien on cheques paid into an overdrawn account.

19.   Holder in Due Course. At this point it will be useful to return to holders in due course in preparation for the following example. The subject is complicated so no apologies are made for some repetition.

a.   If there is a defect on a bill, for example fraud or theft, a transferee will take free from the defect and get a better title than the transferor provided he is a holder in due course.

b.   By *S.29.* a holder in due course is a holder who has taken a bill — complete and regular on the face of it; before it was overdue; without notice of previous dishonour; in good faith; for value; and without notice of any defect at the time of negotiation.

c.   A payee cannot be a holder in due course since a bill is not negotiated to him.

d. A person deriving title through a holder in due course has the same rights as the holder in due course as regards parties prior to the holder in due course, even though he knows of the defect, unless he was himself a party to the defect, for example a party to a fraud.

20. Example on Consideration, Holder for Value and Holder in Due Course

a. *Facts*. A draws a bearer cheque on B Bank and gives it to C as part of a transaction. It is stolen by D. These and the subsequent events can be expressed as follows.

$$
\frac{\text{A}}{\text{B Bank}} \xrightarrow{\quad \text{Value} \quad} \text{C} \parallel \text{D} \xrightarrow{\quad \text{Gift} \quad} \text{E} \xrightarrow{\quad \text{Value} \quad} \text{F} \xrightarrow{\quad \text{Gift} \quad} \text{G}
$$

Stolen by D

b. *Points arising:*

i. D became the holder (because it is a bearer cheque) although C is the true owner.

ii. E is not a holder in due course (because he has not given value), but although it was a gift he is a holder for value because *S.27(1)* states that an antecedent debt or liability is deemed valuable consideration and C gave value.

iii. Because E is not a holder in due course the cheque is not free from its prior defect and E therefore takes it subject to C's right of restoration.

iv. F gave value, and provided he satisfies the other requirements he is a holder in due course. He is therefore the owner of the cheque and he would not have to restore it to C.

v. G is not a holder in due course, because he has not given value, but provided G is not implicated in D's theft he has the same rights as a holder in due course.

NEGOTIATION AND INDORSEMENT

21. Negotiation

a. A bill is negotiated when it is transferred from one person to another in such a manner as to constitute the transferee the holder of the bill.

b. A bill may be negotiated either

i. If it is payable to *bearer*, by delivery; or

ii. If it is payable to *order*, by indorsement of the holder completed by delivery.

297

c.   If the holder of an *order* bill transfers it for *value* without indorsement, then the transferee acquires the same title as the transferor had in the bill, plus the right to have the transferor's indorsement *(S.31)*. The indorsement does not relate back to the date of the defective transfer. Thus if there is a defect, for example fraud on the bill, the transferee will not be a holder in due course unless he was still unaware of the defect at the time of the indorsement.

d.   The indorsement must be written on the bill itself, and signed by the indorser. The simple signature of the indorser is sufficient.

e.   The indorsement must be of the entire bill. A partial indorsement, ie purporting to transfer to the indorsee part of the amount payable, does not operate as a negotiation.

22. Kinds of Indorsement

a.   *In blank.* ie By simple signature of the indorser without specifying any indorsee. A bill so indorsed becomes payable to bearer.

b.   *Special.* ie Specifying the person to whom the bill is payable. That person must indorse if he wishes to transfer the bill. The bill remains an order bill.

c.   *Restrictive.* ie Prohibiting further negotiation of the bill. For example "Pay X only".

d.   *Conditional.* If a bill purports to be indorsed conditionally, the condition may be disregarded by the payer, and payment to the indorsee is valid whether the condition has been fulfilled or not.

e.   *Qualified.* ie With the addition of a provision excluding or limiting the indorser's own liability to the holder.

LIABILITY

23. Drawer and Indorser

a.   By *S.55(1)* the drawer of a bill undertakes that on due presentment the bill will be paid, and that if dishonoured he will compensate the holder and any indorser who is compelled to pay it, provided the requisite proceedings on dishonour are taken.

b.   By *S.55(2)* a similar undertaking is given by an indorser in favour of the holder and indorsers subsequent to himself.

24. Transferor by Delivery.
Where the holder of a bill payable to *bearer* negotiates it by delivery without indorsing it he is called a *"transferor by delivery"*. Note that:-

a.   He is not liable on the bill, not having signed it he is not even a party to it.

298

b.   However by *S.58.* he warrants to his *immediate transferee* if the transfer is for *value*:-

   i.   The the bill is what it purports to be, ie a valid bill;

   ii.   That he has the right to transfer it; and

   iii.   That at the time of the transfer he is not aware of any fact which renders it valueless.

25. Example on Liability

a.   *Facts:* A draws an order cheque on B Bank in favour of C. C indorses it in blank, (converting it to a bearer cheque), and transfers it for value to D. It is then transferred for value to E and from him to F. When F presents the cheque at B Bank it is dishonoured. The facts can be represented as follows:-

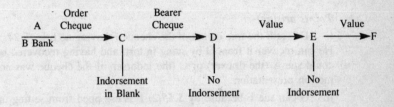

b.   *Points arising:-*

   i.   F can sue A under *S.55(1)* and C under *S.55(2)*.

   ii.   He cannot sue D because D has not signed the cheque and because he is not D's immediate transferee.

   iii.   F cannot sue E on the cheque, but he will be able to sue him on *S.58.* if he can prove that E has broken one of the 3 warranties. Thus if E knew at the time of the transfer that the cheque was valueless he will be liable.

   NB. F need not give notice of dishonour since A has drawn a cheque rather than a bill of exchange.

FORGERY AND FICTITIOUS PAYEES

26. The *basic rule* is that a forged or unauthorised signature on a bill is wholly inoperative and any person taking such a bill has not title to it and is unable to sue on it (*S.24.*).

In **VINDEN v HUGHES (1905)** a fraudulent clerk represented to his employer (P) that money was owed to certain customers who were *well known* to the employer. The employer drew the cheques. The clerk then forged the indorsements of the customers and negotiated the cheques to D who took them in good faith and for value. It was held that P could recover the amounts of the cheques because the forged indorsements were of no effect.

27. There is a *statutory exception* to the above basic rule *S.55(2)* states that an indorser is precluded from denying to a holder in due course the genuineness and regularity in all respects of the drawer's signature and all previous indorsements.

28. Example on Forged Indorsements

a. *Facts:* These can be represented as follows:-

b. *Points arising:-*

i.   D is still the true owner of the cheque F having no title *(S.24.)*. He can recover it from G by suing in tort, and having recovered he could sue A (the drawer) or C (the indorser) if the cheque was not met on presentation.

ii.   G can sue F because by *S.55(2)* F is estopped from setting up the forgery of D's indorsement.

iii.   The double line operates as a barrier. No rights of action can be transferred across the barrier although the parties on either side have rights amongst themselves.

29. Common Law Estoppel. In addition to the statutory estoppel in *S.55(2)* a party may be estopped at common law from setting up a forgery of his own signature.

In **GREENWOOD v MARTINS BANK (1933)** a husband (H) discovered that his wife (W) had been drawing from his account by forging his signature. To avoid publicity he did not tell the bank. He subsequently discovered that W's explanation of her forgeries was untrue and he threatened to reveal what she had done to the bank, whereupon W committed suicide. He then brought an action against the bank reclaiming the money which it had paid under the forged cheques. His action failed. He was estopped because of his failure to report the forgeries as soon as he had discovered them. This led the bank to believe that the payments were authorised, and it did not therefore sue W during her lifetime, which would have enabled it to recover some of the money. The bank had therefore been adversely affected by H's omission.

30. Fictitious Payee

a. By *S.7(3)* where the payee is a fictitious or non-existing person the bill may be treated as payable to bearer.

b.   This provision is important where a person "forges" the indorsement of the non-existing person. Since the bill is treated as payable to bearer the forged indorsement is superfluous since no indorsement is required to transfer a bearer bill. In contrast, as shown above, a forged indorsement on an order bill makes the bill wholly inoperative. The following case should be contrasted with **VINDEN v HUGHES (1905)**, **(26.** above).

In **CLUTTON v ATTENBOROUGH (1897)** a fraudulent clerk wrote a cheque in favour of G. Brett, a name which he *invented*. He persuaded his employer (P) to sign the cheque by falsely representing that G. Brett had done work for the firm. The clerk "forged" G. Brett's indorsement and negotiated the cheque to D, who obtained payment from P's bank. It was held that since the payee was non-existing the cheque may be treated as payable to bearer, the forged indorsement was therefore superfluous and did not render the cheque inoperative. D was therefore a holder in due course and was entitled to retain the money. The difference between this case and Vinden v Hughes is that in Vinden v Hughes the payees were *well known* to the employer. In Clutton v Attenborough the payee was *fictitious*.

DISCHARGE

31.   Presentation for Payment

a.   If a bill falls due for payment on a particular day it must be presented on that day otherwise the drawer and indorsers are discharged.

In **YEOMAN CREDIT v GREGORY (1963)** a bill was presented to the acceptor for payment one day late. It was held that the defendant indorser was discharged from liability.

b.   In the case of a bill payable *on demand* it must be presented for payment within a reasonable time of issue to render the drawer liable, and within a reasonable time of indorsement to render an indorser liable. If not so presented they are discharged *(S.45.)*.

32.   Notice of Dishonour

a.   When a bill has been dishonoured by non-payment, notice of dishonour must be given to the drawer and to each indorser, otherwise they are discharged *(S.48.)*.

b.   Notice may be written or oral, and it must be given within a reasonable time. A reasonable time is the day after the dishonour if the parties live in the same postal district. If they live in different postal districts then the notice should be sent off on the day after the dishonour of the bill.

33.   Payment in Due Course

a.   A bill is discharged when all rights of action on it are extinguished. The usual method is by *payment in due course*.

b. By *S.59.* this means payment in good faith to the holder at or after maturity without the drawee or acceptor having notice that the holder's title is defective. For example:-

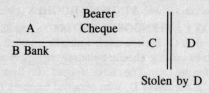

If D obtains payment from B Bank the bank can debit A's account, unless it knew D's title was defective.

c. In the following example the bill would not be discharged:-

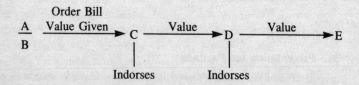

If the bill is dishonoured by B, E may obtain payment from D *(S.55(2))*, but this payment does not discharge the bill because rights still subsist between B, C and D.

34. Material Alteration

a. A bill may also be discharged by material alteration. By *S.64.* if a bill is materially altered, for example its amount or its date, it is void, except as against a party who made authorised, or assented to the alteration, and subsequent indorsers.

b. If the alteration is *not apparent* a holder in due course may enforce the cheque is originally drawn against parties prior to the alteration.

c. *S.64.* does not apply to accidental alteration or damage.

In **HONG KONG AND SHANGHAI BANK v LO LEE SHI (1928)** A banknote (which is a negotiable instrument) was washed while in the pocket of a garment, so that parts of it were illegible. It was held that this accidental damage was not a material alteration, and since its identity as a note of the bank could be established, the holder was entitled to recover from the bank the amount for which the note had been issued.

35. Example on Material Alteration

a. *Facts:* A draws a cheque for £50 on B Bank in favour of C. C fraudulently (and visibly) alters the cheque to £150 and indorses it to D who indorses it to E:-

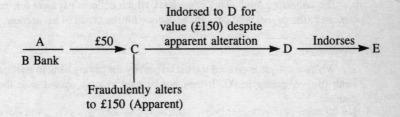

b. *Points arising:-*

i.   E has no rights against A or B Bank because the cheque is void as against them *(S.64.)*.

ii.   E can sue C and D on their indorsements (C being the person who made the alteration, and D being a subsequent indorser).

iii.   If the alteration were *not apparent* E would be a holder in due course, and he could therefore sue A and B Bank for £50 as well as C and D for £150. This would be useful if C and D were both insolvent.

CHEQUES

36. This chapter has so far been concerned with rules applicable to all types of bills of exchange (including cheques). Paragraphs **36.** to **46.** are concerned with rules which only apply to cheques. Refer back to paragraph **7.** to revise the definition of a cheque.

37. The Differences between Cheques and Other Bills.

a.   Acceptance does not apply. Thus the holder cannot sue the banker on whom it is drawn for non-payment. (Remember that in the case of a bill of exchange the drawee "accepts" the bill by signing his name on the bill. He is then primarily liable to pay).

b.   The holder rarely has to give notice of dishonour to the drawer of a cheque. (The drawer will know that it will be dishonoured).

c.   A banker may be protected against a forged or unauthorised indorsement of a cheque drawn on him, *(S.60.)*, (see below). There is no corresponding protection for the drawee of other bills.

d.   The drawer of a cheque is under a duty *to his banker* to exercise reasonable care when drawing the cheque, (see below). The drawer of any other bill owes no corresponding duty.

e.   Crossings only apply to cheques.

38.   Terminology

a.   The *drawee* is the *banker* on whom the cheque is drawn. It is also referred to as the *paying bank*.

b.   The *collecting bank*. This is the bank which collects payment for its customer (the payee) who pays in the cheque for the credit of his account.

39.   Crossings

a.   Where a cheque is crossed it must be paid by the paying bank to another bank (the collecting bank). It may not be paid as cash passed over the counter.

b.   Types:-

i.   *General crossing.* ie / / plus optional "and co". − The cheque can only be paid to another banker.

ii.   *Special crossing.* ie The name of the bank is written across the front. It must be paid to that bank only.

iii.   *"Not negotiable"*. These words may be added to a general or special crossing. The cheque is still transferable, but it is not negotiable, ie the transferee cannot get a better title than the transferor, he cannot become a holder in due course.

iv.   *"A/c payee"*. This marking is not mentioned in the Act. Therefore the cheque remains a negotiable instrument. However in practice the collecting bank will not collect it except for the payee.

v.   *"Not transferable"*. This prevents transfer and negotiation. The cheque will either be crossed "Not Transferable" or carry the order "Pay X Only".

c.   Where a paying bank pays in contravention of a crossing it is liable to the true owner of the cheque for the resulting loss.

40.   Cheque as a Receipt

a.   By *S.3. CHEQUES ACT 1957* an *unindorsed* cheque which appears to have been paid by the banker on whom it is drawn is evidence of receipt by the payee of the sum payable by the cheque.

b.   A paid *indorsed* cheque has always been regarded as prima facie evidence of payment. The effect of *S.3.* is therefore to give a paid unindorsed cheque the same evidential value.

41.   Relationship between Banker and Customer.
The relationship is a simple contractual relationship of debtor and creditor with the added obligation of honouring the customer's cheques to the extent to which he is in credit or to the extent of any agreed overdraft.

42. Duties of the Customer

    a. To indemnify the bank against authorised payments made on his behalf.

    b. To take reasonable care when drawing cheques to prevent alteration of the amount.

In **LONDON JOINT STOCK BANK v MACMILLAN (1918)** a clerk prepared a cheque for M's signature. He wrote £2 in figures, and left the space for the words blank. M signed the cheque. The clerk then altered the figures to £120 and wrote "One hundred and twenty pounds" in the space provided for words, and obtained payment from M's bank. It was held that the loss was due to a breach of duty by M, and the bank could therefore debit M's account.

Contrast **SLINGSBY v DISTRICT BANK (1931)** Executors drew a cheque in favour of "X and Co." leaving a gap between the payee's name and the printed words "or order". A fraudulent clerk then altered the cheque by writing in the gap "Per Y and Z". He then indorsed the cheque and obtained payment. It was held that the executors were not negligent in leaving a gap after the name of the payee. The bank were therefore unable to debit the executors' account.

    c. To inform the bank of any forgeries of which he is aware. — **GREENWOOD v MARTIN'S BANK (1933)** (see **29.**).

43. Duties of the Banker

    a. To take reasonable care in its conduct of the customer's business.

    b. To honour cheques. If a banker wrongly refuses to honour a cheque the customer, if he is a trader, can claim substantial damages without proof of loss. Other customers can only claim nominal damages unless actual loss is proved (**GIBBONS v WESTMINSTER BANK (1938)**). The main instances when the duty to honour ends are:-

    i. On countermand of payment. — Actual notice must be given to the correct branch of the bank.

    ii. On receipt of notice of the customer's death or mental disorder.

    iii. On notice of an act of bankruptcy by the customer, or on liquidation if the customer is a company.

    c. Duty of secrecy. This duty extends to all information acquired in his character as banker and not merely the state of the account. The duty does not end with the closing of the account. It does end:-

    i. When disclosure is under compulsion of law;

In **BARCLAYS BANK v TAYLOR (1989)** it was held that the Bank was not in breach of its duty of confidentiality by complying with an order under S.9. Police and Criminal Evidence Act 1984 for the disclosure of a customer's accounts to the police. Furthermore the Bank was under no duty to oppose the application by the police, nor inform the customer that an order for disclosure had been made.

ii. When there is a public duty to disclose, for example if the country is at war and the customer's account indicates that he is trading with the enemy;

iii. Where the interest of the bank requires disclosure, for example where the banker is suing on an overdraft;

iv. Where the customer expressly or impliedly consents, for example if he gives his banker's name as a reference;

d. To collect for customer's account cheques paid in by the customer.

44. Payment Without Authority. If a banker pays a cheque without authority, for examply if the customer's signature is forged, or the cheque is void for material alteration, prima facie the banker cannot debit his customer's account. The exceptions to this rule are when the customer is himself in breach of his duties to the banker.

45. Protection of the Paying Bank

a. Subject to the provisions below if a banker collects payment of a valid cheque for a person who has no title to it, both the paying banker and the collecting banker, although they acted innocently, are prima facie liable to the true owner for conversion of the cheque, the measure of damages being its face value.

b. By *S.59.* payment to a holder in good faith, without notice that his title is defective constitutes a valid payment, discharges the cheque, and absolves the banker from liability. It entitles him to debit the customer's account. − This is "payment in due course". This section provides a defence if the bank pays the bearer of a bearer cheque, but no defence if it pays an order cheque with a forged or unauthorised indorsement, because such a person is not the holder, and therefore payment would not be payment in due course. *S.60.* provides for this situation.

c. By *S.60.* where a banker pays a cheque drawn on him in good faith and in the ordinary course of business, he is not prejudiced by the fact that an *indorsement* was forged or made without authority, and he is deemed to have paid the cheque in due course. For example:-

306

F obtains payment from B Bank. If the bank pay in good faith, and in the ordinary course of business, they are not prejudiced by the forged indorsement *(S.60.)*. Consequently:-

i.   They can debit A's account.

ii.   They are not liable in conversion to the true owner, C.

iii. C cannot sue A, because payment in due course discharges the drawer.

iv.   C can sue E or F for conversion.

v.   If F has to account to C then F can sue E under *S.55(2)*, with the result that the loss is borne by the victim of the fraud, E. E's sole rights are against D.

d.   By *S.80.* a banker who pays a cheque in good faith, without negligence, and in accordance with the crossing shall be entitled to the same rights, and to be placed in the same position as if payment of the cheque had been made to the true owner. For example A draws a cheque on X Bank in favour of Smith. Smith recieves the cheque and crosses it generally. The cheque is stolen by T who goes to Y Bank and opens an account in Smith's name and pays in the cheque. Y Bank present the cheque to X Bank who pay in good faith, and without negligence. Although T had no title *S.80.* protects X Bank (the paying bank) from liability to the real Smith, who is also barred from suing A. As with the *S.60.* example the loss falls on the victim of the fraud.

e.   By *S.1. CHEQUES ACT 1957* where a banker in good faith and in the ordinary course of business pays a cheque drawn on him which is not indorsed, he does not in doing so incur any liability by reason only of the absence of, or irregularity in, indorsement, and he is deemed to have paid in due course. The Committee of London Clearing Bankers (in effect all English bankers) have decided that although this provision dispenses with the legal necessity of a banker requiring to see the payee's indorsement in all cases, bankers will in practice insist upon the payee's indorsement except when a cheque is paid into a bank for the credit of the payee's account. Thus a paying banker will require the payee's indorsement before cashing a cheque over the counter. It follows that a banker disregarding this practice would not be acting in the ordinary course of business.

f.   None of the above sections give protection where the *drawer's* signature is *forged*, or where a cheque is void for *material alteration*. In such cases a banker cannot generally debit his customer's account.

46. Protection of the Collecting Bank. A banker who collects payment of a valid cheque for a person who is not the true owner can be sued in conversion. He can only escape liability in two cases:-

a.   By *S.4. CHEQUES ACT 1957* a banker will be protected where bona fide, and without negligence it receives payment for a customer, or on crediting his account receives payment for itself. Note that:-

i.   A banker is not negligent merely because of the absence of or irregularity in indorsement.

ii.   "Customer" means a person with an account at the bank.

iii.   The bank must disprove negligence. If the circumstances are suspicious and should have put the bank on inquiry then it may be liable, for example if an employee pays into his private account a cheque payable to his employer, but indorsed in favour of the employee, as in **LLOYDS BANK v SAVORY (1933)**.

b.   Sometimes a collecting banker can claim to be a holder in due course or a holder for value as well as an agent for collection, for example where it has agreed to allow a customer to draw against the cheque before it has been cleared, or if the cheque has been paid in by the customer to reduce an overdraft. To cover such cases *S.2. CHEQUES ACT 1957* provides that where a banker gives value for, or has a lien on, a cheque payable to order which the holder delivers to him for collection without indorsing it, he has the same rights as if the holder had indorsed it in blank. ie He can claim to have title to the cheque as a holder in due course. The interpretation of *S.2.* was considered in the following case:-

In **WESTMINSTER BANK v ZANG (1966)** Z drew a cheque in favour of T. T asked his bank to credit T Ltd's account with the amount of the cheque since T Ltd's account was overdrawn. The cheque was dishonoured and the bank returned it to T so that he could sue Z. T started the action, but he later discontinued it and returned the cheque to the bank. The bank then sued Z claiming to be holders in due course. The bank's claim failed. The House of Lords held that:-

i.   Since the words "for collection" appeared in the Act without qualification it was acceptable for the holder of a cheque, without indorsing it, to pay it into the account of another person.

ii.   However the bank had not given value because it was still able to charge interest on the overdraft which should have been reduced by the cheque.

PROMISSORY NOTES

47.   A promissory note is defined by *S.83(1)* as:-

"An unconditional promise in writing made by one person to another signed by the maker, engaging to pay, on demand or at a fixed or determinable future time, a sum certain in money to, or to the order of, a specified person or to bearer."

Note that:-

a.   Most of the terminology resembles that used to define a bill of exchange.

b.   The Act requires a *promise*. Therefore a mere acknowledgement that a debt is due, for example an IOU is not a promissory note.

c.   Although the promise must be unconditional it is not invalidated by reason only that it contains a pledge of collateral security with authority to sell or dispose thereof *(S.83(3))*.

48.   A promissory note may be drawn as follows:-

> London 2nd January 1988
>
> Three months after date (or on demand) I promise to pay S or order (or bearer) the sum of Two Thousand Pounds (£2000), value received.
>
> Signed: B

Note that:-

a.   B is the *"maker"* and S is the *"payee"*.

b.   A bill of exchange has 3 parties, whereas there are only 2 parties to a promissory note. It is however possible for a promissory note to have two or more makers.

49.   The rules relating to bills of exchange in general apply to promissory notes. Thus, for example the maker has primary liability on the note and indorsers are in effect sureties. Acceptance does not however apply to promissory notes.

50.   Bank Notes

a.   Bank notes are promissory notes issued by a banker, payable to bearer on demand.

b.   They differ from ordinary promissory notes in two ways:-

i.   They are always payable to bearer without indorsement; and

ii.   They are legal tender.

c.   The general rules relating to bills of exchange do not necessarily apply to banknotes. For example if a banknote is altered, whether apparently or not, it is void.

36 Insurance

PRINCIPLES OF INSURANCE LAW

1. The Contract of Insurance

a. Insurance is a contract whereby the insurer, in return for a sum of money called the premium, contracts with the insured to pay a specified sum on the happening of a specific event, for example death or accident, or to indemnify the insured against any loss caused by the risk insured against, for example fire.

b. It differs from a wager in that, although risk is the essence of the contract, the insured takes out insurance to *guard against* the risk of loss, whereas in a wager the contract itself *creates* the risk. In insurance the insured must therefore have some interest apart from the contract, ie an insurable interest.

c. Many insurance contracts provide that the answers submitted by the insured in his proposal form are "the basis of the contract". This has the effect that all the terms of the contract are treated as conditions and the insurers will be able to avoid liability if the proposal form is incorrect, even if the wrong answer was given innocently and does not relate to a material fact. For example:-

In **DAWSONS v BONNIN (1922)** In response to a question on a proposal form as to where a lorry would be garaged, the proposer inadvertently inserted the wrong address. The lorry was later lost due to fire and a claim was made under the policy. It was held that since the proposal form was expressed to be "the basis of the contract", all answers were conditions, the inaccuracy of which entitled the insurer to avoid the policy, even if, as in this case, the answer to the question did not affect the premium charged.

2. The Principle of Good Faith

a. All contracts of insurance are uberrimae fidei. They are therefore voidable at the option of the insurer for non-disclosure of any material fact which was known, or ought to have been known, to the insured at the time of making the contract.

b. A fact is material if it would influence the judgement of a prudent insurer in deciding whether to accept the risk, and if so at what premium and on what conditions.

In **LONDON ASSURANCE v MANSEL (1879)** D failed to disclose that several insurance companies had declined proposals to insure his life. This was held to be a material factor which should have been disclosed. Rescission of the contract was therefore granted.

c. A policy of insurance, like any other contract is voidable for misrepresentation, whether innocent or fraudulent. The insurer however can only avoid if the misrepresentation is materially and substantially false.

3. Insurable Interest

a. Insurable interest means that the insured must be so circumstanced in relation to the subject matter of the insurance as to benefit by its existence or be prejudiced by its destruction. **(LUCENA v CRAUFURD (1806))**. Thus, for example a person has an insurable interest in his property and in his own life or in that of his wife.

b. The common law does not require the insured to have an insurable interest. However:-

i. If the contract is one of indemnity (see below) an insured who has no interest at the time of the loss will have no claim − he loses nothing, therefore no indemnity is necessary.

ii. Any policy in which the insured, at the time of the policy has no insurable interest and no expectation of acquiring one is a wager, and void under the *GAMING ACT 1845*.

iii. The *LIFE ASSURANCE ACT 1774* provides that any insurance on the life of a person is void unless the person taking out the policy has an insurable interest in the life insured. Despite its name this Act also applies to personal accident and fire insurance policies.

The effect of i.-iii. above is that an insurable interest must be present in all contracts of insurance. What "insurable interest" means in relation to specific types of insurance contract is considered below under the appropriate heading.

4. Indemnity

a. An indemnity policy is one under which the insured will be compensated (ie indemnified) for his actual loss so far as it does not exceed the sum insured. For example if X insures his house for £20,000 and it is burnt down, if £5,000 will restore it, then he may claim £5,000 and no more. If it will cost £40,000 to restore it, then he may claim £20,000.

b. A "valued policy" may however agree the measure of indemnity at the time when the policy is issued instead of waiting until the time of the loss. Such a contract is valid unless the over-valuation is so gross as to amount to a wager. The insured can recover the agreed value if the loss is total. If the loss is partial he can recover such proportion of the agreed value as is represented by the depreciation in the actual value. For example:-

In **ELCOCK v THOMSON (1949)** a house was insured against fire. In the policy its value was agreed at £106,850. The house was damaged in a fire. In fact its actual value before the fire was £18,000 and after the fire was £12,600, ie the depreciation in actual value was £5,400. The court therefore held that the insured was entitled to recover:-

311

$$\frac{5,400}{18,000} \quad \times \quad 106,850 \quad = \quad £32,055$$

c.   The insured can never recover more than the sum for which the property is insured. For example:-

In **DARRELL v TIBBITTS (1880)** a house was damaged by a gas explosion. The landlord recovered £750 from insurers. The tenant was however obliged under the terms of his lease to repair the damage. He did this with money received from the local authority (whose negligence caused the explosion). It was held that the insurers could recover the £750 paid to the landlord because clearly he had suffered no loss. To allow him to keep the money would be to award him double compensation.

d.   Provided the policy is not a "valued policy" the measure of indemnity is:-

i.   In the event of total loss, not the cost price, but the market value of the property at the time and place of the loss. For example:-

In **LEPPARD v EXCESS INSURANCE CO (1979)** a cottage was insured for £10,000, this sum being stated to be the amount necessary to replace the property in its existing form if it was completely destroyed. When the cottage was destroyed the insured claimed £10,000. The Court of Appeal however only awarded him the market value of the cottage at the time of its destruction, namely £3,000.

ii.   In the event of partial loss, the cost of repairs.

e.   If the property is under-insured, (ie insured for less than its market value), the insurer is still liable for a partial loss up to the full limit of the sum insured. Some policies guard against this by including a "subject to average" clause, whereby if the amount insured is less than the value the insurers are only liable for that proportion of the actual loss which the sum insured bears to the value of the property. For example the market value of X's house is £20,000, but it is only insured for £10,000. If X suffers fire damage to the extent of £5,000, he can only recover £2,500 from the insurer.

f.   All contracts of insurance are contracts of indemnity except:-

i.   Life assurance.

ii.   Insurance against accident to, or illness of, the insured himself.

5.   Subrogation

a.   If the contract is one of indemnity the insurers have a right of subrogation, ie having paid the insured his compensation, they are permitted to take over any rights that the insured has against the person who caused the loss. The insurers bring the action in the name of the insured, who must lend his name in return for a promise that he will not be liable for

312

cost. The insurers are said to "step into the shoes" of the insured, ie they are subrogated to his rights. For example A has insured his property against damage by fire with X Ltd. A fire is caused by B's negligence. X Ltd must pay A under the policy, but they are then entitled to sue B in negligence. If they recover the damages from B which exceed the amount they have had to pay to A, the excess recieved belongs to A.

b.   If the insured renounces or compromises any right of action he has against a third party, he must repay to the insurers the benefit of which he has thereby deprived them.

In **PHOENIX ASSURANCE v SPOONER (1905)** D's premises were insured against fire with P. The Local Authority then issued a compulsory purchase notice, but before the purchase had been completed the premises were destroyed by fire. The Local Authority then completed the purchase having agreed with D to pay a sum which reflected the fact that D had received some money from P. In addition it was agreed that the Local Authority would indemnify D against any claim brought by P. When P did claim it was held that, since fire insurance is a contract of indemnity, P was entitled to all the rights that D had against the Local Authority, and this included a right to the full market value of the property. Since D had accepted less than the market value (because she had received some insurance money) she had deprived P of their opportunity to obtain the market value from the Local Authority. D therefore had to pay compensation to P, but could re-claim the amount paid from the Local Authority under her agreement with them.

6.   Contribution

a.   Where there is more than one policy enforceable at the time of loss covering the same subject matter, risk and interest the insured may recover the total loss from either insurer.

b.   Any insurer who pays more than his share may claim a contribution from the others in proportion to the sum insured with each.

7.   Risk

a.   Loss resulting from negligence is covered.

In **HARRIS v POLAND (1942)** The insured deliberately hid her jewellery in the grate of her fireplace. Later, having forgotten this, she lit the fire, and damaged her jewellery. Her claim succeeded even though she had been negligent and despite the fact that the fire had not escaped from its usual boundaries.

b.   Clearly loss resulting from negligence is precisely what motor vehicle insurance is designed to cover. A claim will in fact lie even if the driving is so negligent that it amounts to a criminal offence.

c.   A loss will not be covered if it is a loss of profits or if it is caused by:-

    i.   The insured's own wilful misconduct. (The burden of proving this lies on the insurer).

    ii.   Ordinary wear and tear.

TYPES OF INSURANCE CONTRACT

8.   Life Assurance

a.   A life assurance contract is one by which the insurer in return for either a lump sum or annual payments over a specified period, undertakes to pay the person for whose benefit the insurance is made, a sum of money on the death of the person whose life is insured. The term *"assurance"* is used where the event concerned *must* occur, in this case death. The term *"insurance"* is used when the event *may* occur, for example an accident or theft.

b.   *Insurable interest:-*

    i.   The interest must be a pecuniary interest, and must exist at the date of the contract but need not continue until the date of the death. Thus a man may take out a policy on the life of his wife, and even if they divorce he may claim under the policy when his former wife dies.

    ii.   A person may insure his own life for his own benefit for any sum he wishes, even though he intends when insuring to assign the policy to another person.

    iii.   Spouses have an unlimited insurable interest in each others lives, but other relatives, such as father and son, have no insurable interest in the lives of each other.

    iv.   A creditor has an insurable interest in the life of the debtor up to the amount of the debt at the date of insurance.

    v.   An employee has an insurable interest in his employer's life to the extent of his wages, and an employer may insure against the loss of his employee's services through death.

c.   *Suicide:-*

    i.   If the insured is insane when he commits suicide the insurance money is recoverable unless the policy otherwise provides.

    ii.   If the insured is sane the position is unclear. Prior to 1961 suicide was a crime, and since it is contrary to public policy to allow a person to profit from his crime the insurance money could not be recovered by his personal representatives. Suicide is no longer a crime, however it is probable that the money is irrecoverable, because money is not generally payable under a policy when the insured deliberately brings about the event insured against.

314

d. *Assignment:-*

    i.   Assignment means that the right to receive the policy money is transferred from the person originally entitled to the asignee.

    ii.   The assignee need not have an insurable interest in the policy.

    iii.   The assignee must protect his interest in the policy by notifying the insurers.

    iv.   The assignee has a right to sue the insurers, if necessary, for the policy money.

9. Fire Insurance

a.   A fire insurance contract gives the insured an indemnity covering loss caused by fire during a specified period.

    i.   "Fire" means ignition and not merely overheating.

    ii.   "Loss caused by fire" does not merely include items burned, it could include damage caused by the water used to fight the fire.

b.   Clearly the insured cannot recover if he deliberately starts the fire, but if the loss is merely caused by his negligence this does not defeat his claim. − **HARRIS v POLAND (1942)** (See **7.** above).

c.   In contrast to life assurance, since the contract is one of indemnity, the insurable interest must exist not only when the contract is made, but also when the loss occurs. Any legal or equitable interest in the subject matter suffices as an insurable interest. For example an interest as an owner, tenant, mortgage, trustee, beneficiary, or personal representative. However a shareholder has no interest in and cannot insure the property of a company, even if it is a "one-man" company. − **MACAURA v NORTHERN ASSURANCE CO. (1925)** (Chapter 11).

d.   Restoration of the building.

    i.   At common law the insured was not bound to use money received from the insurance company to reinstate the property. He was entitled to be indemnified in cash which he could use as he wished.

    ii.   However the *FIRES PREVENTION (METROPOLIS) ACT 1774*, which despite its name applies throughout the country, provides that any person, (for example a tenant), interested in a building destroyed by fire can require the insurer to spend the insurance money on the reinstatement of the building.

10. Motor Vehicle Insurance

a.   Under the *ROAD TRAFFIC ACT 1972* a motorist must insure against any liability he may incur as a result of causing the death or injury of a third party. The third party has a right to sue the insurers direct despite the general privity of contract rule.

b.   If the user of a motor vehicle is not insured against liability for causing injury to third parties both the owner and the user have committed a criminal offence. In addition to their criminal liability any person who does not have the required compulsory insurance is liable to pay damages for breach of statutory duty if there is no other remedy available to the injured party.

In **MONK v WARBEY (1935)** D lent his car to a friend. The friend's driver drove negligently causing injury to P. The friend was not covered by insurance and D's policy only applied when the owner was driving it. D was therefore liable to pay damages to P for breach of statutory duty.

c.   A provision in the policy which purports to exclude the insurer's liability to indemnify the insured because of his age, physical or mental condition, the condition of his vehicle, or the number of passengers carried is void. However a limitation as to user, for example for "private" purposes only, will prevent a third party from recovering damages from the insurer if he is injured while the car is being used in another way, for example as a taxi.

d.   Unsatisfied judgements. − In 1946 motor vehicle insurers agreed to set up the Motor Insurers Bureau (M.I.B.). The M.I.B. will satisfy a judgement where the driver does not have the compulsory cover, because for example he had not taken out a policy, or the insurers have gone into liquidation. The conditions are:-

 i.   Notice of proceedings is given to the M.I.B. before, or within 7 days after their commencement, and

 ii.   The liability is one that is required to be covered by the Road Traffic Act.

e.   The M.I.B. has also agreed to compensate "hit and run" victims if

 i.   Neither the owner nor driver can be traced.

 ii.   On the balance of probabilities the owner or driver would be liable to compensate the victim.

 iii.   The victim was a compulsory risk within the meaning of the Road Traffic Act.

 iv.   The accident was not a deliberate attempt to run down the victim, and

 v.   The claim is made in writing within three years of the accident.

11. Insurance Against Theft. The principles applicable to life and fire insurance also apply to theft. For example:-

In **ROSELODGE v CASTLE (1966)** When insuring their stock against theft diamond merchants failed to disclose that the sales manager had a previous conviction for smuggling diamonds. It was held that this amounted to non-disclosure of a material fact, and the insurers could avoid the claim, even though the sales manager was not the thief.

316

12. Accident Insurance

a. Life assurance policies usually also cover personal injury to the policy holder.

b. A person who does not have life assurance may either insure himself against personal injury or insure against liability arising from injuries to third parties. He will not however be able to claim under a liability policy in respect of a deliberate unlawful act by himself.

In **GRAY v BARR (1971)** D shot and killed Gray in a fight. He was acquitted of both murder and manslaughter but Gray's personal representatives made a claim against him under the *FATAL ACCIDENTS ACT*. D sought an indemnity under his accident liability policy in respect of any damages he might have to pay. It was held that even if the death was an "accident" within the terms of the policy, the policy would not cover accidents which occurred as a result of threatening unlawful violence with a loaded gun.

c. An injured third party may sue the insurer direct if the insured is bankrupt, or if the insured is a company which has gone into liquidation.

13. Employers' Compulsory Insurance.
The *EMPLOYERS' LIABILITY (COMPULSORY INSURANCE) ACT 1969* makes it compulsory for every employer (except nationalised industries and local authorities) to insure himself against liability for injury or disease sustained by his employees and arising in the course of their employment.

37 Carriage of Goods

CARRIAGE ON LAND

1. Carriers of goods by road or rail may be classified as either "private" or "common".

2. Private Carriers

a.   A private carrier is one who reserves the right to accept or reject requests for carriage whether or not this vehicle is full.

b.   A private carrier is (subject to any express terms of the contract) only liable for loss or damage if he has caused it negligently.

3. Common Carriers

a.   A common carrier is one who offers to carry goods or passengers for anyone who wishes to engage him. He cannot refuse custom offered to him at a fair price unless

  i.   He has no space, because his vehicles are full, or

  ii.   The goods are of a kind which he does not profess to convey, or

  iii.   The destination is not on his normal route, or

  iv.   The goods are not properly packed, or are of a dangerous type.

b.   The law imposes a greater obligation upon common carriers regarding the goods than it does upon a private carrier. In effect a common carrier's liability is that of an insurer. Thus, subject to any expressly agreed exemption clauses, he is liable for any loss or damage, even if it is not his fault. This strict liability rule has five exceptions:-

  i.   Act of God. ie Loss due directly and exclusively to natural causes without human intervention, and which could not be reasonably foreseen and guarded against.

  ii.   Act of the Queen's enemies. – ie A hostile foreign government, and not merely robbers or violent demonstrators.

  iii.   Negligence of the consignor, for example if the packing is defective.

  iv.   Inherent vice in the goods.

  In **BLOWER v GREAT WESTERN RAILWAY (1872)** A railway company agreed to carry a bullock. During the journey the animal escaped from its truck and was killed. It was held that the escape was due to the strength of the animal itself and not the negligence of the company. They were not found to be liable.

  v.   Seizure under a legal process.

c.   A common carrier is only liable in relation to passengers if he is negligent.

4. Rights and Duties of a Common Carrier

a. *Rights.* A carrier can demand reasonable payment in advance, and he may refuse to carry goods which are not properly packed. A carrier has a lien on goods carried for his charges.

b. *Duties:-*

   i. He must carry the goods without unnecessary delay or deviation from his normal route.

   ii. He must deliver the goods within a reasonable time at the destination specified by the consignor unless the consignee instructs him to deliver them elsewhere.

   iii. He must, on arrival at the destination, keep the goods for collection by the consignee within a reasonable time.

c. *Exclusion of liability.* At common law the carrier was able to exclude or limit his liability in a special contract with his customer, usually by means of a notice displayed at his place of business. The *CARRIERS ACT 1830* modified the carrier's rights as follows:-

   i. When certain articles exceeding £10 in value are delivered to a carrier, he will not be liable for loss or damage to such articles unless their value has been declared to him, and any increased charges have been paid, or agreed to be paid. The specified articles include gold, silver, watches, coins, banknotes, paintings, and furs.

   ii. The carrier cannot exclude or limit his liability merely by a public notice, although he may do so by means of a clause in a contract of carriage.

5. Carriage by Road

a. Most carriers use the standard conditions of carriage of the Road Haulage Association, which expressly state that they are not common carriers.

b. The *TRANSPORT (LONDON) ACT 1969* provides that the London Transport Executive is not a common carrier.

c. As private carriers the above bodies in theory have unlimited power to limit or exclude their liability. In practice there are several statutory restrictions on this power. The most important is the *ROAD TRAFFIC ACT 1960* which prohibits any exclusion or limitation of liability for death or physical injury caused to passengers of a public service vehicle.

6. Carriage by Rail

a. The British Railways Board is not a common carrier. – The *TRANSPORT ACT 1962*.

b. If a carriage is at the *Board's risk*, then their liability is similar to that of a common carrier, except that the list of excepted events is longer, and liability is limited to £800 per ton on the gross weight of the goods, or a proportionate part of £800 if part only of the consignment is lost.

c.   If a carriage is at the *owner's risk* (and carried therefore at a cheaper rate) the Board is not liable unless the loss was due to the wilful neglect of the Board or its employees.

CARRIAGE BY SEA

7.   A contract to carry goods by sea is known as a contract of affreightment. There are two types of contract of affreightment:-

a.   A bill of lading, where the goods form part only of the cargo of the ship.

b.   A charterparty, which consists of renting the whole ship.

8.   Bill of Lading

a.   This is a document signed by the shipowner, stating that certain goods have been shipped on a particular vessel, and setting out the terms on which the goods have been delivered to and received by the shipowner.

b.   A bill of lading, when signed and handed to the captain, is:-

i.   Evidence of the terms of the contract of carriage;

ii.   A receipt given by the carrier for the goods delivered to him; and

iii.   A document of title to those goods.

c.   The *CARRIAGE OF GOODS BY SEA ACT 1971* implies several terms into every bill of lading, for example.

i.   That care has been taken to ensure that the ship is seaworthy and properly equipped.

ii.   That the carrier will carefully load, keep and discharge the goods.

iii.   That in the event of loss or damage notice in writing must be given to the carrier before or at the time of removal of the goods, unless the loss or damage is not apparent, in which case written notice must be given within three days of discharge of the goods − otherwise removal of the goods is prima facie evidence of delivery of them as described in the bill of lading.

d.   A bill of lading is a quasi-negotiable instrument in that it can be transferred by delivery, but the transferee, whether or not he gives value, cannot acquire a better title to it than the transferor.

9.   Charterparties

a.   There are two types of charterparty:-

i.   A voyage charterparty, under which the ship is chartered for a particular voyage, and

ii.   A time charterparty, under which the ship is chartered for a specified period.

320

b.   The charterer usually only obtains the use of the ship. Possession and control remain with the owner, who is liable to pay the crew.

c.   Since the charterer hires the whole ship failure to provide a complete cargo will render him liable to pay "dead freight", ie a payment for the unoccupied space.

d.   The terms of the charterparty usually provide for the charterer to load and unload the ship within a specified number of "lay days". If no time is specified this obligation must be carried out within a reasonable time. Failure to do so will render the charterer liable in liquidated damages for the delay caused to the shipowner. These damages are known as demurrage.

e.   The implied terms of the *CARRIAGE OF GOODS BY SEA ACT 1971* do not apply to charterparties unless they are specifically incorporated into the agreement. Other express terms often included exempt the owner from liability in the event of, for example war damage, ice, or fire.

10.   Implied Undertakings by the Carrier. In the absence of express provision to the contrary, the Courts will imply the following conditions into every contract of carriage of goods by sea:-

a.   That the ship is seaworthy, ie that the particular ship is able to undertake the voyage and carry the agreed cargo.

b.   That there will be no unnecessary deviation from the agreed route. − Deviation to save a life is permitted but, in the absence of an express term to the contrary, deviation to save property is not allowed.

In **SCARAMANGA v STAMP (1880)** A ship in the course of a voyage went to the aid of another ship in distress. Although life was not in danger the distressed ship was taken in tow and as a result the assisting ship became stranded. It was held that since the deviation was not necessary for the purpose of saving life the shipowners had to pay compensation to the owners of the cargo on the stranded vessel.

c.   That the voyage will commence and proceed without any unnecessary delay.

11.   Freight

a.   Freight is the price paid to the carrier. At common law freight is only payable when the carrier has delivered the goods, and the goods are of the same nature and description as when they were shipped. Sometimes a contract will contain a clause providing that freight is payable before delivery. This is called *"advance freight"*. The term *"lump sum freight"* describes a payment to be made for the use of the whole ship. It is payable even though the carrier does not ship any goods.

b.   Where freight is payable on delivery the carrier has a lien on the goods until the freight is paid.

12. Average

a. *Particular average.* Normally any loss sustained during the course of a voyage to the ship or the cargo must be carried by the particular interest which incurs the loss. This is known as "particular average", for example if the ship is damaged in a storm the loss must be borne by the shipowner alone.

b. *General average.* This is where part of the cargo is deliberately sacrificed in order to preserve the remaining cargo. In such circumstances all parties whose goods were saved by the sacrifice must contribute to the loss suffered by the owners of the goods sacrificed. A contribution may be claimed if the following conditions are satisfied:-

i.　The sacrifice must have been made to avoid a real danger which was common to all interests involved;

ii.　It must have been a voluntary and reasonably necessary sacrifice;

iii.　As a result of the action the interest called upon to contribute must have been saved wholly or in part; and

iv.　The common danger must not have arisen because of the fault of the party claiming the contribution.

CARRIAGE BY AIR

13. The *CARRIAGE BY AIR ACT 1961* determines the contractual principles of carriage between the UK and other countries.

14. Limits of Liability

a.　Death or injury to a passenger:- 250,000 gold francs (£11,750), unless a higher figure has been agreed by special contract. The maximum limit for carriage between two points in the UK is 875,000 gold francs (£40,950).

b.　Loss of baggage or cargo:- 250 gold francs per kilogram (£11.70p) unless the value has been declared by the consignor and additional charge paid.

c.　Loss of goods to which the passenger himself takes charge:- 5,000 gold francs per passenger (£234).

15. Defences

a.　That the carrier or his servants took all necessary steps to avoid the damage, or that it was impossible to take such steps.

b.　The damage was caused by the negligence of the person who suffered the loss, ie contributory negligence.

38 Lien and Bailment

LIEN

1. A lien is the right to detain the goods of another until a claim has been satisfied. There are three types of lien:-

    a. Possessory;

    b. Equitable; and

    c. Maritime.

2. Possessory Lien. A possessory lien applies when a person is in possession of another person's goods and may retain them until a claim is satisfied, for example a shoe-repairer may retain shoes until the repair bill is paid. To be effective possession is essential and it must be lawful and continuous. A possessory lien may be *general* or *particular*.

    a. *General lien.* This gives the right to the person in possession to retain the goods until *any* debt has been paid, whether or not the debt is in respect of the goods. This lien may be an express term in the contract by Common Law, or by well-established usage. Bankers, solicitors, auctioneers, factors, and stockbrokers have a general lien by usage.

    b. *Particular lien.* This gives the person in possession the right to retain the goods only in connection with the particular debt. Such a lien may arise under contract or may be given under Common Law or Statute, for example carriers (for freight due on goods carried), garages (for repairs), unpaid sellers (for the price of the goods sold), and innkeepers (for amounts owed in respect of a particular visit).

    c. The right of lien is not affected by the rights of third parties of which the person exercising the right of lien is ignorant.

    In **ALBEMARLE SUPPLY CO v HINDE & CO (1927)** a garage repaired taxi-cabs for a person who held them under a HP agreement. The agreement forbade the hirer to create a lien on the taxis, but the garage proprietor was unaware of this. It was held that the garage could exercise a lien over the vehicle despite the clause in the HP agreement.

    d. There is no general right to sell the goods held under a lien, but one may be given by statute. For example the *TORTS (INTERFERENCE WITH GOODS) ACT 1977*, subject to certain conditions, gives a bailee a statutory right of sale (see **7.** below).

    e. A possessory lien is extinguished by:-

        i.   Losing possession of the goods.

        ii. Payment or tender of the amount claimed.

        iii. Abandonment of the right of lien.

iv.   If the creditor takes security for the debt, in which case, by inference, he waives his right of lien.

3.   Equitable Lien. This is a right to have certain property applied for the payment of specific liabilities. Possession of the property is unnecessary. The lien is enforced by applying to the Court for an order for sale. Examples include:

a.   The right of a partner on dissolution of the firm to have the firm's assets applied in payment of the firm's liabilities.

b.   The right a company has over its members' shares for sums due from them in respect of those shares.

4.   Maritime Lien. This is the right to have a ship or its cargo sold and the proceeds applied in satisfaction of any debt due to the person having the lien. Such a lien may arise from salvage claims and claims for damages where a collision is caused by negligence. The master and crew have a lien in respect of unpaid wages. A maritime lien is not dependent on possession and is enforced by application to the Court for an order for sale.

BAILMENT

5.   Introduction

a.   A bailment is a delivery of goods by one person to another for some limited purpose, on condition that when the purpose has been accomplished the goods shall be returned.

b.   The consideration in a contract of bailment is the bailor's parting with possession of his goods. Consequently a bailment is a simple contract, even if no money changes hands.

c.   The owner of goods bailed is called the *"Bailor"* and the party to whom they are entrusted is known as the *"Bailee"*.

d.   Bailment may take many forms, such as the deposit of goods in a cloakroom or left luggage office for safe custody, and can also involve being in possession of goods to be repaired or cleaned. Bailment only involves goods, it has no application to land.

6.   The Duties of the Bailee

a.   *To take reasonable care of the goods*

i.   The standard of care will depend on the circumstances of the case, but if goods are damaged the burden will be upon the bailee to prove he has not been negligent. If it is proved all reasonable care has been taken by the bailee he will not be liable for damage caused to the goods.

ii.   A loss caused by an act which is fundamentally inconsistent with the terms of the contact of bailment (even though the act is not negligent) will fall on the bailee.

iii. If the goods are hired the bailor impliedly warrants the goods are fit for the purpose hired. The bailee must take reasonable care and use them in accordance with the terms of the contract. He is not liable for loss by robbery or accidental fire occasioned without negligence.

iv. Should goods be loaned for use, for example a lawnmower to the next door neighbour, the bailee is entitled to use the goods loaned and is not liable for fair wear and tear unless he deviates from the conditions of the contract.

b. *To return the goods*

i. The goods must be returned in accordance with the contract and failure to do this by the bailee will render him liable for the loss.

ii. The bailee will be liable for loss of goods which are stolen by servants of the bailee.

iii. It is the duty of the bailee to inform the bailor should third parties make a claim to the goods.

7. The Bailee's Right to Sell. Under the *TORTS (INTERFERENCE WITH GOODS) ACT 1977* if the bailor fails to take delivery of the goods and to pay the bailee's charges, the bailee may sell, having given notice to the bailor of his intention. After the sale the bailee must account to the bailor for the proceeds of sale less the costs of the sale and the amount owed to the bailee in respect of the goods.

8. The Duties of the Bailor

a. If the goods are bailed for a particular purpose of which the bailor knows (for example the hire of a car), he is under a duty to disclose any defect rendering the goods unsuitable for that purpose. He impliedly warrants the fitness of any goods hired in this way, and owes a duty of reasonable care in this respect.

b. In other bailments the bailor generally owes no duty of care, save to warn the bailee if goods are dangerous, for example when explosives are deposited in a cloakroom.

39 Bankruptcy

1.   **Introduction.** The law of bankruptcy governs the situation where, when a person is unable to pay his creditors, his property is distributed among them pro rata (with certain exceptions). The law also provides for the discharge (ie release from future liability) of the bankrupt person in certain circumstances. The rules relating to bankruptcy are contained in the *INSOLVENCY ACT 1986*.

2.   **Terminology**

   a.   *Adjudication order.* This is the Court order which makes the debtor "bankrupt" and causes his property to vest in a trustee for the benefit of his creditors.

   b.   *"The debtor"* and *"The bankrupt".* When referring to a person before the adjudication order is made he should be designated *"the debtor"*; subsequently he is referred to as *"the bankrupt"*.

   c.   *"Bankruptcy"* must be carefully distinguished from *"Insolvency"*. The former term should only be applied after the making of the adjudication order. Insolvency means that a person is unable to pay his debts as they fall due.

3.   **The Petition.** A petition for a bankruptcy order to be made against an individual may be presented to the court by, for example:-

   a.   The individual himself;

   b.   The Official Petitioner where a criminal bankruptcy order has been made;

   c.   A creditor, or jointly by two or more providing:-

   i.   The amount of the debt is at least £750;

   ii.   The debt is a liquidated sum payable either immediately or at some certain future time, and is unsecured; or

   iii.   It appears that the debtor is either unable to pay or has no reasonable prospect of being able to pay.

4.   **Receivership**

   a.   The court may, if it is shown to be necessary for the protection of the debtor's property, appoint the official receiver to be the interim receiver of the debtor's property. This is after the petition and before the bankruptcy order.

   b.   The debtor is required to give an interim receiver an inventory of his property and any other information which the interim receiver shall reasonably require to carry out his function.

   c.   The receiver's function is to protect the debtor's property and he may sell or otherwise dispose of any of the bankrupt's goods which are perishable or whose value is likely to diminish. He may summon a meeting of the bankrupt's creditors.

d.   It is the duty of the official receiver to investigate the conduct and affairs of a bankrupt and make such a report to the court as he thinks fit.

5.   Ascertainment and Investigation of a Bankrupt's Affairs.

When a bankruptcy order has been made, other than on the bankrupt's petition, the bankrupt must submit a Statement of Affairs to the official receiver. The statement of affairs includes for example, his assets, liabilities and a list of creditors.

6.   Public Examination of the Bankrupt.

The official receiver may at any time before discharge of the bankrupt apply to the court for public examination of the bankrupt in regard to his affairs, dealings, property and causes of his failure.

7.   The Trustee in Bankruptcy

a.   The trustee is usually appointed by a general meeting of the bankrupt's creditors, but may be appointed by the Secretary of State or the court. Until a trustee is appointed the official receiver is in control.

b.   It is usual for a trustee to work under supervision of a committee of creditors.

c.   The *INSOLVENCY ACT 1986* specifies in great detail the powers, duties and responsibilities of the trustee. Some powers may only be exercised with the santion of the committee, for example carrying on the business of the bankrupt, or mortgaging any of the property of the bankrupt to raise money to pay his debts. Other powers may be exercised without sanction, for example selling any property of the bankrupt. In general the duty of the trustee is to realise the property of the bankrupt and to discharge the liabilities in respect of which the creditors have proved.

d.   The trustee is entitled to such remuneration as is fixed by the creditors or the committee of creditors. He must, of course, keep accounts which are subject to audit by the committee of creditors.

8.   The Property of the Bankrupt.

The property of the bankrupt vests in the trustee, subject to the following exceptions:-

a.   Such tools, books, vehicles and other items of equipment as are necessary to the bankrupt for his personal use in his employment or business.

b.   Such clothing, bedding, furniture, etc. as are necessary for satisfying the basic domestic needs of the bankrupt and his family.

c.   Property held by the bankrupt as a trustee for any other person.

d.   Rights of action for personal injury.

e.   Old age pensions and other payments granted under statutory provisions, for example the *SOCIAL SECURITY ACT 1975*. The trustee may make an application to appropriate part of these payments as and when required.

9.   Claims of Creditors

a.   Before the trustee distributes the money collected as a result of the realisation of the bankrupt's property he will require evidence of the creditors' claims. This evidence consists of proofs which must be submitted by creditors before their claims will be submitted.

b.   A debt may be proved by delivering or sending through the post an affidavit verifying the debt, (if required by the official receiver), or otherwise an unsworn claim. The claim must give full details of the debt and specify the vouchers, if any, by which the debt can be substantiated. If the creditor holds security that fact must be stated in the proof, otherwise the security will be deemed to have been surrendered.

c.   *Provable debts*

i.   Subject to the exceptions mentioned below, all debts and liabilities, present or future, certain or contingent, to which the debtor is subject at the date of the receiving order, or to which he may become subject before his discharge by means of any obligation incurred before the date of the receiving order, are provable.

ii.   If the debt is contingent, ie dependent on the happening of some future event, the trustee must assess its value and make allwance for it. If the creditor disagrees with the assessment he can appeal to court.

d.   *Non-provable debts*

i.   Demands in the nature of unliquidated damages arising *otherwise* than by reason of a contract, promise or breach of trust. (Such demands would therefore usually arise out of a tortious act of the debtor).

ii.   Debts which, in the opinion of the court, cannot be fairly estimated.

iii.   Debts unenforceable at law, for example debts founded on an illegal consideration or statute barred debts.

e.   *Secured creditors.* A secured creditor is a person holding a mortgage, charge or lien on the property of the debtor, or any part thereof, as a security for a debt due to him from the debtor. In the bankruptcy of the debtor there are 4 courses of action available to him. He may:-

i.   Surrender his security and prove for the full amount of the debt;

ii.   Retain his security and not prove at all;

iii.   Realise the security, proving for the balance still outstanding, if any, or accounting for any surplus;

iv.   Estimate the value of his security and prove for the difference.

A fully secured creditor would almost certainly take no action. The facts would appear in the statement of affairs. The trustee would have to decide whether to pay the debt in full and sell the security for the benefit of the estate, or allow the creditor to retain the security in full satisfaction for the debt.

f.   *Interest on debts.* Some classes of debts carry interest at law. In other cases the parties may have agreed that interest is payable. The proof in respect of such debts should include details of the interest due up to the date of the receiving order. Interest cannot be claimed for a period after the receiving order since one effect of the order is to stop interest running.

g.   *Set-off.* Where a creditor is himself under an obligation to the estate as a result of his dealings with the debtor he may set off the amount owed by him against the amount due to him and prove for the net amount. The debts must be due between the same parties. Thus a joint debt owing by a partnership cannot be set off against a separate debt owing to one of the partners. Set-off is only allowed in respect of dealings which result in a money payment, and not for example where specific goods are to be returned.

10.   Distribution of Assets. Upon realisation of the assets, and after payment of the costs connected with realisation, the trustee must apply the proceeds in the following order:-

a.   Costs of administration, for example his own remuneration.

b.   Debts having special priority, (pre-preferential debts), for example funeral expenses of a deceased debtor.

c.   Debts having general priority, (preferential debts). These include:-

   i.   Income tax due for 12 months.

   ii.   VAT for the period of 6 months.

   iii.   Car tax due.

   iv.   Betting duty.

   v.   Social Security contributions.

   vii.   Amounts owed to employees up to four months subject to a limit of £800 in any one case.

   viii.   Holiday remuneration.

   ix.   Repayment of any sum advanced for payment of any of the above.

Preferential debts rank equally, and in the event of the estate being unable to satisfy all the claims they abate equally, ie each creditor receives an equal proportion of the amount owed to him.

d.   Unsecured creditors. Like preferential debts unsecured debts rank and abate equally.

    e.   Creditors for interest.

    f.   Deferred debts, for example debts between husband and wife.

    g.   Any surplus is returned to the debtor.

11. Discharge of the Bankrupt. In the case of bankruptcy as a result of a criminal bankruptcy order, or a person who has been an undischarged bankrupt in the past 15 years, the bankrupt must obtain discharge by court order after 5 years. Otherwise, where a certificate for the summary administration of the bankrupt's estate has been issued, the bankrupt is automatically discharged after 2 years and in any other case, 3 years. An undischarged bankrupt is under the following disabilities:-

    a.   He cannot act as the director of any company, or directly or indirectly take part in the management of any company, except by leave of the court by which he was adjudged bankrupt.

    b.   He cannot act as a receiver or manager of the property of a company on behalf of debenture-holders, unless he is appointed by order of the court.

    c.   He cannot be elected to either House of Parliament.

    d.   He cannot be appointed or act as a Justice of the Peace or a member of a local authority or other public body.

    e.   He cannot act as a solicitor.

40 Patents, Copyright, Trade Marks and Passing Off

INTRODUCTION

1. In order to encourage new inventions and original works and to protect the goodwill of those who have built up a business the law gives statutory protection to patents, designs, copyright and trade marks. These rights are governed by the *COPYRIGHT, DESIGNS AND PATENTS ACT 1988* and the *PATENTS ACT 1977* (as amended). In addition the economic tort of *"passing-off"* prevents a person from conducting himself so that customers will mistake his goods, services or business for that of someone else. This branch of law is known as *intellectual property law*.

DESIGNS

2. Design Right

a. A *design right* is a new property right created under the 1988 Act. Hardware is automatically protected and does not need to be registered. The right subsists in an original design. It does not apply to the following:-

    i. Method of construction.

    ii. Interface (enabling the article to be placed in or against another article in order that either article may perform its function).

    iii. Surface decoration.

b. *Duration.* The design right expires 15 years from the end of the calendar year in which first recorded in a design document or an article was made to the design. If the design was made available for sale or hire within 5 years from first being recorded or an article being made, expiry is 10 years from the end of the year in which this occurred. Designs registered with the Registered Designs Act 1949 expire 10 years from the 12th January 1988 (commencement date of the 1988 Act).

c. *Remedies for infringement.* The following remedies are available:-

    i. Damages.

    ii. Order for delivery-up. The articles delivered up would be disposed of by forfeiture to the design right owner or by destruction.

PATENTS

3. Definition

A patent is the name given to a bundle of monopoly rights which give the patentee the exclusive right to exploit the invention for a given period of time. It is a right to stop others, an inventor does not need a positive right to exploit his own invention.

4. Applying for a Patent

a.   An application is made to the Patent Office. If the invention has been made by an employee in the course of his employment, the employer owns the invention and may apply for a patent with the inventor's consent. Alternatively a joint application may be made, or the employee may apply, in which case the grant will be subject to the employer's interest.

b.   At the Patent Office a document called a *"Complete Specification"* is filed. This contains a description of the article, process or machine, including working instructions and a statement of *"claims"* which define the scope of the invention for which the inventor seeks his monopoly. It is against these claims that any infringement is judged.

c.   The Patent Office carries out *"research"* to test for novelty. According to the result of this search the applicant may decide to abandon or modify his application or request an *examination* by a qualified Patent Office examiner. The main task of the examiner is to see that the claims of the specification describe things that are not only new, but also inventive. Once the examiner is satisfied the specification is published and for 3 months afterwards any interested party can object by notice to the Patent Office.

d.   In the event of no opposition or failure of objections the *"Letters Patent"* will be sealed and the patentee can sue in the High Court (or in some cases the County Court) for any infringement.

e.   Once granted the patent covers the UK and is in force for 4 years, and it can be renewed annually for a further 16 years, after which it can be extended by an application to the High Court for a further 5 or 10 years.

5. International Application Procedure

An application at the British Patent Office will only result in the grant of a British Patent. Until recently an applicant who wanted protection in other countries had to file applications in each country for which a patent was required. This was costly and resulted in the application being examined with varying degress of thoroughness in each country. Two systems now exist to minimise the need for separate national applications.

a.   The Patent Co-Operation Treaty (in operation since 1978) provides for the filing of a single application designating the countries for which the applicant seeks protection. A single search is carried out and the application is then sent to each of the designated countries for separate examination as a national application according to their local laws.

b.   The European Patent Convention (in operation since 1978) to which EEC member states (except Greece) and some other European countries belong, provides for an application to be filed at the European Patent Office in Munich. The application is searched and examined at the European Patent Office and if the invention satisfies the requirements of the Convention separate national patents are granted for the specified countries.

6. Patentability

Patents must fulfil the following requirements specified in the *PATENTS ACT 1977*:-

a. It must be a *patentable* invention which is capable of industrial application. The Act does not define what is patentable, instead it lists a number of things that are not patentable inventions, for example:-

i. Discoveries, scientific theories or mathematical methods;

ii. Literary, dramatic, musical or artistic works;

iii. Schemes, rules or methods for performing a mental act, playing a game, doing business or programming a computer;

iv. The presentation of information.

b. *Novelty*. The invention must be new, ie it must not have been made available to the public anywhere in the world by written or oral description, by use or in any other way.

c. *Inventive steps*. An invention involves an inventive step if it is not obvious to a person skilled in the art, having regard to state of the art knowledge.

7. Employee Inventions

Since most inventions are made by company employees, the question of rights to the invention are important. The Act provides that an invention made in the course of employment shall belong to the employer, but it also establishes a statutory award scheme to compensate employees for inventions made on behalf of their employers. The award will ensure a fair share to the employee having regard to the benefit derived by the employer. Any contract term which diminishes the employee's rights under the Act is void.

8. Ownership, Assignment and Licensing

a. A patent, or an application for a patent, is personal property, but it is not a chose in action.

b. An assignment must be in writing and signed by both parties, otherwise it is void.

c. Licensing is a method of developing a patent whereby the patentee gives permission for the sale or manufacture of the patented article, subject to express conditions.

9. Licences of Right for Drugs

The 1988 Act brings in legislation in respect of "licences of right" for drugs. The intention is to bring the law in Great Britain into agreement with the laws of nearly all other countries. It was considered in the public interest that there should be the right of free use of inventions for the manufacture of food and medicine. Patents may be taken out for these purposes but the patents would not be used to restrain manufacture of them.

In the case of a patent for drugs, without waiting for the 3 year period applicable to other patents, a licence could be had by any person interested on such terms as the comptroller thought fit to secure that drugs should be available to the public at the lowest prices consistent with the patentees deriving a reasonable advantage from their patent rights. The applicant for a licence of right of this nature may make his application in the 16th year of the patent.

10. Infringement

a.   There are two questions in relation to infringement:-

i.   Does the scope of the invention as defined in the claims cover the product or process concerned?

ii.   Is the defendant's conduct prohibited by the Act.

b.   The Act provides that a person infringes a patent if he does any of the following:-

i.   If the invention is a product, he makes, disposes of, uses or imports the product, or keeps it for disposal or otherwise;

ii.   If the invention is a process, he uses it or offers it for use, when he knows or should know that there would be an infringement, or if he disposes of, uses, imports or keeps any product obtained by means of that process;

iii.   Supplies means essential for putting an invention into effect to a person not entitled to work the patent, when he knows, or should know, that the means are suitable and that they are intended to be used to put the invention into effect.

c.   An inventor whose patent is infringed is entitled to an injunction, delivery of the infringing articles and damages, which may be assessed on a loss of profits or royalty basis. He will also be given a "certificate of contested validity" which entitles him to larger costs in any future infringement action. If the patentee loses the grant of the patent may be revoked or the specifications may be found not wide enough to cover the defendant's product or process.

COPYRIGHT

11. Definition

Copyright protects the independent skill, labour and effort which has been expended in producing work and prevents others from helping themselves to too large a portion of that skill, labour and effort. Unlike a patent, a copyright is not a monopoly, it is a right of protection against copying. Copyright is acquired by bringing a work into existence. There is no requirement of, nor provision for, registration.

12. Statutory Protection

a. *Subsistence of copyright.* Works eligible for copyright protection are put into three groups:-

    i.   Literary, dramatic, musical or artistic works.

    ii.   Sound recordings, films broadcasts or cable programmes.

    iii. Typographical arrangement of published editions.

(a computer program is treated as a literary work).

b. *Artistic works.* The following are protected:-

    i.   Paintings, drawings, sculptures, engravings and photographs, *irrespective of artistic quality.*

    ii.   Works of architecture, being either buildings or models of buildings.

    iii. Works of artistic craftsmanship, not included in the above categories.

The phrase "irrespective of artistic quality" has enabled the courts to hold that engineering production drawings are entitled to copyright.

c. *Ownership.* The 1988 Act simplifies the provisions regarding ownership of copyright. The only case where the copyright in a literary, dramatic or musical work does not initially rest in the author is where the work is made by an employee in the course of his employment in which case the employer is the first owner of the copyright unless there is some agreement to the contrary. The Act also introduces a concept of a literary, dramatic, musical or artistic work which is computer generated in circumstances in which there is no human author. The author is taken to be the person by whom arrangements necessary for creation of the work are undertaken.

d. *Duration.* The rule that where copyright in literary, dramatic or musical works which had not been released to the public before the author's death would subsist until 50 years after release has been changed to fall into line with such works which had been released prior to the author's death, ie, to 50 years after the date of death.

e. *Rights of the copyright owner.* The copyright in a work is the exclusive right to do the following acts in the U.K.

    i.   Copy the work. (Copying includes storing in any medium by electronic means)

    ii.   Issue copies to the public.

    iii. Perform, show or play the work in public.

    iv. Broadcast or include in a cable programme service.

    v.   Make an adaptation of the work.

Copyright in the typographical arrangement of a published edition includes not only the right to copy the work but also the right to issue copies to the public.

The 1988 Act introduces the moral rights of an author as follows:-

i.   *Paternity right.* An author of a literary, dramatic, musical or artistic work or the director of a film has a right to be identified as author or director in certain circumstances.

ii.   *Right of integrity.* An author has the right not to have his work subjected to derogatory treatment amounting to distortion or mutilation of the work or which is otherwise prejudicial to the honour or reputation of the author or director.

These two rights subsist throughout the duration of the copyright.

iii.   *Privacy.* A person who commissions a photograph or film for private or domestic purposes has a right not to have:-
  (1) copies issued to the public
  (2) the work exhibited in public
  (3) the work broadcast or included in a cable programme.

An entitled person may waive the above rights.

13. Indirect Copying

Copying a product which has been manufactured from drawings amounts to indirectly copying the drawings and is an infringement of copyright.

In **BERSTEIN v SIDNEY MURRAY (1981)** a dress designer saw P's design at an exhibition and later marketed dresses which were a copy of P's both in materials and design. It was held that although the dresses themselves were not protected by copyright D had indirectly copied the sketches made by P.

Contrast **BRITISH LEYLAND v ARMSTRONG PATENTS (1986)** where D declined to obtain a licence from P to produce spare parts for BL cars, but nevertheless produced replacement exhaust pipes by copying the shape and dimensions of the original. P alleged that D had by indirect copying infringed the copyright in P's original drawings of the exhaust system. The High Court and Court of Appeal granted an injunction in favour of P, but the House of Lords reversed this decision. It was held that although exhaust pipes were purely functional articles which were neither patentable nor a registrable design, the replacements produced by D were clearly recognisable as copies of P's drawings in which artistic copyright subsisted. Therefore D had infringed P's copyright *but* car owners had an inherent right to repair their cars in the most economical way possible and must have access to a free market for spares. P was not entitled to derogate or interfere with that right by asserting their copyright against a person manufacturing parts solely for repair.

Manufacturers have protested that this decision amounts to a "pirates charter" in that it allows a producer of spares to copy the original design of an article and sell it at a cheaper price than the manufacturer. This is very significant for companies such as British Leyland, where the market for spares is near to £1,000 million per annum. The spare parts industry has welcomed the decision as a liberalisation of the market of considerable benefit to the consumer.

14. Restricted Acts

a.   The acts restricted by copyright in artistic work are:-

i.   Reproducing the work in any material form, including converting a two-dimensional work into a three dimensional work and vice versa.

ii.   Publishing the work, including television broadcasts.

There will be no infringement with regard to drawings if the article is not regarded by non-experts as a reproduction.

b.   There is no copyright in a name because of the improbability that a name could amount to an original work.

15. Infringement

a.   Infringement occurs when a person, without the consent of the copyright owner, contravenes the rights of the copyright owner. Secondary infringement will occur if:-

i.   A person, without permission, transmits a work by means of a telecommunication system if he knows that infringing copies will be made on reception.

ii.   A person supplies a copy of a sound recording or film, knowing or believing that the recipient will make infringing copies.

b.   *Electronic infringement of copyright.* The 1988 Act introduces measures for copyright protection in respect of the latest forms of technology which have an impact on the copyright system.

Where copies of a protected work are issued to the public in an electronic form which is "copy protected" any person who makes or trades in, or advertises any device specifically designed to circumvent the copy protection or who publishes information intended to help persons to circumvent it commits an infringement of copyright.

Copyright is also infringed by a person who dishonestly receives a programme either broadcast or distributed by cable transmitted from the UK with the intention of avoiding payment.

c.   *Remedies for infringement.* The following remedies are available:-

i.   Injunction.

ii.   Damages.

iii.   Order for delivery-up.

iv.   Account for profit.

The 1988 Act makes it a criminal offence if a person knew or had reason to believe that copyright would be infringed in the event of making or dealing with infringing articles.

16. Licensing

a.   The 1988 Act renames the Performing Right Tribunal — the Copyright

Tribunal and gives the Secretary of State additional powers of supervision over and regulation of the licensing of right.

b.   The new regime of control will operate where rights are either licensed pursuant to a licensing scheme or licensed by a licensing body. A licensing scheme is defined as a scheme setting out:-

i.   The classes of case in which the operator of the scheme is willing to grant copyright licences, and,

ii.   The terms on which licences would be granted in those classes.

c.   A licensing body is a society or other organisation which has as a main object the negotiation or granting of copyright licences and whose objects include the granting of licences covering works of more than one author.

d.   A copyright licence means a licence to do or authorise the doing of any of the acts restricted by copyright.

The following disputes may be referred to the Tribunal:-

i.   Over the terms of a scheme proposed to be operated by a licensing body.

ii.   Over the terms of a scheme already in operation.

iii.   In respect of a scheme already subject to an order by the tribunal.

iv.   Between a person who claims to be covered by a scheme but complains that the operator of the scheme has either refused a licence or offered one on unreasonable terms.

The Tribunal's jurisdiction over licences from licensing bodies is with respect to disputes concerning licences proposed, granted or withheld by a licensing body but not pursuant to a licensing scheme, eg. a dispute between the Performing Rights Society and the BBC would be appropriate in this case.

17. Performances

The 1988 Act repealed the Performers' Protection Acts 1958-1972.

a.   *Persons Protected.* The following persons are protected:-

i.   Those who act, sing, deliver, declaim, play in or otherwise perform literary, dramatic, musical or artistic works.

ii.   Those having recording rights in relation to a performance.

b.   *Rights of action.* Performers and persons having recording rights have civil rights of action for damages, an injunction, that illicit recordings be delivered up or the seizure of illicit recordings exposed for sale or hire. The seizure remedy is subject to the safeguards that the police must be given advance notice, only premises with public access may be entered and force may not be used. In addition to civil remedies performers are also protected by penal provisions.

338

c.   *The Copyright Tribunal.* The Tribunal is given a limited jurisdiction with respect to performances, ie, a person wishing to make a recording from an existing recording may apply to the Tribunal where:-

    i.   The identity of the performer cannot be ascertained or

    ii.   The performer unreasonably withholds consent.

d.   *Extent of rights.* The rights last for 50 years from the day when the performance took place.

TRADE MARKS

18. Definition

a.   A trade mark is a mark used in relation to goods or services so as to indicate a connection in the course of trade between the goods and some person having a right to use the mark.

b.   "Mark" includes a device, brand, heading, label, ticket, name, signature, word, letter, numeral or any combination thereof.

c.   The commercial purpose of a trade mark is to distinguish the goods or services of a company from those of its competitors. Many trade marks indicate quality and induce customers to buy the goods.

d.   The legal purpose of a trade mark is to prevent others from using the mark and thus benefitting from the goodwill attached to the mark.

e.   Life patents, trade marks constitute "industrial property". However trade marks are concerned with commercial features and sales, rather than the technical features which are crucial to patents. While the life of a patent is limited to 20 years a trade mark can be renewed indefinitely. Another difference is that the cost of registering, renewing and enforcing trade mark rights is much less expensive than for patents.

f.   The law on trade marks is contained in the *TRADE MARKS ACT 1938* as amended by the *TRADE DESCRIPTIONS ACT 1968* and the *TRADE MARKS (AMENDMENT) ACT 1984.*

19. Registration

Registration at the Patent Office confers a statutory monopoly on the use of the mark and a registered owner may sue for infringement. To qualify as sufficiently distinctive for registration the 1938 Act requires one of the following particulars to be present:-

a.   The name of the company, individual or firm represented in a special or particular manner.

b.   The signature of the applicant for registration, or some predecessor in business.

c.   An invented word or words (for example Coca Cola, Bovril, Formica, Harpic).

    d. A word or words having no direct reference to the character or quality of the goods, and not constituting a geographical name or surname.

    e. Any other distinctive mark.

A trade mark will only be registered if it shows a trade connection between the mark owner and his goods or services and provided it distinguishes the goods or services from those of others. A mark in common usage cannot be sufficiently distinctive.

    In **YORKSHIRE COPPER WORKS' APPLICATION (1954)** registration of ''Yorkshire'' as a trade mark was refused although the applicants had shown that the trade regarded it as referring exclusively to their product.

20. Infringement

    a. Infringement occurs when any person, without permission, uses in the court of a trade, a mark identical to the registered mark or so similar as to be likely to deceive or cause confusion. Infringement also occurs if a person compares his goods with those of a trade mark owner and refers to the latters goods by the trade mark, for example a comparative price list setting out the traders brand and comparing it with a famous name product

    b. When considering whether marks are similar the idea conveyed by the mark must be looked at as well as any physical similarity.

    In **TAW v NOTEK (1951)** P used a drawing of a car in the shape of a cat's body with the eyes as headlamps as their trade mark. D used the head of a cat with the eyes as car headlamps. It was held that although the drawings were visually dissimilar the idea was the same, so P's trade mark had been infringed.

    c. When infringement occurs the plaintiff is entitled to an injunction and damages on an account of profits and to an order for destruction or modification of the offending goods.

    d. Where goods are sold that infringe a trade mark title to those goods will not pass and the seller will be in breach of the implied condition in *S.12. SALE OF GOODS ACT 1979*. See **NIBLETT v CONFECTIONERS' MATERIALS CO. (1921)** (Chapter 33.15).

PASSING OFF

21. Definition

Passing off is a tort. X will commit a tort, against Y if he passes off his goods or business as those of Y. Y need not prove that X acted intentionally, or with intent to deceive. Nor does he have to prove that anyone was actually deceived, if deception was likely. There is also no requirement for Y to prove damage.

22. Types of Passing Off

    a. Passing off is usually committed by imitating the appearance of the plaintiff's goods, or by selling them under the same or a similar name. If the name used by the plaintiff merely describes his goods then generally no action will lie. However it is possible for a name that was originally only descriptive to come to signify goods produced by the plaintiff. It is also possible for a word to lose its trade meaning and become merely descriptive.

b.   The tort may be committed by applying the name of the locality in which the plaintiff produces goods to the defendant's goods.

In **BOLLINGER v COSTA BRAVA WINE CO. (1961)** P, who manufactured champagne brough an action against D who were describing their product as "Spanish champagne". It was held that the word "champagne" was generally regarded as referring exclusively to wine produced in the Champagne region of France and even with the prefix "Spanish" purchasers could be misled. An injunction was granted to prevent D using the name.

c.   A person may usually carry on business under his own name, unless he does so fraudulently. But he must not mark his goods with a name (even his own name) if this will have the effect of passing off those goods as goods of another.

d.   Passing-off may be committed by using another person's name or trade name.

In **HINES v WINNICK (1947)** P broadcast with a band called "Dr Crock and the Crackpots". After he left the programme D gave the same name to a replacement band. It was held that the public were likely to be misled and an injunction was granted.

e.   It is not necessary for the defendant's trade to be identical to that of the plaintiff if there is sufficient similarity to mislead the public.

In **HARRODS LTD v R. HARRODS LTD (1923)** the famous Knightsbridge store successfully prevented a money-lending company from trading under the Harrods name. Although the nature of their business was different there was sufficient likelihood that the public would assume that they were connected.

In contrast there have been many cases where a plaintiff has failed to prevent the use of a similar name because the likelihood of confusion or loss of business did not exist. For example the owners of "Wombles" books and television programmes could not prevent a company from leasing "Wombles" rubbish skips and a Mr. Albert Edward Hall was allowed to continue to use the name the "Albert Hall Orchestra" despite an objection from the proprietor of the Royal Albert Hall.

341

f.   False advertising is not generally passing off, but it may be in exceptional circumstances.

In **MASSON SEELEY v EMBOSSOTYPE MANUFACTURING (1924)** D copied P's catalogue in such a way that the public would believe that the goods offered were P's goods. D's goods were however inferior to P's goods. It was held that this was passing off.

"Switch selling" does not amount to passing off.

In **RIMA ELECTRIC v ROLLS RAZOR (1965)** D advertised so as to lead the public to believe that they could buy "Magicair" hairdryers for 5 guineas. However they had no Magicair hairdryers so they offered other makes to enquirers. It was held that this was not passing off.

g.   *Reverse passing-off.* Usually passing-off occurs when the defendant holds out his goods as being those of the plaintiff. However passing-off may also occur when the defendant holds out the plaintiff's goods as being his own, hence the "reverse" passing off.

In **BRISTOL CONSERVATORIES v CONSERVATORIES CUSTOM BUILT (1989)** D showed prospective customers photographs of P's ornamental conservatories, which they held out as being examples of their own goods and workmanship. If the customer placed an order, he would then be supplied with a conservatory manufactured by D. In this case the Court of Appeal was concerned only with D's motion to strike out P's statement of claim as disclosing no reasonable cause of action. However on the facts as alleged the Court held that there was a triable issue.

23. Remedies

The plaintiff may obtain an injunction and/or damages. Damages will reflect lost profit (if any) plus loss of goodwill and reputation.

COURSEWORK QUESTIONS 25-32
COMMERCIAL LAW

25.   *Linda comes home from work to find that her husband Brian, in her absence has entered into a hire-purchase contract with a door-to-door salesman for £1,200 for double-glazing. She seeks your advice on whether he can avoid the contract. She would also like to know the main differences between a hire-purchase contract and a credit sale agreement.*

26.   a.   *'The relationship between principal and agent creates obligations for both parties.'*
      Discuss the nature of the agent's obligations to the principal and the remedies available to the principal if these are not fulfilled.

                                                              (12 marks)

b. Paul asks Alan to sell two word processors for him for not less than
£600 each, for an agreed commission of 5%. Alan purchases one of
the processors himself, without disclosing this to Paul, and pays Paul
£600. Alan sells the other to Terry for £700 and pays over another £650
to Paul, stating that this was the selling price.
Paul has now discovered the full facts about these transactions and seeks
your advice as to possible remedies. Advise Paul.

(8 marks)
(20 marks)
CIMA Stage 1 May 1987

27. a. Discuss the meaning of negotiability and explain the main
characteristics of bills of exchange and promissory notes.

(10 marks)

b. What is the extent of the protection afforded by the law to:
i. a paying banker who pays a cheque to a person who is not its
rightful owner, and
ii. a collecting banker who collects a cheque for a person who is
not its rightful owner?

(10 marks)
(20 marks)
ACCA Level 1 December 1984

28. a. Compare a charterparty with a bill of lading. Is a bill of lading a
negotiable instrument?

b. Jenny has her jewellery insured with X Ltd for £10,000 and with
Y Ltd for £6,000. Her house is burgled and jewellery to the value of
£3,000 is stolen. She claims this amount from Y Ltd. How much can
Y Ltd claim as a contribution from X Ltd?

29. a. State the rules which govern the passing of property in a contract
for the sale of goods, and explain why it is important to ascertain the
time at which the property in goods passes from the seller to the buyer.
(12 marks)

b. H delivers by lorry a consignment of goods which he has contracted
to sell to J. The goods are unloaded in J's yard by the lorry driver. Later
that day J examines the goods and discovers they do not comply with
the contract description.
Advise J.
(8 marks)
(20 marks)
ACCA Level 1 December 1984

30. *Sparks buys old radios, reconditions them and then re-sells them at a cheap price. He always attaches a note stating that they are second hand and that they are bought at the purchaser's risk with no liability on Sparks' part. Some are sold to market traders and others directly to the public.*

In repairing a number of sets, Sparks uses some faulty wiring with the following results:

a. *Watt, who bought a set from a trader in Barchester market, receives an electric shock.*

b. *Volt, who bought a set from Sparks, suffers damage to furniture when the radio causes a fire.*

c. *Ampere, Volt's wife, is burned when she attempts to put out the fire.*

Advise Sparks.

CIMA Foundation May 1981

31. *As a general rule where goods are sold by a person who is not their owner, and who does not sell them under the authority or with the consent of the owner, the buyer acquires no better title to the goods than the seller had.*

Outline the principal exceptions and qualifications to this rule.

ICSA Stage 2 June 1986

32. a. *In relation to cheques explain the types of crossing that may appear. What is the legal effect of such crossings?*

(12 marks)

b. *M signed a cheque and crossed it "not negotiable". He instructed N, his company accountant, to fill in a certain amount on the cheque and so fill in O's name as payee. The accountant owed a personal debt to P so he filled in a different amount from that authorised and made the cheque payable to P. P cashed the cheque in settlement of N's debt. Advise M.*

(8 marks)

(20 marks)

ACCA Level 1 June 1985

PART V   LABOUR LAW

Throughout this section on Labour Law the following abbreviations are used:-

Employment Act 1980	– EA 1980
Employment Act 1982	– EA 1982
Employment Protection Act 1975	– EPA 1975
Employment Protection (Consolidation) Act 1978	– EPCA 1978
Health & Safety at Work Act 1974	– HSAWA 1974
Trade Union Act 1984	– TUA 1984
Trade Union & Labour Relations Act 1974	– TULRA 1974
Employment Act 1988	– EA 1988
Employment Act 1989	– EA 1989
Employment Act 1990	– EA 1990

41 The Contract of Employment

INTRODUCTION

1. In this chapter the form of contract of employment is considered, the distinction between a contract of employment and that of an independent contractor, and the statutory requirement to provide written particulars of the contract, etc.

FORM OF CONTRACT

2. A contract of employment, to be legally binding must fulfil all the normal contractual requirements, ie

a. *Offer and acceptance.* There must be offer and acceptance. The offer must contain the terms of the contract or indicate where they may be found. No particular form is required, the contract may be oral, or in writing.

b. *Consideration.* The consideration is the employer's promise to pay the agreed wages in return for the employee's promise to perform a particular task. Generally speaking the courts would not be concerned with the adequacy of the consideration, although there is legislation aimed at protecting certain classes of low paid workers.

In **ROBERTS v SMITH (1859)** an employee accepted his employer's terms in regard to remuneration, ie "it is entirely left to me to give unto you such sum of money as I may deem right".

c. *Capacity.* There is some restriction on the contractual capacity of minors. Protection is given both under common law and statute, (**DE FRANCESCO v BARNUM (1890)**). (See Chapter 16.3.). Protection is also given to women, disabled persons and ethnic minorities.

d. *Legality.* A contract of employment must not be tainted with illegality, eg a contract which deliberately seeks to defraud the Inland Revenue.

In **CORBY v MORRISON (1980)** the employee received, not only a gross wage in accordance with a wages council order but also an extra £5. This additional payment was not subject to income tax or social security deductions, neither was it shown on the pay envelope. It was held that the whole contract was illegal on the grounds of defrauding the Inland Revenue.

Contrast **DAVIDSON v PILLAY (1974)**. Mrs. D managed a shop and each week took her wages from the till without deducting tax. It was held that D was not aware of the illegality. Only if the employer is guilty of knowingly committing an illegal act to which the employee is not a party may the employee claim under the contract.

However, a legal contract, performed illegally, eg where an employer

347

contravenes the *WAGES ACT 1986*, will not be void on the grounds of illegality.

3. Details of the Contract. The contract may be oral, in writing or by the conduct of the parties. The terms of the contract may be oral, in writing, implied by common law (eg the employee's duty of obedience, the employer's duty to provide work). There are also many statutory requirements affecting the contract of employment. Collective agreements, ie agreements between trade unions and employers associations, may be incorporated into a contract of employment. Terms may also be given in other places, eg works rule books or notice boards. These sources of contractual terms are detailed at the end of this chapter.

DISTINGUISHING THE TYPE OF RELATIONSHIP

4. Where there is a contract of employment there is the relationship of employer and employee. This relationship imposes certain rights and duties on each party. It is important to distinguish whether a relationship is that of employer/employee or employer/independent contractor, etc, for several reasons. There are obligations at common law, eg an employer's vicarious liability for the torts of his employee. There are many statutory rights and liabilities which make the distinction important, eg redundancy and unfair dismissal under the *EPCA 1978*, and social security benefits under the *SOCIAL SECURITY ACT 1975*. Over the years certain "tests" have been incorporated into common law which have arisen from particular cases in which the relationships were distinguished.

5. In the past reliance was placed on what was termed the "control test". The control test was defined in **YEWENS v NOAKES (1880).**

> "A servant is a person subject to the command of his master as to the manner in which he shall do his work."

Nevertheless, in most legal "general rules" there are some deviations, the control test goes on to say, that the greater the amount of control — the stronger the case for suggesting that it is a contract of service. However in many occupations of a skilled or professional nature, the employer exercises little control over the way in which work is carried out. In today's society often the relationship is impersonal, as with a corporate employer. It can be seen from this that a single test may not be sufficient to answer the problem. Other tests have been devised and given such names as the "Integration Test" and the "Multiple Test". Generally courts would ask the following questions in deciding the nature of the relationship:

   a. *What does the contract say?* Does the contract call the worker an employee? If the employer does not want it to be construed as a contract of service he should state in the contract:

   i.   It is a contract for services.

   ii. That the worker is to be classed as an independent contractor and shall be personally liable to third parties for any damage or injury arising out of work.

However, even this is not conclusive as the courts will look at the reality of the situation:

In **YOUNG & WOODS LTD v WEST (1980)** the employee (a skilled sheet metal worker) was given the choice of employment as either an employee or as a self-employed person. No income tax was deducted by his employer and he paid his own social security contributions. Upon dismissal he claimed compensation for unfair dismissal (open only to an employee). Whilst the court accepted the intention of the parties was made in good faith it looked beyond this to the reality of the situation and held that W was not in business on his own and therefore he was an employee and entitled to compensation.

In **FERGUSON v DAWSON (1978)** the worker was employed as part of the "lump" labour force in the building industry. He gave a false name when signing on and no tax or insurance deductions were made by the contractor who engaged him. In order to claim compensation from his employer for an injury sustained at work the worker had to show that he was on a contract of service. It was held that despite the contract which said he was self-employed, in reality he was an employee.

Contrast **BRITISH SCHOOL OF MOTORING v SOCIAL SERVICES SECRETARY (1978)** BSM organised its business so that although it found its pupils, supplied and maintained the car and paid expenses, the instructor was not committed to a set number of hours and was paid on a commission basis with no guaranteed remuneration. It was held that there were no provisions which contradicted the contract's term that the instructor was self-employed.

b. *Does the contract read like a contract of employment?* If the contract includes not only wages, but other details regarding holidays, superannuation, pension, sick benefits, injury benefits and hours of work, then prima facie the worker is an employee. If the contract is to undertake some particular task, then, prima facie it is a contract for services.

c. *What measure of control is exercised over the work?* This was the traditional test. "The greater the amount of direct control exercised over the person rendering the services by the person contracting for them, the stronger the grounds for considering it to be a contract of service." Conversely, the greater the degree of independence of such control the greater the probability that the services rendered are of a professional nature and that the contract is not one of personal service. However, control in itself can never be the sole deciding factor.

349

6. Whilst none of the foregoing questions may be sufficient in themselves, the use of all of them, or a combination of them will help to solve the problem of distinguishing between contracts of service and contracts for services. The following cases give examples of some court decisions in this matter.

a. *Integration test.* This asks if the work, although done for the business, is integrated into it or only an accessory to it.

In **WHITTAKER v M.P.N.I. (1967)** a trapeze artist engaged by a circus also performed other duties, eg acting as an usherette during other performances. Having fallen during her act she claimed industrial injury benefit. It was held that although the circus had no control over the artist during the act, this was integrated into other duties and was therefore a contract of service.

Contrast **WESTALL RICHARDSON LTD v ROULSON (1954)** an "outworker" in the cutlery industry who rented a workshop in a factory to polish cutlery manufactured in the factory was held to be self-employed in view of the independence he enjoyed, even though he formed an integral part of the business carried on in the factory.

b. *The economic reality or multiple test.* Courts will take into account many considerations when deciding on the employer/employee relationship, eg power of selection, payment, right of dismissal, right of control, hours and regularity of work, limited location of work, degree of personal business risk undertaken by the employee, whether income tax is deducted by the employer, etc.

In **READY-MIXED CONCRETE (SOUTH EAST) LTD v M.P.N.I. (1969)** each driver of the company was financially assisted to buy his own vehicle. The vehicle had to be painted in the company's colours. The drivers had to wear the company uniform and be available for work when required. They were paid a mileage rate for work done for the company. It was held that the drivers were not employees but independent contractors as they were operating at their own financial risk.

c. *The organisation test.* It has been decided in several cases involving persons undergoing hospital treatment that the employer shall be responsible for the acts of both employee and contractor where the third party (patient) entrusts himself to the organisation as a whole.

In **CASSIDY v MINISTRY OF HEALTH (1951)** a patient lost the use of some fingers owing to the negligence of the surgeon, and sued the hospital for damages. It was held that although the surgeon was not an employee of the Hospital Board, the plaintiff was entitled to damages as he entrusted himself to the organisation as a whole.

d. *Part-time employees.* The amount of work given is not a deciding factor. A person working part-time may be an employee.

In **MARKET INVESTIGATIONS LTD v MINISTRY OF SOCIAL SECURITY (1969)** a married woman was intermittently engaged by a market research company to act as an interviewer for a fixed remuneration. She was given detailed instructions. It was held that she was an employee.

Contrast **WILLY SCHEIDEGGER SWISS TYPEWRITING SCHOOL (LONDON) v MINISTRY OF SOCIAL SECURITY (1968)** a sales representative of typewriters and typewriting courses whose sole remuneration was a commission on sales with no expenses paid was deemed to be an independent contractor.

e. *Effect of continuous service over a period of time.*

In **NETHERMERE (ST NEOTS) LTD v TAVERNA and GARDINER (1984)** Mrs T and Mrs G were employed by N Ltd as "homeworkers" manufacuring boys trousers. They worked whenever needed and let the company know when they were taking a holiday. They rarely refused work and gave warning when not wanting it. They submitted regular time-sheets and were paid the same rate of pay as the factory workers. The work was an essential part of the factory's production. The machines used were provided by the company. It was held that there may be a contract of service if, over a continuous period of regular giving and taking of work in accordance with the parties expectation, obligations have been established on the part of the company to provide work and on the part of the homeworker to accept it.

IMPORTANCE OF THE RELATIONSHIP BETWEEN EMPLOYER AND EMPLOYEE

7. An employer is usually responsible for the wrongful acts of his employees, committed in the course of employment. He is not usually responsible for the wrongful acts committed by independent contractors but is liable for damage to third parties in the following circumstances:

a. *Negligent selection.* Where the employer is negligent in selecting the contractor, ie he does not ascertain the contractor's competence to do that particular job.

351

b. *Negligently gives instructions.* Where an employer issues, authorises or ratifies a negligent order or instruction, the third party has a good claim against the employer.

c. *Strict liability.* This usually refers to the employer's statutory duty in relation to the fencing of machinery under the *FACTORIES ACT 1961*. Other instances where the employer is liable for the wrongful acts of independent contractors and cannot use the defence that he did not perform the task himself are as follows:

  i. *Withdrawal of support from a neighbours land.* Where the activities of a contractor working on the employers land does something so as to cause subsidence on a neighbours land.

  ii. *Work carried out on or near to a highway.* Because of the obvious danger to members of the public using the highway.

  iii. *The rule in Rylands v Fletcher.* Where dangerous or unpleasant substances escape onto a neighbours land or property. In the above case water seeped onto Ryland's land through a mineshaft. (See Chapter 27.2.).

  iv. *Nuisance.* Where dust and noise inevitable from an extensive building or construction operation affect neighbouring property or persons.

  v. *Acts causing fire or explosion.* Extra hazardous acts which, by their very nature involve, in the eyes of the law, danger to others, eg where implements such as flame-bearing equipment or explosives are necessary or incidental to the work being performed.

  vi. *Contractor breaks the law.* If the employer engages a contractor to perform an unlawful task he cannot evade liability for any resultant damage.

  vii. *Safety of employees.* An employer cannot escape liability for a breach of his duty to provide safe working conditions, etc, by delegating this duty to an independent contractor.

8. Other implications are as follows:

a. *Social Security Acts.* Entitlement to benefits and rates of contributions payable depend on whether a person is an employee or an independent contractor.

b. *Other Statutes.* An employer has legal and financial responsibilities for an employee but not an independent contractor under various statutes, eg *TULRA 1974* and *EPCA 1978, EQUAL PAY ACT 1970*. The employer would be liable for, eg. compensation for unfair dismissal, redundancy payments, maternity payments, etc. In addition the employer would be responsible for deducting income tax and national insurance contributions from the wages of an employee, and paying statutory sick pay.

c.   ***Common law duties.*** An employer has duties under common law as outlined in Chapter 43.

d.   ***Employer's bankruptcy.*** If an employer becomes bankrupt or, in the case of a company goes into liquidation an employee will be a preferential creditor with regard to arrears of pay.

LOANED EMPLOYEES

9.   Under the Control Test judges have often had to decide which of two employers was responsible where one has lent an employee to the other. The general rule is that control remains with the original employer, under the rule that personal service contracts cannot be assigned (employees are not chattels).

In **MERSEY DOCKS & HARBOUR BOARD v COGGINS & GRIFFITH (LIVERPOOL) LTD (1946)** the Harbour Board lent the defendant company a crane plus an operator. The contract specified that the defendants would be the employer, but the Harbour Board retained ultimate right to employ, pay wages and dismiss. It was held that the Harbour Board was still the employer despite the terms of the contract. The actual circumstances should be considered.

10.   The general rule can be rebutted, but the original employer must prove transfer of control. This transfer is more readily inferred when an employee is lent on his own, without equipment.

In **GARRARD v SOUTHEY & CO (1952)** G lent S two electricians for work on a factory. G retained right of dismissal and paid them. The electricians were supervised by S's foreman, a skilled electrician. One of the electricians was injured. It was held that control had passed to S who was thus responsible for provision of safe equipment.

Denning L J suggested that where a skilled man or a man together with machinery or tools is lent, such transference "rarely if ever" takes place but "does sometimes take place" with unskilled workers.

WRITTEN PARTICULARS

11.   *EPCA 1978* (S.1.) requires an employer to provide his employees with a written statement of the terms of his employment within 13 weeks of starting work. The statement is not a contract of service, merely a statement of facts of the basic terms of employment.

"The written statement is not the contract and is not even conclusive evidence of the terms of the contract" (per **Lord Parker C J** in **TURRIFF CONSTRUCTION LTD v BRYANT (1967)**.

In **MARTIN v SOLUS SCHALL (1979)** the written statement of terms said the employee "will be expected to work such overtime as is necessary to ensure continuity of service". It was held that this must be regarded as a contractual obligation since otherwise the words would be meaningless.

12. The statement must contain the following particulars:

    a. Names of employer and employee.

    b. Date the employment began.

    c. Scale of remuneration, or the method of calculation including eg, overtime pay.

    d. The intervals at which remuneration is made.

    e. Terms relating to hours of work.

    f. Terms relating to:

        i.   Entitlement to holidays.

        ii. Payment for periods of holidays, including sufficient information to enable the employee to calculate holiday entitlement and holiday pay on termination of employment.

        iii. Incapacity for work owing to sickness or injury, including provision for sick pay.

        iv. Pensions.

        v.   Length of notice on termination for both employer and employee. If for a fixed term, the date of expiry of the contract.

        vi. A statement showing if a contracting-out certificate is in force under the *SOCIAL SECURITY PENSIONS ACT 1975*.

13. An additional note to the written statement must:

    a. Specify the person to whom the employee can apply if he has a grievance, and how application can be made;

    b. Explain the subsequent steps in any grievance procedure which may be available to him.

This note applies to an employer with more than 20 employees.

14. Disciplinary Rules. Details of any disciplinary rules applying to the employee must be given, or reference made to a document in which the rules are contained.

15. Appeal Against Disciplinary Decisions. If an employee is not satisfied with a disciplinary decision relating to himself he must be made aware of the name of a person to whom he can appeal.

16. Job Title. The title of the job which employee is employed to do must be given.

17. Date Service Began. The statement must show if any service with a previous employer counts as part of the employee's continuous service.

18. For any of the particulars referred to above the written statement may refer the employee to a document or documents which he has reasonable opportunity of reading in the course of his employment, or are reasonably accessible to him in some other way.

EXEMPTIONS

19. The written statement is not necessary where:

a. The employee works for less than 16 hours per week (an employee with 5 years service or more will be deemed to have continuous service if he works 8 or more house per week, and needs a written statement).

b. Employees normally work abroad.

c. An employee returns on the same terms within 6 months of leaving if he previously had a written statement.

d. Employees are Crown servants.

e. The details are contained in a written contract of employment.

CHANGES TO CONDITIONS OF EMPLOYMENT

20. Any agreed changes to the conditions of employment must be notified to the employee within one month of the change taking place. The notification must be by means of a written statement. If a copy of the statement is not left with the employee the employer must preserve the statement and ensure that the employee has reasonable opportunities of reading it in the course of employment.

21. If an employee has not been given written notice as the Act provides or thinks that his notice is incorrect he can apply to an industrial tribunal, who can order that he be given a correct notice. The written statement is evidence although not conclusive evidence of the terms of employment, it is essential, therefore, that it should be correct.

VARIATION TO THE EMPLOYMENT CONTRACT

22. Generally speaking a contract cannot be varied unilaterally. However contracts of employment tend to have considerable flexibility. In the absence of written particulars, terms may be implied as follows:-

a. *Implied in fact.* A term may be implied because it lends business efficacy to the contract:

In **McCAFFREY v A.E. JEAVONS & CO LTD (1967)** an employee described as a "travelling man" in the construction industry was deemed contractually bound to work anywhere in the UK.

In **BRISTOL GARAGE (BRIGHTON) LTD v LOWEN (1979)** L worked at a garage as a petrol-pump attendant. There were a series of cash deficiencies and the employer concluded they were due to dishonesty and deducted the amount from his employees' pay. The contract of employment allowed deduction for deficiencies. An industrial tribunal held that business efficiency required an implied exception in case of loss due to fire and theft since employees would not have agreed to have such losses made up from their pay.

b. ***Implied by custom and practice.*** An employee enters into a contract of employment on terms implied by custom and practice in the trade, industry or locality provided those customs are well-known and reasonable:

In **SAGAR v RIDEHALGH (1931)** Romer L J stated that the employee "entering the employer's service upon the same terms as the other weavers employed by them must be deemed to have subjected himself to those terms whatever they might turn out to be."

Occasionally a long-standing term in a collective agreement will be deemed to have become established by custom and practice.

c. ***Terms implied by law.*** Some terms may be implied at common law or statute. The terms implied by common law are the implied duties of an employee and employer outlined in Chapters 42 and 43. Terms implied by statute include, eg minimum wage legislation which provides for a certain minimum wage regardless of any express provision in the contract to the contrary, and the "equality clause" in the *EQUAL PAY ACT 1970* which is deemed to be read into contracts of employment even without an award by a statutory body.

23. Terms may be incorporated into a contract of employment in the following ways:-

a. ***Express terms.*** Sometimes what was intended as the statutory written statement of particulars appears as a written contract of employment:-

In **GASCOL CONVERSIONS LTD v MERCER (1974)**, the written particulars required by statute was headed "Contract of Employment". The document included a receipt to be signed by the employee and retained by the employer. It was held that the document was a signed, written contract, the express terms of which could not be altered by implication.

b. ***Collective agreements.*** Terms in collective agreement may be incorporated into contracts of employment:

In **JOEL v CAMMELL LAIRD SHIPREPAIRERS LTD (1969)** a collective agreement related to transfers of employees between ship repair and ship building. It was held to be incorporated into the contract of employment because the employees concerned had indicated that they were aware of the provision.

In **ROBERTSON v BRITISH GAS (1983)** meter readers and collectors employed by North Thames Gas received an incentive bonus of about £400 per month. The scheme was negotiated by their union and was referred to in the written statement of terms of each employee. Management gave the union 6 months notice to terminate the agreement. The union members successfully argued in the Appeal Court that this was a breach of contract.

c. ***Other documents.***

SECRETARY OF STATE FOR EMPLOYMENT v A.S.L.E.F. (No. 2) (1972). This case involved railwaymen "working to rule" and by strict observance of the railway rules bringing the railways to a standstill. The court held that a work to rule was a breach of the individual employee's contract of employment because:-

i.   There was an implied term that an employee should not wilfully disrupt his employer's undertaking.

ii.   in this instance it involved refusal to work obligatory overtime.

iii.   the *employer's* rule book contained instructions the employee was obliged by his contract to obey.

Contrast **BRITISH LEYLAND (UK) LTD v McQUILKEN (1978).** An agreement with trade unions on closure of a department provided that employees should be interviewed to ascertain preference for future employment. It was held that the agreement was a long-term policy plan not incorporated into individual contracts of employment.

42 The Common Law Duties of an Employee

INTRODUCTION

1. The duties of an employee are governed by the terms of his contract. In the absence of any express or implied terms his duties will be determined under Common Law. Contravention of any of these duties may give an employer the right to dismiss the employee.

IMPLIED DUTIES

2. The following are circumstances in which the courts have held employees to have implied duties towards their employers:

a. *Indemnity*. Where the employer suffers some loss because of his liability for the wrongful act of his employee, the employee may be liable to indemnify (compensate) his employer;

In **LISTER v ROMFORD ICE & COLD STORAGE LTD (1957)** L was a driver employed by the company. His father, a driver's mate, assisted L. Due to L's negligence his father was injured and claimed damages against the company. The company in turn claimed that L should indemnify it against the loss suffered. It was held that L should indemnify the company due to his negligence.

It was suggested in **GREGORY v FORD (1951)** that there was an implication that an employer would take out the statutory third-party vehicle insurance. It could, accordingly be said that the employer had undertaken to insure himself and not to claim an indemnity. In the Lister case it was held that there was no duty implied in a contract of employment that the employer should take out insurance and not claim indemnity from an employee. As a result of this case a committee was set up to deal with its implications. Subsequently all members of the British Insurance Association agreed that they would not require the employer to claim indemnity from the employee unless there was evidence of collusion or wilful misconduct on the employee's part.

b. *Misconduct*. The employee must not misconduct himself. The term misconduct includes insolence, persistent laziness, immorality, dishonesty and drunkenness. Misconduct will justify summary dismissal if it directly interferes with the business of the employer, or the employee's ability to perform his services.

In **PEPPER v WEBB (1969)** a gardener who behaved in a surly manner, showed disinterest in the garden, refused to perform certain tasks in the garden and was insolent to his employer was held to have been dismissed justifiably.

Contrast **WILSON v RACHER (1974)** a gardener was dismissed for swearing at his employer, on one occasion. It was held that this was an exceptional outburst from an otherwise competent and diligent employee who had been provoked by his employer. Therefore there were no grounds for dismissal.

c. *Personal service.* The employee must not allow others outside the scope of his employer's control to perform his tasks.

In **ILKIW v SAMUELS (1963)** a lorry driver allowed another person to drive his lorry. He did this against express instructions from his employer and without enquiry as to the other person's ability to handle his vehicle. As a result, a third party was injured. The employer was liable because of the negligence of his own driver (the person responsible for the operation of the lorry).

d. *Loyalty and good faith.* The employee must not accept bribes or make secret profits. Similar to the duties of an agent to his principal, see Chapter 32.

In **BOSTON DEEP SEA FISHING CO v ANSELL (1888)** whilst employed as managing director with the plaintiff company Ansell contracted with a shipbuilding company for supply of ships, taking a secret commission. It was held that Ansell's action was a breach of his duty to his employer.

c. *Interests of the employer.* The employee must do nothing to harm his employer's interests, even in his spare time:

In **HIVAC v PARK ROYAL SCIENTIFIC INSTRUMENTS LTD (1946)** employees of the plaintiff worked for the defendants (a rival firm) in their spare time. It was proved that they also passed on trade secrets. It was held that H would be granted an injunction restraining them from working for PR.

In **BARTLETT v SHOE LEATHER RECORD (1960)**. The plaintiff, an editor, worked for a newspaper and a fashion trade journal in his spare-time. Although not writing on the same subject it was held that he would not be able to give of his best by reason of his spare-time activities.

An employee should do nothing to cause his employer to lose confidence in him:

In **SINCLAIR v NEIGHBOUR (1967)** a betting-shop manager "borrowed" £15 from the till, intending to replace it the following day, although he knew his employer would not approve. The employer discovered the employee's act and dismissed him without notice. It was held that dismissal was justified.

f. *Careful service.* An employee must exercise due care and skill in the performance of his duties. Where he claims that he has the ability to do the work undertaken, besides having the ability, he must also perform the tasks diligently and efficiently.

In **HARMER v CORNELIUS (1858)** a person who was given a job as a scene painter had never painted scenes and was incompetent. He was held to have been justifiably dismissed without notice.

In **SUPERLUX v PLAISTED (1958)** the defendant, a vacuum-cleaner salesman left his van outside his home overnight. Several cleaners were stolen. It was held that his breach of the duty of careful service justified dismissal.

An employee who is negligent can be sued for his negligence by his employer or by a third party who suffers loss as a result. However, some relief may be granted under the *LAW REFORM (CONTRIBUTORY NEGLIGENCE) ACT 1945*.

i.   If an employer suffers loss and sues his employee, the employee may claim contributory negligence on the grounds that he had not received sufficient instructions or supervision from the employer.

ii.   Where a third party suffers loss or damage due to an employee's negligent act, the injured party may sue either the employee or the employer (the employer is more likely to be in a position to pay damages). The employer may in mitigation plead contributory negligence against the employee. This does not absolve the tort, but merely apportions some of the blame. The total costs are apportioned between the employer and employee according to their degree of fault.

In **JONES v MANCHESTER CORPORATION (1948)** the case concerned a negligent doctor and anaesthetist, both very inexperienced, left in charge of an emergency ward with no one to supervise. A patient suffered an injury as a result and was awarded damages which were apportioned, 20% against the doctor and anaeathetist and 80% against the hospital.

g.   *Account for property and gain.* An employee must account for any money or property belonging to his employer, and any gains made thereon.

In **READING v ATTORNEY GENERAL (1951)** a sergeant in the British Army in Egypt agreed to accompany lorries carrying illicit spirits. He was paid £20,000 so that his presence in uniform would ensure that the vehicles were not searched. It was held that as he made his profit through the use of his position, he had to account to the Crown as his employer. (The sergeant was not strictly an agent, but he was held to have a fiduciary relationship with his employer similar to a principal/agent relationship.)

h.   *Trade secrecy.* The employee must maintain secrecy over his employer's affairs during the time of his employment. If the employer wishes to extend this beyond the period of employment it would be advisable to insert a suitable clause in the contract of employment. The employee is under an obligation to his employers not to disclose confidential information obtained by him in the course of, and as a result of his employment. This duty applies both during employment and afterwards if the employee seeks to use such information to the detriment of his employer.

In **ROBB v GREEN (1895)**. An employee who copied down a list of customers intending to use it after leaving employment, was restrained from doing so.

Restraint of trade clauses.

Often an employer will wish to protect his trade secrets from disclosure by an employee when the employee leaves his service, and not leave it to the employee's common law duty of fidelity. The employer will do this by including in the contract of employment a clause placing some restriction on future employment, ie a restraint of trade clause. This important aspect of employment law is discussed in Chapter 19.18.

In **BENTS BREWERY CO LTD v HOGAN (1945)** a trade union official invited certain employees to disclose particulars of the total amount of the sales made and the wages paid at the branches of the company in which they were employed. It was held that if any employee gave that information he would commit a breach of contract, and the trade union official would be liable for inducing such breach.

However, an employee may disclose information if it is such that it is in the public interest to disclose it. Furthermore it should be disclosed to one who has a proper interest to receive it:

In **INITIAL SERVICES LTD v PUTTERILL (1968)** P was sales manager of the company which operated a laundry. He left their employment and took with him some documents relating to the company which he passed on to a national newspaper. The newspaper subsequently published articles alleging that there was profiteering in the laundry industry. The company sought an injunction against their former employee, but were unsuccessful since if the allegations were true there were arrangements in the industry which should have been registered under the *RESTRICTIVE TRADE PRACTICES ACT 1976*.

i. *Inventions.* It is the duty of the employee to disclose all inventions made using the facilities of the employer.

In **BRITISH SYPHON COMPANY LTD v HOMEWOOD (1956)** H was employed as a technical adviser and was asked to design a soda syphon, which he did, but he patented the syphon in his own name. It was held that the patent right belonged to the employer.

Statutory provision has been made with regard to employees' inventions by the *PATENTS ACT 1977*, which largely restates the common law position. This is that an invention belongs to the employer if made in the normal course of duties under the circumstances in which it might be expected an invention to result. In addition it is deemed to belong to the employer if the invention results from special duties assigned to the employee under circumstances in which an invention might reasonably be expected to result. However, in all other cases, even where the invention occurs in the course of employment, using the employer's materials but where an invention cannot reasonably be expected it will be deemed to belong to the employee.

j.   *Obedience.*

i.   The employee must obey all lawful and justifiable orders given by his employer in the ordinary course of business.

ii.   An employee only undertakes to perform those tasks to which he has agreed in his contract of employment. An employer may not require him to do other tasks, however reasonable, unless the contract is wide enough to permit this. This applies to both the nature of the work and to the location.

In **PRICE v MOUAT (1862)** a lace dealer was asked to card lace. This was not a task he had undertaken and he was justified in refusing, as it would have involved a lowering of his status.

In **O'BRIEN v ASSOCIATED FIRE ALARMS (1968)** an employee in a Liverpool factory was required to work in Barrow. It was held that such a request was outside the scope of the contract.

iii.   In some circumstances an employee will be justified in refusing a task, even though it is in the contract of employment:

In **OTTOMAN BANK v CHAKARIAN (1930)** C refused to move to a branch of the bank situated in a country in which his life would have been in danger. It was held that his refusal was justified.

iv.   The duty of obedience is mitigated where the employee does not show a wilful flouting of the essential conditions of the contract:

In **LAWS v LONDON CHRONICLE (1959)** L was secretary to an advertising manager. She followed him when he walked out of an editorial conference despite an order from the managing director to remain. It was held that L could not be summarily dismissed because her disobedience was an isolated instance and did not show an intention to repudiate her contract of service.

k.   *Notice.* The employee must give proper notice of termination of his services according to the terms of his contract, the custom of the trade or statute *(EPCA 1978)*. (See Chapter 47.3).

Note: The foregoing are examples of occasions where an employee's duties to his employer have been implied at common law. However it is not necessarily an exhaustive list. Generally courts will not imply unreasonable terms and will justify the implication of any terms they do imply, eg in **SECRETARY OF STATE FOR EMPLOYMENT v A.S.L.E.F. (1972)** Lord Denning concluded that every contract of employment should contain an obligation on the employee not to wilfully disrupt his employer's undertaking.

43 Duties of an Employer

INTRODUCTION

1. The duties which an employer has to his employees are set out in various Statutes and also under Common Law. This chapter is concerned with those duties which are implied under Common Law in the absence of other terms expressed in the contract of service and statutory duties to give time off work and make disclosure of information. We consider also an employers duties to persons other than employees, ie, visitors to his premises and third parties who suffer injury or loss due to the actions of his employees.

COMMON LAW DUTIES

2. **Work.** The employer is not obliged to provide work for his employees except in the following circumstances:

a. Where employment is essential to provide a reputation for future employment. This was originally considered to be in the case of actors:

In **CLAYTON AND WALLER v OLIVER (1930)** an actor was engaged for the leading role in a show. The management engaged someone else but agreed to pay the actor for his lost wages; however he also sued for loss of reputation. It was held that he was entitled to damages.

This principle was also extended to journalists and skilled workers.

In **COLLIER v SUNDAY REFEREE (1940)** Collier, a sub-editor was able to claim damages in accordance with the ruling given in the Clayton and Waller v Oliver case.

In **LANGSTON v AUEW (1974)** L resigned from the AUEW in 1972 and was suspended on full pay for nearly two years. He succeeded in his claim, as a skilled man, for the right to work.

b. Where remuneration depends on the amount of work, eg sales commission, the employer will be obliged to provide the work to enable commission to be earned:

In **TURNER v GOLDSMITH (1891)** G a shirt manufacturer agreed to employ T for 5 years. T's job was to solicit for orders for such goods as manufactured or sold by G as G should send to T by sample. After two years G's factory burnt down. G tried to discontinue T's contract. It was held that T was entitled to damages based on the amount of commission he would have earned in the remaining three years.

In **DEVONALD v ROSSER & SONS (1906)** the court decided that an employer was obliged to provide work for pieceworkers whose pay depended upon performance.

363

3. Pay. The employers common law duties with regard to pay are considered in Chapter 44.

4. Indemnity. An employer must indemnify his employee where the employee has incurred a liability whilst acting on the employer's behalf, except where:

    a. The employee knew that he was doing an unlawful act.

    b. The employee knew that the employer had no right to give the order in question.

        In **BURROWS v RHODES (1899)** the defendants were the organisers of the Jameson raid. They induced the plaintiff to re-enlist in the armed forces of the British South Africa Company, this they did by means of a fraudulent statement. The plaintiff believed that the venture in which he was to take part was lawful. It was held that he was entitled to damages from his employers for injuries received.

5. Equipment and Premises (Safety). The employer must take reasonable care to make his premises safe. Examples of unsafe premises include structural defects, bad ventilation, unsafe insulation, slippery floors or staircases, etc. Some specific areas are covered by statute, eg the necessity to maintain safe means of access.

Equipment includes plant, tools and materials, ie all those things with which a person may be expected to work must be of a safe nature. Many of these things are governed by various statutes, eg the *HSAWA 1974*, the *FACTORIES ACT 1961*, the *EMPLOYERS LIABILITY (DEFECTIVE EQUIPMENT) ACT 1969*. Plant, tools and equipment supplied by the employer must be reasonably safe and the employer fails in this duty in the following circumstances:-

    a. He fails to supply suitable equipment and the employee is forced to improvise:

        In **LOVELLS v BLUNDELL (1944)** workers overhauling a ship's boiler needed planks, none were provided and there was not a supervisor to advise. They found a plank lying about and used it. The plank broke and they sued the firm for not providing a safe system of work. It was held that the firm was liable.

    b. He provides defective equipment knowingly, or which he should have known on a reasonable examination. The onus is on the employer to inspect equipment.

        In **BAXTER v ST HELENA GROUP HOSPITAL MANAGEMENT COMMITTEE (1972)** a nurse sat on a chair which collapsed due to woodworm and she suffered a back injury. It was held that the hospital was liable as the chair should have been inspected.

    c. He fails to remedy defects which have been brought to his notice.

        In **MONAGHAN v RHODES (1920)** a stevedore's labourer fell off an unsafe rope ladder leading to the hold of a ship. He had already drawn the foreman's attention to its danger.

d. But "reasonableness" is all that is required:

In **LATIMER v AEC (1953)** a factory floor became flooded owing to a storm, and the water, when mixed with oil, made the floor slippery. The employer dried the floor and spread sawdust, but L slipped and was injured. It was held that the employer had taken all reasonable precautions and was not liable for the injury.

Note: The employer's failure to take reasonable steps to ensure the safety of his employees may be a breach of a fundamental term of the contract entitling the employee to resign and claim constructive dismissal.

In **BRITISH AIRCRAFT CORPN v AUSTIN (1978)** it was held that there was an implied term in the contract of employment that the employer would not behave intolerably. In this case it was regarded as intolerable that the employer failed to investigate the possibility of purchasing special eye protectors which would accommodate the employee's own spectacles.

GENERAL NOTES ON SAFETY

6. The employer must take reasonable care not to subject his employees to unnecessary risk. The requirements of safety on one hand and production on the other must sometimes conflict. By the test of "reasonableness" judges have brought widely accepted ideas of fairness to assess the merits of a case. The standard of reasonableness indicates that there cannot be a guarantee of absolute safety. Some considerations which would be taken into account are:-

a. *Inherent risk.* All work carries some risk and an employer would not be liable for events outside his control provided he had not been negligent. (**MITCHIE v SHENLEY (1952)** a case involving a nurse who was injured by a mental patient).

b. *Reasonably foreseeable.* If the danger could be reduced or eliminated the question is whether or not the employer was negligent in failing to do so.

In **DOUGHTY v TURNER MFG CO (1964)** an asbestos cover fell into a cauldron of molten metal. There was an explosion and the plaintiff, an employee standing by, was injured by molten metal. It was held that the explosion and hence the injuries were not reasonably foreseeable, therefore the employer was not liable.

c. *Obviousness of risk.* The more obvious the danger the more likely the law is to impose liability on the employer for failing to prevent the accident.

d. *Seriousness of risk.* This depends partly on the probability of an accident occurring but partly also on the gravity of the results if it does occur. The greater the risk the greater is the liability of the employer, and the more thorough are the precautions he should take.

e. *Cost.* The magnitude of the risk has to be weighed against other factors, particularly against the expense involved in safety measures and the necessity of carrying out the work in hand. The law would think it unreasonable to force employers to spend vast sums avoiding some slight chance of an accident.

In **HAWES v RAILWAY EXECUTIVE (1952)** an employee was electrocuted while carrying out repair work. It was held that the only foolproof safe system was for the current to be turned off in the region, the cost of which was too great compared with the risk of injury. .

A REASONABLY SAFE SYSTEM OF WORK

7. There is the requirement for an employer to provide a "reasonably safe system of work". Formerly just a common law duty, the duty is now incorporated into the *HSAWA 1974*. A safe system consists of:-

a. *Reasonably safe work-fellows.* If an employer knows or ought to know (perhaps because of complaints) that employees are a danger to others he is obliged to remove the danger. Employers are held liable for the conduct of known bullies or practical jokers.

In **HUDSON v RIDGE MFG CO LTD (1957)** an employee of a firm was known for his practical jokes. A fellow employee suffered injury as a result of one of these practical jokes, and sued the firm for damages. It was held that the firm was liable for not providing a safe system of work.

Contrast **SMITH v CROSSLEY BROTHERS LTD (1951)** where two apprentices, by way of a practical joke, injected compressed air into the body of a third apprentice. It was held, on the evidence, that such an action could not reasonably be foreseen, there was no failure in the duty of supervision, and the employers were not liable.

b. *Training of employees.* Employees must be instructed in the choice of proper equipment and the correct method of working.

In **BROWN v JOHN MILLS & CO LTD (1970)** Brown was new at his job, which was polishing brass nuts. He polished the nuts by the use of emery cloth wrapped around his finger whilst the nuts were secured in a lathe turning at high speed. He was injured. He had not been properly instructed in the correct method of working. It was held that the company was liable.

c. *Effective arrangements with regard to safety apparatus.*

i. Arrangements must be made for the provision and use of safety apparatus which will reduce the danger to the absolute minimum. No employee, even though experienced, must be left to look after his own safety.

In **GENERAL CLEANING CONTRACTORS v CHRISTMAS (1953)** a window cleaner employed by a firm fell from a ledge while attempting to clean the windows, it was normal practice to stand on the ledge to clean windows. It was held that even though normal practice, this method was not a reasonably safe system of work, and the firm was liable.

ii.   Safety apparatus must be available at the place it is required.

In **FINCH v TELEGRAPH CONSTRUCTION & MAINTENANCE CO (1949)** the plaintiff was injured when metal flew into his eye from a grinding operation. Goggles were provided but the workman did not know where to find them. It was held that the company was liable.

iii.   It is not necessary to stand over experienced workers instructed in safety systems to ensure they are used.

In **WOODS v DURABLE SUITES (1933)** W contracted dermatitis due to working with glue. He had been instructed in the precautions to be taken to prevent dermatitis. It was held that the employer was not liable as the employee was experienced, and the employer was not bound to stand over such a worker of full age to ensure that he took the precautions.

However the employer must take all reasonable measures, including warning of dangers, and persuasion to use the safety equipment.

In **QUALCAST LTD v HAYNES (1959)** molten metal splashed onto the foot of an experienced moulder. He knew that protective clothing was available but did not wear it. It was held that the employer was not responsible for failing to bring pressure to bear on his employee.

Contrast **BUX v SLOUGH METALS LTD (1970)** where B, a die caster, was injured when molten metal flew into his eyes. The company had complied with statutory safety regulations in providing suitable goggles for its foundry workers, but B was not wearing goggles at the time of the accident. The court held that the company were in breach of their common law duty to take reasonable steps for B's safety. They should have made a rule, enforced by supervision, that goggles should be worn. The non-use of goggles by workers had been reported but no management action taken. There were posters in the factory, but no campaign to get the men to wear goggles.

Contrast **JAMES v HEPWORTH & GRANDAGE LTD (1967)** where the plaintiff, who could neither read nor write, had been employed by the defendants for four years, the last six months of which he had been working at a job involving molten metal. In an accident he had molten metal splashed on his foot and claimed damages, alleging the non-provision of safety spats. A prominent notice stated that spats were available and should be used. It was held that there was no legal obligation upon the employers of an illiterate workman to find out whether or not he could read.

367

d. ***Proper co-ordination***. When safety depends on co-ordination of the work of a number of departments the employer must ensure that such co-ordination exists.

In **SWORD v CAMERON (1839)** employees were working in a quarry in which blasting operations were being carried out. They were not given sufficient time to get clear before an explosion took place. It was held that the employer had failed in his duty to provide a safe system of work with regard to proper co-ordination.

e. ***Suitable working conditions***. Suitable working conditions must be provided. General conditions under which work is carried on must, so far as reasonable care can ensure, be such as are consistent with safety.

In **McGHEE v N.C.B. (1971)** M worked in a brick-making plant. No washing facilities were provided. M had to cycle several miles to his home after work. He contracted dermatitis. It was held that the ailment was mainly attributable to the employer's failure to provide suitable working conditions.

But the employer is not liable when he does not control the premises:

In **CILIA v H.M. JAMES & SONS (1954)** during the installation of plumbing a plumber's mate was electrocuted due to defective electrical wiring in the building. It was held that the employer was not liable as the building was not in his occupation.

f. ***Sufficient men for the task***. It is the employer's duty to ensure that there are sufficient employees to perform a task.

In **HARDAKER v HUBY (1962)** the employer was liable for not providing a plumber with a mate to help in carrying a bath upstairs.

LIMITATIONS ON THE EMPLOYER'S DUTIES

8. The following show the extent of the employer's duties with regard to safety provisions.

a. ***Reasonable safety is all that is required.***

i.   Where there are generally accepted safety measures in a particular trade there would be a prima facie breach of duty if the employer failed to take them. However, it may well be that an accepted trade practice is a bad practice and the employer may be liable if he neglects to take precautions even though trade practice has been complied with.

In **POTEC v EDINBURGH CORPORATION (1964)** the plaintiff's job was to stand on a platform at a refuse depot over a deep trench keeping the refuse moving with a long pole. He fell into the trench and contended that there should have been a guard rail. Such rails were not provided at other depots because of overwhelming evidence that a guard rail would impede the use of the pole. It was held that the employer was not liable.

Contrast **CAVANAGH v ULSTER WEAVING CO LTD (1959)** where C fell whilst going down a ladder on a sloping roof. Common practice was that no handrail was provided. It was held that although trade practice had been complied with, it was not conclusive proof that the employer had met his obligations at law and he was liable.

ii.   Where there are unusual circumstances special safety measures should be taken:

In **PARIS v STEPNEY BOROUGH COUNCIL (1951)** P a garage mechanic with one eye, lost his other eye in an accident. No goggles had been provided. It was held that whilst goggles were not usually provided, the employer should have provided them in this case because of the greater risk to eyesight involved.

However, the employer must be aware of the special circumstances:

In **CORK v KIRBY MACLEAN LTD (1952)** the plaintiff suffered injury caused partly by a breach of statutory duty by his employers and partly by reason of a fall caused by an epileptic fit. It was held that he was contributorily negligent by failing to notify his employer that he suffered from epilepsy. Consequently his damages were reduced by half.

iii.   Whilst the employer must do everything reasonable to protect the employee from injury he need not go so far as to refuse to continue to employ an adult worker because the work is likely to endanger him. If an employer were to conceal risk or fail to give an employee enough information for him to assess the risk, then there may be liability.

In **WITHERS v PERRY CHAIN CO LTD (1961)** W contracted dermatitis due to working in greasy conditions. She was moved to another job considered free from this hazard. However she continued to suffer attacks of the ailment and was off work for long periods. It was held that the employer was not negligent in allowing W to continue at work as the only alternative would have been to dismiss her.

iv.   The burden of proof is on the plaintiff who must show that:

    a.   The defendant (employer) was in breach of his duty to take care, and

    b.   This breach was the *direct* cause of the plaintiff's (employee's) injuries:

In **McWILLIAMS v SIR WILLIAM ARROL (1962)** the employer failed to provide safety harness for the employee who fell to his death because of the lack of a harness. Evidence was produced to show that the employee would not have worn a harness even if it had been provided. The employer was not liable.

b.   *Provision of tools.* Under the *EMPLOYERS' LIABILITY (DEFECTIVE EQUIPMENT) ACT 1969*, should any tools supplied to the employee prove to be defective in any way, thus causing injury to the user, the employer shall be liable to the employee. The employer's remedy is to sue the manufacturer.

c. *Protection of the employee's property*. The employer's common law duty for safety extends only to the employee's person and not his property. Under the *FACTORIES ACT 1961*, however, the employer has a duty to provide suitable accommodation for clothing not worn during normal working hours. Additionally there may be a tortious liability on the basis of a duty owed by occupiers to lawful visitors. Tucker L J said in **DEYONG v SHENBURN (1946)** that there is no reason why an employer knowing his servant has placed property in his care shall not be under a duty, as a neighbour, to take reasonable care of it. Furthermore there may be an express contractual duty.

In **EDWARDS v WEST HERTS HOSPITAL COMMITTEE (1957)** a resident surgeon had personal property stolen from his room at the hostel where he lived. There were no security arrangements at the hostel. It was held that the employers had no liability for the safety of employees personal possessions.

Contrast **McCARTHY v DAILY MIRROR (1949)** where an employee had clothing stolen from a peg. It was held that this was not "adequate accommodation" which was required to be provided for employees' clothing under the *FACTORIES ACT*.

REFERENCES AND TESTIMONIALS

9. Obligation to Give References. An employer is not obliged to give references to his employees:

In **GALLEAR v J.F. WATSON & SON LTD (1979)** a dismissed employee claimed compensation for the failure of his employers to give him a reference. It was held that there is no implied duty to provide a reference and therefore there was no entitlement to compensation.

However, if an employer does give a reference he may be liable to a charge of defamation of character if any statement tends to lower the employee "in the eyes of right-thinking people".

10. Action by the Plaintiff and Defendant. The law relating to defamation including the action to be taken by the plaintiff and the defences open to the defendant, is outlined in Chapter 30.

11. Qualified Privilege. Generally an employer would claim that a reference he gave was subject to qualified privilege, ie, being made in good faith by a person who has a legal, social or moral duty to make it, to a person who has a similar interest or duty to receive it (ie a subsequent employer). The success of this defence depends on the statement having been made carefully, honestly and without malice.

12. Untrue References

a. If an employer knowingly recommends an employee in terms which he knows to be false, the subsequent misconduct of the employee will render his former employer liable for damages in the tort of deceit.

b. However, if the misstatement is negligent the recipient may take action for negligent misrepresentation. **HEDLEY BYRNE & CO LTD v HELLER & PARTNERS LTD (1964).**

In **McNALLY v WELLTRADE INTERNATIONAL LTD (1978)** the employer was held liable in damages for negligent misrepresentation when he led the employee to believe that the job in Libya to which the employee was being sent was within the employee's capabilities.

13. *REHABILITATION OF OFFENDERS ACT 1974.* Under this Act a person's convictions will not be subject to disclosure after a lapse of time. Some more serious offences are not subject to non-disclosure. The effect of this in regard to references is that an employer is not bound to disclose a spent conviction to another subsequent employer, and will consequently not be liable to action in deceit.

EMPLOYER'S DUTY TO PERSONS OTHER THAN EMPLOYEES
(See also Chapter 26.10-26.17)

14. The employer (as occupier of premises) has only the duty of common care to see that a visitor will be reasonably safe in using the premises for the purpose for which he is invited or permitted by the owner to be there. "Common care" is a duty to take such care as in all the circumstances is reasonable. A "visitor" is anyone who has express or implied permission of the occupier to be on the premises. This is in contrast to a "trespasser", one who enters premises or land without permission (if continued acts of trespass are ignored it could be implied that the person was a "visitor").

However, there is also a statutory duty under the *HSAWA 1974* for an employer to give information about potential dangers on his premises to *all persons* working on the premises.

In **R. v SWAN HUNTER SHIPBUILDERS LTD (1981)** eight men were killed when a fire broke out on HMS Glasgow. The fire was especially intense because the vessel was badly ventilated and oxygen had escaped from a hose kit left by an employee of a firm of sub-contractors. It was held that the sub-contractors had not been given sufficient information about the dangers of oxygen enrichment in confined spaces, nor, such instruction as was necessary to ensure the safety of all the workers on the vessel, no matter by whom they were employed.

NB. Contravention of the *HSAWA 1974* gives rise to criminal liability.

a. The occupier is entitled to assume that the visitor will guard against the normal hazards of his own trade, ie where the visitor is performing work on the premises, **ROLES v NATHAN (1963)**. In this case a sweep was poisoned by dangerous fumes in a chimney.

b.   The occupier must, however, give suitable warnings of "traps", ie, slippery floors, steep staircases, etc.

c.   The occupier will be liable if the visitor's possessions are stolen, only where the occupier can be proved to be negligent.

d.   Where a visitor is injured through the negligence of an independent contractor working on the premises, the contractor will be liable. However, the burden of proof is on the occupier to give "beyond reasonable doubt" facts to show that it was the fault of the contractor. (**O'CONNOR v SWAN & EDGAR (1963)**. The contractors were liable when a ceiling under repair fell and injured a shopper).

e.   The position of a person other than a "visitor" is covered by the *OCCUPIERS LIABILITY ACT 1984* (see Chapter 26.16).

VICARIOUS LIABILITY

15.   Where a person is injured by another the rule at common law is that the injured party may sue the actual wrongdoer. Where the wrongdoer is an employee the injured party also has an action against the employer. This is "vicarious liability", ie, although the employer did not personally commit the wrong, he may be held responsible for all those who are employed by him. The third party will usually sue the employer as he is usually in a better financial position to meet a claim for damages.

16.   Vicarious liability arises in two ways. Firstly by an employer authorising a wrongful act. Secondly, although the employer did not authorise the act the employee performed it in the course of employment. This may appear to be unfair, but the view is taken that, by employing a person, the employer makes it possible for him to commit the wrong. It is regarded as a normal business risk undertaken by the employer for which he would be wise to take out insurance.

17.   Circumstances of Vicarious Liability. The following are cases in which attempts have been made to clarify the position. Generally speaking the employer is deemed to be liable for the acts of an employee committed in the course of employment during contractual hours of work and whilst he is performing a task for which he is employed:

a.   The employee carries out an authorised task, but in a *wrongful manner:*
    In **L.C.C. v CATTERMOLES GARAGE (1953)** an employee was employed to remove vehicles that blocked the garage entrance. As he had no licence he was instructed to push them by hand. On one occasion he drove a vehicle and caused an accident. It was held that the employers were liable for the damages as the employee had done what he was employed to do, albeit in an unauthorised manner.

b.   The employee commits a wrongful act that was *expressly forbidden:*
LIMPUS v LONDON GENERAL OMNIBUS CO (1862) (See Chapter 25).

c.   The employee commits a *wilful wrong*, even though it was a *criminal offence:* **LLOYD v GRACE, SMITH & CO (1912)** (See Chapter 25).

d.   The employee acts *negligently:*

In **CENTURY INSURANCE v N IRELAND ROAD TRANSPORT BOARD (1942)** a lorry driver was smoking whilst transferring petrol from his tanker to a store. A fire resulted. It was held that the driver's employer was vicariously liable.

Contrast **WILLIAMS v JONES (1865)** where the defendant's employee was making a sign-board in a shed the floor of which was littered with wood-shavings. He lit his pipe and the shed burned down. It was held that the employer was not liable as the act was not deemed to be negligent.

In the Century Insurance case there was an element of danger and lighting a cigarette amounted to negligence. In the second case lighting a pipe was not necessarily negligent in relation to the making of a sign-board.

e.   The employee *wrongfully permits another* to perform his duties: **ILKIW v SAMUELS (1963)** (See Chapter 42.2.).

f.   The employee makes a mistake.

In **BAYLEY v MANCHESTER, SHEFFIELD & LINCOLN-SHIRE RAILWAY CO (1872)** B, a passenger, was forcibly ejected from a train onto the platform by a zealous porter who believed him (wrongly) to be on the wrong train. It was held that the company was vicariously liable for the injury caused by their employee's mistake.

18. Acts committed in an emergency, in the protection of the employers' property, are classed as being in the course of employment.

In **POLAND v JOHN PARR & SONS (1927)** an employee struck a boy whom he thought was stealing from his employer's wagon. The employer was liable. He would not have been liable if the carter's act had been so excessive as to take it out of the class of authorised acts.

19. Employers are not liable for the acts of their employees which are done outside the course of employment, even though they are closely connected with employment:

In **WARREN v HENLYS LTD (1948)** a petrol pump attendant engaged in a fight with a customer over payment. It was held that the employer was not liable as the matter had become personal, outside the course of employment.

20. When an employee uses his employer's property for purposes of his own unconnected with his employment the employer will not be liable even though he gave consent for the use of his property.

373

In **HILTON v THOMAS BURTON LTD (1961)** employees who were allowed to use their employer's van for reasonable purposes used it to drive to a cafe whilst they awaited their normal finishing time. On the way back there was an accident due to negligent driving. It was held that the employer was not liable as the employees were acting outside the course of employment — "on a frolic of their own".

21. Lifts Given in Employer's Vehicle. The following cases are examples of court decisions on this matter:

In **TWINE v BEAN'S EXPRESS (1946)** a driver employed by the defendants gave a lift to a person who was killed due to the employee's negligent driving. The employee had been expressly forbidden to give lifts and a notice to this effect was displayed in the vehicle. It was held that the employer was not vicariously liable as the driver's action was outside the scope of his employment and the injured person was deemed to be a trespasser.

In **YOUNG v EDWARD BOX & CO LTD (1951)** Young was a workman employed by the defendants. He was responsible for getting himself to and from his workplace. However due to the inadequacy of public transport on Sundays it had become the practice to get a lift in his employer's vehicle. Young was injured in the course of one of these journeys.

It was held that the employer was liable as the plaintiff's driver and foreman had concurred to the lifts and this was within the ostensible authority of the foreman. Thus the plaintiff had become a licensee and was not a trespasser.

However, Denning, L J dissenting said

> "The liability of the owner does not depend on whether the passenger was a trespasser or not; it depends on whether the driver was acting within the scope of his employment."

Contrast **ROSE v PLENTY (1976)** (See Chapter 25).

22. Acts for the Exclusive Benefit of the Employee. If an act is not only forbidden but done for the exclusive benefit of the employee, the employer is not liable.

In **RAND v CRAIG (1919)** carters employed by the defendant took rubbish to land owned by the plaintiff and tipped it there, instead of onto a dump provided by their employer which was further off. They did this so they could carry more loads and earn more money.

Contrast **PERFORMING RIGHTS SOCIETY v MITCHELL & BOOKER LTD (1924)** where the plaintiffs accused M & B of infringing copyrights by performance of certain dance music in their dance hall. The band had a clause in its contract forbidding the infringement of copyright and M & B tried to claim that they did so for their own benefit. It was held that the band infringed the copyright in the course of employment and for the benefit of the dance hall.

374

TIME OFF WORK

23. Trade Unions Duties. By *S.27, EPCA 1978* an employer is obliged to permit an employee who is an official of an independent trade union recognised by him, for collective bargaining purposes, to take time off during working hours to:

    a. Carry out official duties which are concerned with industrial relations between his employer and employees; or

    b. Undergo training in aspects of industrial relations which is:

        i.   Relevant to the carrying out of those duties; and

        ii. Approved by the TUC or by the independent trade unions of which he is an official.

24. The amount of time off which an employee may be permitted to take, the occasions and conditions governing such time off are to be tested on the grounds of reasonableness taking into account the guidelines laid down in the ACAS Code of Practice No. 3 on time off for trade union duties and activities.

25. The trade union official taking time off work to perform his duties is entitled to his normal remuneration from his employer. Where remuneration varies according to the amount of work done, remuneration is calculated according to average hourly earnings for the work.

26. Where an employer fails to permit the employee to take time off or fails to pay the normal remuneration the employee may make a complaint to an industrial tribunal within 3 months of the alleged failure complained of. The industrial tribunal, if it finds the complaint well-founded, will make a declaration to that effect and may additionally award compensation for any loss suffered by the complainant.

27. Trade Union Activities. An employer is similarly obliged to permit an employee of his, who is a member of an independent trade union recognised by him for the purpose of collective bargaining, to take time off during working hours for the purpose of taking part in certain trade union activities. The activities are defined as:

    a. Any activities of the trade union of which the employee is a member; and

    b. Any activities in relation to which the employee is acting as a representative of such a union;

excluding activities which themselves consist of industrial action whether or not in contemplation of furtherance of a trade dispute.

28. The amount of, occasions and conditions governing such time off are again tested on the grounds of reasonableness by reference to the guidelines laid down in the **ACAS Code of Practice**.

In **SOOD v GEC ELLIOTT PROCESS AUTOMATION LTD (1984)**
S, a trade union official complained that GEC had failed to allow him time
off for trade union activities. The activities consisted of membership of a
committee the function of which was to exchange information and experience
among union members. It did not have negotiating rights with GEC. It was
held that the time off must be to enable the official to carry out his duties relating
to a matter which arose in relation between employees and management. These
activities did not qualify.

29. The employee is not, however, entitled to remuneration for any time which
he takes off to participate in trade union activities.

30. A similar remedy, nevertheless exists, in that an employee within the
statutory definition may make a complaint to an industrial tribunal which can
make a declaration and order compensation as appropriate.

31. Public Duties. Under the provisions of *S.29, EPCA 1978* an employer
is obliged to permit an employee time off, without remuneration, during working
hours for the purposes of performing any of the following public duties:

    a. A Justice of the Peace;

    b. A member of a local authority;

    c. A member of a statutory tribunal;

    d. A member of, in England and Wales, a Regional Health Authority
or Area Health Authority or, in Scotland, a Health Board;

    e. A member of, in England and Wales, the managing or governing body
of an educational establishment maintained by a local education authority,
or, in Scotland, a school or college council or the governing body of a
central institution or a college of education; or

    f. A member of, in England and Wales, a water authority or, in Scotland,
river purification board.

32. The amount of time off which an employee shall be permitted to take in
respect of public duties and the occasions on which and any conditions subject
to which time off be so taken are those that are reasonable in all the circumstances
having regard, in particular, to:

    a. How much time off is required for the performance of the duties of
the office or as a member of the body in question, and how much time
off is required for the performance of the particular duty;

    b. How much time off the employee has already been permitted for the
performance of any relevant public duty, union duty or activity;

    c. The circumstances of the employer's business and the effect of the
employee's absence on the running of that business.

33. The employee, similarly, has a right of complaint to an industrial tribunal where an employer fails to permit time off to be taken. An industrial tribunal, however, does not have the power to impose conditions upon the parties as to the way in which time off shall be taken or to specify the amount of time off which should be allowed.

34. To Look for Work or Make Arrangements for Training. *S.31, EPCA 1978* gives a right to an employee who is dismissed for redundancy, and who will at the date of dismissal have completed two years' employment, to be allowed reasonable time off during working hours to look for new employment or make arrangements for training for future employment. Such time off is not limited merely to attending for a specific interview.

35. If an employer unreasonably refuses to allow an employee time off when obliged to do so under the *EPCA*, the employee is entitled to be paid the remuneration to which he would have been entitled if he had been allowed time off in addition to his normal remuneration.

36. Where an employer has unreasonably refused the employee time off or has failed to pay him in lieu, the employee may complain to an industrial tribunal. If the tribunal find the complaint well-founded the employer may be made liable to pay:

    a.   Remuneration for the period of absence; or

    b.   Remuneration for the period during which the employee should have been permitted time off; or both

When both these provisions are applicable, the aggregate amount of the employer's liability may not exceed two-fifths of a week's pay of the applicant employee.

Note: This provision would appear to suggest that the employer's duty to give reasonable time off is limited to no more than two days since that is the maximum penalty which may be invoked against an employer who refused to permit time off and who refuses payment in lieu.

37. For Ante-Natal Care. An employee has a statutory right under the *EPCA 1978* as amended by the *FA 1980* not to be unreasonably refused paid time off during working hours to keep an appointment for ante-natal care prescribed by a registered medical practitioner, registered midwife or registered health visitor. This right is accorded to all pregnant employees irrespective of hours worked weekly or length of service. Except in the case of the first appointment the right to time off is specifically linked with attendance at appointments and the employer may require the employee to produce a certificate stating that she is pregnant and documentary evidence that an appointment has been made.

38. An employee may present a complaint to an industrial tribunal if her employer has unreasonably refused time off for ante-natal care or if he has failed to pay her the whole or part of any remuneration to which she is statutorily entitled. Where the tribunal finds the complaint well-founded it may make a declaration to that effect and order the employer to:

a. Pay to the employee an amount equal to the remuneration to which she would have been entitled if the employer had not unreasonably refused time off; or

b. Pay the employee the whole or part of any remuneration to which she is entitled by virtue of having taking time off and for which the employer has failed to pay her.

39. Safety Representatives. The Safety Representatives and Safety Committees Regulations 1977 issued under the provisions of the *HSAWA 1974* oblige an employer to permit a safety representative to take such time off with pay during the employee's working hours as is necessary for the purpose of:

a. Performing his functions as a safety representative; and

b. Undergoing such training in aspects of those functions as may be reasonable in all the circumstances having regard to any relevant provisions of the code of practice issued by the Health and Safety Commission on "Time off for the Training of Safety Representatives".

40. Where an employer refuses a safety representative time off for these purposes or fails to pay him for the time taken, the safety representative may present a complaint to an industrial tribunal. Where the tribunal finds the complaint well-founded it may make an award of a just and equitable amount and in the case of a complaint based upon the employer's failure to pay remuneration due, the tribunal can order that amount to be paid to the safety representative.

41. In all cases where a complaint is made to an industrial tribunal relating to an employer's duty to permit time off, the complaint must be presented within three months of the date when the alleged failure occurred, or within such further period as the tribunal considers reasonable in a case where it is satisfied that it was not reasonably practicable for the complaint to be presented within the three month period.

DISCLOSURE OF INFORMATION

42. *EMPLOYMENT PROTECTION ACT 1975*

a. *Duty to disclose. S.17, EPA 1975* provides that an independent trade union recognised by an employer for collective bargaining purposes may request either orally, or if required by the employer, in writing:

i.   Information without which the trade union representatives would be to a material extent impeded in carrying on with the employer such collective bargaining, and

ii.   Information which it would be in accordance with good industrial relations practice that the employer should disclose to the trade union representatives for the purposes of collective bargaining.

The collective bargaining must be about matters and in relation to descriptions of workers in respect of which the trade union is recognised by the employer. Moreover, the employer's obligation extends to information relating to an associated employer.

b. *Exceptions. S.18, EPA 1975* specifically exempts the employer from disclosing information:

 i.   Which would be against the interests of national security; or

 ii. Which he could not disclose without contravening a prohibition imposed by or under an enactment; or

 iii. Which has been communicated to the employer in confidence, or which the employer has otherwise obtained in consequence of the confidence reposed in him by another person; or

 iv. Relating specifically to an individual, unless he has consented to its being disclosed; or

 v.   Which would cause substantial injury to the employer's undertaking for reasons other than its effect on collective bargaining; or

 vi. Obtained by the employer for the purpose of bringing, prosecuting or defending any legal proceedings.

Additionally, an employer is not required:

 i.   To produce, or allow inspection of, any document (other than a document prepared for the purpose of conveying or confirming the information) or to make a copy of or extracts from any document; or

 ii. To compile or assemble any information where the compilation or assembly would involve an amount of work or expenditure out of reasonable proportion to the value of the information in the conduct of collective bargaining.

c. *Code of practice.* The ACAS Code No. 2 gives guidance on the above disclosure requirements by suggesting examples of information relating to an employer's undertaking which could be relevant in some collective bargaining situations. It is not an exhaustive list.

 i.   *Pay and benefits.* principles and structure of payment systems; job evaluation systems and grading criteria; earnings and hours analysed according to work-group, grade, plant, sex, outworkers and homeworkers, department or division, giving, where appropriate, distributions and make-up of pay showing any additions to basic rate or salary; total pay bill; details of fringe benefits and non-wage labour costs.

 ii. *Conditions of service.* Policies on recruitment, redeployment, redundancy, training, equal opportunity, and promotion; appraisal systems; health, welfare and safety matters.

 iii. *Manpower.* Numbers employed analysed according to grade, department, location, age and sex; labour turnover; absenteeism; over-

379

time and short-time; manning standards; planned changes in work methods, materials, equipment or organisation; available manpower plans; investment plans.

iv.   *Performance.* Productivity and efficiency date; savings from increased productivity and output; return on capital invested; sale and state of order book.

v.   *Financial.* Cost structures; gross and net profits; allocation of profits; details of government financial assistance; transfer prices; loans to parent or subsidiary companies and interest charged.

d.   *Failure to disclose.* Where an employer fails to comply with a request for information the trade union may present a complaint, may refer the matter to the ACAS. Alternatively, and where the ACAS has failed in its attempt at conciliation, the CAC will proceed to hear and determine the complaint. If the CAC finds the complaint wholly or partly well-founded, it may make a declaration specifying;

i.   The information in respect of which the CAC finds that the complaint is well-founded;

ii.   The date (or, if more than one, the earliest date) on which the employer refused or failed to disclose the information or to confirm it in writing; and

iii.   A period (not being less than one week from the date of the declaration) within which the employer must disclose the information or confirm it in writing.

e.   *Continued failure to disclose.* Under the *EPA 1975 (S.20-21)* are set out the rules for the occasions where the employer still refuses to disclose the information requested by the trade union. In such circumstances, the trade union may present a further complaint to the CAC and also a claim for improved terms and conditions of employment of employees of a description specified in the original request for information. If the further complaint is upheld, the CAC can then make an award of terms and conditions specified in the claim or other terms and conditions which the CAC considers appropriate. This then becomes an implied term of the individual employee's contract of employment which may be enforced in the civil courts by an action for breach of contract.

43.   *HEALTH AND SAFETY AT WORK ACT 1974, S.2, HSAWA 1974* obliges employers:

a.   To provide their employees with such information as is necessary to ensure their health and safety at work (this requirement is tested on the basis of what information could have reasonably been discovered or known by the employer and therefore disclosed); and

b.   To prepare, and bring to the notice of all their employees, a written statement of their general policy regarding health and safety at work of their employees and the organisations and arrangements for the implementation of that policy. Moreover, any revision of this written statement must also be brought to the notice of employees.

Failure to provide the above information is a criminal offence carrying a summary fine of up to £1,000 and an unlimited fine on conviction on indictment.

44. Additionally, safety representatives under the Safety Representatives and Safety Committees Regulations 1977 are entitled to inspect and take copies of any document which their employer is legally obliged to keep (except health records of identifiable individuals). Moreover, the employer is obliged to provide safety representatives with any information in his possession relating to health, safety or welfare which will enable the representatives to fulfil their functions except:

a. Any information the disclosure of which would be against the interests of national security; or

b. Any information which he could not disclose without contravening a prohibition imposed by or under some enactment; or

c. Any information relating specifically to an individual, unless the individual has consented to the disclosure; or

d. Any information the disclosure of which would, for reasons other than its effect on health, safety or welfare at work, cause substantial injury to the employer's undertaking or, where the information was supplied to the employer by some other person, to the undertaking of that other person; or

e. Any information obtained by the employer for the purpose of bringing, prosecuting or defending any legal proceedings.

44 Wages

INTRODUCTION

1. The contract of employment usually gives details of the amount of wages to be paid, payment during absence from work, method of payment, etc. In the absence of express terms other terms have been implied by the courts. In addition a body of statute law has arisen governing such things as deductions from pay, etc. The law is reluctant to fix rates of pay, leaving it to negotiation between the employer and employee, or trade union. However whilst there is no general minimum wage level, wages councils attempt to protect some sections of low paid workers. In this Chapter we consider the common law duties of an employer to an employee and the statutory requirements with regard to wages.

WAGES – COMMON LAW

2. The following are the employer's duties to his employees in the absence of express provision in the contract of employment.

    a. *Amount of pay.* The employer must pay the agreed remuneration or what is reasonable in the circumstances.

    b. *Availability of work.* Wages must be paid even though employees cannot work because no work is available. Time workers are paid for being ready, willing and able to work for their agreed hours.

    In **TURNER v SAWDON & CO (1901)** it was held that the employer had a duty only to pay wages, not to provide work to a man employed as a salesman.

    c. *Piece workers.* Piece workers are also paid for being ready, willing and able. It is up to the employer to find them work. (**DEVONALD v ROSSER (1906)**).

    In **MINNEVITCH v CAFE DE PARIS (LONDRES) LTD (1936)** musicians were employed under a contract including a clause to the effect that they would not be paid if they did not play. It was held that the clause implied that they were not entitled to receive pay for such performances their employer thought fit to cancel. This was not valid – it was up to the employer to find the musicians work to enable them to earn their remuneration.

    d. If there is no work available due to circumstances outside the control of the employer, then he is under no obligation to pay his employees. Each case must be examined in the light of the circumstances:

    In **BROWNING v CRUMLIN VALLEY COLLIERIES LTD (1916)** a mine became unsafe due to flooding and work stopped. It was held that the circumstances were outside the employer's control and there was therefore no need to pay wages.

Contrast **JONES v HARRY SHERMAN (1969)** where due to an outbreak of foot and mouth disease racing was cancelled and a turf accountant did not need so many employees. It was held that the right to "lay-off" could not be implied into a contract of employment at fixed or guaranteed periodic wages.

e. *Overtime.* Overtime is payable when expressly agreed in the contract, or is customary. Where the overtime is expressed as obligatory the employer must provide overtime and the employee must serve it.

f. *Discretionary payments.* An employee cannot claim, as a right, a payment which has always been stated "to be within the managements discretion" however often and regularly it may have been paid:

In **GRIEVE v IMPERIAL TOBACCO CO LTD (1963)** part of an annual gift was withheld from G after he took part in a strike. It was held that the company was entitled to withhold a gratuitous payment, despite the argument that it had become a term of the contract.

However, a contractual bonus which has been earned cannot legally be withheld.

g. *Payment during illness.* Payments during periods when an employee is absent due to illness will depend on the custom of the trade or industry, or of individual firms. In the absence of any agreement or custom the following will apply:

i. There is an implied right to receive payment:

In **ORMAN v SAVILLE SPORTSWEAR LTD (1960)** the plaintiff, a production manager, had been off work ill for ten weeks. It was held that there was an implied term in his contract that he should be entitled to pay during sickness. It was considered that if there had been an express term that he would not be entitled. Orman would not have accepted the contract.

ii. The implied right can successfully be rebutted where the conduct of the employee shows that his right has been foregone.

In **O'GRADY v SAPER LTD (1940)** the plaintiff, a doorman at a cinema, had never previously received pay during illness. He claimed pay after seeing the report of another case. It was held that he was not entitled, as the conduct of the parties showed that there was an implied term excluding payment during illness.

iii. An employer may expressly exclude his liability from paying wages during sickness:

In **PETRIE v MACFISHERIES LTD (1940)** a notice on the wall stated that payments made during sickness were ex-gratia payments, and indicated the amounts usually paid. It was held that the clause showed that payments were not made as of right during sickness.

h.   *Suspension without pay*. The power to suspend an employee without pay must be provided for expressly or implicitly by contract. Suspension without pay in the absence of contractual power will amount to a repudiatory breach of contract of employment (ie. constructive dismissal).

WAGES ACT 1986

3.   The *WAGES ACT 1986* reformed the law on payment of wages, removing out-dated restrictions (contained in the Truck Acts) and introduced new protection for employees. The Act simplified the law and put manual and non-manual workers on the same basis. In addition it reformed the law on wages councils.

4.   **Deductions from Pay.** Deductions from an employee's pay will be unlawful unless:-

a.   Authorised by statute, eg income tax, national insurance contributions, or under the *ATTACHMENT OF EARNINGS ACT 1971*.

b.   Agreed in the contract of employment, or,

c.   Agreed in advance by the employee in writing.

d.   An employer may not receive payment from an employee unless in accordance with a, b and c above.

e.   An employer may make deductions from wages or receive payments in respect of:-

i.   Overpayment of wages or expenses

ii.   Disciplinary proceedings in respect of a statutory provision

iii. Payment to a third person if agreed in writing by the employee

iv.   The employee's participation in a strike or other industrial action

v.   An order by a court or tribunal.

Editorial Note. But see chapter 54 para 73b for changes brought about by E.A. 1988.

5.   **Retail Employment.** In the event of employees in the retail trade who suffer deductions from their pay on account of stock or cash deficiencies, any deduction will be limited to 10% of wages. The same limit will apply to any payment required by an employer.

6.   **Complaints to an Industrial Tribunal.** An employee who considers he has been subjected to an unlawful deduction may go to an industrial tribunal.

EQUAL PAY ACT 1970

7.   **Purpose.** The *EQUAL PAY ACT 1970* (as amended by the *SEX DISCRIMINATION ACT 1975*) has the object of eliminating discrimination between men and women in regard to pay and other conditions of employment (eg overtime, bonus, output and piecework payments, holidays and sick leave entitlement).

8.   Persons Covered. The Act extends to all persons under a contract of employment, full or part-time, irrespective of age or length of service. Sex discrimination is forbidden in regard to all terms of employment, except:-

    a.   Where the work is wholly or mainly outside Great Britain,

    b.   Members of the armed forces,

    c.   Where statute law requires discrimination,

    d.   A woman may enjoy privileges in respect of pregnancy and childbirth,

    e.   In provisions for death or retirement.

9.   Right to Equal Treatment. The Act requires that every term in an employee's contract must not be less favourable than the terms in the contract of an employee of the opposite sex with regard to pay or other terms. This applies providing the work they are doing is:-

    a.   The same, or

    b.   Of a broadly similar nature, or

    c.   Although the work is different has been rated of equal value under a job evaluation exercise.

    In **DUGDALE & OTHERS v KRAFT FOODS LTD (1976)** Mrs Dugdale and other women claimed unfair discrimination under the Equal Pay Act as they received lower basic rates of pay than men who worked on a night shift and on Sundays (women precluded under the Factories Act). The woman did work which was broadly similar to the men. The tribunal held that merely because the men worked at a different time did not constitute a difference of practical importance. Therefore the women should receive the same basic pay as men.

    d.   The *EQUAL PAY (AMENDMENT) REGULATION 1983*. This regulation provides for equal pay for equal value, following the judgement of the European Court of Justice that our legislation does not fully implement the EC Directive which provides for equal pay for men and women for work to which equal value is attributed. An industrial tribunal has to commission a report by an independant expert in order to deal with an application for an award of equal pay for work which is not similar nor already rated as equivalent, but which is claimed to be of equal value in terms of the demands made on the workers.

    In **HAYWARD v CAMMEL LAIRD (1984)** H was a cook employed in a shipyard. An industrial tribunal held that her work was of equal value to the company as men employed at the yard in other trades and she was therefore entitled to equal pay.

10.   An "equality clause" is written into every contract of employment. If a term in a contract is inconsistent with the "equality clause" then that term is ineffectual.

11. The comparison of jobs may be made only with an employee of the opposite sex employed with the same employer or another establishment owned by the same employer, or which is a member of the same group of companies.

12. Difference in Rate of Pay. Where it has been established that an employee is entitled to equal treatment under paras a. b. and c. above, the employer would be liable unless he could prove that the variation in pay was genuinely due to a "material difference". For example, the higher pay may be due to longer service or higher productivity or because an employee has moved from a higher paid job to a lower, but his higher rate of pay has been preserved (this is known as "red circling").

In **METHUEN v COW INDUSTRIAL POLYMERS LTD (1980)** a female employee sought equality with a man who was performing the same clerical job as herself, although receiving higher pay. The employers established that the man had been transferred from the shop floor because of age and sickness but his previous income and status had been preserved. It was held that the difference was due to a "material difference" ie, the protection of his income and position, and nothing to do with sex.

In **COOMES (HOLDINGS) LTD v SHIELDS (1978)** the employer owned a string of betting shops. In some shops the male employees were paid more than female employees, because of anticipated trouble from customers. It was held that the deterrent function of the male staff was not a genuine difference as all males received the higher rate regardless of performance of this function.

In **CAPPER PASS LTD v LAWTON (1977)** a female cook sought equal pay with male chefs. She worked in the directors' dining room preparing up to 20 lunches a day, whilst the male chefs worked in the company's canteen preparing 350 meals a day. It was held that she was employed on "like work" and should therefore receive equal basic pay for a 40 hours week. The Act did not intend that too minute an examination of comparative work should be done.

13. Reference to an Industrial Tribunal

a.   A woman believing that she has a right to equal treatment for any of the reasons under the Act may refer her claim to an industrial tribunal. If the tribunal finds the complaint well-founded, it can make an order. In addition the Secretary of State may apply for an order where it appears to him that an employee has a claim for equal treatment but is is not reasonable to expect the employee to make a complaint.

b.   Reference may be made, either during employment or within 6 months of termination.

c.   Arrears of pay may be claimed for up to 2 years before the date of reference to the tribunal. Damages in respect of non-cash benefits may be claimed for the same period.

14. European Community Law Article 119 of the Treaty of Rome provides that women shall be accorded equal treatment for like work with men. This is superimposed on our own legislation. Where there is a conflict or where there is a gap in our own legislation the European Community law takes precedence. The interpreter of EEC law is the European Court, it is then incumbent on our own courts to apply that law.

In **McCARTHYS LTD v SMITH (No. 2) (1980)** a female worker claimed equal pay with her predecessor, a man. The case went to the European Court which ruled that, under Article 119, provided there is not a long gap between the end of one and the beginning of the other, a woman is entitled to equal pay with her predecessor.

15. Part Time Workers. Discrimination against part-time workers was challenged in the European Court.

In **JENKINS v KINGSGATE (1981)** in a textile factory all the men worked 40 hours a week and all except a few women worked 30 hours. The part-timers got an hourly rate of pay 10% less than those on full-time. They claimed equality. The employers said the differential was justified by the need to discourage absenteeism, increase productivity and use the plant to the full. The European Court held that working shorter hours is not itself a material difference justifying unequal pay. However a differential can be justified if it fulfils the stated needs of the employer (productivity, etc.) which are non-discriminatory.

WAGES COUNCILS

16. Purpose. Wages and other conditions of employment are determined in certain industries by wages councils. The industries concerned are those without an effective body to negotiate on their behalf because of non-unionism or weak trade unions. Examples of this type of industry are the retailing and catering industries. The present law is contained in the *WAGES ACT 1986* which repealed the *WAGES COUNCILS ACT 1979* but allowed the continuance of existing councils established under that Act.

17. Abolition or Variation of Scope of Wages Councils. The Secretary of State may at any time, by order, abolish or vary the scope of operation of any wages council. Before making such an order the Secretary of State shall consider:-

a. The current levels of remuneration of workers in relation to whom the wages councils would cease to operate or begin to operate as a result of the order, and,

b. Any other matters considered appropriate, and shall consult such persons and organisations he considers appropriate.

18. Composition of a Wages Council. A wages council shall consist of:-

a. Such numbers of persons representing employers and workers respectively as may be specified by the Secretary of State and,

b. Not more than 5 independent persons as appointed by the Secretary of State.

Those appointed (under a. above) to represent employers shall be appointed by an employers' association, and those to represent workers by a trade union.

19. Functions. A wages council may make an order setting:-

a. A single minimum hourly rate of pay;

b. A single overtime rate;

c. A limit to the amount which may be charged for accommodation if this would take pay below the legal minimum;

for all or any of the workers in relation to whom the council operates.

Notes:

i. The application of wages orders is limited to workers aged 21 or over.

ii. Any order made must be publicised. Enforcement is by officers appointed by the Secretary of State.

iii. No deductions may be made from wages fixed by a wages council, except those that are lawful under the *WAGES ACT 1986.*

(a) Income tax under PAYE.

(b) National Insurance contributions.

(c) Superannuation or thrift scheme contributions at the written request of the worker.

(d) Deductions under written contracts as provided for in the *WAGES ACT 1986.*

iv. Where minimum rates of pay are laid down by a wages council such terms become substituted in the contract of employment for any less beneficial terms in the contract.

v. Wages Councils will have to consider the effect on employment of their decisions.

20. Enforcement. The employer of any worker to whom a wages council order applies is required to keep records showing:-

a. Whether or not the terms of the order is being complied with in respect of remuneration, and;

b. The amount of deductions made for provision of living accommodation by the employer.

An employer who fails to keep adequate or true records, or obstructs an officer appointed by the Secretary of State shall be liable to criminal proceedings and, on conviction, to a fine.

If it appears to an officer that a sum is due to a worker in respect of payment to him of wages lower than that specified in a wages order, the officer may institute civil proceedings to recover that sum.

GUARANTEE PAYMENTS *(EPCA S. 12-18)*

21. Guarantee Payments ensure that employees who are laid-off will receive some payment during that time.

22. Entitlement. Employees will be entitled to five days payment in any three month period at a maximum daily rate specified from time to time (£13.65 at 1st April 1991). This is paid when an employee is laid off work for a whole day.

23. Calculation. The three month periods start on the 1st of February, May, August and November. The rate is calculated as:

Normal hours per day $\times$ The rate per hour.

The statutory requirement is any amount which satisfies the above up to the maximum of £13.65 (ie the daily guarantee payment would be less if the employee had a low weekly wage).

24. Eligibility. To be eligible an employee must:

    a.   Have at least one month continuous service when the lay-off occurs.

    b.   Be laid-off for the whole of his normal working hours.

    c.   Be laid-off because of an occurrence preventing his employer providing him with work (apart from a dispute involving employees of the same or an associated employer).

    d.   Not have unreasonably refused an offer of alternative employment.

    e.   Be available for work.

25. Exemption. Employees who are covered by a collective agreement or a wages order with a provision for guaranteed pay may be exempted from the statutory requirements.

26. Failure to Make Payment. Where an employer fails to make an entitled guarantee payment an industrial tribunal can order him to make it.

MEDICAL SUSPENSION *(EPCA S. 19-22)*

27. Payment during medical suspension was introduced by the *EPA 1975* to enable an employee to receive compensation when not actually sick or disabled.

28. Entitlement. An employer may suspend an employee on medical grounds, (eg, when he may be exposed to radiation or lead poisoning). During such suspension an employee is entitled to receive his pay, and may do so for a maximum period of 26 weeks.

29. Eligibility. To be eligible an employee must:

    a. Have at least one month continuous service

    b. Have not refused reasonably suitable alternative employment

    c. Be available for work should he be required.

30. Dismissal. If the employer dismisses an employee instead of suspending him on medical grounds the employee will have the right to a claim for unfair dismissal. He need have only four weeks' continuous service to quality (*not* the normal 2 years).

31. Temporary Replacements. An employer may engage temporary replacements for those medically suspended. However, he must make the temporary nature of the employment clear at the outset and offer alternative employment on termination if that is possible.

32. Failure to Make Payment. Where an employer fails to make an entitled medical suspension payment an industrial tribunal can order him to make it.

INSOLVENCY *(EPCA S.21)*

33. The *EPCA 1978* provides protection for employees in respect of amounts owing to them at the time an employer goes bankrupt or into receivership.

34. Amounts due under the Act for, eg time-off or medical suspension will also be regarded as wages for preferential payment.

35. If the sum owed cannot be met by the liquidator or receiver the employee may apply for payment to be made from the Redundancy Fund.

36. The maximum recoverable from the liquidator is limited to 8 weeks arrears of wages subject to a maximum at present of £800. If the amount owing cannot be met by the liquidator the excess (plus other sums, ie. wages in lieu of notice, holiday remuneration (maximum 6 weeks) and unfair dismissal compensation) may be claimed from the Redundancy Fund up to a maximum of £198 per week (subject to review by the Secretary of State).

37. Unpaid employer contributions to occupational pensions funds up to a maximum of twelve months may be paid from the Redundancy Fund.

38. Any amount due in respect of a maternity payment may be obtained from the Maternity Pay Fund.

PAY STATEMENTS *(EPCA S.8)*

39. The *EPCA 1978* gave every employee the right to a written itemised pay statement. The statement must include:

    a. Gross amount of wages.

    b. Deductions which vary with the wage, eg, Income Tax.

    c.   Total fixed deductions, eg, trade union subscriptions.

    d.   Net wages payable.

40. Failure to notify deductions makes the employer liable to pay the employee a sum equal to the amount of 13 weeks deductions, on a tribunal finding.

41. In **MILSOM v LEICESTERSHIRE C.C. (1978)** M was advanced £111 for exam fees on the basis that if he failed or resigned within a year he would pay the money back in a lump sum. He gave notice but objected to paying back the money all at once. His employers deducted the £111 from his salary under the heading of "miscellaneous deductions". This was deemed not to be a properly itemised pay statement and therefore the deduction was unlawful. As M suffered no financial loss the employers were ordered to pay him a nominal sum of £25.

42. Standing Statement. Provided that the employer has given in writing a standing statement of fixed deductions, there is no need to itemise fixed deductions on an employee's pay statement, but simply to state the total amount of the deductions. The standing statement should give the following information:

    a.   The amount of each deduction,

    b.   The intervals at which the deduction is to be made, and,

    c.   The purpose for which it is made.

This statement must be renewed after a period of 12 months.

45 Maternity Rights

INTRODUCTION

1. The *EPCA* gives employees the right not to be dismissed by reason of pregnancy, a right to maternity pay and leave, and a right to return to work after maternity leave. The chapter outlines the main statutory provisions.

DISMISSAL *(EPCA S.34)*

2. Dismissal for reasons of pregnancy will automatically be deemed unfair unless the employer can show:

    a. The woman had become incapable of adequately doing the job, or,

    b. For the woman to have continued working, when pregnant, would have resulted in the contravention of a duty imposed by law, and

    c. No reasonable alternative job is available.

The woman must have been employed for at least 2 years.

QUALIFICATIONS (Maternity Pay and Right to Return to Work)

3. An employee must fulfil the following conditions in order to qualify for maternity pay and have a right to return to work: *(S.35)*

    a. She continues to be employed by her employer (whether or not she is actually at work) until immediately before the 11th week before her confinement.

    In **SATCHWELL SUNVIC LTD v SECRETARY OF STATE (1979)** an employee gave notice to leave work 12 weeks before her expected date of confinement and stated that she intended to return. She was paid her full 6 weeks maternity pay. The Secretary of State refused to pay rebate on the grounds that she had not continued to be employed until the beginning of the 11th week before confinement. It was held that the term "continued to be employed" means no more than being under a contract. It does not matter that she is not at work. The contract continued until she resigned.

    b. She has been employed for at least 2 years at the beginning of that 11th week.

    c. She gives notice to her employer at least 21 days before her absence begins, or if that is not reasonably practicable, as soon as it is reasonably practicable that:

    i.   She will be absent from work because of pregnancy or confinement, and

    ii.   She intends to return to work with her employer (if this is the case).

4.   An employee who has been dismissed for a reason stated in paragraph 2 above shall be entited to her maternity rights even though she ceased to be employed before the beginning of the 11th week. This is provided she would have been continuously employed for two years if it had not been for her dismissal.

5.   **Medical Certiticate.** An employee shall not be entitled to maternity rights unless, if requested to do so by her employer, she produces a medical certificate stating the expected week of confinement.

MATERNITY PAY *(S.36)*

6.   **Duration.** An employee shall be entitled to 6 weeks maternity pay for a period during which she is absent from work due to pregnancy or confinement.

7.   **Amount.** The employer will be responsible for making Statutory Maternity Pay payment to his employees which he will recover from National Insurance contributions as for Statutory Sick Pay. This was introduced by the Social Security Act 1986. The amount of maternity pay shall be 9/10ths of a week's pay.

8.   **Complaints to Tribunal.** An employee may present a complaint to an industrial tribunal if her employer fails to make the maternity payment to which she is entitled.

9.   The tribunal will not consider a claim after the lapse of 3 months from the end of the 6 weeks period of maternity pay entitlement.

10. The tribunal will consider a claim made after 3 months if it is satisfied that it was not reasonably practicable for the complaint to be made within the period. *(S.46)*

11. **Contractual Remuneration.** Where an employee receives any payment by way of contractual remuneration for a period when she would have received maternity payment, any sum paid reduces her entitlement to maternity pay.

12. **Payments to Employees from the Maternity Fund.** If an employee claims that her employer has failed to make her maternity payment after:

    a.   She has taken all reasonable steps to recover the money, or

    b.   Her employer is insolvent.

She may be granted payment direct from the Maternity Pay Fund.

RIGHT TO RETURN TO WORK

13. An employee has the right to return to work with her employer after an absence caused by pregnancy or confinement as follows: *(S.48)*

    a. Right to return is at any time before the end of 29 weeks which begins with the week in which her confinement begins.

    b. In the job in which she was employed in the original contract of service.

    c. On terms and conditions not less favourable to those she would have enjoyed had she not been absent for this reason.

If it is not "reasonably practicable" for the employer to give her back her old job he may offer her a suitable alternative job instead. If she unreasonably refuses this she loses her rights.

In **BOVEY v BOARD OF GOVERNORS OF HOSPITAL FOR SICK CHILDREN (1978)** before commencement of her maternity leave the employee intimated to her employer that she was doubtful as to her ability to return to full-time employment but would wish to return part-time. The employer would allow her to return to part-time work only on the basis of a basic rate of pay. It was held that if the employee chose to return to the part-time job she could not dictate her own terms as it was an alternative offer to which she had no contractual right.

    Notes:

        i. The "job" refers to the nature of her work, not the exact position she vacated.

        ii. Conditions "not less favourable" refer to seniority, pension and other rights. The employment prior to her absence shall be counted as continuous with the period afterwards.

        iii. An "alternative job" is considered suitable if the work is suitable and appropriate for the employee. Its terms (including capacity and place of work) must be not substantially less favourable to her than those of her original job.

14. Exemptions. If the employer has five or fewer employees and it is not reasonably practicable either to give her back her old job or offer her a suitable alternative, the employer can refuse to allow her to return to work. The employee then has no further claim against her employer. *(S.56)*

15. Confirmation of Return to Work. On or after the 49th day from the beginning of her expected week of confinement (or the date of her confinement) the employer can write to the employee asking her to confirm her intention to return. The employer must inform her that if she fails to reply she will lose her right to return. The employee must reply to the request within 14 days (or if that is not reasonably practicable, as soon as reasonably practicable). *(S.35)*

In **NU-SWIFT INTERNATIONAL LTD v MALLINSON (1978)** the employee failed to inform her employer of her desire to return to work until after the due date. The reason given was that she had been unable to make up her mind due to anxiety over the birth. It was held that this was not a good reason for failure to notify the employer. He had a right to know in time so as to make the necessary arrangements.

16. Intention to Return to Work. The employee must give her employer at least 21 days notice in writing of her intention to return to work.

17; Failure to Permit Return. If an employer prevents a woman from returning and unfair dismissal is alleged, the following defences may be used;

    a. Redundancy. ie, the job had disappeared (but alternative employment must be offered if possible).

    b. An event occurred during the woman's absence which the employer considered justified fair dismissal.

ANTE-NATAL CARE *(S.31A)*

18. Pregnant employees can have time off with pay during working hours to attend ante-natal clinics.

19. Apart from the first appointment, the employer can require the employee to produce a certificate of pregnancy and appointment card.

20. If the employer fails to comply with his obligations the employee can apply to an industrial tribunal which can grant her compensation. If time off has been refused the amount of compensation will be the sum she would have received if the time off had been granted. If the time off has been granted but without pay the compensation will be the pay which ought to have been paid to her.

21. This right is not dependent on the employee's length of service, ie she can have time off on the first day of her employment. It also does not depend on the number of hours per week that the employee works.

46 Discrimination

INTRODUCTION

1. The problems of discrimination against certain classes of employees are tackled by the *SEX DISCRIMINATION ACTS 1975 and 1986* and the *RACE RELATIONS ACT 1976.* In addition European Community law exists in this field. Although the scope of these statutes is greater than merely that of employment this chapter outlines the main provisions of the Acts only insofar as they affect discrimination in the matter of employment.

SEX DISCRIMINATION ACT 1975

2. **Forms of Discrimination.** There are three forms of discrimination covered by the Act. They are direct discrimination, indirect discrimination and discrimination by victimisation. Discrimination arises where an employer or prospective employer treats a woman less favourably that he would treat a man (or vice versa). The Act also relates to discrimination against married persons.

   a. *Direct discrimination.* This has been equated with "intentional" discrimination. Intention is most difficult to prove, but complainants need only provide facts which show prima facie evidence of intentional discrimination. If the inference of direct discrimination can be arrived at from the evidence produced by the complainant then the motive for the discrimination is immaterial:

   In **GRIEG v COMMUNITY INDUSTRY (1979)** a young girl applied for a job with an organisation whose purpose was to relieve unemployment amongst juveniles. She was refused employment in a particular activity because she would have been the only girl in a group of men, and emotional problems were anticipated. It was held to be sex discrimination, even though the motives were honourable.

   In **GUBALA v CROMPTON PARKINSON LTD (1977)** Mrs Gubala was made redundant in preference to a male colleague of the same seniority. The employer admitted that he had been influenced by the fact that the man was older and had a mortgage whereas Mrs G's husband worked. It was held that this was a case of unlawful discrimination.

   In **PEAKE v AUTOMOTIVE PRODUCTS LTD (1977)** a male employee complained that there was sex discrimination as women were allowed to leave work five minutes earlier than men to avoid the crush at the factory gates. His complaint was, at first upheld. On appeal the decision was reversed on the grounds that this was a minor act of chivalry. Furthermore it was in the interests of safety and therefore there was no unlawful discrimination.

   b. *Indirect discrimination.* This occurs where the same conditions apply equally to both sexes, but because of the nature of the conditions it is more

396

difficult for one group to qualify than the other and this discrimination
cannot be justified. For example, if a height requirement were to be fixed
at six feet there would be relatively few women capable of qualifying.
Similarly if a shoe size of five should be set, few men would qualify.

In **STEEL v UNION OF POST OFFICE WORKERS AND GPO
(1978)** prior to the Sex Discrimination Act women could only be
"Temporary" full-time postmen. After the Act was passed women could
become full-time postmen but walks and rounds were allocated on the basis
of service as a full-time postman. It was held that failure to make the allocation on length of service irrespective of whether it was temporary or not
was discriminatory.

In **PRICE v CIVIL SERVICE COMMISSION (1977)** the requirement that applicants for employment should be between the ages of seventeen and half and twenty-eight was held to be unlawful discrimination
because, in practice, the demands of maternity prevented a considerable
proportion of women from availability.

In **POWELL v ELY-KYNOCH LTD (1981)** an agreement was in
existence whereby the first employees to go if redundancies were needed
would be the part-time employees. This was held to be discriminatory as
family commitments meant that all the part-time workers were women who
would be unable to comply with the condition of full-time work in order
to keep their jobs.

In **MACGREGOR WALLCOVERINGS LTD v TURTON (1977)**
a scheme whereby employees over 60 who were made redundant received an extra 10 weeks pay was held to contravene the Sex Discrimination
Act as it precluded women (who retired at 60) from qualifying. It therefore
did not give women equal rights with men to benefits.

In **WRIGHT v RUGBY CC (1984)** Rugby Council refused to allow
Mrs Wright to work times which fitted in with care of her baby. It was
held to be sex discrimination as it was a circumstance under which a far
greater proportion of women than men would be affected.

c. *Victimisation.* This occurs when less favourable treatment is given
to a person because that person has brought proceedings under the Sex
Discrimination Act or Equal Pay Act, or has given evidence or made allegations with regard to these Acts. This does not apply when the person who
is victimised does not act in good faith (eg, makes false allegations).

3. Scope of the Act. The Act makes discrimination on the grounds of sex
unlawful in employment, training and related matters. It is unlawful for an
employer to discriminate against a person on the grounds of sex or marital status
in relation to employment with regards to contracts of employment and in
contracts for services. This covers all contracts, irrespective of an employee's
age or service, apart from:

a. Employment wholly or mainly outside Great Britain.

b. Employment in a private household if there could be a reasonable objection to someone of a particular sex having the degree of physical or social contact with a person living in the home, or the knowledge of such a person's private affairs, which the job is likely to entail.

4. **Recruitment.** It is unlawful to discriminate when recruiting employees:

a. In the arrangements an employer makes for deciding who should be offered a job, for example, instructions given to a personnel officer.

b. In relation to terms offered, for example, pay, and holidays.

c. By deliberately refusing employment, on the grounds of sex.

5. **Treatment of Present Employees.** Discrimination against employees on the matter of opportunities for promotion, transfer, training and any other benefits is unlawful.

6. **Pregnancy, Childbirth, Death and Retirement.** In these matters it is not unlawful to discriminate by:

a. Giving a special treatment to women in respect of pregnancy and childbirth, and,

b. An employer making special provisions in regard to death or retirement, unless the employer discriminates against a woman in respect of opportunities for promotion, transfer or training.

7. **Genuine Occupational Qualification.** Discrimination is not unlawful where a person's sex is a genuine occupational qualification for a job. A person's sex is regarded as a genuine occupational qualification where:

a. The essential nature of the job calls for a man (or woman) for reasons of physiology (excluding physical strength or stamina), eg, modelling clothes, bunny-girls.

b. Considerations of decency or privacy, eg, because of likely physical contact (clothing sales assistant), or because it involves use of sanitary facilities (lavatory attendant).

c. The nature of location of the establishment makes it impracticable, eg, on an oil rig, or ship where separate sleeping and sanitary facilities do not exist.

d. In a single-sex establishment, eg, a single-sex hospital. It is reasonable to restrict employment to persons of the same sex as that of the establishment.

e. The job-holder provides a personal service, eg, where a person of a particular sex is more acceptable, eg, social worker, masseuse.

f. Where the law requires it, eg, the restriction on a woman resuming work within 4 weeks of giving birth, and exposure to lead.

In **PAGE v FREIGHT HIRE (TANK HAULAGE) LTD (1981)** the applicant, a 23 year-old divorcee was removed by her employer from haulage work involving the chemical dimethylformide on the ground that the substance was a danger to women of child-bearing age. The employer claimed that he was required to do this under the general duty to safeguard the health and safety of his employees imposed by *S.2* of the *HSAWA 1974*. The EAT held that the employer had acted lawfully.

8.   Discrimination Against Contract Workers. It is unlawful to discriminate against the employees of an independent contractor. The contractor himself is liable in regard to the selection of his employees. The "principal" is liable for discrimination in the terms of the contract with the independent contractor or the provision of facilities to contract workers.

In **RICE v FON-A-CAR (1980)** taxis were owned and maintained by the driver but run by a firm to whom the owner paid a weekly sum in return for business. The driver obtained permission to employ a relief driver for his night shift but, when the firm learned it was a woman, they told him to dismiss her, which he did. It was held that the driver did not supply contract labour nor provide services for the purpose of finding employment for women, and consequently the Act did not apply.

9.   Collective Agreements. Any term in a collective agreement or in an employer's rules for his employees which would result in a breach of the SDA or Equal Pay Act will be void. The same applies to any rule made by an organisation of employers or workers or trade association or body which confers qualifications. The voiding of discriminatory terms and rules will not impair employees' rights under their contracts of employment.

10.   Miscellaneous. The Act also applies to partnerships, trade unions and employers organisations, professional and trade bodies. It also applies to vocational training bodies apart from midwifery, to the police and prison service.

11.   Complaints. A person who has been discriminated against may apply to an industrial tribunal where the employer must attempt to justify his action. Application must be made within 3 months of the act of discrimination, or if it is a continuing discrimination, from when it ceases. The time limit may be extended by the tribunal if it is considered just and equitable to do so.

12.   The Equal Opportunities Commission. This body is required to work towards the elimination of discrimination, to promote equality and to keep the Sex Discrimination Act under review. It has the following functions:

a.   Conduct formal investigations into cases where it believes that conduct contravenes either the Sex Distrimination Act or the Equal Pay Act. It may issue a "non-discrimination notice", requiring the employer to act in accordance with its terms.

b.   Seek a declaration from the tribunal that an employer is engaging in discriminatory practices, or an advertisement is discriminatory, or that he has instructed someone over whom he has control to discriminate, or he is pressurising another to discriminate.

c.   Assist an individual in preparing or presenting her case.

13.   European Community Law. Article 119 of the Treaty of Rome provides that women shall be accorded equal treatment for like work with men. This is superimposed on our own legislation. Where there is conflict or where there is a gap in our own legislation the European Community law takes precedence. The interpreter of EC law is the European Court, it is then incumbent on our own courts to apply that law.

14.   Burden of Proof. The burden of proof in discrimination cases rests with the applicant. In order to assist with determination of the facts a form of questionnaire has been prepared by the Secretary of State. This can be served on the employer for answering. The reply should enable the person with the grievance to decide whether or not he has a reasonable case. Although the employer is not bound to reply to the questionnaire if he fails to do so an adverse inference may be taken.

15.   Sexual Harassment. Sexual harassment is not specifically recognised in the SDA but conduct of this nature towards a woman could amount to discrimination on the grounds of sex since she would be treated less favourably than a man would be or subjected to a detriment that a man would not be. Resignation following sexual harassment would result in a claim for constructive dismissal (see Chapter 47.15).

RACE RELATIONS ACT 1976

16.   Under this Act it is an offence for an employer to discriminate against an employee on account of his colour, race, ethnic or national origin. Discrimination consists of treating an employee less favourably than he treats other employees.

17.   Scope. The Act covers discrimination in advertising for an employee, engaging or dismissing him or in his conditions of employment (eg opportunities for training and promotion).

ZARCZYNSKA v LEVY (1978) a white student got a part-time job in an East London public house. She was told not to serve blacks. She objected to this and was sacked. She complained to the CRE which supported her appeal. The EAT said she was treated less favourably than a person who went along with the colour bar and was therefore discriminated against on racial grounds.

18.   Exceptions. It is lawful in certain circumstances to discriminate, they are:

a.   Employment in a private household.

b.   Employment abroad.

c. Employment on ships or aircraft.

d. Jobs requiring certain attributes specially possessed by a person of a certain nationality.

e. Discrimination to secure a balance of different racial groups in a place of employment.

In the latter case an employer would have to show that he was acting in good faith and produce evidence showing the range and level of jobs filled by employees of different ethnic groups.

19. Trade Unions, Employers Organisations, etc. Trade Unions, Employers' Organisations and others concerned with trades or professions must not discriminate in the following ways:

a. Admission to membership.

b. Grant of benefits to members.

c. Expulsion.

20. Liability for Employee's Discrimination. An employer is vicariously liable for racial discrimination by an employee done in the course of his employment. This is regardless of whether or not the employer approved or had knowledge of it. In court proceedings the employer would have to show that he took all such steps as were reasonably practicable to prevent such discrimination.

21. Burden of Proof. The burden of proof is upon the applicant, however, as with sex discrimination a questionnaire may be served on the employer.

22. Commission for Racial Equality. This body has the same duties and powers as the Equal Opportunities Commission.

COURSEWORK QUESTIONS 33-38
LABOUR LAW

33. a. There are certain requirements essential for the validity of all contracts. Explain, with examples, how these apply to the formation of contracts of employment.

b. When Eric is engaged as a machine operator he does not disclose that he has defective eyesight. He is injured when part of the machine breaks away because it has not been properly maintained. A person with good eyesight might have seen the forthcoming danger in time to take avoiding action.

Discuss Eric's claim for damages against his employer.

CIMA Foundation November 1982

34. *Supercabs Limited, which operates a fleet of taxis, engages Clutch as a driver. The company provides and maintains the taxi and pays for the petrol. Clutch promises to work only for the company. However, Clutch does not receive a wage but instead is paid a commission on the earnings he collects. The journeys that he makes and the hours that he works are left entirely to his discretion.*

    a. Discuss whether Clutch is an employee or an independent contractor.

    b. Explain why the existence of a contract of employment in this case might be of importance.

CIMA Foundation May 1983

35. *Your employer owns and operates a chain of garages. Advise him on the legal position with regard to the actions of the following employees:*

    a. Albert, a mechanic, is carrying out repairs for payment in his spare time.

    b. Bernard, a supervisor, has invented a device that will reduce the cost of servicing cars and offers to sell it to his employer.

    c. Charles, a salesman, has taken a present from a customer who felt that he had been given a good price for his old car as part-exchange for a new car.

    d. Doris, a secretary, asks for a reference for a new job for which she is applying.

CIMA Foundation May 1981

36. *Outline the implied duties of an employer towards his workers.*

CIMA Foundation November 1984

37. *Write a short memorandum for the female members of staff setting out the chief legal protection and rights they now enjoy as such.*

ICSA December 1979

38. *Discuss the extent to which free bargaining between employer and worker regarding wages has been affected by statutory intervention.*

CIMA Foundation May 1985

47 Termination of Contracts of Employment

INTRODUCTION

1. Under common law, termination of a contract of employment can arise in several ways. The principal ways are:

  a. By agreement between the employer and employee;

  b. By an act of either party of sufficient gravity to terminate the contract without notice;

  c. By operation of the law, eg, death, dissolution of a partnership, appointment of a receiver, compulsory winding-up of a company or frustration;

  d. By an act of either party terminating the contract with notice.

In this chapter we will consider termination with notice, termination by operation of the law, wrongful dismissal and unfair dismissal.

TERMINATION WITH NOTICE

2. The usual method of terminating a contract is for the employer to give a period of notice, determined as follows:

  a. Where the contract is for a fixed term — on completion of that term.

  b. It may be ascertained by custom of the trade.

  c. The contract may state the period — subject to the minimum under *S.49. EPCA 1978.*

NOTICE — *S.49, EPCA 1978*

3. The notice required to be given by an employer to terminate the contract of employment of a person who has been continuously employed for four weeks or more shall be:

  a. Not less than one week if his period of continuous employment is less than two years;

  b. Not less than one week for each year of continuous employment if his period of employment is two years or more but less than twelve years; and

  c. Not less than twelve weeks if his period of continuous employment is twelve years or more.

4. The employment must be of a continuous nature; periods of sickness are reckonable, but not periods of strikes. (See Chapter 48.7)

5. The following categories of employee do not have the right to be given the statutory minimum period of notice:

a. Employees engaged in work wholly or mainly outside Great Britain. However such periods, whilst not counting towards service, do not break its continuity.

b. Employees in employment under a contract made in contemplation of the performance of a specific task which is not expected to last for more than three months and which in fact lasts no longer than that time.

c. Certain seamen and dock workers.

6. The employee, in the absence of any other term in the contract, is required to give one week's notice after he has been employed for four weeks or more. When an employee has contracted to give a longer period of notice and fails to do so, the employer cannot seek a court order to compel him to continue working. However, in rare cases, an employer may claim damages for any loss caused by the employee's premature departure.

7. Any employer may generally pay wages in lieu of notice unless the employee's reputation is involved. (**CLAYTON AND WALLER v OLIVER (1930)**) (Chapter 43.2).

BY OPERATION OF THE LAW

8. a. *Death*. Death of either the employer or the employee will end the contract.

b. *Dissolution of a partnership*. Such an event will end a contract of employment and may give rise to wrongful dismissal, but:

In **BRACE v CALDER (1895)** the plaintiff was employed by a partnership. There was a change in the membership of the partnership which automatically results in dissolution. The plaintiff was offered re-engagement on the same terms by the remaining partners but refused. It was held that he was entitled to nominal damages as he had failed to mitigate his loss.

c. *Sale of a business*. As contracts of employment (ie of personal service) cannot be assigned, the sale of a business constitutes the "death" of one employer and the "birth" of another. An employee cannot be transferred to the new employer against his will.

In **NOKES v DONCASTER AMALGAMATED COLLIERIES LTD (1940)** two coal-mining companies had been amalgamated so that all the assets etc., of one had been transferred to the other. N had been employed by the colliery which had been merged into the other. He was absent from work, an action which would constitute a breach of contract to an empoloyee of the new company. It was held that his contract of employment had not been automatically transferred on amalgamation of the two companies.

If he wishes to treat the contract as terminated he will only be awarded nominal damages for dismissal. It is because of this fundamental principle of English law that complicated statutory rules have been devised to safeguard the continuity of employment and other statutory rights of employees in the event of the transfer of a business, or the transfer of an employee to an associated employer. (See Transfer of Undertakings (Protection of Employment) Regs 1981 – Chapter 47 para 25 d.).

d.   *Winding up of a company.* An order for compulsory winding up will operate to terminate the contracts of employment of all the company's employees (employees may have a right to claim damages for wrongful dismissal). However, a resolution for voluntary winding up does not automatically terminate employees' contracts of employment. The liquidator may carry on the business or he may close it down and thus terminate the employment contracts. In these circumstances an employee has no right to terminate his contract without notice and claim damages unless it is obvious that the company will be unable to fulfil its obligation under the contract.

e.   *Bankruptcy.* Bankruptcy or insolvency of either party will terminate the contract if the solvency of the party concerned is an essential element of the relationship.

f.   *Frustration.* A contract of employment will be frustrated when either party is incapable of performing his part of the contract due to circumstances beyond his control. Frustration is not dependent upon the conduct of the parties to the contract and therefore there is no dismissal. The employee cannot claim wrongful or unfair dismissal. Frustrating events are:

i.   *Illness.* Sickness may be a frustrating event if it renders future performance impossible or fundamentally different from that envisaged by the parties when they entered into the contract:

In **CONDOR v BARRON KNIGHTS (1966)** P was the drummer in a pop group. Owing to illness he was forbidden by his doctor from performing more than a few nights per week. Since the nature of the work required him to be present seven nights a week the contract was held to be frustrated.

Contrast **STOREY v FULHAM STEEL WORKS (1907)** where a manager on a five years contract was absent owing to illness for five months and was dismissed. It was held that in this case the period of illness did not frustrate the contract because of the nature of the contract. However an employer would not be expected to keep a job open indefinitely.

Further indication as to the criteria to be applied in deciding whether or not a contract of employment is frustrated has been given in more recent cases, as follows:

In **MARSHALL v HARLAND & WOLFF LTD (1972)** the

Court held that the industrial tribunal should take the following points into account when considering whether or not a contract of employment is frustrated by sickness or injury:

(a)   The terms of the contract (including sick pay),

(b)   The duration of the contract in the absence of sickness,

(c)   The nature of the employment,

(d)   The nature of the incapacity, its duration and the prospects of recovery.

(e)   The period served in employment up to the time of the sickness.

In addition, when considering whether it is reasonable for an employer to keep open an employee's position the following should be taken into account (**EGG STORES (STAMFORD HILL) LTD v LEBOVICI (1977)**):

(a)   The need for the work to be done and the requirement for a replacement,

(b)   Whether wages have continued to be paid,

(c)   The acts and statements of the employer, including dismissal or failure to dismiss the employee,

(d)   Whether it is reasonable for the employer to wait longer before replacing the employee.

ii.   *Imprisonment.* A contract of employment may be frustrated by a period of imprisonment:

In **HARE v MURPHY BROS LTD (1974)** Hare received a 12 months' prison sentence for an assault not connected with his employment. It was held that although the offence may not be a frustrating event (being self-induced) the prison sentence frustrated the contract, being an unforeseen event and delaying return to work for so long that the contract was brought to an end.

The contract is frustrated from the time of the sentence regardless that the employee appeals against the sentence and even if the appeal is successful.

WRONGFUL DISMISSAL

9.   If an employee is unjustifiably dismissed he has a claim in damages at common law. A claim for wrongful dismissal may be carried on concurrently with a claim for unfair dismissal under the *EPCA*.

10.   Contract of Indefinite Duration. Where a contract is of an indefinite duration it may be terminated by notice on either side. Notice must be at least as long as that laid down in the *EPCA*. If the parties intend the period of notice to be greater than the statutory period and this is not expressly stated in the contract, the courts may decide on what is reasonable in the circumstances. This depends on, eg, the status, skills and length of service of the employee. Some examples of court decisions in the past in this respect are:- twelve months for the chief engineer of an ocean liner (**SAVAGE v BRITISH INDIA STEAM NAVIGATION CO LTD (1930)**), six months for a journalist (**BAUMAN v HULTON PRESS LTD (1952)**), three months for a company director (**JAMES v THOS H KENT & CO LTD (1951)**) and one month for an advertising and canvassing agent (**HISCOX v BATCHELOR (1867)**).

11. If the employer dismisses an employee without notice the employee may take action for wrongful dismissal, unless the dismissal results from certain actions of the employee.

12. A Fixed Term Contract. A contract of employment will be regarded as one of a fixed term if it states the maximum duration of the contract, even if provision is made for notice to be given before this by either party. It is not a fixed contract if it has no definite end, ie based upon some uncertain future event. A contract for the completion of a particular task is not a fixed term contract.

13. Action by the Employee. The employer may terminate a contract of employment without notice if the employee acts in such a manner as to show repudiation of the contract. The circumstances can be summarised as being:

a. *Misconduct.* Where the conduct of the employee interferes with the proper performance of his duties, even outside working house, eg drunkenness, immorality, insubordination.

b. *Disobedience.* Disobedience of a lawful order may justify dismissal, but this may be mitigated if it is only a single act which is not a wilful flouting of authority.

c. *Negligence.* Negligence, to warrant dismissal, must be a single act of a serious nature, or habitual minor acts.

Details of the above circumstances, with case law, are outlined in Chapter 42.

Since the introduction of statutory unfair dismissal employees must be given a clear indication of the type of conduct which the employer regards as warranting summary dismissal. Moreover the misconduct must be gross or grave, seen in the light of all the circumstances of the case.

In **MARTIN v YORKSHIRE IMPERIAL METALS LTD (1978)** dismissal was for tying down one of two levers (designed as a safety device to occupy both hands of an operative) which activated a machine. The operative admitted to being aware that interference with the safety device would lead to dismissal without warning. It was held that the dismissal was fair.

Contrast **LADBROKE RACING LTD v ARNOTT (1979)** where the Employment Appeal Tribunal (EAT) held that warning of liability to summary dismissal could not be justification for summary dismissal for a minor offence.

CONSTRUCTIVE DISMISSAL

14. A contract of employment may be terminated by an employer's repudiatory conduct. For there to be a repudiation by the employer he must by his act or omission be guilty of either a fundamental breach of the contract or a breach of a fundamental term of the contract. The term may be express or implied:

In **MARRIOTT v OXFORD AND DISTRICT CO-OPERATIVE SOCIETY LTD (1970)** M (an electrical supervisor) was informed that because of a reduction in the size of his department his post had been made redundant and his salary and status would be reduced. M protested but continued to work under the new conditions for a few weeks until he found alternative employment. It was held that his contract had been terminated unilaterally by his employer. The fact that he had stayed on for a few weeks did not signify his agreement to the change.

In **COLEMAN v BALDWIN (1977)** the buyer in a green-grocery business had the bulk and the most interesting part of his work removed from him, which left only repetitive and boring duties. This occurred without any agreement. It was held that there was a fundamental breach of contract entitling the employee to leave. It was unfair because no attempt had been made to negotiate with him.

15. For the purposes of redundancy and unfair dismissal the *EPCA (S.55 and 83)* gives statutory force to the doctrine of constructive dismissal by declaring that an employee shall be treated as dismissed by his employer if the employee terminates the contract, with or without notice, in circumstances such that he is entitled to terminate it without notice by reason of the employer's conduct. Examples of the courts interpretation are given below:

In **WESTERN EXCAVATING (EEC) LTD v SHARP (1978)** an employee left his employment because his employer would not give him an advance of pay. It was held that this was not a fundamental breach of contract. The employee could not leave on some "equitable test" based on the employer's "unreasonable conduct".

However, in **BRITISH AIRCRAFT CORPORATION LTD v AUSTIN (1978)** it was suggested that a term might be implied in a contract of employment that employers shall act in accordance with good industrial relations practice.

In **WIGAN BOROUGH COUNCIL v DAVIES (1979)** D, an employee at an old peoples' home was "sent to Coventry" by fellow employees following her impropriety. It was not possible to move her to another job. D left and claimed constructive dismissal. It was held that the employer had been in breach of the contractual obligation to give her support to enable her to carry out her duties free from harassment.

In **ISLE OF WIGHT TOURIST BOARD v COOMBES (1976)** a Director made a remark to his secretary about another employee that she was an intolerable bitch on a Monday morning. The employee left and claimed constructive dismissal. It was held that there was a fundamental alteration to the trust and respect the relationship required.

REMEDIES FOR WRONGFUL DISMISSAL

16. Damages. To claim damages for wrongful dismissal the employee must prove:

    a. Where he was engaged on a fixed term − that he was dismissed before the expiry of the term.

    b. Where the contract stipulates a period of notice − that the dismissal was without such notice.

    c. That the notice given was less than that required by the *EPCA 1978*.

    d. That dismissal was without just cause.

17. Assessment of Damages

    a. Damages should cover such loss as may be fairly considered to arise naturally from the breach and also for any loss which was reasonably foreseeable as likely to arise from the breach. Generally the amount awarded should compensate for the monetary loss for the period of notice entitlement.

    b. The amount should cover the following:

        i. Wages,

        ii. Gratuities,

        iii. Commission,

        iv. Publicity and reputation (Actors, etc.),

        v. Difficulty in obtaining future employment in cases where narrow specialisation has occurred.

Damages are not recoverable for the manner in which the dismissal took place (**ADDIS v GRAMOPHONE CO (1909)**), nor for hurt feelings, in **BRITISH GUIANA CREDIT CORPN v DA SILVA (1965)** the employee unsuccessfully claimed additional damages in respect of "humiliation, embarrassment and loss of reputation".

18. Deductions from Damages. A dismissed employee must mitigate his loss, (**BRACE v CALDER (1895)**). In assessment of damages the court would take the following into account:

    a. Income tax liability,

    b. Unemployment benefit received by the employee,

    c. National insurance contributions payable,

    d. Unfair dismissal compensation received,

    e. Redundancy payment received.

19. Other Remedies. Other remedies, apart from damages are:

a.   *Quantum meruit.* This is an equitable remedy compelling the defendant to pay for performance done and already accepted.

b.   *Injunction.* A court will not normally grant an injunction which has the effect of requiring specific performance of a contract for personal services owing to the voluntary nature of contracts of employment and the difficulty of the supervision of the enforcement of this remedy.

In **PAGE ONE RECORDS v BRITTON (1968)** an injunction was sought against a pop group (the "Troggs") which would require the group to honour a promise to employ a certain person as manager. The injunction was refused as it was held that a manager had duties of a "personal and fiduciary" nature and in this particular case the pop group had lost confidence in the person.

However sometimes an injunction will be granted restraining an employee from working for a rival employer, eg **WARNER BROS. PICTURES INC v NELSON (1937)**. (See Chapter 21.11).

An injunction may be granted in exceptional cases:

In **HILL v C.A. PARSONS LTD (1972)** the court granted the employee an injunction restraining his employer from terminating his employment. The employer had been influenced by union pressure to dismiss the employee, and the court considered it a "highly exceptional case".

UNFAIR DISMISSAL

20.   The law relating to unfair dismissal is contained in the *EPCA 1978*. The rights apply to those working on a contract of service.

21. Excluded Categories. The following categories of employees are excluded from the unfair dismissal provisions:

a.   Those with less than 2 years continuous service.

b.   Those who have reached the recognised retirement age of the undertaking, or the statutory retirement age, or, in the event of the absence of a normal retirement age, the age of 65 (this applies to both men and women).

Note: categories a. and b. will not be excluded from claiming compensation if the dismissal was as a result of the exercise of their individual rights (joining or refusing to joint a trade union).

c.   Those normally employed for less than 16 hours a week, or 8 hours if they have 5 years service;

d.   Share fishermen;

e.   Those ordinarily working outside Great Britain;

f.   Those on fixed term contracts of two years or more which contain a clause waiving these rights;

g.   Employees covered by an approved scheme (collective agreement) relating to compensation for unfair dismissal.

22.   The Meaning of "Dismissal". "Dismissal" is deemed to have occurred in the following situations:- *(S.55)*

a.   Where the employee's contract of employment is terminated, with or without notice (ie voluntary resignation is not "dismissal");

b.   Where the employee is employed under a fixed term contract which is not renewed;

c.   Where the employer is in breach of contract, in circumstances such that the employee is entitled to regard the contract as repudiated, ie "constructive dismissal".

d.   Failure to permit a female employee to return to work after confinement.

Note: The employee must prove "dismissal".

23.   Compensation for Unfair Dismissal. The right not to be "unfairly" dismissed is applicable regardless of whether or not the employer has given the statutory amount of notice. The concept of unfair dismissal goes some way towards acknowledging the property right an employee has in his job.

The onus is on the employer to prove that the dismissal was fair. He must satisfy the tribunal that there was a valid reason for the dismissal, ie any one of the following reasons:-

a.   *Lack of capability or qualifications.* Capability is assessed by reference to skill, aptitude, health or any other physical or mental quality. Qualification refers to any degree, diploma or other academic, technical or professional qualification relevant to the position which the employee held.

In **WINTERHALTER GASTRONOM v WEBB (1973)** a sales director was held to have been fairly dismissed where his employers established that he had not achieved the standard of sales which the company was entitled to expect from its sales director, notwithstanding the difficulties under which he was working.

Contrast **EARL v SLATER & WHEELER (AIRLYNE) LTD (1972)** where a planning and estimating engineer was dismissed, after several warnings, for inadequate performance. He was dismissed after a spell of absence when it was discovered that contracts were behind time. On his return to work he was handed a letter dismissing him summarily. The court found the dismissal to be unfair as the employee was not given an opportunity to explain the deficiencies in his work.

Generally an employee should be given an opportunity to state his case, but failure to do so does not necessarily render dismissal unfair:

411

In **TAYLOR v ALIDAIR LTD (1978)** an airline pilot made one single, but serious mistake on landing his aircraft. His dismissal was held to be fair even though he had been given no opportunity to state his case prior to dismissal.

b. *The conduct of the employee.* Examples of misconduct which have been held to justify dismissal include: dishonesty (even suspected dishonesty), breach of safety regulations, conviction of a criminial offence, sexual aberrations, fighting with fellow-employees, disclosing information to a competing firm, etc.

In **NEEFJES v CRYSTAL PRODUCTS CO LTD (1972)** the employee assaulted a fellow-employee and was dismissed. He had been warned in writing several months earlier that he would be dismissed in the event of further complaints as to his conduct. It was held that he was fairly dismissed.

An employee may refuse to obey an unreasonable order:

In **MORRISH v HENLYS (FOLKESTONE) LTD (1973)** a stores driver objected when the manager altered the record of the amount of diesel oil drawn by the employee. The manager explained that alteration of the record was done in order to cover any discrepancies in the account. He was dismissed when he continued to object. It was held that the dismissal was unfair, as his objection to the falsification of the account was not unreasonable.

Conduct outside working hours may also amount to a valid reason for dismissal if it affects his employer's business adversely:

In **SINGH v LONDON COUNTY BUS SERVICES LTD (1976)** the employee drove a one-man-operated bus. He was convicted of offences of dishonesty committed outside his employment. It was held that misconduct does not have to occur in the course of employment, or at the employee's place of work, or even connected with work to justify dismissal, so long as it somehow affects the employee when he is doing his work or is thought likely to do so.

In **CREFFIELD v BBC (1975)** a film cameraman was dismissed following his conviction of indecently assaulting a thirteen year old girl. His dismissal was held to be fair as the employer could not be selective in sending the employee on assignments and it might be apprehensive about sending the employee on assignments in a responsible position in the future.

c. *If the employee is redundant.* Provided there is no unfair discrimination and the proper procedures are carried out, an employee who is dismissed because of redundancy will not succeed in a claim for unfair dismissal.

In **HEATHCOTE v NORTH WESTERN ELECTRICITY BOARD (1974)** the employee held the position of driver's mate, classed as a labourer. He was dismissed for redundancy because the board decided there was no longer any need for drivers' mates. Selection was made on the basis of last in, first out. However, selection was confined to the transport section and not the whole of the business. It was held that this was not the correct approach. As the employee was in a class of lesser-skilled worker selection should have been made from the whole concern.

d.   *If the employee could not continue to work in that position without contravening a statutory restriction.*

In **FEARN v TAYFIELD MOTOR CO LTD (1975)** the employee was engaged as a vehicle supervisor, part of his duties including the requirement to drive vehicles. He was convicted of careless driving and failing to stop after an accident and was disqualified from driving for twelve months. His dismissal was held to be fair as he could no longer legally do the job he was employed to do.

e.   *Some other substantial reason.* The National Industrial Relations Court in considering the case of **RS COMPONENTS LTD v IRWIN (1973)** said

"There are not only legal but also practical objections to a narrow construction of *'some other reason'*. Parliament may well have intended to set out the common reasons for a dismissal but can hardly have hoped to produce an exhaustive catalogue of all the circumstances in which a company would be justified in terminating the services of an employee'.

Some examples are:-

i.   Where personality conflicts gave rise to hostility and tension between employees began to have a detrimental effect on the employer's business **TREGANOWAN v ROBERT KNEE & CO LTD (1975)**;

ii.   Failure to accede to a request by the employer to work at times other than those provided in the contract **KNIGHTON v HENRY RHODES LTD (1974)**;

iii.   Where an employee refuses to sign an undertaking that on leaving the employment he would not compete with the employer **GLENDINNING v PILKINGTON BROS LTD (1973)**;

iv.   Where an employee moves to an unreasonable distance from his work, despite a company rule that employees must live within reasonable travelling distance **FARR v HOVERINGHAM GRAVEL LTD (1972)**.

v.   When an employee is a danger to other workers **MORTIBOY v ROLLS ROYCE (1983)**.

Even if the employer can show that an employee was dismissed for any of the above reasons, or some other substantial reason he must have acted "reasonably" in dismissing the employee.

The decision is left to the tribunal which would take into account all circumstances including the size and administrative resources of the undertaking, and decide the question on the grounds of equity and the substantial merits of the case.

24. Codes of Practice. In determining whether or not an employer has acted reasonably or not the tribunal may examine the procedures followed by the employer. Guidance as to the fairness of a procedure can be obtained from the Codes of Practice. Two codes have been issued, they are: the *1972 INDUSTRIAL RELATIONS CODE OF PRACTICE* and the *1977 CODE OF PRACTICE — DISCIPLINARY PRACTICE AND PROCEDURES IN EMPLOYMENT*. The Codes are a guide with the purpose of promoting good industrial relations. If an employer fails to observe any provision of the codes he will not be thereby liable to any proceedings, but the industrial tribunal can take the codes into account in any proceedings brought against the employer. Procedural fairness requires the employer to:

    a.   Hold a reasonable investigation into the matters alleged;

    b.   Give the employee reasonable warning;

    c.   Give an adequate hearing and the employee's explanation;

    d.   If practicable, provide an appeal procedure.

25. Presumption of Unfair Dismissal. Dismissal is presumed to be unfair in the following circumstances: *(S. 59, 60)*

    a.   The employee was selected for redundancy whilst other employees in a similar position were retained and either:

        i.   The selection was in contravention of an agreed or customary arrangement relating to redundancy (eg last in, first out) or

        ii.   The reason for the selective dismissal was in connection with the trade union membership or activities of the employee;

    b.   If the employee was dismissed because she was pregnant, or for any reason connected with her pregnancy;

    c.   If the employee was selected for dismissal on grounds of race or sex.

    d.   *TRANSFER OF UNDERTAKINGS (PROTECTION OF EMPLOYMENT) REGULATIONS 1981.* When an undertaking is transferred from one person to another every contract of employment is automatically transferred. If either the transferor or transferee dismisses any employee for a reason connected with the transfer the dismissal is unfair. Dismissal, however, will not be unfair if it is caused by economic, technical or organisational reasons incidental to the transfer and these reasons entail changes in the workforce of either the transferor or transferee. On the other hand an employee need not accept a transfer if there is a substantial change in his working conditions or the change of employer leads to a significant change, to the detriment of the employee.

    In **SHIPP v D. J. CATERING LTD (1982)** dismissal in order to reduce manning levels under new management was held by an industrial tribunal to be fair — the dismissal being economic grounds for changes in the workforce.

26. Dismissal in Other Circumstances. The following are the rules of unfair dismissal in other situations:

a. *Unfair dismissal in connection with trade union membership or activities.*

The dismissal of an employee shall be regarded as unfair if the reason for dismissal is that the employee:-

i.   Was or proposed to become a member of an independent trade union, or

ii.   Had taken part or proposed to take part in the activities of an independent trade union, or

iii.   Was not a member of any trade union or had refused or proposed to refuse to become or remain a member.

b. *Dismissal during a strike.* If an employee is dismissed for taking part in a strike the tribunal has no jurisdiction to decide whether the dismissal was fair or unfair unless it was a case of selective dismissal, ie

i.   Others taking the same action were not dismissed, or

ii.   Any of the strikers has, within three months, been offered re-engagement, but the complainant has not been offered re-engagement, and the reason is the complainant's membership or non-membership of a trade union or union activities.

iii.   There may be selective dismissal of employees taking part in an unofficial strike or other unofficial action.

c. *Dismissal during a lock-out.* Dismissal following a lock-out is fair if the employee is offered re-engagement from the date of resumption of work, and refuses. Dismissal is unfair if re-engagement is not offered.

d. *Industrial pressure.* If an employer dismisses an employee because of threats of strike action by other employees no account shall be taken of this measure in deciding whether the dismissal was fair or unfair.

27. Written Statement of Reasons for Dismissal. Employees with 26 weeks service have a right to a written statement of the reasons for their dismissal, subject to the following conditions: *(S.53)*

a.   The entitlement to a statement does not depend on whether or not the dismissal is fair;

b.   It must be supplied by the employer within 14 days of the request;

c.   Failure to provide a statement within 14 days, or the provision of one with "inadequate or untrue" reasons gives the right of a complaint to an industrial tribunal within 3 months of dismissal;

d.   The statement has the protection of "qualified privilege", ie the employer will not be liable for defamatory statements unless malice can be proved.

REMEDIES FOR UNFAIR DISMISSAL

28. Reinstatement and Re-engagement. An unfairly dismissed employee has the right to state whether he wishes to be reinstated or re-engaged. In reinstatement the employee is treated in all respects as if he had not been dismissed. Any pay, pension and seniority must be restored to him and he must be given any pay arrears and any other lost benefits. In re-engagement the employee may be employed in a different job provided it is suitable. The terms and conditions may differ from the previous ones. Re-engagement may be by a new employer, eg a successor to the former employer. Damages may be awarded in respect of loss of benefits arising between the dismissal and re-engagement. *(S. 71, 72)*

29. The tribunal may make a recommendation to reinstatement taking into account the extent to which the employee contributed to his own dismissal and the practicability of reinstatement (eg his fellow-employees' attitude). Alternatively the tribunal can recommend re-engagement.

30. If an employer fails to comply with a recommendation for reinstatement or re-engagement he may be liable to pay "punitive" compensation in addition to compensation based on actual loss suffered by the employee.

31. Compensation. Any compensation which may be awarded is based on the following factors: *(S.74)*

    a. The immediate loss of wages, if any;

    b. Compensation for future loss of wages;

    c. The loss of statutory protection from unfair dismissal and redundancy until the employee has been continuously employed for the new qualifying period.

32. Compensation may be reduced if there is contributory fault on the part of the employee:

In **ROBERTSON v SECURICOR TRANSPORT LTD (1972)** an employee was dismissed for carelessness in signing a receipt for a missing container. It was held that he was unfairly dismissed as his employer had not acted reasonably by treating this one act of negligence as sufficient to justify dismissal. However the employee's compensation was reduced by 50% because of his contributory fault.

33. Reduction in Basic Award. There are two circumstances under which a tribunal could reduce the basic award of compensation:

    a. Where the employee has unreasonably refused an offer of reinstatement which would have had the effect if accepted of reinstating him in all respects as if he had not been dismissed;

    b. Where the tribunal considers that the employee's conduct before the dismissal was such that it would be just and equitable to reduce the basic award. This refers to conduct which was not the reason for the dismissal, but came to light afterwards.

In **DEVIS & SONS LTD v ATKINS (1977)** the employee was dismissed for alleged incompetence, with six weeks notice and £6,000 compensation. Afterwards, it came to light that he had been accepting secret commissions. His employers refused to pay the compensation and treated him as summarily dismissed. It was held that this was unfair dismissal as only information known at the time of dismissal is relevant to determine whether it is fair.

34. Amount of Compensation

a.   *Basic award*. The minimum award is two weeks pay up to a maximum of £198 per week. The amount of basic award will normally depend on the employee's service and be calculated in a manner similar to that for redundancy pay.

below the age of 22 years	— ½ weeks pay	for each
between 22 and 41 years	— 1 weeks pay	year of
over the age of 41 years	— 1½ weeks pay	service

The maximum payable is for 20 years employment, ie,

$$20 \times £198 \times 1½ = £5,940$$

b.   *The compensatory award*. The compensatory award is the amount the tribunal considers just and equitable in all the circumstances, based on the financial loss suffered. Compensation is normally assessed under the following headings:

  i.   Immediate loss of wages

  ii.   Future loss of earnings

  iii.   Loss of "perks", eg use of company car

  iv.   Loss of benefits in kind

  v.   Pension rights

  vi.   Loss of statutory rights.

The maximum is £8,925 or such other sum decided by the Secretary of State. A tribunal may reduce the amount of compensation by the amount it considers just and equitable if the unfairly dismissed has caused or contributed to his dismissal.

c.   *Additional awards*. Additional compensation may be awarded where an employer fails to comply with a recommendation for reinstatement or re-engagement as follows: *(S. 71, 76)*

  i.   If the employee is dismissed on grounds of sex or race discrimination the award will be not less than 26 or more than 52 weeks pay at £198 per week with a maximum of £8,925.

  ii.   In any other case the additional compensation will be not less than 13, or more than 26 weeks pay.

d. ***Maximum payable.*** The maximum compensation payable, therefore, is:

£ 5,940	–	basic award
£ 8,925	–	compensatory award
£ 8,925	–	additional award
£23,790		

e. ***Rules for compensation where unfair dismissal is connected with trade union membership or activities.***

A new basic award with a minimum payment of £2,520 was introduced by the *EA 1982* in respect of an employee unfairly dismissed because of his membership or non-membership of a trade union. In addition such an employee will receive the old compensatory award and if he has requested reinstatement or re-engagement a new special award.

The *EA 1982* introduced a special award for cases where an employee has been unfairly dismissed on the grounds of union membership or non-membership, ie,

i. Where reinstatement or re-engagement is requested but the tribunal does not make such an order the special award will be one weeks pay multiplied by 104, or £12,550 whichever is greater, but with a maximum of £25,040.

ii. If reinstatement or re-engagement is ordered but the employer refuses and cannot show that it was impracticable for him to comply the special award shall be one weeks pay multiplied by 156, or £18,795 whichever is greater, but with no maximum amount.

The special award may be reduced as a result of an employee's conduct before dismissal.

f. ***Duty to mitigate loss.*** The employee is under a duty to mitigate his loss. He must show that he has made active attempts to seek alternative employment.

35. Compensation – Awards against Third Parties. The *EPCA 1978* as amended by the *EA 1980* and the *EA 1982* permits unfair dismissal damages to be passed on to a trade union or other party which has exercised pressure directly or indirectly to bring about the dismissal of an employee *(S. 76A)*, as follows:-

a. If in proceedings before an industrial tribunal an employee or employer claims that:-

i. The employer was induced to dismiss the complainant by pressure exerted on the employer by a trade union or other person by calling or organising a strike or other industrial action, and

ii. The pressure was exercised because the employee was not a member of a trade union the employer or employee may request the tribunal to direct that the person who he claimed exercised the pressure be joined in the proceedings.

b.   Where the tribunal makes an award of compensation the award may be made against the other person or partly against that person and partly against the employer as considered just and equitable.

36.   Complaints to Industrial Tribunals. An employee who considers that he has been unfairly dismissed may complain to an industrial tribunal from the time he receives notice. An appeal lies from an industrial tribunal on a point of law to the Employment Appeal Tribunal. Appeals lie from the EAT to the Court of Appeal, and from there to the House of Lords.

ACTION SHORT OF DISMISSAL

37.   Under the *TULRA 1974* and the *EPCA 1978* every employee has the right as an individual not to be penalised for, or deterred or prevented from joining an independent trade union or taking part in its activities at an appropriate time by an action short of dismissal by the employer. *(S.23)*

38.   There is some doubt as to the scope of the action short of dismissal, ie whether it relates to threats against an employee for his union activities, or whether it is applicable to actual measures taken against him:

In **BRASSINGTON v CAULDON WHOLESALE LTD (1978)** the employer told his employees that if they voted in an ACAS ballot on trade union recognition he would close the business, thus dismissing the employees. The EAT said that it was open to argument whether a threat constituted "action", noting that the threat of industrial action is distinguished from that of taking industrial action.

Contrast **CARTER v WILTSHIRE COUNTY COUNCIL (1979)** where the employer threatened disciplinary action if a meeting of an unrecognised union took place. It was held that this threat infringed the statutory right of freedom from action short of dismissal.

39.   Under the *EA 1980* the right of an employee not to have action short of dismissal taken against him has been extended to cover compulsion to join any trade union. Where a closed shop operates those employees who are protected from unfair dismissal for not being a member of a trade union specified in the closed shop agreement will also have the right not to have action short of dismissal taken against them by their employer to compel them to join the union.

40.   Under the *EA 1982* an employee has the right not to have action short of dismissal taken against him in order to enforce a requirement to make one or more payments (to a charity) as a consequence of his failure to become or remain a member of a trade union. In addition any deductions made by the employer which is attributable to the employee failing to become or remain a member of a trade union will be deemed to be action short of dismissal.

48 Redundancy

INTRODUCTION

1. In certain circumstances an employee may receive compensation for the loss of his job. The amount of compensation is related to the age, length of service and average weekly earnings of the redundant employee. The purpose of the redundancy payments scheme is to compensate for loss of security and to encourage employees to accept redundancy without damaging industrial relations.

2. A Redundancy Fund is established, financed by contributions collected with the employers' National Insurance payments. The fund is used to make redundancy payments in the event of an employer being unable to pay due to insolvency.

3. Disputes about entitlement to payment, etc are settled by industrial tribunals.

4. The law relating to redundancy payments is contained in the *EPA 1975* and *EPCA 1978*. References in this Chapter are to the EPCA unless otherwise stated.

CONDITIONS FOR PAYMENT

5. For a person to be entitled to redundancy payment he must have been:

    a. An employee;

    b. Continuously employed for the requisite period;

    c. Dismissed; and

    d. Dismissed by reason of redundancy.

6. **"Employee"** is defined as "an individual who has entered into or works under (or, where the employment has ceased, worked under) a contract of employment". In cases where the employer disputes that the applicant was an employee, it is for the applicant to prove that he was in fact an employee.

7. **Continuous Employment for the Requisite Period.** The applicant must have been continuously employed for a period of two years ending with the relevant date. The general rule in computing the period of employment is that any week in which the employee has been employed for 16 hours or more shall count, but an employee with 5 years service or more will be deemed to have continuous employment if he worked for more than 8 hours per week. The following events do not break continuity:

    a. *Change in job with the same employer.*

    b. *Change in ownership of the business.* When a business that is wholly or partly carried on in the UK is transferred from one person to another the *TRANSFER OF UNDERTAKINGS (PROTECTION OF EMPLOY-MENT) REGULATIONS* 1981 impose the following obligation on the transferor and transferee:

i. Every contract of employment is automatically transferred to the transferee employer. Thus the employee cannot claim that he has been dismissed or made redundant.

ii. Dismissal by reason of the transfer of the business will be unfair unless it is caused by economic, technical or organisational reasons incidental to the transfer. This situation may give rise to redundancies.

iii. An employee need not accept a transfer if either there is a substantial change in his working conditions or the change of employer leads to a significant change, to the detriment of the employee.

iv. The employer is required to inform any recognised trade union sufficiently in advance of the transfer to enable consultation to take place, even if no redundancies are expected.

If only the assets of the business are taken on and an employee is offered work on the same premises there may not be a transfer of ''the business'.

In **WOODHOUSE v PETER BROTHERHOOD (1972)** W had been employed by Crossley Engines Ltd for 40 years. In 1965 the plant was bought by PB Ltd. W continued to work for the company. There was no transfer of trade name, customers or goodwill and an entirely new product was produced. In 1971 W was made redundant. It was held that W was entitled to only 6 years redundancy pay as a change in business and trade had occurred in 1965.

The Regulations apply where there is a *change of employer*, eg,

i. Where the whole or part of a sole trader's business, or a partnership, is sold as a going concern,

ii. Where two companies cease to exist and combine to form a third,

iii. Where a company, or part of its business, is bought by another, provided this is done by the second company purchasing the assets and the business (and not the shares only) of the company being transferred.

Most transfers of businesses are brought about by share transfers and are not covered by the Regulations as there is no change of employer, ie, the original company is still the employer although control may have changed.

c. *Engagement by an associated employer.* Where an employee is taken into the employment of an associated company his period of employment with the first company counts as a period of employment with the associated company. Two companies are associated if one has control (directly or indirectly) of the other or if both are controlled (directly or indirectly) by a third person.

421

In **ZARB v BRITISH & BRAZILIAN PRODUCE CO LTD (1978)** Z was a canteen worker employed by Total Staff (Recruitment) Ltd. The defendant took over the running of the canteen and Z became employed by them. It was held that the two companies were associated employers. The same two people controlled more than 50% of shares in each company. The case brought out the fact that a group of persons who act together can share control.

d.   *Absence.* Periods of absence from work for reasons of sickness, injury, absence due to pregnancy or confinement of less than 26 weeks, or temporary cessation of work count as periods of employment. Additionally, where an employee exercises her right to return to work after an absence due to pregnancy or confinement, the whole period of absence will count as continuous employment notwithstanding that it is longer than 26 weeks.

e.   *Strikes.* The continuity of employment is not destroyed by participation in a strike. However, any week during any part of which the employee is on strike is not counted in the computation of the number of weeks of employment.

f.   *Lock outs.* A period in which an employee is locked out by his employer does not break continuity of employment.

g.   *Working temporarily abroad.* An employee may work abroad temporarily for up to 26 weeks without breaking his contract of employment, but the time abroad does not count towards computation of the length of continuous service.

h.   *Dismissal followed by re-instatement or re-engagement.* Where an employer reinstates or re-engages an employee after he has been dismissed the continuity of employment is maintained if the action was taken as a result of an application to an industrial tribunal by the employee or as a result of an agreement brought about by a conciliation officer.

Notes:

1.   The "relevant date" is generally the date on which the employee actually ceased to work. However, where less than the statutory minimum period of notice is given, the relevant date is calculated as the date on which the minimum period of notice would have expired had it been given. If an employee is given pay in lieu of notice the relevant date is the day of dismissal.

In **SLATER v JOHN SWAIN & SON LTD (1981)** S was made redundant at the age of 64 years and 8 months with 12 weeks pay in lieu of notice. His redundancy payment was reduced by 11/12ths to take into account the period between his 64th birthday and the end of the last week for which he was paid. He claimed that only 8/12ths were deductable. It was held that the date of actual termination was the "relevant date" for this purpose and not the date at which any notice given would have expired. S's claim was upheld.

But an employer cannot prevent an employee from having the necessary qualifying period by dismissing him without notice, or with pay in lieu of notice, where to have given him proper notice would have given him the qualifying length of employment. Additionally, an employee exercising her right to return to work after a pregnancy will be deemed to have been continuously employed up to her notified date of return if she is not permitted to return to work by the employer.

2. Temporary cessation of work is a matter of fact in each case:

In **BENTLEY ENGINEERING CO LTD v CROWN (1976)** C was employed by X Co. from 1948 to 1963 when he became redundant. He obtained employment elsewhere. In 1965 he became employed by Bentley Eng. Co. (an associated company of X Co.) C was subsequently made redundant again and claimed payment on the basis of continuous employment from 1948. It was held that the period 1963 to 1965 should be regarded as temporary cessation of work. Regard was especially taken of the length of service before and after the cessation.

Contrast **WISHART v NATIONAL COAL BOARD (1974)** where W was employed by the NCB. He left and subsequently returned. During his absence he remained a member of the NCB's pension scheme (for NCB employees only). It was held that W was regarded as in NCB employment by custom or arrangement for the purposes of the pension scheme. He was therefore to be regarded as in continuous employment for redundancy payments.

8.   The Meaning of Dismissal. By *S.83* an employee will be taken to be dismissed by his employer if:

a.   The contract under which he is employed by the employer is terminated by the employer, whether it is terminated by notice or not; or

b.   Where under that contract he is employed for a fixed term which expires without being renewed under the same contract; or

c.   The employee terminates the contract with or without notice where his employer's conduct is such as to justify the employee leaving without notice (constructive dismissal).

There is no dismissal, and therefore no redundancy payment where an employee leaves voluntarily or where the contract is frustrated:

In **MORTON SUNDOUR FABRICS LTD v SHAW (1966)** S was employed in the company's velvet department. He was notified that his job in that department was likely to end in some months time. S found a job elsewhere and left MSF Ltd. It was held that S was not entitled to a redundancy payment as he had left voluntarily without having had notice from his employer.

423

9. Redundancy Must be the Reason for Dismissal. Redundancy is defined by *S.81* as the dismissal of an employee wholly or mainly on account of:

a. The fact that his employer has ceased, or intends to cease, to carry on the business for the purposes of which the employee was employed by him, or he ceased, or intends to cease, to carry on that business in the place where the employee was so employed; or

b. The fact that the requirements of that business for employees to carry out work of a particular kind in the place where he was so employed, have ceased or diminished or are expected to cease or diminish.

10. The following cases illustrate how the statutory definition of "redundancy" has been interpreted:

In **EUROPEAN CHEFS v CURRELL LTD (1971)** a pastry cook was dismissed because the requirement for his specialty (eclairs and meringues) had ceased and there became a requirement to produce Continental pastries, for which another person was taken into employment. It was held that the pastry cook was entitled to redundancy payment as *the need for a cook of his type had ceased*.

In **VAUX & ASSOCIATED BREWERIES v WARD (1969)** a quiet public house was converted into a discotheque. The landlord dismissed the 57 year old barmaid as he required a younger person (a "Bunny Girl") to attract customers. It was held that there was no entitlement to redundancy payment as *there had been no change in the nature of the particular work being done*.

In **LESNEY PRODUCTS & CO LTD v NOLAN (1977)** a reorganisation entailed elimination of the night shift. The night shift employees received redundancy payments. A double day shift system was introduced and all day shift workers were offered employment on it. Those who refused the offer were dismissed. It was held that they were not entitled to redundancy payments as *there had been no diminution in requirement for a type of worker*, just a reorganisation in the interests of efficiency.

In **UK ATOMIC ENERGY AUTHORITY v CLAYDON (1974)** the employee was obliged by his contract to move anywhere in the UK as required by his employer. *The need for fewer employees at one plant did not constitute a diminution at his place of employment* as his place of employment was "anywhere in the UK".

In **NORTH RIDING GARAGES v BUTTERWICK (1967)** B had been employed at a garage for 30 years as a workshop manager, which mainly involved a mechanic's work. When the garage came under new ownership B was required to deal with administrative as well as technical matters. B found that he could not adapt to the new situation, and was dismissed. He claimed redundancy payment but failed as it was held that there had been no diminution in requirement for a workshop manager.

In **HINDLE v PERCIVAL BOATS LTD (1969)** H was dismissed on the ground that his work was too thorough to be economical. He was a highly skilled carpenter who had spent his working life building boats and his employer's business had moved from wooden hulled to fibreglass boats. The company still employed woodworkers to instal wooden furniture. It was held that dismissal was not due to redundancy as the employers still required woodworkers.

In **SINGH v HIGGS & HILL LTD (1976)** S was employed as site engineer on the permanent staff. He was given notice of redundancy when the senior engineers' work on the site was nearing its end. It was held that fluctuation in requirement for employees as the work on one site ran down and another worked up could be deemed as a cessation or diminution of requirement, for the purposes of redundancy payment. Furthermore, no distinction could be made between permanent and temporary staff and the employers were not expected to foresee in March that another engineer would be required in July.

In **O'HARE v ROTOPRINT LTD (1980)** in anticipation of increased sales the employers took on additional personnel. The increased work failed to materialise and the staff was reduced back to its original level. It was held that *there was no cessation or diminution of work*, and a redundancy payment was inadmissible.

In **CHAPMAN v GOONVEAN AND ROSTOWRACK CHINA CLAY CO LTD (1973)** the company provided free transport for employees living 30 miles from the works. The transport was discontinued when demand fell so as to make it uneconomical. Employees who could not then get to work gave notice. It was held that there was no redundancy as the *requirement for employees had not diminished*.

In **BROMBY & HOARE LTD v EVANS (1972)** the company's business had been increasing but found it more economical to use self-employed workers rather than its own men. As a consequence two workers were dismissed. It was held that they were entitled to redundancy payments as *the company's need for employees had diminished*.

In **EXEC. OF EVEREST v COX (1980)** a canteen manageress of a firm with a concession at a police station was offered suitable employment elsewhere when the concession came to an end. She refused because the company taking over the work led her to believe she would be employed by them, but in the event she was not. It was held that she was entitled to redundancy payment as her conduct was not unreasonable at the time she took the decision.

In **J. STOTT & SON LTD v STOKES (1971)** the employee, an alleged troublemaker was sacked for absenting himself from a site when he should have been working. He claimed it was a cover-up for redundancy. It was held that as it was proved the dismissal was due to conduct entitling the employer to sack him summarily, then even though a redundancy situation existed, the employee was not entitled to redundancy pay.

425

SPECIAL CONDITIONS FOR LAY-OFF AND SHORT-TIME

11. *S.87-89* make provision for piece workers who are laid off or put on short time to claim a redundancy payment. An employee is considered to be laid off in any week during which he receives no payment under his contract of employment by reason of there being no work of any kind provided by his employer, although he is available for work. Short time is a week in which less than half a week's pay is earned.

12. The employee must give written notice to his employer of his intention to claim a redundancy payment, within four weeks of:

    a. The end of a continuous period of lay-off or short time of 4 or more weeks duration; or

    b. The end of a period of six weeks lay-off or short time out of thirteen weeks (where not more than three weeks are consecutive).

13. The employee must then terminate his contract of employment by giving one week's notice or such longer period as contractually agreed. If notice to terminate is not given before or at the same time as his notice of intention to claim, it must be given within the following time limits:

    a. If the employer does not serve a counter-notice (claiming that work will be available) within three weeks of the expiry of the employee's notice of claim.

    b. Where the employer serves a counter-notice and subsequently withdraws it, within three weeks of the date of withdrawal.

    c. Where a tribunal has determined a right to claim after the employer has served a counter-notice, within three weeks after notification of the tribunal decision.

14. The employer may rebut the claim by serving on the employee a counter-notice if he reasonably expects to be able to provide the employee with a period of employment of not less than 13 weeks during which he would not be laid off or kept on short time. Such a period of employment must be expected to begin not later than four weeks from the date of service of the employee's notice.

15. The employee may pursue his claim, after service of a counter-notice, by taking the matter before an industrial tribunal which will determine whether the employer has reasonable grounds for serving the counter-notice.

In **NEEPSEND STEEL & TOOL CORPN v VAUGHAN (1972)** in order to cancel the effect of lay-offs or short time an employee must be offered work of a kind he is employed to do. This is not a case of a "suitable alternative offer" of work.

EXCLUSIONS FROM THE RIGHT TO A REDUNDANCY PAYMENT

16. The following employees are not entitled to a redundancy payment:

a.   Employees who have not completed at least two years' continuous employment with their employer.

b.   Employees who have reached the age of 65.

c.   Civil servants and other public employees.

d.   Persons employed as a domestic servant by someone to whom they are related.

e.   Share fishermen.

f.   Persons on a fixed term contract who have agreed in writing to exclude any right to a redundancy payment. (This is the only circumstance in which the statutory right to a redundancy payment may be excluded by a term in the contract of employment).

g.   Employees who are summarily dismissed for misconduct or if notice is given and is accompanied by a statement in writing that the employer would be entitled to terminate the contract without notice by reason of the employee's conduct. This provision does not apply where the dismissal is for taking part in a strike.

h.   Employees who, after having been given notice of dismissal for redundancy, accept oral or written offers of further employment on the same or similar conditions.

i.   Employees who unreasonably refuse oral or written offers of further employment on the same or similar conditions. Where the offer of continued employment is on different terms and conditions, the employee must be permitted a trial period of up to four weeks in which to decide whether the job is suitable.

j.   Persons outside Great Britain on the relevant date, unless they are ordinarily employed in Great Britain.

k.   Persons ordinarily employed outside Great Britain unless they are at the relevant date in Great Britain in accordance with their employer's instructions.

(The non-entitlement to persons outside GB does not apply to persons employed as master or seamen in a British ship who are ordinarily resident in GB.)

Note: *Suitable Alternative Offer and Reasonable Rejection.* Whether an offer of alternative employment is suitable or not must be determined objectively. If an employee's wages or status are considerably reduced, this will not normally amount to a suitable alternative. Even if the offer is suitable, an employee may not be barred from compensation if he can show that his refusal to accept it was not unreasonable in the circumstances. The latter is a subjective test, and may depend on personal or financial circumstances.

In **TAYLOR v KENT COUNTY COUNCIL (1969)** T was headmaster of a boys' school. The school was amalgamated with a girls' school and new head appointed over the combined school. T was offered employment in a pool of teachers, standing in for short periods in understaffed schools. He would retain his current salary. It was held that T was entitled to redundancy pay as he was being offered something substantially different, particularly in regard to status.

CALCULATION OF REDUNDANCY PAYMENTS

17.   The amount of the payment is related to the employee's length of continuous employment, age and gross average wage.

18.   Continuous Employment. This is employment on a contract of employment excluding the following:

   a.   Any week when the employee was on strike.

   b.   Any week before the employee's 18th birthday.

   c.   Any week when the employee was employed outside GB and no employer's contribution was payable in respect of that week.

19.   Employee's Age. The amount of redundancy payment is calculated on the following basis:

18 to 21 years of age	− ½ weeks pay	for each
22 to 40	− 1 weeks pay	year of
41 to 64	− 1½ weeks pay	service

Where an employee is made redundant in the year of retirement, the amount payable is reduced by one-twelfth for each month by which the age of the employee approaches retirement, this lower age limit does not count for calculation of the basic award for unfair dismissal.

20.   Calculation of Redundancy Pay. The maximum number of years to be taken into account is 20 and the maximum amount of a week's pay permitted in calculating the payment is currently £198 (from 1 Apr 91). This may be varied by the Secretary of State. The maximum payment is therefore £5,940 ie 20 x £198 x 1½.

EMPLOYMENT PROTECTION ACT 1975 (EPA)

21.   Notification of Redundancies. The employer has a duty under the *EPA* to notify both recognised trade unions and the Secretary of State for Employment of forthcoming redundancies.

22.   Notification to Trade Unions. An employer proposing to dismiss as redundant any employee of a class in respect of which he recognises a trade union must consult with the representatives of that union at the earliest opportunity, and in any event comply with the following timings:

   a.   Where it is proposed to dismiss 100 or more employees at one establishment within a period of 90 days or less, notification must be given at least 90 days before the first of the dismissals takes effect.

   b.   Where it is proposed to dismiss 10 or more, but less than 100 within a period of 30 days or less, notification must be given at least 30 days before the first of the dismissals takes effect.

The employer must begin consultations with the trade union representatives before giving individual notices of dismissal.

In **NATIONAL UNION OF TEACHERS v AVON COUNTY COUNCIL (1978)** the employers issued dismissal notices to some of their teachers on 28 October 1976. Consultation over redundancies with the recognised independent union was not started until 29 October 1976. It was held that the employer failed to comply with *S.99, EPA*, in that individual notices of dismissal should not have been issued before consultations begin.

23.   Consultation. For the purposes of consultation, the employer must disclose in writing to the trade union representatives the following:

   a.   Reasons for the proposed redundancies.

   b.   The number and description of the employees involved.

   c.   The total number in that category employed at the establishment.

   d.   The proposed method of selection for redundancy.

   e.   The proposed method of carrying out the dismissals.

24. The employer must consider any representations made by the trade union, reply to those representations and where he rejects any of them, state his reasons. Failure to consult may render the employer liable to a claim for unfair dismissal and a complaint by the trade union to an industrial tribunal.

25.   The Protective Award. Where a trade union makes a complaint, which is upheld by the tribunal, the tribunal may make a protective award. In this case the employer will have to pay remuneration to the specified employees for a protected period. This is the period beginning with the date on which the first of the dismissals take effect, or the date of the award whichever is the earlier.

The maximum awards permitted are:

a.   Up to 90 days' pay where a minimum of 90 days' notice should have been given;

b.   Up to 30 days' pay where a minimum of 30 days' notice should have been given; or

c.   Up to 28 days' pay in any other case.

In **JOSHUA WILSON & BROS. v USDAW (1978)**. The EAT made a protection award of 40 days because it found that on 31 January 1977 the employees were told that they were being made redundant as from 26 February, since the warehouse in which they were working was closing down. The employers recognised the independent union for collective bargaining purposes and there were no special circumstances in which the employers could claim exemption from their duty to consult the union.

26.   Any payment made by an employer to an employee in respect of any period covered by a protective award will offset the protective award.

27.   An employer who fails to consult with the trade union may use as a defence that special circumstances existed which made it impracticable to consult. Nevertheless he must show that he has taken steps to comply as are reasonably practicable.

28.   An employee himself cannot apply for a protective award but may complain to an industrial tribunal if he fails to receive full payment of any such award.

29.   Notification to the Department of Employment. The employer also has a duty to notify the D of E when he proposes to dismiss as redundant. The requirements are as for trade unions, given in paragraph **25.** a. and b.

30.   Failure to notify the D of E may lead to a fine.

MISCELLANEOUS PROVISIONS

31.   Death of Employer. Where the employer dies the employee is deemed to be dismissed and may claim a redundancy payment from his employer's personal representative, unless the business is carried on and re-engagement is offered and takes effect within 8 weeks.

32.   Death of Employee. Where the employee dies, any unresolved claims which are pending will survive him.

33.   Insolvency of Employer. A redundant employee may claim payment out of the Redundancy Fund where his employer is unable to make payment on the grounds of insolvency.

34.   Employee Leaving Before Expiry of Notice. A redundant employee wishing to leave before expiry of his notice may do so if he notifies his employer in writing and the employer has no objection. If the employer objects he must notify the employee of his objection and his intention to contest the redundancy payment.

35. Strikes During Notice. If, whilst serving notice due to redundancy, an employee is dismissed for going on strike he is still entitled to a redundancy payment. The employer may require him to return to work to complete the days lost due to the strike.

36. Written Statement. On making any redundancy payment, except as a result of a tribunal decision, the employer must give the employee a written statement indicating how the payment has been calculated.

37. Time Limit for Claims. Employees are not entitled to a redundancy payment after 6 months from the date of redundancy unless:-

    a. The payment has been agreed and paid;

    b. The employee has made a claim for payment in writing;

    c. A question as to the right of the employee to the payment, or to the amount, has been referred to an industrial tribunal;

    d. A complaint of unfair dismissal has been presented by the employee to an industrial tribunal.

An industrial tribunal may order a redundancy payment in respect of a late claim if it considers it "just and equitable". However, after one year has elapsed a claim will not be considered.

38. Exemption Orders. The Secretary of State for Employment may exempt employers from liability to make redundancy payments under the *EPCA* where they have similar or more advantageous agreements with their employees or with trade unions representing them.

49 Social Security

INTRODUCTION

1. The law in respect of Social Security benefits is mainly contained in the *SOCIAL SECURITY ACT 1975* and the *SOCIAL SECURITY & HOUSING BENEFIT ACT 1982*. The employment-related benefits covered in this Study are in respect of disablement benefits, unemployment, sickness and invalidity. The right to unemployment and sickness benefit depends on payment of a minimum number of weekly national insurance contributions.

INDUSTRIAL INJURIES

2. Where an employee suffers injury at work he may claim damages for his employer's negligence. If, however, the injury results without negligence on the part of his employer, apart from private insurance his only avenue for compensation may be through the Social Security Act in the form of sickness or disablement benefit. Prior to the *SOCIAL SECURITY & HOUSING BENEFIT ACT 1982* industrial injuries benefit was payable if an employee was absent from work due to an industrial injury which complied with the rules. The current position is that an industrial injury resulting in absence from work will give entitlement to sickness benefit. However the criteria for determining whether or not an injury is resulting from an accident in the course of, and arising out of employment is important for the purpose of disablement benefits and, where the claimant has insufficient contributions for entitlement to sickness benefit within the normal rules.

3. **Exemptions from the Scheme.** In the following circumstances there is no entitlement to claim benefits for injuries under the Act.

    a. Where employment is of a casual nature, eg, assistance to a farmer at harvest-time. (This does not refer to part-time work.)

    b. Employment by one's spouse, or employment on household duties by a near relative.

    c. Self-employed persons.

4. **Risks Insured Against.** The Act insures against the following risks:

    a. Personal injury caused by an accident "arising out of" employment.

    b. A disease, or personal injury, not caused by accident, but arising from the nature of the person's employment. (The distinction between a. and b. is between an unforeseen single event and exposure to conditions over a period of time.)

Note:

    1. "Injury" includes mental as well as physical injuries. In **YATES v SOUTH KIRBY COLLIERIES LTD (1910)** it was stated that "Nervous

432

shock due to an accident which causes incapacity is as much personal injury by accident as a broken leg''.

2.   The term "accident" is construed as being an unlooked-for mishap or an untoward event which is not expected or designed. Over-exertion causing a rupture was held to be an accident, and a draught causing a chill.

Where there has been a progressive deterioration of health resulting in personal injury it will not generally be regarded as an accident, eg a doctor who contracted tuberculosis as a result of prolonged exposure to bacilli over a long period of time. However, a trainee nurse who contracted infantile paralysis within seven days of nursing a patient was held to have suffered an industrial accident.

Other court decisions are as follows:

In **BRINTON v TURVEY (1905)** a workman was sorting out wool when a bacillus entered his eye and resulted in anthrax from which he died. It was held to be an accident although the employee actually died from a disease.

In **TRIM JOINT DISTRICT SCHOOL BOARD OF MANAGE-MENT v KELLY (1914)** a schoolmaster at an industrial school was killed by the premeditated act of pupils he was supervising in the school yard. It was held to be an "accident" even though it was a premeditated act by third parties.

Even suicide may be regarded as an industrial accident if it can be shown to be causally related to the injury, eg a miner who was almost blinded and in great pain committed suicide; it was held that he died as a result of an industrial accident. However an employee who committed suicide because he was told he would have to remain off work for a lengthy period was held not to have died as a result of an accident.

5.   **"In the Course of Employment".** This refers to the time element of employment and includes:

a.   The contractual hours of work and reasonable periods before and after those hours, eg, time to change clothes at the beginning and end of work.

b.   Interruptions in contractual hours, eg, authorised breaks for meals eaten on the premises, teabreaks, etc.

In **R v INDUSTRIAL INJURIES COMMISSION Ex Parte AEU (1966)** smoking was prohibited in a factory except in booths provided, during the 10 minutes teabreak. An employee was injured while waiting outside a booth, but after the teabreak had finished. It was held that the injury was outside the course of employment.

c.   Travelling to and from work as a passenger in a vehicle supplied by the employer. However, it was decided in **VANDYKE v FENDER (1970)** that such a claim will only succeed where the employee is obliged to travel by this method, ie, where such travel is part of the contract of service.

433

6.   "Arising Out of Employment". This refers to the reasons for the accident, as follows:

a.   Performing a task for which he was employed, or one which is incidental to his employment, ie if an employee is injured whilst working on a different machine, without authority, he would not be entitled to benefit.

b.   A task performed in an unauthorised manner, but for the benefit of the employer, will be deemed to arise out of employment. A miner, injured whilst travelling to the coal-face on a coal wagon, contrary to regulations, was entitled to benefit.

c.   Accidents occurring during emergencies are deemed to have arisen out of employment, eg, an employee injured whilst fighting a fire.

d.   Accidents to which the claimant has not contributed are deemed to have arisen out of employment when due to:

i.   *Another person's conduct,* ie sky-larking, negligence or a criminal act. A collector of insurance premiums was robbed and injured, it was held to be an accident in the course of employment. A foreman was struck by an employee whom he reprimanded and it was held to be an accident in the course of employment.

ii.   *The presence of an animal* (including bird, fish or insect).

e.   Events not arising out of employment include:

i.   *Assault,* as a result of a quarrel not connected with work, eg a workman who asked another for assistance which was refused called the other a "lazy swine" and had some teeth knocked out as a result. It was held that the truculent attitude of the injured workman converted the dispute into a personal quarrel.

ii.   *Common risks* (eg street accidents), eg an employee who is injured in a street accident after leaving work is regarded as a member of the public. However a person employed as a messenger injured in this manner whilst on his employer's business would be regarded as having suffered an injury in the course and arising out of his employment. This would be the case also, where an employee was injured whilst travelling to or from work in a manner prescribed in his contract of employment where the vehicle is operated by or on behalf of his employer and not in the ordinary course of a public transport service.

iii.   *Unauthorised acts,* where an employee carries out a task he is not employed to do, eg a Post Office worker was injured whilst putting up Christmas decorations at a post office. He had been asked to do this task by his immediate superior, and there was no objection from his employers. Nevertheless he was not entitled to benefit.

However, a colliery worker injured whilst going to the canteen to buy a replacement bootlace, necessary before he could start work, was entitled to benefit.

434

iv.   *Games,* even authorised games, eg a police constable who was injured whilst playing for his county police team, on his rest day was not entitled to benefit, even though his participation was beneficial, eg to the police "image". However the member of a fire brigade injured during recreational training would be regarded as having suffered an injury arising out of his employment, as recreational training is a normal part of a fireman's duty.

7.   Industrial Diseases. In addition to accidents, the following may be included in the scheme:

a.   Selected diseases, eg Asbestosis, and,

b.   Personal injuries arising from the nature of the employment, ie, prolonged exposure to certain working conditions.

c.   To claim the benefit the employee must prove:

i.   He has the disease;

ii.   That he was employed in the particular occupation during the time the disease was contracted.

8.   Benefits

a.   *Industrial disablement benefit.*

i.   There is no maximum period of payment.

ii.   The benefit is claimed where:

a.   The employee will be capable of work despite some permanent injury suffered (eg. lost fingers).

b.   Sickness benefit having expired, there remains some lasting effect of the injury, and the employee is still incapable of work.

b.   *Industrial death benefit.*

i.   Paid to the widowed dependant spouse (male or female) or exceptionally to parents.

ii.   Death must have resulted from an accident or industrial disease.

c.   *Disqualification from benefit.* An employee may be disqualified from receiving benefit for a maximum of six weeks under the following circumstances:

i.   Industrial Injury Benefit (now sickness benefit) may be withheld where the claimant does not attend for medical examination and treatment when required to do so.

ii.   Disablement Benefit may be withheld where the claimant does not attend:

a.   for medical examination and treatment when required to do so, or

b.   a suitable course of vocational training or rehabilitation approved by the Department of Employment.

UNEMPLOYMENT BENEFIT

9.   The *SOCIAL SECURITY ACT 1975* gives the rules under which an employee who loses his job may be assisted by payment of unemployment benefit. Entitlement depends on payment of contributions to a specified standard, provided he is not in gainful employment, but is available for employment if require.

10.   Disqualification

a.   *Trade disputes.* A claimant is disqualified from benefit when he is unemployed owing to a trade dispute (eg, a strike) at his place of employment, unless he can show that:

i.   He was not participating in the dispute, or,

ii.   He had obtained employment elsewhere and was subsequently unemployed for a reason other than a trade dispute. Benefit is payable only from the date of subsequent unemployment.

In **PUNTON AND ANOTHER v M.P.N.I. (1963)** the case involved a demarcation dispute in a shipyard between platers and shipwrights (skilled workers belonging to different trade unions). The plaintiffs were semi-skilled platers' assistants belonging to a different union. Their claim for unemployment benefit for the period of the dispute was rejected. It was held that the plaintiffs had failed to prove that they were not directly involved in the dispute. Since a plater and a plater's assistant work as a team the platers' assistants had as great an interest in the type and volume of work as the platers themselves.

b.   *Other causes.* Disqualification for a maximum of 6 weeks may occur under the following circumstances:

i.   Leaving employment voluntarily, without "just cause" (the onus is on the employee to establish that he had just cause for leaving). Examples of just cause would be serious domestic problems, difficulties in travelling to work and leaving to go to another job which fails to materialise. Leaving employment on voluntary redundancy is regarded as a "just cause".

ii.   Dismissal owing to misconduct. The test of misconduct is whether it would lead a reasonable employer to terminate the claimant's employment. However proceedings at an industrial tribunal or court are not conclusive as far as determining social security benefits are concerned. For example, in one case a shop manager was acquitted for embezzlement yet was disqualified from unemployment benefit. He had been dismissed when the cash was found to be missing from the till, but despite the acquittal, the loss showed that he was incompetent to handle money.

iii.   Failure (without just cause) to apply for employment of which he had been informed, or to accept employment offered to him.

iv.   Neglect to take "reasonable opportunity of suitable employment".

v.   Failure to take a recommended course of training.

c.   *Suitable employment.* The following are not regarded as being suitable employment:

i.   A vacancy arising from a trade dispute (ie, an unemployed person cannot be expected to take over the work of a striker).

ii.   Where conditions of employment are less favourable than those generally observed, or to which the claimant is accustomed.

iii.   Work of a different kind, unless a reasonable time has elapsed since his last employment.

iv.   Work which may cause deterioration to health.

v.   Work involving excessive travelling, thus causing financial hardship to his family.

As the period of unemployment increases the claimant has a greater obligation to accept employment of a different kind.

SICKNESS BENEFIT

11.   Entitlement. Employees are entitled to sickness benefit subject to the same conditions as for unemployment benefit.

A person is entitled to claim if he is incapable of work through illness or disablement.

12.   Disqualification. A maximum of 6 weeks disqualification may be imposed for the following reasons:

a.   Incapable of work because of own misconduct.

b.   Refusal or failure to undergo medical treatment without "just cause".

c.   Retarding recovery owing to own misconduct.

d.   Following gainful employment on medical advice.

13.   Invalidity Benefit. Invalidity benefit normally replaces sickness benefit when this has been paid for 168 working days and the incapacity continues. It consists of Invalidity Pension and Invalidity Allowance. The latter is payable in conjunction with Invalidity Pension when the claimant has become chronically sick more than 5 years before the statutory retirement age.

The benefit is paid until the statutory retirement age, or the incapacity ceases, whichever is sooner.

ADMINISTRATION OF BENEFITS

14.   The Secretary of State for Health and Social Security has overall responsibility for the administration of Social Security benefits. However, the day-to-day administration falls upon the local officers of the DHSS. The system for claims is outlined below:

a.   All claims are dealt with initially by local insurance officers of the DHSS. All claims are against the State, not the employer, and there is no appeal to the courts of law except as indicated below.

b.   The claimant may appeal against the local insurance officer's decision to the Local Appeal Tribunal, and thence to the National Insurance Commissioner.

c.   The local insurance officer may refer medical questions to the Local Medical Board and, if rejected, the claimant may appeal to the Medical Appeal Tribunal. Industrial Injuries cases may be referred to the Industrial Injuries Commission.

d.   The local insurance officer must refer "special questions" to the Secretary of State, eg,

>   i.   Whether a person is or was in insurable employment.
>
>   ii.   Whether a person is exempt from paying contributions.
>
>   iii. Who is liable to pay the employer's contributions.
>
>   iv.   Rate of contribution payable.

STATUTORY SICK PAY

15. Under the *SOCIAL SECURITY AND HOUSING BENEFIT ACT 1982* employers took over almost total responsibility for payment of sickness benefit to employees. The employer will pay the employee direct for the first 28 weeks of sickness in each tax year. It is illegal to pay SSP on top of a contractual payment.

16. Entitlement to SSP will depend on three tests as follows:

a.   *Incapacity for work.*

>   i.   The employer must be satisfied that the employee is incapable of doing work under the contract of employment.
>
>   ii.   There must be a period of incapacity of at least four consecutive days including Sunday.

b.   *Entitlement to SSP.* The following are excluded in respect of SSP:

>   i.   employees over state pensionable age.
>
>   ii.   employees with contracts of less than three calendar months.
>
>   iii. employees with earnings less than lower earnings level set for payment of N.I. contributions.
>
>   iv.   employees who are sick within 8 weeks of receiving other State benefits.
>
>   v.   new employees who have done no work for the new employer.
>
>   vi.   if there is a trade dispute and the employee cannot prove that he was not involved in the dispute.

vii. during the 11 weeks before the expected date of confinement (maternity) and 6 weeks after.

viii. maximum entitlement already reached (28 weeks in each tax year).

ix. illness in an European Community country counts as for the UK.

x. if the employee is detained in legal custody.

c. **Days which count.** SSP is only payable for qualifying days. The first 3 qualifying days are "waiting days".

50 Industrial Injuries – Employer's Liability

INTRODUCTION

1. An employer has a responsibility for the safety of his employees whilst at work. This responsibility includes common law and statutory duties. The duties of the employer are discussed in Chapters 43 and 44. If an employee suffers injury at work he may be entitled to claim compensation from his employer. In this chapter we consider the courses and remedies open to an employee injured at work, and an employer's defences. In addition the subjects of fatal accidents and limitation of action by lapse of time are covered.

COMMON LAW

2. **Action by an Employee.** If an employee suffers injury as a result of the failure of his employer's common law duties of safety the employee must prove the following if he wishes to claim damages:

   a. There was a duty imposed on the employer, ie, the common law duty to provide a safe system of work, safe premises, etc, and

   b. The employer failed to carry out his duties in a reasonable manner. This action is on the grounds of negligence, and

   c. The employee suffered an injury as a *direct* result of the breach. It is possible that an injury suffered by an employee may not be as a direct result of his employer's breach of duty, ie the fault may lie with the employee (**McWILLIAMS v SIR WM ARROL (1962)**) or the chain of causation may have been broken **QUINN v BURCH BROTHERS LTD (1966)**. A breach of contract to supply plant to a sub-contractor was not a "cause" of the sub-contractor being injured by using makeshift equipment, but just the "opportunity" or "occasion".

   If there are several reasons for the occurrence of an accident the court will single out the root cause and base judgement on this.

   In **DAVIES v MANN (1842)** a vehicle ran into a donkey which was tethered in the middle of the road, in broad daylight. It was held that whilst the animal would not have been run over if it had not been there, the root cause of the accident was negligent driving.

3. **Employer's Defences.** An employer may attempt to refute his employee's action by raising the following defences:

   a. *Deny the breach of duty.* For example the employer may show that the claimant was acting outside the course of employment when injured, eg he was on "a frolic of his own". Or he may show that he had used all reasonable care, eg in making all efforts to persuade his employee to use safety equipment. **WOODS v DURABLE SUITES LTD (1953)**.

b.   *Plead "Volenti non fit injuria".* Literally this means "That to which a man consents cannot be considered an injury". The nature of this defence is that in a dangerous employment situation the employee is not only aware of the risk, but freely takes the risk. This defence is normally applicable to jobs with high inherent dangers. There must be no pressure on the employee to take the risk (eg the threat of loss of his job), and the employer must prove that the employee willingly agreed to the risk.

BOWATER v ROWLEY REGIS CORPORATION (1944) (See Chapter 24.3c).

Contrast **BOLT v WM MOSS & SONS LTD (1966)** where a workman, expressly informed of the danger, persisted in performing a task in a dangerous manner (having a painter's moveable scaffold moved whilst remaining on it). It was held that volenti was a good defence because the task was undertaken entirely with full knowledge of the risk.

ICI LTD v SHATWELL (1964) (See Chapter 24.3b).

c.   *Plead contributory negligence.* This defence, whilst admitting a breach of duty, attempts to secure a reduction in any damages awarded because of the employee's own negligence. "Contributory negligence" was introduced by the *LAW REFORM (CONTRIBUTORY NEGLIGENCE) ACT 1945*. This is not merely carelessness or inadvertence as an employer has a greater degree of responsibility for the employee's safety than he does for himself. It is more in the nature of a deliberate flouting of safety regulations.

In awards of contributory negligence the motive would be taken into account, eg, if the employee was acting in the employer's best interest the negligence attributable to the employee would tend to be lower.

In **SHILTON v HUGHES-JOHNSON (1963)** an employee was injured whilst investigating a fault in a press without first switching off the machine, as to do so would have stopped all production. It was held that the employee was contributorily negligent, but as he had acted in the best interest of the employer by not causing a stoppage of production, the amount of contributory negligence was reduced.

d.   *Deny the existence of an employer/employee relationship.* This would generally be a good defence unless the injury arose as a result of the employer's breach of duty of common care to visitors, as the occupier of premises.

e.   *Rely on an exemption clause in the contract of service.* This would be extremely rare, relating only to very risky jobs, eg circus acts. An exemption clause for accidents which are no fault of the employer is still valid. However a clause which purports to exempt an employer for liability for an accident caused by his own or the employee's negligence is invalid

441

under the *UNFAIR CONTRACT TERMS ACT 1977*. The Act states that liability for personal injury through negligence cannot be excluded or restricted by any contract term or notice.

STATUTE

4.   In order to claim damages for an employer's breach of a statutory duty, eg under the Factories Act, the employee must prove:

a.   The employer failed to comply with the statutory duty, eg failure to fence a dangerous piece of machinery,

b.   The employee was injured as a result of the breach, and

c.   The injury was of a class the duty was designed to prevent.

Generally statutory duties are specific and well defined, and are thus easier to prove than breaches of common law duties. In some cases statutory duties of care are "absolute" whereas the common law duties tend to require only "reasonable" care.

5.   **The Employer's Defences.** An employer may bring the following defences to counter an allegation of breach of statutory duty:

a.   Deny the breach.

b.   Allege contributory negligence.

c.   Deny employer/employee relationship. This defence would not be valid against all breaches of statutory duty as some sections of, eg, the Factories Act make an employer liable to "all persons working on the premises", ie, including independent contractors.

Note:

1.   The employer cannot exclude statutory duties in a contract of service.

2.   The statutes exist to protect the employee, therefore volenti non fit injuria cannot be pleaded.

FATAL ACCIDENTS

6.   The *FATAL ACCIDENTS ACT 1976* (amended by the *ADMINISTRATION OF JUSTICE ACT 1983*) gives certain rights to the dependants in the circumstances where an employee dies due to an employer's breach of duty such as would have given the deceased employee a right to an action for damages if he had lived.

7.   **Definition of "Dependant".** In the Act a dependant means:

a.   The wife or husband of the deceased.

b.   The parent or grandparent of the deceased.

c.   A child or grandchild of the deceased.

d.   A brother, sister, aunt or uncle of the deceased.

e.   A son or daughter of the brother, sister, aunt or uncle of the deceased.

The Act also includes step-children and illegitimate children.

8.   Persons Entitled to Bring the Action. In the first place action should be taken by the executor or administrator of the deceased. In the event of there being no executor or administrator or if the action is not commenced within six months after death the action may be taken by, and in the name of, all or any of the dependants. However, only one action may be taken in respect of the subject matter of the complaint.

9.   Assessment of Damages

a.   Damages awarded may be divided amongst the dependants as directed.

b.   In the case of damages awarded to a widow, no account shall be taken of her remarriage or her prospects for remarriage.

c.   Damages may be awarded in respect of funeral expenses.

d.   Damages may be awarded in respect of bereavement, which may only be paid for the benefit of the wife or husband of the deceased or in the case of an unmarried child, his parents.

e.   Damages will not be reduced by any financial benefits received by the dependants on account of insurance money, pensions, or benefits received in respect of social security or payment by a trade union or friendly society.

f.   Any saving to the injured person attributable to his maintenance at public expense in a hospital or other institution shall be set off against loss of income attributable to his injuries.

Note: The estate may claim for other than loss of earnings under the *LAW REFORM (MISCELLANEOUS PROVISIONS) ACT 1934*, eg, pain and loss of amenities. However any damages awarded under this Act would be subject to reduction for contributory negligence.

THE LIMITATION ACT 1980

10. The *LIMITATION ACT 1980* lays down time limits and other rules for the bringing of actions in respect of wrongs causing personal injuries or death.

a.   No action may be brought after the expiration of three years from:

i.   The date on which the cause of action arose; or,

ii.   The date of the plaintiff's knowledge, if the extent of the injury is not immediately apparent.

b.   If a claim is made under the *FATAL ACCIDENTS ACT 1976* no action may be brought after the expiration of three years from:

i.   The date of death; or,

443

ii.   The date of knowledge of the person for whose benefit the action is brought, whichever is the later.

11.   Reference to a plaintiff's date of knowledge is a reference to the date on which he first had knowledge of the following facts:

a.   The injury was significant (sufficiently serious to justify proceedings).

b.   The injury was attributable to the act of alleged negligence or breach of duty.

c.   The identity of the defendant (eg, in the case of vicarious liability or, for example, a "hit and run" driver).

A person's knowledge includes his own observable knowledge or facts ascertainable with the help of medical or other expert advice.

12.   The court may override the time limit if it considers it equitable to do so, taking into account, eg, the reasons for the plaintiff's delay, eg, the nature of the injury being such that the plaintiff is incapable of making judgements.

ASSESSMENT OF DAMAGES

13.   Damages may be awarded under two general headings, ie Special and General damages.

a.   *Special damages.* These are awarded on the basis of an estimated loss of earnings. This includes not only loss of present earnings, but an estimate of future loss. It would take into account the employee's age, his position and his earnings potential.

b.   *General damages.* These are at the discretion of the court and include such things as, loss of expectation of life, pain and suffering, expenses, loss of faculties and loss of enjoyment of life. In past cases general damages have been awarded where an employee has become sexually impotent due to an accident, and where an employee has lost the ability to enjoy his recreational pursuits, eg, darts playing or dancing.

14.   Any damages awarded will be reduced by, eg, contributory negligence, a proportion of any benefits received under the Social Security Acts and an estimated amount of income tax which would have been payable on future earnings.

51 The Factories Act 1961

INTRODUCTION

1. The *FACTORIES ACT 1961* places certain statutory obligations on employers for the safety, health and welfare of their employees. The factory occupier, usually the employer, has the responsibility for compliance with the Act. If he fails to comply with the Act he may face a criminal prosecution brought by the factories inspector. In addition he may face a civil action for damages by an injured employee.

DEFINITION OF A FACTORY

2. It is important to define a factory as the Act covers only such premises. The definition is given in *S.175 (1)*. An outline is given below.

   a. Any premises in which, or within the precincts of which, persons are employed in manual labour in any process for or incidental to:

      i. The making of any article or part of any article, or

      ii. The altering, repairing, ornamenting, finishing, cleaning or washing, or the breaking up or demolition of any article, or the adapting for sale of any article or

      iii. The slaughtering of animals, or

      iv. The confinement of such animals while awaiting slaughter at other premises, and

   b. Being premises in which, or within the precincts of which, the work is carried on by way of trade or for the purposes of gain and to once over which the employer of the persons employed therein has the right of access or control.

DEVELOPMENT OF *S.175 (1)*

3. The definition of a factory has been interpreted as follows:

   a. *Premises.* No type of building is debarred from being considered a factory by its characteristics, etc. In fact, from the definition above, a factory need not be a building, eg, it may be a building site.

   b. *Manual labour.* A place cannot be a factory unless it is one in which manual labour is performed. Some court decisions are as follows:

      i. A workshop attached to a shop is not automatically debarred from being considered a factory.

      In **HOARE v GREEN (ROBERT) LTD (1907)** the case concerned a florist's shop. In a room behind the shop employees made wreaths, bouquets, etc. It was held to be a factory.

ii.   The amount of physical effort is irrelevant.

In **FULLERS LTD v SQUARE (1901)** the packing of sweets into a box, which was then sold retail, was held to be manual labour but,

iii.   The manual labour must not be merely incidental to the main purposes of the premises.

In **JOYCE v BOOTS CASH CHEMISTS (SOUTHERN) LTD (1950)** a porter in a shop was engaged in manual labour. It was held that this was merely incidental to the main purposes of the premises.

c.   *Adapting for sale.* This has been defined as ''something done to the article which, in some way makes it, in itself, a little different from what it was before.''

d.   *Trade or gain.*

i.   Trade includes sale of goods or supplying of services.

ii.   Premises of the Crown or of any public authority shall not be excluded only by reason that they do not operate for trade or gain. However, H.M. Prisons are not factories.

e.   *Other instances.*

i.   Repair sheds for repairing factory equipment are parts of a factory.

ii.   A workers' canteen is part of the factory, but an administrative staff canteen is not.

MAIN PROVISIONS OF THE ACT

4.   General Health Provisions. An outline of the general health provisions of the Factories Act is given below:

a.   *Cleanliness.* Every factory must be kept in a clean state and free from effluvia arising from drains, etc. Accumulations of dirt and refuse must be removed daily. All floors, walls and ceilings of the factory must be washed within certain periods of time. There is also provision for repainting.

b.   *Overcrowding.* Each person must be allowed 400 cubic foot in each workroom and a notice posted in every workroom specifying the number of persons who may be employed therein.

c.   *Temperature.* A reasonable temperature must be maintained. What is ''reasonable'' depends on such circumstances as the nature of the process and time of the year.

d.   *Ventilation.* Each workroom must be adequately ventilated by circulation of fresh air.

e.   *Lighting.* Sufficient and suitable lighting must be maintained in every part of a factory in which persons are working or passing. Windows and skylights must be kept clean.

f.   *Floor drainage.* If the process is one that makes floors wet, there must be adequate means of draining.

g.   *Sanitary conveniences.* Sufficient and suitable sanitary conveniences must be provided, with separate accommodation where persons of both sexes are employed. The conveniences must be kept clean and well-lit and ventilated.

SAFETY

5.   This is one of the most important areas covered by the Factories Act, and the student should be completely familiar with all provisions and the more important cases to which this area has given rise.

6.   Fencing. The Act demands that certain kinds of machinery must be securely fenced:

a.   Every flywheel directly connected to a prime mover and every moving part of a prime mover. (A prime mover is machinery from which power originates.)

b.   Every part of transmission machinery.

c.   Every dangerous part of any machinery ("A part of machinery is dangerous if it is a possible cause of injury to anybody acting in a way in which a human being may be reasonably expected to act in circumstances which may be reasonably expected to occur.")

7.   Case Law on Fencing of Machinery. The rules on fencing have been amplified by case law as follows:

a.   The accident must be one which could reasonably have been foreseen:

In **CARR v MERCANTILE PRODUCE CO LTD (1949)** a girl working a macaroni-making machine put her hand inside it and was injured. To do this she had to force her hand through a narrow aperture. It was held that the employers were not liable as such an accident was not reasonably foreseeable.

b.   The duty to fence is absolute and cannot be set aside because of impracticability.

In **JOHN SUMMERS & SONS LTD v FROST (1955)** an employee injured his hand when it came into contact with a revolving grindstone. If the stone had been completely fenced it could not have been used. It was held that impracticability was not a good reason for the failure to fence, as the duty was an absolute one.

447

c.   The Minister may exempt specific machinery from the fencing regulations (where fencing would render the machine unusable if completely guarded).

d.   Where a machine is guarded, such guard must be secure and proof against foreseeable contingencies.

In **BURNS v J TERRY & SONS LTD (1951)** the transmission machinery on a cocoa-grinding machine was fenced below and on the sides, but not above. B tried to clear beans from a shelf above the machine. He did this by placing a ladder against the machine, but did not switch it off. He was injured when his arm came into contact with the transmission machinery. It was held that the machine was securely fenced as the accident could not have been foreseen.

e.   The fencing provisions are designed to prevent the worker from coming into contact with the machine. They do not apply to parts of the machine flying out.

f.   Although there is no general liability concerning danger from materials used in the machine, the Minister may make specific regulations in this respect.

In **BULLOCK v POWER (1956)** an employee was killed when struck by a backlash from wire being stretched. It was held that unless special provisions regarding these material had been issued by the factory inspector, the firm would not be liable, under the Factories Act.

g.   The duty to fence applies only to machinery in use in the factory, not to machinery under construction or accepted for repairs.

In **PARVIN v MORTON MACHINE CO LTD (1952)** a boy was injured whilst cleaning a dough-brake made in his employer's factory. The machine had not been fenced. It was held that as it had been manufactured in the factory, the duty to fence did not apply.

h.   The duty to guard machinery exists in relation to all persons employed or working on the premises − whether they have any business near a machine or not.

In **UDDIN v ASSOCIATED PORTLAND CEMENT (1965)** U, an employee, entered a room containing unguarded machinery in an upper part of the factory. He had no right to enter this part of the premises, and did so in order to catch a pigeon roosting there. U was injured by the machinery. It was held that the company was liable as the fact that there were warning notices did not excuse their duty to fence the machine, and even workers "on a frolic of their own" could rely on the protection of the Act.

i.   All fences/guards must be maintained in place and in good order (except for necessary cleaning).

j.   It is an offence to sell or hire new machines which are not guarded.

8.   Means of Access

a.   All means of access must be sound, well maintained, protected by hand-rails or fences where applicable, and kept free from obstruction as far as is reasonably practicable.

In **BRAHAM v J LYONS & CO (1962)** B, employed in J.L.'s sausage department fell and was injured when she stepped on a slippery substance on the floor. J.L's employed two men permanently to clean the floor. It was held that the company was not liable as it had taken all reasonable measures to keep the floor free from such substances.

b.   Obstructions should be moved by the occupier, but again reasonable action only is required of him.

In **LEVESLEY v THOMAS FIRTH & JOHN BROWN LTD (1953)** L, an employee, tripped over a piece of metal lying on the floor and was injured. The object had fallen off a lorry a short time before the accident. It was held that the company was not liable as the obstruction was transient and could not have been foreseen.

c.   Persons included under these provisions are all persons working in the factory (including employees of independent contractors), but not persons who have no business there.

d.   Confined places particularly where dangerous fumes may be present, must have suitable means of egress; if necessary breathing apparatus and a belt with a rope attached must be available.

9.   Other Special Safety Provisions

a.   Fencing or securing of vessels containing dangerous liquids.

b.   Hoists and lifts must be of sound construction and well maintained. (Examinations at 6 monthly intervals are reported to the District Inspector and entered in the General Register). They must also be properly enclosed, equipped with interlocking safety doors, and carry notices denoting maximum working loads.

c.   Similar provisions apply to cranes (except that minimum period of inspection is 14 months).

10.   Miscellaneous Regulations.
The responsibility for observance of provisions of the Act rests primarily on the occupier of the factory.

a.   Exemption from any liability can only be gained if he can show:

i.   He has used all diligence to enforce the Act, and the offence has been committed by another person.

ii.   That the other person committed the offence without consent, or connivance (eg, if the machines were hired from a third party on whom the duty to guard would fall).

449

b.   Persons employed in the factory would also be guilty of an offence if they wilfully misuse or interfere with appliances, etc, provided by the Act, or wilfully commit acts which would endanger themselves or others.

ENFORCEMENT OF THE ACT

11.   Inspectorate. The responsibility for enforcing the provisions of the Act rests mainly with the Factory Inspector. In addition to the powers listed below the Factory Inspector has been given other powers under the HSAWA, eg, to issue improvement notices.

An inspector of factories may:

a.   Enter, inspect and examine a factory at all reasonable times of day or night, when he has reason to believe anyone is employed there, or enter, by day, any place which he believes is a factory. He may take a constable with him if he thinks he may be seriously obstructed in his work. It is an offence for the occupier to obstruct the inspector in his duties.

b.   Require the production of statutory registers, and other documents for inspection.

c.   Make examinations and inquiries as necessary regarding young persons employed therein.

d.   Require any person to render information concerning the identity of the occupier.

e.   Obtain signed declarations from anyone he has reason to believe has been employed in the factory within the previous two months.

f.   Conduct or defend proceedings before a court providing he has written authority from the Minister.

52 Health and Safety at Work Act 1974

INTRODUCTION

1.   The *HEALTH AND SAFETY AT WORK ACT 1974* was based on the recommendations of the Robens Committee of Enquiry on Safety and Health at Work. Statutes involving safety at work, eg, the *FACTORIES ACT 1961* and the *OFFICES, SHOPS AND RAILWAY PREMISES ACT 1963* left many persons outside safety legislation, eg, those employed in education, leisure activities, etc. The *HSAWA* is intended to provide for reasonable safety at all places of employment. The Act covers not only persons at work (including the self-employed) but also the general public. The only excluded category is that of domestic employment. The HSAWA has been amended by the Consumer Protection Act 1987. The main amendments are concerned with the inclusion of the obligations for safety on the manufacturers, suppliers, importers and installers of fairground equipment, and powers of customs officers to detain articles and substances.

2.   In due course most of the existing health and safety legislation will be replaced by a system of Regulations and approved Codes of Practice. The Act set up a Health and Safety Commission and a Health and Safety Executive to be responsible for the enforcement of the Act through the Factory Inspectorate. However, the Secretary of State is responsible for the promulgation of the necessary regulations and Codes of Practice.

3.   The essential difference between a Regulation and a Code of Practice is that the former is legally enforceable, but the latter is not. Regulations will be supplemented by Codes of Practice and these may be used as evidence that statutory requirements have been contravened. For further amplification of Codes of Practice see Chapter 53, para 3.e.

GENERAL DUTIES OF EMPLOYERS TO THEIR EMPLOYEES

4.   Health, Safety and Welfare. Under *S.2.* of the Act it is the duty of an employer to ensure, so far as is reasonably practicable the health, safety and welfare at work of all his employees. This duty covers the following aspects:-

   a.   The provision of plant and systems of work that are safe and without risks to health.

   b.   Arrangements for ensuring safety and absence of risks to health in connection with the use, handling, storage and transport of articles and substances.

   c.   The provision of such information, instruction, training and supervision as is necessary to ensure the health and safety at work of his employees.

   d.   With regards to any place of work under the employer's control. He must maintain it in a safe condition and without risks to health, and provide safe means of access to and egress from his premises.

e.   The provision and maintenance of a working environment that is safe, without risk to health and with adequate facilities and arrangements for his employees' welfare.

The above duties are not absolute but require the employer to exercise "reasonable care". Thus they accord with an employer's common law duties toward his employees.

5.   Information and Consultation. An employer must comply with the following provision with regard to the supply of information and consultation with trade unions:-

a.   Provide a written statement of safety policy, eg, accident procedure, action on outbreak of fire, safety training. An establishment with fewer than five employees is exempt from this provision.

b.   Where the appointment is made of a safety representative by a recognised trade union or other employees he shall represent the employees in consultations with the employer.

c.   The employer must consult any such representatives with a view to the making and maintenance of arrangements for enabling their effective cooperation in promoting, developing and monitoring measures to ensure the health and safety at work of the employees.

d.   Appoint a safety committee on the request of two or more safety representatives.

DUTIES TO PERSONS OTHER THAN EMPLOYEES

6.   The following duties are imposed on employers and self-employed persons for the safety and health of their employees *(S.3.)*:-

a.   An employer and a self-employed person shall conduct his under-taking in such a manner that persons other than employees are not exposed to risks to their health or safety.

b.   The also have the duty to give information to persons other than employees, who may be affected by the way the business is carried out. Such information will detail aspects of the way in which the business is carried out which may affect their health or safety.

DUTIES OF PERSONS IN CONTROL OF PREMISES *(S.4, 5)*

7.   Health and Safety. The Act provides that a person who has control of any work premises owes a general duty of care to persons other than his employees who are working there.

8.   His duty shall be to ensure, as far as is reasonably practicable that the premises and means of access to and egress from, and any plant or substance in the premises are safe and without risks to health.

Similar provisions are laid down in the *OCCUPIERS LIABILITY ACT 1957*. However contravention of the Occupiers Liability Act is a civil offence, contravention of the *HSAWA* is a criminal offence.

9.   Harmful Emissions. A person who has control of a business where noxious or offensive fumes are involved must do his best to prevent these fumes from entering the atmosphere, and to render them harmless if they are emitted.

DUTIES OF MANUFACTURERS AND INSTALLERS *(S.6.)*

10. The Act requires anyone who designs, manufactures, imports or supplies an article or substance for use at work to ensure that such article or substance is safe when used in accordance with the instructions issued by them.

11. The duty extends to the provision of instructions for the user and the carrying out of any necessary testing, inspection and research to ensure compliance with the obligations of safety.

12. Those who install plant have a duty to ensure it is safely installed.

DUTIES OF EMPLOYEES *(S.7.)*

13. An employee has the following duties:-

a.   To act, in the course of employment, with due care for the health and safety of himself, other workers and other persons who may be affected by his acts or omissions at work (ie, the general public).

b.   To observe the provision of the Act insofar as it concerns him and is under his control.

c.   To cooperate with his employer to enable compliance with the requirements of the Act.

GENERAL DUTIES

14. The Act makes provision for the following general duties:-

a.   No person shall interfere with or misuse anything provided under any statutory provision in the interests of health, safety and welfare, eg safety clothing, washing facilities. *(S.8.)*

b.   An employer shall not levy a charge on his employees for anything provided to meet the legal requirements. *(S.9.)*

HEALTH AND SAFETY COMMISSION *(S.10-14)*

15. The Act made provision for the setting up of two corporate bodies, the Health and Safety Commission and the Health and Safety Executive.

16. Composition of the Commission. The Commission is comprised of a Chairman and not less than six but not more than eight members appointed by the Secretary of State: three after consultation with employers' organisations, three after consultation with the TUC and two others appointed from local authorities.

17. Composition of the Executive. The Executive will consist of three persons: the Director is appointed by the Commission and approved by the Secretary of State and the two others are appointed by the Commission after consultation with the Director.

18. Functions of the Commission. The Commission has the following functions:-

    a. To ensure provision for the health, safety and satisfactory working environment of persons during the course of work. This excludes domestic and agricultural operatives work and certain activities of transport workers.

    b. To secure provision against hazards to the safety and health of the public from industrial, etc activities.

    c. To advise Government Departments and to promote safety education and training.

    d. To prepare and enforce regulations and codes.

    e. To investigate any hazardous situation, accident or occurrence.

    f. To delay inquests pending investigation of fatal accidents, to authorise a representative to be present at inquests, with the power to examine witnesses and request a report from the coroner.

    g. To charge fees for, eg, providing advisory work.

    h. To appoint independent persons or committees if considered necessary, to assist and advise the Commission in its work.

19. Functions of the Executive. The Executive has the following duties:-

    a. To exercise such of the Commission's functions as it delegates to it,

    b. To make adequate arrangements for the enforcement of the relevant statutory provisions except insofar as the Secretary of State has conferred the duty of enforcement upon some other authority.

REGULATIONS AND CODES OF PRACTICE *(S.16, 17)*

20. The Secretary of State, after consultation with the Commission, has the power to make "health and safety regulations". Such regulations may:-

    a. Repeal any of the existing statutory provisions, eg the *FACTORIES ACT 1961*.

    b. Exclude or modify any of the foregoing duties, or statutory provisions.

c.   Impose requirements by reference to the approval of the Commission.

d.   Provide for exceptions from any of the relevant statutory provisions.

21.   If a person does not observe any particular approved code of practice it does not mean he will be open to criminal proceedings, but a relevant code of practice is admissible as evidence where there are criminal proceedings.

22.   Authorities Responsible for Enforcement. The Secretary of State may make local authorities responsible for enforcement of the Act, including the current Acts, scheduled for replacement. *(S.18.)*

23.   Local authorities already have safety and health enforcement duties under existing regulations.

24.   Guidance will be given by the Commission. Where technical assistance is required it will be provided, as far as possible by the central organisation.

25.   Provision is made for closer and more effective cooperation between the health and safety organisation and other bodies, ie, the local authorities, the fire authorities and the local planning authorities.

HEALTH AND SAFETY INSPECTORS

26.   Enforcing powers have authority to appoint inspectors, who have the following powers:- *(S.19, 20)*

a.   To enter (accompanied by any person he considers necessary) any place where it is considered the Act will apply. This includes any premises on which he has reason to believe activities are being carried out which could endanger public safety.

b.   To enquire into the causes and assist enquiries on any safety situation. He can demand either oral or written information.

c.   If a qualified medical practitioner he may carry out medical examinations he considers necessary.

d.   To examine, search any premises, plant, materials, equipment, records or any other documents and take samples, measurements, recordings, copies and conduct tests.

e.   To demand facilities and assistance from any person if it is considered necessary.

27.   Enforcement. An inspector is empowered to issue:-

a.   *Improvement notices.* These are to meet a situation where there is contravention of a regulation but no imminent, serious risk of injury is involved. They require remedial action to be taken within a specified time, to comply with the requirements of the Act or to implement non-statutory codes and standards where the inspector considers this to be appropriate. *(S.21.)*

b. ***Prohibition notices.*** An inspector may serve a prohibition notice upon a person who is in control of activities which, in the inspector's opinion, involve a risk of serious personal injury. The prohibition notice will state the inspector's opinion that there is a risk of this nature, specify the matters which in his opinion give rise to the risk, and direct that the activities to which the notice relates shall not be carried on, by or under the control of the person on whom the notice is served unless the matters specified in the notice have been remedied. A direction contained in a prohibition notice when the risk of personal injury is imminent shall take effect:

a. at the end of the period specified in the notice, or

b. if the notice so declares, immediately.

28. Right of Appeal. There is a right of appeal against an improvement or prohibition notice. This should be made to an industrial tribunal within 21 days. Pending the appeal, improvement notices will be held in abeyance but prohibition notices will remain in force unless the employer satisfies the tribunal by an application prior to the hearing that it should not do so. *(S.24.)*

OFFENCES *(S.33.)*

29. It is an offence for a person:-

a. To fail to discharge a duty as outlined in paragraphs **4.** to **14.** above.

b. To wilfully interfere with anything provided for health, safety and welfare.

c. To contravene any health and safety regulation.

d. To contravene any requirement imposed by an inspector.

e. To contravene any requirements made by an improvement or prohibition notice.

f. To intentionally obstruct an inspector in the performance of his duties.

g. To intentionally make a false entry in any book, notice or document required to be kept by law.

30. Penalties. For most of the offences the maximum penalty is £1,000. However some offences are triable by the Crown Court and a convicted person is liable to imprisonment for a term not exceeding two years or an unlimited fine or both.

31. Offences Due to the Fault of Another Person. Where a person is accused of an offence, but this is due to another person, the other person shall be guilty of the offence. *(S.36.)*

32. Offences by a Body Corporate. Where an offence committed by a body corporate is proved to have been committed with the consent, agreement or neglect of any company officer, then the officer as well as the body corporate shall be guilty of the offence. *(S.37.)*

33. Onus on Proving Limits of "Practicability". If a person is accused of an offence involving failure to comply with statutory provisions of the Act as far as is reasonably practicable he has to prove that it was not practicable to do more than he had done in the situation and he had been as practicable as possible to meet the duty, ie, the onus is on the employer. *(S.40.)*

SAFETY REPRESENTATIVES AND SAFETY COMMITTEES

34. Regulations and Codes of Practice with regard to safety representatives and safety committees became effective on 1 October 1978.

SAFETY REPRESENTATIVES

35. Appointment. A recognised trade union:-

a. Appoints safety representatives where one or more members are employed. Normally more than two years' service with the company or with a similar industry is required.

b. Notifies the employer in writing of the names.

c. Notifies employers when an appointment is terminated.

36. Functions. The functions of a safety representative are:-

a. To represent employees in discussions with management.

b. Investigate potential hazards.

c. Investigate complaints.

d. Inspect the workplace at three-monthly intervals, or more often after agreement with the employer.

e. Carry out inspections after an accident, dangerous occurrence or notifiable industrial disease.

f. Receive information from Health and Safety Inspectors.

g. Attend meetings of safety committees.

37. Inspections. Safety representatives have the authority to inspect the workplace:-

a. After giving the employer reasonable written notice and a three-month interval has passed.

b. If there has been a substantial change of work within the three-month interval.

c. If there has been a notifiable accident, dangerous occurrence or industrial disease in the workplace.

d. Inspect any document which is required to be kept by law except a medical examination report of an identifiable employee.

38.   Notifiable Accidents, Dangerous Occurrences and Notifiable Diseases.

a.   An immediate inspection takes place when there has been a notifiable accident or dangerous occurrence.

b.   Written or verbal notification to be given to management by the safety representative.

c.   Employer shall provide all facilities.

d.   Although independent inspections are allowable, nothing shall prevent the employer or his representative from being present at the workplace.

Note: **"Accident and Dangerous Occurrences"**. Accidents and dangerous occurrences are those which are listed in the Notification of Accidents and Dangerous Occurrences Regulations 1980, and which are notifiable to the Health and Safety Executive. They include, inter alia, accidents involving personal injury which result in employees being absent for more than three days, and such occurrences as the overturning of cranes, boiler explosions, building collapses, explosions or fires causing damage and leading to suspension of work for at least five hours, and gassing accidents.

39.   Information from an Employer. Safety representatives have the right to inspect any relevant document kept under the Act for health, safety and welfare. The exceptions are:-

a.   Information against the interests of national security.

b.   Information relating specifically to an individual without his consent.

c.   Information, the disclosure of which, for reasons other than health and safety at work could cause substantial injury to the employer's undertaking.

d.   Information obtained for legal proceedings.

40.   Payments and Time Off for Safety Representatives. An employer shall permit a safety representative to take such time off with pay during the employee's working hours as shall be necessary to enable the safety representative to:-

a.   Perform his functions under the Act.

b.   Undergo training to enable him to perform these functions.

41.   Industrial tribunals. Complaints may be made to an industrial tribunal if the safety representative is not paid or is not given time off for safety matters. The complaint must be made within three months of the date the failure took place. If the complaint is justified, the tribunal can order the employer to pay compensation.

SAFETY COMMITTEES

42.   Establishment. An employer must establish a safety committee conforming to these requirements:-

a.   Safety representatives have been appointed and at least two request a safety committee in writing.

b.   Employer and safety representatives and trade union representatives consult to determine the composition of the committee.

c.   A notice must be posted in a place where it can be read.

d.   The committee shall be formed within three months.

43.   Functions. The committee will meet for discussion. Topics for discussion may include:-

a.   The investigation of individual accidents and cases of notifiable diseases.

b.   The study of accident statistics and trends.

c.   Examination of safety audit reports.

d.   Consideration of safety representatives' reports.

e.   Assist in the development of works safety rules and safe systems of work.

f.   Periodic inspection of the workplace, its plant, equipment and amenities.

g.   Publicity and communication effectiveness.

h.   Keeping adequate records of the proceedings and activities of the committee.

53 Institutions and Tribunals

INTRODUCTION

1. The *EMPLOYMENT PROTECTION ACT 1975* (EPA) set up a number of statutory bodies described as the "machinery for promoting the improvement of industrial relations". The constitution and functions of these statutory bodies are explained in this chapter. The jurisdictions of the Industrial Tribunal and the Employment Appeal Tribunal are also explained for the purpose of completing the students overall view of the machinery available for settling industrial disputes.

THE ADVISORY, CONCILIATION AND ARBITRATION SERVICE (ACAS)

2. *S.1, EPA* specifically charges ACAS with the general duty of promoting the improvement of industrial relations, and in particular of encouraging the extension of collective bargaining and the development and, where necessary, reform of collective bargaining machinery. ACAS is directed by a council appointed by the Secretary of State for Employment. The council consists of a full time chairman and nine other members. In appointing six of the nine members the Secretary of State is required to consult employers' organisations as regards three appointments and workers' organisations as regards three. This ensures that a balance between workers' and employers' interests is maintained.

3. Principal Functions. ACAS has five principal functions:

a. *Conciliation*

    i.   Where a trade dispute exists or is anticipated, ACAS may offer to assist in bringing about a settlement either with or without the consent of the parties.

    To achieve this, ACAS may either appoint an independent person or one of its own officers as a Conciliation Officer. No charge may be made for such assistance. Moreover, during the course of conciliation the parties should be encouraged to use any existing procedures for the resolution of the dispute.

    ii. Conciliation Officers appointed by ACAS are required to endeavour to promote a settlement of any complaint presented to an industrial tribunal in respect of:

        (a)   Unfair Dismissal
        (b)   Sex or Race Discrimination
        (c)   Itemised Pay Statements
        (d)   Guarantee Payments
        (e)   Medical Suspension Payments
        (f)   Trade Union Membership and Activities
        (g)   Time off work

(h) Maternity Rights
(i) Written Statement of Reasons for Dismissal
(j) Redundancy Consultations
(k) Protective Awards

Where a conciliation officer succeeds in bringing about an agreement between the parties, it is recorded in writing and is legally binding on the parties. The Court of Appeal has held that where the conciliation officer has formally recorded any agreement and the parties have signed it, the employee is precluded from presenting a complaint to an Industrial Tribunal. **MOORE v DUPORT FURNITURE PRODUCTS LTD AND ACAS (1980)**

b. *Arbitration.* The EPA provides for ACAS, at the request of one or more parties to a dispute and with the consent of all the parties in dispute, to refer any or all of the matters in dispute for settlement by arbitration of:

i. An independent arbitrator who may not be an officer or servant of ACAS; or

ii. The Central Arbitration Committee.

It is the duty of ACAS to ensure that existing conciliation procedures have been exhausted before referring a matter for arbitration, unless there is some special reason which justifies arbitration. However the arbitrator's award is not legally binding upon the parties because Part I, *ARBITRATION ACT 1950* is specifically excluded. The report of the arbitrator may be published by ACAS providing all the parties consent.

c. *Advice.* ACAS has the discretionary power to offer advice to employers, workers and their organisations on any matter concerned with industrial relations or employment policies, including the following:

i. The organisation of workers or employers for the purpose of collective bargaining;

ii. The recognition of trade unions by employers;

iii. Machinery for the negotiation of terms and conditions of employment, and for joint consultation;

iv. Procedures for avoiding and settling disputes and workers' grievances;

v. Questions relating to communication between employers and workers;

vi. Facilities for officials of trade unions;

vii. Procedures relating to the termination of employment;

viii. Disciplinary matters;

ix. Manpower planning, labour turnover and absenteeism;

x. Recruitment, retention, promotion and vocational training of workers;

xi. Payment systems, including job evaluation and equal pay.

Such advise may be given either on the initiative of ACAS itself or upon the request of an interested party. The advice so given may be published by ACAS without the consent of any other party, but it must be of a general nature and without reference to specific employers or employees.

d.   *Inquiry*. ACAS may, if it thinks fit, inquire into any question relating to industrial relations generally or to industrial relations in any particular industry or in any particular undertaking or part of an undertaking. The findings of such an inquiry may be published in ACAS consider publication to be desirable for the improvement of industrial relations, but only after consulting all the parties concerned and taking account of their views.

e.   *Codes of practice*. The original code of practice was published by the Secretary of State for Employment under powers conferred by the *INDUSTRIAL RELATIONS ACT 1971* with the specific purpose of giving practical guidance upon the four general principles set out in Section 1 of that Act, namely:-

    i.   Freely conducted collective bargaining;

    ii.   Orderly procedures for settling disputes;

    iii.   Free association of workers and employers;

    iv.   Freedom and security for workers.

This code of practice has been retained, and in addition the following codes have been issued by ACAS, under the EPCA.

    i.   Disciplinary Practice and Procedures in Employment;

    ii.   Disclosure of Information to Trade Unions for Collective Bargaining Purposes;

    iii.   Time off for Trade Union Duties and Activities.

Additionally ACAS has a general power under the EPA to issue codes of practice to give practical guidance for promoting the improvement of industrial relations. Since 1 August 1980 the Secretary of State is also empowered, after consulting ACAS and gaining the approval of both Houses of Parliament, to issue Codes of Practice. Two codes have been issued by the Secretary of State on:

    i.   Picketing; and

    ii.   The Closed Shop.

Codes issued under the *HSAWA* are:

    i.   Time off work with pay for safety representatives to carry out their statutory functions and undergo training.

    ii.   Disclosure of relevant information to safety representatives on matters such as dangers relating to machinery used at work.

The provisions of a code of practice are not legally binding upon employers. Failure to observe provisions cannot of itself lead to a criminal penalty or civil liability. Nevertheless, in any proceedings before an industrial tribunal or the CAC a code of practice is admissible in evidence. The employer's compliance or otherwise is taken into account.

THE CENTRAL ARBITRATION COMMITTEE (CAC)

4.   The CAC was established under the EPA to replace the Industrial Arbitration Board. The Secretary of State is responsible for appointing the members of the CAC and its chairman and deputy chairman. ACAS must be consulted with regard to the appointment of the chairman and his deputies. ACAS nominates persons as members who are experienced in industrial relations, ensuring that both employers' and workers' representatives serve on the Committee.

5.   Jurisdiction. The main jurisdictions of the CAC are as follows:

a.   A voluntary jurisdiction in matters referred by ACAS in connection with a trade dispute. An award under this jurisdiction will only be binding upon the parties insofar as it is incorporated into individual employment contracts with the agreement of the parties.

b.   A statutory jurisdiction regarding a complaint that an employer has failed to disclose to a trade union information under the *EPA* in respect of the findings of a Statutory Joint Industrial Council.

c.   Statutory jurisdiction derived from the *EPA* in respect of the findings of a Statutory Joint Industrial Council.

d.   A jurisdiction arising from various statutes where financial assistance or licence is provided by Central or Local government.

6.   Appeals. There is no procedure for appeal against an award made by the CAC but if it can be shown to have exceeded its powers or acted in breach of natural justice, its decisions may be challenged in the High Court.

THE CERTIFICATION OFFICER (CO)

7.   The CO is appointed by the Secretary of State under the *EPA* and has assumed the functions of the former Registrar of Friendly Societies in addition to duties set out in the *EPA*. The principal functions of the CO are:

a.   Duties in connection with the listing and certification of independent trade unions and the monitoring of their annual returns and accounts.

b.   The exercise of powers under the *TRADE UNION ACT 1913*, concerning the political fund rules of trade unions.

c.   The handling of complaints relating to amalgamations of trade unions under the *TRADE UNION (AMALGAMATIONS) ACT 1964*.

Provision is made for appeal from certain decisions of the CO to go before the Employment Appeal Tribunal (see para **12.**).

INDUSTRIAL TRIBUNALS

8.   Industrial tribunals were established under the *INDUSTRIAL TRAINING ACT 1964* for the purpose of resolving disputes between employers and Training Boards arising out of the liability to pay a training levy. Since 1964 the industrial tribunal has assumed many other statutory jurisdictions and have emerged as "labour courts". The tribunals have some 30 separate statutory jurisdictions covering virtually every individual employment right which has been created by statute.

9.   Advantages. The advantages of bringing a case before an industrial tribunal are:

   a.   The procedure is far simpler than for a case in the County Court.

   b.   The interval of time between commencing proceedings and the hearing is about 9 or 10 weeks, compared with many months or even years in the ordinary courts.

   c.   The formality of tribunals is considerably relaxed being designed to put the parties at ease; procedural rules are interpreted flexibly and the rules of evidence which apply in the ordinary courts are not binding on the tribunal.

   d.   They are relatively inexpensive, in comparison with the ordinary courts since legal representation is not encouraged by the rule that costs may only be awarded the losing party where the complaint is frivolous or vexatious.

10.   Claims. A person wishing to bring a claim before an industrial tribunal is called the "applicant" and he commences proceedings by lodging an Originating Notice of Application at the Central Offices of industrial tribunals (COIT). The COIT then serves a copy of the application on the defendant who is known as the Respondent who has 14 days in which to return his answer in the form of a Respondent's Notice of Appearance. The COIT is also required to notify Conciliation Officers, designated by ACAS, of the claim. These officers have a statutory duty to endeavour to promote a settlement even in the absence of a request from either party, providing there is a reasonable prospect of success. In cases where the CO has been unable to achieve a settlement, the tribunal chairman has powers to order the giving of particulars by one party to the other, the attendance of witnesses and the production of documents. A tribunal may order an applicant to pay a deposit of up to £150 as a condition of proceeding with his claim.

11.   Composition. Industrial tribunals sit in about 80 different centres through Britain, each tribunal consisting of a chairman, who must be a barrister or solicitor of not less than 7 years' standing, and 2 panel members one representing employees' interests and the other employers' interests. Panels of each category of member are nominated; the chairman being appointed by the Secretary of State after consultation with employers' and employees' organisations.

EMPLOYMENT APPEAL TRIBUNAL (EAT)

12. The EAT was established under the *EPA* to hear appeals from industrial tribunals. An appeal to the EAT may be made on a question of law arising from any decision of an industrial tribunal under:

    a. The Equal Pay Act 1970;

    b. The Sex Discrimination Acts 1975 and 1986;

    c. The Employment Protection Act 1975;

    d. The Race Relations Act 1976;

    e. The Employment Protection (Consolidation) Act 1978;

    f. The Employment Act 1980;

    g. The Wages Act 1986.

Additionally, the EAT hears appeals on questions of law from decisions of the CO under the *TRADE UNION ACT 1913* and the *TRADE UNION (AMALGAMATIONS) ACT 1964*, and on questions of fact and law under the *TULRA* and *EPA* (relating to listing and independence of trade unions), and unfair exclusion or expulsion from a trade union.

13. Appeals. An appeal generally lies only on an error of law. In order to succeed the appellant must show:

    a. The tribunal misdirected itself in law, or misunderstood the law or misapplied the law; or

    b. That there is no evidence to support the tribunal's findings of fact; or

    c. That the decision was "perverse" (ie no reasonable tribunal could have reached such a decision).

14. Composition. The EAT is composed of High Court and Court of Session Judges and appointed members who must have industrial relations knowledge or experience. Each appeal is heard by one judge and between 2 and 4 appointed members.

15. Further Appeals. A decision of the EAT may, with leave, be appealed to the Court of Appeal, and with further leave, to the House of Lords. Such appeals must, however, be on a point of law. On some matters, eg sex discrimination cases may be referred to the European Court of Justice.

54 Trade Unions

INTRODUCTION

1.   In this chapter we shall consider the status of trade unions and the liabilities and rights of unions and their members under current legislation.

HISTORICAL BACKGROUND

2.   The trade union movement arose out of workers associating together with the common aim of improving their pay and conditions of work. Under the common law such associations were considered illegal as being restraint of trade. Moreover, the earliest statute law *(COMBINATION ACT 1800)* imposed a criminal punishment upon workers associating together. The *TRADE UNION ACT 1871* bestowed upon trade unions a degree of legal status by a system of registration. This was never the same as the separate legal entity accorded associations registered under the Companies Acts. Nevertheless, the courts strove to infer certain characteristics attributable to a separate legal status:

In **TAFF VALE RAILWAY CO v AMALGAMATED SOCIETY OF RAILWAY SERVANTS (1902)** some of the company's employees had been persuaded (by the union officials) to leave their employment in breach of their contracts of service. The company sued the union and officials. It was held that the union, although not a legal entity, was responsible for the wrongs committed on its behalf.

Contrast **BONSOR v MUSICIANS' UNION (1956)** when Bonsor, a union member, was expelled for non-payment of subscriptions and was, as a result, unable to obtain musical engagements. The court held that the expulsion was unlawful as the power to expel was vested in the branch committee but in this case had been carried out by the district secretary. An injunction was granted restraining the union from acting on the expulsion.

3.   The *TRADE DISPUTES ACT 1906* was passed to reverse the decision in the **TAFF VALE** case, thus providing trade unions with absolute immunity from liability in tort. Such immunity was extended to individual members by the *TRADE DISPUTES ACT 1965*.

4.   The *INDUSTRIAL RELATIONS ACT 1971* repealed the *TRADE DISPUTES ACTS* and sought to amend the status of trade unions and their liability in tort.

5.   The legal status and liability of trade unions is now statutorily defined in the *TULRA 1974*.

STATUTORY DEFINITION

6.   A trade union is an organisation (whether permanent or temporary) which either:

a.   Consists wholly or mainly of workers and is an organisation whose principal purposes include the regulation of relations between workers and employers or employers' associations; or

b.   Consists wholly or mainly of:-

i.   Constituent or affiliated organisations which fulfil the conditions specified in para **6.** a. or

ii.   Representatives of such constituent or affiliated organisations;

and in either case is an organisation whose principal purposes include the regulation of relations between workers and employers or between workers and employers' associations, or include the regulation of relations between its constituent or affiliated organisations.

LEGAL CAPACITY

7.   A trade union which is not a special register body is not to be treated as though it were a body corporate, but the *TULRA* nevertheless gives a trade union some characteristics of legal personality so that it can:

a.   Make contracts;

b.   Own property, though it must be vested in trustees;

c.   Sue or be sued in its own name in proceedings relating to property or founded in contract or tort or any other cause of action (subject to the immunity in tort provided by the *TULRA*).

e.   Be subject to judgements, orders or awards, in proceedings brought against it.

Special Register Body means an organisation whose name was entered in the special register maintained under the *INDUSTRIAL RELATIONS ACT 1971, and* which is a company registered under the Companies Act or is incorporated by charter or letters patent. Registration in this way was limited, and no new organisation can now be added to the list. Bodies so registered include the Royal College of Nursing and the British Medical Association.

8.   Additionally immunity is provided from the restraint of trade doctrine. The restrictions on the freedom of labour that a trade union may impose would undoubtedly be considered as an unreasonable restraint of trade at common law. **HORNBY v CLOSE (1867).**

IMMUNITY IN TORT

9.   The *TULRA* gave immunity to trade unions and employers' associations in respect of certain torts. This immunity has been curtailed by the *EA 1982 (S.15)*. Action in tort may be brought against a trade union if a person suffers loss due to unlawful industrial action organised by its officials. It will be liable for actions inducing breach of contract (or threats to do so) or actions for conspiracy when not done in contemplation or furtherance of a trade dispute if that action is authorised or endorsed by a responsible person of the union, ie. the principal executive committee, any other person empowered by the rules of the union to authorise or endorse such action, the president or general secretary, an employed official, or any committee to whom an employed official regularly reports. The Act makes provision for exemption from liability if the action is repudiated. (See para. 60c. for limitation of damages).

Note: For a discussion of the meaning of "an act done in contemplation or furtherance of a trade dispute" see para **50.**

TRADE UNION AFFAIRS

10. Listing of Trade Unions. An association of employees which falls within the statutory definition of a trade union is entitled to have its name entered on a list of trade unions. This list is maintained by the CO. In order to be listed a trade union must:

a. Pay the requisite fee;

b. Submit a copy of its rules;

c. State the address of its head or main office;

d. Submit a list of its officers; and

e. State the name under which it is known.

11. The CO has the following powers in relation to the list, subject to a right of appeal on questions of both fact and law to the EAT:

a. To prevent the use of a misleading name;

b. Removal of a trade union if it no longer appears to be a union within the statutory definition;

c. Removal of a trade union from the list upon the specific request of that union;

d. Removal where a trade union has ceased to exist;

e. The issue of a certificate of listing, which is evidence of trade union status.

12. The purpose of the certificate of listing is twofold:

a. It is proof of the trade union's status without which it would be unable to obtain tax relief on its provident fund income; and,

b. It is a prerequisite for obtaining a certificate of independence.

13. Certificate of Independence. A listed trade union may apply to the CO for a certificate that it is independent. The certificate is conclusive evidence of a trade union's independence.

14. Definition of Independence. An independent trade union is one which:

a.   Is not under the domination or control of an employer or a group of employers or of one or more employers' associations; and

b.   Is not liable to interference by an employer or any such group or association (arising out of the provision of financial of material support or by any other means) tending towards such control.

15. In **BLUE CIRCLE STAFF ASSOCIATION v CERTIFICATION OFFICER (1977)** the EAT adopted the criteria of indpendence formulated by the CO, namely:

a.   Absence of direct subsidy from the employer;

b.   Sufficient absence of other material support from the employer;

c.   Sufficient absence of interference by the employer such as liable to occur when the union is small, weak and receiving help from the employer;

d.   Absence of rules exposing the association to control by the employer;

e.   Evidence sufficient to rebut the likelihood that a single company union is liable to interference by the employer;

f.   A recent history showing sufficient development of independence;

g.   An organisational pattern providing evidence of independance by its size and recruiting ability, the competence and experience of its officers and the fact that it is not run by people near the top of the company;

h.   A robust attitude in negotiation.

16. The importance of the certificate of independence lies in the statutory requirement that a union must be independent in order to:

a.   Enforce rights to information;

b.   Allow individuals to claim protection for trade union membership and activities;

c.   Allow individuals to claim time off for union activities;

d.   Claim consultation in respect of redundancies;

e.   Make union membership agreements in a form which allows the employer fairly to dismiss non-members;

f.   Obtain planning information under the *INDUSTRY ACT 1975*;

g.   Appoint safety representatives under regulations issued under the *HASAW 1974*.

h.   Be consulted about contracting-out of occupational pension schemes under the *SOCIAL SECURITY PENSIONS ACT 1975*;

    i.   Take advantage of the financial assistance available for conducting union ballots;

    j.   To be able to use employer's premises for the purpose of a secret ballot.

The absence of a certificate of independence will not in itself prevent a trade union exercising the above rights, but in the event of the union's independence being challenged any proceedings would be stayed until the CO had issued or refused a certificate.

17. Additionally, the CO may withdraw a certificate at any time if he is of the opinion that the union is no longer independent. The CO must, in coming to such a decision, take into account any relevant information submitted to him by any person. Appeal lies to the EAT.

18. The CO is also required to keep a register of independent trade unions which is open to inspection by the public, free of charge, at all reasonable hours.

RECOGNITION

19. For an independent trade union to exercise the rights set out in para **16.** a. c. d. g. h. and j., it must be one which is "recognised" by the employer for the purposes of collective bargaining. Recognition must now be achieved voluntarily through the conciliation procedures of *S.2, EPA* may still be exercised by ACAS on application of either party, or otherwise if in the view of ACAS it can achieve a settlement to a dispute.

20. Recognition for collective bargaining purposes may be either express or implied. For recognition to be implied the alleged acts of recognition must be clear and unequivocal and involve a course of conduct or a period of time. **NATIONAL UNION OF GOLD, SILVER AND ALLIED TRADES v ALBURY BROS. (1979).**

ANNUAL RETURNS AND ACCOUNTS

21. Detailed requirements with regard to the keeping of accounts, making of annual returns, appointment of auditors and the qualified examination of an report on members' superannuation schemes are contained in the TULRA.

    a. *Duty to keep accounting records.* Every trade union must keep proper accounting records so as to give a true and fair view of the state of its affairs and to explain its transactions, and in particular:

        i.   Cause to be kept proper accounting records with respect to its transactions and its assets and liabilities; and

        ii.   Establish and maintain a satisfactory system of control of its accounting records, its cash holdings and all its receipts and remittances.

    b. *The Annual Return.* A return must be made in each calendar year to the CO, containing:

i.   Revenue accounts indicating the income and expenditure of the trade union for the period to which the return relates;

ii.   A balance sheet as at the end of that period;

iii.   Such other accounts (if any) as the CO may require;

iv.   A copy of the rules of the trade union as in force at the end of the period;

v.   A note of all changes in the officers of the union and any change in the address of the head or main office of the union during the period to which the return relates;

vi.   A copy of the auditors report.

c.   *Appointment of auditors.* Trade unions must appoint auditors to audit the annual accounts. Generally, such auditors must be qualified to act as auditors of a company incorporated under the Companies Acts. The auditors are required to report on the accounts stating whether, in their opinion, the accounts give a true and fair view of the matters to which they relate.

d.   *Members' superannuation schemes.* Before such a scheme is commenced:

i.   The proposals for the scheme must have been examined by an appropriately qualified actuary; and

ii.   A copy of a report made to the trade union by the actuary on the results of his examination, signed by the actuary, must have been sent to the CO.

22. The CO must keep available for public inspection copies of all annual returns. Every trade union must, on the request of any person supply a copy of its rules and latest annual return, for which it may make a reasonable charge.

AMALGAMATION

23. A statutory procedure for the amalgamation of trade unions has existed since 1876. The current procedure is contained in the *TRADE UNION (AMALGAMATIONS) ACT 1964* which provides two methods by which a merger of trade unions may be achieved:

a.   By an agreed Instrument of Amalgamation which must contain certain matters (a guidance pamphlet is available from the CO), and obtain the consent of more than 50 per cent of the members of each union voting by ballot.

b.   By a Transfer of Engagements which involves the transference by one union of all its obligations and assets to the other whilst still retaining its nominal identity. In this method only the members of the transfer union are required to vote and a simple majority of those voting by ballot will suffice.

24. The Act lays down procedural requirements, which in some cases must first be approved by the CO, for the notice informing members of the proposals and for the conduct of the ballot. Additionally there are grounds for complaint, by any member of the unions concerned, to the CO and a right of appeal on questions of law to the EAT.

THE POLITICAL FUND

25. The issue of financing a political activity by a trade union in 1910 was considered illegal because the statutory definition at that time required that the union's principal object be the regulation of relations between workers and employees.

In **AMALGAMATED SOCIETY OF RAILWAY SERVANTS v OSBORNE (1910)** the House of Lords held that the funding of Labour Party MP's was not within the statutory objects of a trade union.

The *TRADE UNION ACT 1913* effectively overruled this decision by permitting a trade union to have any lawful objects. This provision is implied in the *TULRA 1974* which states that the principal purpose of the union need only "include" the regulation of relations between workers and employers.

26. Nevertheless the *TRADE UNION ACT 1913* provides a detailed procedure for maintenance and conduct of a political fund for the protection of the dissident minority.

    a. There must be a secret ballot of the membership of the trade union to approve the establishment of a political fund.

    b. The fund must be financed by a political levy and in no other way.

    c. After approval by a simple majority of those voting in the ballot at a. the union must incorporate in its rules special rules, approved by the CO for the conduct of the fund.

    d. Members of the union must have the right to contract out and to suffer no discrimination by doing so, except in the control of the fund.

    e. The political fund may only be used to promote certain political objects:

        i.   Payment of expenses incurred by a candidate or prospective candidate for election to Parliament or any other public office.

        ii. Holding of meetings and the distribution of literature in support of such candidates or prospective candidates;

        iii. Maintenance of a person who is a Member of Parliament or holds any other public office;

        iv. Registration of electors or the selection of a candidate for Parliament or any other public office;

        v.   Holding of political meetings of any kind or the general distribution of political literature, unless the main purpose of these is the furtherance of the statutory objects of the union.

    f. Complaints regarding any breach of the political fund provisions are dealt with by the CO with a right of appeal to the EAT.

TRADE UNION BALLOTS

27. Specific provision is made in the *EA 1980* for the financing and holding of secret ballots by trade unions.

  a. *Financial assistance in respect of secret ballots.* The Secretary of State is empowered to make regulations providing for financial assistance to be given to independent trade unions holding a secret ballot within the following purposes:

    i.   Obtaining a decision or ascertaining the views of members as to the calling or ending of a strike or other industrial action;

    ii.   Carrying out an election provided for by the rules of the union;

    iii.   Electing a worker who is a member of a trade union to be a representative of other members also employed by his employer;

    iv.   Amending the rules of a trade union;

    v.   Obtaining a decision in accordance with the *TRADE UNION (AMALGAMATIONS) ACT 1964* on a resolution to approve an instrument of amalgamation or transfer.

  b. *Secret ballots on employer's premises.* An employer with more than 20 workers, has a statutory duty to permit the use of his premises, so far as is reasonably practicable, for the purpose of giving those workers employed by him and who are members of the union a convenient opportunity of voting. This duty only exists where the request is made by an independent trade union recognised by the employer for the purpose of collective bargaining and where the ballot is in respect of at least one of the questions set out in sub. para. a. above. Moreover, the proposals for the conduct of the ballot must be such as to secure so far as reasonably practicable, that those voting may do so in secret. Where an employer is in breach of this duty the trade union concerned may complain to an industrial tribunal which has the power to award compensation to be paid by the employer to the union. Appeal on a question of law lies to the EAT.

28. Postal Ballot. The regulations so far issued only provide for financial assistance to be given in the case of a postal ballot and contain detailed conditions to ensure that payment is not made if the CO is not satisfied that the ballot was properly and fairly held.

  a. The ballot must be conducted so as to secure as far as reasonably practicable, that those voting may do so in secret;

  b. Those voting must be required to do so by marking a voting paper;

  c. Those voting must be required to return the voting papers individually by post to the union or to a person responsible for counting the votes;

  d. The voting paper must contain only questions within the prescribed purposes at para. **27.** a. above. Moreover, as regards election of officers, only the positions of president, chairman, secretary, treasurer executive committee member or other positions whereby the person elected becomes an employee of the union are permitted under heads ii. and iii.

e.   Payments under the scheme will generally cover the cost of printing stationery and postage and will be made by the CO upon application of the union after the expenditure has been incurred.

TRADE UNION MEMBERSHIP

29.   Rules. The only statutory regulation of Trade Union rules is as follows:

a.   *S.2 TULRA 1974* provides that no rule of a trade union shall be unlawful or unenforceable by reason only that it is in restraint of trade; and

b.   *S.4 EA 1980* provides that where a closed shop agreement exists, an actual or prospective employee is entitled not to have his application for union membership unreasonably refused, and not to be unreasonably expelled from the union. This right is specifically stated to be in addition to any common law right that may exist.

The effect of these statutory provisions is examined below under the headings of Exclusion and Expulsion from membership.

30.   Exclusion from Membership. A person who has been excluded from a trade union may have a right of action in the following circumstances:

a.   *Eligibility.* Following the dicta in **BOULTING v ASSOCIATION OF CINEMATOGRAPH, TELEVISION AND ALLIED TECHNICIANS (1963)** an applicant could probably obtain a declaration of his eligibility for membership if that was the reason for refusal. Where however the applicant is ineligible for membership under the rules the courts would not be prepared to strike out the rule for reasons other than restraint of trade and any admission to membership contrary to the rules would be ultra vires.

In **FARAMUS v FILM ARTISTES' ASSOCIATION (1964)** the union had a rule disqualifying from membership any applicant who had been convicted of a criminal offence. F had been convicted of a trivial offence several years before admission to membership. He did not declare the fact. He was removed from membership eight years after admission on the grounds that his membership had never been valid. The House of Lords held that:

i.   F had never been validly elected a member;

ii.   The rule did not constitute unreasonable restraint of trade, and

iii.   The rules prescribing qualifications for union membership cannot be invalidated on the grounds of "unreasonableness", or being contrary to natural justice.

b.   *Actionable conspiracy.* Where officials of a trade union refuse an applicant admission, it may be possible to show that those officials are guilty of a conspiracy to injure the applicant.

In **CROFTER HAND WOVEN HARRIS TWEED CO LTD v VEITCH (1942)** V was an official of a union to which the dockers of Stornoway and most of the workers in the spinning mills on the island of Lewis belonged. The plaintiffs were producers of tweed cloth on Lewis and they used mainland yarn (at a cheaper rate than that produced on Lewis). V in combination with the owners of the island spinning mills instructed the dockers not to handle the mainland yarn. It was held that V and others were not guilty of conspiracy since their actions had been motivated by a desire to protect their own lawful interests and not to injure the plaintiffs.

In **HUNTLEY v THORNTON AND OTHERS (1957)** district officials regarded Huntley as properly expelled from the union (for refusing to obey an order to strike) despite the order of the national executive committee that he should be re-instated. The action was taken to ensure that he would not obtain employment and was connected with a personal quarrel. The court held that the officials had committed the tort of conspiracy as their motive was to injure the plaintiff, not as a furtherance of a trade dispute.

c.   *Requirement of the rules.* Where a cause of action for conspiracy is not present, an excluded applicant may have a right to have his application properly considered unless the rules provide for arbitrary exclusion. This would certainly be the case where an entrance fee is paid on application and not returned when membership is subsequently refused. Such a requirement would impose a contractual duty to act honestly and in good faith, upon the officials and the trade union.

d.   *The right to work.* In so far as the concept of a "right to work" exists, as distinct from an application of the concept of restraint of trade to the individual, the following cases indicate that the concept may be used to found a cause of action and indeed to strike out a trade union rule.

In **NAGLE v FIELDEN (1966)** the plaintiff, a woman, had her application for a trainers license turned down by the Jockey Club on the grounds of sex. Without such license she could not train horses to run on the flat. She sought and was granted an injunction ordering the license to be granted on the grounds that she was being unjustly excluded from the "right to work" at her chosen trade or profession.

In **EDWARDS v S.O.G.A.T. (1971)** the plaintiff's employers omitted to deduct his union dues from his salary and as a result his membership was automatically terminated. The termination was after six weeks, and without appeal, in accordance with union rules. As a closed shop was in operation Edwards lost his job. It was held that the rule was invalid as being "an unwarranted encroachment on a man's right to work". The point was also made that the rules were possibly in restraint of trade. Additionally, the dicta in **McINNES v ONSLOW FANE (1978)** would seem to suggest that a trade union, as a quasi-public body, owes a potential applicant a duty to act fairly, in some circumstances.

e.   *S.4, EA 1980.* This gives an applicant a right not to have his application for membership of a specified trade union unreasonably refused where a closed shop agreement is in force. This right is specifically stated to be in addition to any other existing rights. Indeed, the code of practice expresses a preference for voluntary rather than legal procedures. Thus, the Independent Review Committee of the TUC will continue to function hearing cases in respect of affiliated trade unions. The question of whether the trade union has acted reasonably is to be tested in accordance with equity and the substantial merits of the case, analogous with the reasonableness test for unfair dismissal. Moreover, it is specifically provided that compliance with the rules does not of itself establish that the trade union has acted reasonably, nor does a breach automatically demonstrate unreasonableness. The code of practice gives further guidance in that it requires trade union rules to clearly state the grounds for rejecting the applicant and such rules to comply with natural justice.

31.   Expulsion from Membership. A person who has been expelled from trade union membership has similar common law rights and may challenge his expulsion under one or more of the following grounds:

a.   *Power to expel.* There must be an express power of expulsion contained in the trade union rules. Moreover, the courts tend to interpret such rules strictly as illustrated in the following cases:

In **LEE v SHOWMANS' GUILD OF GREAT BRITAIN (1952)** the plaintiff was charged with "unfair competition" under a union rule. He was fined by an area committee. Lee failed to pay the fine and was expelled in accordance with union rules. He applied for an injunction to prevent implementation of the expulsion. The Court of Appeal held that the courts should examine the decisions of domestic tribunals with regard to their observation of the law. In addition the courts should consider the correct interpretation of the rules. In this case it was held that Lee could not properly have been found guilty of "unfair competition" and the committee finding was, therefore, unjust.

In **ESTERMAN v N.A.L.G.O. (1974)** the plaintiff volunteered to assist returning officers in certain local authority elections, contrary to union orders. She sought an injunction to prevent her branch committee from considering her expulsion on the grounds of disobedience. The rule in question permitted expulsion if the local committee found that the member was "guilty of conduct which rendered him unfit for membership". The court confirmed that it would not interfere with the decision of a local tribunal unless it was satisfied that no reasonable tribunal could uphold such a decision. In this particular case it was considered that it would be impossible in the circumstances to convict a member of conduct rendering him unfit to belong to the union. Some reasons given were: the

dubious nature of an order concerning the spare-time activities of a member
and the ethics of attempting to wreck local elections.

b.   *Natural justice.* The principles of natural justice involved in expulsion cases are firstly, that the member must be notified of the charge against
him and be given an opportunity to answer the charge; and secondly that
he has a right to be heard by an unbiased tribunal.

c.   *The penalty.* Additionally, the Courts may intervene in cases where
the penalty is excessive. **BURN v NATIONAL AMALGAMATED
LABOURERS UNION OF GREAT BRITAIN AND IRELAND (1920).**

d.   *S.4 EA 1980.* Where a closed shop agreement is in force, every person
who is in such employment has a statutory right not to be unreasonably
expelled from a specific trade union. This is similar to the right not to
be unreasonably excluded from a trade union discussed at **30.** e. above,
and the rules of interpretation and the effect of the code of practice also
apply. Additionally, it is specifically provided that where the rules provide
for automatic forfeiture of membership, such as non-payment of union
dues, this will be treated as an expulsion.

32.   Compensation for Unreasonable Exclusion or Expulsion. In addition
to any common law action, the *EA 1980* provides for a complaint to be made
to the industrial tribunal in a situation where a person is unreasonably excluded or expelled from a trade union in circumstances where he either is, or is
seeking to be, employed by an employer who has entered into a union membership agreement, and it is the practice for employees to belong to a union in
accordance with that agreement. The ultimate remedy of the industrial tribunal
will of course be compensation since a person could not be forced upon any
particular trade union.

33.   When a tribunal finds an applicant's case well founded it makes a declaration that the exclusion or expulsion was unreasonble. There is a right of appeal
from the tribunal's decision to the EAT on questions of both law and fact.

34.   For the applicant to obtain compensation a further application to either
the industrial tribunal or the EAT must be made, at least four weeks after and
within six months after the declaration as follows:

a.   *Industrial Tribunal.* If at the time of the application for compensation the applicant has been admitted or re-admitted to membership of the
union against which he made the complaint, the industrial tribunal may
award such amount as it considers appropriate for the purpose of compensating the applicant for the loss sustained by him in consequence of
the exclusion or expulsion which was the subject of the complaint. Such
compensation is payable by the trade union concerned and may not exceed
an amount equal to thirty times the current maximum amount of a week's
pay for the purposes of calculating the basic award in unfair dismissal cases
plus an amount equal to the current maximum compensatory award.

b.   ***Employment Appeal Tribunal.*** On the other hand, if the applicant has not been admitted or re-admitted to trade union membership at the time of the application for compensation it will be made to the EAT which can award compensation of such amount as it considers just and equitable in all the circumstances. The maximum compensation that the EAT can award is the limit of the industrial tribunal plus a sum equal to fifty-two times the maximum amount of a week's pay for the purposes of calculating additional awards of compensation in unfair dismissal cases.

35.   Participation in Trade Union Affairs. The right of the individual member to participate in the affairs of his trade union may be conveniently classified under two headings.

a.   ***Positive rights.*** Other than the two statutory rights (of voting where a trade union proposes to establish a political fund and where it proposes to amalgamate with another trade union) the positive right of the trade union member to participate in his trade union affairs by attending meetings, voting, seeking office, attending delegate conferences etc, is merely a matter of construction of the contract established by the rules of the trade union.

In **BREEN v AEU (1971)** the plaintiff sought a declaration that the decision of a union's district committee to refuse to endorse his election as a shop steward was void as being contrary to the requirements of natural justice. The union claimed that natural justice was inapplicable as the committee's function was not judicial. It was held that natural justice, ie the need to act fairly was applicable. However in this particular instance the facts indicated that the committee's decision was not biased.

b.   ***Negative rights.*** The member also has a right to restrain any trade union action which is not permitted by its constitution subject to the rule in **FOSS v HARBOTTLE (1843)**. This again is a question of the individual enforcing his right under the contract of membership to prevent the trade union acting in breach of its rules.

In **EDWARDS v HALLIWELL (1950)** an ultra vires resolution to increase members' subscriptions.

In **HODGSON v NALGO (1972)** an executive council instruction to delegates attending a TUC conference to vote in favour of Britain joining the EEC contrary to NALGO policy.

Note: The rule in **FOSS v HARBOTTLE** in this context provides for a minority to restrain a trade union action where it is acting ultra vires. The courts will not permit a minority action to proceed where the action is intra vires though lacking some formality which can be ratified by the appropriate body.

COLLECTIVE AGREEMENTS

36.   Statutory Definition. *S.29-30, TULRA 1974* define a collective agreement as any agreement or arrangement made by or on behalf of one or more trade unions and one or more employer or employers' association and relating to one or more of the following matters:

a. Terms and conditions of employment, or the physical conditions in which any workers are required to work;

b. Engagement or non-engagement, or termination or suspension of employment or the duties of employment, of one or more workers;

c. Allocation of work or the duties of employment as between workers or groups of workers;

d. Matters of discipline;

e. The membership or non-membership of a trade union on the part of a worker;

f. Facilities for officials of trade unions; and

g. Machinery for negotiation or consultation, and other procedures, relating to any of the above matters, including the recognition by employers or employers' associations of the right of a trade union to represent workers in any such negotiation or consultation or in the carrying out of such procedures.

37. Enforceability. *S.18, TULRA 1974* provides that any collective agreement made before 1 December 1971 or after 15 September 1974 shall be presumed not to have been intended by the parties to be a legally enforceable contract unless the agreement is in writing, and contains a provision which (however expressed) states that the parties intended that the agreement shall be a legally enforceable contract.

38. If a collective agreement contains a provision which states that the parties intend that only one or more parts of the agreement shall be a legally enforceable contract, then it will have this effect.

39. The extent to which a collective agreement may be enforced by or against those workers who are covered by it is a question of whether it has been expressly incorporated, in whole or in part into the contract of employment.

40. The Collective Agreement and Common Law. The collective agreement is the product of a generally voluntary system of negotiation of terms, and conditions of employment. This is reflected in the presumption as to non-enforceability unless the parties take positive steps to make the agreement legally binding. This presumption, however, applies only to those agreements which fall within the statutory definition. The common law will apply in the case of agreements not conforming to the statutory definition, but it is uncertain what provision is made under common law. There are three possibilities:

a. It is suggested that there is a general presumption of legal enforceability as there is with any other commercial agreement.

b. There is the view of the Donovan Commission that collective agreements are not enforceable because the parties do not intend to create legal relations.

c. In the only recent case raising the issue of enforceability, the Court held that the particular agreements were not enforceable because of the nature and wording of the agreements. The case is no authority, therefore, for adopting a general view of non-enforceability.

It rather suggests that collective agreements are of such a divers nature that it is impossible to adopt a universal rule and that each must be considered on the facts at the time. Moreover, some collective agreements do not fulfil a contractual function, and others are too vague to be enforceable. **FORD MOTOR CO LTD v AMALGAMATED UNION OF ENGINEERING & FOUNDRY WORKERS (1969)**.

41. "No Strike" Clauses. The *TULRA 1974* provides that any terms of a collective agreement which prohibit or restrict the right of workers to engage in a strike or other industrial action, or have the effect of prohibiting or restricting that right, shall not form part of any contract between any worker and the person for whom he works unless the agreement:

a.   Is in writing; and

b.   Contains a provision expressly stating that those terms shall or may be incorporated in such a contract; and

c.   Is reasonably accessible at his place of work to the worker to whom it applies and is available for him to consult during working hours; and

d.   Is one where each trade union which is a party to the agreement is an independent trade union;

and unless the contract with the worker expressly or impliedly incorporates those terms in the contract.

42. The effect of this provision is governed by the provision of *S.16, TULRA 1974* that no court shall, whether by way of an order for specific performance or an injunction restraining a breach of, or threatened breach of a contract of employment, compel an employee to do any work or attend at any place for the doing of any work.

43. The effect of a "no strike" clause complying with the statutory provisions is therefore limited to circumstances where, for example, procedural requirements like consultation must be exhausted before taking strike action. In such circumstances an injunction could be granted in order that the proper procedure be followed.

INDUSTRIAL ACTION

44. Historical Background. The *COMBINATION ACT 1800* made any industrial action by employees illegal. The *TRADES DISPUTES ACT 1906* gave protection to employees participating in industrial action as a result of the case of **TAFF VALE RAILWAY COMPANY v AMALGAMATED SOCIETY OF RAILWAY SERVANTS (1901)**. The immunity of individuals was broadened by the *TRADE DISPUTES ACT 1965* as a result of **ROOKES v BARNARD (1964)** where it was held that intimidation (ie, threatening to break a contract of employment by striking) was an actionable tort.

45. The *INDUSTRIAL RELATIONS ACT 1971* changed the liability for industrial action for a period until the *TULRA 1974* restored the position of immunity which existed prior to 1971.

46. The Present Law Relating to Immunity in Tort. The *TULRA (S.13)* as amended by the *EA 1982* provides that an act done by a person in contemplation or furtherance of a trade dispute shall not be actionable in tort on the ground only,

    a.   That it induces another person to break a contract or interferes or induces any other person to interfere with its performance; or

    b.   That it consists in his threatening that a contract (whether one to which he is a party or not) will be broken or its performance interfered with, or that he will induce another person to break a contract or to interfere with its performance.

Note: An agreement or combination by two or more persons to do or procure the doing of any act in contemplation or furtherance of a trade dispute shall not be actionable in tort if the act is one which, if done without any such agreement or combination, would not be actionable in tort.

47. Trade Dispute. This is defined by the *TULRA (S.29)* as amended by the *EA 1982* as a dispute between workers and their employer which is related wholly or mainly with one or more of the following:

    a.   Terms and conditions of employment, or the physical conditions in which any workers are required to work;

    b.   Engagement or non-engagement, or termination or suspension of employment or the duties of employment, of one or more workers;

    c.   Allocation of work or the duties of employment as between workers or groups of workers;

    d.   Matters of discipline;

    e.   The membership or non-membership of a trade union on the part of a worker;

    f.   Facilities for officials of trade unions; and

    g.   Machinery for negotiation or consultation, and other procedures, relating to any of the above matters, including the recognition by employers or employers' associations of the right of a trade union to represent workers in any such negotiation or consultation or in the carrying out of such procedures.

48. Acts in Contemplation of Furtherance of a Trade Dispute. The statutory immunity only applies where industrial action is taken in contemplation or furtherance of a trade dispute. This is traditionally called the *"Golden Formula"* and has recently been subjected to considerable scrutiny by the courts. The following criteria must be satisfied in order to gain the protection of the golden formula:

    a.   There must be a dispute.

    In **BBC v HEARN (1977)** the refusal of technicians to transmit television pictures of the FA Cup Final to South Africa was held not to be a trade dispute.

b.   The dispute must fall within the statutory definition of a trade dispute.

In **J.T. STRATFORD & SONS LTD v LINDLEY (1965)** the plaintiffs hired out barges. A trade union imposed an embargo on the company because one of the company's subsidiaries refused to recognise the union. Members of the union would not return the barges which had been hired out thus rendering the hirers in breach of contract. The company's business was brought to a standstill. The company was granted an injunction against the union as no trade dispute as then defined was shown to exist.

c.   The dispute must be between the parties mentioned in paragraph **47.** above. **BEAVERBROOK NEWSPAPERS LTD v KEYS (1980)**.

d.   The action must be in contemplation or furtherance of the dispute. **EXPRESS NEWSPAPERS LTD v MACSHANE (1980)**.

49. Strikes. The *EPCA 1978* defines a strike for the purpose of computing continuous employment as a cessation of work by a body of persons employed acting in combination, or a concerted refusal of any number of persons employed to continue to work for an employer in consequence of a dispute, done as a means of compelling their employer or any person or body of persons employed, or to aid other employees in compelling their employer or any person or body of persons employed, to accept or not to accept terms or conditions of or affecting employment.

50. In **TRAMP SHIPPING CORPN v GREENWICH MARINE INC (1975)** Lord Denning defined a strike as a concerted stoppage of work by men done with a view to improving their wages or conditions of employment, or giving vent to a grievance or making a protest about something or other, or supporting or sympathising with other workmen in such endeavour.

51.   There is no right to strike recognised by British law, though immunity from the consequences is conferred under the law, provided the strike is for a proper purpose. There would seem little argument to contradict the view that a strike is merely one form of industrial action.

52. Picketing. *S.16, EA 1980* contains the law on peaceful picketing. Lawful picketing must be:

a.   In contemplation or furtherance of a trade dispute; and

b.   Only at the following specified places:

i.   At or near his own place of work, or

ii.   If his last employment was terminated in connection with a trade dispute, at or near his former workplace, or

iii.   If he does not work at any one place or if the place is in a location such that attendance there for picketing is impracticable, any premises of his employer from which he works or from which his work is administered, or

iv.   If he is an official of a trade union, at or near the place of work or former place of work of a member of that union whom he is accompanying and whom he represents; and

c.   For the purpose only of peacefully obtaining or communicating information or peacefully persuading any person to work or abstain from working.

53.   Where picketing extends outside the limits imposed by the *EA 1980* the persons concerned may not claim the legal immunity from actions in tort provided by *S.13, TULRA 1974.* (See para. **46.** above)

54.   Additionally, even where picketing falls within the conditions described in para **54.** above immunity will only be effective if:

a.   The picketing does not constitute secondary industrial action; or

b.   The employer of the pickets is a party to the trade dispute or, if not, the actions of the pickets fall within the gateways for lawful secondary action.

55.   Secondary Action.   By the provisions of *S.17, EA 1980* the immunity from legal proceedings in tort conferred by the *TULRA 1974* is not available when the industrial action consists of inducing a breach of a commercial contract (ie a contract which is not a contract of employment) by means of secondary action outside the permitted thresholds. There is secondary action in relation to a trade dispute when a person:

a.   Induces another to break a contract of employment or interferes or induces another to interfere with its performance, or

b.   Threatens that a contract of employment under which he or another is employed will be broken or its performance interfered with, or that he will induce another to break a contract of employment or to interfere with its performance,

if the employer under the contract of employment is not a party to the trade dispute.

In **MARINA SHIPPING LTD v LAUGHTON AND ANOTHER (1981)** a blacking action by officials of the International Transport Workers Federation against a Maltese ship was declared unlawful in the Court of Appeal. The court held that for such secondary action to be lawful under the *EA 1980* a contract would have to exist between the shipowners and the port authority supplying the services. No such contract had been entered into by the owners, or by the ship's master on their behalf.

In **SHAH v SOGAT 82 (1984)** members of SOGAT picketed the premises of the "Stockport Messenger" a place which was not the pickets' place of work. It was held that the action was unlawful secondary picketing and an injunction was imposed. The plaintiff also successfully claimed damages for loss of revenue.

56.   The following are the instances when secondary action may be within the scope of immunity conferred by the *TULRA 1974*:

a.   *The general rule*

i.   The principal purpose of the secondary action must be directly to prevent or disrupt the supply, during the dispute, of goods and services between an employer party to the dispute and the employer subject to the secondary action.

ii.   The action must directly prevent or disrupt supply. Thus, action taken against the employer supplying goods to the primary employer would be lawful but if supply was routed through a middleman action against the supplier may be unlawful.

iii.   The action must aim to disrupt or prevent a current supply. If there is no supply then action at the suppliers place of business may be unlawful.

iv.   The supply between primary and secondary employer which is disrupted must be in pursuance of a contract between them subsisting at the time of the secondary action.

v.   Finally there is an objective test; the secondary action must be likely to achieve the above purposes.

b.   *Associated employers.* The general rule applies but is extended to cover associated employers where:

i.   The secondary action is taken against an employer associated with an employer who is a party to the dispute and the goods or services are in substitution for those which would have been supplied by the employer in dispute.

ii.   The secondary action is taken against an employer associated with an employer who is a supplier of an employer party to the dispute and the goods or services are in substitution for those which would have been supplied by the primary supplier.

c.   *Secondary picketing.* Where secondary action takes the form of picketing it is lawful only if it is done in the course of attendance permitted (see para. **54.** above).

d.   *Employers' associations.* An employer affected by a dispute between an employers' association and a union is treated as a party to the dispute only if he is:

i.   A member of the association, and

ii.   Is represented in the dispute by the association.

EDITOR'S NOTE: See *EA 1990* for changes to the law in respect of secondary action.

57. Acts to Compel Trade Union Membership. *S.18, EA 1980* further provides that industrial action aimed at compelling workers to join a trade union is outside the ambit of *S.13, TULRA 1974* in certain circumstances. There is no immunity from liability in tort:

a.   Where a person induces or threatens to induce an employee to break his contract of employment, or interferes with or threatens interference with performance by an employee of his contract of employment, for the purpose of compelling workers to join a particular trade union, where the workers being compelled are employed neither by the same employer nor at the same place of work as that employee.

b.   The *EA 1982* provides that any term in a contract for the supply of goods or services is void in so far as it purports to require that the whole or part of the work is to be done by persons who are members of a trade union. Thus, union-only or non-union only labour contracts are void.

58.   Employers' Remedies. The rights and remedies of an employer who is or has been the target of industrial action are discussed under the following headings:

a.   *Remuneration of employees.* Industrial action by employees may constitute a breach, termination or suspension of the contract of employment dependent upon the terms of the contract. Similarly, the giving of notice of intention to take industrial action may be construed as anticipatory breach or repudiatory action or merely as an intention to suspend the contract. In any event it would seem that the employer has no duty to remunerate employees participating in industrial action unless he has expressly or impliedly contracted to do so.

b.   *Dismissal of employees.* Where industrial action may be construed as a breach of the contract of employment, the employer may dismiss all employees participating in the industrial action. For unfair dismissal provision see Chapter 47 para. **26.**

c.   *Damages.* The employer may have a right to claim damages in tort against workers participating in industrial action for which immunity is not provided by statute. Moreover, a claim for damages in tort may also be impossible against trade unions and their officials. The *EA 1982 (S.16)* sets out limits on damages which may be awarded against trade unions for certain torts. The limits depend on the total membership of a particular union, eg, £10,000 for less than 5,000 members to £250,000 for 100,000 or more. These limits do not apply in cases of personal injury caused by negligence, nuisance or breach of duty, nor for breach of duty connected with the ownership, occupation, possession, control or use of property.

d.   *Injunction.* Where the industrial action is not in contemplation or furtherance of a trade dispute the employer can seek an injunction to restrain such action. The courts, however, will not grant an injunction where its effect is to compel employees to work.

e.   *Conciliation.* In the interests of promoting good industrial relations the best solution to industrial action that the employer have available is conciliation and if necessary with the assistance of ACAS.

59.   Effect of Industrial Action on Employees' Rights. The consequences for employees participating in industrial action (whether or not in furtherance of a trade dispute) are discussed under the following headings:

a.   *Remuneration.* As indicated in the preceding paragraph the employee loses his right to receive remuneration during the industrial action.

b.   *Social security benefits.* An employee is not entitled to unemployment benefit for any period during which he is participating in industrial action. He may, however, be entitled to supplementary benefit in respect of his dependants.

c.   *Guarantee payments.* Employees engaged in industrial action are not entitled to guarantee payments under the terms of the *EPCA 1978.*

d.   *Unfair dismissal.* An employee dismissed because of his participation in industrial action will only be considered as unfairly dismissed in the circumstances outlined in chapter 47, para. **26.**

e.   *Continuous employment.* For the purposes of redundancy and unfair dismissal, absence due to participation in a strike does not break the continuity of employment, but the period of absence does not count in the computation of the period of continuous employment.

TRADE UNION ACT 1984

60.   The *TU ACT 1984* has introduced rules for the use of ballots in election of the governing bodies of trade unions, before strike action and in the use of funds on political matters.

61.   Secret Ballots for Election of Principal Executive Committees. The Act requires that all voting members of a trade union's executive committee will be elected by secret postal ballot at least once every five years. All members of the trade union in question must be given a voting entitlement except those who are precluded by the union rules and those in the following classes:-

a.   Members who are not in employment

b.   Members in arrears with union subscriptions

c.   Apprentices, trainees, students or new members.

62.   Workplace Ballot. Alternatively a workplace ballot may be allowed if it is:-

a.   Secret and free from interference or constraint

b.   Provides a convenient method of voting to members without incurring cost to themselves (eg by forfeiting overtime in order to vote)

c.   Voting is by ballot paper and votes are fairly and accurately counted.

63.   Names and Addresses of Members. Every trade union is required to compile and maintain a register of the names and addresses of its members.

64.   Failure to Comply with Provisions. Application to the Certification Office or the Court may be made within one year by any member alleging that a trade union has failed to comply with any of the foregoing provisions.

65.   Enforcement Order. The court may make an "enforcement order", imposing on the trade union one or more of the following provisions:-

a.   To secure the holding of an election

b.   To take other steps to remedy the union's failure

c.   To abstain from certain specified acts.

66. Secret Ballot Before Industrial Action. A trade union must hold a secret ballot not more than four weeks before taking strikes or other industrial actions to ascertain the wishes of the majority of their members. In the event of failure to do so the union will lose any immunity in tort.

67. Method of Voting. The ballot must be conducted by post or at the workplace and involve the marking of a ballot paper. The ballot must be secret and followed by announcement of the voting figures to the members concerned.

68. Entitlement to Vote. Entitlement to vote must be given equally to trade union members who it is believed will be called upon to take industrial action, and to no others.

In **AUSTIN ROVER v TGWU (1984)** the TGWU called a strike after a vote on a show of hands. The plaintiff alleged that the strike was unlawful as it had not been preceded by a secret ballot. It was held that the strike was illegal and should be called off pending the holding of a ballot.

69. Political Funds and Objects. Any trade union which has adopted a political fund resolution under the *TU ACT 1913* must pass a new resolution by means of a secret ballot of all its members if it wishes to continue to spend money on party political matters. The ballot must be carried out at intervals of not more than ten years.

EMPLOYMENT ACT 1988

70. The Employment Act 1988 increased the rights of individual employees in respect of their employment and as trade union members. The following is a summary of the main provisions of the Act.

EMPLOYMENT RIGHTS

71. a. **Right not to belong to a Trade Union.** No employee is obliged to join or remain a member of a trade union. Prior to this Act certain employees could be fairly dismissed for not belonging to a trade union if they worked in an approved "closed shop" (union membership agreement). All statutory protection for the closed shop has been removed and dismissal of any employee for not belonging to trade union is automatically unfair irrespective of whether or not they worked in a "closed shop".

b. **Right to have "check-off" stopped.** Check-off is the term for an arrangement under which trade union subscriptions are deducted by an employer from an individual's wages and paid over directly to the union. The Act gives individuals who inform their employer that they have left, or are leaving, the union the right to have check-off arrangements stopped.

The employee must notify his employer in writing, either:-

    i.   That his membership of the union has ended, or will end, on a specified date and that the union is aware of that fact, or

    ii.   That any notice of resignation that he has given to the union has expired, or will expire on a specified date. The notification is referred to in the Act as a certificate.

An employer who receives a certificate must stop deducting union subscriptions from the date specified in it. The individual's right to have check-off stopped overrides any arrangement with the union. The employer does not, therefore, need to obtain the union's authorisation before stopping check-off.

The continued deduction of union subscriptions will be unlawful. The employee can apply to an industrial tribunal under Part I of the Wages Act 1986 for a declaration that unlawful deductions have been made, and for a refund of the money unlawfully deducted.

TRADE UNION RIGHTS

72. a.   **Unjustifiable discipline.** The Act gives union members the right not to be unjustifiably disciplined by their union. Discipline will be unjustifiable for such conduct as working during a strike or making an assertion that their union has broken its rules. Members may complain to an industrial tribunal and obtain compensation. Individuals who work in a closed shop also have the right not to be unreasonably expelled from their union. Where expulsion is for conduct which is protected and so constitutes unjustifiable discipline an individual may not complain of unjustifiable discipline but may complain to a tribunal about unreasonable expulsion from a closed shop which is automatically treated as unreasonable expulsion.

It will be unjustifiable discipline if a union to which an individual previously belonged advises another union not to accept him because of conduct protected by the Act as constituting "unjustifiable discipline". The individual retains the right to apply to a tribunal on the grounds that his exclusion by the "new" union was unreasonable. The tribunal would automatically find any such exclusion to have been unreasonable.

b.   **Right to inspect accounts.** A trade union is required to keep its accounting records available for six years from 1 January following the end of the period to which they relate.

Any member of a trade union may request access to the records in respect of any period during which he was a member. Access must be permitted within 28 days of the request. The member is entitled to take an accountant with him and to take copies and extracts of the records. The trade union may make a charge for reasonable administrative expenses.

c.   **Right to a ballot before industrial action.** If a trade union calls a strike or other industrial action without the support of a proper ballot, a member may apply to the court for an order to have the endorsement of the action withdrawn by the union.

d.   **Political fund ballots.** If a trade union member complains that a ballot on the political fund was taken otherwise than in accordance with the rules approved by the Certification Officer, or there has been a failure to comply with those rules he may apply to the Certification Officer or the court for a declaration. The application must be made within one year from the date when the result of the ballot was announced.

e.   **Remedies against trustees.** A trade union member may apply to the court for an order if he considers that the trustees of the union's property are permitting an unlawful application of the property, or are complying with an unlawful direction given to them under the union's rules.

f.   **Indemnification of unlawful conduct.** Property of a trade union may not be applied in indemnifying a person in respect of a penalty imposed on him for a relevant offence or for contempt of court. If the union unreasonably fails to make a claim for recovery of the payment any member may apply to the court for authority to bring proceedings on behalf of the union and at its expense.

COMMISSIONER FOR THE RIGHTS OF TRADE UNION MEMBERS

73. The Act creates this new post. The Commissioner will be appointed by the Secretary of State and will hold office for five years.

The functions of the Commissioner will be to assist a trade union member who is taking legal action against his trade union. The actions appropriate are those authorised under various employment statutes, eg, failure to call a ballot on industrial action or to restrain the application of union funds for unlawful political purposes.

EMPLOYMENT ACT 1989

74. The aim of the EA 1989 is to "create a freer and more efficient market for jobs". In pursuance of this aim the Act has made a number of repeals and amendments to existing protective legislation. The following are the main provisions, in outline. The changes have been incorporated into the appropriate places in this text-book.

a.   The Act removed restrictions on womens' working hours in industrial employment (some restrictions are retained in respect of protection of women in pregnancy).

b.   Removal of controls in respect of children below minimum school-leaving age.

c.   Amendments to individual employment rights affecting:-

  i.   right to written statement of terms and conditions of employment.

  ii.   written statement of the reasons for dismissal.

  iii.   right to pursue a claim for unfair dismissal.

  iv.   shop steward's right to paid leave for industrial relations and training purposes.

EMPLOYMENT ACT 1990

75. The main changes brought in by the EA 1990 are in three areas of employment law, ie, the pre-entry closed shop, industrial action and the powers of the Commissioner for the Rights of Trade Union Members. The following are brief details of the changes:-

PRE-ENTRY CLOSED SHOP

76. The Act effectively made the pre-entry closed shop redundant by making it unlawful to refuse employment on the grounds of union membership.

a.   Unfair recruitment, ie, by making as a pre-requisite for employment either joining or leaving a union.

b.   An "employment agency" is subject to the conditions of a. above.

c.   A person who claims to have been unlawfully refused employment may complain to an industrial tribunal within 3 months.

d.   The complaint may be against an employer and employment agency jointly, and in addition a trade union.

BALLOTS

77. The Act introduces new requirements for industrial action ballots as follows:-

a.   The self-employed must be included in a ballot taken with a view to industrial action.

b.   An industrial action ballot ceases to be effective at the end of 4 weeks from the date of the ballot, ie it will be unlawful to initiate industrial action without a fresh ballot.

c.   Unions must appoint independent scrutineers to supervise the conduct of political fund and union election ballots.

INDUSTRIAL ACTION

78. The following are the three main points on the Act's provisions on industrial action:-

a.   **Secondary Action**

i.   Liability for secondary action arises where the action induces a breach of contract of employment regardless of whether a commercial contract is also broken.

ii.   Unlawful secondary action also covers the contract of a self-employed person.

iii.   There is now only one "gateway" to legality of secondary action. This is where the action consists of peaceful picketing as defined in the TULRA S.15.

b.   **Liability for unofficial action.** The Act makes the union instead of officials liable for unofficial industrial action, even though the action was not authorised by the union or even if it was forbidden by the union's rule book.

c.   **Repudiation.** The act of a committee or shop steward will not be regarded as having been authorised or endorsed by a union if it is repudiated by the principal executive committee (PEC) or the president or general secretary of the union as soon as is reasonably practicable after coming to the knowledge of any of them.

d.   **Selective dismissal during normal unofficial action.** An employer is permitted the selective dismissal of employees who are participating in unofficial action. An employee so dismissed has no right to complain of unfair dismissal.

COMMISSIONER FOR THE RIGHTS OF TRADE UNION MEMBERS

79. The Act extends the powers of the Commissioner to cover assistance to union members arising out of an alleged breach or threatened breach of the union's rules. Assistance may be provided, inter alia, in relation to:-

a.   Appointment or removal, etc, from any office in the union.

b.   Disciplinary proceedings.

c.   Authorising or endorsing industrial action.

COURSEWORK QUESTIONS 39-45
LABOUR LAW

39.   a.   Discuss the circumstances that legally justify the summary dismissal of an employee.

b.   Albert, a waiter, was summarily dismissed when he slipped on a wet floor and dropped a tray of plates. After he had left his employer, it was discovered that he had been taking money regularly from the till. Advise Albert.

CIMA Foundation November 1983

40.   A former employee is entitled to redundancy payment when he has been dismissed. Explain whether the following are dismissals for this purpose.

a.   A is employed for a two-year fixed term contract which expires and is not renewed.

b.   B is warned that his firm will close in the near future. He therefore finds a job elsewhere and leaves his present post.

c.   C leaves his job after his employer has asked him to take risks for which he is neither employed nor prepared to take.

d.   D's job comes to an end but he agrees to try another job for six weeks to see if he likes it. After three weeks he leaves.

e.   E has been away from work through illness for over a year. He is now told that his job has ended.

CIMA Foundation May 1983

41.   Martin brings an action against his employer for injuries received whilst operating a machine which is unguarded in contravention of the Factories Act 1961. Examine, in turn, the validity of the following defences:

a.   That it was not possible to guard the machine securely.

b.   That Martin was injured by a broken camshaft which flew out from the machine.

c.   *That Martin had removed the guard.*

d.   *That Martin was injured by the wire which the machine was processing, and not the machine itself.*

e.   *That Martin shouldn't have been anywhere near the machine, which was in a normally locked room. Martin had obtained the key from a keyboard.*

f.   *That the machine was not part of the factory equipment but a product which was being tested.*

g.   *That Martin was not a regular employee, but was brought in from time to time to test and repair the machines.*

h.   *That Martin had climbed on to the machine during lunch break to retrieve a football which had lodged there during a game.*

42.   Explain the term "safety representative". What powers does a safety representative have?

ICSA December 1978

43.   a.   A claim for unfair dismissal will fail if the dismissal is deemed to be fair. What reasons may be put forward by an employer to justify the dismissal?

b.   *Thirty employees at a small engineering factory went on strike in support of a wage claim. Orders were lost during the strike and, after a settlement had been reached, the employer re-engaged twenty of the employees and said that there was no work for the other ten. It is alleged that the employer has used the situation to dismiss those employees likely to cause trouble, including the union representative. To what extent is a claim for unfair dismissal likely to succeed?*

CIMA Foundation May 1982

44.   a.   Explain how the statutory rights of an employee are affected by the length of his employment.   *(14 marks)*

b.   *Charles has been employed for five years as a labourer in a factory used for the manufacture of furniture. The factory is bought by another furniture manufacturing company which closes down most of the manufacturing processes. It uses the space for storage of its products. The employment of Charles is continued but, three months later, he is dismissed as redundant.*
Consider whether Charles' length of service entitles him to compensation.   *(6 marks)*
                                    (20 marks)

CIMA Foundation November 1985

Introduction to Appendices 1 and 2

1. The questions and answers in these two appendices serve 3 purposes:-

   a. They illustrate the style and structure of legal answers.

   b. They are a valuable means of self-testing.

   c. They provide an incentive to practice.

2. The way to use these answers is:-

   a. First attempt the question. Your attempt may be a "timed" answer, ie written in 30-35 minutes without the aid of notes or textbooks, or a "model" answer, ie an examintion-length answer prepared in as much time as necessary, using all available resources.

   b. Then, and only then, read the suggested answer. You can then critically assess your own answer, perhaps awarding yourself a mark, or even re-writing the answer if you consider your attempt very poor.

3. The authors would like to make it clear that although many of the questions have been selected from past ACCA, CIMA and ICSA examination papers the solutions have been prepared by the authors and do not represent the official solutions of the examining boards concerned.

Appendix 1

SUGGESTED ANSWERS TO
COURSEWORK QUESTIONS 1-8
THE ENGLISH LEGAL SYSTEM

1. Prior to 1066 there existed a primitive legal system based on local custom. The effect of the Norman conquest was to set in motion the unification of these local customs into one system of law with the King at its head. The system was common to all men, and for this reason was known as "common law". The ascendancy of the King's Courts over the local courts took about 300 years, during which the King gradually assumed control through his travelling justices. The growth of the King's Courts was resisted by the local barons, landowners and sheriffs whose jurisdiction and revenue was being reduced.

At the same time as the King's justices were dealing with criminal matters and supervising local administration, the King himself had established the Curia Regis (King's Court). It consisted of the King and his tenants-in-chief. Although called a court it had legislative, administrative and judicial functions. It was therefore the predecessor of Parliament as well as the courts. In medieval times a pattern developed whereby courts separated from the Curia Regis and eventually acquired a jurisdiction separate from it. In about 1140 the Court of Exchequer became a separate court. It dealt with the collection of royal revenue and disputes over debts. Soon afterwards the Court of Common Pleas was formed. It exercised jurisdiction over the disputes concerning land. The final court to break from the Curia Regis was the King's Bench. It was created in 1268. It had a varied civil jurisdiction, and appellate jurisdiction. These three courts survived until 1875. The influence of the King himself gradually declined although he retained a residual judicial power which led to other courts deriving their jurisdiction from him, notably The Court of Chancery, (1474-1875) and The Star Chamber (approximately 1500-1640).

Over the years the common law grew into a rigid and often harsh system. "Fictions" to some extent mitigated this, for example the fictitious valuation of stolen property at less than one shilling, thus reducing the offence from a felony to a misdemeanour for which the penalties were less severe. Fictions were not however capable of remedying all the defects of the common law. For example (i) The plaintiff either had to fit his action into the framework of an existing writ, for example trespass, or else show that it was similar to such a writ. If he could do neither he had no remedy; (ii) In civil actions the only remedy which the common law courts could grant was an award of damages; and (iii) Rules of procedure were complex, and any slight breach of these rules could leave a plaintiff, who had a good case without a remedy. The practice grew in such cases of dissatisfied litigants petitioning the King to exercise his prerogative power in their favour. The King, through his

Chancellor, eventually set up the Court of Chancery to deal with these petitions.

It became independent of the King in 1474. If there was any conflict between the Common Law Courts and the Court of Chancery the "equity" of the Court of Chancery prevailed.

The system outlined above was heavily criticised in the 19th century. The separate existence of the Common Law Courts and the Court of Chancery led to the criticism that one court was set up to do injustice and another to stop it. Procedure was slow, expensive, complex, and generally out of date, and some courts, for example the High Court of Admiralty, and the ecclesiastical courts, had their own individual procedures. In addition the court structure, and system of appeals needed a complete overhaul.

The most important reforms of the 19th century were brought about by the *JUDICATURE ACTS OF 1873-1875*, which came into operation together in 1875. Their main reform was to create a new Supreme Court of Judicature to which was transferred the jurisdiction of all the superior Common Law Courts and the Court of Chancery. The Supreme Court was divided into two parts, the High Court, and the Court of Appeal. The Judicature Acts thus fused the administration (but not the content) of common law and equity. They also enacted the established principle that in all cases of conflict the rules of equity shall prevail. These reforms also simplified procedure by abolishing the existing forms of action and introducing new procedural rules. Thus a plaintiff could frame his case in his own words, rather than those of a particular form of action, and he did not need to fear losing his case because of a purely technical error.

2. The term "sources of law" has several different meanings. There are the historical sources, namely common law and equity; literary sources, for example law reports; and legal sources. Legal sources are the most important. They are sources from which rules must originate before judges will consider that they are bound to apply those rules. There are three legal sources — legislation, judicial precedent, and custom.

Legislation is the name given to rules enacted by the Queen in Parliament. Each piece of legislation is contained in a statute (or Act of Parliament). The purposes of legislation are to change or clarify existing law, or create new rules. To achieve these purposes some statutes will repeal earlier statutes, others will consolidate all previous statutes on one topic into one Act, whilst codifying statutes enact all of the law on a particular subject. Many modern statutes are concerned with the day to day running of society, for example consumer protection statutes such as the *CONSUMER CREDIT ACT 1974*, and the *RENT ACT 1974*. Legislation is the supreme source of law because Parliament may enact or repeal any law it chooses, and if there is a conflict between legislation and custom or precedent then legislation prevails. In addition a statute never becomes obsolete, it retains the force of law until it is repealed by another statute.

In recent years there has been an increasing tendency for Parliament to confer on persons or bodies, for example Ministers in charge of government departments, power to make regulations for specified purposes. These regulations are known as delegated legislation, and they have the same legal effect as an Act of Parliament. The main advantages of delegated legislation are that it saves the time of Parliament, and it enables experts to deal with local or technical matters. On the other hand it must be carefully controlled since it is less open to public scrutiny, and it removes direct control from the hands of elected representatives.

The third type of legislation is the regulations, directives, and decisions emanating from the Institutions of the European Economic Community, ie The Council of Ministers, The Commission and The European Court. It is a condition of membership of the EEC that this community legislation be observed in member states.

Judicial precedents are the decisions of judges. A judge is bound to follow a rule of law formulated by his predecessor if the material facts of the case are the same, and if the earlier judgement was given in a court of superior, or in some cases equal, status. This system is necessary to maintain an element of certainty in the law. The earlier judgement may either be a ruling on the interpretation of a statute, or it may be a decision on a general principle of common law or equity. Traditionally the function of a judge is not to make law, but to apply law in accordance with existing rules. Sometimes however this is not possible, for example if a statute is to be interpreted for the first time, or if there is no existing precedent. In such cases judges must make law. Precedent is therefore a very important source of law.

The least important of the three legal sources is custom. In order to be a source of law the custom must be confined to a particular locality such as a county or parish, and it must be an exception to the common law. If a local custom is to be incorporated into the law it must be proved to exist in Court. It is then said to be "judicially noticed" and will be enforced by other courts.

3. Laymen are involved primarily in the administration of criminal justice.

Magistrates courts are composed of lay justices. Three justices usually sit. They are advised on the law by a qualified Clerk to the Justices. There is no jury. Any person may apply, or be proposed, to be a magistrate. Selection is made by a Lord Chancellor's advisory committee, of which there is one per county. Committee membership, and selection criteria are secret.

The reason for the involvement of lay justices is basically historical. The origin of the modern Justice of the Peace can be traced back to the *STATUTE OF LABOURS 1361*. This provided for the appointment of lay justices and compelled them to hold sessions in each county four times a year. Lay justices would not have survived without good reason. Their involvement today has several advantages. Firstly lay participation in the legal process reduces the remoteness of the law from the public. Secondly the system is cheap, since magistrates are not paid. It nevertheless appears to attract high quality personnel, although they tend to be drawn from a narrow background, being predominantly male, middle aged and middle class. Thirdly lay magistrates reduce the pressure on professional lawyers, leaving them to hear the more serious offences and most civil cases. Finally, although not legally qualified, magistrates may be better qualified in other respects. They may be for example, better qualified to hear children's cases. Lay magistrates also reduce the risk of the child perceiving himself as a young criminal.

The second major area of lay participation is the jury. Jurors are summoned by the Lord Chancellor, and selection is by random ballot. Any registered elector, (some professions such as lawyers and doctors excepted), between 18 and 65 may be summoned. The jury sits in secret, it does not give a reason for its verdict, and a majority of 10-2 is necessary for a conviction. The reason for lay juries is also historical. They first evolved in the 13th century to replace trial by ordeal, which the Church condemned in 1215. Originally the jury merely informed the judge what the local customs were, but by the 15th century their function had changed from witnesses to judges of fact. Most civil and criminal cases were tried by jury until 1854. Today the jury has been abolished in most civil cases, although a person over the age of 16 has the right to demand trial by jury in the Crown Court if he is accused of an indictable (serious) offence. Despite the fact that only a small minority of criminal defendants are tried by jury the right to such a trial is still regarded as fundamental in all cases involving major criminal charges. The jury has its critics, who argue that jurors can be taken in by skilled speeches, and are not experienced in weighing evidence. There is also recent evidence of a disturbingly high incidence of "questionable" convictions and acquittals. (Baldwin and McConville 1979).

It is however clear that the jury enjoys the confidence of the public, the judiciary, lawyers and the police. Its defenders argue that it is the best means of establishing the truth, and it clearly serves an important political function by involving laymen in the administration of justice. Most important it is a safeguard of liberty. Lord Devlin has written:-

"No tyrant could afford to leave a subject's freedom in the hands of 12 of his countrymen. So that trial by jury is more than an instrument of justice and more than one wheel of the constitution: It is the lamp that shows that freedom lives".

Finally it should be noted that laymen are involved in other aspects of the administration of justice. For example a lay trade union representative will sit on an industrial tribunal, and many arbitrators are specialist laymen rather than lawyers.

4. a. Statute law refers to laws enacted by Parliament. A statute is an Act of Parliament, the term is not used to refer to delegated legislation or EEC legislation. Acts of Parliament are the supreme source of law because

   i.   they cannot be questioned by the courts

   ii. they can change the common law

   iii. they can expressly or impliedly repeal earlier statutes. (The only thing that Parliament cannot do is bind its successors.)

The main advantages of statute law are:-

   i.   It is democratic since it is made by elected representatives who can take public opinion into account when making new law.

    ii.   It is written down, readily accessible, and its meaning is generally clear.

    iii.   It can be used to formalise uncertain areas of common law for example the *SUPPLY OF GOODS AND SERVICES ACT 1982*.

Disadvantages of statute law include:-

    i.   If the meaning of a statute is uncertain any doubt will not be resolved until another Act is passed or the courts are called upon to interpret the statute.

    ii.   Passing an Act of Parliament is a relatively slow process and Parliamentary time is very limited, thus relatively few major pieces of legislation are passed each year.

    iii.   Case law deals with actual events, statute law anticipates factual situations. Sometimes a statute will not cover all the intended situations.

b.   The basic rule of interpretation is known as the literal rule. This states that the words used must be given their literal or usual meaning even if the result appears to be contrary to the intentions of the legislature. For example in **FISHER v BELL (1961)**, a shopkeeper who displayed "flick knives" in his window was found not guilty of "offering for sale" an offensive weapon because an exhibition of goods in a shop window does not constitute an offer. His conduct was however clearly of the type which Parliament intended to punish.

If the legislature's words, interpreted literally, are capable of alternative meanings the literal rule clearly cannot be applied. In such cases the Court may resort to the approach to interpretation known as the golden rule. This states that the literal rule must be followed unless to do so produces an absurd result. For example in **RE SIGSWORTH (1935)** the golden rule was applied to prevent a murderer from inheriting on the intestacy of his victim although he was, as her son, the only person entitled to her estate on a literal interpretation of the *ADMINISTRATION OF ESTATES ACT 1925*.

The third approach to interpretation is known as the mischief rule (or the rule in Heydon's Case). The rule is that where a statute was passed to remedy a mischief the court must adopt the interpretation which will have the effect of correcting the mischief in question. For example a "single woman" for the purpose of affiliation proceedings is a woman with no husband to support her, not necessarily an unmarried woman, since the mischief which the Act was passed to remedy is the possibility of a woman having an illegitimate child with no means of supporting it.

In addition to the above three approaches to interpretation there exists several rules of interpretation and construction. Firstly, the statute must be read as a whole, each section being read in the light of every other section, and in particular in the light of an interpretation section (if any). Secondly, where general words follow two or more particular words they must be confined to a meaning of the same kind as the particular words.

For example "cats, dogs and other animals" means other domestic animals. This is known as the eiusdem generis rule. Thirdly, there is a rule that penal provisions are construed narrowly. Thus where there is ambiguity or uncertainty a criminal statute will be interpreted in favour of the individual. Finally, unless there are clear words to the contrary it will be presumed that a statute (i) is not retrospective, (ii) does not alter the law, (iii) does not deprive a person of a right vested in him before the statute came into operation, (iv) does not bind the Crown, and (v) does not oust the jurisdiction of courts.

5. The law recognises two types of full legal person: natural persons and corporations. A corporation is an artificial legal entity which comes into existence once the formalities for its creation have been complied with.

The main feature of all corporations is that they are separate entities distinct from their members. This was established in **SALOMON v SALOMON AND CO (1897)**, where the majority shareholder in a family company was able to sue his company to recover a loan, thus gaining prior claim to the company's assets over the general unsecured trade creditors. The creditors claimed that they should have priority because Salomon and the company were basically the same person. This claim failed.

Some of the other consequences of incorporation are:- (i) A company may own property. Consequently its property is distinct from that of the members. Therefore the members have no insurable interest in the property of the corporation. (ii) It can make contracts, sue, and be sued in its own name, and (iii) it has perpetual succession, ie its existence is not affected by the death of some or even all of its members.

In some circumstances the law will ignore the fact that the corporation and its members are separate legal entities. For example if an individual uses a corporation as a means of avoiding a valid restraint of trade clause entered into by him personally the corporation may be held bound by the clause. This is because the courts will not allow a corporation to be used by an individual as a means of avoiding his legal obligations. Also if it appears that business has been carried on with intent to defraud creditors the members who are party to the fraud may be held personally liable for the company's debts.

The quoted statement is therefore basically correct, although there are several statutory and case law exceptions whereby the law "lifts the veil of incorporation" and regards the corporation and its members as the same legal person.

There are two basic types of corporation, corporations sole and corporations aggregate.

A corporation sole is an official position which is filled by one person who is replaced from time to time. Examples include the Crown in its public capacity, the Treasury Solicitor, and the Public Trustee. The monarchy became a corporation sole because of recognition by the common law. Today corporations sole can be created only be statute.

A corporation aggregate is a legal person formed by a group of natural persons. There are three types namely Chartered Corporations, Statutory Corporations and Registered Companies.

The prerogative powers of the monarch have been reduced over the years, but there still remains the power to create corporations by Royal Charter. At one time trading companies such as the Hudson's Bay Company were created by Royal Charter. More recently the power has been confined to non-commercial corporations and was used to create, for example The Law Society, The Institute of Chartered Accountants, and The British Broadcasting Corporation. The procedure is for the organisation to petition the Privy Council, asking for a Charter and outlining the powers it requires. If the Privy Council considers that the organisation is appropriate they will advise the Crown to grant a charter.

A corporation may also be created by a particular statute. Public corporation are usually formed in this way. For example the *TRANSPORT ACT 1962* created The British Railways Board.

The *COMPANIES ACT 1985* provides for the registration of unlimited companies, companies limited by guarantee, and companies limited by shares. The latter are by far the most numerous, being the predominant type of business organisation in modern society. To form a registered company the promoters of the company must deliver to the Registrar of Companies a registration fee and certain documentation including details of the constitution which is to regulate the internal and external affairs of the proposed company, and details of the first directors and secretary of the company.

6. Magistrates' courts are composed of unqualified and unpaid Justices of the Peace. Three magistrates usually sit, without a jury. They have first instance jurisdiction over both civil and criminal cases.

Magistrates criminal jurisdiction mainly concerns summary offences (all of which are statutory). The maximum penalty that can be imposed is a fine of £1,000 or 6 months imprisonment. Most summary convictions are for motoring offences, and in total about 1.5 million people are convicted each year.

Magistrates also have jurisdiction over certain indictable offences, although an accused over 16 may demand the right to a jury trial. In practice most indictable offences are either tried in Magistrates or Juvenile Courts, but the accused, if found guilty may be sent to the Crown Court for sentence if the magistrates consider that he deserves a greater punishment than they have power to impose.

A further criminal function of magistrates concerns committal proceedings. A person cannot be tried on indictment before a jury unless he is first brought before one or more magistrates so that they can hold a preliminary examination to decide whether or not a reasonable case can be made out against him. If such a "prima facie" case is established he will be committed for trial in the Crown Court.

Children (under 14) and young persons (14-16) also have their cases heard by magistrates. Three magistrates drawn from a special panel, and including one man and one woman hear the case in private. The court may make a supervision, care, guardianship, or hospital order. These orders are not regarded as convictions.

Magistrates also have a varied, but limited, civil jurisdiction. This includes the recovery of certain civil debts such as income tax, gas bills and council rates. Also, by virtue of the *DOMESTIC PROCEEDINGS AND MAGISTRATES' COURTS ACT 1978* they may hear such matters as affiliation, adoption and guardianship. In matrimonial proceedings they may make, for example, orders for periodic payments for the benefit of either spouse of a child of the family, or orders for custody or access.

Magistrates' courts are very important for two reasons:-

Firstly they deal with the vast majority of the country's criminal offences. The system is cheap, since magistrates are unpaid, and it is quick. In 1957 procedure was expedited by the introduction of new rules enabling persons to plead guilty to minor summary offences by post.

Secondly it involves the public in the legal process. This has several important advantages. − It reduces the remoteness of the public from the law; it reduces the pressure on professional judges, allowing them to hear more serious cases; and it enables persons with special qualifications to hear children's cases. Such persons may be better qualified than judges to deal with children. They also reduce the danger of the child perceiving himself as a young criminal.

Criticisms have however been aimed at magistrates. Firstly because they are predominantly white, male, middle aged and middle class they are unrepresentative of the general population. Secondly because of the pressure of work they do not probe adequately into the facts of each case, and are rather too willing to accept police evidence.

The advantages nevertheless outweigh the disadvantages. Magistrates courts are a well-established and important part of the English legal system.

7.   A trust is a relationship in which a person called a trustee, in whom the legal title of property for the benefit of another person called a beneficiary. The essence of a trust is confidence placed in the trustee by the settlor (the person who conveyed his property to the trustee to hold for the beneficiary). Since the settlor has placed his confidence in the trustee, the trustee has an obligation to act in accordance with the settlor's wishes. This obligation is recognised by equity and can be enforced by a beneficiary, even though he was not a party to the creation of the trust.

There are several methods by which a trust may come into existence.

The most common would be where the settlor creates an express trust, which may be either private in nature of public (usually by deed) that he is the trustee of property or to convey (by deed or by will) his property to a trustee to hold for the beneficiary. Where he creates a trust of land to take effect inter vivos (within his lifetime) the terms must be contained in written evidence signed by the settlor. Trusts of pure personalty to take effect inter vivos may be created verbally. Trusts which are to arise on the settlor's death must be created by will. Whichever method is used it is a requirement that the "3 certainties" are present. The first is certainty of words, ie the words used must show a clear intention to create a trust. Secondly there must be certainty of subject matter, ie the trust must define the extent of the trust property. Finally there must be certainty of objects, ie the beneficiaries themselves must be adequately identified.

A trust may also be created by implication, ie from the presumed intention of the owner of the property. For example if A pays for property which is conveyed by the vendor to B the general rule is that B is presumed to hold the property as trustee for A.

Finally a trust may be imposed by equity on grounds of conscience independently of any presumed intention. For example if a stranger to the trust knowingly receives trust property, being aware that it has been transferred to him in breach of trust, he will hold the property for the beneficiaries on what is known as a constructive trust.

The main functions and duties of trustees are as follows. Firstly they must reduce the trust property into possession, ie obtain control of the trust property. They must then take such care of the property as an ordinary prudent man would take of his own property. In particular they must only invest trust funds in investments authorised by the *TRUSTEE INVESTMENTS ACT 1961*. They must also keep proper accounts and produce them to the beneficiaries when required. Secondly a trustee must not delegate his duties. This is expressed by the maxim "delegatus non potest delegare" (a delegate must not delegate). There are however exceptions, for example by *S.23. TRUSTEE ACT 1925* a trustee may appoint a solicitor or other agent to do any act required in the carrying out of the trust. Thirdly a trustee must not profit from the trust, by for example purchasing the trust property for himself. He may however receive such remuneration as is granted by the trust instrument or agreed by the beneficiaries. Finally the trustee must distribute the trust property to the persons entitled to it.

8.   Property is anything that can be owned. English law recognises two basic kinds of property namely real property, which consists of freehold land, and personal property, which is any other property, including leasehold land.

Property is classified as real or personal according to the right of action that used to have to be followed to claim a right to such property. If a person was dispossessed of freehold land he had a right "in rem" (ie in "the thing") and he could claim back the thing lost be bringing a real action. If a person was dispossessed of any other property he only had a right "in personam". ie he only had a right against the person who dispossessed him which he could enforce by means of a personal action. The distinction between real and personal actions has long since ceased to exist but the method of classification that it gave rise to is still used.

Real property, ie freehold land, is one of only two legal estates which may exist in land (the other being a term of years absolute, ie a lease). The correct name for this legal estate is the fee simple absolute in possession. This means an estate capable of being inherited, and able to pass to any person under a will or on an intestacy. It must not be subject to any conditions and the owner must be entitled to physical possession.

There are several types of personal property. Leasehold interests in land are known as chattels real, whereas all other personal property is known as chattels personal or pure personalty. (The word "chattel" is derived from cattle). Chattels personal are further sub-divided into choses in action and choses in possession. A chose in action is a property right which can only be protected by legal action, for example a patent, copyright, or shares in a limited company. A chose in possession is property which can be protected by physical control, for example a car, book, or pen.

It is interesting to note that although leasehold land has been classified as personal property, the courts since the 15th century have allowed a person dispossessed of such land to bring a real action to eject the trespasser. Thus leasehold land was in this respect similar to freehold land and became known as chattels real. Since the *LAW OF PROPERTY ACT 1925* leasehold property has been treated in all respects as real property.

An important modern distinction between real property (and leasehold land) and personal property, is the method by which such property must be transferred. Freehold land must be transferred by deed. Leases for more than 3 years must be granted by deed, even a gift of land must be by deed. In contrast ownership of a chose in possession can usually be transferred by mere delivery, either actual delivery, ie handing over the thing itself, or constructive delivery, for example handing over the keys to a warehouse where the goods are kept. Choses in action may be assigned at law under *S.136. LAW OF PROPERTY ACT 1925*. This section requires that the assignment is in writing and signed by the assignor. The whole of the interest must be transferred to the assignee and where a debt is assigned written notice must be given to the debtor.

There is also a distinction with regards to the creation of real and personal property. Personal property can be created in various ways, for example an artist may paint a picture, a cat may have a kitten or an inventor may be granted a patent. Real property cannot really be created at all. Freehold land may be split and transferred to several people to create new legal estates and leasehold land may revert to freehold at the end of the term of the lease, but the historical origin of freehold land precludes the creation of real property in any literal sense.

SUGGESTED ANSWERS TO COURSEWORK QUESTIONS 9-16 THE LAW OF CONTRACT

9. a. Certain restrictions in agreements are normally accepted as part of the modern pattern of trade, and will not usually be nullified by the courts.

For example, a restraint by a brewer in a lease of a public house tying it to the brewer.

Other contracts involving a restriction on the freedom of an individual to trade are prima facie void, and will not be upheld unless they are shown to be reasonable in the interests of both parties and the public.

If the restraint is to be reasonable between the parties it must be no wider than is reasonably necessary to protect an interest of the covenantee which requires protection. With regard to the public the court must consider the agreement as a whole including the area and duration of the restraint.

The 4 main categories of contracts in restraint of trade which may be upheld as being reasonable are as follows:-

i. Restraints imposed on ex-employees. − As between employer and employee the only interests which the employer is entitled to protect are his trade secrets and business connections. In considering whether it is reasonable to prevent misuse of such knowledge and influence the area and time of the restraint are particularly relevant. Thus in **MASON v PROVIDENT CLOTHING CO (1913)**, a clothing company's canvasser was restrained from working in a similar post within 25 miles of London. This restraint was held to be void since the area was too wide, being about 1,000 times as large as the area in which he was employed. However a worldwide covenant against solicitation of customers may be valid, **PLOWMAN v ASH (1964)**.

The reasonableness of the duration of the restraint depends on the type of business to be protected. If it is one to which clients are likely to resort of a long time, a lifetime restraint may be valid. Thus in **FITCH v DEWES (1921)**, a lifetime restraint, preventing a solicitor's managing clerk from practising within 7 miles of his principal's office, was upheld.

ii. Restraints imposed on the vendor of a business. − A distinction must be drawn between restraints imposed by an employer on his employee, which if aimed at competition as such are always void, and restraints imposed on the sale of goodwill, or as between partners, which within limits may validly prevent competition. Furthermore the restraint is more likely to be upheld because the parties are on an equal footing. − The vendor cannot get a fair price unless he agrees not to compete, nor can the purchaser get the benefit of his purchase.

iii. Restraints arising from agreements between traders. − The common law regarded such restraints leniently. However, since they were often contrary to the public interest, protection has been given by statute, including the *RESTRICTIVE TRADE PRACTICES ACT 1976*. The theme of the Act is that all such agreements which are not shown to be in the public interest under a specified "gateway" are illegal. An example of an acceptable restraint would be that it reduced the risk of injury to the public.

iv.   Solus agreements, − ie where a trader agrees to restrict his orders to one supplier. Such a restraint may be one of the terms of a mortgage. Duration is the most important factor in assessing the legality of solus agreements. In **ESSO PETROL v HARPER'S GARAGE (1967)** a 4½ year restraint was upheld, whereas in **PETROFINA v MARTIN (1966)** a 12 year restraint was declared void.

b.   If a restraint on an ex-employee is to be upheld the duration and area covered must not be unreasonable. Furthermore the employer may only protect his confidential information and business contacts, he may not impose a blanket restriction on competition or the subsequent employment of his ex-employee. In each situation the outcome would be as follows:-

i.   Both the duration and area covered are unreasonable. In such cases the court will not re-write the clause to validate the restraint. In **GREER v SKETCHLEY (1978)** a nationwide restraint imposed by a company which only operated in London and the Midlands was held to be unreasonably wide and unenforceable since it included areas in which the company did not operate. The court was not prepared to interpret the clause so that it would only apply to London and the Midlands.

ii.   Blackacres may be able to prevent Alec from canvassing present customers by, for example, using the company's mailing list, but they could not prevent canvassing of "future customers" since this would be an attempt to prevent competition. (The term "future customers" may in any case be too uncertain to be enforceable). The court would be unlikely to sever the reference to future customers so as to render the remainder of the clause valid.

iii.   This could not be enforced it is far too wide and it specifically seeks to prevent competition.

10.   a.   i.   There are two types of injunction. A *prohibitory* injunction restrains the defendant from committing a future breach. Such an injunction would be appropriate to prevent breach of a negative stipulation in a contract. For example in **WARNER BROS v NELSON (1936)** an actress agreed to act for the plaintiffs for a period of time, and promised that during that time she would not act for anyone else without the plaintiff's written consent. She was restrained by injunction from breaking this promise.

The second type of injunction is a *mandatory* injunction. This is an order compelling the defendant to take action to undo a breach of contract. For example he may be ordered to take down an advertising sign erected in breach of contract.

When deciding whether to award a mandatory injunction the court will be concerned with the "balance of convenience". ie The injunction will not be granted if the prejudice to the defendant in having to restore the original position heavily outweighs the advantage that such restoration will give to the plaintiff. In contrast when awarding a prohibitory injunction the court will not be concerned with the "balance of convenience" and an injunction cannot therefore be resisted on the grounds that observance of the restriction will be burdensome on the defendant or that the breach would cause little harm to the plaintiff.

ii.   With the exception of the enforcement of a specific obligation to pay money the common law did not recognise either injunction or specific performance. Specific performance is an equitable remedy and, as such, is subject to many restrictions:-

Firstly specific performance is a discretionary remedy. Therefore it will not be awarded if it would cause severe hardship to the defendant. For example in **DENNE v LIGHT (1857)** the court refused to order specific performance against the buyer of farm land which was completely surrounded by land belonging to other people over which there was no right of way. Similarly specific performance would not be awarded of a contract which was obtained by unfair means.

Secondly specific performance is not awarded where damages would be an adequate remedy. It is accepted by the courts that a buyer of land or a house is not adequately compensated by damages, and he can therefore get specific performance. On the basis of the maxim "equality is equity" the vendor can also claim specific performance even though his only claim is for money. Damages are also inadequate where there is a sale of unique goods, (see b. i. below).

Thirdly it must be available to either party. Thus, since specific performance will not be awarded against an infant, it will not be granted to him.

Finally specific performance is not available in respect of certain types of contract, for example a contract which requires extensive supervision, such as a building contract.

b.   i.   John is in breach of contract for refusing to give the painting to Dave. Dave's possible remedies are damages and specific performance. Where there is a contract for the sale of specific goods (as in this case) *S.52. SALE OF GOODS ACT 1979* gives the court a discretion to order specific performance. This discretion is however sparingly exercised. For example in **COHEN v ROCHE (1927)** the court refused to grant specific performance to the buyer of Hellpewhite chairs on the grounds that they were "ordinary articles of commerce and of no special interest".

Dave's case is slightly different since a painting is a unique item. In such cases the plaintiff will clearly not be able to obtain a satisfactory substitute. Thus for many years the courts have been prepared to award specific performance of contracts for the sale of heirlooms or works of art.

ii.   Since specific performance is an equitable remedy, it will be granted only when its award is consistent with the maxims of equity. One such maxim is "equality is equity". Thus a person who undertakes to render personal services cannot claim specific performance since the remedy is not available against him, and for the same reason an infant cannot claim specific performance. (**FLIGHT v BOLLAND (1828)**).

Thus, if Dave were a minor, specific performance would not be granted, and even though damages would be difficult to assess Dave would be restricted to the remedy of damages.

11. a.   The courts will imply 3 types of terms into contracts. Firstly terms which are so obvious that the parties must have intended them to be included. These are called terms implied in fact. Secondly terms which are implied to maintain a standards of behaviour, even though the parties may not have intended them to be included. These are called terms implied in law. Finally terms implied by custom.

THE MOORCOCK (1889), is the leading case on terms implied in fact. D, who were wharf owners contracted to allow P to unload their ship at the wharf. The ship grounded at low water, and was damaged by settling on a ridge of hard ground. D were held to be in breach of an implied term that the wharf was safe. The impled term must be both obvious and necessary to give "business efficacy" to the contract, the courts will not imply a term merely because it is reasonable to do so.

Terms implied in law cover many classes of contract. Thus in a contract of employment the employee impliedly undertakes, for example, to faithfully serve his employer, and that he is reasonably skilled. The employer impliedly undertakes that he will not require the employee to do an unlawful act, and that he will provide safe premises. Similarly in a tenancy agreement the landlord impliedly covenants that his tenant shall have quiet possession, and the tenant impliedly agrees not to commit waste.

With regard to custom the parties are presumed to have contracted by reference to the customs of their trade. Thus in **BRITISH CRANE HIRE v IPSWICH PLANT HIRE (1974)** the owner of a crane hired it to a contractor who was engaged in the same business. It was held that the hirer was bound by the owner's usual terms even though they had not been communicated to him at the time the contract was made.

The most important statutory implied terms are now contained in the *SALE OF GOODS ACT 1979*. The Act implies conditions:-

a.   That the seller has a right to sell *(S.12.)*.
b.   That if a sale is by description, the goods shall correspond with the description *(S.13.)*.
c.   That the goods supplied are of merchantable quality, and fit for the purpose for which they are required *(S.14.)*.
d.   That where the goods are sold by sample the bulk will correspond with the sample. *(S.15.)*.

b.   The extent to which implied terms may be excluded is as follows:-

Terms implied by the courts may be excluded, although following the *UNFAIR CONTRACT TERMS ACT 1977* the exemption clause would have to satisfy the Act's requirement of reasonableness. The same principles would apply to a term implied by custom. However a clause excluding such an implied term would almost certainly be held to be reasonable.

The *UNFAIR CONTRACT TERMS ACT* (as amended) also governs the extent to which *S.12-15 SALE OF GOODS ACT 1979* can be excluded. *S.12.* cannot be excluded in any sale. *S.13-15* cannot be excluded in a consumer sale but can be excluded in a non-consumer sale if the exemption clause is reasonable. A person deals as a consumer if

i.   He neither makes the contract in the course of a business, nor holds himself out as doing so, and

ii.   The other party does make the contract in the course of a business, and

iii.   The goods are of a type ordinarily supplied for private use or consumption.

12. a.   A person who alleges that he has been the victim of a misrepresentation will have a remedy if either a fraudulent or innocent misrepresentation has been committed and neither a defence nor a "bar" prevents him claiming his remedy.

A misrepresentation is an untrue statement of fact which is one of the causes which induces the contract. A fraudulent misrepresentation is a statement which is known to be false, or made without belief in its truth, or recklessly, not caring whether it is true or false. (**DERRY v PEEK (1889)**). A misrepresentation is innocent if the maker of the statement honestly believes it to be true.

A fraudulent misrepresentation makes a contract voidable, and whether or not it is avoided, it gives the innocent party a right to damages in tort for deceit.

A statutory remedy for misrepresentation is now provided by *S.2(1) MISREPRESENTATION ACT 1967* whereby the innocent party has a right to damages if he has suffered loss. However if the maker of the statement proves that he had reasonable grounds for believing, and in fact did believe, up to the time the contract was made, that the facts represented were true, then he has a defence.

The equitable remedy of rescission is also available where there has been an innocent misrepresentation. Since the 1967 Act this remedy is no longer lost if the representation is incorporated into the contract *(S.1.)*. In addition *S.2(2)* of the Act gives the court a discretion to award damages in lieu of rescission if it thinks it equitable to do so. These damages may be awarded even if the *S.2(1)* defence of reasonable belief is available.

The remedy of rescission, or damages in lieu, may not be awarded if any of the bars apply. The bars are:-

i.   Impossibility of restoration to the pre-contract situation, for example if the subject matter of the contract has deteriorated.

ii.   Affirmation. − If the innocent party, with knowledge of his right to rescind, affirms the contract.

iii.   The intervention of third party rights.

iv.   Lapse of time. − Where the misrepresentation is fraudulent lapse of time does not itself bar rescission because time only begins to run from discovery of the truth. An example concerning innocent misrepresentation is **LEAF v INTERNATIONAL GALLERIES (1950)**, where the plaintiff was induced to buy a painting by an innocent misrepresentation that it was by John Constable. 5 years later he discovered the truth and immediately claimed rescission. He could not therefore have affirmed the contract but his claim was held to be barred by lapse of time.

b.   The general rule is that a party is under no duty to disclose material facts known to him but not to the other party. Thus in **FLETCHER v KRELL (1872)**, it was held that a person who applied for the post of governess did not need to disclose the fact that she was a divorcee. A person must however disclose facts that falsify an earlier statement made by him. In **WITH v O'FLANAGAN (1936)**, a doctor who wished to sell his practice stated in January, at the start of negotiations, that it was worth £2,000 per year. He then fell ill and by May, when the contract was signed, the practice was almost worthless. The contract was set aside on the ground that the doctor should have communicated this change of circumstances to the purchaser.

Ivan cannot however base any claim on **WITH v O'FLANAGAN** since the case is only relevant if a later event falsifies an earlier representation. Since there is no "later event" Ivan is restricted to arguing that the statement, although literally true, was misleading. It is difficult to succeed in such a claim. In **NOTTS PATENT BRICK AND TILE COMPANY v BUTLER (1886)** a solicitor stated that he was not aware of any restrictive covenants affecting some land. He did not say that this was because he had failed to read the relevant documents. The plaintiff was successful. However in Ivan's case there is no authority to suggest that he would succeed. It is not a contract uberrimae fidei, there is no special relationship between Ivan and Henry and the facts are not especially unusual. If Ivan had asked for more detailed information presumably it would have been given. It is therefore suggested that the general rule of caveat emptor (let the buyer beware) applies, leaving Ivan without a remedy.

13.   a.   The general rule is that mistake does not affect the validity of a contract. For example if X purchases an imitation leather briefcase in the mistaken belief that it is real leather he cannot return it to the shop and claim his money back. There are several common law and equitable exceptions to this general rule.

If a common law exception applies the mistake is said to be "operative" and the contract is void. This will occur:-

i.   When the parties make a mistake as to the existence of the subject matter. For example in **GALLOWAY v GALLOWAY (1914)** a separation deed between a man and woman who mistakenly thought they were married to each other was held to be void because it purported to deal with a marriage which did not exist.

ii.   When there is a mistake as to the possibility of performing the contract. For example in **COOPER v PHIBBS (1867)** a person took a lease of land which, unknown to either party, already belonged to him. The lease was set aside since it was impossible to perform.

iii.   When there is a mistake as to the identity (not the quality) of the subject matter. ie Where A intends to sell "Product X", but B intends to buy "Product Y".

iv.   When there is a mistake as to the identity of the other party. Such a mistake cannot be made if the parties deal face to face. Furthermore the innocent party must be led to believe that he is dealing with another existing person. The contract will not be void if he believes that he has made a contract with a person who in fact does not exist.

v.   When a person makes a mistake as to the terms of the contract of which the other party is aware. In **HARTOG v COLIN AND SHIELDS (1939)** a seller of skins mistakenly offered them at a price per pound instead of per piece. The buyer, knowing of the mistake, accepted the offer, but later failed in his attempt to sue for non delivery.

The equitable remedies for mistake are rescission and rectification. Both are confined to fairly narrow limits. Rescission will only be granted if the party seeking to rescind was not at fault and provided justice can be done to the other party by imposing conditions. In **SOLLE v BUTCHER (1950)** a flat was let for £250 per annum. The parties thought the flat was free from rent control, but this was not the case and it was subject to standard rent of £140 per annum. If the lessor had known this he could, before granting the lease, have increased the rent to about £250 per annum because of work done by him to the flat. The tenant claimed that the standard rent should apply and he sought repayment of the excess he had paid. The lessor claimed rescission of the lease. Rescission was granted, but since it was unjust to turn the tenant out of the flat the court gave him the option of staying on if he paid the standard rent plus the amount by which the landlord could have increased it, had he been aware of the position when he granted the lease. Rectification may be granted where a clear agreement between the parties has been incorrectly reduced into writing. The court will rectify the written document so that it reflects the true agreement of the parties.

Thus it can be seen that the effect of a mistake on the validity of a contract depends on the type of mistake that has been made.

b.   The general rule where a document is signed is that a person will be bound even if he has not read the document, although this will not be the case if the other party misrepresented the terms of the document as in **CURTIS v CHEMICAL CLEANING COMPANY (1951)**. This is one application of the general rule that mistake does not invalidate a contract. In David's case if he was handed the contract and specifically told that it covered him for "all risks", no mention being made of the fire certificates, then David may have a slim chance of success provided fire certificate clauses are not usually included in such contracts. However the clause is probably not unusual and David is presumably a businessman from whom a reasonable level of competence would be expected. It is therefore most unlikely that he would get relief from his mistake. Since insurance companies generally specify that all terms are conditions ERC would be entitled to refuse to compensate David. It would make no difference if the precautions required by any fire certificate would not have prevented the loss.

14.   a.   The basic rule is that if a person contracts to do something, he is not discharged if performance proves to be impossible. This harsh rule is mitigated by the doctrine of frustration which, if it applies, automatically discharges the contract.

Frustration occurs:-

i.   If the whole basis of the contract is a thing which is destroyed. In **TAYLOR v CALDWELL (1863)**, D contracted to let a music hall to P for 4 days. Before the first day the music hall was accidentally burnt down. P claimed damages, but it was held that the contract was frustrated by the destruction of the hall.

ii.   If either party to a contract of personal service dies, becomes seriously ill, or is called up for military service. In **MORGAN v MANSER (1948)** a music hall artiste employed a manager for 10 years from 1938. The artiste was called-up in 1940 and demobilised in 1946. It was held that the contract was frustrated since in 1940 it was likely that the artiste would be in the army for a long time.

iii.   If the whole basis of the contract is the occurrence of an event which does not occur. In **KRELL v HENRY (1903)**, D hired a flat in Pall Mall to view the coronation procession. The procession was then cancelled due to the King's ill health. Because the rent was very high, and the letting was for only one day the contract was construed as one to provide a room for a specific purpose, and it was held to be frustrated when the procession was cancelled. In contrast in **HERNE BAY STEAMBOAT CO v HUTTON (1903)**, the hire of a boat to view an inspection of the fleet by the King was not frustrated when the King's inspection was cancelled since it was construed merely as a contract to hire a boat.

iv.   If the government prohibits performance of the contract for so long that to maintain it would impose fundamentally different obligations from those bargained for, or if performance of the main object of the contract becomes illegal.

A contract will not be frustrated if the parties have provided for the event which has occurred, or if the frustration is "self-induced", ie due to the conduct of one of the parties. Nor will a contract be frustrated merely because it becomes unexpectedly more expensive. For example in **DAVIS CONTRACTORS v FAREHAM UDC (1956)** the plaintiff agreed to build 78 houses at a price of £94,000 in 8 months. Labour shortages caused the work to take 22 months at a cost to the plaintiff of £115,000. It was held that the contract was not frustrated. For frustration to apply performance must become radically different from that bargained for.

b.   i.   A contract may be discharged even though it is not literally impossible to perform if later events destroy "some basic, though tacit assumption on which the parties have contracted" (**LINDSAY PARKINSON v COMMISSIONERS OF WORKS (1949)**). This is the basis of the decision in **KRELL v HENRY (1903)**. However the various "coronation cases" are the only cases where the principle has been the sole reason for the decision. Normally a person cannot rely on frustration merely because supervening events prevent him using the subject matter in the way that he originally contemplated. Thus in **AMALGAMATED INVESTMENT AND PROPERTY CO v JOHN WALKER (1977)** a person who contracted to buy property for re-development could not rely on frustration when, between contract and completion the buildings were listed as being of special architectural and historic interest so that development became impossible and the property lost much of its value.

It is fairly clear therefore that Bill will not be able to cancel his reservation without committing a breach of contract.

ii.   A contract may be discharged by frustration if the person required for its performance ceases to be available, for example **MORGAN v MANSER (1948)**. One relevant factor is the ratio between the probable length of interruption and the contract period. In contrast to the above case in **NORDMAN v RAYNER AND STURGES (1916)** a long-term agency agreement was not frustrated when the agent was interned, since his internment was not likely to last very long and in fact only lasted one month. Another relevant factor is the importance of the delay, having regard to the nature of the contract. Thus in **ROBINSON v DAVIDSON (1871)** it was held that a contract to play in a concert on a particular day was frustrated by the performer's illness on that day. If a person's unavailability is brought about by his own deliberate act the contract will be broken rather than frustrated, although it was suggested in **HARE v MURPHY BROTHERS (1974)** that if an employee commits a crime for which he is imprisoned the contract is frustrated. This case however seems to be inconsistent with the rule that frustration must not be self induced.

Peter's position is therefore not at all clear. It is suggested that since his unavailability is his own fault the contract has been discharged by breach rather than frustration. Peter will not be able to claim compensation for the OK Club's refusal to engage him. In fact he will have to pay damages to them as a result of his non-appearance on the 1st and 2nd of June.

15. a.   A rule exists that consideration need not be adequate but it must be sufficient. ie It must be something of value in the eyes of the law, although not necessarily of proportionate value to the "thing" given in return. Some "things" although arguably of some value are not regarded as valuable consideration. Thus in **PINNEL'S CASE (1602)** it was stated that payment on the day that a debt is due of less than the full amount of the debt is not consideration for a promise to release the balance. This rule was approved by the House of Lords in **FOAKES v BEER (1884)**. − F owed B a judgement debt of about £2,100. F asked for time to pay and a written agreement was entered into whereby F would make an immediate payment of £500 and the rest by stated instalments. In return B agreed not to take "any proceedings whatsoever" on the judgement. After the full sum had been paid B claimed £360 for interest and the court upheld the claim.

The scope of the rule is however limited by the following factors:-

i.   Consideration for the creditor's promise to accept part payment can be provided if the debtor does an act which he was not bound by the contract to do. For example early payment of a smaller sum at the creditor's request is consideration for a promise to release the balance.

ii.   If payment is made by a third party and accepted by the creditor the debtor will have a good defence if sued for the balance. In **HIRACHAND PUNAMCHAND v TEMPLE (1911)** the father of a young man who was indebted to money lenders sent them a smaller sum of money "in full settlement" of his son's debt. The money lenders accepted this payment and then sued the sone for the balance. Their claim failed.

iii.   Where the debtor makes a composition agreement with all his creditors, (ie he agrees to pay each creditor an equal proportion of what is owed to them), a creditor who accepts a payment cannot sue for the balance of his debt.

iv.   Finally equity has mitigated the hardship that could be caused to a person who relies on a promise that a debt will not be enforced in full. The principle is known as equitable estoppel. It may be expressed as follows:-

If X, a party to a legal relationship, promises Y, the other party, that he (X) will not insist on his full rights under that relationship, and this promise is intended to be acted upon by Y, and is in fact acted upon, the X is estopped (stopped because of his own previous conduct) from bringing an action against Y which is inconsistent with his promise, even if Y gives no consideration. ie Y can use the principle of equitable estoppel as a defence against X should X attempt to enforce his original rights. In **CENTRAL LONDON PROPERTY TRUST v HIGH TREES HOUSE (1947)** the plaintiff leased a block flats from the defendant. Due to the war he was unable to sub-let the flats, and so the plaintiff agreed to accept half rent. 6 months after the war the plaintiff claimed the full rent for the post-war period. This claim succeeded. However the court also considered whether the plaintiff would have succeeded if he had claimed the full rent back to the start of the war. Denning, J. (as he then was), said that he would not have been successful because he would have been estopped in equity from going back on his promise.

b. i.   A person does not provide consideration by merely promising to do what can already be legally demanded (**STILK v MYRICK (1809)**). However in this case a variation of the contract has been agreed, there is consideration for that variation i.e. extra remuneration in return for extra distance. D would be successful in his action to recover the agreed extra remuneration.

ii.   There is some authority for the view that where D is bound to do something for F, D may rely on his performance of that act as consideration for a new promise made by G to D. For example in **SCOTSON v PEGG (1861)** A agreed to deliver coal to B, or to B's order. B ordered A to deliver it to C. C promised A that he would unload the coal. It was held that A could enforce C's promise because A's delivery of the coal was consideration for C's promise, despite the fact that A was already bound by his contract with B to deliver to C.

The facts of the problem resemble Scotson v Pegg, although a promise to "assist with unloading" is more vague than a promise to unload. Thus despite the existence of contrary authority, for example **PFIZER v MINISTRY OF HEALTH (1965)** it is likely that Scotson's case would be followed.

16. a.   A contract is illegal as being contrary to public policy if it purports to oust the jurisdiction of the court. For example in **HYMAN v HYMAN (1929)** a husband as part of a separation agreement promised to pay his wife an allowance in return for the wife's promise not to apply to the court for maintenance. It was held that the agreement was void and the wife could apply for maintenance.

Problems are most likely to arise where arbitration clauses are involved. Such clauses are valid if they merely provide that the parties shall resort to arbitration before going to court. For example in **SCOTT v AVERY (1855)** an insurance policy provided that the insured should not be entitled to maintain any action on his policy until the dispute had been decided by arbitrators, and then only for such sum as the arbitrators shall award. The clause was held to be valid since it did not oust the jurisdiction of the court, it merely laid down the stage at which the jurisdiction arose and the nature of the cause of action. In contrast in **CZARNIKOW v ROTH, SCHMIDT (1922)** a contract which provided that no party could require the arbitrator to state a case for the opinion of the court on any point of law was void.

A contract which purports to oust the jurisdiction of the court must be distinguished from a promise which is "binding in honour only". Such contracts are unenforceable but they do not purport to take away the right of the court to say so.

b. An agreement will not be a contract if it is too vague or clearly incomplete. For example in **SCAMMELL v OUSTON (1941)** an agreement to buy goods "on hire purchase" was too vague to be enforced because there were so many different types of hire purchase agreement. Vague agreements may however be resolved by reference to previous dealing between the parties. It is therefore suggested that since the parties have already entered into a lease, it would be implied that the option is to renew on similar terms, subject to a reasonable increase in rent.

It had however been held that an option to renew a lease is a "privilege", which if granted on condition that certain terms and conditions are complied with, will not be enforceable even if there is only a minor breach of such terms. In **WEST COUNTRY CLEANERS v SALY (1966)** an option to renew a lease "providing all covenants herein contained have been duly observed and performed" could not be enforced by a tenant who committed a minor breach (failure to paint the interior of the premises) even though the lessor was not seriously prejudiced by the breach.

c. In a contract for the sale of goods the price may be fixed by the contract, it may be left to be fixed in a manner agreed by the contract or it may be determined by the course of dealing between the parties. If it is not so determined the buyer must pay a reasonable price *(S.8. SALE OF GOODS ACT 1979)*. Thus an agreement will not necessarily fail for uncertainty merely because no price is mentioned, (although combined with other factors this could contribute to the failure of an agreement). The validity of arbitration clauses has been discussed in a. above. It is most likely that this particular arbitration clause, and the agreement as a whole is valid.

d. An offer may be accepted by conduct. However in such cases it is implicit in the offer that conduct *may* be the method of acceptance, not that it *must* be. Where the conduct in question is silence the general rule is that an offeree who does nothing on receipt of an offer which states that it may be accepted by silence is not bound. In **FELTHOUSE v BINDLEY (1863)** a prospective purchaser wrote to the seller "If I hear no more about him I consider the horse is mine at £30 15s." It was held that the seller's silence was not an acceptance. The reason for the basic rule is that if a person does not wish to accept an offer, it is undesirable to put him to the trouble and expense of rejecting it.

SUGGESTED ANSWERS TO COURSEWORK QUESTIONS 17-24 THE LAW OF TORTS

17. a. The general rule is that if the plaintiff is to succeed in a negligence action he must prove that the defendant has broken his duty of care. An exception occurs when the maxim res ipsa loquitur (the thing speaks for itself) applies. In **SCOTT v LONDON AND ST CATHERINE DOCKS (1865)** it was stated that the maxim applies where

> "the thing is shown to be under the management of the defendant, and the accident is such as in the ordinary course of things does not happen if those who have the management use proper care"

In such cases there is prima facie evidence of a breach of duty. The burden of proof is then shifted to the defendant who must prove that he did show reasonable care. Th existence of res ipsa loquitur does not therefore guarantee success for the plaintiff, it is merely a rule of evidence.

For example in **WARD v TESCO STORES (1976)** an accident occurred due to a spillage of yoghurt on a shop floor. It was held that the facts placed a burden of proof upon the shopowners to show that it did not occur because of lack of care on their part. They were unable to do this and the plaintiff therefore succeeded.

b. Harry should consider the possibility of a negligence claim brought against him by Susan. Susan would have to show that Harry owed her a duty of care. She would be able to do this since a road user owes a duty to fellow road users. Susan would also be able to show that she had suffered damage. Susan's difficulty would be in proving that Harry has broken the duty of care since she is in no position to know why the car crashed.

The facts however infer negligence. It can be seen that the passage quoted in a. above will apply. "Res ipsa loquitur" will therefore shift the burden of proof from Susan to Harry.. Thus if he is to avoid liability Harry must show that he has not broken his duty of care. He will be able to do this if he can show that he exercised the care and skill that a reasonable car driver would have exercised. This is an objective test. It therefore may not be sufficient if Harry merely proves that he has done his best.

It is clearly not possible to give any conclusion on the facts given. There are many possible explanations for the brakes failure, for example a negligent service at a local garage. Harry will however be presumed by the court to be negligent unless he can provide an alternative explanation indicating that he was not at fault.

18. a. A public nuisance is an unlawful act which endangers the health, safety, or comfort of the public (or some section of it), or obstructs the exercise of a common right. Examples are the sale of contaminated food, or obstruction of the highway. Principles of "give and take" are relevant to the definition of nuisance. Thus, for example, a temporary highway obstruction of moderate size may be permissible.

A private nuisance is an unlawful interference with the use or enjoyment of another person's land. It may consist of actual injury to property as where fumes kill shrubs, or it may be an interference with health or comfort, for example noise, smoke, or smells.

Public nuisance differs from private nuisance in that (i) it is a crime as well as a civil wrong; (ii) an isolated act may be a public nuisance; (iii) it need not involve interference with the use or enjoyment of land; (iv) several people must be affected; (v) a right to commit a public nuisance cannot be acquired by long use; and (vi) it is an unlawful activity, whereas private nuisance is only an unlawful interference, the activity itself normally being lawful.

b. Both noise and vibrations potentially fall within the definition of private nuisance stated above. However it does not follow that such harm always constitutes a nuisance, regard must be had to the principle of "give and take" between neighbours. It may be relevant to consider for example how far the act complained of is excessive, its duration and whether the defendant has shown only lack of care. For example in **ANDRAE v SELFRIDGE (1938)** a hotel owner recovered damages from the defendant who was demolishing the adjoining premises. Although building and demolition do not usually constitute a nuisance, since they are socially desirable, if the amount of noise and dust created is unnecessarily great, a nuisance will be committed.

It thus appears that the residents will have a good chance of success if they sue A.P. Ltd for private nuisance. They should claim an injunction to prevent the factory from operating until the noise and vibrations have been prevented, and damages for any loss suffered.

In respect of the damage to his house Mr Evans cannot sue for private nuisance since it was an isolated act which caused the damage. He should sue A.P. Ltd for negligence. He would be able to show that he is owed a duty of care, and that he has suffered damage. He would not need to show that the company had broken their duty of care since res ipsa loquitur would apply and shift the burden of proof to A.P. Ltd who whould have to show that the accident did not occur due to their lack of care. It seems

517

probable that they would not be able to show this. Mr Evans is also therefore likely to succeed.

19. a. In **HEDLEY BYRNE v HELLER (1963)** P asked D for a bank reference about a mutual client. The reference was satisfactory and P granted the client credit. Shortly afterwards the client went into liquidation owing P over £17,000. It was held that D owed P a duty of care because P relied on the skill and judgement of D, and D knew or ought to have known of this reliance. Although D had broken their duty they were not held to be liable because the reference was given with a disclaimer of responsibility. This case is important because it shows that an advisor may be liable in negligence if he gives unsound advice which results in financial loss, even if his advice is given gratuitously.

Thus unless Albert's advice was given with a disclaimer of responsibility, Thomas will probably have a remedy.

b. In **RONDEL v WORSLEY (1969)** the plaintiff, who had been convicted of causing grievous bodily harm sued his barrister, claiming that he would not have been convicted if his case had been conducted properly. It was held that no action could be brought against the barrister. The main reason for the decision is that an action against the barrister would amount to a re-trial of the original case, and this would not be in the public interest. Thomas therefore cannot sue Bernard.

c. Charles will be liable to Thomas if he:-

   i.   Owed him a duty of care,

   ii. Broke the duty of care, and

   iii. Thomas suffered damage, which was not too remote, as a result of the breach of duty.

   i. and iii. above are present. The problem will be to establish a breach of duty by Charles. If he is to do this Thomas will have to show that Charles did not act as a reasonable car driver. It seems likely that he will be aided by the rule of evidence known as "res ipsa loquitur" (the thing speaks for itself). This applies where the "thing" is under the control of the defendant and the accident is such as in the ordinary course of events does not occur if proper care is taken. If the maxim applies the burden of proof is shifted to the defendant who must show that he did exercise proper care. For example in **RICHLEY v FAULL (1965)** where the facts were similar to those stated in the question res ipsa loquitur was held to apply, and since the defendant could not give a satisfactory explanation he was held to be liable. This does not necessarily mean that Charles will be liable, there may be many satisfactory explanations for the skid which are consistent with Charles acting as a reasonable driver, for example the car may have been serviced incorrectly, or Charles may have swerved and skidded to avoid a pedestrian.

d. Generally a plaintiff will be entitled to compensation for damage suffered if the damage is the reasonably foreseeable result of the negligent act. However, even though nervous shock is often reasonably forseeable, the courts are reluctant to apply the general principle of forseeability to such cases. There are two reasons for this, firstly such injury would be far more easy to fake than physical injury, secondly it would vastly increase the potential claimants in a particular case, putting pressure on the legal system and causing substantial increases in insurance premiums. Damages for nervous shock are therefore usually limited to situations where the plaintiff actually witnesses the death or serious injury of a close relative. Furthermore the shock must be in the nature of a psychiatric illness, mere grief and sorrow do not entitle the plaintiff to damages. It is therefore clear that Thomas will not be able to sue David.

20. a.   Libel and slander are the two torts that comprise defamation. A defamatory statement is a false statement that tends to injure the plaintiff's reputation or causes him to be shunned by ordinary members of society.

Libel is defamation in a permanent form or a statement made for general reception. It includes writing, pictures and waxworks. Radio, television and theatrical performances are libel by virtue of statute *(DEFAMATION ACT 1952* and *THEATRES ACT 1968)*. Slander is a defamatory statement that lacks permanence, for example words or gestures.

The distinction is important for two reasons. Firstly libel is a crime where as slander is not. Secondly libel is actionable per se (i.e. without the need to prove loss). Slander is only actionable per se in the following cases:-

  i.   If it imputes a crime punishable by imprisonment.

  ii.   If it imputes certain diseases e.g. aids.

  iii.   If it imputes unchastity or adultery in a women (but not a man).

  iv.   If it calculated to damage the plaintiff in any trade, office or profession held or carried on by him.

b.   If Quip is to succeed in a defamation action he must prove:

  i.   That the statement is defamatory i.e. it is false and would tend to lower the plaintiff in the estimation of right thinking members of society or make them shun or avoid that person.

  ii.   That the statement refers to him.

  iii.   That the statement was published i.e. communicated to at least one person other than him.

In this case the words (if taken literally) are clearly defamatory unless Red has actually sold secrets to the Russians. Quip's defence would be that such language is commonplace in political debate and that "sold out" refers to a state of mind rather than acceptance of money, consequently Red's reputation would not suffer. However it is suggested that this defence would not succeed. Concerning classification as libel or slander, tape recordings present a problem since there is no case on them, however it is more likely to be libel and this would certainly be the case if the tape were broadcast.

21. Strict liability which arises without fault, ie the defendant need not have acted either intentionally or negligently. The best known examples of strict liability arise under the rule in **RYLANDS v FLETCHER (1868)** and where there is a breach of statutory duty. Liability without fault is also placed on a master (employer) when he is made vicariously liable for the torts of his servant (employee), although such liability is not normally referred to as "strict liability".

The facts of **RYLANDS v FLETCHER** were that the defendant, a mill owner, employed independent contractors to construct a reservoir on his land. During the work the contractors found disused mine shafts which, unknown to them, connected with the plaintiffs mine under adjoining land. The contractors failed to seal these shafts, so when the reservoir was filled with water the water escaped via the shafts and flooded the plaintiffs mine. The defendant was held liable. In his judgement Blackburn J said

"The person who for his own purposes brings on his lands and collects and keeps there anything likely to do mischief if it escapes, must keep it at his peril, and if he does not do so is prima facie liable for all the damage which is the natural consequence of its escape."

The judgement made it clear that even though the defendant employed competent workmen and did not himself know of the disused mine shafts, he was nevertheless personally liable and not merely vicariously liable for the contractors' negligence.

The rule applies to such other things as chemicals, gas and animals. Two points must however be noted. Firstly there must be a non-natural use of the land, ie something which brings an increased danger to others. Secondly there must be an escape beyond the boundaries of the defendant's land.

Although liability is strict some defences are available. The defendant will have a defence if he can prove that the escape was caused by the plaintiff, by act of God, or by a third party over whom he had no control. He will also have a defence if the accumulation was made with the plaintiff's consent or with absolute statutory authority.

The term "breach of statutory duty" refers to situations where a civil action in tort will be possible for breach of an apparently criminal statute. The breach of duty will sometimes coincide with common law negligence. Other statutes have the effect of defining the standard of reasonable conduct expected from a person. Sometimes the statutory duty will be absolute, ie even a non-negligent failure to comply with the statute will be a breach of duty. Only in such cases can liability truly be described as strict.

In general if a plaintiff is to succeed in an action for breach of statutory duty he must show:-

a. That Parliament intended that a civil action should be for breach of the statute;

b. That the duty was imposed on the defendant;

c. That the defendant broke his duty; and

d. That the plaintiff suffered harm as a result of the breach of duty, provided such harm was not too remote.

If the above requirements are proved the only defence which could help the defendant is that the plaintiff has been guilty of contributory negligence.

22. a. A nuisance is an unlawful interference with the use or enjoyment of another person's land. In contrast to trespass the interference is indirect rather than direct. At one time the courts held that a person could not be liable in nuisance for failure to act in connection with a condition naturally arising on his land for example in **PONTARDAWE RDC v MOORE-GWYN (1929)** the defendant was held not libel when there was a natural fall of rocks from his land onto the plaintiff's land. However in **DAVEY v HARROW CORPORATION (1958)**, a case which involved encroaching tree roots, the defendant was held liable. It therefore seems clear that Mr A will be liable in nuisance (even if he did not plant the tree). It is also possible that he would be liable if sued for negligence.

b. Trespass to land is the direct interference with a possession of another person's land without lawful authority. It includes entering on land, remaining on land after permission to stay has been withdrawn or placing objects on land. Moving the boundary fence onto Mrs Barker's land is a clear trespass to land. Mrs Barker would be able to obtain a court order that the fence be restored to its correct position. In addition the court would make an award of damages. If the fence actually belongs to Mrs Barker rather than Mr Adams there would also be a trespass to goods.

c. Entry onto Mrs Barker's land to dig the hole is clearly trespass. Once the soil has been detached it ceases to be land and becomes goods. By removing the soil Mr Adams commits a trespass to goods as well as the tort of conversion. Conversion is a dealing with the plaintiff's goods which is a denial of the plaintiff's right to use and possess those goods. Any measure of damages related to the market value of the soil would probably be inappropriate. Mrs Barker should seek an injunction prohibiting any further trespass and sufficient damages to enable the land to be restored to its original state.

23. a. One of the general defences to a tort action is remoteness of damage. ie That the loss suffered by the plaintiff is not sufficiently closely linked to the defendant's tort because the loss is not reasonably foreseeable. (**THE WAGON MOUND (1961)**).

A novus actus interveniens is one factor which may break this link. It is an unforeseeable incident which changes the course of events. It could either be an act of the plaintiff himself, or of a third party over whom the defendant had no control. For example in **HOGAN v BENTINCK COLLIERIES (1949)** an employee sustained a broken thumb due to his employer's negligence. Acting on bad advice he had it amputated. It was held that the unreasonable amputation was a novus actus interveniens and therefore the plaintiff could only recover damages for a broken thumb.

There are however situations when an action which is arguably a novus actus interveniens will not break the link between the plaintiff and the defendant. For example in **SCOTT v SHEPHERD (1773)** a lighted squib was thrown onto a stall in a market place, and from there to another stall, and from there to Shepherd, whom it injured. It was held that the onward throwing was not a novus actus interveniens since it was an instinctive and foreseeable act done in the "agony" of the emergency created by the defendant's tort. The same is true when the intervening act is a rescue. For example in **HAYNES v HARWOOD (1935)** a boy caused a horse to bolt into a crowded street. A policeman was injured whilst trying to bring the horse to a halt. His negligence action succeeded, since the defence of volenti cannot be invoked against a rescuer, nor could it be claimed that his act was a novus actus interveniens since the act of rescue was foreseeable.

If a novus actus interveniens is proved by the defendant it will enable the defence of remoteness to be invoked. This will not enable the defendant to avoid primary liability but it will enable him to avoid payment of some or all of the damages claimed by the plaintiff.

b. i.   In an attempt to limit the award of damages AB Ltd should plead that the error by the surgeon was a novus actus interveniens. Although mistakes are occasionally made in hospitals such serious errors are rare. In addition, the actions of the surgeon are entirely out of AB Ltd's control. The situation is very similar to **HOGAN v BENTINCK COLLIERIES**. The defence will succeed, and AB Ltd's liability will be confined to compensation for Arthur's broken leg.

ii.   AB Ltd will again plead novus actus interveniens. In this case, however, success is in more doubt. It is reasonably well known that if a person is injured, and a fracture is suspected, it is best to leave him until medical help arrives. Many people, however, either do not realise this, or forget it in the "heat" of the moment, and inflict greater injury on a person by trying to help him to his feet, or by pulling him out of wreckage. It is suggested that such action, although unwise, is reasonably foreseeable, and would not therefore amount to a novus actus interveniens.

If this suggestion were not accepted by the court Arthur would have two further chances of success. Firstly he could claim that AB Ltd was negligent (for a second time) in failing to provide a system of supervision which prevented such unwise action by employees. Secondly if Arthur could prove that the employees were themselves negligent, AB Ltd as their employer may be held vicariously liable for their tort.

On balance it seems that AB Ltd will be unable to avoid full liability for Arthur's injuries.

24. There is no generally accepted definition of a tort, although several writers have put forward suggestions. Probably the most well known of these suggestions was given by Professor Winfield. He stated that:-

"Tortious liability arises from the breach of a duty primarily fixed by the law: such duty is towards persons generally and its breach is redressible by an action for unliquidated damages".

This definition illustrates two of the differences between contract, tort and crime. Firstly in contract liability is imposed by the parties themselves, in crime liability is imposed by the state, whereas in tort liability is imposed by the law. Secondly tort damages are unliquidated, ie the amount awarded to a successful plaintiff is fixed by the court. In contract damages are usually unliquidated, but they may be liquidated, ie fixed by the parties themselves. Damages are not relevant to crime since the purpose of criminal proceedings is to protect the community and punish the offender rather than to compensate the injured party.

The above definition does not however explain the functions and purposes of the law of torts. Basically the law of torts is concerned with adjusting the losses which must inevitably result from the increasing number of different activities of persons living in a common society. The diversity of these activities, and of the interests protected, means that no basic principle can underlie this branch of the law. The law of torts protects a wide variety of interests from behaviour such as intentionally or negligently causing physical injury to another, interfering with his enjoyment of land and injuring his reputation. In each case the law categorises such behaviour is wrongful, it recognises an interest which needs to be protected, and it allows a civil action to be brought by the person against whom the wrong was committed.

The lack of a basic underlying principle means that a tort cannot be defined by reference to the tort itself, but only by reference to the consequences that follow from it. Thus the same act may be both a tort and a breach of contract. For example if a taxi driver crashes he may commit the tort of negligence and he will break his contractual obligation to deliver the passenger to his destination. In many cases it will make no difference whether an action is brought in contract or in tort. However in some cases it will be significant because, for example, the rules for remoteness, limitation, and infants' liability are different in contract and tort.

Another difference between contract and tort is that contract only protects one interest, but this may be any interest which is capable of being, and which is chosen as, the subject matter of the contract. The interests protected by the law of torts are (as already stated) very diverse, but they are limited. There are some interests which the law of torts adequately protects, for example personal security and property, but there are other interests which the law of torts excludes. Thus in general it does not protect economic security in that damages are not awarded where negligence results in mere economic loss.

The main difference between crime and tort is one of purpose. Even so there is a considerable overlap between criminal and tortious liability and behaviour. Thus for example the taxi driver referred to above may also have committed a crime of dangerous driving, a thief will commit both the crime of theft and the tort of conversion, a person who commits a criminal fraud may be sued in tort for deceit, and libel is both a crime and a tort. In one tort, namely breach of statutory duty, liability actually depends upon proof that a crime has been committed.

SUGGESTED ANSWERS TO COURSEWORK QUESTIONS 25-32 COMMERCIAL LAW

25. The hirer's rights of cancellation are at present contained in the *CONSUMER CREDIT ACT 1974*.

When a hirer signs a hire purchase agreement at a place other than the place of business of the owner, creditor or person acting on their behalf he may serve a notice of cancellation of the agreement on the owner or his agent at any time before the end of the 5th day following the day on which he receives the ''second statutory copy'' of the agreement. (When an agreement is signed at the hirer's home the ''first statutory copy'' must be sent to him by post within 7 days after making the agreement). Both statutory copies must contain a statement of the hirer's right of cancellation, and must specify the name and address of a person to whom notice of cancellation may be given.

The effect of service of notice of cancellation is to rescind the hire-purchase agreement. The hirer is under no obligation to redeliver the goods except at his own premises and in response to a written and signed request. Until collection he is under an obligation to take reasonable care of them. On service of a notice of cancellation any payment made by the hirer under the agreement is recoverable.

Thus unless Linda has run out of time under the above rules, she has a statutory right to cancel the agreement.

The difference between a hire-purchase and a credit sale agreement is as follows. In a hire-purchase agreement the consumer hires the goods, and after payment of a specified number of hire instalments he is given an option to buy the goods for eg £1. Alternatively the ownership of the goods may pass automatically when he pays, for example, the 24th monthly instalment. Hire-purchase agreements are often tripartite arrangements. ie If the consumer wishes to take goods on hire-purchase the dealer sells the goods to a finance company for cash. The finance company (now the owner) then hires the goods to the consumer, and the rights and obligations then exist between the finance company and the consumer, rather than the dealer and the consumer. It is important to note that under a hire-purchase agreement title does not pass to the consumer at once. He remains a hirer. He does not become the owner until all the instalments have been paid. He therefore cannot pass title to the goods.

A credit sale agreement is an agreement for the sale of goods, the purchase price being payable by 5 or more instalments, not being a conditional sale agreement. Under such agreements the ownership of the goods passes to the buyer at once, and he may therefore pass on good title to another person. (A conditional sale, which is referred to in the above definition, is an agreement for the sale of goods whereby the price is payable by instalments and ownership remains with the seller until fulfilment of all conditions governing payment of instalments and other matters specified in the agreement).

The main difference therefore concerns the basic nature of the agreement. As the names imply, under one the consumer hires the goods, under the other he buys the goods. All other differences result from this fundamental difference.

26. a. The agent's obligations to the principal are contractual in nature. They consist of any expressly agreed obligations, plus certain duties implies by law. The main obligations are as follows:-

i. To obey the principal's lawful instructions.

ii. To act with reasonable care and skill, i.e. the level of skill normally expected from a person carrying on the agent's type of business.

iii. To act personally, i.e. without any delegation to a sub-agent, although agents may instruct their own employees to do necessary acts to fulfil the agency agreement.

iv. To act in good faith and for the benefit of the principal. This is probably the most important obligation. It has several aspects. For example an agent must disclose any conflict between his own and the principal's interests. He must not use his position to secure a benefit for himself (a secret profit), he must keep his money separate from the principal's money and he must disclose any information relevant to the performance of his duties as an agent. Thus in **KEPPEL v WHEELER (1927)** an estate agent was obliged to inform the person for whom he was acting of better offers for his house even though the principal had accepted an offer "subject to contract".

If there is a serious breach of duty (express or implied) the principal may terminate the agreement. Any loss can be recovered together with any secret profit that the agent had made (even if the principal could not have made the profit himself).

b. An agent has a duty not to allow his interest to conflict with those of his principal for example in **ARMSTRONG v JACKSON (1917)** a stockbroker (the agent) was employed to purchase shares for the principal. In fact he sold his own shares to him. It was held that there was a conflict

525

of interest since his duty as a buyer was to obtain the lowest price but his interest as a seller was to sell at the highest price. Alan is in breach. Paul may therefore recover the first word processor from him. Since this would terminate the agency agreement in respect of that machine the 5% commission would clearly not be payable.

In his dealing with the second word processor Alan has made a secret profit. Such a breach of his obligations is sufficiently serious to entitle Paul to terminate the agency agreement without notice or compensation. Paul would be entitled to recover the £50 undisclosed profit and would not be obliged to pay Alan any commission.

27.   a.   A right of action under a contract is known as a chose in action, for example a debt, patent, copyright or insurance policy. Personal tangible property cannot be a chose in action. Usually an assignment of a chose in action, for example a debt, must be in writing, signed by the assignor and written notice must be given to the debtor. The effect is that the asignee can then sue the debtor, however he can never have any better title than the assignor. Negotiability is a concept that applies to a particular class of chose in action, including for example bills of exchange, cheques, bank notes and banker's drafts. The characteristics of a negotiable instrument are:-

i.   Title can be passed by delivery or delivery and indorsement.

ii.   Title passes free of defects provided the transferee took in good faith for value and without notice of any defects.

iii.   Notice of the transfer need not be given to the person obliged to pay.

A bill of exchange is "an unconditional order in writing addressed by one person to another, requiring the person to whom it is addressed to pay on demand, or at a fixed or determinable future time, a sum certain in money to, or to the order of, a specified person or to bearer" *S.3 BILLS OF EXCHANGE ACT 1882*. Most aspects of this definition are self explanatory, however "unconditional" means that as between drawer and drawee the bill cannot require any act other than the payment of money. In **BAVINS v LONDON AND SOUTH WESTERN BANK (1900)** the direction to the drawer was to pay "on the attached receipt being signed" this imposed a condition on the drawee, so the instrument was not a bill. "Fixed or determinable future time" means a fixed period after date or sight ("sight" means when the drawee signifies acceptance) or a fixed period after the occurrence of a specified event that is certain to happen (although the time of happening may be uncertain).

A promissory note is "an unconditional promise in writing made by one person to another signed by the maker, engaging to pay, on demand or at a fixed or determinable future time, a sum certain in money to, or to the order of, a specified person or to bearer" *S.83 BILLS OF EXCHANGE ACT 1882*. In contrast to a bill, which has a drawer, drawee and payee, a promisory note has only two parties, the maker and the payee. With a bill the drawer (who writes the bill) will not be the person to pay (the drawee to whom it is addressed must pay). In contrast the person who writes the promisory note will be the debtor. A promisory note requires a promise not a mere acknowledgement. Therefore an IOU is not a promisory note. The most common example is a bank note.

b.   If a banker collects payment of a valid cheque for a person who has no title to it, both the paying and collecting banker are prima facie liable to the true owner for conversion of the cheque.

The paying bank is therefore given the following statutory protection. By *S.59 BILLS OF EXCHANGE ACT* payment to the holder in good faith without notice of any defect is a valid payment and absolves the bank from any liability. By *S.60 BILLS OF EXCHANGE ACT* if payment is made in good faith in the ordinary course of business the bank is not prejudiced by any forged indorsements. By *S.80 BILLS OF EXCHANGE ACT* payment of a crossed cheque in good faith without negligence discharges the banker from liability. By *S.1 CHEQUES ACT 1957* where a banker in good faith and in the ordinary course of business pays a cheque which is not indorsed or is irregularly indorsed, he does not incur any liability by reason only of the absence or irregularity of indorsement.

The collecting bank is protected as follows. By *S.4 CHEQUES ACT 1957* a banker has protection if bona fide, without negligence it receives payment for a customer, or on crediting his account receives payment for itself. By *S.2 CHEQUES ACT 1957* when a banker gives value or has a lien on a cheque payable to order which the holder delivers to the banker for collection without indorsing it, the banker has the same rights as if the holder had indorsed in blank i.e. he can claim title as a holder in due course.

28. a.   A charterparty is a documentary by which the owner lets his ship, or part of it to the charterer, or undertakes that it shall be used to carry a cargo for him. There are two types of charterparty — a voyage charterparty, under which the ship is chartered for a particular voyage, and a time charterparty, under which the ship is chartered for specific period.

A bill of lading is a document signed by the shipowner which states that certain goods have been shipped on a particular vessel, and setting out the terms on which the goods have been delivered to and received by the shipowner. It is (i) evidence of the contents of the contract of affreightment; (ii) a receipt given by the carrier for the goods delivered to him; and (iii) a document of title to those goods.

Every contract for the carriage of goods by sea, whether by charterparty or by bill of lading contains (subject to any express terms to the contrary) three implied conditions — ie that the ship is seaworthy; that there will be no unnecessary deviation from the agreed route; and that the voyage will commence and proceed without unnecessary delay.

There are several differences between charterparties and bills of lading. For example the *CARRIAGE OF GOODS BY SEA ACT 1971* implies terms that the carrier must carefully load, keep, and discharge the goods, and the shipper must give notice in writing to the carrier if there is any damage to his goods either at the time of removal, or if the damage is not apparent, within 3 days of removal. − If he does not do so, removal of the goods will constitute conclusive evidence that the goods were as described in the bill of lading at the time of delivery. These implied terms of the 1971 Act do not apply to charterparties unless they are expressly included.

A second difference between a bill of lading and a charterparty is that a charterparty may operate as a demise of the whole ship. Thus instead of the charterer merely obtaining the use of ths ship, he obtains use, possession, and control of the ship. The master and the crew will become the employees of the charterer for the period of the charter. Such charterparties are described as charterparties by demise. In contrast a shipper of goods under a bill of lading never has control and possession of the ship.

A bill of lading is a document of title to the goods and is transferred by indorsement. An indorsee has the same rights and liabilities in respect of the goods as though the bill of lading had been made with himself. It is not however a negotiable instrument because a transferee obtains no better title than the transferor. − In the case of a negotiable instrument the holder in due course may have a good title notwithstanding any defect in the title of the person from who he received it. A bill of lading is thus a quasi-negotiable instrument in that the title passes by indorsement and delivery, but the holder's title is subject to the defects in title (if any) of a previous holder.

b.   Where two or more indemnity policies have been taken out with different insurers in respect of the same interest in the same subject matter and the total amount of the insurance exceeds the total value of the loss, the insured may recover the total loss from any insurer. However the insurer who pays can claim a contribution from the other insurer in proportion to the amount for which he (the other insurer) is liable, provided the loss arises from a risk which is common to both policies.

The amount that Y Ltd can claim from X Ltd is therefore £1,875. This is calculated as follows:-

Total Insurance Cover = £16,000   (£10,000 + £6,000)

Amount covered by X Ltd = £10,000

Loss = £3,000

Y Ltd can therefore recover $\dfrac{10}{16}$ of £3,000 = £1,875

X Ltd will, of course, have to bear the rest of the loss, ie 6/16 of £3,000 which equals £1,125.

29.   a.   "Property" means title to goods, it does not mean possession. The basic rule is that property in specific or ascertained goods passes when the parties intend it to pass *(S.17 SALE OF GOODS ACT 1979)*. Consequently a seller may protect himself from a buyer's insolvency by reserving title to the goods, i.e. specifying that where the goods have been sold on credit and delivered to the buyer, the property will not pass until the buyer has paid for them (**AIV v ROMALPA (1976)**). The basic rule for unascertained goods (i.e. goods defined by description and not identified until after the contract is made) is that no property passes until they are ascertained *(S.16 SGA)*.

If neither the terms of the contract nor the conduct of the parties indicate their intention the property passes in accordance with the rules in *S.18 SGA*. By Rule 1 where there is an unconditional contract for the sale of specific goods in a deliverable state the property passes when the contract is made. Thus in **TARLING v BAXTER (1827)** B purchased a haystack. Before he took it away it was destroyed by fire. B was held liable to pay for the haystack because the property passed when the contract was made. By Rule 2 where the contract is for specific goods and the seller is bound to do something to the goods to put them into a deliverable state, the property does not pass until this has been done and the buyer has notice thereof. By Rule 3 where the specific goods are in a deliverable state but the seller still has to do something such as weighing, measuring or testing the goods, the property does not pass until such act has been done and the buyer has notice thereof. By Rule 4 where goods are delivered on approval or on sale or return the property passes:-

i.   When the buyer signifies his acceptance to the seller or;

ii.   When he does any other act adopting the transacting; or

iii. If he retains the goods beyond the agreed time or if no time was agreed beyond a reasonable time.

By Rule 5 where there is a contract for the sale of unascertained or future goods by description the property passes when goods of that description and in a deliverable state are unconditionally appropriated to the contract by one party with the consent of the other. A seller who delivers goods to the buyer or to a carrier for transmission, without reserving a right of disposal is deemed to have unconditionally appropriated goods to the contract.

It is important to ascertain when property passes because:-

i.   Unless otherwise agreed the risk passes with the property *(S.20 SGA)*.

ii.   Once the property has passed the seller can sue for the price.

iii. If the seller resells the goods after the property has passed to the buyer the second buyer will not acquire title unless he is protected by an exception to the "nemo dat" rule. The same principles apply if a buyer re-sells goods before he has title to them

b.   In a contract for the sale of goods it is the duty of the seller to deliver the goods and unless there is a contrary provision the place of delivery is the seller's place of business. Delivery is defined as "voluntary transfer of possession from one person to another" *(S.61 SGA)*. In this case it seems clear that the place of delivery has been agreed as J's place of business.

By *S.13 SGA* where goods are sold by description there is an implied condition that the goods will correspond with the description. J's remedies will depend on:-

    i.   Whether he has accepted the goods, since if he has done so he will be limited to damages for breach of warranty *(S.11 (4) SGA)*. However J will not be deemed to have accepted until he has had a reasonable opportunity to examine them to ensure conformity with the contract *(S.34 SGA)*. Since he examined the goods on the day of delivery J would not be deemed to have accepted prior to that examination.

    ii.   The nature of H's breach. For example if a larger quantity has been delivered (description includes quantity) then J may accept or reject the whole, or accept the contract goods and reject the rest. If the mis-description relates to the quality J would have the usual options available to a person suffering a breach of condition. He can treat the contract as at an end and/or claim damages.

30. The following provisions are relevant to Sparks:-

S.14(2) SALE OF GOODS ACT 1979 states a basic rule that where goods are sold in the course of a business there is an implied condition that those goods are of merchantable quality. *S.14(6)* provides that goods are of merchantable quality if they are as fit for the purpose or purposes for which goods of that kind are commonly bought as is reasonable to expect having regard to the description applied to them, the price (if relevant), and all other relevant circumstances.

S.14(3) SGA 1979 states that where goods are sold in the course of a business and the buyer makes known to the seller the purpose for which the goods are being bought there is an implied condition that the goods are reasonably fit for that purpose, except where the circumstances show that the buyer does not rely, or that it is unreasonable for him to rely on the skill and judgement of the seller.

It is clear that although Sparks' goods are "cheap" and "second-hand" the wiring defect is so serious that the radios do not work at all. Sparks is therefore in breach of both *S.14(2)* and *S.14(3)*. The effectiveness of his exemption clause therefore be relevant.

S.6. UNFAIR CONTRACT TERMS ACT 1977 states that in consumer sale *S.13-15 SGA* cannot be excluded and in a non-consumer sale they can only be excluded if the exemption clause is reasonable. *S.12 UCTA 1977* provides that a person deals as a consumer if

    i.   He neither makes the contract in the course of a business nor holds himself out as doing so, and

    ii.   The other party does make the contract in the course of a business, and

iii. The goods are of a type ordinarily supplied for private use and consumption.

The above statements are relevant to all 3 cases. Each is now considered in turn.

The contractual exemption is not directly relevant to Watt's case since there is no contractual link (ie privity) between Watt and Sparks. Watt may however sue the trader, who may in turn sue Sparks. Since Sparks' sale to the trader is a non-consumer sale the exemption clause will be effective if it is reasonable. It is suggested that having regard to the fact that the radios are "cheap" and "second-hand", and since Sparks and the trader are in the same line of business, the exemption clause would be held to be reasonable. Sparks therefore has no contractual liability to Watt or the trader. Sparks will however be liable to Watt for negligence. — He owes him a duty of care, he has broken the duty by failing to act with reasonable care and skill, and Watt has suffered damage which is not too remote.

It appears that Volt has dealt as a consumer in his contract with Sparks. Sparks' exemption clause is therefore ineffective. It is clear that the damage to the furniture by fire would be foreseeable as the probable result of Sparks' breach of contract. Volt's loss is therefore not too remote and he would succeed if he sued for breach of contract. He would also succeed if he sued for negligence. An action for negligence would be preferable for Volt if remoteness were thought to be a crucial issue since the tort test for remoteness is "reasonable foreseeability" which is rather more generous to the plaintiff than the contract test mentioned above.

Ampere's situation is in some respects similar to that of Watt. She cannot sue Sparks for breach of contract because there is no privity between them. She may however sue for negligence. Sparks' only possible defence would be remoteness (volenti, ie consent, is not available against a rescuer). A loss will be too remote if it is not a reasonably foreseeable result of the tort. Ampere's injury would probably be held to be reasonably foreseeable. It is likely that she will be able to succeed in a negligence action against Sparks.

31. The basic rule stated in the question is correct, even if a person purchases in good faith and without knowledge of the lack of title he acquires no title and can be sued in conversion by the owner. The purpose of this rule is to protect ownership. However this conflicts with another principle, namely that a person who buys goods in good faith should be protected. The law therefore admits both general and specific exceptions to the basic rule.

The first general exception is where the seller is the owner's agent. In such cases the buyer obtains a good title. He will also obtain a good title if the owner is precluded by his conduct (ie estopped) from denying the seller's authority to sell. The other general exception is where a sale is made under a common law or statutory power of sale or under a court order.

The special exceptions to the basic rule are as follows:-

By *S.22 SALE OF GOODS ACT 1979* if a person buys goods in good faith in an open, public and legally constituted market (a market overt), or in a shop in the City of London, he will acquire a good title provided the sale takes place between sunrise and sunset.

By *S.23 SGA 1979* where a seller of goods has a voidable title which has not been avoided at the time of sale, the buyer acquires a good title provided he buys in good faith without notice of the seller's defect in title.

Under *S.2 FACTORS ACT 1889* any sale, pledge, or other disposition by a mercantile agent in possession of goods or documents of title with the consent of the owner, and in the mercantile agent's ordinary course of business, to a bona-fide purchaser for value without notice of any defect in his authority, is as valid as if expressly authorised by the owner.

A mercantile agent is an agent, having in the customary course of his business authority to sell or raise money on the security of goods. The definition includes an auctioneer or broker, but not a clerk or warehouseman.

By *S.24 SGA 1979* where a person having sold goods continues in possession of them or documents of title to them, the delivery or transfer by him, or by a mercantile agent acting for him, of the goods or documents is as valid as if authorised by the owner, provided the second buyer takes in good faith without notice of the previous sale. — The seller need not remain in possession as seller, he may remain in possession as, for example, hirer or trespasser as in **WORCESTER WORKS FINANCE v COODEN ENGINEERING (1971)**.

S.25 SGA 1979 gives similar protection to *S.24* in the case of a person taking delivery from someone who has agreed to buy and has obtained possession of the goods or documents of title with the consent of the seller. The usual sequence is firstly an agreement to sell (ie no property passes) but the buyer is given possession. Secondly a "sale" by the buyer and delivery to a third party who takes in good faith.

It is clear that the law always has a difficult task when it has to apportion loss between two innocent parties. Proposals for reform have been made. In 1966 the Law Reform Committee published a report entitled "Report on the Transfer of Title to Chattels". It contained many proposals for reform. For example it recommended that *S.22 SGA 1893* (now *S.22 SGA 1979*) be repealed and replaced by a provision enabling a person who buys in good faith at retail trade premises or at a public auction to obtain good title. To date only one of the proposals of the Committee has been implemented. This reflects the difficulties encountered when trying to resolve the conflict between the owner and the bona fide purchaser referred to at the state of this answer.

32. a. Where a cheque is crossed it must be paid by the paying bank to the collecting bank. It may not be paid as cash over the counter. This would act as a hindrance to a person who dishonestly obtains the cheque since he cannot obtain cash for it, but must pay it into an account, meanwhile the cheque may have been stopped. The types of crossing are as follows:-

A general crossing consists of two transverse parallel lines with an optional "and company" or "and co.". The cheque will only be paid by the paying bank through another bank.

A special crossing also includes the name of a particular banker. The cheque will then only be paid by the paying bank to the bank named. Although usually present the two parallel lines are not needed for a special crossing.

A cheque may be crossed "not negotiable" by adding these words to a general or special crossing. This means that a transferee of a cheque can never get a better title than the transferor, because a cheque must be negotiated if the transferee is to become a holder in due course.

Where a cheque is crossed "not transferable" the cheque can be neither transferred nor negotiated. A cheque will be not transferable if it is crossed as such or if it carried the order "Pay X Only".

Finally a cheque may be crossed "Account Payee". This type of crossing is not mentioned in the *BILLS OF EXCHANGE ACT 1882* but it nevertheless gives some protection to the true owner of the cheque. Its effect is to put the collecting bank under a duty to make inquiry to see that it collects for the payee named on the cheque or that its customer has the payee's authority. Therefore if the bank does not make such inquiry it will be liable if it collects for someone other than the true owner. A bank may therefore collect for someone other than the true owner only if that other person has the owner's authority and the bank has confirmed this by inquiry. A cheque crossed "Account Payee" is still negotiable. Therefore it would be advisable to combine this cross with "not negotiable".

b. Two general principles of contract are relevant to this question. Firstly N as agent for M has apparent authority to pass cheques. In order to protect third parties the law allows apparent authority to override any lack of actual authority. Secondly when a person signs a document then, unless there has been fraud or misrepresentation, that person will be bound. In M's case there was no fraud or misrepresentation at the time he signed. He intended to sign a cheque, he was no doubt aware that he was taking a risk when signing a blank cheque. The validity of his signature is not affected by the subsequent acts that his carelessness facilitated.

If P took the cheque in good faith and for value he will be entitled to keep the money that he has drawn. The fact that it was crossed "not negotiable" is irrelevant when payment is made to the payee. M will also not be able to recover from the paying bank provided it paid in good faith in the ordinary course of business (which is likely) *S.59 BILLS OF EXCHANGE ACT*. M's only remedy is to try to recover from N. He may also terminate N's agency contract without any need to pay compensation.

SUGGESTED ANSWERS TO COURSEWORK QUESTIONS 33-45 LABOUR LAW

33. a. For any agreement to become a legal, enforceable contract the following elements must be present:

i. **Offer and acceptance.** A contract of employment comes into existence only when a valid offer is accepted in all its terms. A newspaper advertisement would not be an offer of employment, but an invitation to interested parties to make further enquiries. Eventually an offer emerges, after negotiations, with definite terms. Usually the offer is made by the employer and must be accepted without qualification. The contract of employment may be oral, but it is better if the terms are in writing. Under the *EPCA 1978* an employer must provide an employee with a written statement of the terms of employment with 13 weeks of commencement.

ii. **Consideration.** A valid contract must have consideration. The employer promises to provide work and pay wages, and the employee promises to carry out the work in accordance with the contract. Consideration has been defined as "some right, interest, profit or benefit accruing to one party or some forbearance, detriment, loss or responsibility given, suffered or undertaken by the other".

iii. **Contractual capacity.** Both parties must have the capacity to bind themselves in a valid contract. Certain persons have a limitation on their capacity to contract, eg, minors, drunken persons and persons of unsound mind. In order to be enforceable a contract with a person under the age of 18 years must be, on the whole, for his benefit. If the contract is not beneficial the minor can avoid it if he wishes, either before he reaches his majority or a reasonable time afterwards.

iv. **Genuineness of agreement.** The validity of the contract may be affected if there is a lack of consensus ad idem in the shape of mistake, misrepresentation, duress or undue influence. If an employee makes misrepresentations with regard to his qualifications, etc, the contract becomes voidable at the option of the employer.

v. **Legality.** The contract must not contain any element of illegality or be contrary to public policy. Contracts in restraint of trade are prima facie illegal as are agreements which attempt to avoid the payment of income tax.

vi. **Legal intent.** The parties must intend to create legal relations with each other, ie, enforceable in a court of law. This would be presumed in the case of a contract of employment.

b. An employer has a duty under common law and the *HSAWA 1974* to provide a safe system of work on his premises. An employee, injured as a result of his employer's breach of this duty, may claim damages in tort. The duty is one of "reasonable care" to prevent injuries that are "reasonably foreseeable".

The duty includes the provision of safe premises, plant and machinery. In this case the failure of the machine is due to poor maintenance. There is, therefore, a breach of duty. However, Eric failed to inform his employer of his defective eyesight. The employer may allege contributory negligence on Eric's part and thus have the damages reduced. Alternatively the defence of "volenti non fit injuria" may be used. As the employer was unaware of Eric's disability he owes him no special care **(PARIS v STEPNEY BOROUGH COUNCIL)**. **CORK v KIRBY McLEAN** would be an appropriate case in this instance.

34. a. The distinction between a person on a contract of service (employee) and a contract for services (independent contractor) is often a difficult question to decide. It is based on the facts of any particular case and over the years several "tests" have been advocated to distinguish between the two positions. Whilst the wording of a contract may be taken into account this is not conclusive evidence as in **FERGUSON v DAWSON (1978)**.

Based upon the facts that commission and not a wage is paid, and he decides on his own hours of work and the journeys he makes, Clutch would appear to be an independent contractor. However Clutch's cab is owned and maintained by Supercabs Ltd, thus he is not in business on his own account. In addition Clutch has agreed to work only for the company, ie, a "restraint of trade" clause, normally connected with a contract of service. These would indicate a contract of service. Other factors would be taken into account such as whether or not Clutch is left to make his own arrangements in respect of PAYE and national insurance.

b. In law the relationship between an employer and an employee or independent contractor decides their rights and liabilities as follows:-

i. Certain statutory provisions apply only to employees, eg, the *EPCA 1978* in respect of redundancy payments, unfair dismissal, guarantee payments, written details of the terms of employment.

ii. An employer must make deductions for income tax and national insurance contributions in the case of an employee, and himself make an employer's contribution.

iii. An employee is entitled to certain Social Security benefits under the *SOCIAL SECURITY ACT 1975* and the *SOCIAL SECURITY & HOUSING BENEFITS ACT 1982*. An employer is also obliged to make Statutory Sick Payments.

iv. An employer will be vicariously liable for the torts of employees, but in general, not for those of an independent contractor.

v. An employer has certain common law duties to his employees in respect of work, pay, indemnity and provision of a safe system of work.

vi. An employee also has common law duties to his employer, eg, loyalty and good faith, obedience, good conduct, etc.

vii. If his employer goes into liquidation an employee becomes a preferential creditor for arrears of pay which puts him in a stronger position than an independent contractor.

35. a. Unless there is a stipulation in an employee's contract of employment forbidding the performance of work in his spare time, an employee may perform such work provided it does not harm his employer's interests. In this case it would appear that A's spare-time activities may be to his employer's detriment, ie in the loss of work. In common law an employee has a duty of loyalty and good faith and therefore A's employers may possibly obtain an injunction preventing his spare-time activity or, if he persists, there may be grounds for dismissal.

In **HIVAC v PARK ROYAL SCIENTIFIC INSTRUMENTS LTD**, employees of the plaintiff worked for the defendants (a rival firm) in their spare time. H was granted an injunction preventing this.

b. It is the duty of an employee to disclose all inventions made, using the facilities of the employer.

In **BRITISH SYPHON COMPANY LTD v HOMEWOOD**, H was employed as a technical adviser and was asked to design a soda syphon, which he did, but patented it in his own name. It was held that the patent right belonged to the employer.

However, B, in his position as a supervisor, may not be expected to produce an invention. In this case he may fall under the *PATENTS ACT 1977* provision that, even where an invention occurs in the course of employment, using the employer's materials, but where an invention cannot reasonably be expected, it will be deemed to belong to the employee. Otherwise, if B's employer does establish a claim over the invention, it may still be possible for B to make a claim for compensation under the *PATENTS ACT* if either the invention belonged to the employer and proved to be of 'outstanding benefit', or if it belonged to the employee who assigned it to his employer but received inadequate benefits.

c. An employee owes a duty of loyalty and good faith to his employer and thus may not accept bribes or make secret profits. In effect the customer is willing to dispose of his old car for less than C has allowed him in part exchange, so that the price should have been reduced and the benefit passed on to the employer. The employer may recover the bribe from C, dismiss him without notice and repudiate the contract made with the customer.

d. An employer is under no obligation to give a reference or testimonial, **GALLEAR v J.F. WATSON & SON LTD (1979)**. However, if an employer does give a reference he may be liable to a charge of defamation of character if any statement tends to lower the employee "in the eyes of right-thinking people". The employer may be liable for damages in tort on the grounds of either slander if the statement is made verbally, or libel if made in a more permanent form. The employer may use the defences of justification, ie the statement was substantially true, or qualified privilege. If the employer knowingly recommends an employee in terms which he knows to be false, the subsequent misconduct of the employee will render his former employer liable for damages in the tort of deceit.

If the mis-statement is negligent the employer may be liable for negligent misrepresentation (**HEDLEY BYRNE & CO LTD v HELLER & PARTNERS (1964)**).

36. a. The common law duties owed by an employer to his employee in the absence of any specific provisions in the contract of service are as follows:

i. A duty to pay the agreed remuneration.

ii. A duty to indemnify the employee in respect of all losses, liabilities and expenses incurred by the latter in carrying out orders, unless the employee knew that the act was unlawful.

iii. A duty to provide for the reasonable safety of his employees. This consists of provision of safe premises and equipment and a "reasonably safe system of work". The latter comprises:

a. Care in the choice of safe and competent workmen.
b. Provision of safety equipment.
c. The giving of proper training.
d. Proper co-ordination where more than one department is responsible for co-ordinating safety arrangements.
e. Provision of suitable working conditions, with adequate washing facilities.

iv. The employer is under no implied duty to provide work, except:
a. Where the employee would lose the opportunity to increase his reputation by publicity if no work were provided (eg, with actors and journalists), and
b. Where the remuneration depends upon the amount of work performed, eg, where he is paid partly by commission on sales.

v. There is no duty to safeguard the employee's property.

vi. An employer is not bound to give his employee a reference or testimonial.

37. a. *THE EQUAL PAY ACT 1970* implies an equality clause in every woman's contract of employment, provided that the contract does not already include such a clause. This clause operates in any situation where a woman is engaged on like work or on work rated as equivalent to work done by a man.

The clause operates (a) to include in her contract a beneficial term in a man's contract which is absent from hers, and (b) to modify her contract so that its terms are no less favourable than those in a man's contract.

A woman is regarded as employed on like work with men if, but only if, her work and theirs is of the same or a broadly similar nature and the differences (if any) between the things she does and the things they do are not of practical importance in relation to the performance of her contract of employment. In making this comparison, the nature and extent of the differences and the frequency or otherwise with which such differences occur in practice will be taken into account.

b.   A woman may not be discriminated against on grounds of sex or marital status *(SEX DISCRIMINATION ACT 1975)*. Discrimination means that the employer treats a woman less favourable than he treats a man or treats her less favourably because she is married.

The Act forbids discrimination at every stage of employment, viz, in advertising vacancies, engagement, promotion, transfer, other benefits and dismissal. However an employer may discriminate in giving special treatment to women in respect of pregnancy and childbirth.

c.   Under the *EMPLOYMENT PROTECTION (CONSOLIDATION) ACT 1978* as amended by the *EMPLOYMENT ACT 1980* an employee with not less than two years' continuous employment who is absent from work wholly or partly because of pregnancy or confinement is entitled to maternity payment and to return to work afterwards. These rights arise only if she continues to be employed (whether or not she is actually at work) until immediately before the beginning of the eleventh week before the expected week of confinement.

In addition if she is dismissed because of her pregnancy the dismissal will be deemed unfair unless it can be shown that:

i.   She had become incapable of doing the job,

ii.   To have continued working would have contravened the law, and

iii.   No reasonable alternative job is available.

An employee is also entitled to time off with pay during working hours to attend ante-natal clinics.

The maximum maternity payment is for a period of six weeks and is nine-tenths of a week's pay reduced by the amount of maternity allowance under the Social Security legislation.

The European Economic Community law provides that women shall be accorded equal treatment for like work with men.

38. Normally wages are fixed by agreement between employers and employees or by collective bargaining between trade unions and employers associations. Statutory intervention occurs in the following ways:

a.   *Wages Councils.* Under the *WAGES COUNCILS ACT 1979* (an Act which consolidated former legislation on this topic), wages and other conditions of employment were determined by wages councils for certain industries. The industries were those in which it was considered the employees had no effective negotiating power due to being non-unionised or with weak unions. Although the 1979 Act was repealed by the *WAGES ACT 1986* existing councils are allowed to continue. The Secretary of State may, however, abolish or alter the scope of existing councils. A wages order made by a wages council may determine:-

i.   Minimum hourly rates of pay,

ii.   Overtime rates,

iii.   Limits to the amount charged for accommodation.

The orders apply only to employees aged 21 or over. In the case of disputes between a wages council and employers' representatives there is provision for conciliation by ACAS and eventually arbitration by the CAC.

b.   *The Wages Act 1986.* This Act repealed the Truck Acts and introduced new protection for employees in respect of deductions from pay. Certain deductions are made lawful and others are specified as unlawful under the Act. A special provision is made for employees in the retail trade in respect of deductions for stock or cash deficiencies. An employee who considers his employer has contravened the Act may complain to an industrial tribunal.

c.   *The Equal Pay Act 1970.* This Act has the object of eliminating discrimination between men and women in regard to pay and other conditions of employment.

d.   *Guarantee Payments.* Under the *EPCA 1978* in certain circumstances an employee who is laid-off may receive a guarantee payment which ensures that he receives some payment during this time.

e.   *Medical Suspension.* Under the *EPCA 1978* an employee who is suspended because he is endangered by exposure to radiation or lead poisoning may be entitled to his pay during this time.

39.   a.   An employee may be dismissed summarily, ie, without notice or payment of wages in lieu if he commits a breach of his contract of service so serious as to constitute a fundamental breach of the contract.

   i.   *Misconduct.* Where the conduct of the employee interferes with the proper performance of his duties, eg. persistent laziness, insubordination, dishonesty. This may even apply to misconduct outside working hours if it affects his work, eg. excessive drinking..

   ii.   *Incompetence.* An employee is bound to perform his work with the skill he claims to possess. Particularly if his incompetence is such that it endangers his fellow employees the employer is under an obligation to remove that danger.

   iii.   *Negligence.* Dismissal for negligence may be justified if it constitutes even one act of serious nature, or there may be a series of minor acts of negligence.

   iv.   *Disobedience.* Disobedience of a lawful order may justify dismissal, but this may be mitigated if it is only a single act which is not a wilful flouting of authority. An employee may be justified in refusing to obey an order which puts him in physical danger not contemplated in the service contract. (**OTTOMAN BANK v CHAKARIAN (1938)**).

   v.   *Good faith.* An employee has a duty of loyalty and good faith to his employer. Thus he is bound to account for any profit made by him due to his position and not to harm his employer's interests by working for a rival (**HIVAC v PARK ROYAL SCIENTIFIC INSTRUMENTS LTD (1946)**).

vi.   *Illness.* Illness can give good grounds for summary dismissal if it frustrates the purpose of the contract, eg. **CONDOR v BARRON KNIGHTS (1966)**.

b.   Albert may claim under common law for wrongful dismissal or for unfair dismissal under the *EPCA 1978*. The dismissal will be deemed to be wrongful if the employer cannot show good reason for dismissal without notice or wages in lieu. As the wet floor was presumably the employer's fault, Albert could not be said to be incompetent or negligent. Theft, although discovered after dismissal would support justification for dismissal (**DEVIS v ATKINS (1977)**.

It would appear that Albert would be wiser to claim unfair dismissal, the rules for which give the remedies of re-instatement, re-engagement or compensation. In the case of unfair dismissal the employer cannot rely on circumstances of which he became aware after dismissal. It is unlikely that Albert's employer would contemplate re-instatement or re-engagement and therefore compensation would be claimed. This consists of a basic award, a compensatory award and an additional award. Under the *EA 1980* the basic award may be reduced because of conduct which was not the reason for the dismissal but came to light afterwards.

40.   a.   If a fixed term contract expires without being renewed an employee is normally regarded as dismissed and is entitled to a redundancy payment. However, an employee must have at least 2 years continuous service to be entitled to a redundancy payment and therefore in a fixed term contract of over 2 years redundancy payment entitlement can be excluded by agreement of both parties before expiry of the contract.

b.   If the employer agrees B may leave employment before expiry of his notice without jeopardising his claim to redundancy payment. If the employer objects in writing the case would go to an industrial tribunal for settlement.

c.   If an employer changes the conditions of employment so as to make them fundamentally different to the original contract and intolerable to the employee, the employee may leave and consider himself to have been constructively dismissed. In this case he may claim damages for wrongful dismissal under common law, statutory compensation for unfair dismissal, or a redundancy payment if his job has ceased to exist.

d.   An employer may make an employee an oral or written offer before the old job ends to re-engage him in suitable alternative work. The employee is entitled to a six week trial period in the new job. If the job is unsuitable the employee may terminate his contract either at the end of, or at any time during the trial period and claim redundancy payment. If the new work is suitable the employee may be debarred from payment.

e. It is probable that E's illness for a year has frustrated the purpose of his contract of employment in which case the contract would be automatically terminated with no entitlement to a redundancy payment. If the job has ceased to exist before the contract is terminated E may be entitled to a redundancy payment.

41. a. The obligation of Martin's employer under the *FACTORIES ACT 1961* is to ensure that the machine is "securely fenced". It imposes an absolute obligation, and it is no defence to say that it is impracticable to fence the machine or that the machine, if securely fenced, will become useless.

b. It has generally been decided (eg in **SPARROW v FAIREY AVIATION (1961)**) that machines must be guarded in order to prevent the employee from coming into contact with the machine, not the machine coming into contact with the employee. Parts of a machine flying out and hitting the employee do not, of themselves, render the employer liable under the Act.

c. In **ROSS v ASSOCIATED PORTLAND CEMENT (1961)**, it was held that the employer could avoid liability to the actual offender if he (the employer) could show that the conduct of the offender was the sole cause of the breach of statutory duty and the resulting damage to him. Martin's employer is under a duty (1) to provide a secure fence, and (2) to give Martin proper instructions. If he has done this he is not responsible for Martin's disobedience.

A duty is imposed by *S.143(1)* on employees to use any means or appliance provided for their safety, and *S.143(2)* provides that no employee shall wilfully or without reasonable cause do anything likely to endanger himself or others. Martin would seem to be in breach of his duty.

d. The fence is intended to keep the worker out, not to keep the machine or its product in, **CLOSE v STEEL CO OF WALES (1961)**. The employer would seem to have a good defence against Martin's action. However, where there is a known tendency to ejection of machine or material, failure to guard against injury to workmen may afford a cause of action.

e. In **UDDIN v ASSOCIATED PORTLAND CEMENT CO (1965)**, it was held that, where a machine was not guarded because it was maintained in a place where employees were not working — or indeed forbidden to go — there could be no defence for an employer if an employee disobeyed orders and was subsequently injured by the unguarded machine. Warning notices are not considered to be sufficient safeguards. This only applies to persons "employed or working on the premises" — not to any other visitor.

f. In **PARVIN v MORTON MACHINE CO (1952)**, it was held that the term "machinery" as used in the fencing sections of the Act does not include machinery which is a product of the factory. In this case a dough-brake had been made in the factory and a young person was injured when the guard was removed for an adjustment. He was held unable to recover for breach of statutory duty.

g.   If the Court considered that the "irregularity" of Martin's employment constituted regarding him as an independent contractor, it may decide that there was no *contract of service* in operation, but instead a *contract for services*. In this case, the employer has no responsibility under common law principles for injury where no employer/employee relationship exists. However, the Act is specifically designed to protect persons employed or working on the premises. Martin would therefore appear to have a good case.

h.   In this case, as in e. above, the Act is intended to protect all employees, not just careful ones so that this in itself is no good defence. However, the employer's liability is limited to what is *reasonable* and *foreseeable*, and it might well be held that all reasonable precautions had been taken in this case. (**BURNS v J. TERRY & SONS (1951)**).

42.   The *HEALTH AND SAFETY AT WORK ACT 1974* imposes a general duty on employers to ensure as far as is reasonably practicable the health, safety and welfare at work of all employees. The employer must for this purpose consult employees on joint action, he must consult with safety representatives, and in certain circumstances establish Safety committees.

The *SAFETY REPRESENTATIVES AND SAFETY COMMITTEE REGULATIONS 1977* which came into force on 1st October 1978 recognise that safety is the responsibility of both employees and employer. The number of safety representatives is not prescribed, but clearly depends on factors such as the number of employees, the variety of occupations, the size of the workplace, the existence of shift systems, and the degree of danger. Safety representatives are therefore the channel through which employees play their part in cooperating with the employer to carry out the health and safety policy.

Their powers are:

a.   To investigate hazards, accidents and complaints by employees and make representations to the employer thereon;

b.   To make representations, usually in writing, to the employer on general matters affecting health, safety and welfare;

c.   To consult with inspectors and to receive information from them;

d.   To attend meetings of safety committees;

e.   To make inspections of the workplace (a) quarterly, (b) specially when there is any substantial change in conditions, and (c) specially following any notifiable accident or disease;

f.   To inspect and copy any relevant documents which the employer is required to keep;

g. Together with at least one other safety representative, to request the employer to establish safety committees, when the employer must do so within three months following consultation with representatives of recognised trade unions.

43. a. The following reasons may be put forward by an employer to justify dismissal. The provisions are contained in the *EPCA 1978* and the *EA 1982*.

i. *Lack of capability or qualifications*. Capability refers to skill, aptitude, health or any other physical or mental quality. Qualification refers to any formal technical or professional qualification relevant to the position which the employee held.

ii. *The conduct of the employee*. Examples of misconduct which have been held to justify dismissal include: dishonesty (even suspected dishonesty), breach of safety regulations, conviction of a criminal offence, sexual aberrations, fighting with fellow-employees, disclosing information to a competing firm and disobedience.

iii. *If the employee is redundant*. Provided there is no unfair discrimination and the proper procedures are carried out, an employee who is dismissed because of redundancy will not succeed in a claim for unfair dismissal.

iv. *If the employee could not continue to work in that position without contravening a statutory restriction*.

v. *Some other substantial reason*.

vi. *Transfer of undertaking*. Generally dismissal in connection with the transfer of an undertaking is presumed to be unfair. However, this is not so when the dismissal is caused by economic, technical or organisational reasons incidental to the transfer. (Transfer of Undertakings (Protection of Employment) Regulations 1981.)

Even if the employer can show that an employee was dismissed for any of the above reasons he must have acted reasonably. The decision as to the reasonableness of the dismissal is left to the Industrial Tribunal, which would take into account all circumstances including the size and administrative resources of the undertaking, and decide the question on the grounds of equity and the substantial merits of the case. The Tribunal may examine the procedures followed by the employer. Guidance can be obtained from the Codes of Practice.

b. If an employee is dismissed for taking part in a strike the tribunal has no jurisdiction to decide whether the dismissal was fair or unfair unless it was a case of selective dismissal, ie:

i. Others taking the same action were not dismissed, or

ii. Any of the strikers has, within three months, been offered re-engagement, but the complainant has not been offered re-engagement, and the reason is the complainant's membership or non-membership of a trade union or union activities.

If the strike lasted longer than three months the employer is at liberty to re-engage the employees he wishes to re-engage. If the strike is less than three months duration there may be claims for unfair dismissal by the ten employees who were not re-engaged. The grounds for complaint would be that the employees had been dismissed for taking part in the activities of an independent trade union.

If successful the employees may be awarded compensation under the following headings:

a. *Basic award.* This will be dependant upon the employee's service, with a minimum of £2,520 in respect of dismissal in connection with trade union membership or activities.

b. *Compensatory award.* This is based on the financial loss suffered eg. immediate and future loss of earnings and pension rights.

c. *Additional award.* This is based on a formula laid down in the *EA 1982*, which takes into account the weekly wage (up to a maximum figure) multiplied by a certain number of weeks. This is in the nature of a punitive award given by reason of the failure of the employer to comply with a tribunal's recommendation to reinstate or re-engage an employee.

The question does state that orders were lost during the strike and that the employer stated that there was no work for the ten employees. This may indicate a redundancy situation. However dismissals in respect of redundancy would be unfair if the employer used unfair discrimination in his selection and did not follow the proper procedures.

44. a. The statutory rights of an employee are contained in the *EPCA 1978*. The rights are affected by the length of his employment in the following ways:

i. *Minimum weekly hours.* An employees' statutory rights are dependent upon his number of continuous weeks service. Qualifying weeks are those in which he works at least 16 hours. If he serves over 5 years the requirement is 8 hours.

ii. *Notice.* Once an employee has completed 4 weeks service he is entitled to one weeks notice. After this notice depends on further continuous service up to a maximum of 12 weeks for 12 years service.

iii. *Written terms.* An employer must provide his employees with a written statement of the terms of employment within 13 weeks of them commencing employment.

iv. *Guarantee payments.* Employees with one months service who are laid off may be entitled to guarantee payments.

v. *Maternity rights.* An employee with 2 years continuous service becomes entitled to certain maternity rights, including maternity leave and maternity pay. An employee with one years service may not be fairly dismissed on account of pregnancy.

vi. *Unfair dismissal.* An employee becomes protected by the rules for unfair dismissal after 2 years continuous service. The calculation of the basic award and additional award for unfair dismissal is based on continuous service (a maximum of 20 years to count).

vii. *Redundancy.* An employee must have 2 years continuous service before becoming entitled to redundancy pay. Payment is based on number of years service with a maximum of 20 to count.

viii. *"Continuous service".* Normally, in order to count for the various rights an employee's service must be with the same employer. However the following do not break continuity:

    (a) Change in ownership of a business, provided the business is transferred as a going concern.

    (b) Work with an "associated employer".

In addition the following events do not break continuity:

    (a) Period of absence for up to 26 weeks on account of sickness, injury, pregnancy, temporary cessation of work and working abroad.

    (b) Lock-outs.

    (c) Dismissal followed by re-instatement or re-engagement.

b.   Charles requires 2 years continuous service for an entitlement to redundancy pay. However he has only 3 months with the new employer. He will be entitled only if the 5 years with his previous employer can be counted.

Continuity is not broken if the business is taken over as a going concern and it is not merely a transfer of the assets.

In Charles' case it would appear that there is mainly a transfer of assets, the buildings now being used mainly for storage and not manufacture. Charles may have an entitlement if he continues to work in the part of the premises still concerned with manufacturing.

Another possibility is that the new employer has agreed to count the previous service.

If there has been a transfer of assets only, Charles would not be helped by the Transfer of Undertakings (Protection of Employment) Regulations 1981.

Otherwise Charles may claim against his previous employer as it is still within the time limit of 6 months.

Appendix 2

REVISION QUESTIONS AND ANSWERS
QUESTIONS

1. Compare and contrast common law and equity.

2. a. Discuss whether legislation is the supreme source of English Law today. (10 marks)

    b. Explain the methods used by judges when faced with ambiguous statutory provisions. (10 marks)
    ACCA Pilot Paper for Level 1 1981

3. Explain what is meant by the "doctrine of precedent" in English Law, and distinguish between the ratio decidendi and obiter dicta of a case. When can a judge refuse to follow a binding precedent?
    ACCA Level 1 December 1985

4. Many industrial and commercial disputes are today settled by administrative tribunals.

    a. What is an administrative tribunal?

    b. Why are tribunals established?

    c. How are tribunals controlled?
    CIMA Foundation May 1984

5. Explain, with reasons, whether Eric Ltd is contractually bound in each of the following situations.

    a. It promises to sell a delivery van to Frank who is given seven days to make up his mind. Four days later it sells the van elsewhere for a better price. On the eighth day it receives a letter from Frank who has heard of this subsequent sale. Frank states that he accepts the offer of Eric Ltd. (4 marks)

    b. It promises to sell a very valuable machine to George for £5. (4 marks)

    c. It promises to sell goods to Henry at a price to be fixed later. (4 marks)

    d. It receives unsolicited goods through the post with a notice saying that it will be assumed that Eric Ltd has bought them unless it returns them within seven days. Eric Ltd takes no action. (4 marks)

    e. After Ivan has painted Eric Ltd's office, it promises to pay Ivan £500. (4 marks)
    CIMA Stage 1 Specimen Paper 1986

6. a. Describe the rules governing remoteness of damage and the measure of damages in the law of contract. (10 marks)

    b. H promised to deliver goods to I on a specified date.
    There was a term in the contract which provided for the payment of

liquidated damages of £500 in the event of a breach of contract.

H delivered goods of the right quality and quantity but two weeks late. I accepted the goods. Later I decided to sue H for breach of contract and to claim £500 damages.

Advise I.

(10 marks)
(20 marks)
ACCA Level 1 June 1987

7. David, aged 17, asks your advice as to whether or not he is bound by the following contracts.

a. John a tailor, provides him with a new suit on credit.

b. He borrows £50 from Harry to buy books for his studies. He spends £30 on books and £20 on a party for his friends.

c. He takes a 3 year lease of a flat at £1,000 per annum.

d. He orders a sports car, valued at £3,000. By giving his age as 21 he persuades the seller to deliver it before any payment is made.

ACCA Foundation December 1978

8. Explain what is meant by anticipatory breach of contract, and discuss the remedies available to the party not at fault.

ACCA Foundation December 1977

9. a. What are the essential elements in the tort of negligence?

b. Betty left her car on the top of a hill without applying the handbrake. Doris, in her car, pulled up behind Betty's car in a careless manner just touching Betty's rear bumper as she drew to a halt. This action set Betty's car in motion down the hill and into Fred's parked car, which is severely damaged. Advise Fred.

10. a. Explain what must be proved by the plaintiff if he is to succeed in an action for defamation.

b. Mary is a well known judge at cat shows. One evening, while drinking in a bar, Carol is overheard to say to the barman "Mary as a cat judge is no better than her mother was". People who knew Mary's mother knew that she was a very dishonest person. Advise Mary of her chance of success if she were to sue Carol in defamation.

11. Mr. Thomas is the owner of 16 Grove Gardens, a private house, which is being converted. The builders whom he has employed for this purpose have erected scaffolding in the passage-way between 16 Grove Gardens and its neighbour, 14 Grove Gardens, which belongs to Mrs. Watts. One night a burglar climbs the scaffolding, breaks into 14 Grove Gardens, and steals a quantity of jewellery belonging to Mrs. Watts. Mrs. Watts is not insured for the loss of her jewellery, and so she is suing Mr. Thomas and the builders for the value of the jewellery, £5,000, claiming that they were each negligent in erecting, or allowing the erecting of, the scaffolding in such a way as to permit this loss to occur.

Advise Mr. Thomas as to his liability, if any.

ICSA Part 1 December 1986

12. a. In what circumstances is an employer liable for the wrongful acts of his employees? (14 marks)

b. Eric, an accountant, is sent by his employer to audit the accounts of a client. Eric's instructions prohibit him from giving any advice on the investment of surplus funds. However, he does give such advice carelessly and, in acting upon it, the client suffers loss.

To what extent is the employer liable for this loss?

(6 marks)
(20 marks)
CIMA Foundation May 1986

13. It has been said that "The basic principle behind every passing off action is that no man is entitled to represent that his goods or his business are the goods or business of another".

Explain and illustrate this statement.

ICSA Part 2 June 1986

14. a. Distinguish between

i.   Agency of necessity, and

ii. Agency by ratification.

b. Arthur is authorised to sell goods for Percy at a price not less than £800. Since trade is bad he offers to sell to Thomas for £700. Thomas accepts the offer but then changes his mind and states that he no longer wants the goods. Later Percy ratifies the sale at the lower price and seeks to hold Thomas liable on the contract.

Advise Thomas.

CIMA Foundation May 1981

15. a. In relation to bills of exchange explain what is meant by:

i.   an indorsement;

ii. a holder in due course;

iii. acceptance for honour. (12 marks)

b. A drew a cheque for £100 payable to B as payment for goods. B specially indorsed the cheque to C. C specially indorsed this cheque to D in payment of his rent. D paid the cheque into his bank and it was returned marked, 'refer to drawer'.

State with reasons who is liable to D on the cheque. (8 marks)

(20 marks)
ACCA Level 1 December 1985

16. a. Marion has six children under ten. She bought 50 packets of a new brand of washing powder from Smith's shop at 50p a packet. Three of Marion's children develop a severe rash after wearing clothes washed in the powder. Tests show that the powder would cause similar rashes to 30% of children. Marion wants to return the remaining 49 packets and claim compensation from Smith for her children's injuries. Advise Marion.

(8 marks)

b. What remedies are available to the creditor if the debtor defaults on payments under a hire purchase agreement? (12 marks)

ACCA Pilot Paper for Level 1 1981

17. a. "The common law demands that employers should take reasonable care to lay down a reasonably safe system of work." (**GENERAL CLEANING CONTRACTORS LIMITED v CHRISTMAS (1953) per Lord Oaksey.**) What is meant by "reasonable care"?

b. T was injured whilst polishing a component in a lathe. He was doing this by holding a piece of emery paper in his fingers instead of using the polishing stick provided. Although this was admitted to be a dangerous practice, evidence was produced to show that this was also a practice generally used in the industry which most employees had adopted. Discuss T's claim against his employer.

18. A worker who has been dismissed may have a right to various claims and benefits. What are these?

19. a. To what extent, if at all, will the transfer of a business from one employer to another affect employees' rights to redundancy payments?

b. Fogy is employed as an office manager. His employer gradually installs a number of new office machines, the operation of which Fogy does not understand, nor does he make any attempt to do so. Eventually he is dismissed.

Advise Fogy on his possible right to redundancy payment.

How, if at all, would your advice differ, if, before dismissal, the employer had offered him the managership of another office which had not been so mechanised?

CIMA Foundation November 1980

20. a. Explain the distinction between the common law right of a worker to claim damages from his employer for wrongful dismissal and the statutory right to claim compensation for unfair dismissal.

b. What must an employer prove in order to defeat an allegation of unfair dismissal?

21. Sparks is employed by Power and Co as an electrician. Whilst carrying out certain repairs at the department store of Harridges, Sparks lights a cigarette and throws away the lighted match. This badly damages the fur coat of Mrs.

549

Lamb, a customer. Can Mrs. Lamb sue Sparks, or Power and Co., or Harridges? Would your answer be different if Sparks had been forbidden to smoke during the course of his work?

22. Explain, with reasons, whether or not a claim for sickness or industrial disablement benefit is likely to succeed in each of the following situations:

a.   A trade union meeting is held on the firm's premises during normal working hours with the employer's permission. K attends this meeting and become involved in an argument with another employee. The latter loses his temper and strikes K who thereby receives a broken nose.

b.   L, a bus driver, is travelling to work on a bus which is being used to carry football supporters. He is standing on the platform, contrary to the company rules, and has not paid a fare, a practice accepted but not expressly authorised. The bus stops suddenly and L is thrown off, thereby receiving a broken leg.

c.   M visits the works canteen during a meal break. After eating his dinner, he falls asleep. This causes him to fall of his chair and to strike his head on the table.

d.   An employee, P, on passing his employer's premises late at night discovers an attempted robbery. He intervenes and is injured.

e.   During a tea break in the factory yard, an apprentice, Q, was practising for the Work's team's big football match, and suffers a broken leg.

f.   Having spent five minutes washing and changing, R is knocked down by the Managing Director's Rolls Royce, whilst walking to the main gate to "clock out" at midday on Saturday.

g.   On the same day, R's friend S, who is in a hurry to get home, is knocked down by a lorry belonging to the firm, while crossing the main road outside the gate in order to catch the special bus laid on for suburban workers by the firm.

23.   Consider the right to claim unemployment benefit in each of the following cases:

a.   Alan and his fellow workers strike for higher wages. During the strike, Alan obtains a temporary job at his local garage but then loses his work when the person he is replacing returns after illness.

b.   Brian is laid off when the workers in another part of the factory strike and production is stopped.

c.   Cecil leaves his employment after an argument with his employer.

d.   David loses his job with a heavy engineering firm which closes its factory. He is offered a course of training which will fit him for work as a machinist in a factory which has just opened in the district making ladies' underwear. He refuses to undergo the training.

e.   Elsie is laid off when her employer closes down. She is offered a similar position in another town at a higher rate of pay. She refuses on the grounds that she is living with her aged mother who is dependent upon her.

24. a.   Discuss the defences open to an employer to defeat or mitigate a claim for damages brought by an employee who has been injured by an accident at work.

b.   What allegations must be made and proved by the employee to win his action?

c.   Jones was employed by the Old Loaf Baking Company as a delivery man. When he was on his round the van he was driving ran into a telegraph pole and Jones was injured. The employer, when sued by Jones, pleads:

i.   That Jones knew the brakes were defective, and

ii.   That he was driving too fast having regard to the state of the brakes.

Discuss the validity of these defences.

25. What legal provisions exist to protect workers from injuries arising out of the use of dangerous machinery?

Martin is employed by D.S. Mills Limited. One day during working hours he went to see his friend, Norman, who worked in another department of the company, about a private matter. Martin dropped a packet of cigarettes and, as he bent over to pick it up, his clothing became caught in the machinery. Martin was seriously injured as also was Norman who tried to pull him clear.

Advise D.S. Mills Limited.

CIMA Foundation May 1980

26. Write a short memorandum for a factory owner setting out the law on:

a.   Allowable time off work; and

b.   The provision of holidays.

ICSA Part 3 December 1980

ANSWERS

1.   Neither common law nor equity can be concisely defined. Broadly speaking, however, common law was the first system to develop. It was based on local customs, which were extended throughout the country by the King's itinerant justices, and it was interpreted in the rigid common law atmosphere of the King's Courts, ie the Courts of Exchequer, Common Pleas, and King's Bench.

Equity developed later as a "gloss" on the common law. It was administered in a separate Court of Chancery and interpreted in an atmosphere where principles of justice and conscience played a more important part than rigid rules of procedure. These principles are embodied in the maxims of equity, for example, "he who comes to equity must come with clean hands". This means that a plaintiff seeking an equitable remedy must have acted morally correctly in his past dealing with the defendant.

The similarities between common law and equity can be summarised as follows:-

Firstly both common law and equity are law. In ordinary language "equity" means natural justice, but although inspired by these ideas, equity no longer represents the flexible concept of natural justice. It is now "nothing else than a particular branch of the law of England" — Glanville Williams.

Secondly common law and equity have both developed in an English context. They are not imported systems and have only been subject to minimal foreign influence.

Thirdly both have been partly embodied in statute, for example the *SALE OF GOODS ACT 1979* (common law) and the *TRUSTEE ACT 1925* (equity). Also since the *JUDICATURE ACTS OF 1873-1875* both have been administered in the same courts.

Finally both rely on the doctrine of judicial precedent.

There are a number of differences between common law and equity:-

Historically each system had different procedural rules since, until 1875, they were administered in separate courts. In the common law courts an action was commenced by the issue of a writ, whereas in the Court of Chancery an action was commenced by a petition. This allowed a greater scope to the plaintiff.

The most important difference is that common law was constructed as a complete and independent system, whereas equity developed to remedy the defects of the common law and would be meaningless if considered in isolation, since it pre-supposes the existence of common law. For example the doctrine of equitable estoppel in contract developed as an exception to the arguably harsh rule of **PINNEL'S CASE (1602)**.

Although the administration of common law and equity has now been fused, their content nevertheless remains separate. Thus to say that a rule or remedy is "equitable" means that it must be interpreted in an equitable atmosphere, and that the attendant maxims of equity apply. Thus the equitable remedies, for example specific performance, and rescission are discretionary, whereas the common law remedy of damages exists if a wrong is proved. An example of the exercise of this discretion was **MILLER v JACKSON (1976)** where although the plaintiff "won" the case the injunction he sought was refused.

Finally the 1875 Act enacted that in cases of conflict between common law and equity the rules of equity shall prevail. For example the equitable rule that time is not of the essence of a contract prevails over the common law rule which states that it is.

2.   a.   The evidence for the proposition that parliamentary legislation is the supreme source of law is overwhelmingly strong. It may be summarised in 3 statements:-

i.   No court may question the validity of an Act of Parliament. In **CHENEY v CONN (1968)** the plaintiff objected to his tax assessment under the *FINANCE ACT 1964* because the government was spending part of the tax collected on making nuclear weapons. He alleged this was contrary to the *GENERAL CONVENTIONS ACT 1957* and in conflict with international law. The court however held that the 1964 Act gave clear authority to collect the taxes and being more recent it prevailed over the 1957 Act. It was said by Ungoed-Thomas J that
   "It is not for the court to say that a parliamentary enactment, the highest law in this country, is illegal".

ii.   A statute may be passed to vary or revoke the common law or even to retrospectively reverse a judicial decision. — The *WAR DAMAGE ACT 1965* operated to remove vested rights to compensation from the Crown and was controversially expressed to apply to proceedings commenced before the Act came into force. It thus reversed the decision of the House of Lords in **BURMAH OIL v LORD ADVOCATE (1965)**.

iii.   An Act of Parliament may expressly or impliedly repeal an earlier statute. For example in **VAUXHALL ESTATES v LIVERPOOL CORPORATION (1932)** if compensation for compulsory purchase were assessed under an Act of 1919 the plaintiffs would receive £2,370, whereas if it were assessed under an Act of 1925 they would only receive £1,133. Furthermore the 1919 Act provided that any Act inconsistent with it would have no effect. It was held that this provision did not apply to subsequent Acts, ie Parliament cannot bind it successors. The 1925 Act impliedly repealed the 1919 Act so far as it was inconsistent with it, and the plaintiffs therefore received £1,133.

Thus the will of elected representatives prevails over the views of appointed judges. However the importance of the judiciary in relation to legislation should not be underestimated for two reasons. Firstly delegated legislation can be set aside by judges on the ground that the subordinate legislative body has exceeded its powers. Secondly all legislation must be interpreted by judges.

An ambiguous statement is one that may be interpreted in more than one way. In such cases it will not be possible for judges to adopt the usual approach to statutory interpretation ie the literal rule. In such cases the courts adopt the approach to interpretation known as the "golden rule". ie The words of a statute must be interpreted according to their natural, ordinary and grammatical meaning, but only to the extent that this does not produce an absurd result. Thus where a statute permits two or more literal interpretations the court must adopt the interpretation which produces the least absurd result. For example *S.57 OFFENCES AGAINST THE PERSON ACT 1861* provides that

"Whosoever, being married, shall *marry* any other person during the life of the former husband or wife"

– shall be guilty of bigamy. The problem is that "marry" could be construed to mean (i) make a valid marriage, or (ii) go through a ceremony of marriage. Since a person who is married cannot make a valid marriage interpretation (i) above would produce an absurd result. "Marry" is therefore construed to mean "go through a ceremony of marriage".

The golden rule is also sometimes applied where a statute is capable of only one literal meaning and that meaning is rejected in favour of a more sensible construction. This is a more controversial application of the golden rule. However the question is restricted to "ambiguity" and in such situations application of the golden rule is a necessity.

3. The traditional function of a judge is not to make law but to decide cases in accordance with existing rules. These rules are contained in statutes and in the judgements of his predecessors. These past judgements (deciding both the meaning of statutes and principles of common law and equity) are known as precedents. The modern doctrine of precedent is about 120 years old. Its inception was due to two factors. Firstly the introduction of professional and methodical law reporting in 1865 when the Council of Law Reporting was formed. Secondly the Judicature Acts of 1873 and 1875 which established a clear court hierarchy.

If a precedent is to be binding two requirements must be satisfied. Firstly it must be a ratio decidendi statement and secondly the court must have a superior, or in some cases equal, status to the court considering the statement at a later date. If these requirements are met and the material facts as found are the same, the court is bound to apply the rule of law stated in the earlier judgement.

"Ratio decidendi" literally means "reason for deciding". Walker and Walker (The English Legal System) however provide a more detailed and descriptive definition.

"The ratio decidendi may be defined as the statement of law applied to the legal problems raised by the facts as found upon which the decision is based".

In some cases the court may have difficulty "isolating" the ratio decidendi, particularly if several judges (for example in the House of Lords) have given different reasons for reaching the same decision.

"Obiter dicta" statements are statements made by the way. Either they are not based on facts as found, (for example the statements made in **HEDLEY BYRNE v HELLER (1963)** concerning liability for negligent statements) or they do not provide the basis for the decision, for example a dissenting judgement. Obiter dicta statements are persuasive rather than binding precedents.

In general, the decision of a court binds its own future judges and judges in lower courts. However, following a statement by the Lord Chancellor in

1966, the House of Lords may depart from its own previous decisions in exeptional circumstances.

In **YOUNG v BRISTOL AEROPLANE CO (1944)** it was held that the civil division of the Court of Appeal is bound by its own previous decisions unless its previous decision conflicts with a later House of Lords judgement; or there are two conflicting Court of Appeal decisions — in which case it may choose which one to follow; or if the earlier decision was given per incuriam. "Per incuriam" means though lack of care because some relevant statute or precedent was not brought before the court.

The criminal division of the Court of Appeal regards itself as bound by its own decisions and by decisions of the civil division of the Court of Appeal subject to the exceptions contained in Young's case. However it will not be bound by its own previous decision if it would cause injustice to the appellant, because the need for attaining justice exceeds the desirability of certainty. This was stated by Lord Goddard C.J. in **R v TAYLOR (1950)** and adopted in **R v GOULD (1968)**.

County courts and magistrates courts are not bound by their own previous decisions since they are not sufficiently authoritative, there are too many of them, and they are rarely reported.

4.   a.   During the 20th century there has been a significant increase in administrative justice dispensed in tribunals which are outside the ordinary court system. These tribunals assist in the administration of Acts of Parliament and delegated legislation, and determine may of the disputes that arise from the operation of such legislation.

Some of these tribunals resolve disputes between individuals and the state, for example the Lands Tribunal deals with disputes concerning the compensation payable on compulsory acquisition of land by public authorities; National Insurance Tribunals deal with disputes about family allowances and national insurance contributions; and National Health Service Tribunals deal with dissatisfied NHS patients. Other tribunals deal with disputes between individuals. These "domestic" tribunals are often concerned with the regulation of certain professions and trades, for example the Disciplinary Committee of the General Medical Council and the Solicitors' Disciplinary Tribunal.

b.   Tribunals are established because they have several advantages over the courts as a method of resolving disputes:-

Firstly tribunals specialise in a particular field, and use as decision-takers persons with specialised knowledge or experience. Thus doctors sit on tribunals which assess the degree of disability in National Insurance claims, and employers and trade unionists sit on social security tribunals because their knowledge of labour practice is considered valuable.

Secondly tribunals are as informal as is consistent with the orderly conduct of their affairs. An attempt is usually made to create an atmosphere where people who appear in person will not be ill at ease or nervous. In contrast the physical layout of courts, the judges' robes, and the modes of address, can damage the self-confidence of a person appearing in court.

Thirdly tribunals are cheaper than courts. Civil courts generally charge fees, tribunals do not. In addition those appearing before tribunals can be represented by persons other than lawyers, and this also helps to keep costs down, although if a lawyer is required he will have to be paid, and there is as yet no legal aid except in the Lands Tribunal and the Employment Appeal Tribunal. Also a person who loses a case before a tribunal does not have to pay the costs of the other side.

Finally tribunals generally act speedily and meet by appointment. Court hearings generally cannot be arranged as quickly, and although a date is normally given for the hearing a time of day is rarely stated.

Tribunals also have disadvantages. For example some tribunals do not give reasons for their decisions, and others hear cases in private. It is however clear that they are more suitable than the courts for the resolution of many types of disputes, and in many cases they are therefore preferred by both the state and the individual.

c.   The Queen's Bench Division of the High Court exercises supervisory control over tribunals by means of the prerogative orders of mandamus, prohibition, and certiorari. Mandamus is an order compelling the performance of a duty by a person or body of persons. Prohibition is an order to prevent something being done. Certiorari is an order to bring before the High Court a case which has been adjudicated upon or which is in progress. In each case the court will be concerned to see that the principles of natural justice have been observed. ie That no person should be a judge of his own case, that both sides should be given a fair chance to state their views, and that the facts were fully investigated. In some cases the order may be sought because it is alleged that the tribunal has acted ultra vires (beyond its powers) in which case its action will be declared void.

The issue of the prerogative orders is the usual method of supervisory control, but these orders only lie against statutory tribunals and do not extend to tribunals exercising a voluntary jurisdiction. A person dissatisfied with the decision of a voluntary tribunal may however invoke the supervisory jurisdiction of the High Court by bringing an action against the officers of the tribunal claiming an injunction or a declaration as to his rights.

An application for a prerogative order is not the same as an appeal. An appeal to the High Court will be possible if allowed by statute, (there is no common law right of appeal). *S.13 TRIBUNALS AND INQUIRIES ACT 1971* provides for any party to appeal or to require the tribunal to state a case on a point of law to the Queen's Bench Division of the High Court. Other statutes provide a right of appeal to various branches of the Supreme Court.

5.   a.   An offer may be revoked at any time before acceptance, even if there was a promise to keep the offer open for a fixed period, unless the offeree

gave consideration for such an option to purchase. In this case there is no indication that F has given consideration. However to be effective revocation must be communicated. Usually the offeror will communicate, but if the offeree knows that the offer has been revoked he cannot accept. Thus knowledge of the sale received via a reliable third party will effectively communicate revocation (**DICKINSON v DODDS (1876)**). If for any reason the revocation was not effective, F's acceptance would probably be valid, since although it was received on the 8th day, it must have been posted before the end of 7 days. The postal rule applies provided the post was contemplated by the parties as the mode of acceptance and the letter was properly addressed, stamped and posted.

b. A promise is only binding if given in return for another promise or thing. This element of value (something for something) is known as consideration. The court will not enforce a promise if nothing is given in return. The court is not however concerned that the thing given be of similar value to the benefit received, for example in **THOMAS v THOMAS (1842)** an annual rent of £1 per year for a house was upheld. Money is always "something" as far as the courts are concerned. The courts will therefore uphold the sale to G at £5 whatever the value of the machine.

c. *S.8 SGA 1979* states that if an agreement for the sale of goods does not specify a price then a reasonable price will be payable. The court may therefore uphold the contract if it provides for the price to be fixed by reference to arbitration, previous dealing between the parties, or a prevailing market price. However if the contract merely provides that the price will be fixed by future agreement then it is likely to be void for uncertainty. For example in **KINGS MOTORS (OXFORD) v LAX (1969)** an option in a lease for a further period of years at such rent as may be reached by agreement was held to be void.

d. It is not possible for an offeror to stipulate that the offeree's silence will amount to acceptance (**FELTHOUSE v BINDLEY (1863)**). This would contravene the rule that acceptance must be communicated and will be most unfair to the offeree. Furthermore a person who receives unsolicited goods is entitled to treat them as a gift if the sender fails to take them within six months, or some earlier date if the recipient gives notice to the sender *(UNSOLICITED GOODS AND SERVICES ACT 1971)*.

e. Consideration must not be past, i.e. the act put forward as consideration must not be complete before any promise to pay is made, because then such a promise would amount to giving something for nothing. A promise to pay for completed work is not enforceable. However if Eric Limited requested the work then Ivan could rely on an implied promise to pay, and the promise to pay £500 could be regarded as fixing the price of an existing agreement.

6. a. A claim for damages raises two questions. Firstly is the loss sufficiently closely related to the breach (ie remoteness of damage) and secondly what measure of damages should the plaintiff receive in respect of loss which is not too remote?

The test for remoteness was formulated in **HADLEY v BAXENDALE (1854)** – Damages are recoverable if the loss is the natural result of the breach itself, or if it was foreseeable by both parties as the probable result of the breach.

For example in **INTERNATIONAL MINERALS AND CHEMICALS CORPORATION v HELM (1986)** a debt was due to be paid to an American plaintiff in Belgian francs. Between the due date and judgement date the value of Belgian francs as against US dollars had fallen by 40%. It was held that this loss was recoverable since D knew that such a loss was not an improbable consequence of their default.

Concerning measure of damages the general rule is that the plaintiff recovers his actual loss. ie He is placed in the same position as if the contract had been performed. This rule makes it clear that the plaintiff can recover for loss of anticipated profit. Where the breach of contract amounts to non-acceptance or non-delivery of goods *S.50* and *S.51 SALE OF GOODS ACT 1979* provide that where there is an available market the measure of damages is the difference between the contract price and the market price on the date fixed for acceptance or delivery or, if no date was fixed, at the time of refusal to accept or deliver.

The general rule is subject to the plaintiff's duty to mitigate. ie The plaintiff cannot recover for any loss that he ought to have avoided. For example in **JAMAL v MOOLLA DAWOOD (1916)** it was held that a seller of shares who kept them after the buyer's breach could not recover the extra loss that he suffered as a result of a later fall in market price.

In some cases the courts may award speculative damages, ie damages for loss of opportunity. For example in **MANUBENS v LEON (1919)** damages were awarded for the loss of a chance of earning tips and in **CHAPLIN v HICKS (1911)** for the loss of a chance of taking part in a beauty contest. However in **SAPWELL v BASS (1910)** D broke a contract that his stallion would serve P's mare. P failed to recover damages for the loss of the foals that may have been born, the court considering that such damages would be too speculative.

There are many other factors that affect the amount of damages awarded, for example the plaintiff's liability to tax, and the amount of inconvenience or annoyance that he has suffered (**JARVIS v SWAN TOURS (1973)**). In addition the parties may have themselves fixed the amount to be paid on a breach. Such an agreed damages clause will be upheld by the courts if it is a genuine pre-estimate of the loss, but not if it is a clause designed to penalise a breach.

b. Failure to deliver goods on the contract date will amount to a breach of warranty unless the contract specifically states that time is of the essence.

Breach of warranty entitles the innocent party to damages, it does not allow him to treat the contract as at an end. If the parties specify the damages in the contract, the court will uphold the clause provided it is a genuine estimate of the loss, it does not matter if the actual loss is more or less than the sum specified. The court will not uphold a specified sum that is out of all proportion to the maximum possible loss. Such a sum would be regarded as a penalty, from which equity grants relief.

It is not possible to give a firm conclusion to this problem for two reasons. Firstly it is not possible to assess whether or not £500 is an excessive sum. Secondly we do not know how much time passed between the breach and I's decision to sue, although the limitation period for an action on a simple contract is 6 years. It is possible that I waited to see whether any market price for the goods rose or fell. However even if the price rose between the contract delivery date and the actual delivery date (resulting in an extra profit for I) he would probably still be able to claim the liquidated damages because there would have been a significant chance that the price would have fallen. Such conduct may be immoral, but the clause would not necessarily be a penalty. It is not relevant that I "accepted" the goods since he has to accept where there is only a breach of warranty.

7. a. *S.3 SALE OF GOODS ACT 1979* states that an infant (a person aged under 18) must pay a reasonable price for necessaries sold and delivered. *S.3* also defines necessaries as "goods suitable to the condition in life of such minor and to his actual requirements at the time of sale or delivery".

Suits are clearly capable of being necessaries, but whether the particular suit is in fact a necessary in this case will depend on the quality of the suit in relation to David's position in life. For example an expensive "Savile Row" suit would be regarded as a luxury for the son of a poor man. It will also depend on whether or not David is already adequately supplied. In **NASH v INMAN (1908)** a tailor's claim for the price of clothes supplied failed because the father gave evidence that his son already had an adequate supply of clothes. Finally it does not matter that the sale is on credit, since the time of payment is not relevant in deciding whether or not a sale has been made, the requirement of the section is merely that the goods have been "sold and delivered", ie the adult must have performed his part of the bargain if he is to stand a chance of success.

Common law provides that a contract for the repayment of money lent to an infant is void. This has always been the rule at common law, but equitable relief is available. Thus a person who lends money to an infant can recover such part of the loan as was actually used by the infant to discharge his liability for necessaries supplied to him. The lender is said to be subrogated to the rights of the seller, ie he takes his place.

Thus, provided the books are necessaries, (which seems likely), Harry will be able to recover £30 from David. Harry will not be able to recover the other £20 since it was not spent on necessaries.

c. Contracts concerning land which involve infants are voidable, ie the contract binds both parties, but the infant can escape liability by repudiating before majority or within a reasonable time thereafter. The other party cannot repudiate.

David is therefore not bound by the lease. He will not however be able to recover any rent which he has already paid unless there has been a total failure of consideration. He will also remain liable to pay rent which fell due before repudiation.

There is one early case (**LOWE v GRIFFITH (1835)**) which suggested that an infant lessee is only liable for rent if the premises let are necessary, in which case he would presumably not be able to repudiate. There is however no other authority for this proposition and it is probably not the law. In fact the opposite is true in that the infant is liable unless he repudiates even if the lease is disadvantageous to him.

d. The question concerns the situation where an infant obtains non-necessary goods by fraud. (The sports car is almost certainly not a necessary). At common law the infant need not pay the price. Similarly equity will not enforce a contract against an infant merely because he is guilty of fraud. Equity will however undo the contract by ordering the infant to restore the property obtained under it. David is therefore not bound by the contract, but he will have to return the car.

8. One of the parties to a contract may, before the date fixed for performance say that he will not perform, or incapacitate himself from performing. This conduct is called "anticipatory breach". The innocent party then has a choice. He may attempt to keep the contract alive and press for performance, or he can "accept" the breach and claim his remedy.

If he accepts the breach he may claim damages at once, before the time fixed for performance. This was established in **HOCHSTER v DE LA TOUR (1853)**, where D agreed to employ P as a courier for 3 months commencing on June 1st. Before this date D told P that his services would not be required. It was held that P could sue for damages immediately, he did not have to wait until June 1st. This ability to sue immediately is particularly useful when a plaintiff has paid in advance for future performance, since if such a person were compelled to wait until the time fixed for performance to recover his money his ability to make an alternative contract may be reduced. The rule also has the effect of helping to minimise the total loss since the plaintiff has an incentive to abandon the contract and thus avoid an extra loss that may be suffered while waiting for performance. The difficulty which arises when a plaintiff sues immediately is that damages may be made more difficult to quantify, since where there is an available market for the goods the measure of damages is (prima facie) the difference between the market price and the contract price on the date fixed for performance. Clearly if the trial takes place before that date the market price will not be known.

If the innocent party chooses not to accept the breach he retains the right to enforce the other party's obligations, and clearly such conduct has the advantage that he may secure performance of the contract without the need to resort to legal action. Furthermore he may at a later date change his mind and accept the breach unless to do so would prejudice the other party (who may by now have made an attempt to perform the contract). A party who chooses not to accept the breach cannot get damages until the date fixed for performance. In the meantime he runs the risk that the contract is frustrated, in which case he would lose his right of action. For example in **AVERY v BOWDEN (1855)** D chartered a ship from P to carry goods from Odessa. The charter allowed 45 days for loading. During that time D's agent told the captain (P's agent) that he had no cargo, but the captain pressed for performance. Before the 45 days expired the Crimean War broke out. It was held that the charter-party was discharged by frustration, and P's right of action was extinguished.

9. a. The essential elements in the tort of negligence are:-

   i.   A duty of care owed by the defendant to the plaintiff.

   ii. Breach of that duty of care, and

   iii. Damage caused to the plaintiff as a reasonably foreseeable result of the breach.

The test used by the courts to determine whether a duty of care is owed was established in **DONOGHUE v STEVENSON (1932)**. Lord Atkin said that a person owes a duty of care to his neighbour, and that his neighbour is anyone who he can reasonably foresee will be injured by his acts or omissions. The test was applied in deciding that a manufacturer owes a duty of care to any person who consumes his goods, and not merely to the purchaser.

In some cases a person who is arguably within the "neighbour" test will not, for reasons of public policy, receive compensation. − For example where the loss suffered is merely economic, or in some cases where the plaintiff suffers a nervous shock.

The standard for determining whether the duty of care is broken is objective. ie The court will assess whether the defendant exercised the care that a reasonable person in the defendant's position, and with the defendant's knowledge would have exercised. The defendant will not discharge his duty merely by doing his best. The standard of care therefore varies with the circumstances. Thus if the defendant is faced with an emergency as in **WATT v HERTFORDSHIRE CC (1954)** a lower standard will be required. In this case a fireman was injured when lifting equipment slipped while being rushed to an accident in a vehicle that was not equipped to carry it. It was not a breach of duty to use the vehicle since to do so saved time that was vital to the accident victim. The known characteristics of the party at risk are also relevant. In **PARIS v STEPNEY B.C. (1951)** it was held to be a breach of duty of care when goggles were not supplied to a one-eyed vehicle welder, even though it would not have been a breach to fail to supply a two-eyed man. The reason was that loss of a person's only eye is far more serious that the loss of one of two good eyes. Examples of other relevant factors are the magnitude of the foreseeable risk, and the ease or difficulty of preventing the injury. ie If an injury can be easily guarded against then action should be taken even if the risk of injury is slight. However if the same injury could only be prevented with comparative difficulty, failure to take precautions is less likely to be a breach of duty.

The third requirement, ie damage, must be either physical injury to the plaintiff's person or property, or economic loss consequential upon physical injury, such as loss of wages. Mere economic loss, ie loss of profit cannot be recovered (**WELLER v FOOT AND MOUTH DISEASE RESEARCH INSTITUTE (1965)**), unless it is the result of a negligent statement, which satisfies the more restrictive tests established in **HEDLEY BYRNE v HELLER (1963)**.

b.   Fred should consider suing both Betty and Doris in negligence. If he is to succeed he must prove the three essential elements stated above.

He would satisfy the first requirement — the "neighbour test", since as a road user it is reasonably foreseeable that he will be affected by the acts or omissions of other road users. The second requirement would also be satisfied since neither Betty nor Doris have achieved the standard required of a reasonable car driver since a reasonable car driver would not park at the top of a hill without putting on the handbrake, nor would he hit stationary vehicle. The third requirement of damage is also clearly satisfied. A prima facie case of negligence could therefore be made out against either Betty or Doris and they would only be able to escape liability if a defence could be successfully pleaded.

Of the various defences available only remoteness may be of help. Both Betty and Doris would claim that the other's conduct was a novus actus interveniens. It is unlikely that either would succeed for two reasons. Firstly because each is a substantial cause of the accident. If the "but for" test of causation is applied, ie the question is asked "Would the accident have happened but for the defendant's conduct?", then it is clear that the answer for both Betty and Doris is "No it would not have happened". Both Betty and Doris have therefore caused the accident. Secondly it would be contrary to public policy to allow Fred to go uncompensated where some fault clearly exists.

Fred would therefore have an equal and substantial chance of success if he were to sue either Betty or Doris.

10.   a.   If a person is to succeed in a defamation action he must prove three things:-

Firstly the statement must be shown to be defamatory, ie Words that tend to lower the plaintiff in the estimation of right-thinking members of society generally or which tend to make them shun or avoid that person. In **SIM v STRETCH (1936)**, it was held that a telegram reading: —

> "Edith has resumed her services with us today. Please send her possessions, and the money you borrowed, also her wages"

did not defame the recipient. The plaintiff claimed that the telegram indicated that he was so short of money that he could not pay a servant's wages, and that he had to borrow from her. The court however said that where a statement has a number of good interpretations it would be unreasonable to seize on the bad interpretation to give a defamatory sense to the statement — this is not what a "right-thinking member of society" would do.

It is also insufficient if the plaintiff is only lowered in the estimation of section of society. In **BYRNE v DEANE (1937)**, a notice posted on the wall of a clubhouse referred to a member who had informed the police that the club were operating an illegal gaming machine. This clearly lowered Byrne in the estimation of his fellow members, but it was not held to be defamatory since a person who supplies such information ought not be less well-thought of by persons generally.

A statement is defamatory if it reflects on a person's trading or professional ability, if it imputes dishonesty or criminalty, or if it imputes unchastity in a woman.

A statement is also defamatory if it imputes certain diseases, eg cancer, or if it suggests that the plaintiff has been raped as in **YOUSSOUPOFF v M.G.M. PICTURES (1934)**. In such cases the traditional definition stated above is inadequate since it fails to appreciate that the reaction of society may be irrational in that the plaintiff may be shunned when he has suffered a misfortune rather than committed as misdeed.

In some cases the words may not be prima facie defamatory. The plaintiff will then have to prove an innuendo if he is to succeed. An innuendo is a statement by the plaintiff of a special meaning that he attributes to otherwise innocent words. In **TOLLEY v J.S. FRY (1931)**, a chocolate manufacturer used an amateur golfer's name and picture in an advertisement without the golfer's consent. The advertisement was not itself defamatory. The plaintiff however alleged that reasonable people would think that he had been paid for the use of his name, and that he was not a genuine amateur. He successfully proved this innuendo and won his libel action.

The second requirement is that the statement refers to the plaintiff. This may be shown even though the plaintiff is not named. In **J'ANSON v STEWARD (1787)**, the description:-

> "He has but one eye, and is well known to all persons acquainted with the name of a certain noble circumnavigator"

was held to be sufficient reference to the plaintiff who had one eye and a name similar to that of a famous admiral.

Thirdly the plaintiff must show that the statement was published ie communicated to at least one person other than himself. The defendant will have a defence if he proves that publication was the result of an act which could not reasonably foresee.

In addition to the above basic requirements, where slander is not actionable per se, the plaintiff will have to prove that he has suffered loss capable of monetary evaluation. Libel, on the other hand, is actionable per se.

Finally, if it is to be defamatory, the statement must be false. The plaintiff does not however have to prove its falseness. The burden is placed on the defendant to prove its truth, and thus avail himself of the defence of justification.

b. If Mary is to succeed she must prove the three basic requirements of defamation stated above. In addition Mary will have to prove damage (unless she is a professional cat judge) since the spoken word, ie slander, is not actionable per se.

It seems clear that the second and third requirements of reference and publication are satisfied. In contrast it appears unlikely that loss has been suffered since on the facts given there has only been publication to a barman, who is probably not influential in the world of cat judges. It will however be assumed that some loss has resulted, otherwise Mary's case would fail without consideration of the first requirement.

If Mary is to show that Carol's statement is defamatory she must prove an innuendo. Here the words used say nothing about Mary's standard as cat judge unless the standard of her mother as a cat judge is also known, (whether she is honest is irrelevant). If Mary's mother was excellent it would not be defamatory to merely say that Mary was no better than her mother, since this would leave room for Mary to be very good. If however Mary's mother was known to be a very poor cat judge, then the statement is defamatory if it is made to persons who know of the standard of Mary's mother, and provided it is untrue.

Mary will therefore have to prove that her mother was a poor cat judge and that the barman knew this if she is to show that the statement is defamatory. Since the standard of Mary's mother is not a given fact no firm conclusion can be reached. It is however clear that statements such as Carol's are not usually complimentary. Therefore even if the barman did not know Mary or her mother he would probably assume that neither of them were good cat judges.

11. To succeed in a negligence action Mrs Watts must show:-
    i.   That she is owed a duty of care;
    ii. The duty of care has been broken;
    iii. That she has suffered damage that is reasonably foreseeable.

In order to determine whether a duty is owed the courts will apply the "neighbour test" laid down by Lord Atkin in **DONOGHUE v STEVENSON (1932)**. A duty is owed to anyone who we can reasonably foresee will be injured by our acts or omissions.

The duty of care will be broken if the plaintiff fails to act as a reasonable person in the defendant's position and with the defendant's knowledge. This test makes all the circumstances relevant, for example the magnitude of the foreseeable risk. Thus in **LATIMER v AEC (1953)** a factory floor had been flooded. D had done everything possible to dry the floor and the chance of someone slipping and sustaining a serious injury was very slight. Nevertheless P slipped and was injured. D was held not liable for failing to close the factory. The third requirement is damage. This must be physical injury or financial loss consequential upon physical injury. Mere economic loss does not qualify. In this case there are three possible issues:-

i.   Is Mr Thomas personally liable in negligence?
ii.   Are the builders liable in negligence?
iii. Is Mr Thomas vicariously liable for negligence by the builders?

Concerning Mr Thomas' liability it seems likely that a duty is owed to Mrs Watts. The main issue is whether it has been broken. In **PERL v CAMDEN BOROUGH COUNCIL (1983)** P leased retail premises from D, who owned the adjoining property. D's premises did not have a front door lock and unauthorised persons were often seen there and several burglaries had taken place. Despite complaints D did nothing. Later intruders gained access to D's premises, knocked a hole in the wall and stole P's goods. The Court of Appeal reversed the High Court and held that D was not liable. There is no duty to control the acts of an independent third party in the absence of some special relationship between the defendant and the third party. In particular there is no duty upon an occupier of property to prevent others from entering his premises and thereby gaining access to neighbouring property – Goff L.J. It is therefore clear that Mrs W could not succeed against Mr T, scaffolding would be even more difficult to secure against unauthorised use than a front door. Mr T is not in breach of duty.

The same arguments would apply to the builders. They would not be held liable for the improper use of their scaffolding by an independent third party. Imposition of such a liability would "lead to the most startling and far reaching consequences". Oliver L.J. in Perl's case.

Since the builders were not negligent the question or Mr T's vicarious liability does not arise. However it is suggested that the builders are independent contractors who would therefore be liable for their own negligence. They have been engaged to produce a given result and presumably Mr T is not supervising them on a step by step basis.

12. a. Vicarious liability means liability for the torts of others, and it arises because of a relationship between the parties. The relationship may be either employer/independent contractor, or employer/employee (master/servant). A parent is not vicariously liable for his child's torts.

The general rule is that the employer is not liable for the torts of his servant. A person is a servant if the employer retains the right to control not only the work he does, but also the way in which he does it. This classic test is often unsuitable for professional servants such as doctors. Here it may be necessary to consider such criteria as payment of salaries and the power of dismissal.

If the master is to be vicariously liable, the servant's tort must be committed within the course of his employment. − The tortious act must be a wrongful way of going what the employee is employed to do. It may be negligent, fraudulent, or even forbidden provided it is within the scope of his employment. In **ROSE v PLENTY (1976)**, a notice at a milk depot, addressed to the milkmen stated:

> "Children must not in any circumstances be employed by you in the performance of your duties"

Contrary to this instruction the defendant employed a small boy who was later injured due to the defendant's negligent driving. Since the boy was the means by which the defendant did his job the employers were held liable despite their clear instruction that boys should not be employed by milkmen.

In contrast in **BEARD v LONDON GENERAL OMNIBUS CO (1900)**, a bus conductor attempted to turn a bus around at the end of its route and in doing so caused an accident. His employers were not liable since he was employed only to collect fares, and not to drive buses.

Where the master is vicariously liable, the servant is generally also liable, but if a blameless master is held vicariously liable a term is implied in the servant's contract that he will indemnify the master. − **LISTER v ROMFORD ICE (1957)**.

b. Firstly it must be pointed out that Eric appears to have been negligent. In **HEDLEY BYRNE v HELLER (1963)** it was held that an advisor may be liable in negligence if he gives unsound advice which results in financial loss, even if the advice is given gratuitiously, although the advisor has a defence if he gave a disclaimer of liability. To establish the employer's liability it must be decided whether the advice was given in the course of Eric's employment. It has already been shown in **ROSE v PLENTY** that a prohibition on particular conduct does not necessarily take such conduct outside the scope of employment. It is more relevant to look at the conduct itself. In this case the employer would no doubt claim that auditing accounts and giving investment advice are two completely different activities. However this distinction is unlikely to be appreciated by a lay client, who would probably regard accountants as experts on a whole range of financial matters. Accountants should be aware of this reliance and conduct themselves accordingly (in fact this is the probable reason for their prohibition on giving advice). It is therefore suggested that Eric's employers would be held vicariously liable for his negligence.

13. By his conduct a trader may not lead customers to mistake his business services or goods for those of another. A person is liable in the tort of passing off if when selling, or offering his goods or services in an area where he competes with the plaintiff, he represents them as being those of the plaintiff in a manner likely to deceive members of the public. Thus passing off may consist of using the plaintiff's trade mark, business name, product "get-up", or he may simply supply his own goods when he receives an order for the plaintiff's goods. An action for passing off will lie even when the defendant is innocent and relief may be granted without proof of actual damage if there is a likelihood of future damage.

The main methods of passing off are:-

a.   Marketing a product as that of the plaintiff. For example in **VOKES v EVANS AND MARBLE ARCH MOTOR SUPPLIES (1931)** D acquired windscreen wipers direct from P's sub-contractors and passed them off as their own. D was held liable.

b.   Using the plaintiff's name or trade name. For example in **HINES v WINNICK (1947)** P, who had broadcast under the name "Dr Crock and the Crackpots" successfully prevented the radio programme from using the same name for a replacement band. The trade name may be derived from an area in which the goods are manufactured. Thus a successful action was brought to protect the name "Champagne" (**BOLLINGER v COSTA BRAVA WINE CO (1961)**). Also in **HARRODS v R HARRODS (1923)** an action was successfully brought against a money lending company which used the same name as a famous Knightsbridge store. However a remedy will not be available if, despite a similarity of name, there is no possibility of confusion or loss. Thus, for example the makers of "Zoom" ice lollies could not obtain an injunction to prevent the sale of "Zoom" bubble gum.

c.   Imitating the appearance of the plaintiff's goods. The courts are more likely to grant an injunction if the decorative rather than the functional aspect of the goods has been imitated.

d.   Selling inferior goods of the plaintiff, so that buyers are led to believe that the low grade goods are typical of the plaintiff's goods. For example Gillette successfully prevented a dealer from selling used Gillette razor blades as "genuine".

Thus the statement quoted is basically true and if successful in his action the plaintiff may obtain an injunction and/or damages. The damages will compensate him for any lost profit. Loss of goodwill and reputation will also be taken into account.

14. a.   A person who acts to save the property of another, or gives him some other form of assistance, may as a matter of law be regarded as an agent of necessity. For example a person who goes to the aid of a ship at sea and saves life or property is entitled to a reward. The amount of the reward is at the discretion of the court. The doctrine of agency of necessity is confined to fairly narrow limits. In general 3 conditions must be satisfied:-

i.   There must be an emergency, making it necessary for the agent to act as he did;

ii.   It must be impossible to get instructions from his principal; and

iii.   The agent must act in good faith in the interests of all the parties.

These conditions were fulfilled in **GREAT NORTHERN RAILWAY v SWAFFIELD (1874)** where the railway company succeeded in claiming the cost of feeding and stabling a horse from the owner, who had failed to collect it when it arrived at its destination.

A principal may acquire rights and liabilities by ratifying his agent's unauthorised act. They following conditions must be satisfied:-

i.   The agent must purport to act on behalf of the principal;

ii.   The principal must have contractual capacity at the date of both the contract and the ratification. Where the principal is a company it must have been incorporated at the time of the contract (**KELNER v BAXTER (1866)**).

iii.   The principal must have full knowledge of the relevant facts or be prepared to ratify in any event. For example in **FITZMAURICE v BAYLEY (1856)** a principal in effect said to a third party − I don't know what my agent has agreed to do, but I must support him. It was held that he had ratified. Although he did not know that the agent had exceeded his authority he had agreed to take the risk.

It can therefore be seen that the main difference between creation of agency of necessity and agency by ratification is that agency of necessity is created by operation of law without the agreement of the principal, whereas agency by ratification can only be created with the knowledge and consent of the principal.

b.   The effect of ratification by a principal of the unauthorised act of the agent is to put the parties in the position they would have been in if the agent's act had been authorised from the start. Thus the agent's authority relates back to the time of the unauthorised act. In **BOLTON PARTNERS v LAMBERT (1888)** the managing director of a company, acting without authority, accepted an offer by the defendant for the purchase of company property. The defendant later withdrew his offer, but the company then ratified the manager's acceptance. It was held that the defendant was bound.

The above case has been criticised in that it puts the third party in an unfair position since the principal may repudiate or ratify as he pleases, and may keep the third party waiting, (but only for a reasonable time), while he decides what to do. On the other hand it has been argued that there is no undue hardship to the third party since if the principal ratifies the third party gets what he bargained for, and if he does not ratify he may sue the agent for breach of warranty of authority.

It is therefore clear that provided Percy ratifies within a reasonable time, (the period would be considerably shortened if Thomas were to inform Percy that he wished to withdraw), Thomas will be liable on the contract.

15. a.   i.   One of the fundamental characteristics of a bill of exchange is the ability to transfer its title. The act of transferring title to a bill is known as negotiation. A bill payable to bearer is negotiated by delivery, a bill payable to order is negotiated by the indorsement of the holder and delivery. By indorsing a bill the indorsor promises that the bill will be accepted and paid and that if it is dishonoured he will compensate the holder and subsequent indorsors *(S.53 BILLS OF EXCHANGE ACT 1882)*.

Where negotiation requires an indorsement it must be written on the bill itself and signed by the indorsor. It must also be an indorsement of the whole bill. A indorsement in blank is the simple signature of the indorsor. This converts the bill to a bearer bill. A special indorsement names the person to whom it is payable. The bill remains an order bill. A restrictive indorsement prevents further negotiation of the bill.

ii.   If there is a defect on a bill, for example fraud or theft, a transferee will take free from the defect and get a better title than the transferor provided he is a holder in due course or a later transferee who has acquired title from such a holder.

By *S.29 BILLS OF EXCHANGE AGE 1882* a holder in due course is a holder who has taken a bill:-

i.   Complete and regular on the fact of it;

ii.   Before it was overdue;

iii.   Without notice of previous dishonour;

iv.   In good faith;

v.   For value;

vi.   Without notice of any defect at the time of negotiation.

It is clear from the definition that a payee cannot be a holder in due course since a bill is not negotiated to him. Every holder of a bill is prima facie deemed to be a holder in due course.

iii.   Where a bill has been dishonoured by non acceptance it may, with the consent of the holder, be accepted for the honour of any person liable on the bill (who may, for example, be insolvent). The acceptor for honour promises that he will, on due presentment pay the bill if it is not paid by the drawee/acceptor, provided the bill has been protested for non payment and that he has been notified of these events.

b.   A cheque is a bill of exchange drawn on a banker payable on demand *S.73 BILLS OF EXCHANGE ACT 1882*. Therefore the rules in the Act apply to cheques.

By *S.55(1) BILLS OF EXCHANGE ACT 1882* the drawer undertakes that on due presentment the bill will be paid, and that if dishonoured he will compensate the holder and any indorsor who is compelled to pay it, provided the requisite procedures on dishonour are taken. By *S.55 (2)* a similar undertaking is given by an indorsor in favour of the holder and indorsor's subsequent to himself. Notice of dishonour may be written or oral. It must be given to the drawer and each indorsor otherwise they are discharged *(S.48 BEA)*. The notice must be given or sent off on the day after the cheque was dishonoured. Having given notice of dishonour D may proceed against A, B, or C under *S.55*. C may then proceed against B and B against A since D's notice to A also operates for the benefit of B and C. The paying banker will not incur liability because (in contrast to bills of exchange) a cheque is not accepted.

16. a. *S.14(2) SALE OF GOODS ACT 1979* states that where goods are sold in the course of a business there is an implied condition that those goods are of merchantable quality.

S.14(3) SGA 1979 which also applies where goods are sold in the course of a business states that there is an implied condition that the goods are fit for their putpose. In Marion's case there is no need to make known the purpose for which the goods will be used since it is obvious. If a person is abnormally sensitive to the particular goods and does not disclose this fact to the seller, the seller will not be liable. In **GRIFFITHS v PETER CONWAY (1939)** a woman with an abnormally sensitive skin bought a Harris Tweed coat without disclosing this fact to the seller. She contracted dermatitis from the coat, but the seller was not held liable since a normal person would not have been affected.

Although a condition which only affects 30% of children could not be regarded as "normal" is nevertheless a sufficiently high percentage of persons to make it clear that Smith is definitely in breach of the condition implied by *S.14(3)* and probably in breach of *S.14(2)* as well.

Marion may therefore return the goods and recover the price paid. If she has suffered any other foreseeable loss, for example loss of wages as a result of taking time off work to nurse her children, or medical expenses, she will also be able to recover that loss. She will not personally be able to claim for the discomfort suffered by her children, but they could sue the manufacturer for negligence.

b. At common law the debtor would be liable for all arrears. In addition the creditor will usually have reserved a right to terminate the agreement and re-possess the goods. Whether the debtor will also be liable for any loss of profit that the creditor suffers will depend on whether the debtor has repudiated the agreement or not. If he has the creditor may recover his loss of profit. In **YEOMAN CREDIT v WARAGOWSKI (1961)** the measure of damages was held to be £434 7s 0d (hire purchase price) less (i) £205 (received on resale of goods); (ii) £72 (initial payment); (iii) £60 4s 6d (arrears of payments already recovered); and (iv) £1 (payable on exercise of option to purchase). This equals £96 2s 6d ie the finance company received:-

£	s.	d.	
205	—	—	(Resale proceeds)
72	—	—	(Initial payment)
60	4	6	(Arrears recovered)
96	2	6	(Damages)
433	7	0	

They therefore recovered their loss of profits. (They did not recover the £1 payable on the exercise of the option to purchase. This accounts for the difference between the hire purchase price and the total of the sums received).

Where the debtor has not repudiated the agreement, but is merely in arrears with a few instalments, and the creditor exercises a contractual right to terminate the creditor may only claim the amount of the instalments in arrears plus damages for any failure by the debtor to take reasonable care of the goods plus the costs of the re-possession (**FINANCINGS v BALDOCK (1963)**).

The above common law rules must be read subject to *S.87* and *88 CONSUMER CREDIT ACT 1974* which provides that when a debtor defaults the creditor may not take any action until he has served a "default notice" on the debtor specifying the nature of the breach, what action is required to remedy the breach, and what sum if any is payable as compensation. The debtor cannot take any further action until 7 days after service of the notice.

The debtor is also protected by *S.90 CCA 1974* which provides that once one-third or more of the total price of the goods has been paid the creditor cannot recover possession except on an order of the court. In addition if the creditor wishes to repossess any goods which are situated on the debtor's premises he must obtain a court order. This is particularly relevant if the goods are not protected under *S.90*.

Jurisdiction over consumer credit agreements is exercised by the County Court, which has wide powers to vary the agreement made by the parties. For example it may make a "time order", allowing the debtor extra time to pay for the goods, or a "return order" under which the goods are handed back to the creditor, or "transfer order" which involves giving part of the goods to the debtor and returning the rest to the creditor. Finally if the court feels that a credit agreement is extortionate it may re-open the agreement so as to do justice between the parties and it may, for example, relieve the debtor from liability to go on paying for the goods or it may order the return of money already paid.

17. a. At common law the employer is not under a strict duty to provide for the safety of his employees. He is required to take reasonable care, ie, he must take careful and prudent steps for their safety. What is reasonable care depends on the circumstances of the case and is a question of fact. Some of the criteria used include the foreseeability of injury, the seriousness of possible injury, the obviousness of the risk and the cost of safety measures in relation to the likelihood of injury. The employer is at fault if he omits precautions common to the particular trade, or which in the circumstances it was folly to neglect. **(PARIS v STEPNEY BOROUGH COUNCIL (1951))**.

Reasonable care must be exercised in relation to:

i.   The condition of the premises.

ii. The provision of plant, tools and equipment.

iii. Laying down of a safe system of work, which includes safe workmen, proper training, provision of safety equipment, proper co-ordination, and safe working conditions.

An example of reasonableness as to (a) (i) above is in the case of **LATIMER v AEC (1953)**, where a factory floor became slippery after flooding and the employer was held to have complied with his duty by using all the available sand and sawdust to render the floor safe.

b. It is part of the employer's duty to co-ordinate workmen and appliances into a reasonably safe system of work. The installation of a common practice does not alone establish that the employer has met his obligation at common law **(CAVANAGH v ULSTER WEAVING CO (1959))** for an established practice may be an established bad practice. In the circumstances given, the practice is dangerous, and a worker injured as a result of the practice might have a right of action against his employer, as in **BROWN v JOHN MILLS & CO (1970)**.

This case is similar to that in which an inexperienced workman was polishing brass nuts in a lathe using a piece of emery cloth wrapped around his finger, although polishing sticks were provided. His fellow workmates used this dangerous practice. It was held that the employer was liable as he had failed to give proper training and exercise adequate supervision.

Where the employer has laid down a safe system of work and provided the necessary equipment (such as the polishing stick) he must remind his employees to take safety precautions. However, with an experienced workman the employer is not obliged to stand over him. In **QUALCAST v HAYNES (1954)** an experienced workman in a foundry had molten metal splash into his boots, when he was not wearing safety spats. It was held that as the workman was experienced the employer was not bound by law to urge or require employees to wear the safety clothing.

The employer may still be liable if, knowing of the unsafe practice, he permits it to continue. To escape liability the employer should show that he did what he could to ensure that the workers were made aware of the dangerous practice and of the provision of the polishing sticks to safeguard them.

18. a. If a worker is dismissed in breach of contract, he is entitled to damages at common law for wrongful dismissal. This right arises if the worker was entitled to notice, and was wrongly dismissed without notice (unless he had been guilty of such serious misconduct as to justify summary dismissal). The damages would normally be wages for the notice period. If the worker had been employed for a fixed term of, say, five years, damages would normally be his net income for the unexpired portion of his fixed term.

b. Whether or not the worker was in breach of contract, he might secondly be entitled to compensation from his ex-employer for unfair dismissal. To qualify, he must continuously have been employed by his ex-employer for at least two years. If dismissal is to do with trade union membership or activities, these qualifying periods are not necessary. In an unfair dismissal claim before an industrial tribunal, the tribunal must assume that that the dismissal was unfair unless the employer can prove that the sacking was because of (a) incompetence or lack of capability or qualifications, (b) misconduct or to continue to employ would be a breach of a statutory provision. The tribunal must then also be satisfied that, in the circumstances, having regard to equity and the substantial merits of the case, the employer acted reasonably in dismissing the worker. It might not, for example, be reasonable to dismiss a long-standing worker for an isolated and minor piece of misconduct. If dismissal is held unfair, the tribunal can order reinstatement (giving back his old job) or re-engagement (giving a comparable job). If the employer disobeys such an order he cannot be forced to take back the employee, but would have to pay additional compensation. The amount of compensation generally is (a) a basic award, calculated in the same way as a redundancy payment, but subject to reduction if the worker's own misconduct contributed to the dismissal; (b) a compensatory award; and (c) an additional award if the employer has disobeyed a reinstatement or re-engagement order.

c. If the worker is dismissed for redundancy, he may be entitled to a redundancy payment from his employer. To qualify, he must continuously have been employed by his ex-employer for at least two years. He is redundant if dismissal is beause the employer has ceased business, either totally or in the place where the employee was employed, or if the work needed to be done by the worker has ceased or diminished, either generally or in the place of employment. The amount of payment depends on the worker's length of service with his ex-employer. He will receive 1½ weeks' pay for each year since he reached 41, one week's pay for years between 22 and 41, and half a week's pay for years from 18-22. A maximum of 20 years can be taken into account, and 'week's pay' is subject to a maximum amount. If he is unfairly selected for redundancy, a worker can receive both redundancy payment and compensation for unfair dismissal.

d. Whilst unemployed, the worker may be entitled to social security benefits from the State. In order to qualify, he must have paid the required amount in contributions (as deductions from wages) whilst employed. Insurance officers can disqualify claimants for up to six weeks if dismissal was for misconduct, or the worker left voluntarily, or refuses new employment or retraining. Unemployed persons may also be entitled to 'financial help' from state funds in the case of hardship, and in this case no contribution conditions are required.

19. a. The *EMPLOYMENT PROTECTION (CONSOLIDATION) ACT 1978, (S.94)* provides that where a business is transferred from one employer to another continuity of service of an employee is not broken. This principle is confirmed and extended under the *TRANSFER OF UNDERTAKINGS (PROTECTION OF EMPLOYMENT) REGULATIONS 1981*, ie every contract of employment is automatically transferred to the new employer. Dismissal by reason of the transfer is unfair unless it is caused by economic, technical or organisational reasons incidental to the transfer. If these reasons involve a diminution in the number of employees, a redundancy situation will exist. In **SKILLING v READ (1982)** dismissal of a shop assistant by new owners on the grounds that they (a husband and wife partnership) could run the business without Mrs Skilling's assistance was held by an Industrial Tribunal to be fair. They did however uphold a claim for redundancy pay.

b. Fogy may claim to be redundant if the work he is required to do is fundamentally different, ie his original job has effectively ceased. In **SARTIN v CO-OPERATIVE RETAIL SERVICES (1969)** a grocery shop was converted into a supermarket which resulted in a great increase in floor space and turnover. S was manager of the grocery shop but could not cope with the requirements of the new type of business. S was therefore redundant as a new type of manager was required. Contrast **NORTH RIDING GARAGES v BUTTERWICK (1967)** which involved a garage which came under new ownership. B was the workshop manager and was mainly involved in mechanics work. Under the new ownership B was expected to deal with the administration, but could not cope. It was held that he was not redundant as the requirement was still for a workshop manager. It would appear that Fogy's position is similar to the Butterwick case and he would therefore not receive a redundancy payment.

If Fogy was offered suitable new employment on the same terms, and unreasonably refused, or on different terms, or in a separate place, and after a reasonable trial period of not less than 4 weeks, also unreasonably refused, then he would not be entitled to a redundancy payment.

The agreement under the new contract must be in writing stating the date the trial period ends and terms of employment at the end of the trial period. If the employee terminates the contract at the end of the trial period, or before because the work was unsuitable, he would be entitled to a redundancy payment. The same situation applies if the employer terminates on the ground that the employee cannot cope with the new type of work.

20. a. At common law, an employee who is summarily dismissed (ie, dismissed without notice) can maintain an action for damages for wrongful dismissal if the employer was not justified in so dismissing him. Summary dismissal is justified when the employee has broken a condition of his contract, eg, has been guilty of misconduct showing that he has disregarded the essential conditions of the contract. (**LAWS v LONDON CHRONICLE (1959)**). The measure of the damages can never exceed the amount of remuneration he would have received had he been dismissed by notice. Where a fixed-term contract is involved damages may amount to the pay due for the remaining period of the contract.

An employee can always be dismissed by being given the proper notice and being paid during that period, and he has no recourse against his employer if the employer is exercising his contractual right to terminate the contract. The employer's reasons are irrelevant.

The statutory right to claim compensation for unfair dismissal is not concerned with the manner of the dismissal but with the fairness of the dismissal. It protects, for example, against arbitrary dismissal. The statutory provisions are contained in the *EPCA 1978* as amended by the *EAs* of 1980 and 1982 which expressly state that an employee has the right not to be unfairly dismissed by his employer.

An industrial tribunal may make a recommondation to reinstate taking into account the extent to which the employee contributed to his dismissal, and the practicability of reinstatement, eg, the chance of his fellow employees refusing to work with him. Alternatively a recommendation to re-engagement may be made.

Failure to comply with the tribunal's recommendation makes the employer liable to additional damages in addition to a "basic award" calculated as for a redundancy payment and a "compensatory award" based on actual loss suffered.

In the case of failure to make reinstatement or re-engagement where the reason for dismissal is the employee's trade union membership or activities he will be entitled to a special award of compensation under the *EA 1982*.

b. It is for the employer to show the reason for the dismissal and that it justified dismissal. Prior to the *EA 1980* the onus was on the employer to show that in the circumstances he acted reasonably in treating it as a sufficient reason for dismissal. The *EA 1980* amended the law to allow the tribunal to decide the fairness of the dismissal. The tribunal would decide "in accordance with equity and the substantial merits of the case".

Dismissal is fair − and accordingly an allegation of unfair dismissal may be defeated − if the employee was incapable or unqualified to do his work, was guilty of misconduct, his continued employment would have contravened a statute or he was redundant (unless selection for redundancy was for an unfair reason).

Dismissal is not to be regarded as unfair if the reason for dismissal was that the employee took part in a strike or other industrial action, unless it is shown that other employees who struck were not dismissed for taking part, or were offered re-engagement within 3 months but the complainant has not been offered re-engagement and the reason for this is his trade union membership or activities. An employee may be selectively dismissed for taking part in an unofficial strike or other industrial action.

21. a. Mrs. Lamb can sue Sparks for the tort of negligence since it was his negligent act which led directly to the damaging of her fur coat. However, Sparks, an employee, may not be able to compensate Mrs. Lamb adequately and so she should also bring action against his employer.

b. Mrs. Lamb can sue Power and Co. As Sparks' employer, Power and Co are vicariously liable for the misdeeds of their employees which arise out of their employment: **CENTURY INSURANCE CO v N. IRELAND ROAD TRANSPORT BOARD (1942)** in which a lighted match, carelessly thrown away by an employee, ignited a petrol tanker. However, the degree of danger involved in a department store may not be as great as that in the circumstances of the Century Insurance Co case (**WILLIAMS v JONES (1865)**). Although Sparks is working at Harridges, control of their employee would appear to remain with Power and Co, unless Sparks was under the supervision of Harridges' own foreman electrician: **GARRARD v SOUTHEY (1952)**.

c. Mrs. Lamb can sue Harridges:

i. As employer of Sparks, but only if control has passed from Power and Co to Harridges, which is unlikely.

ii. If Harridges were cleaning or repairing the coat they would be in the position of bailees and as such would be liable for the damage even if the wrongful action was not done in the course of Sparks' employment: **MORRIS v C.W. MARTIN & SONS (1965)**. In this case M. sent a fur coat to a furrier for cleaning and the furrier gave it to the defendants who were fur-cleaning specialists. Whilst on the defendants premises it was stolen by an employee. It was held that the defendants were liable to M. in their capacity as bailees to take reasonable care of the goods entrusted to them.

iii. There may be the possibility of an action under the *OCCUPIERS LIABILITY ACT 1957* for Harridges failure in the common duty of care to a visitor. (**O'CONNOR v SWAN & EDGAR (1963)**).

d. It makes no difference whether Sparks has been forbidden to smoke or not. Even though wrongful act was expressly forbidden the employer is liable provided that the act was done in the course of employment: **LIMPUS v LONDON GENERAL OMNIBUS CO (1862)**.

22. a. The injury to K undoubtedly happened "in the course of employment", ie, the time element is satisfied. However, it is likely, in this case, that the cause of the injury would be adjudged not to be arising out of K's employment. Therefore no benefit is claimable.

b. In **VANDYKE v FENDER (1970)** it was held that travelling to and from employment in a vehicle supplied by the employers will be considered to be in the course of employment only where the use of such transport is obligatory. As this is unlikely in this case no benefit can be claimed. If, however, it were a condition of employment that L travel by this bus to work, then he would receive benefit, despite his contravention of the company rules concerning standing on the platform, since injuries which result from a forbidden act arise out of employment if they would do so if they were not forbidden. The payment/non-payment of the fare is immaterial in this case, except insofar as it makes obligation to travel by that transport unlikely.

c. An employee who visits the works canteen on the employer's premises does not take himself out of employment, and an accident to him in that place is deemed to arise out of and in the course of employment. Exceptions could be made if the cause of his falling asleep was attributable to some cause unconnected with his work or the meal or if, by falling asleep, M had overstayed his breaktime (as in **REG v IIC ex parte A.E.U. (1966)**).

d. An employee is bound at common law to protect his employer's property, and in trying to prevent an attempted robbery he is doing an act arising out of his employment. If as a result of acting in this emergency he is injured, he is entitled to benefit.

e. Although within the course of employment an injury sustained whilst playing games, even authorised games, does not qualify an employee for injuries benefit.

f. A person who is injured whilst travelling to or from work is, in general, not entitled to benefit, for the accident does not arise in the course of and out of his employment. On the other hand the course of employment does not begin and end when he clocks on and off. In general, if he is still on the employer's premises he will be entitled to benefit. It has already been held that, if the employee is on a private road or means of access reserved for those having business at the employer's business, the employee will still be entitled to benefit if he sustains an injury.

g. When the employee passes through the main gate of the factory on to the public highway, he takes no greater risk than do other members of the public. He takes himself out of the course of his employment. The special bus he intends to catch may or may not be one within the terms of the Act, but even if it is the section relates only to travelling by that bus, and does not cover crossing a public highway to reach it.

23. a. Under the *SOCIAL SECURITY ACT 1975* Alan is disqualified from receiving unemployment benefit during the period of the strike unless he can establish that he has become bona fide employed elsewhere in the occupation he usually follows or has become regularly engaged in some other occupation. Since Alan obtained what was merely a temporary job, he cannot be brought within either of the exceptions and continues to be disqualified.

b. Brian may claim unemployment benefit if he can show that he does not belong to a grade or class of workers, members of which at his place of work are taking part in the dispute. For this purpose, separate departments on the same premises are treated as separate places of employment and Brian will therefore be successful in his claim.

c. Cecil may be disqualified for a period of up to six weeks if he left his employment voluntarily and without just cause. Whether he had just cause for leaving is a matter to be decided by the appropriate insurance officer on the facts of the case.

d. David can be disqualified for a period of six weeks if he refuses to avail himself of the opportunity of receiving training approved by the Department of Employment for the purpose of returning to regular employment. He will not be required to go on a course of retraining until a reasonable period of unemployment has elapsed and it is clear that he has little hope of fresh employment in his regular occupation.

e. The disqualification of up to six weeks also applies where a person without just cause refuses to accept suitable employment, in Elsie's case, a similar position. However, she may well have just cause in refusing the situation in view of her domestic circumstances. The matter is one for decision by the local insurance officer.

24. a. The defences open to an employer to defeat or mitigate a claim for damages brought by an employee who has been injured by an accident at work are as follows:

i. In an action for breach of common law duty (but not for breach of statutory duty) the employer may plead volenti non fit injuria. This defence asserts that the employee has freely and voluntarily agreed to run the risk of injury from a certain employment and cannot therefore claim damages if he is so injured (**BOLT v WM. MOSS & SONS LTD (1966)**). It is extremely doubtful whether the maxim will ever apply to employments which are not inherently dangerous. If the defence is to succeed in respect of even a risky employment, it is not enough that the employee had full knowledge of the risk he ran; it must also be clearly shown that he agreed that what risk there was should lie on him (eg, by the acceptance of danger money). The defence is not available if the employee protested about the danger or had to be persuaded to take the risk.

ii.   The employer may plead Contributory Negligence, ie, whilst admitting his own negligence, he also alleges negligence on the part of the employee. Under the *LAW REFORM (CONTRIBUTORY NEGLIGENCE) ACT 1945*, the court may then apportion the negligence and resultant loss between the employer and employee, and the latter, if successful in his action, will recover only that proportion of his loss attributable to the employer's negligence; he will not recover the proportion attributable to his own negligence.

iii.   The employer may *not* rely on an exemption clause excluding himself from liability for an employee's death or injury due to his (the employer's) negligence (*UNFAIR CONTRACT TERMS ACT 1977 (S.2)*).

iv.   He may deny that there is an employer/employee relationship in existence at all.

b.   The employee must allege and prove that:

i.   There was a duty imposed upon the employer;

ii.   That the employer failed to carry out his duty in a reasonable manner.

iii.   That he suffered injury as a result of the breach (**McWILLIAMS v SIR WILLIAM ARROL (1962)**).

c.   i.   The mere fact that Jones knew that the brakes of the van were defective is not enough to let the employer succeed in a defence of volenti non fit injuria. To succeed the employer would also have to show that Jones freely and voluntarily agreed that he would accept any resultant risk. His carrying on his job despite the defective brakes is not sufficient evidence of such agreement. (**BOWATER v ROWLEY REGIS CORPORATION (1944)**).

ii.   In his second defence the employer is admitting his own negligence in supplying a van with defective brakes, but alleging that a contributory cause of the accident was Jones' own negligence in driving too fast having regard to the state of the brakes. A great deal must obviously depend on the actual facts, but if Jones did know and did drive too fast in the circumstances, the employer might well succeed in fixing part of the liability for the loss, however small, on Jones himself, and this part of the loss Jones will be unable to recover.

In awards of contributory negligence the court would take into account the employee's motive in taking the risk, ie was the employee acting in the best interests of his employer (**SHILTON v HUGHES-JOHNSON (1970)**).

25. a. The *FACTORIES ACT 1961, S.12.* requires that flywheels directly connected to any prime mover be securely fenced. Under *S.13.* transmission machinery must be securely fenced unless its position or construction render it as safe as if it were fenced. By *S.14.* every dangerous part of any machinery must be securely fenced unless its position or construction render it as safe as if it were fenced. Under *S.16.* fencing and other safeguards must be substantial, and constantly maintained and kept in position while the dangerous parts are in motion or use. The factory provisions are strict, if the machine can only be used unfenced it must not be used (there are some special regulations which make exceptions to this). If these statutory provisions are not complied with the factory owner is criminally liable, and in addition he may be sued at civil law for damages by an injured employee.

The *HEALTH AND SAFETY AT WORK ACT 1974* applies to virtually all premises. Under *S.2.* every employer must ensure so far as is reasonably practicable the health, safety and welfare of all his employees while they are at work. In particular he must provide plant which is safe. There is also responsibility (under *S.6.*) to manufacturers, designers and suppliers of machinery. Under *S.7.* employees must take reasonable care for themselves and others, and co-operate in ensuring that safety requirements are observed. Contravention of this Act constitutes a criminal offence, an injured employee has no right of civil action under the Act.

b. If Mills Ltd is classed as a 'factory' as defined by *S.175(1) FACTORIES ACT 1961*, Martin and Norman may sue for damages for breach of statutory duty, ie failure to fence under *S.14(1)*. The company may also be criminally prosecuted by an inspector of the Health and Safety Executive. In addition, a prohibition notice may be served on the company preventing use of the machine.

Martin may be classed as a trespasser being in a part of the factory away from his normal duties on a private matter. However, in **UDDIN v ASSOCIATED PORTLAND CEMENT (1965)** Uddin was injured by unfenced machinery whilst in a forbidden area of the factory but was still entitled to damages because of the strict liability to fence dangerous machinery. However, Martin's damages may be reduced under the *LAW REFORM (CONTRIBUTORY NEGLIGENCE) ACT 1945*.

Norman may claim damages as it is reasonably foreseeable that he will attempt to rescue a fellow workman in an emergency and an employer owes a duty of care to an employee attempting such a rescue (**HAYNES v HARWOOD (1935)**).

If Mills Ltd is not classed as a factory a claim may be made under common law for the employer's failure to provide a safe system of work.

The claimants must bring their action within 3 years under the *LIMITATION ACT 1980*. Mills Ltd must be insured against such contingencies under the *EMPLOYERS LIABILITY (COMPULSORY INSURANCE) ACT 1969*.

26. a.   A factory owner must allow employees time off work in the following circumstances:-

i.   ***Trade union duties.*** By *S.27. EPCA 1978* an employer is obliged to permit an employee who is an official of an independent trade union recognised by him for collective bargaining purposes, to take reasonable time off (with pay) during working hours to:

a.   Carry out official duties which are concerned with industrial relations between his employer and employees; or

b.   Undergo training in aspects of industrial relations which is relevant to the carrying out of those duties and approved by the TUC or the trade union of which he is an official.

ii.   ***Trade union activities.*** An employer is obliged to permit an employee who is a member of a trade union (as in i.) to take reasonable time off (without pay) during working house to take part in the following trade union activities:

a.   Any activities of the trade union of which the employee is a member; and

b.   Any activities of the trade union of which the employee is acting as a representative of such a union.

This excludes activities which constitute industrial action.

iii.   ***Public duties.*** By *S.29. EPCA 1978* an employer is obliged to permit an employee reasonable time off (without pay), during working hours to perform certain public duties, eg, a Justice of the Peace, a member of a local authority, a member of a statutory tribunal, etc.

The amount of time off allowed will depend on such considerations as, how much time is required to perform the duty, how much time off the employee has already had in respect of the duty and the effect to the employer's business of the employee's absence.

iv.   ***To look for work or make arrangements for training.*** *EPCA 1978*gives the right to an employee who is dismissed for redundancy to be allowed reasonable time off (with pay) during working hours to look for new employment or make arrangements for training for future employment. The employee must have completed two years employment.

v.   ***For ante-natal care.*** An employee has a right under *S.31A. EPCA 1978* to time off (with pay) during working house to keep an appointment for ante-natal care prescribed by a registered health visitor. This right is irrespective of hours worked or length of service. The employer may require the employee to produce documentary evidence of the appointment and a certificate stating that she is pregnant.

vi.   ***Safety representatives.*** The *HEALTH AND SAFETY AT WORK ACT 1974* requires an employer to permit a safety representative to take time off (with pay) during working hours for the purpose of:

    a. Performing his functions as a safety representative; and

    b. Undergoing training.

b. Under the *FACTORIES ACT 1961 (S. 94)* a factory owner must allow the following days as holidays to every young person (under 18 years) employed in the factory:

    i.   Christmas Day, Good Friday and every bank holiday; alternatively these days may be substituted for other weekdays provided a notice to this effect is posted in the factory three weeks before these days;

    ii.   At least half of the days in i. must be allowed between 15 March and 1 October;

    iii. A young person shall not be employed, on a holiday as above, in the factory or about the business of the factory or in any other business carried on by the owner.

Under *S.1. EPCA 1978* The written statement of terms of employment must include any terms relating to holidays, including entitlement and payment, and sufficient information to enable the employee to calculate holiday entitlement and holiday pay on termination of employment.

Appendix 3

QUESTIONS AND DISCUSSION TOPICS WITHOUT ANSWERS

INTRODUCTION

This appendix is designed as a teaching aid for lecturers, therefore the questions are not, in general, selected from past examination papers. Their purpose varies from question to question. They either

> *a. Provide a basis for discussion of topics related to the syllabuses for which the book is written, but not in the "mainstream" of those syllabuses, for example questions 1-4, 11 and 14; or*

> *b. Pose rather more unusual and searching problems than are set in Foundation and Level I examinations. Some of these problems are based on facts which have never apparently been litigated. Others are based on actual cases. For example the facts of question 9 (unlikely though they seem) have occurred twice, and led to litigation in America.*

Lecturers may obtain notes to assist in discussion of these questions by writing to the publishers on college notepaper. There is no charge.

1. Explain the origin of the case name:-

DOE d. CARTER v BARNARD (1849) (Chapter 29.9)

2. What would be the effect of an inconsistency between EEC law and a subsequently passed English statute?

3. Explain the early methods of trial used in the common law courts. To what extent were they influenced by religious beliefs?

4. Describe the scheme for providing legal aid and advice to persons of limited financial means. How effective is Legal Aid?

5. John had been negotiating by post for the purchase of a car from Charles. At 10.00 am Monday John posted a firm letter of acceptance. At 11.00 am the same day John changed his mind and sent the following telegram:-

> "Ignore the postal acceptance that you will receive tomorrow. I don't want the car. John."

Charles received the telegram at 3.00 pm on Monday and immediately sold the car to Philip. At 4.30 pm John changed his mind again, and telephoned Charles to tell him to ignore the telegram. Advise Charles.

6. Refer to the exemption clause in **PHOTO PRODUCTION v SECURICOR TRANSPORT (1980)** (Chapter 18.14). Would the exemption clause quoted in the text satisfy the requirement of reasonableness as laid down by the *UNFAIR CONTRACT TERMS ACT 1977*?

7.   X instructed Y & Co, a firm of estate agents, to sell a house which he owned, and handed over to them drawings of the property which had formed part of a planning application. Y & Co produced particulars of sale which included a clause stating:-

> "X does not give, and neither Y & Co or any person in their employment has any authority to make or give, any representations or warranty whatsoever in relation to this property."

Z, who was interested in purchasing the house, was given the drawings referred to above. They showed that there had been a two storey extension at the back of the house which had recently been demolished because it was dangerous. Z therefore assumed that (subject to planning permission) he would be able to build a two storey extension to replace the previous one. Contracts were then exchanged. Soon afterwards Z discovered that (i) a two storey extension could not be built without obstructing a neighbour's right to light and (ii) the plan shown to him by the agents was inaccurate in that the demolished extension had not been as high as was indicated.

Advise Z.

8.   "There are many contractual undertakings which cannot be categorised as being 'conditions' or 'warranties'. Of such undertakings all that can be predicted is that some breaches will and others will not give rise to an event which will deprive the party not in default of substantially the whole benefit which it was intended that he should obtain."

– Diplock L.J.

Discuss.

9.   John's daughter went into hospital for a minor operation. During the course of the operation the surgeon, Peter, removed the patient's only kidney, believing it to be an ovarian cyst. The patient was immediately linked to a kidney machine and the process of looking for a suitable kidney donor began. After 12 months of fruitless search John volunteered to have one of his own kidneys removed for transplantation to his daughter. After this was done John decided to sue Peter claiming damages for the loss of his kidney. Advise John of his chance of success.

10. Whilst playing on a high bridge Billy, aged 10, lost his balance. He was falling to certain death, but in his fall he came into contact with high tension electricity cables. These cables had been negligently maintained by the Central Electricity Generating Board and Billy was therefore killed by electrocution. Discuss the liability of the Central Electricity Generating Board.

11. Compare the tort system with personal insurance as methods of providing compensation to accident victims.

12. Frank was an employee of A.B. Ltd. In 1973 he was injured at work due to his employer's breach of statutory duty. The injury, which was to his back, meant that Frank could only undertake light work and had to have frequent rests. In 1976 Frank contracted a disease of the spine which was *not* connected with the accident. This disease rendered Frank totally unfit to work. How will this subsequent illness affect Frank's claim for damages for breach of statutory duty.

13. S sells goods to B and receives a cheque in payment of the price. Although the goods are in conformity with the contract B has second thoughts about the wisdom of his purchase and instructs his bank, P, not to pay the cheque. In ignorance of this fact S presents the cheque for payment and P, overlooking the stop order, pays. Can P recover the amount paid from S?

14. What is the legal effect of instructions or warnings as to the use of goods supplied to consumers?

15. A B C Finance Ltd lent Tom £3,000 to buy a car from X Y Z Garage. The credit agreement stipulated that if Tom defaulted in payment of any instalment for a period of a month, then the balance of the loan plus interest would become immediately payable. In fact, although the agreement lasted for 9 months, Tom did not pay a single instalment because he claimed that the car was defective. After a series of malfunctions and attempted repairs Tom finally rejected the car as unfit for its purpose. A B C Finance Ltd wish to recover the full amount of the loan plus interest and accrued interest on Tom's arrears. Advise Tom.

16. Describe the role played by the *TRADE DESCRIPTIONS ACT 1968* in the protection of consumers.

17. Watt, an electrician, has been offered employment by a department store. The store is prepared either (i) to pay him a weekly wage for specific hours of work, or (ii) to pay him as a contractor for each job that he carries out.
   Watt is undecided as to which offer to take. He realises that the first alternative will give him greater security but that the second will probably enable him to earn more money. Advise him further of the legal consequences that will follow from his decision.

18. a.   An employee of your company claims that he is being underpaid. What sources would you examine to ascertain the validity of this claim?

b.   Your company decides that it would be less costly to close the factory for a third week's annual holiday and to maintain production by working an extra three-quarters of an hour on each Monday evening throughout the remainder of the year. Advise on the legal considerations affecting the means by which this proposed change in the terms of employment could be introduced.

19. a.   T Limited is engaged in the demolition of some old houses. Safety headgear is provided for employees but is rarely used. As a result of the negligence of the foreman a fall of bricks causes head injuries to a number of workers which the wearing of safety helmets would have prevented.

b.   Advise T Limited as to its liability in respect of the following injured workers:

   i.   Albert, an experienced demolition worker, who has been employed on this type of work for fifteen years;

   ii.   Bernard, a young man of nineteen, who was only engaged the previous week;

   iii.   Charles, who is known to be deaf and who could have avoided injury if he had heard the warning shout;

   iv.   David, who is also deaf but has not told his employer for fear of losing his job;

   v.   Eric, whose injuries prove to be fatal because of an abnormally thin skull.

20.   Your company employs a number of sales representatives who are paid a basic wage, a commission on sales and a variable annual bonus. You are required to draft a report explaining the extent, if any, to which your company is liable (a) to pay remuneration to these representatives if they are ill, and (b) to provide them with goods to sell if production falls away.

21.   Explain in outline the principal provisions of the *EQUAL PAY ACT 1970.* State the methods by which its provisions can be enforced.

22.   Outline and critically explain two methods by which a minimum standard of pay can be guaranteed for a particular class of worker in an industry.

23.   The employees in the following circumstances are all dismissed. Explain whether or not a claim for unfair dismissal is likely to succeed.

a.   Arthur, where a 'closed shop' operates, refuses to join a trade union.

b.   Brenda has become pregnant.

c.   Charles, a van driver, has been disqualified from driving for three months.

d.   David promised when he was engaged that he would make no claim in the future for unfair dismissal.

24.   a.   A suffers from chronic bronchitis. He is often absent especially during winter. His employer feels that we cannot continue to employ A who is too unreliable.

b.   B is a cashier in a supermarket. His employer learns that he has been found guilty of stealing a car radio from a fellow member of a golf club.

586

The rules of work say that all appearances in the criminal court must be reported to the employer. B has failed to do so.

Write a short note on each of these cases for the employer.

25. Your company has a factory employing 5,000 workers. Orders have fallen away and it is proposed to make 200 workers redundant. You are asked for advice on the possible legal implications of this proposal. You are asked particularly whether your company may keep the decision secret until the last moment for fear of industrial action and whether it is possible to use the opportunity to get rid of some alleged 'trouble-makers' and poor workers.

Draft an appropriate report.

26. a. An accident occurs in your workshop and one of your employees suffers serious injury. He sues you, as his employer, for damages. Explain whether any of the following matters would be a defence.

i. The accident occurred because the foreman, in breach of your express instructions, was operating the machinery at over the recommended speed.

ii. The injured employee had known of the danger but had never complained.

iii. The injured employee had failed to use safety equipment which you had provided, and which was available in the general office about fifty yards from the workshop.

b. To what extent, if at all, will the injured employee be able to claim both damages from you, his employer, and industrial injuries benefits?

27. a. The law which attempts to ensure occupational safety may sometimes be broken if greater output is likely to result. Upon whom will liability fall if such a breach is discovered?

b. Which authorities are responsible for the administration and enforcement of the law relating to occupational safety? Outline the powers and duties of such authorities.

28. Distinguish conciliation, mediation and arbitration. Indicate the extent to which the law requires conciliation to take place.

29. Explain the significance of the phrase "in furtherance of a trade dispute" in the law giving legal protection to trade unions.

Appendix 4

ASSIGNMENTS

1. In January 1990 Kevin was captain of England's football team and generally regarded as a "certainty" to play in the World Cup Finals in Italy in June 1990.

In February 1990 he agreed with Sports Publishers Ltd to write a book giving a personal account of the Finals. His fee would be £25,000. In the same month he also agreed to do a series of television commentaries for the BBC on specific matches involving countries other than England. The contract included a promise by Kevin that he would not be involved in any type of broadcasting in any capacity for any other country.

In April Kevin lost form and was dropped from the team for two consecutive warm-up matches. He reacted by publicly calling the Team Manager "an incompetent fool". He was then told that because of this outburst and his attitude to the Manager he would not even be selected for the 22 man squad. In early May Kevin formed a company called Kick Ltd in which he held 999 shares (his wife held the only other share). The company has just signed a contract with ITV to sell Kevin's commentary services to ITV for all of the matches not already contracted to the BBC.

It is now mid-May, Kevin has just heard from Sports Publishers Ltd that they have cancelled his contract to write a personal account of the Finals, because they want it written from the point of view of a leading player. Kevin still wants to write the book.

The BBC also wish to avoid their contract with him, but whether they avoid it or not, they are determined that he shall not do any commentating for ITV. Kevin wants to work for both of them, but given a choice he would prefer to work for the BBC.

Advise the parties.

2. Memorandum To: Chief Administrative Officer
Central College

From: Principal — Central College

Date: 1st September 1990

I have had several telephone conversations with the Training Director of the Egyptian National Power Company (ENP). We have a "gentlemans agreement" that the College will provide a six month training course in computer aided design for 10 young employees of ENP. The course will include one day per week English tuition provided by our English as a Foreign Language section. We have also agreed to provide whatever help we can with regard to student accommodation. Please prepare a formal draft contract to send to the Training Director of ENP. Thank you.

3. You have been contacted by two of your friends. They have both recently qualified as professional tennis coaches. They want to go into partnership on a equal basis and have asked your advice on what they should include in their partnership agreement.

Write a letter to them giving whatever advice you think appropriate, and pointing out the main matters that should be included in the partnership agreement.

4. In the past 12 months a friend of yours, who lectures at a local college, has published three booklets written by colleagues. He did not have any formal written contract with the authors, only a verbal agreement to pay them 10% of the selling price of each booklet sold. The booklets have all sold well and he is now considering publishing a text book written by another colleague. Your friend feels that authors should enter into a formal contract and seeks your advice on what the contract should contain.

You are asked to write to him advising him of the main things to be included in such a contract.

5. Write a reply to the following letter:

Dear Sir,

Seven months ago I purchased a television set on hire purchase at a price of £320.00. I made a down-payment of £32.00 and I have paid 6 monthly instalments of £12.00. Can I avoid further payment by returning the set to the dealer?

A few days ago my husband Frank signed a hire purchase agreement for a set of Encyclopaedia Britannica. We now realise that this was a terrible mistake. Can we get out of the contract?

Yours faithfully

June Smith

6. A friend of yours has recently purchased a house which he intends to let. His tenants will each have a bedroom and shared use of the dining room, lounge, kitchen and bathroom. Your friend will pay all bills, except heating in the bedrooms. The tenants will pay this by feeding separate gas and electricity meters in each bedroom.

Your friend has asked you to draft him a simple agreement for a weekly tenancy.

7. You are required to advise as to the legal rights and liabilities of persons involved in the following incident on the premises of Cobden Engineering Co. Ltd.

Larkin, a supervisor, told Young, an apprentice that he must wear safety

589

goggles at all times. Larkin gave Young a pair of goggles, the eye pieces of which he had liberally smeared with grease. Young blundered around the workshop and collided with Speedie who was working at his lathe. Speedie had removed the guard from the machine to speed up production. Both Speedie and Young came into contact with the machine and were injured. Helpmann, a fellow worker saw the accident and ran over to switch off the machinery. However, Helpmann's hands were wet and he suffered a severe electric shock. Mrs Nervy, a member of the contract cleaning staff heard Speedie's screams as she worked in the office. She suffered from shock and had a miscarriage. Young and Speedie were taken to the nearby hospital for treatment. Both men were given anti-tetanus injections. Speedie however, was allergic to the anti-tetanus vaccine and died.

8. Your company is concerned about the number of accidents which have occurred at its premises and caused injuries to people who are not employees.

Draft a report outlining the extent to which the company will be liable as occupier if the premises are dangerous.

In addition, explain the company's possible liability for injuries to the following:-

(a) Albert, a member of a group of students on an official visit who fell on a slippery floor.

(b) Bernard, who entered the yard at night and was bitten by a guard dog.

(c) Charles, an electrician, who was called in to repair a fault and electrocuted himself.

(d) David, a boy of nine, who despite warnings, used to walk along the top of the wall and one day slipped and fell off.

9. You are employed in the industrial relations department of your company. Write a report to the Managing Director explaining the legal position in the following cases.

a. There has been a strike at one of the company's plants. It is believed that Allen who has been employed there for 5 years has been the instigator of the strike and the company is considering his dismissal.

b. Another employee, Brown, is known to be recruiting members into a trade union. He has been employed by the company for only 3 weeks.

c. It has been suggested that Caldwell should be dismissed. He has been employed for 27 months during which time he has been away sick for 2 months and on strike for 2 months. However, during the past week he has been late for work on three occasions. Prior to this his work record has been good.

d. Miss Duffy, who is secretary to the Sales Manager, has resigned and walked out of her job. She is claiming compensation for unfair dismissal, alleging that the Sales Manager has, for some time, been making advances to her of a sexual nature (which she has resisted).

e.   Edwards, a skilled employee in the Research & Development Department, has recently been released from prison after serving 18 months of a 4 year sentence for manslaughter. He has applied to be re-instated but has been refused.

f.   Field has been employed as a filing clerk for 10 years. Most of the system has been computerised and the company wishes to train him to operate the system. Field does not believe that he can adapt to this change and refuses to undergo training.

g.   Green, a sales representative, has been dismissed without notice after returning late from his holidays. After the dismissal it has been discovered that he has been taking bribes from customers.

h.   Howard is an Assistant Manager with 20 years of service. Due to re-organisation his position has been cut. Howard has been requested to move to a similar post in the company's plant, 100 miles away. He has refused to move.

Appendix 5

AN OUTLINE OF THE SCOTTISH LEGAL SYSTEM

1. Introduction

Within the British Political System there exists various forms of devolution and decentralisation above the level of Local Government.

a. *Northern Ireland* has a separately elected Parliament at Stormont, a local government structure and a system of courts. Apart from periods of "direct rule" in the 1970s Northern Ireland has been governed partly from Stormont and partly from Westminster, the division of power being laid down in the *GOVERNMENT OF IRELAND ACT 1920* and subsequent Acts.

b. *Wales* is also treated as a distinct area by British central government. There is a Welsh Office and the Secretary of State for Wales is a member of the Cabinet. However there is no Welsh legal system and the identity of Wales is therefore based on language, religion and education rather than on political institutions.

c. *Scotland* falls between Northern Ireland and Wales. It does not have its own Parliament but it does have a number of political and social institutions and a strong constituitional identity. Probably the most important factor contributing to this is the existence of a separate Scottish legal system.

2. The Scottish Legal System

The main features are described below:-

a. *Law making*

Clearly most Acts of Parliament apply throughout the U.K., but between five and ten Acts are passed each parliamentary session which apply exclusively to Scotland. Some of these are the result of recommendations by the Scottish Law Commission. The passage of these Acts through Parliament is scrutinised by several Scottish Committees in the House of Commons. In addition clauses which apply only to Scotland may be tacked on to British legislation.

b. *The Court Structure*

With one exception the court structure is different from and independent of the courts in the rest of Britain. The exception is that the final civil court of appeal is the House of Lords. All other cases must be tried in Scottish courts. Procedure in these courts differs from procedure in England. For example public prosecutions proceed under the direction of procurators-fiscal, rather than the police and the courts may return a verdict of "not proven" rather than just "guilty" or "not guilty". The court structure is as follows:-

Civil Courts	Criminal Courts
House of Lords	Court of Criminal Appeal
Court of Session	High Court of Justiciary
Sheriff Court	Sheriff Court
	District Court

The same judges sit in the Court of Session and the High Court of Justiciary and at present they number about 20. The main local courts are the Sheriff Courts which have a wide jurisdiction in both civil and criminal cases.

c. *Law Officers*

The Scottish legal system is represented in the House of Commons by the Lord Advocate and the Solicitor General for Scotland. The Lord Advocate has a function similar to the Lord Chancellor in England and Wales, however the Lord Advocate is not the head of the Scottish Judiciary, that position is held by the Lord President of the Court of Session.

d. *The Judiciary*

The senior judges sit in the Court of Session and the High Court of Justiciary. Below them are the Sheriffs-principal and the Sheriffs. In Scotland there is a much greater link between law and politics than in England. Often judges are appointed from principal government law officers as political reward. Scottish judges, in court and elsewhere see themselves as public figures. They often sit on important government committees and voice opinions on current affairs. Politics also pays a part in the lower courts where District Courts can have elected councillors as magistrates.

e. *The Legal Profession*

The Scottish Legal profession is different from that in England. It is recruited separately under the control of the Law Society of Scotland and the Faculty of Advocates (the equivalent of barristers) and judges are nearly always Scots. They receive their legal education in Scotland and they are generally not qualified to practice in England.

3. Scottish Law and English Law

All law in Scotland is technically "Scottish" law since it is interpreted in Scottish courts, but in substance most law is "British" since it lays down the same rights and duties for persons throughout the UK. For example civil liberties, ie. the freedom of speech and assembly are the same as in England. Also the growth of the welfare state and of government regulation of the UK economy has resulted in more "British" legislation. The main substantive differences concern private and property law rather than public and commercial law. The exclusively Scottish Acts of Parliament generally concern private matters such as local government and education. There is a different procedure for the sale of land and Scottish "permissive" legislation concerning, for example divorce, homosexuality and licensing is more strict than in England.

4. Conclusion

In 1603 the monarchy of England and Scotland was united. In 1707 the *ACT OF UNION* passed by the parliaments of England and Scotland abolished separate parliaments and replaced them with a single parliament of the United Kingdom (a reform in which bribery and secret diplomacy played a significant part). Nevertheless the present system was not imposed on the Scots as it was on the Welsh. The Act of 1707 guaranteed certain rights, for example free trade with England, and certain institutions, in particular an independent church, legal system and universities. Lawyers, churchmen and educationalists may each claim that their institution is the foundation of Scottish nationality, but it is the legal system which must take priority because it lays down the rights and duties of the others.

Index

600

COMPANY LAW
4th Edition
KR Abbott

This book is intended for anyone studying company law who needs to get a good grasp of the subject in a relatively short period of time. It covers all areas of company law, presenting complex legislation in a clear and readable style and format. This edition incorporates all the relevant provisions of the Companies Act 1989. It also includes, for the first time, 21 short progress tests with answers, and a number of new past questions from recent ACCA and CIMA examination papers. In addition it contains a new short section on European Community Company Law Harmonisation.

COURSES ON WHICH THIS BOOK IS KNOWN TO BE USED:
ACCA; CIMA; ICSA; CIB; AAT; IComA; BTEC HNC/D Business and Finance; BA Business Studies; SSVA Taxation and Law; LLB
On reading lists of ACCA, CIMA and IComA

CONTENTS:

Introduction • History of Company Law • The Modern Company and the European Community • **Incorporation** • Consequences of Incorporation • Promotion • Memorandum of Association • Articles of Association • **Raising and Maintenance of Capital** • Public Offers for Shares • Capital • Dividends • **Company Securities** • Shares • Membership • Debentures • **Company Officers** • Directors • Secretary • **Protection of Investors and Creditors** • Publicity and Accounts • Auditors • Company Meetings • Insider Dealing • Minority Protection • **Reconstructions, Takeovers, Liquidation, Receivership and Administration** • Reconstructions, Mergers and Takeovers • Liquidation • Administration Orders • Receiverships.

REVIEW COMMENTS:

'It's very readable. A good balance to the more substantial reference works and a very valuable alternative to the study manual approach.' 'A clear, concise text with good explanations - it is a core text on the second year of our HND.' **Lecturers**

ISBN: 1 870941 56 X
Extent: 512 pp
Size: 216 × 138 mm

Free Lecturers' Supplement

UNDERSTANDING BUSINESS AND FINANCE
An Active-Learning Approach

Edited by Jill Hussey

P Cox - P Goodwin - M Hall - G Heaven - S Howe - J Hussey - R Hussey - J Jordan - M Sutcliffe

The aim of this book is to provide a course text covering the **whole** of the core subjects of BTEC HNC/D Business and Finance. It will also be of considerable value to business and finance students on other courses.

It satisfies the need for a completely different kind of book which takes into account all the following requirements:

- the variety of ways the BTEC core subjects are implemented
- **all** the themes, knowledge and skills required by the core subjects
- the 'learning by doing', 'problem solving' and 'learning by discussion' approach central to BTEC philosophy
- the tasks and assignments (both topic-based and integrated) **appropriate to the level** of the BTEC Higher Student.

To summarise, it forms a single book that can be recommended by all lecturers on the core subjects.

The book itself **does not try to teach**. Within each specialist area the equivalent of the lecturer's notes (including key facts and formulae) are **listed**, to provide a checklist (for students and lecturers) of the topics that need to be covered. These guidelines are interspersed, as appropriate, with problem-solving activities which students can tackle only when they have acquired the understanding and associated skills. **How** the requisite knowledge and skills are acquired will depend on whether it is better **researched** by the student or **explained** by the lecturer (guidance will be given in the lecturers' supplement).

CONTENTS:

Accounting and Finance • Business Environment • Business Policy • Employee Relations • Marketing • Operations Management • People and Organisations • Quantitative Methods and Information Technology • Business Law • Integrated Assignments.

Free Lecturers' Supplement

ISBN: 1 870941 74 8

Extent: 352 pp

Size: 275 x 215

MANAGEMENT THEORY AND PRACTICE
3rd Edition
GA Cole

This book aims to provide, in one concise volume, the principal ideas and developments in the theory and practice of management as required by business and accountancy students.

This edition revises and updates in such areas as employment law and employee relations and has a number of new chapters, including *Japanese Approaches to Management*.

COURSES ON WHICH THIS BOOK IS KNOWN TO BE USED:
CIMA; ACCA; AAT; IComA; BTEC HNC/D; IIM; BA Business Studies; BA Accounting; MSc Information Technology; BSc Software Engineering; Hotel and Catering Management courses; Chartered Institute of Building; CIB; CIM; IAM; DMS.
On reading lists of CIMA , ACCA and IComA

CONTENTS:

Glossary of Management Terms • Introduction to Management Theory • Classical Theories • Human Relations Theories • Systems Approaches to Management Theory • Management in Practice • Planning • Organising – Leadership and Groups • Control in Management • Marketing Management • Production Management • Personnel Management • Appendices – Guide to Further Reading – Examination Technique – Outline Answers to Examination Questions at Section Ends – Further Examination Questions – Suggested Answers for Lecturers.

REVIEW COMMENTS:

'Excellent textbook for any management student.' 'One of the clearest presentations available.' 'Very clear – excellent chapter design.' 'The right mix of diagrams, charts and reading text ...' 'Our students find your approach to topics and logical progression beneficial and easy to understand.' **Lecturers**

Also available as ELBS edition in member countries at local currency equivalent price of £2.50

ISBN: 1 870941 60 8
Extent: 608 pp
Size: 216 × 138 mm

Free Lecturers' Supplement

PERSONNEL MANAGEMENT
2nd Edition
GA Cole

This book is intended to meet the needs of students and lecturers for an introductory textbook that can offer a variety of learning opportunities in the form of discussion questions, case studies, examination questions and suggested answers.

COURSES ON WHICH THIS BOOK IS KNOWN TO BE USED:
IPM; ICSA; Association of Business Executives; HNC/D Business and Finance; CNAA Diploma in Personnel Management; CNAA Degrees in Business Studies (Personnel Management Options); CIB; Institute of Training and Development; A Level Business Studies.

CONTENTS:

The Scope of Personnel Management • The Personnel Function in Organisations • Personnel Policies and Strategies • **The Organisational Context** • Organisations – Key Issues • Organisation Structures • Leadership • Groups at Work • Motivation Theory • **Planning the Organisation's Manpower** • Manpower Planning • Job Analysis • Job Evaluation • Recruitment • Selection • Job Design • Organisation Development • Retirements, Redundancies and Redeployments • Personnel Records and Administration • **Conditions of Employment** • The Employment Contract • Hours of Work • Payments Systems – Key Issues • Wage Payments Systems • Salary Systems and Employee Benefits • Health, Safety and Welfare • **Employee Development** • Performance Appraisal • Key Theories of Learning • Systematic Training • Training Needs and Training Plans • Designing Training Programmes • Evaluation of Training • Management Development • **Employee Relations** • Introduction to Employee Relations • Formal Communication in Organisations • Collective Bargaining • Disputes and Strikes • Grievances, Discipline and Employee Participation • Employment Law and Personnel Management.

ISBN: 1 870941 16 0

Extent: 508 pp

Size: 216 × 138 mm

Free Lecturers' Supplement

Financial Management
5th edition
R BROCKINGTON

600pp 1990

This book gives a full coverage of the subject of financial managment to the level required by students taking the subject to a professionally qualifying level. It deals with both the basic and more advanced elements of the subject in logical way, helping the student to develop understanding through manageable steps. It contains a large number of worked examples together with exercises and examination questions to enable the student to test understanding.

Courses on which this book is known to be used
ACCA; CIMA; CIPFA; CIB; IMI; DMS; BTEC HNC/D Business Studies; Degree courses; short courses for managers and executives.

CONTENTS

REVIEW EXTRACTS

'...*written in a note format, the style is very clear and the development logical.*'
AUTA

'*Ideal for giving non-accounting students an overall coverage of the subject area.*' '*Good, useful, practical book, reasonably priced.*'
Lecturer

'*Makes very easy reading and understanding of such an involved subject.*'
Student

Free Lecturers' Supplement

Management Theory and Practice
3rd Edition
G A COLE

608pp 1990
(Also available as ELBS edition in member countries at
local currency equivalent price of £2.50)

This book aims to provide, in one concise volume, the principal ideas
and developments in the theory and practice of management as
required by business and accountancy students.

This edition revises and updates in such areas as employment law and
employee relations and has a number of new chapters, including
Japanese Approaches to Management.

Courses on which this book is known to be used
CIMA; ACCA; AAT; BTEC HNC/D; IIM; BA Business Studies; BA
Accounting; MSc Information Technology; BSc Software Engineering;
Hotel and Catering Management courses; CIB; CIM; IAM; DMS.

CONTENTS

LECTURERS' COMMENTS
'*Excellent textbook for any management student.*' '*One of the clearest
presentations available.*' '*Very clear - excellent chapter design.*' '*The right
mix of diagrams, charts and reading text.*' '*Our students find your approach
to topics and logical progression beneficial and easy to understand.*'

Free Lecturers' Supplement